# Career Guide to Industries

# 2008-09 Edition

U.S. Department of Labor
Elaine L. Chao, Secretary

Bureau of Labor Statistics
Keith Hall, Commissioner

January 2008

Bulletin 2701

Suggested citation: Bureau of Labor Statistics, U.S. Department of Labor, *Career Guide to Industries, 2008-09 Edition*, Bulletin 2701. Superintendent of Documents, U.S. Government Printing Office, Washington, DC.

For sale by the Superintendent of Documents, U.S. Government Printing Office
Internet: bookstore.gpo.gov   Phone: toll free (866) 512-1800;   DC area (202) 512-1800
Fax: (202) 512-2104 Mail: Stop IDCC, Washington, DC 20402-0001

ISBN 978-0-16-079905-1

# Preface

This eighth edition of the Career Guide *to Industries* provides valuable information from an industry perspective for persons making career decisions. It is a companion to the Bureau of Labor Statistics 2008-09 edition of the *Occupational Outlook Handbook*, a nationally recognized source of career guidance information for more than five decades. The *Handbook* provides information on careers from an occupational perspective.

The Bureau of Labor Statistics produced the *Career Guide* under the general direction and guidance of Dixie A. Sommers, Assistant Commissioner for Occupational Statistics and Employment Projections, and Kristina J. Shelley, Chief, Division of Occupational Outlook. Chester C. Levine and Jon Sargent, Managers of Occupational Outlook Studies, provided planning and day-to-day direction.

Supervisors overseeing the research and preparation of material were Douglas Braddock, Arlene Dohm, Roger J. Moncarz, and Terry Schau. Occupational analysts who contributed materi-

al were Phillip C. Bastian, Sadie Blanchard, Lauren Csorny, Tamara D. Dillon, Thomas DiVincenzo, Diana Gehlhaus, Samuel L. Greenblatt, Henry T. Kasper, Jonathan W. Kelinson, William S. Lawhorn, C. Brett Lockard, Kevin M. McCarron, Gregory Niemesh, Alice Ramey, Brian Roberts, Patricia Tate, Colleen D. Teixeira, David Terkanian, Nicholas K. Terrell, Michael Wolf, Benjamin Wright, and Ian Wyatt. Data development and computer programming support was provided by Erik A. Savisaar, David Terkanian, and Lynn Shniper under the supervision of Theresa Cosca. Word processing support was provided by Wendy Davis.

Editorial work and cover design was done under the direction of Richard Devens, Chief, Division of BLS Publishing, Office of Publications and Special Studies. Edith Baker, Eugene Becker, Monica Gabor, Anna H. Hill and Lori Pastro provided editorial support. The cover and other art were designed by Keith Tapscott.

---

**Notes**

Many trade associations, professional societies, unions, industrial organizations, and government agencies provide career information that is valuable to counselors and jobseekers. For the convenience of *Career Guide* users, some of these organizations and their Internet addresses are listed at the end of each industry section. Although these references were carefully compiled, the Bureau of Labor Statistics has neither authority nor facilities for investigating the organizations or the informa-

tion or publications that they might send in response to a request, and cannot guarantee the accuracy of such information. The listing of an organization, therefore, does not constitute in any way an endorsement or recommendation by the Bureau, either of the organization and its activities or of the information it may supply. Each organization has sole responsibility for whatever information it may issue.

# Contents

# Information in the *Career Guide to Industries*

What kinds of workers are employed by a particular industry, and what jobs are you qualified for right now? What jobs require special education or training? And, what advancement opportunities do these jobs offer in the long run? The *Career Guide to Industries* addresses these questions and more for 44 diverse industries which, when combined, accounted for about 3 out of 4 wage and salary jobs in 2006.

As a companion to the *Occupational Outlook Handbook,* the *Career Guide* discusses careers from an industry perspective. Why?: Because many career-minded people think in terms of industries rather than occupations. Your personal circumstances may compel you to remain in a specific area, limiting prospective jobs to those offered by the distinctive mix of industries in your State or community. Or, you may be attracted to a particular industry for other reasons—the glamour and travel associated with the air transportation industry, the potential for high earnings in the securities and commodities industry, the appeal of using advanced technology in aerospace manufacturing, or the opportunity to work with children offered by the educational services industry. By focusing on industries, the *Career Guide* provides information that the *Handbook* does not. It shows the relationships between different occupations and how they cooperate within industries to produce goods and bring them to the market or provide services to businesses and the public. Furthermore, some occupations are unique to a particular industry, and are not discussed in the *Handbook*. And, some industries offer specific paths of career advancement that are not addressed in the *Handbook*.

For each industry, the *Career Guide* includes a section with information on each of the following topics, although the information presented within each section varies slightly from industry to industry:

---

**About those NAICS numbers at the beginning of each industry statement**

The numbers in parentheses that appear to the right of each industry title are North American Industry Classification System (NAICS) codes that define the economic activities covered by each industry in the *Career Guide*. These codes are from *North American Industry Classification System, United States 2002,* a manual published by the U. S. Office of Management and Budget. The *NAICS Manual* defines and names industries and establishes a structure for relating industries to one another. All statistics on industries produced by the Federal Government are collected in accordance with the NAICS. The *NAICS Manual* describes the establishment types and goods and services produced in each of the specific industries covered in the *Career Guide*. Readers interested in obtaining more detailed definitions of the industries in the *Career Guide* should consult the *NAICS Manual*, which is available in the reference section of many libraries. The *NAICS Manual* also may be consulted on the Internet at **http://www.census. gov/epcd/www/naics.html**. This edition of the *Career Guide* is the second to be classified according to NAICS. Editions prior to the 2002-03 edition classified industries according to the Standard Industrial Classification (SIC), which is no longer being used by Federal statistical programs

---

## Nature of the Industry

- Describes the goods produced or the services provided by the individual segments of each industry.
- Describes the production processes, and the changes in technology or business practices taking place.

## Working Conditions

- Describes the physical environment in which workers perform their duties, including the hours of work, the frequency of night or weekend work or split shifts, and the physical activities essential to successful job performance.
- Discusses the proportion of part-time workers, rates of job-related injury and illness, and the extent and frequency of travel.

## Employment

- Indicates the number of wage and salary jobs and, where significant, the number of self-employed persons in the industry and data on the age of workers.
- Includes the number of establishments and concentration of industry employment by State, as well as the distribution of establishments and employment in the industry by employment-size class.
- Includes data on other unusual characteristics of industry workers, where significant.

## Occupations in the Industry

- Describes the various jobs and the ways in which each fits into the process of producing goods or delivering services to consumers.
- Provides the current and projected numbers of wage and salary jobs by occupation.

## Training and Advancement

- Details the qualifications required for key occupations and the types of formal education and other training that employers prefer.
- Discusses the training and educational paths of career advancement for key occupations.
- Discusses self-employment opportunities, when relevant.

## Earnings

- Provides data on the average weekly earnings, earnings of key occupations, and employee benefits.
- Lists the principle unions and the proportion of workers who belong to unions or who are covered by union contracts.

## Outlook

- Discusses the projected growth or decline of jobs in the industry and the projected rate of job growth compared with those in the economy as a whole.
- Describes the factors expected to influence employment growth, such as new technology, changing business practices, and demographics.
- May discuss the ease or difficulty of acquiring a job.

---

**Tables in the *Career Guide***
Unless otherwise indicated, the source of data presented in the tables is the Bureau of Labor Statistics.

---

# Career Guide to Industries: Overview and Outlook

The U.S. economy is comprised of industries with diverse characteristics. For each industry covered in the *Career Guide*, detailed information is provided about specific characteristics: The nature of the industry, working conditions, employment, occupational composition, training and advancement requirements, earnings, and job outlook. This chapter provides an overview of these characteristics and the outlook for the various industries and economy as a whole.

## Nature of the Industry

Industries are defined by the processes they use to produce goods and services. Workers in the United States produce and provide a wide variety of products and services and, as a result, the types of industries in the U.S. economy range widely—from agriculture, forestry, and fishing to aerospace manufacturing. Each industry has a unique combination of occupations, production techniques, inputs and outputs, and business characteristics. Understanding the nature of the industry is important because it is this unique combination that determines working conditions, educational requirements, and the job outlook for each of the industries discussed in the *Career Guide*.

Industries consist of many different places of work, called *establishments*. Establishments are physical locations at which people work, such as the branch office of a bank, a gasoline service station, a school, a department store, or a plant that manufactures machinery. Establishments range from large factories and corporate office complexes employing thousands of workers to small community stores, restaurants, professional offices, and service businesses employing only a few workers. Establishments should not be confused with companies or corporations, which are legal entities. Thus, a company or corporation may have a single establishment or more than one establishment. Establishments that use the same or similar processes to produce goods or services are organized together into *industries*. Industries are, in turn, organized together into *industry groups*. These are further organized into *industry subsectors* and then ultimately into *industry sectors*. For the purposes of labor market analysis, the Bureau of Labor Statistics organized industry sectors into *industry supersectors*. A company or corporation could own establishments classified in more than one industry, industry sector, or even industry supersector.

Each industry subsector is made up of a number of industry groups, which are, as mentioned, determined by differences in production processes. An easily recognized example of these distinctions is in the food manufacturing subsector, which is made up of industry groups that produce meat products, preserved fruits and vegetables, bakery items, and dairy products, among others. Each of these industry groups requires workers with varying skills and employs unique production techniques. Another example of these distinctions is found in utilities, which employs workers in establishments that provide electricity, natural gas, and water.

There were almost 8.8 million private business establishments in the United States in 2006. Business establishments in the United States are predominantly small; 60.4 percent of all establishments employed fewer than 5 workers in March 2006.

However, the medium-sized to large establishments employ a greater proportion of all workers. For example, establishments that employed 50 or more workers accounted for only 4.7 percent of all establishments, yet employed 56.5 percent of all workers. The large establishments—those with more than 500 workers—accounted for only 0.2 percent of all establishments, but employed 17.1 percent of all workers. Table 1 presents the percent distribution of employment according to establishment size.

The average size of these establishments varies widely across industries. Most establishments in the construction, wholesale trade, retail trade, finance and insurance, real estate and rental and leasing, and professional, scientific, and technical services industries are small, averaging fewer than 20 employees per establishment. However, wide differences within industries can exist. Hospitals, for example, employ an average of 542.7 workers, while physicians' offices employ an average of 10.3. Similarly, although there is an average of 14.7 employees per establishment for all of retail trade, department stores employ an average of 130.3 people but jewelry stores employ an average of only 5.9.

Establishment size can play a role in the characteristics of each job. Large establishments generally offer workers greater occupational mobility and advancement potential, whereas small establishments may provide their employees with broader experience by requiring them to assume a wider range of responsibilities. Also, small establishments are distributed throughout the Nation—every locality has a few small businesses. Large establishments, in contrast, employ more workers and are less common, but they play a much more prominent role in the economies of the areas in which they are located.

**Table 1. Percent distribution of establishments and employment in all private industries by establishment size, March 2006**

| Establishment size (number of workers) | Establishments | Employment |
|---|---|---|
| **Total** | 100.0 | 100.0 |
| 1 to 4 | 60.4 | 6.8 |
| 5 to 9 | 16.5 | 8.3 |
| 10 to 19 | 10.9 | 11.2 |
| 20 to 49 | 7.6 | 17.3 |
| 50 to 99 | 2.6 | 13.4 |
| 100 to 249 | 1.5 | 16.6 |
| 250 to 499 | 0.4 | 9.4 |
| 500 to 999 | 0.1 | 6.7 |
| 1,000 or more | 0.1 | 10.4 |

## Working Conditions

Just as the goods and services produced in each industry are different, working conditions vary significantly among industries. In some industries, the work setting is quiet, temperature-controlled, and virtually hazard free, while other industries are characterized by noisy, uncomfortable, and sometimes dangerous work environments. Some industries require long workweeks and shift work, but standard 40-hour workweeks are common in many other industries. In still other industries, a lot of the jobs can be seasonal, requiring long hours during busy periods and abbreviated schedules during slower months. Production processes, establishment size, and the physical location of work usually determine these varying conditions.

One of the most telling indicators of working conditions is an industry's injury and illness rate. Overexertion, being struck by an object, and falls on the same level, are among the most common incidents causing work-related injury or illness. In 2006, approximately 4.1 million nonfatal injuries and illnesses were reported throughout private industry. Among major industry divisions, manufacturing had the highest rate of injury and illness—6.0 cases for every 100 full time workers—while financial activities had the lowest rate—1.5 cases. About 5,703 work-related fatalities were reported in 2006; the most common events resulting in fatal injuries were transportation incidents, contact with objects and equipment, assaults and violent acts, and falls.

Work schedules are another important reflection of working conditions, and the operational requirements of each industry lead to large differences in hours worked and in part-time versus full-time status. In food services and drinking places, for example, fully 36.5 percent of employees worked part time in 2006 compared with only 2.0 percent in motor vehicles and motor vehicle equipment manufacturing. Table 2 presents industries having relatively high and low percentages of part-time workers.

Table 2. Part-time workers as a percent of total employment, selected industries, 2006

| Industry | Percent part-time |
| --- | --- |
| **All industries** | 15.4 |
| **Many part-time workers** | |
| Food services and drinking places | 36.5 |
| Grocery stores | 31.9 |
| Clothing, accessories, and general merchandise stores | 36.4 |
| Arts, entertainment, and recreation | 27.2 |
| Child day care services | 26.1 |
| Motion picture and video industries | 23.6 |
| Social assistance, except child day care | 23.6 |
| **Few part-time workers** | |
| Mining | 2.6 |
| Computer and electronic product manufacturing | 2.4 |
| Pharmaceutical and medicine manufacturing | 2.4 |
| Steel manufacturing | 2.1 |
| Motor vehicle and parts manufacturing | 2.0 |
| Utilities | 1.8 |
| Aerospace product and parts manufacturing | 1.8 |

The low proportion of part-time workers in some manufacturing industries often reflects the continuous nature of the production processes that makes it difficult to adapt the volume of production to short-term fluctuations in product demand. Once begun, it is costly to halt these processes; machinery must be tended and materials must be moved continuously. For example, the chemical manufacturing industry produces many different chemical products through controlled chemical reactions. These processes require chemical operators to monitor and adjust the flow of materials into and out of the line of production. Because production may continue 24 hours a day, 7 days a week under the watchful eyes of chemical operators who work in shifts, full-time workers are more likely to be employed. Retail trade and service industries, on the other hand, have seasonal cycles marked by various events that affect the hours worked, such as school openings or important holidays. During busy times of the year, longer hours are common, whereas slack periods lead to cutbacks in

work hours and shorter workweeks. Jobs in these industries are generally appealing to students and others who desire flexible, part-time schedules.

## Employment

The total number of jobs in the United States in 2006 was 150.6 million. This included 12.2 million self-employed workers, 130,000 unpaid workers in family businesses, and 138.3 million wage and salary jobs—including primary and secondary job holders. The total number of jobs is projected to increase to 166.2 million by 2016, and wage and salary jobs are projected to account for almost 153.3 million of them.

As shown in table 3, wage and salary jobs are the vast majority of all jobs, but they are not evenly divided among the various industries. Education, health, and social services had the largest number of jobs in 2006 with almost 29.1 million. The trade supersector was the second largest, with about 21.2 million jobs, followed by professional and business services with 17.6 million jobs in 2006. Manufacturing accounted for roughly 14.2 million jobs in the United States in 2006. Among the industries covered in the *Career Guide*, wage and salary employment ranged from only 154,300 in steel manufacturing to over 13.6 million in health care. The three largest industries—education services, health care, and food services and drinking places—together accounted for 38.5 million jobs, over one-quarter of the Nation's wage and salary employment.

Although workers of all ages are employed in each industry, certain industries tend to possess workers of distinct age groups. For the previously mentioned reasons, retail trade employs a relatively high proportion of younger workers to fill part-time and temporary positions. The manufacturing sector, on the other hand, has a relatively high median age because many jobs in the sector require a number of years to learn and perfect specialized skills that do not easily transfer to other industries. Also, manufacturing employment has been declining, providing fewer opportunities for younger workers to get jobs. As a result, more than one-forth of the workers in retail trade were 24 years of age or younger in 2006, compared with only 8.1 percent of workers in manufacturing. Table 4 contrasts the age distribution of workers in all industries with the distributions in five very different industries.

Employment in some industries is concentrated in a few regions of the country. Such industries often are located near a source of raw or unfinished materials upon which the industry relies. For example, oil and gas extraction jobs are concentrated in Texas, Louisiana, and Oklahoma; many textile mills and products manufacturing jobs are found in North Carolina, South Carolina, and Georgia; and a significant proportion of motor vehicle manufacturing jobs are located in Michigan and Ohio. On the other hand, some industries—such as grocery stores and educational services—have jobs distributed throughout the Nation, reflecting the general population density.

## Occupations in the Industry

The occupations found in each industry depend on the types of services provided or goods produced. For example, because construction companies require skilled trades workers to build and renovate buildings, these companies employ large numbers of carpenters, electricians, plumbers, painters, and sheet metal workers. Other occupations common to construction include construction equipment operators and mechanics, installers, and repairers. Retail trade, on the other hand, displays and sells manufactured goods to consumers. As a result, retail trade employs

**Table 3. Wage and salary employment in industries covered in the Career Guide, 2006 and projected change, 2006-16**
(Employment in thousands)

| Industry | 2006 Employment | 2006 Percent distribution | 2016 Employment | 2016 Percent distribution | 2006-16 Percent change | 2006-16 Employment change |
|---|---|---|---|---|---|---|
| **All industries** | 138,310 | 100.0 | 153,262 | 100.0 | 10.8 | 14,951 |
| **Natural resources, construction, and utilities** | 10,076 | 7.3 | 10,710 | 7.0 | 6.3 | 634 |
| Agriculture, forestry, and fishing | 1,220 | 0.9 | 1,114 | 0.7 | -8.6 | -105 |
| Construction | 7,689 | 5.6 | 8,470 | 5.5 | 10.2 | 781 |
| Mining | 619 | 0.4 | 609 | 0.4 | -1.6 | -10 |
| Utilities | 549 | 0.4 | 518 | 0.3 | -5.7 | -31 |
| **Manufacturing** | 14,197 | 10.3 | 12,695 | 8.3 | -10.6 | -1,503 |
| Aerospace product and parts manufacturing | 472 | 0.3 | 497 | 0.3 | 5.4 | 25 |
| Chemical manufacturing, except drugs | 576 | 0.4 | 486 | 0.3 | -15.7 | -90 |
| Computer and electronic product manufacturing | 1,316 | 1.0 | 1,159 | 0.8 | -12.0 | -157 |
| Food manufacturing | 1,484 | 1.1 | 1,489 | 1.0 | 0.3 | 5 |
| Machinery manufacturing | 1,192 | 0.9 | 1,045 | 0.7 | -12.3 | -146 |
| Motor vehicle and parts manufacturing | 1,070 | 0.8 | 918 | 0.6 | -14.3 | -153 |
| Pharmaceutical and medicine manufacturing | 292 | 0.2 | 362 | 0.2 | 23.7 | 69 |
| Printing | 636 | 0.5 | 497 | 0.3 | -21.8 | -139 |
| Steel manufacturing | 154 | 0.1 | 116 | 0.1 | -25.1 | -39 |
| Textile, textile product, and apparel manufacturing | 595 | 0.4 | 385 | 0.3 | -35.4 | -211 |
| **Trade** | 21,217 | 15.3 | 22,332 | 14.6 | 5.3 | 1,115 |
| Automobile dealers | 1,247 | 0.9 | 1,388 | 0.9 | 11.3 | 141 |
| Clothing, accessory, and general merchandise stores | 4,352 | 3.1 | 4,676 | 3.1 | 7.5 | 324 |
| Grocery stores | 2,463 | 1.8 | 2,479 | 1.6 | 0.7 | 16 |
| Wholesale trade | 5,898 | 4.3 | 6,326 | 4.1 | 7.3 | 428 |
| **Transportation and warehousing** | 4,466 | 3.2 | 4,962 | 3.2 | 11.1 | 496 |
| Air transportation | 487 | 0.4 | 522 | 0.3 | 7.3 | 35 |
| Truck transportation and warehousing | 2,074 | 1.5 | 2,381 | 1.6 | 14.8 | 307 |
| **Information** | 3,055 | 2.2 | 3,267 | 2.1 | 6.9 | 212 |
| Broadcasting | 331 | 0.2 | 362 | 0.2 | 9.3 | 31 |
| Motion picture and video industries | 357 | 0.3 | 396 | 0.3 | 10.9 | 39 |
| Publishing, except software | 660 | 0.5 | 611 | 0.4 | -7.5 | -49 |
| Software publishers | 243 | 0.2 | 321 | 0.2 | 32.0 | 78 |
| Telecommunications | 973 | 0.7 | 1,022 | 0.7 | 5.0 | 49 |
| Internet services providers, web search portals, and data processing services | 383 | 0.3 | 437 | 0.3 | 14.0 | 54 |
| **Financial activities** | 8,363 | 6.1 | 9,570 | 6.2 | 14.4 | 1,207 |
| Banking | 1,825 | 1.3 | 1,899 | 1.2 | 4.0 | 74 |
| Insurance | 2,316 | 1.7 | 2,488 | 1.6 | 7.4 | 172 |
| Securities, commodities, and other investments | 816 | 0.6 | 1,192 | 0.8 | 46.1 | 376 |
| **Professional and business services** | 17,552 | 12.7 | 21,644 | 14.1 | 23.3 | 4,092 |
| Advertising and public relations services | 458 | 0.3 | 520 | 0.3 | 13.6 | 62 |
| Computer systems design and related services | 1,278 | 0.9 | 1,768 | 1.2 | 38.3 | 489 |
| Employment services | 3,657 | 2.6 | 4,348 | 2.8 | 18.9 | 692 |
| Management, scientific, and technical consulting services | 921 | 0.7 | 1,639 | 1.1 | 77.9 | 718 |
| Scientific research and development services | 593 | 0.4 | 649 | 0.4 | 9.4 | 56 |
| **Education, health, and social services** | 29,082 | 21.0 | 34,543 | 22.5 | 18.8 | 5,461 |
| Child day care services | 807 | 0.6 | 1,078 | 0.7 | 33.7 | 272 |
| Educational services | 13,152 | 9.5 | 14,564 | 9.5 | 10.7 | 1,412 |
| Health services | 13,621 | 9.8 | 16,576 | 10.8 | 21.7 | 2,954 |
| Social assistance, except child day care | 1,502 | 1.1 | 2,326 | 1.5 | 54.8 | 823 |
| **Leisure and hospitality** | 13,143 | 9.5 | 15,016 | 9.8 | 14.2 | 1,873 |
| Arts, entertainment, and recreation | 1,927 | 1.4 | 2,522 | 1.6 | 30.9 | 595 |
| Food services and drinking places | 9,383 | 6.8 | 10,407 | 6.8 | 10.9 | 1,024 |
| Hotels and other accommodations | 1,833 | 1.3 | 2,088 | 1.4 | 13.9 | 254 |
| **Government and advocacy, grantmaking, and civic organizations** | 11,210 | 8.1 | 11,895 | 7.8 | 6.1 | 685 |
| Advocacy, grantmaking, and civic organizations | 1,234 | 0.9 | 1,392 | 0.9 | 12.8 | 158 |
| Federal Government | 1,958 | 1.4 | 1,869 | 1.2 | -4.6 | -90 |
| State and local government, except education and health | 8,018 | 5.8 | 8,634 | 5.6 | 7.7 | 617 |

NOTE: May not add to totals due to omission of industries not covered in the Career Guide.

4

**Table 4. Percent distribution of wage and salary workers by age group, selected industries, 2006**

| Industry | Age group | | | |
|---|---|---|---|---|
| | 16 to 24 | 25 to 44 | 45 to 64 | 65 and older |
| **All industries** | 14 | 45 | 37 | 4 |
| Computer systems design and related services | 5 | 63 | 30 | 2 |
| Educational services | 9 | 43 | 45 | 4 |
| Food services and drinking places | 43 | 38 | 17 | 2 |
| Telecommunications | 8 | 53 | 37 | 2 |
| Utilities | 4 | 42 | 54 | 1 |

**Table 6. Total employment and projected change by broad occupational group, 2006-16**
(Employment in thousands)

| Occupational group | Employment, 2006 | Percent change, 2006-16 |
|---|---|---|
| **Total, all occupations** | 150,620 | 10.4 |
| Professional and related occupations | 29,819 | 16.7 |
| Service occupations | 28,950 | 16.7 |
| Office and administrative support occupations | 24,344 | 7.2 |
| Sales and related occupations | 15,985 | 7.6 |
| Management, business, and financial occupations | 15,397 | 10.4 |
| Production occupations | 10,675 | -4.9 |
| Transportation and material moving occupations | 10,233 | 4.5 |
| Construction and extraction occupations | 8,295 | 9.5 |
| Installation, maintenance, and repair occupations | 5,883 | 9.3 |
| Farming, fishing, and forestry occupations | 1,039 | -2.8 |

numerous retail salespersons and other workers, including more than three-fourths of all cashiers. Table 5 shows the industry sectors and the occupational groups that predominate in each.

The Nation's occupational distribution clearly is influenced by its industrial structure, yet there are many occupations, such as general managers or secretaries, that are found in all industries. In fact, some of the largest occupations in the U.S. economy are dispersed across many industries. For example, professional and related occupations is the largest major group of occupations in the Nation while also experiencing the fastest growth rate. (See table 6.) Other large major occupational groups include service occupations, office and administrative support occupations, sales and related occupations, and management, business, and financial occupations.

## Training and Advancement

Workers prepare for employment in many ways, but the most fundamental form of job training in the United States is a high school education. Better than 88 percent of the Nation's workforce possessed a high school diploma or its equivalent in 2006. However, many occupations require more training, so growing numbers of workers pursue additional training or education after high school. In 2006, 28.7 percent of the Nation's workforce reported having completed some college or an associate's degree as their highest level of education, while an additional 30.2

percent continued in their studies and attained a bachelor's or higher degree. In addition to these types of formal education, other sources of qualifying training include formal company-provided training, apprenticeships, informal on-the-job training, correspondence courses, Armed Forces vocational training, and non-work-related training.

The unique combination of training required to succeed in each industry is determined largely by the industry's production process and the mix of occupations it requires. For example, manufacturing employs many machine operators who generally need little formal education after high school, but sometimes complete considerable on-the-job training. In contrast, educational services employs many types of teachers, most of whom require a bachelor's or higher degree. Training requirements by industry sector are shown in table 7.

Persons with no more than a high school diploma accounted for about 64.5 percent of all workers in construction; 62.3 percent in agriculture, forestry, fishing, and hunting; 61.3 percent in accommodation and food services; 58.8 percent in mining; 53.9 percent in administrative and support and waste management

**Table 5. Industry sectors and their largest occupational group, 2006**

| Industry sector | Largest occupational group | Percentage of industry wage and salary jobs |
|---|---|---|
| Agriculture, forestry, fishing, and hunting | Farming, fishing, and forestry occupations | 58.4 |
| Mining | Construction and extraction occupations | 37.8 |
| Construction | Construction and extraction occupations | 66.8 |
| Manufacturing | Production occupations | 52.5 |
| Wholesale trade | Sales and related occupations | 26.3 |
| Retail trade | Sales and related occupations | 54.1 |
| Transportation and warehousing | Transportation and material moving occupations | 59.8 |
| Utilities | Installation, maintenance, and repair occupations | 27.1 |
| Information | Professional and related occupations | 33.3 |
| Finance and insurance | Office and administrative support occupations | 49.8 |
| Real estate and rental and leasing | Sales and related occupations | 24.5 |
| Professional, scientific, and technical services | Professional and related occupations | 45.0 |
| Management of companies and enterprises | Management, business, and financial occupations | 33.1 |
| Administrative and support and waste management and remediation services | Service occupations | 31.4 |
| Educational services, public and private | Professional and related occupations | 67.4 |
| Health care and social assistance | Professional and related occupations | 43.3 |
| Arts, entertainment, and recreation | Service occupations | 58.8 |
| Accommodation and food services | Service occupations | 86.6 |
| Government | Service occupations | 25.0 |

5

**Table 7. Percent distribution of workers by highest grade completed or degree received, by industry sector, 2006**

| Industry sector | High school diploma or less | Some college or associate's degree | Bachelor's or higher degree |
|---|---|---|---|
| All industries........................... | 41.1 | 28.7 | 30.2 |
| Agriculture, forestry, fishing, and hunting........................... | 62.3 | 22.0 | 15.8 |
| Mining............................... | 58.8 | 24.9 | 16.3 |
| Construction .................... | 64.5 | 24.2 | 11.3 |
| Manufacturing.................. | 50.7 | 25.6 | 23.6 |
| Wholesale trade.............. | 43.0 | 29.3 | 27.8 |
| Retail trade ..................... | 50.8 | 32.1 | 17.1 |
| Transportation and warehousing....................... | 52.3 | 32.1 | 15.7 |
| Utilities............................. | 39.3 | 34.4 | 26.3 |
| Information....................... | 25.6 | 31.6 | 42.8 |
| Finance and insurance ........ | 22.7 | 31.0 | 46.3 |
| Real estate and rental and leasing............................. | 33.6 | 32.5 | 33.9 |
| Professional, scientific, and technical services............ | 13.4 | 24.6 | 61.9 |
| Administrative and support and waste management services..... | 53.9 | 28.3 | 17.9 |
| Educational services ................ | 17.3 | 19.2 | 63.5 |
| Health care and social assistance............................. | 29.8 | 34.6 | 35.5 |
| Arts, entertainment, and recreation............................. | 39.5 | 32.1 | 28.3 |
| Accommodation and food services ........................... | 61.3 | 27.8 | 10.9 |

services; and 52.3 in transportation and warehousing. On the other hand, those who had acquired a bachelor's or higher degree accounted for 63.6 percent of all workers in private educational services; 61.9 percent in professional, scientific, and technical services; 46.3 percent in finance and insurance; and 42.8 percent in information.

Education and training also are important factors in the variety of advancement paths found in different industries. Each industry has some unique advancement paths, but workers who complete additional on-the-job training or education generally help their chances of being promoted. In much of the manufacturing sector, for example, production workers who receive training in management and computer skills increase their likelihood of being promoted to supervisory positions. Other factors that impact advancement and that may figure prominently in the industries covered in the *Career Guide* include the size of the establishments, institutionalized career tracks, and the mix of occupations. As a result, persons who seek jobs in particular industries should be aware of how these advancement paths and other factors may later shape their careers.

## Earnings

Like other characteristics, earnings differ by industry as a result of a highly complicated process that reflects a number of factors. For example, earnings may vary due to the nature of the occupations in the industry, average hours worked, geographical location, workers' average age, educational requirements, industry profits, and the degree of union representation of the workforce. In general, wages are highest in metropolitan areas to compensate for the higher cost of living. Also, as would be expected, industries that employ a large proportion of unskilled minimum-wage or part time workers tend to have lower earnings.

The difference in earnings between software publishers and the food services and drinking places industries illustrates how various characteristics of industries can result in great differences in earnings. In software publishers, earnings of all wage and salary workers averaged $1,444 a week in 2006, while in food services and drinking places, earnings of all wage and salary workers averaged only $215 weekly. The difference is large primarily because software publishing establishments employ more highly skilled, full-time workers, while food services and drinking places employ many lower skilled workers on a part time basis. In addition, most workers in software publishing are paid an annual salary, while many workers in food services and drinking places are paid an hourly wage, but many are able to supplement their low hourly wage rate with money they receive

**Table 8. Average weekly earnings of production or nonsupervisory workers on private nonfarm payrolls, selected industries, 2006**

| Industry | Earnings |
|---|---|
| All industries................................................. | $568 |
| **Industries with high earnings** | |
| Software publishers ..................................... | 1,444 |
| Computer systems design and related services .................. | 1,265 |
| Scientific research and development services.................... | 1,136 |
| Utilities............................................................. | 1,136 |
| Aerospace product and parts manufacturing..................... | 1,153 |
| Securities, commodities, and other investments ................ | 1,055 |
| **Industries with low earnings** | |
| Employment services ...................................... | 453 |
| Hotels and other accommodations ..................... | 346 |
| Arts, entertainment, and recreation ................... | 332 |
| Grocery stores.............................................. | 328 |
| Child day care services .................................. | 316 |
| Food services and drinking places ..................... | 215 |

as tips. Table 8 highlights the industries with the highest and lowest average weekly earnings.

Employee benefits, once a minor addition to wages and salaries, continue to grow in diversity and cost. In addition to traditional benefits—paid vacations, life and health insurance, and pensions—many employers now offer various benefits to accommodate the needs of a changing labor force. Such benefits sometimes include childcare, employee assistance programs that provide counseling for personal problems, and wellness programs that encourage exercise, stress management, and self-improvement. Benefits vary among occupational groups, full- and part-time workers, public and private sector workers, regions, unionized and nonunionized workers, and small and large establishments. Data indicate that full-time workers and those in medium-sized and large establishments—those with 100 or more workers—usually receive better benefits than do part-time workers and those in smaller establishments.

Union representation of the workforce varies widely by industry, and it also may play a role in determining earnings and benefits. In 2006, about 13.2 percent of workers throughout the Nation were union members or covered by union contracts. As table 9 demonstrates, union affiliation of workers varies widely by industry. 51.6 percent of the workers in air transportation were union members, the highest rate of all the industries, followed by 37.6 percent in educational services, and 34.4 percent in public administration. Industries with the lowest unionization rate include computer systems design and related services, 1.7 percent: food services and drinking places, 1.5 percent; and internet service providers, web search portals, and data processing

6

**Table 9. Union members and other workers covered by union contracts as a percent of total employment, selected industries, 2006**

| Industry | Percent union members or covered by union contract |
|---|---|
| All industries............................................................ | 13.2 |
| **Industries with high unionization rates** | |
| Air transportation .................................................. | 51.6 |
| Educational services ............................................. | 37.6 |
| Public administration.............................................. | 34.4 |
| Utilities.................................................................. | 31.9 |
| **Industries with low unionization rates** | |
| Computer systems design and related services ...................................................... | 1.7 |
| Food services and drinking places ...................... | .5 |
| Internet service providers, web search portals, and data processing services ........................... | 0.0 |
| Software publishing .............................................. | 0.0 |

services and software publishing, both with virtually no union workers.

## Outlook

Total wage and salary employment in the United States is projected to increase by about 10.8 percent over the 2006-16 period. Employment growth, however, is only one source of job openings. The total number of openings in any industry also depends on the industry's current employment level and its need to replace workers who leave their jobs. Throughout the economy, replacement needs will create more job openings than will employment growth. Employment size is a major determinant of job openings—larger industries generally have larger numbers of workers who must be replaced and provide more openings. The occupational composition of an industry is another factor. Industries with high concentrations of professional, technical, and other jobs that require more formal education—occupations in which workers tend to leave their jobs less frequently—generally have fewer openings resulting from replacement needs. On the other hand, more replacement openings generally occur in industries with high concentrations of service, laborer, and other jobs that require little formal education and have lower wages because workers in these jobs are more likely to leave their occupations.

Employment growth is determined largely by changes in the demand for the goods and services provided by an industry, worker productivity, and foreign competition. Each industry is affected by a different set of variables that determines the number and composition of jobs that will be available. Even within an industry, employment may grow at different rates in different occupations. For example, changes in technology, production methods, and business practices in an industry might eliminate some jobs while creating others. Some industries may be growing rapidly overall, yet opportunities for workers in occupations could be stagnant or even declining because they are adversely affected by technological change. Similarly, employment of some occupations may be declining in the economy as a whole, yet may be increasing in a rapidly growing industry.

As shown above in table 3, employment growth rates over the next decade will vary widely among industries. Natural resources, construction, and utilities are primarily expected to grow due to growth in construction, offsetting job declines in agriculture,

mining, and utilities. Growth in construction employment will stem from new factory construction as existing facilities are modernized; from new school construction, reflecting growth in the school-age population; and from infrastructure improvements, such as road and bridge construction. Employment in agriculture, forestry, and fishing should continue to decrease with consolidation of farm land, increasing worker productivity, and depletion of wild fish stocks. Employment in mining is expected to decline due to the use of new laborsaving technology and with the continued reliance on foreign sources of energy.

Employment in manufacturing is expected to decline overall with some growth in selected manufacturing industries. Employment declines are expected in chemical manufacturing, except drugs; computer and electronic product manufacturing; machinery manufacturing; motor vehicle and parts manufacturing; printing; steel manufacturing; and textile, textile product, and apparel manufacturing. Textile, textile product, and apparel manufacturing is projected to lose about 211,000 jobs over the 2006-16 period—more than any other manufacturing industry—due primarily to increasing imports replacing domestic products.

Employment gains are expected in some manufacturing industries. Small employment gains in food manufacturing are expected, as a growing and ever more diverse population increases the demand for manufactured food products. Employment growth in pharmaceutical and medicine manufacturing is expected as sales of pharmaceuticals increase with growth in the population—particularly among the elderly—and with the introduction of new medicines to the market. Both food and pharmaceutical and medicine manufacturing also have growing export markets. Aerospace product and parts manufacturing is expected to have modest employment increases as well.

Growth in overall employment will result primarily from growth in service-providing industries over the 2006-16 period, almost all of which are expected to have increasing employment. Job growth is expected to be led by health care and educational services—the two largest industries discussed in the *Career Guide*. Large numbers of new jobs also are expected in food services and drinking places; social assistance, except child day care; management, scientific, and technical consulting services; employment services, state and local government, except education and health care; arts entertainment, and recreation; computer systems design and related services; and wholesale trade. When combined, these sectors will account for nearly two-thirds of all new wage and salary jobs across the Nation. Employment growth is expected in many other service-providing industries discussed in the *Career Guide*, but they will result in far fewer numbers of new jobs.

Health care will account for the most new wage and salary jobs, almost 3.0 million over the 2006-16 period. Population growth, advances in medical technologies that increase the number of treatable diseases, and a growing share of the population in older age groups will drive employment growth. General medical and surgical hospitals, public and private—the largest health care industry group—is expected to account for about 691,000 of these new jobs.

Educational services is expected to grow by 10.7 percent over the 2006-16 period, adding about 1.4 million new jobs. A growing emphasis on improving education and making it available to more children and young adults will be the primary factors contributing to employment growth. Employment growth is expected at all levels of education, particularly at the postsecondary level, as children of the baby boomers continue to reach college age, and as more adults pursue continuing education to enhance or update their skills.

Employment in the Nation's fastest growing industry—management, scientific, and technical consulting services—is expected to increase by almost 78 percent, adding another 718,000 jobs over the 2006-16 period. Projected job growth can be attributed primarily to economic growth and to the continuing complexity of business. A growing number of businesses means increased demand for advice in all areas of business operations and planning.

The food services and drinking places industry is expected to add over 1.0 million new jobs over the 2006-16 projection period. Increases in population, dual-income families, and dining sophistication will contribute to job growth. In addition, the increasing diversity of the population will contribute to job growth in food services and drinking places that offer a wider variety of ethnic foods and drinks.

Almost 617,000 new jobs are expected to arise in State and local government, except education and health care, growth of almost 8 percent over the 2006-16 period. Job growth will result primarily from growth in the population and its demand for public services. Additional job growth will result as State and local governments continue to receive greater responsibility from the Federal Government for administering federally funded programs.

Wholesale trade is expected to add over 428,000 new jobs over the coming decade, reflecting growth both in trade and in the overall economy. Most new jobs will be for sales representatives at the wholesale and manufacturing levels. However, industry consolidation and the growth of electronic commerce using the Internet are expected to limit job growth to 7.3 percent over the 2006-16 period, less than the 10.8 percent projected for all industries.

Continual changes in the economy have far-reaching and complex effects on employment in each of the industries covered in the *Career Guide*. Jobseekers should be aware of these changes, keeping alert for developments that can affect job opportunities in industries and the variety of occupations that are found in each industry. For more detailed information on specific occupations, consult the 2008-09 edition of the *Occupational Outlook Handbook*, which provides information on hundreds of occupations.

Career Guide to Industries 2008-09 Edition

# Natural Resources
# Construction
# Utilities

# Agriculture, Forestry, and Fishing

## SIGNIFICANT POINTS

- Although farms generating over $250,000 per year in sales make up less than 10 percent of all farms, they supply three-quarters of all agricultural output.

- Self-employed workers—mostly farmers and fishers—account for 43 percent of the industry's workforce.

- Employment in agriculture, forestry, and fishing is projected to decline, especially among self-employed farmers and ranchers.

## Nature of the Industry

The agriculture, forestry, and fishing industry sector plays a vital role in our economy and our lives. It supplies us and many other countries with a wide variety of food products and non-food products such as fibers, lumber, and nursery items. It contributes positively to our foreign trade balance and it remains one of the Nation's larger industries in terms of total employment. However, technology continues to enable us to produce more of these products with fewer workers, resulting in fewer farms and farmworkers.

*Goods and services.* Agriculture, forestry, and fishing includes two large subsectors—crop production and animal production—plus three smaller subsectors—forestry and logging, fishing, and agricultural support activities. Crop production includes farms that mainly grow crops used for food and fiber, while animal production includes farms and ranches that raise animals for sale or for animal products. The fishing subsector includes mainly fishers that catch fish and shellfish to sell, while the forestry and logging subsector includes establishments that grow, harvest, and sell timber. Agricultural support activities includes establishments that perform any number of agricultural-related activities, such as soil preparation, planting, harvesting, or management on a contract or fee basis.

Establishments in agriculture, forestry, and fishing include farms, ranches, dairies, greenhouses, nurseries, orchards, and hatcheries. The operators, or people who run these agricultural businesses, typically either own the land in production or they lease the land from the owner. But production may also take place in the country's natural habitats and on government-owned lands and waterways, as in the case of logging, cattle-grazing, and fishing.

The vast majority of farms, ranches, and fishing companies are small enterprises, owned and operated by families as their primary or secondary source of income. Although large family farms (those generating more than $250,000 per year in gross annual sales) and corporate farms comprise less than 10 percent of the establishments in the industry, they produce almost three-fourths of all agricultural output. Increasingly, these large farms are being operated for the benefit of large agribusiness firms, which buy most of the product.

*Industry organization.* Agricultural production is the major activity of this industry sector and it consists of two large subsectors, *animal production* and *crop production*. Animal production includes establishments that raise livestock, such as beef cattle, poultry, sheep, and hogs; farms that employ animals to produce products, such as dairies, egg farms, and apiaries (bee farms that produce honey); and animal specialty farms, such as horse farms and aquaculture (fish farms). Crop production includes the growing of grains, such as wheat, corn, and barley; field crops, such as cotton and tobacco; vegetables and melons; fruits and nuts; and horticultural specialties, such as flowers and ornamental plants. Of course, many farms have both crops and livestock, such as those that grow their own animal feed, or have diverse enterprises.

The nature of agricultural work varies, depending on the crops grown, animals being raised and the size of the farm. Although much of the work is now highly mechanized, large numbers of people still are needed to plant and harvest some crops on the larger farms. During the planting, growing, and harvesting seasons, farmers and the workers they employ are busy for long hours, plowing, disking, harrowing, seeding, fertilizing, and harvesting. Vegetables generally are still harvested manually by groups of migrant farmworkers, although new machines have been developed to replace manual labor for some fruit crops. Vegetable growers on large farms of approximately 100 acres or more usually practice "monoculture," large-scale cultivation of one crop on each division of land. Fieldwork on large grain farms—consisting of hundreds, sometimes thousands, of acres—often is done using massive tractors controlled by global positioning system (GPS) technology, and other modern agricultural equipment.

Production of some types of crops and livestock tends to be concentrated in particular regions of the country based on growing conditions and topography. For example, the warm climates of Florida, California, Texas, and Arizona are well suited for citrus fruit production, while Northern States are better suited to growing blueberries, potatoes, and apples. Grains, hogs, and range-fed cattle are major products in the Plains States, where cattle feedlots also are numerous. In the Southwest and West, ranchers raise beef cattle.

Poultry and dairy farms tend to be found in most areas of the country. Most poultry and egg farms are large operations resembling production lines. Although free-range farms allow fowl some time outside during the day for exercise and sunlight, most poultry production involves mainly indoor work, with workers repeatedly performing a limited number of specific tasks. Because of increased mechanization, poultry growers can raise chickens by the thousands—sometimes by the hundreds of thousands—under one roof. Although eggs still are collected manually in some small-scale hatcheries, in larger hatcheries eggs tumble down onto conveyor belts. Machines then wash, sort, and pack the eggs into individual cartons. Workers place the cartons into boxes and stack the boxes onto pallets for shipment.

Aquaculture farmers raise fish and shellfish in salt, brackish, or fresh water, depending on the requirements of the particular species. Farms usually use ponds, floating net pens, raceways, or recirculating systems, but larger fish farms are actually in the sea, relatively close to shore. Workers on aquaculture farms stock, feed, protect, and otherwise manage aquatic life to be sold for consumption or used for recreational fishing.

Horticulture farms raise ornamental plants, bulbs, shrubbery, sod, and flowers. Although much of the work takes place outdoors, in climates with cold seasons, substantial production also takes place in greenhouses or hothouses. The work can be year-round on such farms.

Workers employed in the forestry and logging subsector grow and harvest timber on a long production cycle of 10 years or more, and specialize in different stages of the production cycle. Those engaged in reforestation handle seedlings in specialized nurseries. Workers in timber production remove diseased or damaged trees from timber land, as well as brush and debris that could pose a fire hazard. Besides commercial timber land, they may also work in natural forests or other suitable areas of land that remain available for production over a long duration. Logging workers harvest timber, which becomes lumber for construction, wood products, or paper products. They cut down trees, remove their tops and branches, and cut their trunks into logs of specified length. They usually use a variety of specialized machinery to move logs to loading areas and load them on trucks for transport to papermills and sawmills.

People employed in the fishing subsector harvest fish and shellfish from their natural habitat in fresh water and in tidal areas and the ocean, and depend for their livelihood on a naturally replenishing supply of fish, lobster, shellfish, or other edible marine life. Some full-time and many part-time fishers work on small boats in relatively shallow waters, often in sight of land. Crews are small—usually only one or two people collaborate on all aspects of the fishing operation. Others fish hundreds of miles offshore on large commercial fishing vessels. Navigation and communication are essential for safety of all of those who work on the water, but particularly for those who work far from shore. Large boats, capable of hauling a catch of tens of thousands of pounds of fish, require a crew that includes a captain, or "skipper," a first mate and sometimes a second mate, a boatswain (called a deckboss on some smaller boats), and deckhands to operate the fishing gear, sort and load the catch when it is brought to the deck, and aid in the general operation of the vessel.

The final subsector of agriculture, forestry, and fishing includes companies that provide agricultural support services to establishments in the other subsectors. On farms that primarily grow crops, these activities may include farm management services, soil preparation, planting and cultivating services, as well as crop harvesting and post-harvesting services. Other support services companies provide aerial dusting and spraying of pesticides over a large number of acres. They may also perform post-harvesting tasks to prepare crops for market, including shelling, fumigating, cleaning, grading, grinding, and packaging agricultural products. Typically, such support services are provided to the larger farms that are run more like businesses. As farms get larger, it becomes more economical as well as necessary to hire specialists to perform a range of farm services, from pest management to animal breeding. Establishments providing farm management services manage farms on a contract or fee basis. As more farms are owned by absentee landowners and corporations, farm managers are being hired to run the farms. They make decisions about planting and harvesting as well as do most of the hiring of farmworkers and specialists.

The agricultural support services subsector also includes farm labor contractors who specialize in supplying labor for agricultural production. Farm labor contractors provide and manage temporary farm laborers—often migrant workers—who usually work during peak harvesting times. Contractors may place bids with farmers to harvest labor-intensive crops such as fruit, nuts, or vegetables or perform other short-term tasks. Once the bid is accepted, the contractor, or crew leader, organizes and supervises the laborers as they harvest, load, move, and store the crops.

Establishments that supply support activities for animal production perform services that may include breeding, pedigree record services, boarding horses, livestock spraying, and sheep dipping and shearing. Workers in establishments providing breeding services monitor herd condition and nutrition, evaluate the quality and quantity of forage, recommend adjustments to feeding when necessary, identify the best cattle or other livestock for breeding and calving, advise on livestock pedigrees, inseminate cattle artificially, and feed and care for sires.

*Recent developments.* The agriculture, forestry, and fishing industry sector is being transformed by the implementation of science and technology in almost every phase of the agricultural process. For example, bioengineered crops that are resistant to pests or frost or that can withstand drought conditions enable farmers to produce more food without using costly insecticides and irrigation. The use of GPS in tractors helps farmers to cut the time it takes to plant and harvest a crop and enables more rows of crops to be planted per acre. And the latest science in genetics is being used to breed animals with specific characteristics. The use of modern equipment and technology has changed the way ranching is done. Branding and vaccinating of herds, for example, are largely mechanized; and the use of trucks, portable communications gear, and geopositioning equipment now is common and saves valuable time for ranchers.

Marketing is becoming more important in agriculture. For small farms to make money, many have had to come up with ways to bypass the middleman and sell directly to consumers or other end users. For example, some fruit and vegetable growers use the marketing strategy of "pick-your-own" produce, set up roadside stands, or sell at farmers' markets. More local growers are contracting with nearby restaurants or grocery stores to sell their produce.

Another development is the use of crops, particularly corn, to produce ethanol as a source of energy. The impact of this development on the agriculture industry is not yet known. The rise in the price of corn will no doubt help corn farmers, but may have unintended effects as land used for other crops is taken out of production and replaced with corn, and the rising price of corn causes problems for producers that feed corn to animals and consumers of other corn products. Organic farming, however, provides farmers large and small with tremendous growth opportunities. Its success is shown in the doubling of acreage devoted to it between 2002 and 2005, with more than 4 million acres of both pastureland and crops farmed organically. Sales of organically raised foodstuffs have been growing at approximately 20 percent per year since 1998, and the prospects for more such growth seem all but certain.

## Working Conditions

*Hours.* While the working conditions in this industry sector vary by occupation and setting, there are some characteristics common to most agriculture, forestry, and fishing jobs. Work hours generally vary and the jobs often require longer than an 8-hour day and a 5-day, 40-hour week; work cannot be delayed when crops must be planted and harvested, or when animals must be sheltered and fed. Weekend work generally is the norm, and farmers, agricultural managers, crew leaders, farm-equipment operators, and agricultural workers may work a 6- or 7-day week during planting and harvesting seasons. Graders and sorters may work evenings or weekends because of the perishable nature of the products. Almost 1 out of 4 employees in this industry work variable schedules. Because much of the work is seasonal in nature, many farmworkers must cope with periods of unemployment or obtain short-term jobs in other industries when the farms have no work. Migrant farmworkers, who move from location to location to harvest crops as they ripen, live an unsettled lifestyle, which can be stressful.

Workers on farms that raise other products, particularly animals, have work that must be done all year long. On dairy farms, for example, the cows must be milked and fed every day and their stalls cleaned. Cows may then be taken outside for exercise and grazing. Dairy workers also may plant, harvest, and store crops, such as corn or hay, to feed the cattle through the cold of winter or the drought of summer.

Most workers employed in fishing return to their homes every evening. However, workers on vessels that range far from port may be at sea for days or even weeks. While newer vessels of this type have improved living quarters and amenities, such as television and shower stalls, crews still experience the aggravations of confined conditions, continuous close personal contact, and the absence of family.

*Work Environment.* Agriculture, forestry, and fishing attract people who enjoy working with animals, living an independent lifestyle, or working outdoors on the land. For many, the wide-open physical expanse, the variability of day-to-day work, and the rural setting provide benefits that offset the sometimes hard labor and the risks associated with unseasonable or extreme weather and shifting outlook for revenues.

Much of the work on farms and ranches takes place outdoors, in all kinds of weather, and is physical in nature. Harvesting some types of vegetables, for example, requires manual labor and workers do a lot of bending, stooping, and lifting. Living conditions of contract laborers are guided by regulations to assure minimum standards. The year-round nature of much live-stock production work means that ranch workers must be out in the heat of summer, as well as the cold of winter. Those who work directly with animals risk being bitten or kicked.

Farmers, farm managers, and agricultural workers in crop production risk exposure to pesticides and other potentially hazardous chemicals that are sprayed on crops or plants. Those who work on mechanized farms must take precautions when working with tools and heavy equipment in order to avoid injury.

Forestry and logging jobs are physically demanding and often dangerous, although machinery has eliminated some of the heavy labor. Most logging occupations involve lifting, climbing, clearing brush, felling trees, and other strenuous activities.

Loggers work under unusually hazardous conditions. Falling trees and branches are a constant menace, as are the dangers associated with log-handling operations and the use of sawing equipment, especially delimbing devices. Special care must be taken during strong winds, which can halt operations. Slippery or muddy ground and hidden roots or vines not only reduce efficiency but also present a constant danger, especially in the presence of moving vehicles and machinery. Workers may encounter poisonous plants, brambles, insects, snakes, and heat and humidity. If safety precautions are not taken, the high noise level of sawing and skidding operations over long periods may impair hearing. If workers are to avoid injury, their experience, exercise of caution, and use of proper safety measures and equipment—such as hardhats, eye and ear protection, and safety clothing and boots—are extremely important.

Logging sites are often far from population centers and require long commutes. Some lumber companies set up bunkhouses or camps for employees to stay in overnight.

Fishing operations are conducted under various environmental conditions, depending on the region of the country, the kind of species sought, and the time of year. Storms, fog, and wind may hamper the work of fishing vessels. People employed in fishing work under conditions that can quickly turn from pleasant to wet and hazardous, and help is often not readily available. Work must be performed on decks that are wet and slippery as the result of fish processing operations or ice formation in the winter. Workers must be constantly on guard against entanglement in fishing nets and gear, sudden breakage or malfunction of fishing gear, or being swept overboard. Malfunctioning navigation or communication equipment may lead to collisions with underwater hazards or other vessels and even shipwrecks. Also, when injuries occur, medical treatment beyond simple first aid usually is not available until the vessel can reach port.

Some component industries making up agriculture, forestry, and fishing have some of the highest incidences of illnesses and injuries of any industry. In 2006, the overall industry sector had 6.0 injuries and illnesses per 100 full-time workers, compared with an average of 4.4 throughout private industry. Those working with livestock had significantly higher incidences of work-related illness and injury than those working with crops.

*Employment.* In 2006, agriculture, forestry, and fishing employed a total of 1.2 million wage and salary workers plus an additional 919,000 self-employed and unpaid family workers, making it one of the largest industries in the Nation. Over 80 percent of employment is in crop production and animal production. (See table 1.) Most establishments in agriculture, forestry, and fishing are very small. Nearly 60 percent employ fewer than 4 workers (see chart). Overall, this industry sector is also unusual in that self-employed and unpaid family workers account for such a high proportion of its workforce.

Workers in agriculture, forestry, and fishing tend to be older than workers in other industries. In 2006, 32 percent of workers were aged 55 or older, compared with 17 percent of all workers in all industries.

## Occupations in the Industry

Agriculture, forestry, and fishing is dominated by three large occupations—farmers and ranchers; farm, ranch, and other agricultural managers; and farmworkers. Together these occupations make up almost 95 percent of the industry sector. Among wage and salary workers, the single most common occupation was farmworkers, who made up about 46 percent of the entire

13

**Table 1. Distribution of wage and salary employment in agriculture, forestry, and fishing by detailed industry, 2006**
(Employment in thousands)

| Industry | Employment | Percent |
|---|---|---|
| **Agriculture, forestry, and fishing, total** ........................... | 1,220 | 100.0 |
| Crop production .................................. | 539 | 44.2 |
| Animal production ............................... | 459 | 37.6 |
| Support activities for agriculture and forestry ................................ | 118 | 9.7 |
| Logging ............................................ | 65 | 5.3 |
| Fishing, hunting and trapping .................. | 25 | 2.1 |
| Forestry ........................................... | 14 | 1.1 |

sector (table 2). The industry sector also employs a number of other occupations that help support the industry.

*Management and professional occupations. Farmers and ranchers* are the self-employed owner-operators of establishments that produce agricultural output. They perform many tasks, both production-related and management-related. Along with planting, cultivating, harvesting their crops, and feeding and raising their livestock, farmers and ranchers hire, train, and manage the schedules and supervise the work of farmworkers or farm labor contractors. They assign, monitor, and assess individuals' work. Farmers and ranchers also must perform the bookkeeping for their business and other activities. They keep records of their animals' health, crop rotation, operating expenses, major purchases, as well as pay bills and file taxes. If the farm or ranch has paid employees, its owner or operator may keep all of the paperwork needed to satisfy legal requirements, including payroll records and State and Federal tax records.

Farmers and ranchers must have additional skills to keep a farm or ranch operating. Computer literacy has become as necessary for farmers as it has for many other occupations. In addition, a basic understanding and working knowledge of mechanics, carpentry, plumbing, and electricity are helpful, if not essential, for running an agricultural establishment. Farmers who work large farms make decisions as much as a year in advance about which crop to grow. Therefore, a farmer must be aware of commodity prices in national and international markets to use for guidance, while tracking the costs associated with each particular crop. When dealing in hundreds or thousands of acres of one crop, even small errors in judgment are magnified, so the impact can be substantial. Thus, large-scale farmers strive to keep costs to a minimum in every phase of the operation. Furthermore, risk management of portfolios—the practice of juggling stocks, buying and selling futures, and engaging in other paper deals such as bond trading—is now becoming more important for owner-operators of large commercial farms.

*Farm, ranch, and other agricultural managers* operate farms, ranches, nurseries, timber tracts, and aquaculture operations on a daily basis for the owners. Agricultural managers perform many of the same tasks as do farmers and ranchers. Large commercial farms may have a manager for different operations within the establishment. On smaller farms, one manager may oversee all operations. Managers are responsible for purchasing machinery, seed, fertilizers, herbicides and pesticides, fuel, and labor. They must be aware of any laws that govern the use of such inputs in the farm's locality. Agricultural managers must be knowledgeable about crop rotation, soil testing, and various types of capital improvements necessary to maximize crop yields.

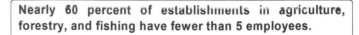

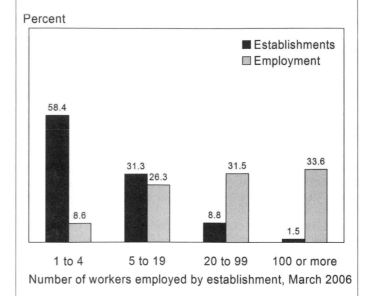

Number of workers employed by establishment, March 2006

*Foresters*, a type of life scientist, manage forested lands for economic, recreational, and conservation purposes. They inventory the type, amount, and location of standing timber, determine the timber's worth, negotiate with purchasers for the timber, and draw up contracts for tree removal and procurement. Foresters determine how to conserve wildlife habitats and creekbeds, preserve water quality and soil stability, and comply with environmental regulations. They also devise plans for planting and growing trees, monitor the trees' growth, and determine the best time for harvesting.

*Farming, fishing, and forestry occupations. Agricultural workers* include occupations that perform a whole spectrum of daily chores involved in crop and livestock production. *Graders and sorters* ensure the quality of the agricultural commodities that reach the market. They grade, sort, or classify unprocessed food and other agricultural products by size, weight, color, or condition. *Farmworkers and laborers, crop, nursery, and greenhouse* manually plant, maintain, and harvest food crops; apply pesticides, herbicides, and fertilizer to crops; and cultivate plants used to beautify landscapes. They prepare nursery acreage or greenhouse beds for planting; water, weed, and spray trees, shrubs, and plants; cut, roll, and stack sod; stake trees; tie, wrap, and pack flowers, plants, shrubs, and trees to fill orders; and dig up or move field-grown and containerized shrubs and trees. Additional duties include planting seedlings, transplanting saplings, and watering and trimming plants.

*Farmworkers, farm and ranch animals* care for farm, ranch, or aquaculture animals that may include cattle, sheep, swine, goats, horses, poultry, finfish, shellfish, and bees. They also tend to animals raised for animal products, such as meat, fur, skins, wool, feathers, eggs, milk, and honey. Duties may include feeding, watering, herding, grazing, castrating, branding, debeaking, weighing, catching, and loading animals. These farmworkers also may maintain records on animals, examine animals to detect diseases and injuries, and assist in birth deliveries and administer medications, vaccinations, or insecticides, as appropriate. Daily duties include cleaning and maintaining animal housing areas. These workers also may repair farm buildings and fences and

**Table 2. Employment of wage and salary workers in agriculture, forestry, and fishing by occupation, 2006 and projected change, 2006-2016.**
(Employment in thousands)

| Occupation | Employment, 2006 Number | Percent | Percent change, 2006-16 |
|---|---|---|---|
| **All occupations** . . . . . . . . . . . . . . . . . . . . | 1,220 | 100.0 | -8.6 |
| **Management, business, and financial occupations** . . . . . . . . . . . . . . . . . . . . . | 254 | 20.8 | -2.2 |
| Top executives . . . . . . . . . . . . . . . . . . . . . | 9 | 0.7 | -25.9 |
| Farm, ranch, and other agricultural managers. . . . . . . . . . . . . . . . . . . . . . . | 228 | 18.7 | 0.3 |
| Accountants and auditors . . . . . . . . . . . | 7 | 0.6 | -28.5 |
| **Professional and related occupations** . . | 21 | 1.7 | -11.8 |
| Life scientists . . . . . . . . . . . . . . . . . . . . . . | 8 | 0.7 | -7.1 |
| Agricultural and food science technicians | 5 | 0.4 | -1.5 |
| . . . . . . . . . . . . . . . . . . . . . . . . . . . . . | | | |
| **Service occupations** | 48 | 4.0 | -12.2 |
| Security guards . . . . . . . . . . . . . . . . . . . . | 5 | 0.4 | -15.3 |
| Building cleaning workers . . . . . . . . . . . | 7 | 0.6 | -19.5 |
| Landscaping and groundskeeping workers . . . . . . . . . . . . | 12 | 1.0 | -22.7 |
| Animal trainers . . . . . . . . . . . . . . . . . . . . | 10 | 0.9 | 4.3 |
| Nonfarm animal caretakers . . . . . . . . . . | 5 | 0.4 | 1.5 |
| **Office and administrative support occupations** . . . . . . . . . . . . . . . . . . . . . | 54 | 4.4 | -23.7 |
| Bookkeeping, accounting, and auditing clerks . . . . . . . . . . . . . . . . . . . | 19 | 1.6 | -21.3 |
| Material recording, scheduling, dispatching, and distributing occupations | 6 | 0.5 | -34.5 |
| Executive secretaries and administrative assistants . . . . . . . . . . . | 6 | 0.5 | -15.7 |
| Secretaries, except legal, medical, and executive . . . . . . . . . . . . | 8 | 0.7 | -25.2 |
| Office clerks, general. . . . . . . . . . . . . . . | 4 | 0.3 | -14.3 |
| **Farming, fishing, and forestry occupations** . . . . . . . . . . . . . . . . . . . . . | 713 | 58.4 | -7.6 |
| First-line supervisors/managers of farming, fishing, and forestry workers. . . | 27 | 2.2 | -11.0 |
| Graders and sorters, agricultural products . . . . . . . . . . . . . . | 13 | 1.0 | -15.5 |
| Agricultural equipment operators . . . . . . | 48 | 3.9 | -9.0 |
| Farmworkers and laborers, crop, nursery, and greenhouse . . . . . . . . . . | 492 | 40.4 | -6.3 |
| Farmworkers, farm and ranch animals . . | 64 | 5.2 | -7.9 |
| Agricultural workers, all other. . . . . . . . . | 12 | 1.0 | -8.6 |
| Fishers and related fishing workers . . . . . | 11 | 0.9 | -22.6 |
| Forest and conservation workers. . . . . . . | 7 | 0.6 | -12.8 |
| Logging workers . . . . . . . . . . . . . . . . . . | 36 | 3.0 | -11.1 |
| **Construction and extraction occupations** . . . . . . . . . . . . . . . . . . . . . | 12 | 1.0 | -22.5 |
| Construction laborers. . . . . . . . . . . . . . . | 4 | 0.3 | -32.2 |
| Operating engineers and other construction equipment operators . . . . . | 4 | 0.3 | -26.1 |
| **Installation, maintenance, and repair occupations** . . . . . . . . . . . . . . . | 16 | 1.3 | -13.7 |
| Heavy vehicle and mobile equipment service technicians and mechanics . . . . | 5 | 0.4 | -17.8 |
| Industrial machinery installation, repair, and maintenance workers. . . . . . . . . . . | 6 | 0.5 | -10.5 |
| **Production occupations** . . . . . . . . . . . . | 26 | 2.1 | -15.2 |
| Food processing occupations . . . . . . . . | 6 | 0.5 | -15.3 |
| Other production occupations . . . . . . . . | 11 | 0.9 | -14.5 |

(continued in next column)

---

(continued from previous column)

**Table 2. Employment of wage and salary workers in agriculture, forestry, and fishing by occupation, 2006 and projected change, 2006-2016.**
(Employment in thousands)

| Occupation | Employment, 2006 Number | Percent | Percent change, 2006-16 |
|---|---|---|---|
| **Transportation and material moving occupations** . . . . . . . . . . . . . . . . . . . . . | 68 | 5.6 | -21.0 |
| Truck drivers, heavy and tractor-trailer . . . . . . | 22 | 1.8 | -17.5 |
| Truck drivers, light or delivery services . . . . . . | 8 | 0.7 | -17.6 |
| Industrial truck and tractor operators . . . . . . . . | 7 | 0.6 | -23.9 |
| Laborers and material movers, hand . . . . . . . . | 22 | 1.8 | -26.0 |
| Packers and packagers, hand. . . . . . . . . . . . . . | 12 | 1.0 | -32.1 |

Note: May not add to totals due to omission of occupations with small employment

haul livestock products to market. On dairy farms, they may operate milking machines and other dairy-processing equipment. *Animal breeders* select and breed animals according to their genealogy, characteristics, and offspring. Usually, these workers need knowledge of the techniques of artificial insemination. Often, they keep the records of these animals' birth cycles and pedigree.

*Forest and conservation workers* perform a variety of tasks to reforest and conserve timber lands and maintain forest facilities, such as roads and campsites. They may plant tree seedlings to reforest timber land areas, remove diseased or undesirable trees, and spray trees with insecticides. They also may clear away brush and debris from trails, roadsides, and camping areas. Other forest and conservation workers work in forest nurseries, sorting out tree seedlings and discarding those that do not meet prescribed standards of root formation, stem development, and foliage condition.

*Fishers and related fishing workers* use nets, fishing rods, or other equipment to catch and trap various types of marine life for human consumption, animal feed, bait, and other uses. Fishing boat captains plan and oversee fishing operations—the fish to be sought, the location of the best fishing grounds, the method of capture, the duration of the trip, and the sale of the catch. First mates are captains' assistants who assume control of the vessel when the captain is off duty. They also must be familiar with navigation requirements and the operation of the vessel and all of its electronic equipment. Boatswains, highly experienced deckhands with supervisory responsibilities, direct the deckhands as they carry out the sailing and fishing operations.

## Training and Advancement
Most jobs in agriculture, forestry, and fishing are learned on the job. The industry sector employs a large number of workers with relatively low levels of educational attainment. Approximately one-quarter of this sector's workforce does not have a high school diploma. However, farmers, ranchers, and agricultural managers who seek to make a living from their work, are increasingly getting college degrees to learn how to run a business and how to take advantage of new agricultural technologies.

*Management, business, and financial occupations.* Becoming a *farmer* generally does not require formal training or credentials. However, knowledge of and expertise in agricultural production are essential to success for prospective farmers. The traditional method for acquiring such knowledge is through growing up on a farm, but this background is becoming less and less common as the percentage of the U.S. population raised on farms continues to dwindle. But even with a farming background, a person considering farming would benefit from a formal postsecondary agricultural education offered by either community colleges or land-grant colleges and universities, found in all of the States and territories. Programs usually incorporate hands-on training to complement the academic subjects. Typical coursework covers the agricultural sciences (crop, dairy, and animal) and business subjects such as accounting, marketing, and farm management. Also, some private organizations help people gain farming skills, particularly if they are interested in more "alternative" types of farming.

Experience and some formal education are necessary for *agricultural managers*. A bachelor's degree in business with a concentration in agriculture provides a good background, and work experience in the various aspects of farm or ranch operations enhances knowledge and develops decision-making skills. The experience of having performed tasks on other farming establishments as a farmworker may save managers valuable time in forming daily or monthly work plans and help them to avoid pitfalls that could result in financial burdens for the farm.

Whether it is gained through experience or formal education, both farmers and agricultural managers need enough technical knowledge of crops, growing conditions, and plant diseases to make sound scientific and business decisions. A rudimentary knowledge of veterinary science, as well as animal husbandry, is important for dairy and livestock farmers, ranchers, and agricultural managers.

It also is crucial for farmers, ranchers, and agricultural managers to stay abreast of the latest developments in agricultural production. They may do this by reviewing agricultural journals that publish information about new cost-cutting procedures, new forms of marketing, or improved production using new techniques. County cooperative extension agencies serve as a link between university and government research programs on the one hand, and farmers and farm managers on the other, providing the latest information on numerous agriculture-related subjects. County cooperative extension agents may demonstrate new animal-breeding techniques, or more environmentally safe methods of fertilizing, for example. Other organizations provide information—through journals, newsletters, and the Internet—on agricultural research and the results of implementing innovative methods and ideas.

*Farming, fishing, and forestry occupations.* Training and education requirements for general *farmworkers* are few. Some experience in farmwork or ranchwork is beneficial, but most tasks can be learned fairly quickly on the job. Advancement for farmworkers is somewhat limited, although motivated and experienced farmworkers may become crew leaders or farm-labor contractors. Also, firsthand knowledge of farm produce is good preparation for grading, sorting, and inspecting, so some farmworkers become agricultural graders and sorters or inspectors. Farmworkers who wish to become independent farmers or ranchers first must buy or lease a plot of land, which can be a substantial financial commitment if one buys instead of leases.

Some private organizations are helping to make farmland available and affordable for new farmers through a variety of institutional innovations. Land Link programs, coordinated by the National Farm Transition Network, operate in 19 States. They help match up young farmers with farmers approaching retirement so that arrangements can be made to pass along their land to young farmers wishing to keep the land under cultivation. Often beginning farmers lease some or all of their farmland. Sometimes, a new farmer will work on a farm for a few years, while the farm owner gradually transfers ownership to the new farmer.

Most *forest, conservation, and logging workers* develop skills and learn to operate the complex machinery through on-the-job training, with instruction coming primarily from experienced workers and logging companies' training. Some trade associations also offer special training programs. Safety training is a vital part of instruction for all logging workers.

Many State forestry and logging associations provide training sessions for fallers, whose jobs require more skill and experience than other positions on the logging team. Sessions may take place in the field, where trainees, under the supervision of an experienced logger, have the opportunity to practice various felling techniques. Fallers learn how to manually cut down extremely large or expensive trees safely and with minimal damage to the felled or surrounding trees. They also may receive training in best management practices, safety, endangered species preservation, reforestation, and business management. Some programs lead to logger certification.

Workers in the fishing industry subsector usually acquire occupational skills on the job, many as members of families involved in fishing activities. No formal academic requirements exist. Operators of large commercial fishing vessels are required to complete a Coast Guard-approved training course. Students can expedite their entrance into these occupations by enrolling in 2-year vocational-technical programs offered by secondary schools. In addition, some community colleges and universities offer fishery technology and related programs that include courses in seamanship, vessel operations, marine safety, navigation, vessel repair and maintenance, health emergencies, and fishing gear technology. Courses include hands-on experience. Secondary and postsecondary programs are normally offered in or near coastal areas.

*Fishers* must be in good health and possess physical strength. Good coordination, mechanical aptitude, and the ability to work under difficult or dangerous conditions are necessary to operate, maintain, and repair equipment and fishing gear. On large vessels, they must be able to work as members of a team. Fishers must be patient, yet always alert, to overcome the boredom of long watches when their vessel is not engaged in fishing operations. The ability to assume any deckhand's functions, on short notice, is important. As supervisors, mates must be able to assume all duties, including the captain's, when necessary. The captain must be highly experienced, mature, and decisive, and must possess the business skills needed to run business operations.

On fishing vessels, most workers begin as deckhands. Deckhands who acquire experience and whose interests are in ship engineering—maintenance and repair of ship engines and equipment—can eventually become licensed chief *engineers* on large commercial vessels, after meeting the Coast Guard's experience, physical, and academic requirements. Experienced, reliable deckhands who display supervisory qualities may become boatswains. Boatswains may become second mates, first mates, and, finally, *captains*. Almost all captains become self-employed, and the overwhelming majority eventually own, or have an interest in, one or more fishing vessels. Some may choose to run a sport or recreational fishing operation. When their seagoing days are over, experienced individuals may work in or, with the necessary capital, own stores selling fishing and marine equipment and supplies.

## Outlook

The agriculture, forestry, and fishing industry sector is expected to continue to produce more with greater efficiency through the use of increasingly productive machinery and greater use of science. Jobs in most parts of the sector are expected to continue to decline.

*Employment change.* Employment in the agriculture, forestry, and fishing is projected to decline 8 percent over the 2006-2016 period. Rising costs, greater productivity, increasing urbanization, and greater imports of food, lumber and fish will cause many workers to leave this industry. In addition, fishers face growing restrictions on where they can fish and how much they can harvest because many fisheries, or fish habitats, have been depleted because of years of overfishing.

Market pressures on the family farm will continue to drive consolidation in the industry, as the more prosperous farms become bigger in order to achieve greater economies of scale, along with a greater portion of farm subsidies. In addition, increasing productivity overall means that it takes less farm labor to produce crops and livestock than in the past. For many farmers, the low prices for many agricultural goods have not kept up with the increasing costs of farming. For those who need to make a living from their farm, these conditions make it difficult for many small farmers to survive.

Employment declines in agriculture, forestry, and fishing, however, are being moderated by other changes taking place in agriculture. Improved prospects for agriculture might be coming from the demand for ethanol. Higher prices for raw petroleum will make the use of this home-grown fuel more economically viable. Ethanol is currently made from corn, and rapid growth in demand for ethanol has led to higher prices for this key grain, improving the income of corn producers and providing incentive for producers of other crops to shift more acreage to corn.

New developments in the marketing of milk and other agricultural produce through farmer-owned and -operated cooperatives hold promise for some dairy and other farms. Furthermore, demand continues to rise for organic farm produce—grown to a large extent on small to medium-sized farms. The production of crops without the use of pesticides and certain chemicals is allowing farms of small acreage to remain economically viable. Also, some Federal, State, and local government programs provide assistance targeted at small farms. For example, some programs allow farmers to sell the development rights to their property to nonprofit organizations pledged to preserving green space. This immediately lowers the market value of the land—and the property taxes levied on it—making farming more affordable.

Employment in aquaculture had been growing steadily in recent years in response to growth in the demand for fish. However, competition from imported farm-raised fish and unsettled regulatory concerns about environmental impacts of fish farms is slowing the growth of aquaculture.

In fishing, increases in imports and efforts to revive many fisheries through stringent limits on fishing activity will continue to lead to employment declines. In certain areas of the country, such as Alaska, prudent management has sustained healthy fisheries that should continue to harvest massive amounts of fish. In other areas, fisheries have been damaged by coastal pollution and depleted by years of overfishing. In these areas there will be fewer jobs for fishers.

The logging subsector also is projected to decline as domestic timber producers continue to face increasing competition from foreign producers who can harvest the same amount of timber at lower cost. As competition increases, the logging industry is expected to continue to consolidate in order to reduce costs, eliminating some jobs. Additionally, increased mechanization of logging operations and improvements in logging equipment will continue to depress demand for many manual timber-cutting and logging workers.

The forestry subsector is also projected to show a decline in wage and salary workers as owners of forested lands are expected to hire fewer people to plant and raise timber stands as landowners find other uses for their lands more profitable. Professionals in the forestry industry will likely turn to self employment as consultants.

*Job prospects.* Jobs in agriculture, forestry, and fishing are expected to become increasingly harder to find and increasingly vulnerable to being eliminated. Employment on many farms will continue to be characterized by low wages and lack of benefits. While employment of self-employed farmers and ranchers is projected to decrease, employment of farm, ranch, and other agricultural managers is expected to remain stable. Thus, as more farms are owned by either corporations or absentee owners, these agricultural managers will play a relatively larger role in the operation of farms. In contrast, the numbers of farmworkers in crops, nurseries, and greenhouses and graders and sorters are expected to decline as technology continues to replace manual labor and as fewer workers seek jobs in this field.

In forestry, those seeking employment may expect some competition as owners of forest lands decide to use the land for other purposes, mainly recreational. Those with degrees in forestry will fare best, as they should be able to find work with consulting firms or in State or local government. Employment in logging is also expected to decline as the sector moves towards greater mechanization, replacing many lower skilled workers with more machinery controlled by a few operators. The best job opportunities will be for those workers with more skills, such as technicians, operators, and mechanics.

## Earnings

*Industry earnings.* In 2006, median earnings for workers in the agriculture, forestry, and fishing industry sector were $443 a week, with a wide range from less than $264 a week for the lowest 10 percent to more than $955 a week for the highest 10 percent. Lower than average earnings are due in part to the low level of skill required for many of the jobs in the industry and to the seasonal nature of the work.

Farm income can vary substantially depending on a number of factors, including: The type of crop or livestock being raised, price fluctuations for various agricultural products, and weather conditions that affect yield. In some cases, government subsidies may supplement a farmer's income. For a growing number of farmers and ranchers, particularly those working on farms for residential and lifestyle reasons, crop or livestock production is not their major occupation or source of income.

*Benefits and union membership.* Benefits in agriculture, forestry, and fishing are known to be generally much lower than those in manufacturing industries or high-tech industries. Those who are self-employed, particularly farmers, fishers, and agricultural managers, must provide for their own health insurance and plan for their own retirements above and beyond Social Security. Few workers in agriculture, forestry, and fishing are represented by unions.

17

**Table 3. Median weekly earnings of the largest occupations in agriculture, forestry, and fishing, 2006**

| Occupation | All industries |
|---|---|
| All occupations ........................................................ | $671 |
| Farm, ranch, and other agricultural managers......................... | 640 |
| Logging workers ...................................................... | 541 |
| Graders and sorters, agricultural products ........................... | 407 |
| Grounds maintenance workers........................................... | 402 |
| Packers and packagers, hand........................................... | 391 |

## Sources of Additional Information

For general information about starting out in farming, contact:
> United States Department of Agriculture, Cooperative State, Research, Education, and Extension Service, 1400 Independence Avenue SW, Stop 2201, Washington, DC 20250-2201. Internet: **http://www.csrees.usda.gov/**

For information about organic farming, horticulture, and internships, contact:
> ATTRA, National Sustainable Agriculture Information Service, P.O. Box 3657, Fayetteville, AR 72702. Internet: **http://attra.ncat.org**

For information on a wide range of topics in agriculture, contact:
> The National Agricultural Library, AFSIC, 10301 Baltimore Ave., Room 132, Beltsville, MD 20705-2351. Internet: **http://www.nal.usda.gov**

For information on a career as a farm manager, contact:
> American Society of Farm Managers and Rural Appraisers, 950 South Cherry St., Suite 508, Denver, CO 80246-2664. Internet: **http://www. asfmra.org**

For information on Land Link Programs, contact:
> The National Farm Transition Network, ISU Extension Outreach Center, 2020 DMACC Boulevard, Ankeny, IA 50021. Internet: **http://www.farmtransition.org/netwpart.html**

For information about State agencies involved in the purchases of development rights of farmland, contact:
> American Farmland Trust, 1200 18th St., NW, Washington, DC 20036. Internet: **http://www.farmland.org**

For information about careers and education resources in agriculture, contact:
> National FFA Organization, The National FFA Center, Attention: Career Information Requests, P.O. Box 68690, Indianapolis, IN 46268-0960. Internet: **http://www.ffa.org**

Information on licensing of fishing vessel captains and mates, and requirements for merchant mariner documentation, is available from the U.S. Coast Guard Marine Inspection Office or Marine Safety Office in your State, or:
> Licensing and Evaluation Branch, National Maritime Center, 4200 Wilson Blvd., Suite 630, Arlington, VA 22203-1804.

Schools of forestry at States' land-grant colleges or universities also should be able to provide useful information.

Information on the following occupations may be found in the 2008-09 *Occupational Outlook Handbook*:

- Agricultural workers
- Bookkeeping, accounting, and auditing clerks
- Conservation scientists and foresters
- Farmers, ranchers, and agricultural managers
- Fishers and fishing vessel operators
- Forest, conservation, and logging workers
- Grounds maintenance workers

# Construction

## SIGNIFICANT POINTS

- Job opportunities are expected to be excellent for experienced workers, particularly for certain occupations.

- Workers have relatively high hourly earnings.

- About 65 percent of establishments employ fewer than 5 people.

- Construction includes a very large number of self-employed workers.

## Nature of the Industry

*Goods and services.* Houses, apartments, factories, offices, schools, roads, and bridges are only some of the products of the construction industry. This industry's activities include the building of new structures, including site preparation, as well as additions and modifications to existing ones. The industry also includes maintenance, repair, and improvements on these structures.

*Industry organization.* The construction industry is divided into three major segments. The *construction of building* segment includes contractors, usually called general contractors, who build residential, industrial, commercial, and other buildings. *Heavy and civil engineering construction contractors* build sewers, roads, highways, bridges, tunnels, and other projects. *Specialty trade contractors* perform specialized activities related to construction such as carpentry, painting, plumbing, and electrical work.

Construction usually is done or coordinated by general contractors, who specialize in one type of construction such as residential or commercial building. They take full responsibility for the complete job, except for specified portions of the work that may be omitted from the general contract. Although general contractors may do a portion of the work with their own crews, they often subcontract most of the work to heavy construction or specialty trade contractors.

Specialty trade contractors usually do the work of only one trade, such as painting, carpentry, or electrical work, or of two or more closely related trades, such as plumbing and heating. Beyond fitting their work to that of the other trades, specialty trade contractors have no responsibility for the structure as a whole. They obtain orders for their work from general contractors, architects, or property owners. Repair work is almost always done on direct order from owners, occupants, architects, or rental agents.

*Recent developments.* Construction is heavily dependent upon business cycles. Changes in interest rates and tax laws affect individual and business decisions related to construction activity. State and local budgets affect road construction and maintenance. Changes in regulations can result in new construction or stop planned projects. The effects of these various influences can be short term or long term.

## Working Conditions

*Hours.* Most employees in this industry work full time, and many work over 40 hours a week. In 2006, about 20 percent of construction workers worked 45 hours or more a week. Construction workers may sometimes work evenings, weekends, and holidays to finish a job or take care of an emergency. Construction workers must often contend with the weather when working outdoors. Rain, snow, or wind may halt construction work. Workers in this industry usually do not get paid if they can't work due to the weather.

*Work Environment.* Workers in this industry need physical stamina because the work frequently requires prolonged standing, bending, stooping, and working in cramped quarters. They also may be required to lift and carry heavy objects. Exposure to weather is common because much of the work is done outside or in partially enclosed structures. Construction workers often work with potentially dangerous tools and equipment amidst a clutter of building materials; some work on temporary scaffolding or at great heights and in bad weather. Consequently, they are more prone to injuries than are workers in other jobs. In 2006, cases of work-related injury and illness were 5.9 per 100

**Table 1. Distribution of wage and salary employment in construction by industry, 2006**
(Employment in thousands)

| Industry | Employment | Percent |
|---|---|---|
| **Construction, total** | 7,689 | 100.0 |
| **Construction of buildings** | 1,806 | 23.5 |
| Residential building | 1,018 | 13.2 |
| Nonresidential building construction | 789 | 10.3 |
| **Heavy and civil engineering construction** | 983 | 12.8 |
| Utility system construction | 426 | 5.5 |
| Highway, street, and bridge construction | 349 | 4.5 |
| Land subdivision | 97 | 1.3 |
| Other heavy and civil engineering construction | 112 | 1.5 |
| **Specialty trade contractors** | 4,900 | 63.7 |
| Building equipment contractors | 2,006 | 26.1 |
| Foundation, structure, and building exterior contractors | 1,132 | 14.7 |
| Building finishing contractors | 1,036 | 13.5 |
| Other specialty trade contractors | 726 | 9.4 |

full-time construction workers, which is significantly higher than the 4.4 rate for the entire private sector. Workers who are employed by foundation, structure, and building exterior contractors experienced the highest injury rates. In response, employers increasingly emphasize safe working conditions and habits that reduce the risk of injuries. To avoid injury, employees wear safety clothing, such as gloves and hardhats, and devices to protect their eyes, mouth, or hearing, as needed.

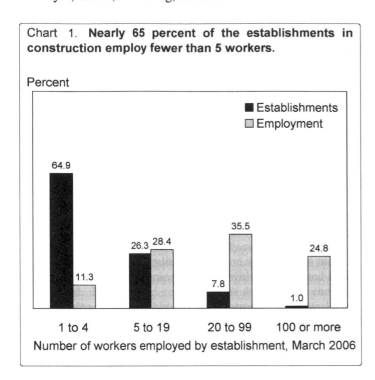

**Chart 1. Nearly 65 percent of the establishments in construction employ fewer than 5 workers.**

Percent

■ Establishments
☐ Employment

Number of workers employed by establishment, March 2006

**Chart 2. Many construction occupations have a substantial percentage of self-employed workers.**

Percentage of self-employed workers by occupation, 2006

## Employment

Construction, with 7.7 million wage and salary jobs and 1.9 million self-employed and unpaid family workers in 2006, was one of the Nation's largest industries. Construction also maintains the most consistent job growth. About 64 percent of wage and salary jobs in construction were in the specialty trades, primarily plumbing, heating, and air conditioning; electrical; and masonry. Around 24 percent of jobs were mostly in residential and nonresidential construction. The rest were in heavy and civil engineering construction (table 1).

Employment in this industry is distributed geographically in much the same way as the Nation's population. There were about 883,000 construction establishments in the United States in 2006: 268,000 were building construction contractors; 64,000 were heavy and civil engineering construction or highway contractors; and 550,000 were specialty trade contractors. Most of these establishments tend to be small; 65 percent employed fewer than 5 workers (chart). About 11 percent of workers are employed by small contractors.

Construction offers more opportunities than most other industries for individuals who want to own and run their own business. The 1.9 million self-employed and unpaid family workers in 2006 performed work directly for property owners or acted as contractors on small jobs, such as additions, remodeling, and maintenance projects. The rate of self-employment varies greatly by individual occupation in the construction trades, partially dependent on the cost of equipment or structure of the work (chart 2).

## Occupations in the Industry

Construction offers a great variety of career opportunities. People with many different talents and educational backgrounds—managers, clerical workers, engineers, truck drivers, trades workers, and construction helpers—find job opportunities in the construction industry (table 2).

*Construction trades occupations.* Most of the workers in construction are *construction trades workers*, which include master, journey, and apprentice craft workers, construction managers, and construction laborers. Most construction trades workers are classified as either structural, finishing, or mechanical workers, with some performing activities of more than one type. *Structural workers* build the main internal and external framework of a structure and can include carpenters; construction equipment operators; brickmasons, blockmasons, and stonemasons; cement masons and concrete finishers; and structural and reinforcing iron and metal workers. *Finishing workers* perform the tasks that give a structure its final appearance and may include carpenters; drywall installers, ceiling tile installers; plasterers and stucco masons; segmental pavers; terrazzo workers; painters and paperhangers; glaziers; roofers; carpet, floor, and tile installers and finishers; and insulation workers. *Mechanical workers* install the equipment and material for basic building operations and may include pipelayers, plumbers, pipefitters, and steamfitters; electricians; sheet metal workers; and heating, air-conditioning, and refrigeration mechanics and installers.

Construction trades workers are employed in a large variety of occupations that are involved in all aspects of the construction industry. *Boilermakers* make, install, and repair boilers, vats, and other large vessels that hold liquids and gases. *Brickmasons, blockmasons, and stonemasons* build and repair walls, floors, partitions, fireplaces, chimneys, and other structures with brick, pre-cast masonry panels, concrete block, stone and other masonry materials. *Carpenters* construct, erect, install, or repair structures and fixtures made of wood, such as framing walls and partitions, putting in doors and windows, building stairs, laying hardwood floors, and hanging kitchen cabinets. *Carpet, floor, and tile installers and finishers* lay floor coverings, apply tile and marble, and sand and finish wood floors in a variety of buildings. *Cement masons, concrete finishers, segmental pavers, and terrazzo workers* smooth and finish poured concrete surfaces and work with cement to create sidewalks, curbs, roadways, or other surfaces. *Construction equipment operators* use machinery that moves construction materials, earth, and other heavy materials and applies asphalt and concrete to roads and other structures. *Drywall installers, ceiling installers and tapers* fasten drywall panels to the inside framework of residential houses and other buildings and prepare these panels for painting by taping and finishing joints and imperfections. *Electricians* install, connect, test, and maintain building electrical systems, which also can include lighting, climate control, security, and communications. *Glaziers* are responsible for selecting, cutting, installing, replacing, and removing all types of glass. *Insulation workers* line and cover structures with insulating materials. *Painters and paperhangers* stain, varnish, and apply other finishes to buildings and other structures and apply decorative coverings to walls and ceilings. *Pipelayers, plumbers, pipefitters, and steamfitters* install, maintain, and repair many different types of pipe systems. They may also install heating and cooling equipment and mechanical control systems. *Plasterers and stucco masons* apply plaster, cement, stucco, and similar materials to interior and exterior walls and ceilings. *Roofers* repair and install roofs made of tar or asphalt and gravel; rubber or thermoplastic; metal; or shingles made of asphalt, slate, fiberglass, wood, tile, or other material. *Sheet metal workers* fabricate, assemble, install, and repair products and equipment made out of sheet metal, such as duct systems; roofs; siding; and drainpipes. *Structural and reinforcing iron and metal workers* place and install iron or steel girders, columns, and other structural members to form completed structures or frameworks of buildings, bridges, and other structures. Lastly, *construction laborers* perform a wide range of physically demanding tasks at building and highway construction sites, such as tunnel and shaft excavation, hazardous waste removal, environmental remediation, and demolition. Many construction trades workers perform their services with the assistance of *helpers*. These workers assist trades workers and perform duties requiring less skill.

***Mechanical and installation occupations.*** The construction industry employs a number of other workers apart from the construction trades. *Elevator installers and repairers* assemble, install, and replace elevators, escalators, moving walkways, and similar equipment in new and old buildings. *Heating, airconditioning, and refrigeration mechanics and installers* install systems that control the temperature, humidity, and the total air quality in residential, commercial, industrial, and other buildings. *Material moving occupations* use machinery to move construction materials, earth, and other heavy materials, and clean vehicles, machinery, and other equipment.

***Managerial occupations.*** *First-line supervisors and managers of construction trades and extraction workers* oversee trades workers and helpers and ensure that work is done well, safely, and according to code. They plan the job and solve problems as they arise. Those with good organizational skills and exceptional supervisory ability may advance to construction management occupations, including *project manager, constructor, field manager,* or *superintendent.* These workers are responsible for getting a project completed on schedule by working with the architect's plans, making sure materials are delivered on time, assigning work, overseeing craft supervisors, and ensuring that

every phase of the project is completed properly and expeditiously. They also resolve problems and see to it that work proceeds without interruptions.

The construction industry employs nearly all of the workers in some construction craft occupations. Other industries, including transportation equipment manufacturing; transportation, communication, and utilities; real estate; wholesale and retail trade; educational services; and State and local government also include large numbers of construction craft occupations (table 3).

## Training and Advancement

Persons can enter the construction industry through a variety of educational and training backgrounds. Those entering construction out of high school usually start as laborers, helpers, or apprentices. While some laborers and helpers can learn their job in a few days, the skills required for many trades worker jobs take years to learn and are usually learned through some combination of classroom instruction and on-the-job training. In a few cases, skills can be learned entirely through informal on-the-job training, but the more education received, generally the more skilled workers become.

Some pre-hire construction courses have recently been developed to create a pool of available workers with the basic knowledge and skills needed by contractors. The first major initiative has been developed along the Gulf Coast by the Business Roundtable, an association of 160 chief executive officers of leading U.S. companies. Qualified applicants will be able to take courses that prepare them to enter construction trades. The training is free for applicants who pass a skills test, are U.S. citizens, and in Mississippi, pass a drug test.

Construction trades workers such as carpenters, bricklayers, plumbers, and other construction trade specialists most often get their formal instruction by attending a local technical or trade school or through an apprenticeship, or other employer-provided training program. In addition, they learn their craft by working with more experienced workers. Most construction trades workers' jobs require proficiency in reading and mathematics. Safety training is also required for most jobs; English language skills are essential for workers to advance within their trade.

Laborers and helpers advance in the construction trades occupations by acquiring experience and skill in various phases of the craft. As they demonstrate ability to perform tasks they are assigned, they move to progressively more challenging work. As their skills broaden, they are allowed to work more independently, and responsibilities and earnings increase. They may qualify for jobs in related, more highly skilled occupations. For example, after several years of experience, painters' helpers may become skilled painters.

Many persons enter the construction trades through apprenticeship programs. Apprenticeships administered by local employers, trade associations, and trade unions provide the most thorough training. Apprenticeships usually last between 3 and 5 years and consist of on-the-job training and 144 hours or more of related classroom instruction each year. However, a number of apprenticeship programs now use competency standards in place of time requirements, making it possible to complete a program in a shorter time. Those who enroll in apprenticeship programs usually are at least 18 years old and in good physical condition. Many employers or programs require applicants to pass background checks.

Depending on the occupation, there may be technical or vocational schools that train students to perform a given occupation's tasks. Those who enter construction from technical or

**Table 2. Employment of wage and salary workers in construction by occupation, 2006 and projected change, 2006-2016.**
(Employment in thousands)

| Occupation | Employment, 2006 Number | Employment, 2006 Percent | Percent change, 2006-16 |
|---|---|---|---|
| **All occupations** | 7,689 | 100.0 | 10.2 |
| **Management, business, and financial occupations** | 583 | 7.6 | 11.6 |
| General and operations managers | 127 | 1.7 | -0.8 |
| Construction managers | 173 | 2.3 | 16.5 |
| Cost estimators | 136 | 1.8 | 19.5 |
| Accountants and auditors | 40 | 0.5 | 9.8 |
| **Professional and related occupations** | 98 | 1.3 | 10.2 |
| Engineers | 40 | 0.5 | 10.7 |
| Drafters, engineering, and mapping technicians | 25 | 0.3 | 8.0 |
| **Service occupations** | 59 | 0.8 | 10.0 |
| Building cleaning workers | 25 | 0.3 | 12.5 |
| **Sales and related occupations** | 154 | 2.0 | 12.0 |
| Sales representatives, services, all other | 37 | 0.5 | 21.6 |
| Sales representatives, wholesale and manufacturing, except technical and scientific products | 62 | 0.8 | 10.7 |
| Other sales and related workers | 35 | 0.5 | 6.0 |
| **Office and administrative support occupations** | 738 | 9.6 | 6.2 |
| First-line supervisors/managers of office and administrative support workers | 38 | 0.5 | 2.7 |
| Bookkeeping, accounting, and auditing clerks | 157 | 2.1 | 10.5 |
| Payroll and timekeeping clerks | 25 | 0.3 | -1.0 |
| Receptionists and information clerks | 43 | 0.6 | 9.8 |
| Material recording, scheduling, dispatching, and distributing occupations | 33 | 0.4 | -0.1 |
| Executive secretaries and administrative assistants | 84 | 1.1 | 10.2 |
| Secretaries, except legal, medical, and executive | 136 | 1.8 | -1.7 |
| Office clerks, general | 179 | 2.3 | 8.9 |
| **Construction and extraction occupations** | 5,139 | 66.8 | 10.4 |
| First-line supervisors/managers of construction trades and extraction workers | 464 | 6.0 | 10.6 |
| Brickmasons and blockmasons | 114 | 1.5 | 10.9 |
| Carpenters | 831 | 10.8 | 11.8 |
| Carpet, floor, and tile installers and finishers | 86 | 1.1 | 7.9 |
| Cement masons and concrete finishers | 204 | 2.6 | 11.4 |
| Construction laborers | 824 | 10.7 | 10.4 |
| Paving, surfacing, and tamping equipment operators | 45 | 0.6 | 9.0 |
| Operating engineers and other construction equipment operators | 263 | 3.4 | 9.1 |
| Drywall installers, ceiling tile installers, and tapers | 182 | 2.4 | 7.4 |
| Tapers | 41 | 0.5 | 7.3 |
| Electricians | 476 | 6.2 | 9.2 |
| Glaziers | 37 | 0.5 | 10.4 |
| Insulation workers, floor, ceiling, and wall | 30 | 0.4 | 7.6 |
| Insulation workers, mechanical | 26 | 0.3 | 8.6 |
| Painters and paperhangers | 221 | 2.9 | 9.0 |
| Pipelayers | 46 | 0.6 | 8.5 |
| Plumbers, pipefitters, and steamfitters | 360 | 4.7 | 12.7 |

(continued in next column)

(Continued from previous column)

**Table 2. Employment of wage and salary workers in construction by occupation, 2006 and projected change, 2006-2016.**
(Employment in thousands)

| Occupation | Employment, 2006 Number | Employment, 2006 Percent | Percent change, 2006-16 |
|---|---|---|---|
| **Construction and extraction occupations (continued)** | | | |
| Plasterers and stucco masons | 50 | 0.6 | 8.2 |
| Reinforcing iron and rebar workers | 29 | 0.4 | 11.9 |
| Roofers | 121 | 1.6 | 16.4 |
| Sheet metal workers | 125 | 1.6 | 10.6 |
| Structural iron and steel workers | 61 | 0.8 | 6.0 |
| Helpers, construction trades | 402 | 5.2 | 9.5 |
| Helpers—Brickmasons, blockmasons, stonemasons, and tile and marble setters | 61 | 0.8 | 11.1 |
| Helpers—Carpenters | 96 | 1.3 | 12.0 |
| Helpers—Electricians | 96 | 1.3 | 6.2 |
| Helpers—Pipelayers, plumbers, pipefitters, and steamfitters | 78 | 1.0 | 12.1 |
| Helpers, construction trades, all other | 26 | 0.3 | 10.7 |
| Other construction and related workers | 84 | 1.1 | 9.4 |
| **Installation, maintenance, and repair occupations** | 535 | 7.0 | 12.1 |
| First-line supervisors/managers of mechanics, installers, and repairers | 42 | 0.5 | 9.2 |
| Telecommunications equipment installers and repairers, except line installers | 24 | 0.3 | 39.6 |
| Miscellaneous electrical and electronic equipment mechanics, installers, and repairers | 34 | 0.4 | 6.8 |
| Mobile heavy equipment mechanics, except engines | 26 | 0.3 | 9.0 |
| Heating, air conditioning, and refrigeration mechanics and installers | 172 | 2.2 | 12.5 |
| Industrial machinery installation, repair, and maintenance workers | 77 | 1.0 | 13.3 |
| Line installers and repairers | 71 | 0.9 | 9.6 |
| **Production occupations** | 101 | 1.3 | 13.1 |
| Welders, cutters, solderers, and brazers | 42 | 0.6 | 17.6 |
| **Transportation and material moving occupations** | 281 | 3.7 | 6.9 |
| Driver/sales workers and truck drivers | 138 | 1.8 | 9.6 |
| Material moving occupations | 130 | 1.7 | 3.8 |

Note: May not add to totals due to omission of occupations with small employment

vocational schools also may complete apprenticeship training; technical or vocational school graduates progress at a somewhat faster pace because they already have had courses such as mathematics, mechanical drawing, and woodworking.

A few occupations have licensing requirements. Crane operators, electricians, plumbers, and heating and air- conditioning mechanics and installers are required to have a license in most States; without a license, a contractor cannot operate in the State. There are often separate licenses for contractors and workers. Other occupations do not have strict licensing requirements but often have voluntary certifications. These certifications provide tangible evidence of knowledge and abilities to potential employers and consumers. Certification is administered by many associations that are related to specific trades, but also are offered by other organizations as well. Licensing and certification requirements include years of work experience and classroom

**Table 3. Percentage of wage and salary workers in construction craft occupations employed in the construction industry, 2006**

| Occupation | Percent |
|---|---|
| Cement masons, concrete finishers, and terrazzo workers | 91.7 |
| Insulation workers | 91.4 |
| Structural iron and steel workers | 84.8 |
| Plasterers and stucco masons | 81.6 |
| Roofers | 77.1 |
| Drywall installers, ceiling tile installers, and tapers | 75.7 |
| Brickmasons, blockmasons, and stonemasons | 71.8 |
| Pipelayers, plumbers, pipefitters, and steamfitters | 71.4 |
| Glaziers | 67.7 |
| Electricians | 67.6 |
| Carpenters | 56.8 |
| Painters and paperhangers | 46.7 |
| Carpet, floor, and tile installers and finishers | 44.1 |

instruction. Licenses and certifications need to be renewed on a regular basis.

To further develop their skills, construction trades workers can work on different projects, such as housing developments, office and industrial buildings, or road construction. Flexibility and a willingness to adopt new techniques, as well as the ability to get along with people, are essential for advancement. Those who are skilled in all facets of the trade and who show good leadership qualities may be promoted to supervisor or construction manager. Construction managers may advance to superintendent of larger projects or go into the business side of construction. Some go into business for themselves as contractors. Those who plan to rise to supervisory positions should have basic Spanish language skills to communicate safety and work instructions to Spanish-speaking construction workers.

Outside the construction industry, construction trades workers may transfer to jobs such as construction building inspector, purchasing agent, sales representative for building supply companies, or technical or vocational school instructor. In order to advance to a management position, additional education and training is recommended.

Managerial personnel usually have a college degree or considerable experience in their specialty. Individuals who enter construction with college degrees usually start as management trainees or as assistants to construction managers. Those who receive degrees in construction science often start as field engineers, schedulers, or cost estimators. College graduates may advance to positions such as assistant manager, construction manager, general superintendent, cost estimator, construction building inspector, general manager or top executive, contractor, or consultant. Although a college education is not always required, administrative jobs usually are filled by those with degrees in business administration, finance, accounting, or similar fields.

Opportunities for workers to form their own firms are better in construction than in many other industries. Construction workers need only a moderate financial investment to become contractors and they can run their businesses from their homes, hiring additional construction workers only as needed for specific projects. The contract construction field, however, is very competitive, and the rate of business turnover is high. Taking courses in business helps to improve the likelihood of success.

## Outlook

Job opportunities are expected to be excellent for experienced workers, particularly for certain occupations.

*Employment change.* The number of wage and salary jobs in the construction industry is expected to grow 10 percent through the year 2016, compared with the 11 percent projected for all industries combined. Employment in this industry depends primarily on the level of construction and remodeling activity which is expected to increase over the coming decade.

Although household growth is expected to slow slightly over the coming decade, the increase will create demand for residential construction, especially in the fastest growing areas in the South and West. Rising numbers of immigrants, as well as the children of the baby boomers, will generate demand for homes and rental apartments. In addition, a desire for larger homes with more amenities will fuel demand for move-up homes, as well as the renovation and expansion of older homes. Townhouses and condominiums in conveniently located suburban and urban settings also are desired types of properties.

Employment is expected to grow faster in nonresidential construction over the decade. Replacement of many industrial plants has been delayed for years, and a large number of structures will have to be replaced or remodeled. Construction of nursing homes and other residential homes for the elderly, as well as all types of healthcare facilities, will be needed to meet the need for more medical treatment facilities, especially by the growing elderly population. Construction of schools will continue to be needed, especially in the South and West where the population is growing the fastest. In other areas, however, replacing and renovating older schools will create jobs.

Employment in heavy and civil engineering construction is projected to increase due to growth in new highway, bridge, and street construction, as well as in maintenance and repairs to prevent further deterioration of the Nation's existing highways and bridges. Voters and legislators in most States and localities continue to approve spending on road construction, which will create jobs over the next decade. Another area of expected growth is in power line and related construction. Even with increased conservation and more efficient appliances, there is an increasing demand for power. New power plant construction and connecting these new facilities to the current power grids will increase demand for workers.

The largest number of new jobs is expected to be created in specialty trades contracting because it is the largest segment of the industry and because it is expected to grow about as fast as the rest of the construction industry. The number of jobs will grow as demand increases for subcontractors in new building and heavy construction, and as more workers are needed to repair and remodel existing homes, which specialty trade contractors are more likely to perform. Home improvement and repair construction is expected to continue even as new home construction slows. Remodeling should provide many new jobs because of a growing stock of old residential and nonresidential buildings. Many older, smaller homes will be remodeled to appeal to more affluent buyers interested in more space and amenities. Remodeling tends to be more labor-intensive than new construction. In addition, the construction industry, as well as all types of businesses and institutions, is increasingly contracting out the services of specialty trades workers instead of keeping these workers on their own payrolls.

The number of job openings in construction may fluctuate from year to year. New construction is usually cut back during periods when the economy is not expanding or interest rates are high. However, it is rare that all segments of the construction industry are down at the same time, allowing workers to switch from building houses to working on office building construction, depending on demand.

23

Although employment in construction trades as a whole is expected to grow about as fast as the industry average, the rate of growth will vary by trade. Employment of boilermakers; roofers; tile and marble setters; and construction and building inspectors is projected to grow faster than the industry average because their specialized services will be in greater demand. On the other hand, employment of carpet installers and floor sanders and finishers is expected to experience little or no growth as the demand for their specialties declines due to lower-cost options and changes in consumer preferences. Employment of rail-track laying and maintenance equipment operators and structural iron and steel workers is expected to grow more slowly than the construction industry as a whole as workers become more productive. Employment of paperhangers and floor layers, except carpet, wood, and hard tile, is expected to decline rapidly due to changes in consumer preferences, lower-cost options, and movement towards tile and prefinished hardwood floors.

Employment of construction managers is expected to grow as a result of the increasing complexity of construction work that needs to be managed, including the need to deal with the proliferation of laws dealing with building construction, worker safety, and environmental issues. Also, the growth of self-employment in this industry is leading to a larger number of managers who own small construction businesses.

*Job prospects.* Job opportunities are expected to be excellent in the construction industry, especially for construction trades workers, due to the need to replace the large number of workers anticipated to leave these occupations over the next decade, coupled with continued job growth. Furthermore, fewer people are expected to enter the construction trades, reflecting "blue collar bias," the perception that non-professional occupations are associated with relatively low status.

Experienced construction workers, and new entrants with a good work history or prior military service, should enjoy the best job prospects. A variety of factors can affect job prospects and competition for positions. Entering specialties requiring specific education, certification, or licensure are likely to improve job prospects for those willing to get the needed certifications, licenses, training, and education. Jobs that cause a worker to be at great heights, are physically demanding, or expose workers to extreme conditions are also more likely to have less competition for positions and often have conditions related to high replacement needs. Occupations that have few training needs are likely to have increased competition and less favorable job prospects.

Certain occupations should have particularly good job opportunities. Because of the difficulty in obtaining certification as a crane operator, some employers have been unable to fill all their construction equipment operator job openings. Electricians, plumbers, pipefitters, and steamfitters are also licensed occupations that should have a favorable outlook due to projected job growth. Roofers should have favorable opportunities due to job growth and difficult working conditions which leads to high replacement needs. Boilermakers; brickmasons, blockmasons and stonemasons; and structural and reinforcing iron and rebar workers should have excellent opportunities because of the skills required to perform their duties and the difficult working conditions. Installation and maintenance occupations—including line installers and heating and air-conditioning mechanics and installers—also should have especially favorable prospects because of a growing stock of homes that will require service to maintain interior systems. Construction managers who have a bachelor's degree in construction science, with an emphasis on construction management, and related work experience in construction management services firms, should have especially good prospects as well. Employment growth among administrative support occupations will continue to be limited by office automation. Construction laborers needing less training should face competition for work due to few barriers to entrance to this occupation. The outlook for carpenters will be heavily dependent upon residential construction activity, which is unlikely to grow as fast as in recent years. Painters should have good opportunities because of demand for their work, while paperhangers should have less favorable opportunities because of the reduced demand for their work.

## Table 4. Average earnings of nonsupervisory workers in construction, 2006

| Industry | Weekly | Hourly |
|---|---|---|
| **Total, private industry** . . . . . . . . . . . . . . . . . . | $568 | $16.76 |
| **Construction, total** . . . . . . . . . . . . . . . . . . | 781 | 20.02 |
| Construction of buildings . . . . . . . . . . . . . . . . . | 760 | 19.73 |
| Nonresidential building construction . . . . . . . . | 855 | 21.23 |
| Residential building . . . . . . . . . . . . . . . . . . . . | 682 | 18.39 |
| **Heavy and civil engineering construction**. . . | 873 | 20.32 |
| Highway, street, and bridge construction. . . . . | 904 | 20.67 |
| Utility system construction. . . . . . . . . . . . . . . . | 878 | 20.52 |
| Other heavy and civil engineering construction . . . . . . . . . . . . . . . . . . . . . . . . . . | 833 | 19.22 |
| Land subdivision . . . . . . . . . . . . . . . . . . . . . . | 688 | 17.84 |
| **Specialty trade contractors** . . . . . . . . . . . . . | 770 | 20.05 |
| Building equipment contractors . . . . . . . . . . . | 848 | 21.62 |
| Other specialty trade contractors. . . . . . . . . . | 768 | 18.77 |
| Building finishing contractors . . . . . . . . . . . . . | 714 | 19.18 |
| Foundation, structure, and building exterior contractors . . . . . . . . . . . . . . . . . . | 694 | 18.95 |

## Earnings

*Industry earnings.* Earnings in construction are higher than the average for all industries (table 4). In 2006, production or non-supervisory workers in construction averaged $20.02 an hour, or about $781 a week. In general, the construction trades workers needing more education and training, such as electricians and plumbers, get paid more than construction trades workers requiring less education and training, including laborers and helpers. Earnings also vary by the worker's education and experience, type of work, complexity of the construction project, and geographic location. Earnings of construction workers often are affected when poor weather prevents them from working. Traditionally, winter is the slack period for construction activity, especially in colder parts of the country, but there is a trend toward more year-round construction even in colder areas. Construction trades are dependent on one another to complete specific parts of a project—especially on large projects—so work delays affecting one trade can delay or stop the work of another trade. Earnings of selected occupations in construction in 2006 appear in table 5.

*Benefits and union membership.* About 15 percent of construction trades workers were union members or covered by union contracts, compared with 13 percent of workers throughout private industry. In general, union workers are paid more than non-

**Table 5. Median hourly earnings of the largest occupations in construction, May 2006**

| Occupation | Construction of buildings | Heavy and civil engineering construction | Specialty trade contractors | All industries |
|---|---|---|---|---|
| Construction managers | $34.59 | $36.90 | $35.54 | $35.43 |
| First-line supervisors/managers of construction trades and extraction workers | 26.23 | 25.96 | 25.77 | 25.89 |
| Plumbers, pipefitters, and steamfitters | 20.82 | 19.15 | 20.45 | 20.56 |
| Electricians | 19.62 | 20.17 | 20.45 | 20.97 |
| Operating engineers and other construction equipment operators | 18.29 | 18.90 | 18.29 | 17.74 |
| Carpenters | 18.07 | 17.97 | 17.50 | 17.57 |
| Cement masons and concrete finishers | 16.29 | 15.94 | 15.75 | 15.70 |
| Painters, construction and maintenance | 15.19 | 14.67 | 14.67 | 15.00 |
| Construction laborers | 13.15 | 13.24 | 12.60 | 12.66 |
| Office clerks, general | 11.03 | 11.08 | 11.02 | 11.40 |

union workers and have better benefits. Many different unions represent the various construction trades and form joint apprenticeship committees with local employers to supervise apprenticeship programs.

## Sources of Additional Information

Information about apprenticeships and training can be obtained from local construction firms and employer associations, the local office of the State employment service or apprenticeship agency, or the Bureau of Apprenticeship and Training, U.S. Department of Labor.

Currently, apprenticeships are available in over 500 occupations registered by the U.S. Department of Labor's National Apprenticeship system. Information on the Labor Department's registered apprenticeship system and links to State apprenticeship programs are available on the Internet at: **http://www.doleta.gov/atels_bat**

For additional information on jobs in the construction industry, contact:

➤ Associated Builders and Contractors, Workforce Development Department, 9th Floor, 4250 North Fairfax Dr., Arlington, VA 22203. Internet: **http://www.trytools.org**

➤ Associated General Contractors of America, Inc., 2300 Wilson Blvd., Suite 400., Arlington, VA 22201. Internet: **http://www.agc.org**

➤ National Association of Home Builders, Home Builders Institute, 1201 15th St. NW., Washington, DC 20005-2800. Internet: **http://www.hbi.org**

➤ National Center for Construction Education and Research, 3600 NW 43rd St., Building G, Gainesville, FL 32606. Internet: **http://www.nccer.org**

Additional information on occupations in construction may be found in the 2008-09 edition of the *Occupational Outlook Handbook*:

- Boilermakers
- Brickmasons, blockmasons, and stonemasons
- Carpenters
- Carpet, floor, and tile installers and finishers
- Cement masons, concrete finishers, segmental pavers, and terrazzo workers
- Construction and building inspectors
- Construction equipment operators
- Construction laborers
- Construction managers
- Drywall installers, ceiling tile installers, and tapers
- Electricians
- Elevator installers and repairers
- Glaziers
- Hazardous materials removal workers
- Heating, air-conditioning, and refrigeration mechanics and installers
- Insulation workers
- Material moving occupations
- Painters and paperhangers
- Pipelayers, plumbers, pipefitters, and steamfitters
- Plasterers and stucco masons
- Roofers
- Sheet metal workers
- Structural and reinforcing iron and metal workers

# Mining

## SIGNIFICANT POINTS

- Employment is projected to decline, but job opportunities in coal mining and nonmetallic mineral mining should be favorable for construction, extraction, and production workers.

- While many mining jobs can be entered directly from high school, the increasing sophistication of equipment and machinery requires a higher level of technical skill.

- Earnings are higher than the average for all industries.

## Nature of the Industry

The United States has been endowed with a wealth of natural resources that have fostered its growth and development. In the past, the discovery of resources such as gold and oil has resulted in major population shifts and rapid growth for formerly remote regions of the country, such as California, Texas, and Alaska. Extraction of these resources, and finding new deposits, is the work of the mining industry, which continues to provide the foundation for local economies in some regions.

*Goods and services.* Products of the mining industry generate the majority of energy used in this country, from electricity in homes to fuel in vehicles. Mined resources also serve as inputs for consumer goods and the processes and services provided by nearly all other industries, particularly in agriculture, manufacturing, transportation, utilities, communication, and construction. Uses of mined materials include coal, oil, and gas for energy, copper for wiring, gold for satellites and sophisticated electronic components, stone and gravel for construction of roads and buildings, and a variety of other minerals as ingredients in medicines and household products.

*Industry organization.* The mining industry contains five main industry segments, which are defined by the resources they produce: oil and gas extraction, coal mining, metal ore mining, nonmetallic mineral mining and quarrying, and support activities for mining.

The oil and gas extraction segment produces the petroleum and natural gas that heat homes, fuel cars, and power factories. Petroleum products are also the raw materials for plastics, chemicals, medicines, fertilizers, and synthetic fibers. Petroleum, commonly called crude oil or just oil, is a liquid formed under ground from the decay of plants and animals over millions of years through extreme heat and pressure. Occasionally, this decaying material becomes trapped under a layer of impermeable rock that prevents it from dispersing and creates a pocket of oil. Similar processes also produce natural gas, which can be found mixed with oil or in separate deposits. Finding and extracting the oil and gas in these pockets is the primary function of this industry segment.

Using a variety of methods, on land and at sea, small crews of specialized workers search for geologic formations that are likely to contain pockets of oil or gas. Sophisticated equipment and advances in computer technology have increased the productivity of exploration. Maps of potential deposits now are made using remote-sensing satellites. Seismic prospecting—a technique based on measuring the time it takes sound waves to travel through underground formations and return to the surface—has revolutionized oil and gas exploration. Computers and advanced software analyze seismic data to provide three-dimensional models of subsurface rock formations. Another method of searching for oil and gas is based on collecting and analyzing core samples of rock, clay, and sand in the earth's layers.

After scientific exploration studies indicate the possible presence of oil, a well must be drilled to prove oil is there. An oil company selects a well site and installs a derrick—a tower-like steel structure—to support the drilling equipment. A hole is drilled deep into the earth until oil or gas is found, or the company abandons the effort. Similar techniques are employed in offshore drilling, except that the drilling equipment is part of a steel platform that either sits on the ocean floor, or floats on the surface and is anchored to the ocean floor. Advancements in directional or horizontal drilling techniques, which allow increased access to potential reserves, have had a significant impact on drilling capabilities. Drilling begins vertically, but the drill bit can be turned so that drilling can continue at an angle of up to 90 degrees. This technique extends the drill's reach, enabling it to reach separate pockets of oil or gas. Because constructing new platforms is costly, this technique commonly is employed by offshore drilling operations.

Once the drilling reaches the oil or gas, extraction can begin as natural pressure forces the oil or gas up through the drill hole to the wellhead, where it enters separation and storage tanks. If natural pressure is not great enough to force the oil to the surface, pumps may be used. In some cases, water, steam, or gas may be injected into the oil deposit to improve recovery. The recovered oil is transported to refineries by pipeline, ship, barge, truck, or railroad. Natural gas usually is transported to processing plants by pipeline. While oil refineries may be many thousands of miles away from the producing fields, gas processing plants typically are near the fields, so that impurities—water, sulfur, and natural gas liquids—can be removed before the gas is piped to customers. The oil refining industry is considered a separate industry, and its activities are not covered here, even though many oil companies both extract and refine oil.

The coal mining industry segment produces coal, a fossil fuel that is used primarily for electric power generation and in the production of steel. Like oil, coal is formed over millions of years from plant and animal matter, but unlike oil, coal is a solid, and therefore miners must go into the earth to recover it. Many coal seams are located close to the surface, however, which makes the extraction of this resource easier.

Surface mining of coal typically uses the method known as strip mining, which is usually more cost-effective than underground mining and requires fewer workers to produce the same quantity of coal. In strip mining, workers use huge earthmoving equipment, such as power shovels or draglines, to scoop off the layers of soil and rock covering the coal seam. Once the coal is exposed, it is broken up by using explosives, and then smaller shovels lift it from the ground and load it into trucks. Mining companies are required by Federal, State, and local laws to restore the mined land after surface mining is completed; as a result, the overburden and topsoil are stored after removal so that they can be replaced and native vegetation replanted.

Underground mining is used when the coal deposit lies deep below the surface of the earth. When developing an underground mine, miners first must dig tunnels deep into the earth near the place where the coal is located. Depending on where the coal seam is in relation to the surface, tunnels may be vertical, horizontal, or sloping. Entries are constructed so that miners can get themselves and their equipment to the ore and carry it out, while allowing fresh air to enter the mine. Once dug to the proper depth, a mine's tunnels interconnect with a network of passageways going in many directions. Using the room-and-pillar method, miners remove sections of the coal as they work the coal seam from the tunnel entrance to the edge of the mine property, leaving columns of coal in place to help support the ceiling together with long steel bolts. This process is then reversed, and the remainder of the ore is extracted, as the miners work their way back out. In the case of longwall mining of coal, self-advancing roof supports, made of hydraulic jacks and metal plates, cover the area being mined. As coal is removed, the entire apparatus advances, allowing the ceiling in the mined area to cave in as the miners work back towards the tunnel entrance. Underground mining does not require as extensive a reclamation process as surface mining; however, mine operators and environmental engineers still must ensure that ground water remains uncontaminated and that abandoned mines do not collapse.

The metal ore mining industry segment covers the extraction of metal ores, primarily gold, silver, iron, copper, lead, and zinc. These naturally occurring minerals have a variety of industrial purposes: gold and silver are primarily used in jewelry and high-end electronics, iron is used to produce steel, copper is the main component of electrical wiring, lead is used in batteries, and zinc is used to coat iron and steel to reduce corrosion and as an alloy in the making of bronze and brass.

Most metals do not exist in concentrated form but rather in small traces in rock called "ore". Indistinguishable from regular rocks to the untrained eye, some ores are currently mined that contain only a fraction of a percent of metal. As a result, a massive amount of rock must be extracted from the ground in order to obtain a useable amount of metal. As a result of this, and because metal ores are less common than coal, metal mines can be much larger than coal mines and operate in more extreme environments—while coal mines are rarely more than a few hundred feet underground, gold mines can be over a mile below the surface.

Like coal mines, metal ore mines are found in both surface and underground varieties, depending on where the ore deposit is located. In addition to strip mining, surface ore mines also use the open-pit mining technique. These mines are huge holes in the ground that are mined by blasting rock from the sides and bottom with explosives, carrying out the broken up material in trucks, and then repeating the process. Open pit mines can grow to be hundreds of feet deep and several miles wide. Underground mining of ore is less common, typically only occurring when rich veins of ore are discovered or mineral prices are high enough to justify the added expense.

A significant amount of processing is needed to convert ore into usable metal. The mining industry includes initial mineral processing and preparation activities that are located together with mines as part of the extraction process. Further processing is classified under the primary metal manufacturing industry.

The nonmetallic mineral mining and quarrying industry segment covers a wide range of mineral extraction. The majority of the industry produces crushed stone, sand, and gravel for use in construction of roads and buildings. Other important minerals produced are clays, primarily for ceramics, water filtration, and cement making; gypsum, the primary material used in wallboard; salt, used in foodstuffs and as an ice remover; phosphate, for use in fertilizers; and sulfur, the main component of sulfuric acid, a major industrial input. Most of these minerals are found in abundance close to the surface, so underground mining is uncommon in this industry segment.

Surface mining for stone is also known as "quarrying". In quarrying operations, workers use machines to extract the stone. Stone—primarily granite and limestone—is quarried by using explosives to break material off from a massive rock surface. The resulting rocks are crushed further and shipped off for the production of asphalt or concrete. Some high-quality stone, such as marble and certain types of granite, is quarried in large blocks, known as dimension stone, and used as a building material by itself.

The final industry segment is support activities for mining. The activities of this industry are often the same as those of the other industry segments, but the work is done by contract companies that specialize in one aspect of resource extraction. For example, the majority of drilling for new oil wells is done by specialty drilling companies; other support companies specialize in exploration for new resource deposits or operation of offshore oil rigs.

***Recent developments.*** Many resources produced by the mining industry, particularly metals, oil, and gas, are relatively rare and are part of a global market that is highly sensitive to changes in prices. During the 1990s, commodity prices were relatively stable at low levels, causing production to stagnate and limiting the creation of new drilling and mining operations. In recent years, prices have increased dramatically, and exploration and production has likewise risen. Coal is less susceptible to world market conditions, but it also has seen price increases in recent years that have led to expanded production. Demand for nonmetallic minerals is primarily affected by the level of activity in the construction industry, particularly the building of new roads and highways.

Employment in the mining industry has been affected significantly by new technology and more sophisticated mining techniques that increase productivity. Most mining machines and control rooms are now automatic or computer-controlled, requiring fewer, if any, human operators. Many mines also operate with other sophisticated technology such as lasers and robotics, which further increases the efficiency of resource extraction. As a result, mine employment has been falling over time, particularly of workers who are involved in the extraction process itself. These new technologies and techniques have also increased specialization in the industry and led to expanded use of contract mining services companies for specific tasks. These companies also allow mining firms to more easily adjust production levels in response to changes in commodity prices.

## Working Conditions

*Hours.* Work schedules in the mining industry can vary widely. Some sites operate 24 hours a day, 7 days a week, particularly in oil and gas extraction and underground mines. This creates the opportunity for some mining workers to work long shifts several days in a row, and then have several days off. The remote location of some sites, such as offshore oil rigs, requires some workers to actually live onsite for weeks at a time, often working 12 hour shifts, followed by an extended leave period onshore. As a result of these conditions, part time opportunities are rare in this industry, but overtime is common; less than 3 percent of workers were part-time employees in 2006, while nearly 4 in 9 worked over 40 hours per week, and 1 in 3 over 50 hours per week. The average work week for a production worker in mining was 46.3 hours.

*Work Environment.* Work environments vary by occupation. Scientists and technicians work in office buildings and laboratories, as do executives and administrative and clerical workers. Engineers and managers usually split their time between offices and the mine or well site, where construction and extraction workers spend most of their time. Geologists who specialize in the exploration of natural resources to locate resource deposits may have to travel for extended periods to remote locations, in all types of climates.

Working conditions in mines, quarries, and well sites can be unusual and sometimes dangerous. Physical strength and stamina are necessary, as the work involves standing for long periods, lifting moderately heavy objects, and climbing and stooping to work with tools that often are oily and dirty. Workers in surface mines, quarries, and wells are subject to rugged outdoor work in all kinds of weather and climates, though some surface mines and quarries shut down in the winter because snow and ice covering the mine site makes work too dangerous. Oil and gas sites, because they are largely automated once deposits have been located, generally operate year round regardless of weather conditions, although offshore oil platforms are evacuated before the onset of dangerous weather, such as hurricanes. Surface mining, however, usually is less hazardous than underground mining.

Underground mines are damp and dark, and some can be very hot and noisy. At times, several inches of water may cover tunnel floors. Although underground mines have electric lights along main pathways, many tunnels are illuminated only by the lights on miner's hats. Workers in mines with very low roofs may have to work on their hands and knees, backs, or stomachs, in confined spaces. In underground mining operations, unique dangers include the possibility of a cave-in, mine fire, explosion, or exposure to harmful gases. In addition, dust generated by drilling in mines still places miners at risk of developing either of two serious lung diseases: pneumoconiosis, also called "black lung disease," from coal dust, or silicosis from rock dust. These days, dust levels in mines are closely monitored and occurrences of lung diseases are rare if proper procedures are followed. Underground miners have the option to have their lungs x-rayed on a periodic basis to monitor for the development of the disease. Workers who develop black lung disease or silicosis may be eligible for Federal aid.

Mine safety is regulated by the Federal Mine Safety and Health Act of 1977 and successive additional legislation, which has resulted in steadily declining rates of mining injuries and illnesses. Increased automation of mining and oil well operations has also reduced the number of workers needed in some of the more dangerous activities. As a result, in 2006, the rate of work-related injury and illness per 100 full-time workers was only 3.5 for the mining industry as a whole, lower than the rate of 4.4 in the entire private sector. Rates for the specific industry sectors were 2.0 in oil and gas extraction, 4.8 in coal mining, 3.1 in metal ore mining, 3.2 in nonmetallic mineral mining and quarrying, and 3.9 in support activities for mining.

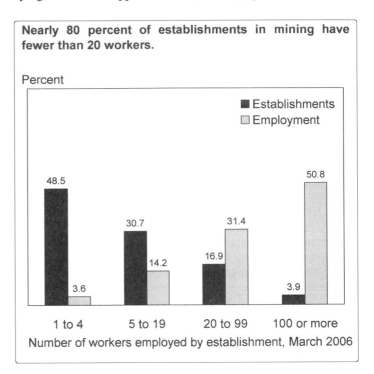

**Nearly 80 percent of establishments in mining have fewer than 20 workers.**

## Employment

There were approximately 619,000 wage and salary jobs in the mining industry in 2006; around 136,000 in oil and gas extraction; 79,000 in coal mining; 33,000 in metal mining; and 110,000 in nonmetallic mineral mining. Not included in these figures are the thousands of Americans who work abroad for U.S. companies conducting mining or drilling operations around the world. In addition to those employed directly by mining companies, there are also 262,000 jobs in the support activities for mining industry segment.

Mining jobs are heavily concentrated in the parts of the country where large resource deposits exist. Almost 3 out of 4 jobs in the oil and gas extraction industry are located in Texas, California, Oklahoma, and Louisiana. Although there were around 1,400 coal mining operations in 26 States in 2005, over two-thirds of all coal mines, and about half of all mine employees, were located in just three States—Kentucky, Pennsylvania, and West Virginia, according to the Energy Information Administration. Other States employing large numbers of coal miners are Alabama, Illinois, Indiana, Virginia, and Wyoming. Metal mining is more prevalent in the West and Southwest, particularly in Arizona, Nevada, and Montana, and iron ore mining in Minnesota and Michigan. Nonmetallic mineral mining is the most widespread, as quarrying of nonmetallic minerals, such as stone, clay, sand, and gravel, is done in nearly every State. In many rural areas, mining operations are the main employer. About 80 percent of mining establishments employ fewer than 20 workers (chart).

## Table 1. Employment of wage and salary workers in mining by occupation, 2006 and projected change, 2006-2016. (Employment in thousands)

| Occupation | Employment, 2006 | | Percent change, 2006-16 |
|---|---|---|---|
| | Number | Percent | |
| **All occupations** | 619 | 100.0 | -1.6 |
| **Management, business, and financial occupations** | 59 | 9.6 | -3.6 |
| Management occupations | 35 | 5.6 | -6.9 |
| Business and financial operations occupations | 25 | 4.0 | 1.0 |
| **Professional and related occupations** | 59 | 9.5 | 2.2 |
| Computer specialists | 8 | 1.3 | 2.8 |
| Engineers | 21 | 3.4 | 4.0 |
| Geoscientists, except hydrologists and geographers | 8 | 1.3 | 4.5 |
| Geological and petroleum technicians | 7 | 1.1 | 3.0 |
| **Office and administrative support occupations** | 60 | 9.6 | -6.5 |
| Financial clerks | 13 | 2.1 | -2.8 |
| Secretaries and administrative assistants | 18 | 2.8 | -7.8 |
| Office clerks, general | 11 | 1.8 | -2.5 |
| **Construction and extraction occupations** | 234 | 37.8 | -2.0 |
| First-line supervisors/managers of construction trades and extraction workers | 22 | 3.6 | -2.0 |
| Construction laborers | 7 | 1.2 | -0.6 |
| Operating engineers and other construction equipment operators | 29 | 4.6 | 2.8 |
| Electricians | 8 | 1.4 | 4.2 |
| Derrick operators, oil and gas | 18 | 2.9 | -6.3 |
| Rotary drill operators, oil and gas | 19 | 3.0 | -6.5 |
| Service unit operators, oil, gas, and mining | 26 | 4.2 | -6.5 |
| Earth drillers, except oil and gas | 6 | 0.9 | -1.3 |
| Continuous mining machine operators | 9 | 1.5 | 3.8 |
| Mine cutting and channeling machine operators | 7 | 1.2 | 3.5 |
| Rock splitters, quarry | 3 | 0.5 | 28.3 |
| Roof bolters, mining | 4 | 0.7 | 1.2 |
| Roustabouts, oil and gas | 39 | 6.4 | -5.3 |
| Helpers—Extraction workers | 19 | 3.1 | -3.1 |
| **Installation, maintenance, and repair occupations** | 50 | 8.0 | 4.8 |
| Mobile heavy equipment mechanics, except engines | 10 | 1.6 | 8.2 |
| Industrial machinery installation, repair, and maintenance workers | 26 | 4.2 | 6.5 |
| **Production occupations** | 53 | 8.6 | -0.5 |
| Welding, soldering, and brazing workers | 6 | 1.0 | 5.2 |
| Petroleum pump system operators, refinery operators, and gaugers | 11 | 1.8 | -3.1 |
| Separating, filtering, clarifying, precipitating, and still machine setters, operators, and tenders | 3 | 0.5 | 4.7 |
| Crushing, grinding, and polishing machine setters, operators, and tenders | 6 | 1.0 | -5.0 |
| Inspectors, testers, sorters, samplers, and weighers | 5 | 0.8 | -7.5 |
| Helpers—Production workers | 5 | 0.8 | -0.5 |
| **Transportation and material moving occupations** | 93 | 15.0 | -3.0 |
| Truck drivers, heavy and tractor-trailer | 28 | 4.5 | 1.5 |
| **Material moving occupations** | 56 | 9.0 | -5.6 |
| Excavating and loading machine and dragline operators | 14 | 2.2 | 3.6 |
| Pumping station operators | 17 | 2.8 | -12.7 |
| Wellhead pumpers | 13 | 2.1 | -13.2 |

Note: May not add to totals due to omission of occupations with small employment

## Occupations in the Industry

The mining industry requires many kinds of workers. In 2006, about half of all workers were employed in *construction and extraction* or *transportation and material-moving* occupations (table 1). Many construction and extraction workers are unique to the mining industry as many of them work with equipment that is only used in resource extraction.

*Professional and related occupations.* Before any mining can actually begin, a deposit of the resource needs to be found. This is the primary work of *geologists* and *geological and petroleum technicians*, who travel around the world using tools such as seismic data and core samples to locate deposits of sufficient size and purity for extraction. *Petroleum engineers* and *mining and geological engineers* then formulate the general plan for how the mining operation will be undertaken. They design, with *drafters and engineering technicians*, the general structure of the well or mine, and the most efficient method of extraction. These engineers generally supervise mine and well activities throughout the entire lifecycle of the project, troubleshooting any problems and ensuring smooth operations. They also work with *environmental engineers*, who ensure that mine or well sites meet stringent Federal, State, and local regulations. Environmental regulations make obtaining permits for new projects increasingly difficult and impose substantial penalties should projects fail to meet standards, making proper environmental remediation a necessity for any mining operation. Environmental engineers also plan reclamation projects when product extraction is complete. Other engineers who ensure smooth working operations include *industrial engineers*, who manage the use of workers and equipment for optimum productivity, and *mechanical engineers*, who ensure that complicated systems for cooling and ventilation are designed and constructed properly.

*Extraction, transportation, and material moving occupations.* The main work of resource extraction is done by the workers who operate the equipment that builds the mine or well and that removes the resource when it is reached. Most occupations are unique to oil and gas extraction, underground mining operations, or surface mining operations.

Most oil field operations are performed by rotary drilling crews of four or five workers. *Rotary drill operators* supervise the crew and operate machinery that controls drilling speed and pressure. *Rotary-rig engine operators* are in charge of engines that provide the power for drilling and hoisting. Second in charge, *derrick operators* work on small platforms high on rigs to help run pipe in and out of well holes and operate the pumps that circulate mud through the pipe. *Rotary-driller helpers*, also known as *roughnecks*, guide the lower ends of pipe to well openings and connect pipe joints and drill bits.

Though not necessarily part of the drilling crew, *roustabouts*, or general laborers, and *helpers* do general oilfield maintenance and construction work, such as cleaning tanks and building roads, throughout the entire life cycle of the oil well. Once the well is complete and operational, *pumpers* operate and maintain the equipment that regulates the flow of oil out of the well.

Most workers involved in gas processing are operators. *Gas treaters* tend automatically controlled treating units that remove water and other impurities from natural gas. *Gas-pumping-station operators* tend compressors that raise the pressure of gas for transmission in pipelines. Both types of workers can be assisted by *gas-compressor operators*.

The workers involved in mining coal, metal, or minerals undergound vary based on the mining method used. In conventional underground mining, typically used currently only when mining metal ores, *drilling-machine operators* drill holes in the ore where the *blasters* place explosives. This potentially dangerous work requires workers to follow safety procedures, such as making sure everyone is clear of the area before the explosives are detonated. After the blast, *loading-machine operators* scoop up the material using a power shovel and deposit it in a truck for transport to the surface. Self contained load-haul-dump machines are also used to both scoop up and transport the ore.

The continuous mining method, used with coal and other soft minerals, eliminates the drilling and blasting operations of conventional mining through the use of a machine called a continuous miner. Traditionally, a *continuous-mining machine operator* sits or lies in a machine's cab and operates levers that cut or rip out ore and load it directly onto a conveyor or shuttle car. However, the use of remote-controlled continuous mining machines—which have increased safety considerably—now allows an operator to control the machine from a distance.

In longwall mining, which is similar to continuous mining, *longwall-machine operators* run large machines with rotating drums that automatically shear ore and load it on a conveyor. At the same time, hydraulic jacks reinforce the roof of the tunnel. As ore is cut, the jacks are hydraulically winched forward, supporting the roof as they move along.

Many other workers are needed to operate safe and efficient underground mines. Before miners are allowed underground, a *mine safety inspector* checks the work area for such hazards as loose roofs, dangerous gases, and inadequate ventilation. If safety standards are not met, the inspector prohibits the mine from operating until conditions are made safe. *Rock-dust machine operators* spray the mine walls and floor to hold down dust, which can be a safety hazard. *Roof bolters* operate the machines that automatically install roof support bolts to prevent roof cave-ins, the biggest cause of mining injuries. *Brattice builders* construct doors, walls, and partitions in tunnel passageways to force air into the work areas.

In surface mining, most miners operate huge machines that either remove the earth above the ore deposit, or dig and load the ore onto trucks. The number of workers required to operate a surface mine depends on the amount of overburden, or earth, above the ore seam. In many surface mines, the overburden is first drilled and blasted. *Overburden stripping operators* or *dragline operators* then scoop the earth away to expose the coal or metal ore. Some draglines are among the largest land machines on earth.

Next, *loading-machine operators* rip the exposed ore from the seam and dump it into trucks to be driven to the preparation plant. *Tractor operators* use bulldozers to move earth and ore and to remove boulders or other obstructions. *Truck drivers* haul ore to railroad sidings or to preparation plants and transport supplies to mines.

Workers at quarries have duties similar to those of surface miners. Using jackhammers and wedges, *rock splitters* remove pieces of stone from a rock mass. *Dredge operators* and *dipper tenders* operate power-driven dredges to mine sand, gravel, and other materials from beneath the surfaces of lakes, rivers, and streams. Using power-driven cranes with dragline buckets, *dragline operators* excavate or move sand, gravel, and other materials.

***Construction, installation, maintenance, and repair occupations.*** Other workers, who are not directly involved in the ex-

traction process, work in and around wells, mines, and quarries. For example, *mechanics* are needed to repair and maintain the wide variety of machinery, and *electricians* are needed to check and install electrical wiring. Mechanical and electrical repair work has become increasingly complex, as machinery and other equipment have become computerized. *Carpenters* construct and maintain benches, bins, and stoppings (barricades to prevent airflow through a tunnel). These workers generally need specialized training to work under unusual conditions. Mechanics in underground mines, for example, may have to repair machines while on their knees, with only their headlamps to illuminate the working area.

## Training and Advancement

There are few formal education requirements for new extraction workers, although a considerable amount of job training and experience is needed before workers can perform most duties or advance to more skilled positions. Skilled maintenance and construction workers usually need several years of vocational training in their field, while workers in professional occupations need at least a bachelor's degree.

*Extraction workers.* Workers in extraction occupations usually must be at least 18 years old, be in good physical condition, and pass a drug test. A high school diploma is not necessarily required, but is usually preferred; some companies also require workers to pass a basic skills test. Most workers start as helpers to experienced workers and learn skills on the job; however, formal training is becoming more important, as more technologically advanced machinery and methods are used. Given the increasing complexity of operations and the sophisticated nature of technology used today, employers now demand a higher level of skill and adaptability, including the ability to work with computers and other more complex equipment. As a result, some employers prefer to hire recent graduates of high school vocational programs in mining or graduates of junior college or technical school programs in mine technology. Such programs usually are found only at schools in mining areas.

Because of the unique dangers in mining operations, workers also need extensive safety training. The Federal Mine Safety and Health Act of 1977 mandates that each U.S. mine have an approved worker training program in health and safety issues. Each plan must include at least 40 hours of basic safety training for new miners with no experience in underground mines, and 24 hours for new miners in surface mines. In addition to new miner training, each miner must receive at least 8 hours of refresher safety training a year, and miners assigned to new jobs must receive safety training relating to their new task. The U.S. Mine Safety and Health Administration (MSHA) also conducts classes on health, safety, and mining methods, and some mining machinery manufacturers offer courses in machine operation and maintenance as well. The MSHA has recently put interactive training materials on its Website, and also has translated many of the training materials into Spanish. Increasingly, mines use more high-tech tools for miner training, such as machinery simulators and virtual reality simulators. By simulating actual mine conditions and emergencies, mine workers are better prepared and companies can instantly assess a mineworker's progress and skills.

As workers gain more experience, they can advance to higher paying jobs requiring greater skill. A mining machine operator's helper, for example, might become an operator, or a roughneck may become a derrick operator. Due to the extreme environment and critical nature of the work, offshore oil crews generally are more experienced than land crews. Many companies will not employ someone who has no knowledge of oilfield operations to work on an offshore rig, so workers who have gained experience as part of a land crew might advance to offshore operations. Positions are usually filled on the basis of seniority and ability. Miners with significant experience or special training also can become mine safety, health, and compliance officers, whose duties include mine safety inspection. According to MSHA, a mine safety, health, and compliance officer needs at least 5 years' experience as a miner, or a degree in mining engineering.

*Construction, maintenance, and repair occupations.* Most skilled occupations in construction or maintenance require several years of vocational training or experience in the occupation. Many schools in areas with mining operations often offer specialized mine technology programs. Enrollment in these programs can lead to a certificate in mine technology after 1 year, an associate degree after 2 years, or a bachelor's degree after 4 years. Courses cover areas such as mine ventilation, roof bolting, and machinery repairs. Specialized training on equipment use and repair may also be provided by equipment manufacturers.

*Professional and related occupations.* For professional positions, a bachelor's degree is required, usually in engineering or one of the physical sciences. A number of colleges and universities have mining schools or departments and programs in mining or oil and gas extraction, particularly those in States with large numbers of mining or oil and gas field operations. Environmental positions require regulatory knowledge and a strong natural science background, or a background in a technical field, such as environmental engineering or hydrology. To date, most environmental professionals have been drawn from the ranks of engineers and scientists who have had experience in the mining industry. Universities and mining schools have introduced more environmental coursework into their programs, and mining firms are hiring professionals from existing environment-related disciplines and training them to meet their companies' needs.

## Outlook

Employment in mining will decrease. The growing U.S. and world economies will continue to demand larger quantities of the raw materials produced by mining, but the increased output will be able to be met by new technologies and new extraction techniques that increase productivity and require fewer workers.

*Employment change.* Wage and salary employment in mining is expected to decline by 2 percent through the year 2016, compared with 11 percent growth projected for the entire economy. Mining production is tied closely with prices and demand for the raw materials produced, and as prices for oil, gas, and metals have risen rapidly in recent years, production and employment in the industry have also grown. Further short-term increases in employment may be likely if prices remain high, but over the course of the projections period, technological advances will increase productivity and cause employment declines in the mining industry as a whole.

Petroleum and natural gas exploration and development in the United States depends upon prices for these resources and the size of accessible reserves. Stable and favorable prices are needed to allow companies enough revenue to expand exploration and production projects. Rising worldwide demand for oil and gas—particularly from developing countries such as India

and China—is likely to cause prices to remain high and generate the needed incentive for oil and gas producers to continue exploring and developing oil and gas reserves, at least in the short run. U.S. reserves of oil and gas should remain adequate to support increased production over the projection period. Many U.S. oil services companies operate in overseas oil and gas fields as well, and are therefore not limited by domestic reserves.

Environmental concerns, accompanied by strict regulation and limited access to protected Federal lands, also continue to have a major impact on this industry. Restrictions on drilling in environmentally sensitive areas and other environmental constraints should continue to limit exploration and development, both onshore and offshore. These factors will cause employment in oil and gas extraction to decline by 2 percent through 2016. However, changes in policy could expand exploration and drilling for oil and natural gas in currently protected areas and add jobs, especially in Alaska and the Federally-controlled Outer Continental Shelf.

Demand for coal will increase as coal remains the primary fuel source for electricity generation. Although environmental concerns exist regarding coal power—burning coal releases pollutants and carbon dioxide—few alternatives exist on a scale large enough to meet the fuel demand of utilities. Natural gas burns cleaner than coal, but coal power plants equipped with scrubbers reduce this disadvantage, and both fuels emit greenhouse gases. Recent increases in the price of natural gas have also caused some electricity producers to delay their conversion to natural gas, which is helping to maintain demand for coal. Future increased use of nuclear power or renewable energy sources, such as solar or wind power, could reduce demand for coal, but over the projection period neither is expected to increase rapidly enough to contribute significantly to U.S. energy supplies.

Advances in mining technology will adversely affect employment in coal mining as new machinery and processes increase worker productivity. Fewer workers are required for operation and maintenance of new mining machines that are operated remotely by computer and that self-diagnose mechanical problems. Productivity in coal mining has increased with advances in longwall and surface mining and improvements in transportation and processing that require fewer workers.

Environmental concerns will continue to affect mining operations. Increasingly, government regulations are restricting access to land and restricting the type of mining that is performed in order to protect native plants and animals and decrease the amount of water and air pollution. As population growth expands further into the countryside, new developments and mine operators are competing for land, and residents are increasing their opposition to nearby mining activities. These concerns, together with depletion of the most accessible coal deposits in the East, will result in a shift in coal production. Coal mining will increase in the Central, and particularly the Western, United States and decrease in the East. Overall, coal mining employment will experience little employment change as rising demand for coal is met with productivity gains from more efficient and automated production operations

Employment in mining for metal ores is expected to grow by about 9 percent through 2016 as continued high prices for metals will lead to increased production. Because metals are used primarily as raw materials by other industries, such as telecommunications, construction, steel, aerospace, and automobile manufacturing, the strength of the metal ore mining industry is greatly affected by the strength of these industries. Most metals are sold and bought in a world market, so demand stems not only from domestic industries but also from fast growing industries in developing countries. Demand from these countries has caused prices for many metals to increase substantially in recent years. This has caused U.S. mining companies to expand production at existing mines and restart production at some mines that were closed in the past when low metal prices made them unprofitable. However, employment growth in metal ore mining will be moderated by many of the same technological advances and environmental concerns as coal mining.

Employment in nonmetallic mineral mining should increase by 6 percent because of continued demand for crushed stone, sand, and gravel used in construction activities. Like the metal ore mining industry, the nonmetallic mineral mining industry is influenced by the strength of the industries that use its outputs in the manufacture of their products. Nonmetallic minerals are used to make concrete and asphalt for road construction and also as materials in residential and nonresidential building construction. The nonmetallic mineral mining industry did not experience the past employment declines of the other mining industries, largely because of demand increases from the fast growing construction industry. The demand for crushed stone and gravel should remain strong over the next few years because of demand for residential housing, roads, and airports, but productivity increases should limit employment growth. Transportation costs for stone, sand, and gravel are high so mining of them is spread across the country and therefore not as susceptible to industry consolidation. This geographical spread, together with the small size of many mines, causes some mines to operate only during warm months. Many workers laid off during the winter find jobs in other industries and must be replaced when the mines reopen. Jobs in nonmetallic mineral mining attract many migrant workers and those looking for summer employment.

*Job prospects.* Despite an overall decline in mining industry employment, job opportunities in most occupations should be very good. Because workers in the mining industry are older than average, some companies may have trouble coping with the loss of many experienced workers to retirement at a time when the industry is expanding production. At the same time, past declines in employment in the industry have dissuaded potential workers from considering employment in the industry, and many colleges and universities have shut down programs designed to train professionals for work in mining. Employment opportunities will be best for those with previous experience and with technical skills, especially qualified professionals and extraction workers who have experience in oil field operations and who can work with new technology.

## Table 2. Average earnings of nonsupervisory workers in mining, 2006

| Industry segment | Weekly | Hourly |
|---|---|---|
| **Total, private industry** . . . . . . . . . . . . . . . . . . | $568 | $16.76 |
| **Mining** . . . . . . . . . . . . . . . . . . . . . . . . . . . . . . | 939 | 20.29 |
| Coal mining . . . . . . . . . . . . . . . . . . . . . . . . . . | 1093 | 22.08 |
| Metal ore mining . . . . . . . . . . . . . . . . . . . . . . | 974 | 22.39 |
| Oil and gas extraction . . . . . . . . . . . . . . . . . . | 921 | 21.40 |
| Support activities for mining . . . . . . . . . . . . . | 921 | 19.65 |
| Nonmetallic mineral mining and quarrying . . . | 863 | 18.74 |

## Earnings

*Industry earnings.* Average earnings of wage and salary workers in mining were significantly higher than the average for all industries. In 2006, production workers, earned $21.40 an hour in oil and gas extraction, $22.08 an hour in coal mining, $22.39 an hour in metal ore mining, and $18.74 an hour in nonmetallic minerals mining, compared to the private industry average of $16.76 an hour (table 2). Earnings in selected occupations in specified mining industries appear in table 3.

*Benefits and union membership.* About 8 percent of mineworkers were union members or were covered by union contracts in 2006, compared with about 12 percent of workers throughout private industry. Most union members were employed in the coal, metal ore, and nonmetallic mineral mining industries, where 19 percent of workers were union members in 2006. Only 1 percent of workers were unionized in the other mining industries. Union coal miners are primarily represented by the United Mine Workers of America (UMWA). The United Steelworkers of America, the International Union of Operating Engineers, and other unions also represent miners.

## Sources of Additional Information

For additional information about careers and training in the mining industry, contact:

➤ American Geological Institute, 4220 King St., Alexandria, VA 22302. Internet: **http://www.agiweb.org**

➤ American Petroleum Institute, 1220 L St. NW, Washington, DC 20005-4070. Internet: **http://www.energyprofessions.org**

➤ Mine Safety and Health Administration, 1100 Wilson Blvd., Arlington, VA 22209-3939. Internet: **http://www.msha.gov**

➤ National Mining Association, 101 Constitution Ave. NW., Suite 500 East., Washington, DC 20001. Internet: **http://www.nma.org**

➤ United Mine Workers of America, 8315 Lee Highway, Fairfax, VA 22031. Internet: **http://www.umwa.org**

## Table 3. Median hourly earnings of the largest occupations in mining, May 2006

| Occupation | Mining, except for oil and gas | Oil and gas extraction | Support activities for mining | All industries |
|---|---|---|---|---|
| General and operations managers | $39.91 | $51.17 | $38.81 | $40.97 |
| First-line supervisors/managers of construction trades and extraction workers | 30.08 | 29.39 | 27.03 | 25.89 |
| Rotary drill operators, oil and gas | - | 19.50 | 18.43 | 18.49 |
| Service unit operators, oil, gas, and mining | - | 17.65 | 15.57 | 15.82 |
| Operating engineers and other construction equipment operators | 17.48 | 19.32 | 15.17 | 17.74 |
| Helpers—extraction workers | 17.20 | 12.13 | 13.87 | 13.79 |
| Truck drivers, heavy and tractor-trailer | 16.03 | 13.93 | 14.67 | 16.85 |
| Excavating and loading machine and dragline operators | 16.02 | - | 14.05 | 15.83 |
| Derrick operators, oil and gas | - | 15.73 | 17.53 | 17.42 |
| Roustabouts, oil and gas | - | 12.65 | 12.47 | 12.36 |

Detailed information on the following occupations in the mining industry may be found in the 2008-09 *Occupational Outlook Handbook:*

- Construction equipment operators
- Engineering and natural sciences managers
- Engineers

- Geoscientists
- Heavy vehicle and mobile equipment service technicians and mechanics
- Industrial machinery mechanics and maintenance workers
- Material-moving occupations
- Occupational health and safety specialists and technicians
- Truck drivers and driver/sales workers

# Utilities

## SIGNIFICANT POINTS

- Almost half of the utilities workforce will be nearing retirement age within the next 10 years, resulting in excellent opportunities for qualified entrants.

- Persons with college training or advanced technical education will have the best opportunities.

- Skills developed in one segment of the industry may not be transferable to other segments because the utilities industry consists of many different companies and products.

- Earnings for production workers are significantly higher than in most other industries.

## Nature of the Industry

*Goods and services.* The simple act of walking into a restroom, turning on the light, and washing your hands, uses the products of perhaps four different utilities. Electricity powers the light, water supply systems provide water for washing, wastewater treatment plants treat the sewage, and natural gas or electricity heats the water. Some government establishments also provide electric, gas, water, and wastewater treatment services and employ a significant number of workers in similar jobs, but they are part of government and not included in this industry. Information concerning government employment in utilities is included in the *Career Guide to Industries* statements on Federal Government and State and local government, except education and health.

*Industry organization.* The utilities sector is comprised of three distinctly different industries.

*Electric power generation, transmission, and distribution.* This segment includes firms engaged in the generation, transmission, and distribution of electric power. Electric plants harness highly pressurized steam, flowing water, or some force of nature to spin the blades of a turbine, which is attached to an electric generator. Coal is the dominant fuel used to generate steam in electric power plants, followed by nuclear power, natural gas, petroleum, and other energy sources. Hydroelectric generators are powered by the release of the tremendous pressure of water existing at the bottom of a dam or near a waterfall. Renewable sources of electric power—including geothermal, wind, and solar energy—are expanding rapidly, but only make up a small percentage of total generation.

Legislative changes and industry competition have created new classes of firms that generate and sell electricity. Some industrial plants have their own electricity-generating facilities, capable of producing more power than they require. Those that sell their excess power to utilities or to other industrial plants are called non-utility generators (NUGs). Independent power producers are a type of NUG that are electricity-generating plants designed to take advantage of both industry deregulation and the latest generating technology to compete directly with utilities for industrial and other wholesale customers.

Transmission lines supported by huge towers connect generating plants with industrial customers and substations. At substations, the electricity's voltage is reduced and made available for household and small business use via distribution lines, which usually are carried by telephone poles.

*Natural gas distribution.* Natural gas, a clear odorless gas, is found underground, often near or associated with crude oil reserves. Exploration and extraction of natural gas is part of the oil and gas extraction industry, covered elsewhere in the *Career Guide to Industries*. Once found and brought to the surface, it is transported throughout the United States, Canada, and Mexico by gas transmission companies using pressurized pipelines. Local distribution companies take natural gas from the pipeline, depressurize it, add its odor, and operate the system that delivers the gas from transmission pipelines to industrial, residential, and commercial customers. Industrial customers, such as chemical and paper manufacturing firms, account for almost a third of natural gas consumption. Electric power plants, residential customers who use gas for heating and cooking, and commercial businesses—such as hospitals and restaurants—account for most of the remaining consumption.

*Water, sewage, and other systems.* Water utilities treat and distribute nearly 34 billion gallons per day to customers nationwide. Water is collected from various sources such as rivers, lakes, and wells. After collection, water is treated, and sold for residential, industrial, agricultural, commercial, and public use. Depending on the population served by the water system, the utility may be a small plant in a rural area that requires the occasional monitoring of a single operator or a huge system of reservoirs, dams, pipelines, and treatment plants requiring the coordinated efforts of hundreds of people. Sewage treatment facilities operate sewer systems or plants that collect, treat, and dispose of waste from homes and industries. Other utilities include steam and air-conditioning supply utilities, which produce and sell steam, heated air, and cooled air.

*Recent developments.* Utilities and the services they provide are so vital to everyday life that they are considered public goods and are typically heavily regulated. Most utility companies that distribute to consumers operate as regulated monopolies because utility distribution tends to require a large investment in plant and equipment and it is generally not desirable to have several competing systems of pipes or power lines in most areas. Since these companies do not face competition, they are regulated by public utility commissions that ensure that companies act in the public interest and set the rates that are charged. However, legislative changes in recent years have established and promoted competition in some parts of the utilities industry. Wholesale providers of electricity now face competition from a number of non-utility generators.

Many utility companies are municipally owned. In the natural gas industry, for example, a majority of the distribution companies in the United States are municipally owned. However, they serve just a fraction of the nationwide customers. Historically, utilities serving large cities had sufficient numbers of customers to justify the large investment in infrastructure needed to run a utility, and so private, investor-owned companies established utility service. In rural areas, where the small number of customers in need of services did not provide an adequate return for private investors, the State or local government, or rural co-operative associations, established utility service.

The various segments of the utilities industry vary in the degree to which their workers are involved in production activities, administration and management, or research and development. Industries such as water supply, that employ relatively few workers, employ more production workers and plant operators. On the other hand, electric utilities generally operate larger plants using very expensive, high technology equipment, and thus employ more professional and technical personnel.

The utilities industry is unique in that urban areas with many inhabitants generally have relatively few utility companies. For example, there were about 52,349 community water systems in the United States in 2006 serving more than 281 million people. The 48,275 smallest water systems served only 52 million people while the 4,074 largest systems served more than 229 million. This shows that economies of scale in the utilities industry allow a few large companies to serve large numbers of customers in metropolitan areas more efficiently than many smaller companies. In fact, some utility companies, predominately serving large metropolitan areas, offer more than one type of utility service to their customers.

Unlike most industries, the utilities industry imports and exports only a small portion of its product. To some degree, this is because of the great difficulty in transporting electricity, freshwater, and natural gas. It is also the result of a national policy that utilities should be self-sufficient, without dependence on imports for the basic services our country requires. However, easing trade restrictions, increased pipeline capacity, and shipping natural gas in liquefied form have made international trade in utilities more feasible, especially with Canada and Mexico.

In 2005, Congress passed a new Energy Policy Act, which is the first major legislation on energy since 1992. This will be a major force in the industry through 2016. It was designed to promote conservation and use of cleaner technologies in energy production through higher efficiency standards and tax credits. It is expected that several new power plants will be built as a result of this legislation, including new clean-burning coal and nuclear facilities.

## Working Conditions

*Hours.* Electricity, gas, and water are used continuously throughout each day. As a result, split, weekend, and night shifts are common for utility workers. The average workweek for production workers in utilities was 41.4 hours in 2006, compared with 33.4 hours for all trade, transportation, and utilities industries, and 33.9 hours for all private industries. Employees often must work overtime to accommodate peaks in demand and to repair damage caused by storms, cold weather, accidents, and other occurrences. The industry employs relatively few part-time workers.

*Work Environment.* The hazards of working with electricity, natural gas, treatment chemicals, and wastes can be substantial, but generally are avoided by following rigorous safety procedures. Protective gear such as rubber gloves and rubber sleeves, non-sparking maintenance equipment, and body suits with breathing devices designed to filter out any harmful fumes are mandatory for work in dangerous environs. Employees also undergo extensive training on working with hazardous materials and utility company safety measures.

In 2006, the utilities industry reported 4.1 cases of work-related injury or illness per 100 full-time workers, compared with an average of 4.4 cases for all private industries.

## Employment

Utilities had 549,000 wage and salary jobs in 2006. Electric power generation, transmission, and distribution provided about 7 in 10 jobs, as shown in table 1.

**Table 1. Distribution of wage and salary employment in nongovernment utilities, 2006**
(Employment in thousands)

| Industry | Employment | Percent |
|---|---|---|
| **Utilities, total** | 549 | 100.0 |
| Electric power generation, transmission, and distribution | 397 | 72.3 |
| Natural gas distribution | 106 | 19.3 |
| Water, sewage, and other systems | 46 | 8.4 |

The diversity of production processes in the utilities industry was reflected in the size of the establishments that made up the industry. For example, the electric power and natural gas distribution sectors consisted of relatively large plants. In 2006, electric power generation, transmission, and distribution plants employed an average of about 49 workers per establishment. On the other hand, the water, sewage, and other systems sector employed an average of only 8 workers per establishment (table 2).

Although many establishments are small, the majority of utilities jobs were in establishments with 100 or more workers (chart).

**Table 2. Nongovernment establishments in utilities and average employment per establishment, 2006**

| Occupation | Number of establishments | Employment per establishment |
|---|---|---|
| **Total, all utilities** | 16,100 | 34 |
| Electric power generation, transmission, and distribution | 8,000 | 49 |
| Natural gas distribution | 2,600 | 40 |
| Water, sewage, and other systems | 5,500 | 8 |

## Occupations in the Industry

About 226,000 jobs—approximately 41 percent of all wage and salary jobs in the utilities industry—were in production or installation, maintenance, and repair occupations in 2006 (table 3). About 21 percent of jobs were in office and administrative support occupations; 14 percent were in professional and related occupations; and 12 percent were in management, business, and financial occupations. The remaining jobs were in construction, transportation, sales, and service occupations.

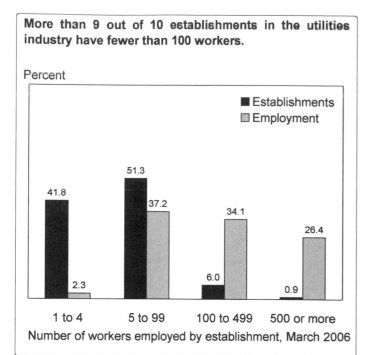

**More than 9 out of 10 establishments in the utilities industry have fewer than 100 workers.**

Percent

- ■ Establishments
- □ Employment

| | 1 to 4 | 5 to 99 | 100 to 499 | 500 or more |
|---|---|---|---|---|
| Establishments | 41.8 | 51.3 | 6.0 | 0.9 |
| Employment | 2.3 | 37.2 | 34.1 | 26.4 |

Number of workers employed by establishment, March 2006

*Production and installation, maintenance, and repair occupations.* Workers in these occupations install and maintain pipelines and powerlines, operate and fix plant machinery, and monitor treatment processes. For example, *electrical powerline installers and repairers* install and repair cables or wires used in electrical power or distribution systems. They install insulators, wooden poles, transformers, and light- or heavy-duty transmission towers. *First-line supervisors and managers* directly supervise and coordinate the activities of production and repair workers. These supervisors coordinate workload and work assignments and help to ensure a safe and productive work environment.

Production occupations include *power plant operators*, *power distributors and dispatchers*, and *water and liquid waste treatment plant operators*. *Power plant operators* control or operate machinery, such as stream-driven turbine generators, to generate electric power, often using control boards or semi-automatic equipment. *Power distributors and dispatchers* coordinate, regulate, or distribute electricity or steam in generating stations, over transmission lines to substations, and over electric power lines. *Water and liquid waste treatment plant and system operators* control the process of treating water or wastewater, take samples of water for testing, and may perform maintenance of treatment plants.

*Industrial machinery mechanics* install, repair, and maintain machinery in power generating stations, gas plants, and water treatment plants. They repair and maintain the mechanical components of generators, waterwheels, water-inlet controls, and piping in generating stations; steam boilers, condensers, pumps, compressors, and similar equipment in gas manufacturing plants; and equipment used to process and distribute water for public and industrial uses.

*General maintenance and repair workers* perform work involving a variety of maintenance skills to keep machines, mechanical equipment, and the structure of an establishment in repair. Generally found in small establishments, these workers have duties that may involve pipefitting, boilermaking, electrical work, carpentry, welding, and installing new equipment.

*Office and administrative support occupations.* These occupations account for about a quarter of jobs in the utilities industry. *Customer service representatives* interview applicants for water, gas, and electric service. They talk with customers by phone or in person and receive orders for installation, activation, discontinuance, or change in service. *General office clerks* may do bookkeeping, typing, office machine operation, and filing. *Utilities meter readers* read electric, gas, water, or steam consumption meters visually or remotely using radio transmitters and record the volume used by residential and industrial customers. Financial clerks, such as *bookkeeping, accounting, and auditing clerks*, compute, classify, and record numerical data to keep financial records complete. They perform any combination of routine calculating, posting, and verifying duties to obtain primary financial data for use in maintaining accounting records.

*Professional and managerial occupations.* Professional and related occupations in this industry include *engineers* and *computer specialists*. *Engineers* develop technologies that allow, for example, utilities to produce and transmit gas and electricity more efficiently and water more cleanly. They also may develop improved methods of landfill or wastewater treatment operations in order to maintain compliance with government regulations. *Computer specialists* develop computer systems to automate utility processes; provide plant simulators for operator training; and improve operator decision making. *Engineering technicians* assist engineers in research activities and may conduct some research independently.

Managers and administrators in the utilities industry plan, organize, direct, and coordinate management activities. They often are responsible for maintaining an adequate supply of electricity, gas, water, steam, or sanitation service.

**Training and Advancement**

Utilities provide career opportunities for persons with varying levels of experience and education. However, because the utilities industry consists of many different companies and products, skills developed in one segment of the industry may not be transferable to other segments.

High school graduates qualify for many entry-level production jobs. In some cases, however, safety and security regulations require higher standards for employment, such as documented proof of the skills and abilities necessary to complete the work. As a result, a degree from a college, university, or technical school may be required. Production workers may start as laborers or in other unskilled jobs and, by going through an apprenticeship program and gaining on-the-job experience, advance into better-paying positions that require greater skills or have greater responsibility.

Substantial advancement is possible even within a single occupation. For example, power plant operators may move up through several levels of responsibility until they reach the highest paying operator jobs. Advancement in production occupations generally requires mastery of advanced skills on the job, usually with some formal training provided by the employer or through additional vocational training at a 2-year technical college or trade school.

Most computer, engineering, and technician jobs require technical education after high school, although opportunities exist for persons with degrees ranging from an associate degree to a doctorate. These workers are usually familiar with company objectives and production methods which, combined with college education, equip them with many of the tools necessary

**Table 3. Employment of wage and salary workers in utilities by occupation, 2006 and projected change, 2006-2016.**
(Employment in thousands)

| Occupation | Employment, 2006 | | Percent change, 2006-16 |
|---|---|---|---|
| | Number | Percent | |
| All occupations ........................................... | 549 | 100.0 | -5.7 |
| **Management, business, and financial occupations**............................... | 66 | 12.1 | -8.7 |
| Top executives .............................................. | 11 | 1.9 | -15.6 |
| Administrative services managers .............. | 2 | 0.4 | -9.7 |
| Financial managers .................................... | 2 | 0.4 | -8.6 |
| Engineering managers ................................ | 4 | 0.8 | -8.2 |
| Buyers and purchasing agents ................... | 4 | 0.7 | -11.2 |
| Human resources, training, and labor relations specialists ................................... | 5 | 1.0 | -5.5 |
| Management analysts.................................. | 5 | 1.0 | -8.9 |
| Business operation specialists, all other..... | 7 | 1.3 | -1.3 |
| Accountants and auditors ........................... | 6 | 1.2 | -8.0 |
| **Professional and related occupations**...... | 78 | 14.3 | -4.4 |
| Computer specialists ................................... | 16 | 2.9 | -1.4 |
| Electrical engineers .................................... | 13 | 2.3 | 0.5 |
| Industrial engineers, including health and safety ......................................................... | 2 | 0.4 | 7.2 |
| Nuclear engineers ...................................... | 4 | 0.8 | 0.2 |
| Electrical and electronic engineering technicians................................................... | 8 | 1.4 | -8.6 |
| Surveying and mapping technicians........... | 3 | 0.5 | -10.0 |
| Nuclear technicians .................................... | 3 | 0.6 | 0.8 |
| **Service occupations**................................... | 7 | 1.3 | -7.1 |
| Security guards............................................ | 3 | 0.6 | -8.8 |
| **Office and administrative support occupations** ............................................... | 116 | 21.1 | -10.3 |
| First-line supervisors/managers of office and administrative support workers .......... | 8 | 1.4 | -13.7 |
| Bill and account collectors ......................... | 4 | 0.7 | -10.0 |
| Billing and posting clerks and machine operators.................................................... | 4 | 0.8 | -15.9 |
| Bookkeeping, accounting, and auditing clerks ......................................................... | 7 | 1.2 | -3.1 |
| Customer service representatives .............. | 30 | 5.5 | -0.8 |
| Dispatchers ................................................. | 4 | 0.7 | -19.0 |
| Meter readers, utilities ............................... | 19 | 3.6 | -16.8 |
| Stock clerks and order fillers...................... | 4 | 0.8 | -24.0 |
| Executive secretaries and administrative assistants................................................... | 8 | 1.5 | -6.9 |
| Secretaries, except legal, medical, and executive.................................................... | 6 | 1.1 | -12.6 |
| Office clerks, general.................................. | 10 | 1.8 | -6.6 |
| **Construction and extraction occupations**.. | 33 | 6.0 | -6.7 |
| Operating engineers and other construction equipment operators................................. | 5 | 0.9 | -6.7 |
| Electricians ................................................. | 8 | 1.5 | -5.2 |
| Pipelayers, plumbers, pipefitters, and steamfitters ............................................... | 10 | 1.7 | -7.8 |
| **Installation, maintenance, and repair occupations** ............................................... | 149 | 27.1 | -3.6 |
| First-line supervisors/managers of mechanics, installers, and repairers ......... | 15 | 2.8 | -8.2 |
| Electrical and electronics repairers, powerhouse, substation, and relay ........... | 17 | 3.0 | -8.3 |
| Vehicle and mobile equipment mechanics, installers, and repairers....................... | 6 | 1.1 | -8.2 |
| Control and valve installers and repairers, except mechanical door........................... | 19 | 3.4 | -4.1 |
| Industrial machinery mechanics ................ | 8 | 1.4 | 6.9 |
| Maintenance and repair workers, general ..... | 11 | 2.0 | -5.4 |
| Electrical power-line installers and repairers . | 57 | 10.4 | 0.4 |

(continued on next column)

(continued from previous column)

**Table 3. Employment of wage and salary workers in utilities by occupation, 2006 and projected change, 2006-2016.**
(Employment in thousands)

| Occupation | Employment, 2006 | | Percent change, 2006-16 |
|---|---|---|---|
| | Number | Percent | |
| **Production occupations** | | | |
| Nuclear power reactor operators ................ | 3 | 0.6 | 10.3 |
| Power distributors and dispatchers............. | 6 | 1.1 | -8.2 |
| Power plant operators................................. | 24 | 4.4 | 0.9 |
| Stationary engineers and boiler operators.. | 4 | 0.7 | -4.5 |
| Water and liquid waste treatment plant and system operators ..................................... | 11 | 2.0 | 26.6 |
| Gas plant operators.................................... | 6 | 1.0 | -6.7 |
| **Transportation and material moving occupations** ............................................... | 12 | 2.2 | -11.8 |

Note: Columns may not add to totals due to omission of occupations with small employment

for advancement to management positions. Graduates of 2-year technical institutes usually fill technician positions. Sometimes, graduates of engineering programs will start as technicians until an opportunity to advance into an engineering position arises.

Managerial jobs generally require a 4-year college degree, although a 2-year technical degree may be sufficient in smaller plants. Managers usually can advance into higher level management jobs without additional formal training outside the workplace.

## Outlook

Employment in utilities is expected to decline, but many job openings will arise because large numbers of many workers in the industry are approaching retirement age and will need to be replaced.

*Employment change.* Wage and salary employment in utilities is expected to decline 6 percent between 2006 and 2016, compared with an increase of about 11 percent for all industries combined. Projected employment change varies by industry segment, as shown in table 4. Although electric power, natural gas and water continue to be essential to everyday life, employment declines will result from the retirement of much of the industry's workforce. While utilities are doing what they can to replace these workers, the wide variety of careers open to people with technical skills will make it difficult for companies to find enough applicants to fill these openings. Utilities will be forced to further automate their systems, negotiate part-time status with retirees and contract with employment services to make up for the difference between the desired number of employees and the number of workers actually available.

Reorganization of electric utilities has increased competition and provided incentives for improved efficiency. This has resulted in extensive cost-cutting and a number of mergers, which have led to a decline in employment over the past several years. This has been accomplished by a combination of layoffs and hiring freezes, which have resulted in an older workforce than in most other industries. Because electric utilities tend to be particularly labor intensive and require technically-minded people who are in high demand in other industries, they will have the most difficulty recruiting enough replacements. Worker attrition will be managed by further automation of systems and more responsibility for workers.

In the gas transmission and distribution industry, regulatory changes have made it possible for wholesale and even some retail buyers to choose their own natural gas providers. While distributors still maintain local monopolies, they are highly regulated and are not allowed to mark up the wholesale price of natural gas. Their revenues are based on distribution fees, which vary based on infrastructure needs rather than actual use of natural gas. These regulatory changes have resulted in several mergers and an emphasis on cost-cutting. As in the area of electric power, this has led to hiring freezes which have resulted in an older workforce. As these people retire, there will not be enough applicants to replace them, forcing the industry to find new ways to fill its needs.

In the water and sewage systems industries, regulatory changes have had the opposite impact. While most water systems remain locally-operated and fairly small in scale, water quality standards for both drinking water and disposal of wastewater have been increased for public health and environmental reasons. While hiring freezes have been less common in water than in other parts of the industry, much of the water workforce is nearing retirement age. Water and sewage systems services are projected to grow slightly, as water systems are expanding rapidly despite the difficulty in securing workers. Employment is projected to increase 18.7 percent from 2006 to 2016.

*Job prospects.* Job prospects for qualified applicants entering the utilities industry are expected to be excellent during the next 10 years. As of 2006, about 55 percent of the utilities industry workforce is over the age of 45 (table 5). Many of these workers will either retire or prepare to retire within the next 10 years. Because on-the-job training is very intensive in many utilities industry occupations, preparing a new workforce will be one of the industry's highest priorities during the next decade.

In general, persons with college training in advanced technology will have the best opportunities in the utilities industry. Computer systems analysts and network systems and data communications analysts are expected to be among the fastest growing occupations in the professional and related occupations group, as plants emphasize automation and productivity. Some

Table 4. Projected employment growth in nongovernment utilities by industry segment, 2006-16

| Industry segment | Percent change |
|---|---|
| **Total, all nongovernment utilities** | -5.7 |
| | |
| Electric power generation, transmission and distribution | -5.3 |
| Natural gas distribution | -17.6 |
| Water, sewage and other systems | 18.7 |

office and administrative support workers, such as utilities meter readers and bookkeeping, accounting, and auditing clerks, are among those adversely affected by increasing automation and outsourcing. Technologies including radio-transmitted meter reading and computerized billing procedures are expected to decrease employment.

New and continuing energy policies also provide investment tax credits for research and development of renewable sources of energy and ways to improve the efficiency of equipment used in electric utilities. As a result, electric utilities will continue to increase the productivity of their plants and workers, resulting in a slowdown in new employment. This slowdown will lead

Table 5. Percent distribution of employment, by age group, 2006

| Age group | Utilities | All industries |
|---|---|---|
| **Total** | 100.0% | 100.0% |
| 16-19 | 0.4 | 4.3 |
| 20-24 | 3.3 | 9.6 |
| 25-34 | 15.5 | 21.5 |
| 35-44 | 26.1 | 23.9 |
| 45-54 | 38.2 | 23.6 |
| 55-64 | 15.3 | 13.4 |
| 65 and older | 1.2 | 3.7 |

to keen competition for some jobs in the industry. However, at the same time, these new technologies will create jobs for highly skilled technical personnel with the education and experience to take advantage of these developments in electric utilities.

## Earnings

*Industry earnings.* Overall, production workers in the utilities industry had average weekly earnings of $27.42 in 2006. Earnings varied by industry segment within utilities (table 6). Average weekly earnings for production workers were higher in natural gas distribution and in electric power generation than in water, sewage, and other systems.

Table 6. Average earnings and hours of production workers in nongovernment utilities by industry segment, 2006

| Industry segment | Earnings | | Weekly hours |
|---|---|---|---|
| | Weekly | Hourly | |
| **Total, private industry** | $568 | $16.76 | 33.9 |
| | | | |
| **Nongovernment utilities** | 1136 | 27.42 | 41.4 |
| Power generation and supply | 1173 | 28.36 | 41.4 |
| Natural gas distribution | 1159 | 27.66 | 41.9 |
| Water, sewage, and other systems | 751 | 18.39 | 40.8 |

Earnings in utilities were generally higher than earnings in other industries. The hourly earnings for production workers in utilities averaged $27.42 in 2006, compared with $16.76 in all private industry. This was due in part to more overtime and weekend work, as utility plant operations must be monitored 24 hours a day. Earnings in selected occupations in utilities appear in table 7.

Table 7. Median hourly earnings of the largest occupations in utilities, May 2006

| Occupation | Utilities | All industries |
|---|---|---|
| Electrical engineers | $37.44 | $36.50 |
| First-line supervisors/managers of mechanics, installers, and repairers | 32.57 | 25.91 |
| Electrical and electronics repairers, powerhouse, substation, and relay | 28.26 | 27.60 |
| Power plant operators | 27.24 | 26.44 |
| Electrical power-line installers and repairers | 26.05 | 24.41 |
| Control and valve installers and repairers, except mechanical door | 25.22 | 21.84 |
| Maintenance and repair workers, general | 21.11 | 15.34 |
| Customer service representatives | 16.89 | 13.62 |
| Water and liquid waste treatment plant and system operators | 16.75 | 17.34 |
| Meter readers, utilities | 16.33 | 14.58 |

***Benefits and union membership.*** Most full-time workers in the utilities industry receive substantial benefits in addition to their salaries or hourly wages. This is particularly true for those workers covered by a collective bargaining agreement. In 2006, about 27.4 percent of workers in utilities were union members or covered by union contracts, more than double the proportion for all industries.

## Sources of Additional Information

General information on employment in the utilities industry is available from local utilities and:

➤ Center for Energy Workforce Development, 701 Pennsylvania Ave. NW, Washington, DC 20004-2696. Internet: **http://www.cewd.org**

Information on employment in electric power generation and distribution is available from:

➤ American Public Power Association, 2301 M St. NW, Washington, DC 20037-1484. Internet: **http://www.appanet.org**
➤ International Brotherhood of Electrical Workers, 1125 15th St. NW, Washington, DC 20005. Internet: **http://www.ibew.org**

Information on employment in natural gas transmission and distribution is available from:

➤ American Public Gas Association, 201 Massachusetts Ave. NE, Suite C-4, Washington, DC 20002. Internet: **http://www.apga.org**

Information on employment in water and wastewater treatment is available from:

➤ American Water Works Association, 6666 West Quincy, Denver, CO 80235. Internet: **http://www.awwa.org**
➤ Water Environment Federation, 601 Wythe St., Alexandria, VA 22314. Internet: **http://www.wef.org**

Detailed information on many key occupations in the utilities industry, including the following, may be found in the 2008-09 edition of the *Occupational Outlook Handbook.*

• Computer scientists and database administrators
• Construction laborers
• Engineering technicians
• Engineers
• Industrial machinery mechanics and maintenance workers
• Line installers and repairers
• Power plant operators, distributors, and dispatchers
• Stationary engineers and boiler operators
• Water and liquid waste treatment plant and system operators

# Manufacturing

# Aerospace Product and Parts Manufacturing

(NAICS 3364)

## SIGNIFICANT POINTS

- Production and professional jobs account for the largest share of employment.

- Earnings are higher, on average, than in most other industries.

- Employment is projected to grow more slowly than in other industries.

- During slowdowns in aerospace manufacturing, production workers are vulnerable to layoffs, while professional workers enjoy more job stability.

## Nature of the Industry

*Goods and services.* The aerospace industry comprises companies producing aircraft, guided missiles, space vehicles, aircraft engines, propulsion units, and related parts. Aircraft overhaul, rebuilding, and conversion also are included.

*Industry organization.* Firms producing transport aircraft make up the largest segment of the civil (nonmilitary) aircraft portion of the industry. Civil transport aircraft are produced for air transportation businesses such as airlines and cargo transportation companies. These aircraft range from small turboprops to wide-body jets and are used to move people and goods all over the world. Another segment of civil aircraft is general aviation aircraft. Aircraft in this segment range from the small two-seaters designed for leisure use to corporate jets used for business transport. Civil helicopters, which make up one of the smallest segments of civil aircraft, are commonly used by police and large city traffic departments, emergency medical services, and businesses such as oil and mining companies that need to transport people to remote worksites.

Aircraft engine manufacturers produce the engines used in civil and military aircraft. These manufacturers design and build engines according to the aircraft design and performance specifications of the aircraft manufacturers. Aircraft manufacturers may use engines designed by different companies on the same type of aircraft.

Military aircraft and helicopters are purchased by governments to meet national defense needs, such as delivering weapons to military targets and transporting troops and equipment around the globe. Some of these aircraft are specifically designed to deliver or guide a powerful array of ordnance to military targets with tremendous maneuverability and low detectability. Other aircraft, such as unmanned aerial vehicles, are produced to gather defense intelligence such as radio signals or to monitor movement on the ground.

Firms producing guided missiles and missile propulsion units sell primarily to military and government organizations. Although missiles are viewed predominantly as offensive weapons, improved guidance systems have led to their use as defensive systems. This part of the industry also produces space vehicles and the rockets for launching them into space. Consumers of spacecraft include the National Aeronautics and Space Administration (NASA), the U.S. Department of Defense (DOD), telecommunications companies, television networks, and news organizations. Firms producing space satellites are discussed with the computer and electronic product manufacturing industry in this publication because satellites are primarily electronic products.

The Federal Government traditionally has been the aerospace industry's biggest customer. The vast majority of Government contracts to purchase aerospace equipment are awarded by DOD. NASA also is a major purchaser of the industry's products and services, mainly for space vehicles and launch services.

The aerospace industry is dominated by a few large firms that contract to produce aircraft with Government and private businesses, usually airline and cargo transportation companies. These large firms, in turn, subcontract with smaller firms to produce specific systems and parts for their vehicles. Government purchases are largely related to defense. Typically, DOD announces its need for military aircraft or missile systems, specifying a multitude of requirements. Large firms specializing in defense products subsequently submit bids, detailing proposed technical solutions and designs, along with cost estimates, hoping to win the contract. Firms also may research and develop materials, electronics, and components relating to their bid, often at their own expense, to improve their chances of winning the contract. Following a negotiation phase, a manufacturer is selected and a prototype is developed and built, then tested and evaluated. If approved by DOD, the craft or system enters production. This process usually takes many years.

*Recent developments.* The way in which commercial and military aircraft are designed, developed, and produced continues to undergo significant change in response to the need to cut costs and deliver products faster. Firms producing commercial aircraft have reduced development time drastically through computer-aided design and drafting (CADD), which allows firms to design and test an entire aircraft, including the individual parts, by computer; the drawings of these parts can be sent electronically to subcontractors who use them to produce the parts. Increasingly, firms bring together teams composed of customers, engineers, and production workers to pool ideas and make decisions concerning the aircraft at every phase of product development. Additionally, the military has changed its design philosophy, using commercially available, off-the-shelf technology when appropriate, rather than developing new customized components.

Commercial airlines and private businesses typically identify their needs for a particular model of new aircraft based on a number of factors, including the routes they fly. After specifying requirements such as range, size, cargo capacity, type of engine, and seating arrangements, the airlines invite manufacturers of civil aircraft and aircraft engines to submit bids. Selection ultimately is based on a manufacturer's ability to deliver reliable aircraft that best fit the purchaser's stated market needs at the lowest cost and at favorable financing terms.

## Working Conditions

*Hours.* The average production employee in aerospace products and parts production worked 43.8 hours a week in 2006, compared with 41.1 hours a week for all manufacturing workers and 33.9 hours a week for workers in all industries. About half of all workers in this industry worked a standard 40 hour week. Part-time work is unusual.

*Work Environment.* Working conditions in aerospace manufacturing facilities vary. Many new plants, in contrast to older facilities, are spacious, well lit, and modern. Specific work environments usually depend on occupation and the age of the production line. Engineers, scientists, and technicians frequently work in office settings or laboratories, although production engineers may spend much of their time with production workers on the factory floor. Production workers, such as welders and other assemblers, may have to cope with high noise levels. Oil, grease, and grime often are present, and some workers may face exposure to volatile organic compounds found in solvents, paints, and coatings. Heavy lifting is required for many production jobs.

The rate of work-related injury and illness in the aerospace products and parts industry was 4.2 per 100 full-time workers in 2006. In comparison, throughout the private sector the rate averaged 4.4 per 100 workers.

## Employment

Aerospace manufacturers employed 472,000 wage and salary workers in 2006. Employment data in this statement do not include aerospace R&D-related workers who work in separate establishments. Under the North American Industry Classification System (NAICS), workers in research and development establishments that are not part of a manufacturing facility are included in a separate industry—research and development in the physical, engineering, and life sciences. This industry is covered in the statement on scientific research and development services elsewhere in the *Career Guide.* Given the importance of R&D work to the aerospace manufacturing industry, however, aerospace-related R&D occupations and issues are discussed in the following sections, even though much of their employment is not included in the employment data in this statement.

In 2006, about 2,900 establishments made up the aerospace industry. In the aerospace parts industry, most establishments were subcontractors that manufacture parts and employ fewer than 100 workers. Nevertheless, 62 percent of the jobs in aerospace manufacturing were in large establishments that employed 1,000 or more workers (chart 1).

The largest numbers of aerospace jobs were in California and Washington, although many also were located in Texas, Kansas, Connecticut, and Arizona.

## Occupations in the Industry

The design and manufacture of the technologically sophisticated products of the aerospace industry require the input and skills of various workers. Production, professional and related, administrative support, and managerial occupations make up the bulk of employment. Those employed in managerial and administrative support occupations manage the design process and factory operations, coordinate the hundreds of thousands of parts that are assembled into an aircraft, and ensure compliance with Federal

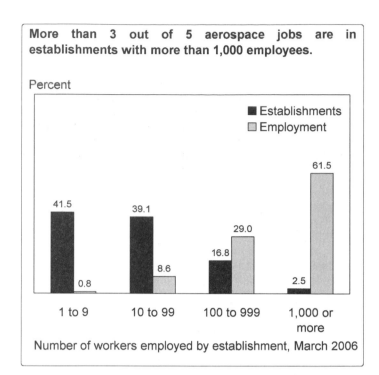

**More than 3 out of 5 aerospace jobs are in establishments with more than 1,000 employees.**

Percent

Number of workers employed by establishment, March 2006

recordkeeping regulations.

The industry invests a great deal of time and money in research and development of aerospace products, and much of the work is performed by professional and related workers, who made up 31 percent of the aerospace workforce in 2006 (table 1). In addition, as mentioned in the previous section, many more aerospace-related professionals work in the scientific research and development services industry.

*Professional and related occupations.* These workers develop new designs and make improvements to existing designs. *Aerospace engineers* are integral members of the teams that research, design, test, and produce aerospace vehicles. Some specialize in areas such as structural design, guidance, navigation and control, and instrumentation and communication. Electrical and electronics and mechanical engineers also contribute to the research for and development and production of aerospace products. For example, *mechanical engineers* help design mechanical components and develop the specific tools and machines needed to produce aircraft, missile, and space vehicle parts, or they may design jet and rocket engines. *Industrial engineers* develop methods of producing complex aerospace products efficiently and solve logistical problems of manufacturing and transporting the sometimes large parts. *Engineering technicians* assist engineers, both in the research and development laboratory and on the manufacturing floor. They may help build prototypes of newly designed products, run tests and experiments, and perform a variety of other technical tasks. One of the earliest users of computer-aided design, the aerospace industry continues to use the latest computer technology. *Computer scientists and systems analysts, database administrators, computer software engineers, computer programmers, computer support specialists,* and *network and computer systems administrators* are responsible for the design, testing, evaluation, and setup of computer systems that are used throughout the industry for design and manufacturing purposes.

*Management, business, and financial occupations.* This occupational group accounted for 17 percent of industry employment in 2006. Many advance to these jobs from professional occupations. Many managers in the aerospace industry have a technical or engineering background and supervise teams of engineers in activities such as testing and research and development. *Industrial production managers* oversee all workers and lower level managers in a factory. They also coordinate all activities related to production. In addition to technical and production managers, *financial managers; purchasing managers, buyers, and purchasing agents; cost estimators;* and *accountants and auditors* are needed to negotiate with customers and subcontractors and to track costs.

*Production, installation, and transportation occupations.* Of all aerospace workers, 40 percent are employed in production; installation, maintenance, and repair; and transportation and material-moving occupations. Many of these jobs are not specific to aerospace and can be found in other manufacturing industries. Many production jobs are open to persons with only a high school education; however, special vocational training after high school is preferred for some of the more highly skilled production jobs. *Aircraft structure, surfaces, rigging, and systems assemblers* usually specialize in one assembly task; hundreds of different assemblers may work at various times on producing a single aircraft. Assemblers may put together parts of airplanes, such as wings or landing gear, or install parts and equipment into the airplane itself. Those involved in assembling aircraft or systems must be skilled in reading and interpreting engineering specifications and instructions. *Machinists* make parts that are needed in numbers too small to mass-produce. Machinists follow blueprints and specifications and are highly skilled with machine tools and metalworking. *Tool and die makers* are responsible for constructing precision tools and metal forms, called dies, which are used to shape metal. Increasingly, as individual components are designed electronically, these highly skilled workers must be able to read electronic blueprints and set up and operate computer-controlled machines. *Inspectors, testers, sorters, samplers, and weighers* perform numerous quality-control and safety checks on aerospace parts throughout the production cycle. Their work is vital to ensure the safety of the aircraft.

*Administrative support, service, and sales occupations.* Most of these jobs can be entered without education beyond high school. Workers in office and administrative support occupations help coordinate the flow of materials to the worksite, draw up orders for supplies, keep records, and help with all of the other paperwork associated with keeping a business functioning. Those in service occupations are employed mostly as guards and janitors and other cleaning and maintenance workers. As a result of the highly technical nature of the products produced by this industry, sales workers are mostly wholesale and manufacturing sales representatives, sales engineers, and sales worker supervisors.

## Training and Advancement

The proportion of workers with education beyond high school is larger in the aerospace industry than the average for all industries. Because employers need well-informed, knowledgeable employees who can keep up with the rapid technological advancements in aerospace manufacturing, the industry provides substantial support for the education and training of its workers. Firms provide onsite, job-related training to upgrade the skills of technicians, production workers, and engineers. Classes teaching computer skills and blueprint reading are common. Some firms reimburse employees for educational expenses at colleges and universities, emphasizing 4-year degrees and postgraduate studies.

The aerospace industry is on the leading edge of technology, constantly striving to create new products and improve existing ones. Many workers are employed in research and development in the aerospace products and parts manufacturing industry. A bachelor's degree in a specialized field, such as engineering, is required for most of these jobs; a master's or doctoral degree is preferred for some. For many technician occupations, however, a 2-year program of technical training after high school is favored.

Production workers may enter the aerospace industry with minimal skills. Mechanical aptitude and good hand-eye coordination usually are necessary. A high school diploma or equivalent is required, and some vocational training in electronics or mechanics also is favored.

Lesser-skilled production workers typically start by being shown how to perform a simple assembly task. Through experience, on-the-job instruction provided by other workers, and brief formal training sessions, they expand their skills. Their pay increases as they advance into more highly skilled or responsible jobs. For example, machinists may take additional training to become numerical tool and process control programmers or tool and die makers. Inspectors usually are promoted from assembly, machine operation, and mechanical occupations.

Because of the reliance on computers and computer-operated equipment, classes in computer skills are common. With training, production workers may be able to advance to supervisory or technician jobs.

To enter some of the more highly skilled production occupations, workers must go through a formal apprenticeship. Machinists and electricians complete apprenticeships that can last as long as 4 years. Apprenticeships usually include classroom instruction and shop training.

Entry-level positions for technicians usually require a degree from a technical school or junior college. Companies sometimes retrain technicians to upgrade their skills or to teach different specialties. They are taught traditional as well as new production technology skills, such as computer-aided design and manufacturing, and statistical process control methods.

## Outlook

*Employment change.* Wage and salary employment in the aerospace product and parts manufacturing industry is expected to grow by 5 percent over the period, 2006-16, slower than the 11-percent growth projected for all industries combined. Employment in the aerospace industry declined in the first half of this decade as a result of a drastic reduction in commercial transport aircraft orders, but an increase in air traffic and the improving financial health of the Nation's airlines have caused this trend to reverse since 2004. The introduction of several major new aircraft in both the civil and military segments of the industry should lead to a substantial increase in production and a moderate increase in employment over the projection period.

The military aircraft and missiles segment of the industry has fared better than the civil segment in recent years and should continue to grow. Concern for the Nation's security has increased the need for military aircraft and military aerospace equipment. Although new employment opportunities in the defense-related sector of the aerospace industry may not reach levels previously attained during the Cold War, employment in this sector is expected to continue rising.

**Table 1. Employment of wage and salary workers in aerospace product and parts manufacturing by occupation, 2006 and projected change, 2006-2016.**

(Employment in thousands)

| Occupation | Employment, 2006 | | Percent change, 2006-16 |
|---|---|---|---|
| | Number | Percent | |
| **All occupations** | 472 | 100.0 | 5.4 |
| | | | |
| **Management, business, and financial occupations** | 81 | 17.2 | 4.9 |
| General and operations managers | 4 | 0.9 | -8.3 |
| Financial managers | 2 | 0.5 | 1.8 |
| Industrial production managers | 5 | 1.0 | 1.8 |
| Engineering managers | 10 | 2.2 | 12.0 |
| Purchasing agents, except wholesale, retail, and farm products | 10 | 2.0 | 1.8 |
| Cost estimators | 2 | 0.5 | 10.0 |
| Human resources, training, and labor relations specialists | 3 | 0.7 | 10.0 |
| Logisticians | 4 | 0.8 | 12.0 |
| Management analysts | 9 | 1.8 | 1.8 |
| Business operation specialists, all other | 9 | 1.9 | 12.0 |
| Accountants and auditors | 4 | 0.9 | 1.8 |
| Budget analysts | 3 | 0.6 | 1.8 |
| | | | |
| **Professional and related occupations** | 147 | 31.2 | 8.9 |
| Computer software engineers, applications | 12 | 2.4 | 22.2 |
| Computer software engineers, systems software | 5 | 1.2 | 12.0 |
| Computer systems analysts | 3 | 0.6 | 12.0 |
| Aerospace engineers | 44 | 9.3 | 6.9 |
| Electrical and electronics engineers | 5 | 1.0 | 1.8 |
| Industrial engineers, including health and safety | 15 | 3.2 | 22.8 |
| Industrial engineers | 15 | 3.1 | 23.7 |
| Mechanical engineers | 11 | 2.3 | 1.8 |
| Engineers, all other | 9 | 1.8 | 1.8 |
| Drafters | 5 | 1.1 | 8.9 |
| Aerospace engineering and operations technicians | 4 | 0.8 | 1.8 |
| Electrical and electronic engineering technicians | 3 | 0.6 | 1.8 |
| Industrial engineering technicians | 7 | 1.5 | 12.0 |
| Engineering technicians, except drafters, all other | 5 | 1.1 | 1.8 |
| | | | |
| **Office and administrative support occupations** | 38 | 8.0 | -3.2 |
| Bookkeeping, accounting, and auditing clerks | 2 | 0.5 | 1.8 |
| Production, planning, and expediting clerks | 7 | 1.6 | 1.8 |
| Shipping, receiving, and traffic clerks | 4 | 0.8 | -2.0 |
| Stock clerks and order fillers | 5 | 1.0 | -14.8 |
| Secretaries and administrative assistants | 8 | 1.8 | -0.6 |
| Office clerks, general | 4 | 0.8 | 0.3 |
| | | | |
| **Installation, maintenance, and repair occupations** | 41 | 8.7 | 14.3 |
| Avionics technicians | 4 | 0.9 | 12.0 |
| Electrical and electronics repairers, commercial and industrial equipment | 2 | 0.5 | 8.6 |
| Aircraft mechanics and service technicians | 21 | 4.4 | 22.2 |
| Industrial machinery mechanics | 2 | 0.5 | 17.1 |
| Maintenance and repair workers, general | 4 | 0.8 | 1.8 |
| | | | |
| **Production occupations** | 141 | 29.9 | 2.5 |
| First-line supervisors/managers of production and operating workers | 9 | 2.0 | 1.8 |
| Aircraft structure, surfaces, rigging, and systems assemblers | 24 | 5.2 | 12.0 |

(continued in next column)

(continued from previous column)

**Table 1. Employment of wage and salary workers in aerospace product and parts manufacturing by occupation, 2006 and projected change, 2006-2016.**

(Employment in thousands)

| Occupation | Employment, 2006 | | Percent change, 2006-16 |
|---|---|---|---|
| | Number | Percent | |
| **Production occupations (continued)** | | | |
| Electrical and electronic equipment assemblers | 4 | 0.8 | -18.5 |
| Team assemblers | 7 | 1.5 | 1.8 |
| Computer-controlled machine tool operators, metal and plastic | 5 | 1.2 | 12.0 |
| Machine tool cutting setters, operators, and tenders, metal and plastic | 12 | 2.6 | -6.5 |
| Machinists | 18 | 3.8 | 6.9 |
| Multiple machine tool setters, operators, and tenders, metal and plastic | 4 | 0.8 | 12.0 |
| Tool and die makers | 3 | 0.7 | 6.9 |
| Welders, cutters, solderers, and brazers | 4 | 0.8 | 8.3 |
| Inspectors, testers, sorters, samplers, and weighers | 16 | 3.5 | -4.0 |

Note: May not add to totals due to omission of occupations with small employment

*Job prospects.* In addition to some growth in employment opportunities for professional workers in the industry, there will be many job openings arising from replacement needs, especially for aerospace engineers. Many engineers who entered the industry in the 1960s are approaching retirement. Among those in the aerospace manufacturing industry, professionals typically enjoy more job stability than do other workers. During slowdowns in production, companies prefer to keep technical teams intact to continue research and development activities in anticipation of new business. Production workers, on the other hand, are particularly vulnerable to layoffs during downturns in the economy, when aircraft orders decline.

Job opportunities in the aerospace product and parts manufacturing industry are also influenced by unique production cycles within the industry in addition to the general cyclical fluctuations of the economy. Job openings in the industry rise rapidly when major new aircraft or systems are in development and production. However, job openings become scarcer after the

**Table 2. Median hourly earnings of the largest occupations in aerospace products and parts manufacturing, May 2006**

| Occupation | Aerospace product and parts manufacturing | All industries |
|---|---|---|
| Engineering managers | $53.38 | $50.69 |
| Computer software engineers, applications | 40.71 | 38.36 |
| Aerospace engineers | 39.91 | 42.12 |
| Mechanical engineers | 36.58 | 33.58 |
| Industrial engineers | 33.75 | 32.99 |
| Purchasing agents, except wholesale, retail, and farm products | 28.55 | 24.39 |
| Aircraft structure, surfaces, rigging, and systems assemblers | 22.18 | 21.83 |
| Aircraft mechanics and service technicians | 21.58 | 22.95 |
| Inspectors, testers, sorters, samplers, and weighers | 20.62 | 14.14 |
| Machinists | 18.46 | 16.71 |

initial production run. Both the civil and military segments of the industry have their own cyclical variations, corresponding to the introduction of major civil aircraft and military aircraft and systems.

Because of past reductions in defense expenditures and intense competition in the commercial aircraft sector, there have been and may continue to be mergers in the industry, resulting in layoffs. Even though the number of large firms performing final assembly of aircraft has been reduced, hundreds of smaller manufacturers and subcontractors will remain in this industry.

## Earnings

*Industry earnings.* Production workers in the aerospace industry earn higher pay than the average for all industries. Weekly earnings for production workers averaged $1,153 in aerospace product parts manufacturing in 2006, compared with $691 in all manufacturing and $568 in all private industry. Above-average earnings reflect, in part, the high levels of skill required by the industry and the need to motivate workers to concentrate on maintaining high quality standards in their work. The earnings may also reflect longer average hours worked each week in the industry. Nonproduction workers, such as engineering managers, engineers, and computer specialists, generally command higher pay because of their advanced education and training (table 2).

*Benefits and union membership.* Workers in the aerospace industry generally receive standard benefits, including health insurance, paid vacation and sick leave, and pension plans.

In 2006, 21 percent of all workers in the aerospace industry were union members or covered by union contracts, compared with about 13 percent of all workers throughout private industry. Some of the major aerospace unions include the International Association of Machinists and Aerospace Workers; the United Automobile, Aerospace, and Agricultural Implement Workers of America; the Society of Professional Engineering Employees in Aerospace (SPEEA); and the International Union of Allied Industrial Workers of America.

## Sources of Additional Information

For additional information about the aerospace product and parts manufacturing industry, contact:

➤ Aerospace Industries Association, 1000 Wilson Blvd., Suite 1700, Arlington, VA 22209. Internet: **http://www.aia-aerospace.org**
➤ American Institute of Aeronautics and Astronautics, 1801 Alexander Bell Dr., Suite 500, Reston, VA 20191. Internet: **http://www.aiaa.org**
➤ Federal Aviation Administration, 800 Independence Ave. SW., Room 810, Washington, DC 20591. Internet: **http://www.faa.gov/education**

Information on the following occupations may be found in the 2008-09 edition of the *Occupational Outlook Handbook*:

- Aircraft and avionics equipment mechanics and service technicians
- Assemblers and fabricators
- Computer programmers
- Computer scientists and database administrators
- Computer software engineers
- Engineering and natural sciences managers
- Engineering technicians
- Engineers
- Inspectors, testers, sorters, samplers, and weighers
- Machine setters, operators, and tenders—metal and plastic
- Machinists

# Chemical Manufacturing, Except Pharmaceutical and Medicine Manufacturing

(NAICS 325, except 3254)

## SIGNIFICANT POINTS

- Employment is projected to decline.

- Workers involved in production and in installation, maintenance, and repair hold more than half of all jobs.

- Earnings are higher than average.

## Nature of the Industry

*Goods and services.* Vital to industries such as construction, motor vehicles, paper, electronics, transportation, agriculture, and pharmaceuticals, chemicals are an essential component of manufacturing. Although some chemical manufacturers produce and sell consumer products such as soap, bleach, and cosmetics, most chemical products are used as intermediate products for other goods.

*Industry organization.* Chemical manufacturing is divided into seven segments, six of which are covered here: basic chemicals; synthetic materials, including resin, synthetic rubber, and artificial and synthetic fibers and filaments; agricultural chemicals, including pesticides, fertilizer, and other agricultural chemicals; paint, coatings, and adhesives; cleaning preparations, including soap, cleaning compounds, and toilet preparations; and other chemical products. The seventh segment, pharmaceutical and medicine manufacturing, is covered in a separate *Career Guide* statement.

The *basic chemicals segment* produces various petrochemicals, gases, dyes, and pigments. Petrochemicals contain carbon and hydrogen and are made primarily from petroleum and natural gas. The production of both organic and inorganic chemicals occurs in this segment. Organic chemicals are used to make a wide range of products, such as dyes, plastics, and pharmaceutical products; however, the majority of these chemicals are used in the production of other chemicals. Industrial inorganic chemicals usually are made from salts, metal compounds, other minerals, and the atmosphere. In addition to producing solid and liquid chemicals, firms involved in inorganic chemical manufacturing produce industrial gases such as oxygen, nitrogen, and helium. Many inorganic chemicals serve as processing ingredients in the manufacture of chemicals, but do not appear in the final products because they are used as catalysts—chemicals that speed up or otherwise aid a reaction.

The *synthetic materials segment* produces a wide variety of finished products as well as raw materials, including common plastic materials such as polyethylene, polypropylene, polyvinyl chloride (PVC), and polystyrene. Among products into which these plastics can be made are loudspeakers, toys, PVC pipes, and beverage bottles. Motor vehicle manufacturers are particularly large users of such products. This industry segment also produces plastic materials used for mixing and blending resins on a custom basis.

The *agricultural chemicals segment*, which employs the fewest workers in the chemical industry, supplies farmers and home gardeners with fertilizers, herbicides, pesticides, and other agricultural chemicals. The segment also includes companies involved in the formulation and preparation of agricultural and household pest control chemicals.

The *paint, coating, and adhesive products segment* includes firms making paints, varnishes, putties, paint removers, sealers, adhesives, glues, and caulking. The construction and furniture industries are large customers of this segment. Other customers range from individuals refurbishing their homes to businesses needing anticorrosive paints that can withstand high temperatures.

The *cleaning preparations segment* is the only segment in which much of the production is geared directly toward consumers. The segment includes firms making soaps, detergents, and cleaning preparations. Cosmetics and toiletries, including perfume, lotion, and toothpaste, also are produced in this segment. Households and businesses use these products in many ways, cleaning everything from babies to bridges.

The *"other chemical" products segment* includes manufacturers of explosives, printing ink, film, toners, matches, and other miscellaneous chemicals. These products are used by consumers or in the manufacture of other products.

Chemicals generally are classified into two groups: basic chemicals and specialty chemicals. Basic chemical manufacturers produce large quantities of basic and relatively inexpensive compounds in large plants, often built specifically to make one chemical. Most basic chemicals are used to make more highly refined chemicals for the production of everyday consumer goods by other industries. Conversely, specialty chemical manufacturers produce smaller quantities of more expensive chemicals that are used less frequently. Specialty chemical manufacturers often supply larger chemical companies on a contract basis. Many traditional chemical manufacturers are divided into two separate entities, one focused on basic and the other on specialty chemicals.

The diversity of products produced by the chemical industry also reflects its component establishments. For example, firms producing synthetic materials operated relatively large plants in 2006. By contrast, manufacturers of paints, coatings, and adhesive products had a greater number of establishments, each employing a much smaller number of workers.

The chemical industry segments vary in the degree to which their workers are involved in production activities, administration and management, and research and development. Industries that make products such as cosmetics or paints that are ready for sale to the final consumer employ more administrative and marketing personnel. Industries that market their products mostly

48

to industrial customers generally employ a greater proportion of precision production workers and a lower proportion of unskilled labor.

***Recent developments.*** Although development of nanotechnology has been slow in chemical manufacturing, research and development in this area has been increasing, and should continue to increase. Advances in nanotechnology in the chemical manufacturing industry could potentially lead to the development of new, safer, and more effective products.

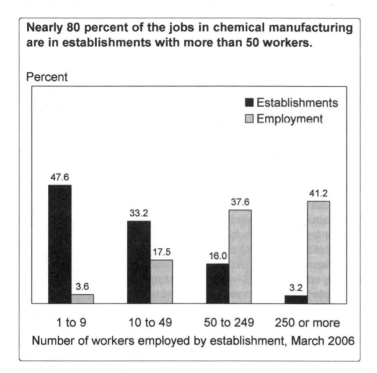

**Nearly 80 percent of the jobs in chemical manufacturing are in establishments with more than 50 workers.**

Percent

■ Establishments
□ Employment

47.6
33.2
17.5
16.0
37.6
3.6
3.2
41.2

1 to 9    10 to 49    50 to 249    250 or more

Number of workers employed by establishment, March 2006

## Working Conditions

***Hours.*** Manufacturing chemicals usually is a continuous process; this means that, once a process has begun, it cannot be stopped when it is time for workers to go home. Split, weekend, and night shifts are common, and workers on such schedules usually are compensated with higher rates of pay. The industry employs relatively few part-time workers.

***Work Environment.*** Most jobs in chemical manufacturing are in large establishments. The largest 19 percent of establishments that employed 50 or more workers in 2006 had 79 percent of the industry's jobs (chart 1). The plants usually are clean, although machines that run constantly sometimes are loud and the interior of many plants can be hot. Hardhats and safety goggles are mandatory and worn throughout the plant.

Hazards in the chemical industry can be substantial, but they generally are avoided through strict safety procedures. Workers are required to have protective gear and extensive knowledge of the dangers associated with the chemicals being handled. Body suits with breathing devices designed to filter out any harmful fumes are mandatory for work in dangerous environments.

In spite of the hazards associated with working with chemicals, extensive worker training in handling hazardous chemicals and chemical company safety measures have resulted in injury

and illness rates for some segments of the chemical industry that are much lower than the average for the manufacturing sector. The chemical industry reported just 2.9 cases of work-related injury or illness per 100 workers, compared with an average of 6.0 cases for all manufacturing industries in 2006.

## Employment

The chemical and allied products industry employed about 576,000 wage and salary workers in 2006.

Chemical firms are concentrated in regions where other manufacturing businesses are located, such as the Great Lakes region near the automotive industry, or the West Coast, near the electronics industry. Chemical plants also are located near the petroleum and natural gas production centers along the Gulf Coast in Texas and Louisiana. Because chemical production processes often use water, and chemicals are primarily exported by ship all over the world, major industrial ports are another common location of chemical plants. California, Illinois, New Jersey, New York, Ohio, Pennsylvania, South Carolina, Tennessee, and Texas had a majority of the establishments in the industry in 2006.

Most segments of the industry had substantial numbers of jobs, as shown in table 1. Under the North American Industry Classification System (NAICS), workers in research and development (R&D) establishments who are not part of a manufacturing facility are included in a separate industry: research and development in the physical, engineering, and life sciences. However, because of the importance of R&D work to the chemical manufacturing industry, chemical-related R&D workers are discussed in this statement but are not included in the employment data.

**Table 1. Distribution of wage and salary employment in chemical manufacturing, except pharmaceutical and medicine manufacturing, by detailed industry, 2006**
(Employment in thousands)

| Industry | Employment | Percent |
|---|---|---|
| **Chemical manufacturing, except pharmaceutical and medicine manufacturing, total** | 576 | 100.0 |
| Basic chemical manufacturing | 148 | 25.7 |
| Soap, cleaning compound, and toilet preparation manufacturing | 113 | 19.6 |
| Resin, synthetic rubber, and artificial synthetic fibers and filaments manufacturing | 105 | 18.2 |
| Paint, coating, and adhesive manufacturing | 67 | 11.6 |
| Pesticide, fertilizer, and other agricultural chemical manufacturing | 39 | 6.8 |
| Other chemical product and preparation manufacturing | 105 | 18.2 |

## Occupations in the Industry

About 54 percent of those employed in the industry worked in production and in installation, maintenance, and repair occupations. Another 12 percent worked in professional and related occupations. Approximately 20 percent worked in management, business, and financial occupations and in office and administrative support occupations, and another 9 percent worked in transportation and material moving occupations (table 2).

*Production occupations.* Workers in production occupations operate and fix plant machinery, transport raw materials, and monitor the production process. Improvements in technology gradually are increasing the level of plant automation, reducing the number of jobs in production occupations. Although high school graduates qualify for most entry-level production jobs, advancement into better paying jobs requiring higher skills or more responsibility usually is possible only with on-the-job training and work experience or through additional vocational training at a 2-year technical college.

*Chemical plant and system operators* monitor the entire production process. From chemical ingredient ratios to chemical reaction rates, the operator is responsible for the efficient operation of the chemical plant. Chemical plant operators generally advance to these positions after having acquired extensive experience and technical training in chemical production processes. Experienced operators sometimes advance to senior supervisory positions.

*Industrial machinery mechanics* and *machinery maintenance workers* keep the sophisticated industrial machinery running smoothly. They typically repair equipment, install machines, or practice preventive maintenance in the plant. Workers advance to these jobs through apprenticeships, through formal vocational training, or by completing in-house training courses.

*Inspectors, testers, sorters, samplers, and weighers* ensure that the production process runs efficiently and that products meet quality standards. They refer problems to plant operators or managers. A high school diploma is sufficient for basic product testing. Complex precision-inspecting positions are filled by those with experience and knowledge of the chemical manufacturing industry's products and production processes.

*Packaging and filling machine operators and tenders* wrap products and fill boxes to prepare the final product for shipment or sale to the wholesaler or consumer. More than half of these jobs are in the soap and cosmetics industry because of the amount of packaging needed for this industry's consumer products. A high school diploma and short-term on-the-job training are the most common level of education and training for this occupation.

*Transportation and material moving workers* use industrial trucks to move materials around the plant or to deliver finished products to customers. For these jobs, employers seek experienced workers with knowledge of chemical hazards, safety procedures, and regulations governing the transport of hazardous chemicals. Learning to operate an industrial truck or tractor can be done with on-the-job training, but previous experience driving a truck and a commercial driver's license generally are required to operate a tractor-trailer carrying chemicals. Some jobs in transportation and material movement are open to workers without experience. Workers in these jobs move raw materials and finished products through the chemical plant and assist motor vehicle operators in loading and unloading raw materials and chemicals. They learn safe ways to handle chemicals on the job and develop skills that enable them to advance to other occupations.

*Professional and related occupations.* Most workers in professional and related occupations have at least a college degree, and many have advanced degrees.

*Chemists* and *materials scientists* carry out research over a wide range of activities, including analyzing materials, preparing new materials or modifying existing ones, studying chemical processes for new or existing products, and formulating cosmet-

**Table 2. Employment of wage and salary workers in chemical manufacturing, except drugs by occupation, 2006 and projected change, 2006-2016**
(Employment in thousands)

| Occupation | Employment, 2006 | | Percent change, 2006-16 |
|---|---|---|---|
| | Number | Percent | |
| **All occupations** | 576 | 100.0 | -15.7 |
| **Management, business, and financial occupations** | 51 | 8.9 | -15.5 |
| Top executives | 11 | 1.9 | -23.0 |
| Marketing and sales managers | 4 | 0.7 | -12.5 |
| Industrial production managers | 8 | 1.3 | -15.1 |
| Engineering managers | 3 | 0.5 | -16.5 |
| Purchasing agents, except wholesale, retail, and farm products | 4 | 0.7 | -13.4 |
| Accountants and auditors | 5 | 0.9 | -13.8 |
| **Professional and related occupations** | 68 | 11.7 | -12.8 |
| Computer specialists | 6 | 1.1 | -9.5 |
| Chemical engineers | 7 | 1.3 | -12.2 |
| Industrial engineers | 5 | 0.9 | 0.6 |
| Chemists | 13 | 2.3 | -13.6 |
| Chemical technicians | 17 | 3.0 | -14.9 |
| **Sales and related occupations** | 20 | 3.5 | -13.1 |
| Sales representatives, wholesale and manufacturing, technical and scientific products | 6 | 1.1 | -14.9 |
| Sales representatives, wholesale and manufacturing, except technical and scientific products | 11 | 1.9 | -12.1 |
| **Office and administrative support occupations** | 63 | 10.9 | -16.8 |
| Bookkeeping, accounting, and auditing clerks | 7 | 1.2 | -13.0 |
| Customer service representatives | 7 | 1.3 | -4.4 |
| Production, planning, and expediting clerks | 6 | 1.0 | -14.7 |
| Shipping, receiving, and traffic clerks | 11 | 1.9 | -16.6 |
| Secretaries and administrative assistants | 11 | 1.9 | -18.6 |
| Office clerks, general | 6 | 1.1 | -14.9 |
| **Construction and extraction occupations** | 6 | 1.1 | -15.4 |
| Electricians | 3 | 0.6 | -13.7 |
| **Installation, maintenance, and repair occupations** | 48 | 8.3 | -11.5 |
| Electrical and electronics repairers, commercial and industrial equipment | 5 | 0.9 | -12.8 |
| Industrial machinery mechanics | 13 | 2.2 | -1.3 |
| Maintenance and repair workers, general | 17 | 3.0 | -15.3 |
| Maintenance workers, machinery | 3 | 0.6 | -16.4 |
| **Production occupations** | 265 | 46.0 | -16.2 |
| First-line supervisors/managers of production and operating workers | 25 | 4.3 | -15.0 |
| Team assemblers | 15 | 2.6 | -14.0 |
| Extruding and drawing machine setters, operators, and tenders, metal and plastic | 5 | 0.9 | -19.1 |
| Machinists | 3 | 0.5 | -10.0 |
| Molding, coremaking, and casting machine setters, operators, and tenders, metal and plastic | 4 | 0.7 | -23.7 |
| Extruding and forming machine setters, operators, and tenders, synthetic and glass fibers | 3 | 0.6 | -27.5 |
| Chemical plant and system operators | 46 | 7.9 | -17.1 |
| Chemical equipment operators and tenders | 24 | 4.2 | -16.0 |
| Separating, filtering, clarifying, precipitating, and still machine setters, operators, and tenders | 6 | 1.1 | -13.4 |

(continued in next column)

(continued from previous column)

**Table 2. Employment of wage and salary workers in chemical manufacturing, except drugs by occupation, 2006 and projected change, 2006-2016.**
(Employment in thousands)

| Occupation | Employment, 2006 Number | Percent | Percent change, 2006-16 |
|---|---|---|---|
| **Production occupations (continued)** | | | |
| Crushing, grinding, polishing, mixing, and blending workers......................................... | 51 | 8.9 | -13.5 |
| Mixing and blending machine setters, operators, and tenders............................. | 50 | 8.7 | -13.3 |
| Extruding, forming, pressing, and compacting machine setters, operators, and tenders................................................ | 7 | 1.2 | -15.0 |
| Inspectors, testers, sorters, samplers, and weighers ............................................ | 14 | 2.5 | -19.3 |
| Packaging and filling machine operators and tenders............................................. | 27 | 4.7 | -18.9 |
| Helpers--Production workers ...................... | 9 | 1.5 | -14.3 |
| Production workers, all other ...................... | 5 | 0.9 | -14.3 |
| **Transportation and material moving occupations** ............................................. | 51 | 8.8 | -20.6 |
| Truck drivers, heavy and tractor-trailer ......... | 7 | 1.2 | -16.1 |
| Industrial truck and tractor operators........... | 10 | 1.8 | -20.4 |
| Laborers and freight, stock, and material movers, hand.............................................. | 11 | 2.0 | -21.8 |
| Packers and packagers, hand...................... | 9 | 1.6 | -26.4 |

Note: Columns may not add to totals due to omission of occupations with small employment

ics, household care products, or paints and coatings. They also try to develop new chemicals for specific applications and new applications for existing chemicals. The most senior chemists sometimes advance to management positions. Although chemical companies hire some chemists with bachelor's degrees, a master's or doctoral degree is becoming more important for chemist jobs.

*Chemical engineers* design equipment and develop processes for manufacturing chemicals on a large scale. They conduct experiments to learn how processes behave and to discover new chemical products and processes. A bachelor's degree is essential for all of these jobs, and a master's degree may be preferred or required for some.

*Engineering* and *science technicians* assist chemists and engineers in research activities and may conduct some research independently. Those with bachelor's degrees in chemistry or graduates of 2-year technical institutes usually fill these positions. Some graduates of engineering programs start as technicians until an opportunity to advance into an engineering position arises.

*Management, business, and financial occupations.* Most managers need a 4-year college degree in addition to experience in the industry. As in other highly technical industries, top managerial positions often are held by those with substantial technical experience. Employment in managerial occupations is expected to decline as companies merge and consolidate operations.

*Engineering managers* conduct cost estimations, perform plant design feasibility studies, and coordinate daily operations. These jobs require a college degree in a technical discipline, such as chemistry or chemical engineering, as well as experience in the industry. Some employees advance from research and development positions to management positions.

*Marketing* and *sales managers* promote sales of chemical products by informing customers of company products and services. A bachelor's degree in marketing, chemistry, or chemical engineering usually is required for these jobs.

*Office and administrative support occupations.* Office and administrative support workers perform office functions such as secretarial duties, bookkeeping, and material records processing, among others. Training beyond high school and familiarity with computers is preferred for these occupations.

**Training and Advancement**
Despite recent reductions in the workforce, the chemical industry offers career opportunities for persons with varying levels of experience and education. Training and advancement differ for the three major categories of occupations.

*Production occupations.* Production workers may start as laborers or in other lesser skilled jobs and, with experience and training, advance into better paying positions that require greater skills or have greater responsibility. Substantial advancement is possible even within a single occupation. For example, *chemical plant and system operators* may move up through several levels of responsibility until they reach the highest paying operator job. Advancement in production occupations usually requires mastery of advanced skills, generally acquired by a combination of on-the-job training and formal training provided by the employer. Some workers advance into supervisory positions.

*Professional and related occupations.* Most jobs in research and development require substantial technical education beyond high school up to a doctorate degree; opportunities exist, however, for persons with a 2-year associate degree. Developing a new product or being awarded a patent brings an increase in pay and prestige but, after a point, advancement may require moving from research and development into management. Researchers usually are familiar with company objectives and production methods, which, combined with college education, equips them with many of the tools necessary for management positions.

*Management, business, and financial occupations.* Managerial jobs usually require a 4-year college degree, though some may require only a 2-year technical degree. Managers can advance into higher level jobs without additional formal training outside the workplace, although competition is keen. In general, advancement into the highest management ranks depends on one's experience and proven ability to handle responsibility in several functional areas. Among larger, multinational firms, international experience is important for career advancement. Also, industry restructuring has left fewer layers of management, intensifying competition for promotions.

**Outlook**
Employment is projected to decline, and applicants for jobs are expected to face keen competition.

*Employment change.* Although output is expected to grow, wage and salary employment in the chemical manufacturing industry, excluding pharmaceuticals and medicine, is projected to decline by 16 percent. The expected decline in employment growth can be attributed to trends affecting the U.S. and global economies. A number of factors will influence chemical industry employment, such as more efficient production processes, increased plant automation, the state of the national and world economy, company mergers and consolidation, increased foreign competition, the shifting of production activities to foreign countries, and environmental health and safety concerns and legislation. Another trend in the chemical industry is the rising demand for specialty chemicals. Chemical companies are finding that, in order to remain competitive, they must differentiate their products and produce specialty chemicals, such as advanced polymers and plastics designed for customer-specific uses—for example, a durable body panel on an automobile.

Improvements in production technology have reduced the need for workers in production; installation, maintenance, and repair; and material moving occupations, which account for large proportions of jobs in the chemical industry. Both the application of computerized controls in standard production and the growing manufacture of specialty chemicals requiring precise, computer-controlled production methods will reduce the need for workers to monitor or directly operate equipment. Although production facilities will be easier to run with the increased use of computerized controls, the new production methods will require workers with a better understanding of the systems.

Foreign competition has been intensifying in most industries, and the chemical industry is no exception. Globalization—the increase in international trade and rapidly expanding foreign production capabilities—should intensify competition. Pressure to reduce costs and streamline production will result in mergers and consolidations of companies both within the United States and abroad. Mergers and consolidations are allowing chemical companies to increase profits by eliminating duplicate tasks and departments and shifting operations to locations in which costs are lowest. U.S. companies are expected to move some production activities to developing countries—in East Asia and Latin America, for example—to take advantage of rapidly expanding markets.

The volatility of crude oil and natural gas prices has impacted the chemical manufacturing industry; the cost of these resources is particularly volatile in the United States. Likewise, prices of chemical feedstocks—like ethane or propane, which are used to produce petrochemicals, plastics, fertilizers, and other products—are expected to remain high. As a result, production of such products may shift overseas, where the costs of feedstocks are lower.

Although the industry is expected to increase spending on research and development, a growing amount of this investment is going overseas, thus limiting employment growth in this segment. In addition, Federal Government investment in research and development has been decreasing, a trend that, if it continues, could further restrict job growth.

The chemical industry invests billions of dollars yearly in technology to reduce pollution and clean up waste sites. Concerns about the costs of waste and hazardous chemicals cleanup, and their effects on the environment, may spur producers to create chemicals with fewer or less dangerous byproducts or with byproducts that can be recycled or disposed of cleanly.

*Selected Industry Segments.* The factors influencing employment in the chemical manufacturing industry will affect different segments of the industry to varying degrees. Only one segment—cleaning preparations, including soap, cleaning compounds, and toilet preparations—is projected to grow. Three segments—other chemical products, basic chemical manufacturing, and synthetic materials—are projected to lose jobs.

*Job prospects.* Individuals seeking employment in the chemical manufacturing industry are expected to face keen competition, particularly those seeking to enter the industry for the first time. For production jobs, opportunities will be best for those with experience and continuing education. For professional and managerial jobs, applicants with experience and an advanced degree should have the best prospects. In addition, some job opportunities will arise from the need to replace workers who transfer to other occupations or who retire or leave the labor force for other reasons.

## Earnings

*Industry earnings.* Earnings in the chemical industry are higher than average. Weekly earnings for all production workers in chemical manufacturing averaged $834 in 2006, compared with $699 in all manufacturing industries. The higher earnings were due, in part, to the chemical industry's practice of assigning more overtime and weekend work, which commands higher hourly rates.

Wages of workers in the chemical industry vary according to occupation, the specific industry segment, and the size of the production plant. Medial hourly earnings of the largest occupations in chemical manufacturing are shown in table 3.

**Table 3. Median hourly earnings of the largest occupations in chemical manufacturing, May 2006**

| Occupation | Chemical manufacturing | All industries |
|---|---|---|
| Chemists | $28.84 | $28.78 |
| First-line supervisors/managers of production and operating workers | 26.65 | 22.74 |
| Chemical plant and system operators | 23.68 | 23.60 |
| Maintenance and repair workers, general | 20.20 | 15.34 |
| Chemical technicians | 20.32 | 18.87 |
| Chemical equipment operators and tenders | 19.26 | 19.37 |
| Inspectors, testers, sorters, samplers, and weighers | 15.40 | 14.14 |
| Mixing and blending machine setters, operators, and tenders | 14.64 | 14.10 |
| Packaging and filling machine operators and tenders | 12.24 | 11.06 |
| Team assemblers | 11.77 | 11.63 |

*Benefits and union membership.* One of the principal unions representing chemical workers was the Paper, Allied-Industrial, Chemical, and Energy (PACE) Workers International Union, which recently merged with the United Steel Workers Union, the new organization kept the name of the later. Another major representative for chemical workers is the International Chemical Workers Union. In 2006, nearly 12 percent of manufacturing workers were union members or covered by union contracts.

## Sources of Additional Information

Additional information on training and careers in the chemical manufacturing industry is available from either of the following organizations:

➤ American Chemical Society, 1155 16th St. N.W., Washington, DC 20036. Internet: **http://www.acs.org**
➤ American Institute of Chemical Engineers, 3 Park Ave., New York, NY 10016-5991. Internet: **http://www.aiche.org**

General industry information and facts are available from:

➤ American Chemistry Council, 1300 Wilson Blvd., Arlington, VA 22209.

Detailed information on many occupations in the chemical manufacturing industry, including the following, may be found in the 2008-09 edition of the *Occupational Outlook Handbook*:

- Chemists and materials scientists

- Engineers
- Industrial production managers
- Inspectors, testers, sorters, samplers, and weighers
- Material moving occupations
- Science technicians

# Computer and Electronic Product Manufacturing

## SIGNIFICANT POINTS

- Employment is projected to decline 12 percent over the 2006-16 period due to productivity improvements, imports, and the movement of some jobs to lower wage countries.

- The industry is characterized by significant research and development activity and rapid technological change.

- Professional and related personnel account for 1 out of 3 workers.

## Nature of the Industry

The computer and electronic product manufacturing industry produces computers, computer-related products, including printers, communications equipment, and home electronic equipment, as well as a wide range of goods used for both commercial and military purposes. In addition, many electronics products or components are incorporated into other industries' products, such as cars, toys, and appliances.

*Goods and services.* This industry differs somewhat from other manufacturing industries in that production workers make up a relatively small proportion of the workforce. Technological innovation characterizes this industry more than most others and, in fact, drives much of the industry's production. This unusually rapid pace of innovation and technological advancement requires a high proportion of engineers, engineering technicians, and other technical workers who carry out extensive research and development. Likewise, the importance of promoting and selling the products manufactured by the various segments of the industry requires knowledgeable marketing and sales workers. American companies in this industry manufacture and assemble many products abroad to take advantage of lower production costs and favorable regulatory environments.

Electronic products contain many intermediate components that are purchased from other manufacturers. Companies producing intermediate components and finished goods regularly choose to locate near each other, because doing so allows companies to receive new products more quickly and lower their inventory costs. It also facilitates joint research and development projects which benefit both companies. As a result of having the skilled workforce that fosters product improvement, several regions of the country have become centers of the electronics industry. The most prominent of these centers is Silicon Valley, a concentration of integrated circuit, software, and computer firms in California's Santa Clara Valley, near San Jose. However, there are several other centers of the industry throughout the country.

Globalization has become a major factor in the electronics manufacturing industry, often making it difficult to distinguish between American and foreign companies. Many American companies are opening plants and development centers overseas and overseas companies are doing the same in the U.S. Many products are being designed in one country, manufactured in another, and assembled in a third. The U.S. electronics industry tends to be focused on high-end products, such as computers and microchips. Even so, many components of final products manufactured in the U.S. are produced elsewhere and shipped to an American plant for final assembly.

Although some of the companies in this industry are very large, most are relatively small. The history of innovation in the industry explains the startup of many small firms. Some companies are involved in design or research and development (R&D), whereas others may simply manufacture components, such as computer chips, under contract for others. Often, an engineer or a physicist will have an innovative idea and set up a new company to develop the associated product. Once developed, the company licenses a production company to produce the product, which is then sold by the original company. Although electronic products can be quite sophisticated, production methods are generally similar, making it possible to manufacture many electronic products or components with a relatively small investment. Furthermore, investors often are willing to put their money behind new companies in this industry because of the history of large paybacks from some successful companies.

Products manufactured in this industry include computers and computer storage devices, such as DVD drives, and computer peripheral equipment, such as printers and scanners; communications equipment—wireless telephones and telephone switching equipment; consumer electronics, such as televisions and audio equipment; and military electronics—for example, radar, communications equipment, guidance for "smart" bombs, and electronic navigation equipment. The industry also includes the manufacture of semiconductor products—better known as computer chips, or integrated circuits—which are key components of computers and many other electronic products. Two of the most significant types of computer chips are microprocessors, which are the central processing units of computers, and memory chips, which store information.

*Industry organization.* The computer and electronic product manufacturing industry has many segments. Companies in the industry are generally classified by what they sell.

*Computer and peripheral manufacturing* is made up of a wide variety of companies that make computers and computer-related products. A relatively large number of companies build computers for home or business use. Most computers are built by a small number of well-known brands, but there are also many small companies that sell their products locally or on the Internet. Because computers are very complex products, they are made up of a wide range of components, such as motherboards, central processing units, graphics cards, hard disk drives, and power supplies. Although some computer manufacturers build some of these products themselves, many of these products are purchased from other companies and assembled as part of the computer. As a result, many finished computers are simply the combination of a number of other products.

Other firms in this industry segment produce computer-related products, known as peripheral equipment. These products include keyboards, mice, printers and scanners. Other peripherals are physically installed in the computer's case, and are generally known as internal peripherals. These include hard disk drives, networking cards, modems, sound cards, and disk drives. Many internal peripherals are prepackaged as part of a computer, although almost all of them can be installed by a technician or experienced computer owner.

The *communications equipment manufacturing* segment of the industry produces a number of devices that simplify communication between individuals or groups. It includes telephones and cellular telephones, as well as equipment used by television and radio stations to transmit information. It should be noted that this does not include computer-related peripherals—such as networking cards or modems—which allow computers to connect to other computers.

*Audio and video equipment manufacturing* is a relatively small industry in the United States and includes companies who produce consumer electronics. These include televisions, stereo receivers, compact disc and DVD players, and other such devices. While these devices are widespread in the U.S., most of them are produced overseas, making employment in this industry relatively small.

*Semiconductor and other electronic component* manufacturers produce a wide variety of integrated circuits, or computer microchips, which power a wide range of electronic products. They also produce a number of other electronic components, such as resistors and capacitors, as well as printed circuit boards. Unlike most of the companies in this industry, these manufacturers start from basic materials such as silicon and copper and produce intermediate products that are only rarely sold directly to consumers. The exceptions to this rule include companies which produce central processing units and memory chips, although even these products are more likely to be pre-installed in a new computer.

Fabrication plants that build semiconductor products, known as "fabs", are fitted with dust-free zones called "cleanrooms". Microchip circuitry is so small and complex that it can be ruined by microscopic particles floating in the air, so semiconductor products must be built by computer-controlled machines in an environment with very little human intervention. Most production workers in this industry segment are actually more involved in evaluating manufacturing methods and testing completed chips. Semiconductor manufacturers also spend an inordinate amount of money on research and development—more than most companies in the entire computer and electronic product manufacturing industry.

The *navigational, measuring, electromedical, and control instruments manufacturing* segment is a diverse group of companies that produce products mainly for industrial, military and health care use. It also includes some consumer products, such as global positioning system (GPS) devices, as well as clocks and watches. This segment is one of the largest in the industry, mainly because the Federal Government puts so much money into defense and health care.

Many of the companies in this segment work as government contractors, producing equipment for military purposes. In some cases, this technology has been adapted for consumer use. For example, GPS technology was originally designed for use by the U.S. Navy, but has been developed into a navigation system that

individuals can use in their cars. There is also a growing health care component of this industry segment. Extensive government funding for research in medical technology has led to a number of important innovations that are being used worldwide in medical care.

*Manufacturing and reproducing magnetic and optical media* is another segment of this industry. Firms in this segment produce blank compact discs, DVDs, and audio and video tape. They produce some of this blank media for sale to consumers, but most of it they use to duplicate on a mass scale audio recordings, videos and movies, software, and other media for distribution to consumers and business users. Establishments in this segment are generally either subsidiaries of companies that create the software, movies, or recordings or are independent firms licensed by such companies as distributors.

*Recent developments.* The rapid pace of innovation in electronics technology makes for a constant demand for newer and faster products and applications. This demand puts a greater emphasis on R&D than is typical in most manufacturing operations. Being the first firm to market a new or better product can mean success for both the product and the firm. Even for many relatively commonplace items, R&D continues to result in better, cheaper products with more desirable features. For example, a company that develops a new kind of computer chip to be used in many brands of computers can earn millions of dollars in sales until a competitor is able to improve on that design. Many employees, therefore, are research scientists, engineers, and technicians whose job it is to continually develop and improve products.

The product design process includes not only the initial design, but also development work, which ensures that the product functions properly and can be manufactured as inexpensively as possible. When a product is manufactured, the components are assembled, usually by soldering them to a printed circuit board by means of automated equipment. Hand assembly of small parts requires both good eyesight and coordination, but because of the cost and precision involved, assembly and packaging are becoming highly automated.

## Working Conditions

*Hours.* About half of all employees work regular 40-hour weeks, but pressure to develop new products ahead of competitors may result in some R&D personnel working extensive overtime to meet deadlines. The competitive nature of the industry makes for an exciting, but sometimes stressful, work environment—especially for those in technical and managerial occupations.

*Work Environment.* In general, those working in computer and electronics manufacturing—even production workers—enjoy relatively good working conditions. In contrast to those in many other manufacturing industries, production workers in this industry usually work in clean and relatively noise-free environments.

In 2006, the rate of work-related injuries and illnesses per 100 full-time workers was 2.0 in the computer and electronic parts manufacturing industry, lower than the average of 4.4 for the private sector. However, some jobs in the industry may present risks. For example, some workers who fabricate integrated circuits and other components may be exposed to hazardous chemicals, and working with small parts may cause eyestrain.

## Employment

The computer and electronic product manufacturing industry employed 1.3 million wage and salary workers in 2006 (table 1). Few workers were self-employed.

**Table 1. Distribution of wage and salary employment in computer and electronic product manufacturing, by detailed industry, 2006** (Employment in thousands)

| Industry | Employment | Percent |
|---|---|---|
| **Computer and electronic product manufacturing, total** | 1,316 | 100.0 |
| Semiconductor and other electronic component manufacturing | 463 | 35.2 |
| Navigational, measuring, electromedical, and control instruments manufacturing | 438 | 33.3 |
| Computer and peripheral equipment manufacturing | 199 | 15.1 |
| Communications equipment manufacturing | 144 | 10.9 |
| Manufacturing and reproducing magnetic and optical media | 41 | 3.1 |
| Audio and visual equipment manufacturing | 32 | 2.4 |

The industry comprised about 19,000 establishments in 2006, many of which were small, employing only 1 or a few workers. Large establishments of 100 or more workers employed the majority—78 percent—of the industry's workforce (chart).

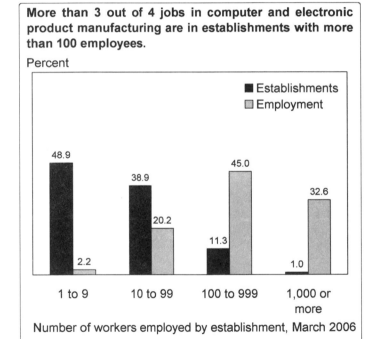

**More than 3 out of 4 jobs in computer and electronic product manufacturing are in establishments with more than 100 employees.**

Percent

- ■ Establishments
- ▨ Employment

| | 1 to 9 | 10 to 99 | 100 to 999 | 1,000 or more |
|---|---|---|---|---|
| Establishments | 48.9 | 38.9 | 11.3 | 1.0 |
| Employment | 2.2 | 20.2 | 45.0 | 32.6 |

Number of workers employed by establishment, March 2006

Companies in this industry also may employ many additional workers in establishments that are part of other industries. Some workers who perform R&D work at separate research establishments that are not actually part of a manufacturing facility in this industry, although owned by the companies in this industry, and so are included in a different industry—research and development in the physical, engineering, and life sciences. However, due to the importance of R&D work to the computer and electronic product manufacturing industry, computer and electronic product-related R&D is discussed here even though a large proportion of the associated workers is not included in this industry.

## Occupations in the Industry

The computer and electronic product manufacturing industry has a diverse workforce mainly composed of professionals, who conduct research and development work, and production workers, who are directly involved in the assembly and testing of the industry's products.

***Professional and related occupations.*** About 1 in every 3 jobs in this industry is in a professional occupation (table 2). About 15 percent of those workers are engineers—predominantly *electrical and electronics engineers* and *computer hardware engineers,* but also many *industrial* and *mechanical engineers.* These workers develop new products and devise better, more efficient production methods. Engineers may coordinate and lead teams developing new products. Others may work with customers to help them make the best use of the products.

*Computer systems analysts, database administrators, and computer scientists* are employed throughout the industry, becoming more dispersed with the increasing computerization of development and production methods. Many new hardware devices are now controlled by software, which has increased the share of computer specialists in this field. Other professionals include *mathematical* and *physical scientists,* and *technical writers.*

About 6 percent of workers are *engineering technicians,* many of whom work closely with engineers. Engineering technicians help develop new products, work in production areas, and sometimes assist customers in installing, maintaining, and repairing equipment. They also may test new products or processes to make sure that everything works correctly.

***Production occupations.*** About 3 out of 10 employees are production workers. About half of those are *assemblers and fabricators,* who place and solder components on circuit boards, or assemble and connect the various parts of electronic devices. *Electrical and electronic equipment assemblers* are responsible for putting together products such as computers and appliances, telecommunications equipment, and even missile control systems. *Semiconductor processors* initiate and control the many automated steps in the process of manufacturing integrated circuits or computer chips. Some assemblers are highly skilled and use their significant experience and training to assemble major components. A skilled assembler may put together an entire subassembly or even an entire product, especially when products are made in relatively small numbers. Other, less skilled assemblers often work on a production line, attaching one or a few parts and continually repeating the same operation. Increasingly, as production work becomes more automated, assemblers and other production workers monitor the machinery that does the assembly work rather than physically assembling products themselves. *Inspectors, testers, sorters, samplers, and weighers* use sophisticated testing machinery to ensure that devices operate as designed.

***Management, business, and financial occupations.*** About 16 percent of the workers in the industry are in management, business, and financial occupations. Top managers in this industry are much more likely to have a technical background than their counterparts in other industries. This is especially true in smaller companies, which often are founded by engineers or other technical professionals who found companies to sell the products they develop.

*Office and administrative support occupations.* About 10 percent of workers in the industry hold office and administrative support jobs. The largest occupation in this group is *secretaries and administrative assistants.*

*Sales and related occupations.* A small number of workers are involved in selling products manufactured by the industry. Sales positions require technical knowledge and abilities; as a result, engineers and technicians may find opportunities in sales or sales support.

## Training and Advancement

Training requirements vary greatly among the different occupations in the computer and electronic products manufacturing industry. Workers in all fields must have strong technical knowledge and an ability to work in teams. In most cases, advancement comes in the form of leadership and increased responsibility.

*Professional and related occupations.* Entry into engineering occupations generally requires at least a bachelor's degree in engineering, although those with 4-year degrees in physics, computer science, or another technical area may qualify as well. Some positions, however, may require a master's or doctorate degree. Most advanced positions require a certain amount of relevant work experience. Computer systems analysts or scientists usually need a degree in computer science or a related field, and in many cases they also must have considerable programming experience.

Training for engineering technicians is available from a number of sources. Although most employers prefer graduates of 2-year postsecondary training schools—usually technical institutes or junior colleges—training in the U.S. Armed Forces or through proprietary schools also may meet employer requirements. Engineering technicians should have an aptitude for math and science. Entry-level technicians may begin working with a more experienced technician or engineer. Advancement opportunities for experienced technicians may include supervisory positions or movement into other production and inspection operations.

Advancement for technical workers comes in a variety of forms, depending on the goals of the individual and the needs of the company. Because companies often are founded by professionals with technical backgrounds, opportunities for advancement into executive or managerial positions may arise for experienced workers who keep up with rapid changes in technology and who possess the business expertise necessary to succeed in a fast-changing economy. Others are not as intrigued by the idea of working in management, and prefer to continue in their technical positions. Top engineers and other technical professionals are often given a great deal of flexibility in their work and offered excellent compensation.

Due to the rapid pace of technological development, technical workers must constantly update their skills and knowledge base to stay abreast. Also, due to the global nature of computer and electronic product manufacturing, knowledge of another language or culture is emerging as a desired qualification for workers in this industry.

**Table 2. Employment of wage and salary workers in computer and electronic product manufacturing by occupation, 2006 and projected change, 2006-2016.**
(Employment in thousands)

| Occupation | Employment, 2006 Number | Employment, 2006 Percent | Percent change, 2006-16 |
|---|---|---|---|
| **All occupations** | 1,316 | 100.0 | -12.0 |
| **Management, business, and financial occupations** | 209 | 15.9 | -11.8 |
| Top executives | 23 | 1.8 | -19.2 |
| Marketing and sales managers | 18 | 1.4 | -13.5 |
| Industrial production managers | 12 | 0.9 | -10.3 |
| Engineering managers | 29 | 2.2 | -8.3 |
| Purchasing agents, except wholesale, retail, and farm products | 20 | 1.5 | -10.7 |
| Accountants and auditors | 14 | 1.1 | -11.7 |
| **Professional and related occupations** | 446 | 33.9 | -7.7 |
| Computer software engineers, applications | 38 | 2.9 | 3.1 |
| Computer software engineers, systems software | 46 | 3.5 | -10.1 |
| Computer support specialists | 14 | 1.1 | -15.5 |
| Computer systems analysts | 13 | 1.0 | -8.8 |
| Aerospace engineers | 14 | 1.1 | 1.0 |
| Computer hardware engineers | 32 | 2.4 | -15.3 |
| Electrical engineers | 34 | 2.6 | -9.2 |
| Electronics engineers, except computer | 36 | 2.7 | -10.7 |
| Industrial engineers | 31 | 2.3 | 8.7 |
| Mechanical engineers | 21 | 1.6 | -8.6 |
| Drafters | 9 | 0.7 | -8.9 |
| Electrical and electronic engineering technicians | 42 | 3.2 | -10.8 |
| Industrial engineering technicians | 15 | 1.1 | -2.8 |
| **Sales and related occupations** | 47 | 3.6 | -12.1 |
| **Office and administrative support occupations** | 133 | 10.1 | -14.2 |
| Bookkeeping, accounting, and auditing clerks | 11 | 0.8 | -9.5 |
| Customer service representatives | 15 | 1.2 | -0.2 |
| Production, planning, and expediting clerks | 15 | 1.1 | -11.1 |
| Shipping, receiving, and traffic clerks | 17 | 1.3 | -14.3 |
| Secretaries and administrative assistants | 22 | 1.7 | -13.0 |
| Office clerks, general | 14 | 1.1 | -14.2 |
| **Installation, maintenance, and repair occupations** | 38 | 2.9 | -6.5 |
| **Production occupations** | 411 | 31.2 | -16.1 |
| First-line supervisors/managers of production and operating workers | 29 | 2.2 | -9.7 |
| Electrical and electronic equipment assemblers | 114 | 8.7 | -29.3 |
| Electromechanical equipment assemblers | 28 | 2.1 | -8.4 |
| Team assemblers | 59 | 4.5 | -8.5 |
| Machinists | 15 | 1.1 | -2.8 |
| Inspectors, testers, sorters, samplers, and weighers | 36 | 2.7 | -15.6 |
| Semiconductor processors | 41 | 3.1 | -13.8 |

Note: Columns may not add to totals due to omission of occupations with small employment

*Production occupations.* Although assembly workers generally need only a high school diploma, assemblers in the computer and electronic product manufacturing industry may need more specialized training or experience than do workers in other manufacturing industries. Precision assembly work can be extremely sophisticated and complex, and some jobs may even require formal technical training. A certificate or associate's degree in semiconductor technology or high-tech manufacturing is good preparation for semiconductor processor operator positions.

Advancement opportunities depend not only on work experience, but also on the level of technical training and the ability to keep up with changing technology. Production workers may advance into more responsible positions, as well as team leadership. Experienced workers may work directly with engineers to determine how production methods can be improved.

*Management, business, and financial occupations.* Managers and executives in this industry tend to be much more technically oriented than in most fields. Because technology is fast-changing, managers and executives must be able to speak intelligently about new developments. They must also be able to work directly with engineers to come up with viable strategies for business development. Many managers in this industry are actually trained as engineers or other technical professionals. Furthermore, many companies in this industry are founded by an inventor or group of inventors who design a new product. Although in many cases these individuals hire others to manage the business, there are still several companies whose CEO is the product inventor.

## Outlook

Employment in the computer and electronic product manufacturing industry is expected to decline over the next decade, but there should still be favorable employment opportunities in certain segments of the industry.

*Employment change.* Wage and salary employment in the computer and electronic product manufacturing industry is expected to decline by 12 percent between 2006 and 2016, compared with a projected increase of 11 percent in all industries. Although the output of this industry is projected to increase more rapidly than that of any other industry, employment will decline as a result of continued rapid productivity growth—the ability of the industry to produce more and better products with fewer employees. Employment also will be adversely affected by continued increases in imports of electronic and computer products, including intermediate products such as components and microchips. Although a great deal of the design work in this industry takes place in the U.S., much of the manufacturing process has been moved overseas.

The projected change in employment over the 2006-16 period varies by industry segment (table 3). Although demand for computers should remain relatively strong worldwide, employment is expected to decline 33.5 percent in computers and peripheral equipment and 13.7 percent in semiconductor and other electronic component manufacturing. Declines in both will be due to the introduction of new technology and automated manufacturing processes, as well as a slowdown in the growth of output in these segments from previously high levels. Further, these segments will continue to face strong foreign competition.

Employment in navigational, measuring, electromedical, and control instruments manufacturing is expected to decline relatively slowly at 4.5 percent due to heavy spending on military and health care electronics. Employment in audio and video equipment manufacturing is expected to decrease by 21.1 percent, due largely to continued import competition as well as improvements in productivity. Employment in communications equipment manufacturing is expected to increase by 0.4 percent despite automation and consolidation among firms in the industry. Employment in the manufacturing and reproduction of magnetic and optical media is expected to decrease by 3.7 percent, because of higher productivity and more efficient production processes.

**Table 3. Projected employment change in computer and electronic product manufacturing by industry segment, 2006-16**

| Industry segment | Percent Change |
|---|---|
| **Computer and electronic product manufacturing, total** .......... | -12.0 |
| Communications equipment .......... | 0.4 |
| Manufacturing and reproducing magnetic and optical media .......... | -3.7 |
| Navigational, measuring, electromedical, and control instruments .......... | -4.5 |
| Semiconductor and other electronic components.......... | -13.7 |
| Audio and video equipment .......... | -21.1 |
| Computer and peripheral equipment .......... | -33.5 |

There should be a smaller decrease in employment among professional and related occupations than among most other occupations in the computer and electronic product manufacturing industry. Despite large numbers of engineering graduates in many foreign countries, many American manufacturers prefer U.S.-based engineering teams because they are believed to have a better knowledge of the domestic market. However, the use of the Internet and other new forms of communication makes it possible for engineers to collaborate over great distances. At the same time, wages have been increasing rapidly among qualified engineers in developing countries. While offshore outsourcing of engineers will probably continue, there should be little danger to American workers, who report very low unemployment.

The computer and electronic product manufacturing industry is characterized by rapid technological advances and has grown faster than most other industries over the past several decades, although rising costs, imports, and the rapid pace of innovation continue to pose challenges. Certain segments of the industry and individual companies often experience problems. For example, the industry occasionally undergoes severe downturns, and individual companies—even those in segments of the industry doing well—can run into trouble because they have not kept up with the latest technological developments or because they have erred in deciding which products to manufacture. Such uncertainties can be expected to continue. In addition, the intensity of foreign competition and the future role of imports remain difficult to project. Import competition has wiped out major parts of the domestic consumer electronics industry, and future effects of such competition depend on trade policies and market forces. The industry is likely to continue to encounter strong competition from imported electronic goods and components from countries throughout Asia and Europe.

Because defense expenditures are expected to increase, sales of military electronics, an important segment of the industry, will likely pick up. Furthermore, firms producing electromedical equipment will continue to expand as new health care breakthroughs are made. Smaller, more powerful computer chips are constantly being developed and incorporated into an even wider array of products, and the semiconductor content of all electronic products will continue to increase. New opportunities will continue to be created by the growth of digital technology, artificial intelligence, and nanotechnology, as well as the expansion of the Internet and the increasing demand for global information networking.

*Job prospects.* Despite the overall projected decrease in employment, many employment opportunities should continue to arise in the industry due to the technological revolutions taking place in computers, semiconductors, and telecommunications, as well as the need to replace the many workers who leave the industry due to retirement or other reasons. Opportunities should be best in research and development. The products of this industry—especially powerful computer chips—will continue to enhance productivity in all areas of the economy.

Prospects are especially good for professional workers, such as engineers. Despite competition from abroad, U.S. companies prefer workers in research and development who have a strong understanding of the domestic marketplace. Although employment in the industry continues to decline, the relatively small number of engineers in the U.S. makes it very difficult for companies to find qualified workers when openings arise. Computer software engineers are also in high demand in this industry because many complicated hardware products will require software. This includes both drivers which help devices interface with computers and software that runs directly on complex devices.

Despite the rapid decline of production jobs, prospects should still be good for qualified workers, especially those with formal training in high-tech manufacturing. Although fewer positions are now available, changes in the nature of the work have meant that workers need to have a higher skill level than before. Many positions require a certificate or associate's degree from a technical school.

## Earnings

*Industry earnings.* Earnings in the computer and electronic product manufacturing industry are generally high; this is partly because many of the lower wage production jobs have been automated or exported to other countries. Average weekly earnings of all production or nonsupervisory workers in the industry were $768, higher than the average of $568 for all industries in 2006 (table 4).

**Table 4. Average earnings of nonsupervisory workers in the computer and electronic product manufacturing industry, 2006**

| Industry segment | Weekly | Hourly |
|---|---|---|
| Total, private industry | $568 | $16.76 |
| **Computer and electronic products** | | |
| manufacturing | 768 | 18.96 |
| Computer and peripheral equipment | 884 | 23.00 |
| Audio and video equipment | 789 | 20.33 |
| Communications equipment | 776 | 18.99 |
| Electronic instruments | 766 | 18.89 |
| Semiconductor and other electronic | | |
| components | 711 | 17.30 |

**Table 5. Median hourly earnings of the largest occupations in computer and electronic product manufacturing, May 2006**

| Occupation | Computer and electronic product manufacturing | All industries |
|---|---|---|
| Computer hardware engineers | $43.75 | $42.54 |
| Computer software engineers, systems software | 43.33 | 41.04 |
| Computer software engineers, applications | 43.16 | 38.36 |
| Electronics engineers, except computer | 39.23 | 38.97 |
| Electrical engineers | 38.54 | 36.50 |
| Electrical and electronic engineering technicians | 22.05 | 24.35 |
| Semiconductor processors | 15.76 | 15.80 |
| Inspectors, testers, sorters, samplers, and weighers | 14.32 | 14.14 |
| Electrical and electronic equipment assemblers | 12.25 | 12.29 |
| Team assemblers | 11.73 | 11.63 |

Earnings in selected occupations in several components of the computer and electronic product manufacturing industry in 2006 appear in table 5.

## Benefits and union membership

Benefits are very good for workers in this industry with companies offering health care and retirement plans at a minimum. Compared with other manufacturing industries, union membership is relatively small.

## Sources of Additional Information

More information on computer and electronic products manufacturing is available from:

➤ American Electronics Association, 5201 Great America Pkwy., Suite 520, Santa Clara, CA 95054. Internet: **http://www.aeanet.org**

➤ The Electronic Industries Alliance, 2500 Wilson Blvd., Arlington, VA 22201. Internet: **http://www.eia.org**

For information on engineering careers within the industry, contact:

➤ IEEE Computer Society, 1730 Massachusetts Ave., N.W., Washington, DC 20036-1992. Internet: **http://www.computer.org**

Information on these occupations may be found in the 2008–09 *Occupational Outlook Handbook*:

- Assemblers and fabricators
- Computer scientists and database administrators
- Computer software engineers
- Engineers
- Engineering and natural sciences managers
- Engineering technicians
- Semiconductor processors

# Food Manufacturing

- Food manufacturing has one of the highest incidences of injury and illness among all industries; animal slaughtering plants have the highest incidence among all food manufacturing industries.

- Production workers account for 54 percent of all jobs.

- Most production jobs require little formal education or training; many can be learned in a few days.

- Unlike many other industries, food manufacturing is not highly sensitive to economic conditions.

## Nature of the Industry

*Goods and services.* Workers in the food manufacturing industry link farmers and other agricultural producers with consumers. They do this by processing raw fruits, vegetables, grains, meats, and dairy products into finished goods ready for the grocer or wholesaler to sell to households, restaurants, or institutional food services.

Food manufacturing workers perform tasks as varied as the many foods we eat. For example, they slaughter, dress, and cut meat or poultry; process milk, cheese, and other dairy products; can and preserve fruits, vegetables, and frozen specialties; manufacture flour, cereal, pet foods, and other grain mill products; make bread, cookies, cakes, and other bakery products; manufacture sugar and candy and other confectionery products; process shortening, margarine, and other fats and oils; and prepare packaged seafood, coffee, potato and corn chips, and peanut butter. Although this list is long, it is not exhaustive. Food manufacturing workers also play a part in delivering numerous other food products to our tables.

Quality control and quality assurance are vital to this industry. The U.S. Department of Agriculture's (USDA) Food Safety and Inspection Service branch oversees all aspects of food manufacturing. In addition, other food safety programs have been adopted recently as issues of chemical and bacterial contamination and new food-borne pathogens remain a public health concern. For example, by applying science-based controls from raw materials to finished products, a food safety program called Hazard Analysis and Critical Control Point focuses on identifying hazards and preventing them from contaminating food in early stages of meat processing. The program relies on individual plants developing and implementing safety measures along with a system to intercept potential contamination points, which is then subject to USDA inspections.

*Industry organization.* About 34 percent of all food manufacturing workers are employed in plants that slaughter and process animals and another 19 percent work in establishments that make bakery goods (table 1). Seafood product preparation and packaging, the smallest sector of the food manufacturing industry, accounts for only 3 percent of all jobs.

## Working Conditions

*Hours.* The average production employee in food manufacturing worked 40.1 hours a week in 2006, compared with 41.1 hours a week for all manufacturing workers and 33.9 hours a week for workers in all industries. Relatively few workers work part time or are on variable schedules. Eighty-six percent worked full time in 2006.

**Table 1. Distribution of wage and salary employment in food manufacturing by industry segment, 2006**
(Employment in thousands)

| Industry segment | 2006 Employment | 2006-16 Percent Change |
|---|---|---|
| **Food manufacturing, total** | 1,484 | 0.3 |
| Animal slaughtering and processing | 509 | 11.8 |
| Bakeries and tortilla manufacturing | 281 | 1.5 |
| Fruit and vegetable preserving and specialty food manufacturing | 177 | -12.3 |
| Dairy product manufacturing | 132 | -3.9 |
| Sugar and confectionery product manufacturing | 75 | -18.0 |
| Grain and oilseed milling | 61 | -15.0 |
| Animal food manufacturing | 50 | -15.5 |
| Seafood product preparation and packaging | 40 | -11.0 |
| Other food manufacturing | 160 | 1.6 |

*Work environment.* Many production jobs in food manufacturing involve repetitive, physically demanding work. Food manufacturing workers are highly susceptible to repetitive-strain injuries to their hands, wrists, and elbows. This type of injury is especially common in meat- and poultry-processing plants. Production workers often stand for long periods and may be required to lift heavy objects or use cutting, slicing, grinding, and other dangerous tools and machines. To deal with difficult working conditions, ergonomic programs have been introduced to cut down on work-related accidents and injuries.

In 2006, there were 7.4 cases of work-related injury or illness per 100 full-time food manufacturing workers, much higher than the rate of 4.4 cases for the private sector as a whole. Injury rates vary significantly among specific food manufacturing industries, ranging from a low of 1.8 per 100 workers in retail bakeries to 12.5 per 100 in animal slaughtering plants, the highest rate in food manufacturing.

In an effort to reduce occupational hazards, many plants have redesigned equipment, increased the use of job rotation, allowed longer or more frequent breaks, and implemented extensive training programs in safe work practices. Furthermore, meat and poultry plants must comply with a wide array of Occupational Safety and Health Administration (OSHA) regulations ensuring a safer work environment. Although injury rates remain high, safety training seminars and workshops have reduced those rates. Some workers wear protective hats or masks, gloves, aprons, and boots. In many companies uniforms and protective clothing are changed daily for reasons of sanitation.

Because of the considerable mechanization in the industry, most food manufacturing plants are noisy, with limited opportunities for interaction among workers. In some highly automated plants, "hands-on" manual work has been replaced by computers and factory automation, resulting in less waste and higher productivity. While much of the basic production—such as trimming, chopping, and sorting—will remain labor intensive for many years to come, automation is increasingly being applied to various functions, including inventory management, product movement, and quality control issues such as packing and inspection.

Working conditions also depend on the type of food being processed. For example, some bakery employees work at night or on weekends and spend much of their shifts near ovens that can be uncomfortably hot. In contrast, workers in dairies and meat-processing plants typically work daylight hours and may experience cold and damp conditions. Some plants, such as those producing processed fruits and vegetables, operate on a seasonal basis, so workers are not guaranteed steady, year-round employment and occasionally travel from region to region seeking work. These plants are increasingly rare, however, as the industry continues to diversify and manufacturing plants produce alternative foods during otherwise inactive periods.

## Employment

In 2006, the food manufacturing industry provided 1.5 million jobs. Almost all employees were wage and salary workers; only a few were self-employed and unpaid family workers.

In 2006, about 28,000 establishments manufactured food, with 89 percent employing fewer than 100 workers (chart).

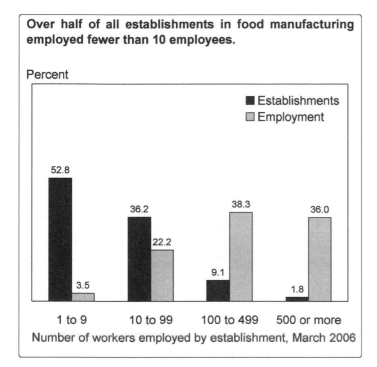

**Over half of all establishments in food manufacturing employed fewer than 10 employees.**

Percent

■ Establishments
▢ Employment

1 to 9: 52.8, 3.5
10 to 99: 36.2, 22.2
100 to 499: 9.1, 38.3
500 or more: 1.8, 36.0

Number of workers employed by establishment, March 2006

Nevertheless, establishments employing 500 or more workers accounted for 36 percent of all jobs.

The employment distribution in this industry varies widely. Animal slaughtering and processing employs the largest proportion of workers. Economic changes in livestock farming and slaughtering plants have changed the industry. Increasingly, fewer, but larger, farms are producing the vast majority of livestock in the United States. Similarly, there are now fewer, but much larger, meat-processing plants, owned by fewer companies—a development that has tended to concentrate employment in a few locations.

Food manufacturing workers are found in all States, although some sectors of the industry are concentrated in certain parts of the country. For example, in 2006, California, Illinois, Iowa, Pennsylvania, and Texas employed 24 percent of all workers in animal slaughtering and processing. That same year, Wisconsin employed 32 percent of all cheese manufacturing workers, and California accounted for 24 percent of fruit and vegetable canning, pickling, and drying workers.

## Occupations in the Industry

The food manufacturing industry employs many different types of workers. More than half, or 54 percent, are production workers, including skilled precision workers and less skilled machine operators and laborers (table 2). Production jobs require manual dexterity, good hand-eye coordination, and, in some sectors of the industry, strength.

Red-meat production is the most labor-intensive food-processing operation. Animals are not uniform in size, and *slaughterers and meatpackers* must slaughter, skin, eviscerate, and cut each carcass into large pieces. They usually do this work by hand, using large, suspended power saws. Increasingly, most plants today require slaughterers and meat packers to further process the large parts by cleaning, salting, and cutting them into tenders and chucks to make them readily available for retail use. Such prepackaged meat products are increasingly preferred by retailers and grocers as they can be easily displayed and sold without the need of a butcher. *Meat, poultry, and fish cutters and trimmers* use handtools to break down the large primary cuts into smaller sizes for shipment to wholesalers and retailers. Such ready to cook meat products are increasingly prepared at processing plants where preparation may now entail filleting; cutting into bite-sized pieces or tenders; preparing and adding vegetables; and applying sauces and flavorings, marinades, or breading. These workers use knives and other handtools for these processes.

*Bakers* mix and bake ingredients according to recipes to produce breads, cakes, pastries, and other goods. Bakers produce goods in large quantities, using mixing machines, ovens, and other equipment.

Many food manufacturing workers use their hands or small handtools to do their jobs. *Cannery workers* perform a variety of routine tasks—such as sorting, grading, washing, trimming, peeling, or slicing—in the canning, freezing, or packaging of food products. *Hand food decorators* apply artistic touches to prepared foods. *Candy molders and marzipan shapers* form sweets into fancy shapes by hand.

As the food manufacturing industry increasingly automates, a growing number of workers are operating machines. For example, *food batchmakers* operate equipment that mixes, blends, or cooks ingredients used in manufacturing various foods, such as cheese, candy, honey, and tomato sauce. *Dairy processing equipment operators* process milk, cream, cheese, and other dairy products. *Cutting and slicing machine operators* slice bacon, bread, cheese, and other foods. *Mixing and blending machine operators* produce dough batter, fruit juices, or spices. *Crushing and grinding machine operators* turn raw grains into cereals, flour, and other milled-grain products, and they produce oils from nuts or seeds. *Extruding and forming machine operators* produce molded food and candy, and *casing finishers and stuffers* make sausage links and similar products. *Bottle packers and bottle fillers* operate machines that fill bottles and jars with preserves, pickles, and other foodstuffs.

*Food cooking machine operators and tenders* steam, deep-fry, boil, or pressure-cook meats, grains, sugar, cheese, or vegetables. *Food and tobacco roasting, baking, and drying machine operators and tenders* operate equipment that roasts grains, nuts, or coffee beans and tend ovens, kilns, dryers, and other equipment that removes moisture from macaroni, coffee beans, cocoa, and grain. *Baking equipment operators* tend ovens that bake bread, pastries, and other products. Some foods—ice cream, frozen specialties, and meat, for example—are placed in freezers or refrigerators by *cooling and freezing equipment operators*. Other workers tend machines and equipment that clean and wash food or food-processing equipment. Some machine operators also clean and maintain machines and perform duties such as checking the weight of foods.

Many other workers are needed to keep food manufacturing plants and equipment in good working order. *Industrial machinery mechanics* repair and maintain production machines and equipment. *Maintenance repairers* perform routine maintenance on machinery, such as changing and lubricating parts. Specialized mechanics include *heating, air-conditioning, and refrigeration mechanics*, *farm equipment mechanics*, and *diesel engine specialists*.

Still other workers directly oversee the quality of the work and of final products. *Supervisors* direct the activities of production workers. *Graders and sorters* of agricultural products, *production inspectors,* and *quality control technicians* evaluate foodstuffs before, during, or after processing.

Food may spoil if not packaged properly or delivered promptly, so packaging and transportation employees play a vital role in the industry. Among these are *freight, stock, and material movers*, who manually move materials; *hand packers and packagers*, who pack bottles and other items as they come off the production line; and *machine feeders and offbearers*, who feed materials into machines and remove goods from the end of the production line. *Industrial truck and tractor operators* drive gasoline or electric-powered vehicles equipped with forklifts, elevated platforms, or trailer hitches to move goods around a storage facility. *Truck drivers* transport and deliver livestock, materials, or merchandise and may load and unload trucks. *Driver/sales workers* drive company vehicles over established routes to deliver and sell goods, such as bakery items, beverages, and vending-machine products.

The food manufacturing industry also employs a variety of managerial and professional workers. Managers include *top executives*, who make policy decisions; *industrial production managers*, who organize, direct, and control the operation of the manufacturing plant; and *advertising, marketing, promotions, public relations, and sales managers*, who direct advertising, sales promotion, and community relations programs.

Engineers, scientists, and technicians are becoming increasingly important as the food manufacturing industry implements new automation and food safety processes. These workers include *industrial engineers,* who plan equipment layout and workflow in manufacturing plants, emphasizing efficiency and safety. Also, *mechanical engineers* plan, design, and oversee the installation of tools, equipment, and machines. *Chemists* perform tests to develop new products and maintain the quality of existing products. *Computer programmers* and *systems analysts* develop computer systems and programs to support management and scientific research. *Food scientists and technologists* work in research laboratories or on production lines to develop new products, test current ones, and control food quality, including minimizing food-borne pathogens.

Finally, many sales workers, including sales *representatives, wholesale and manufacturing*, are needed to sell the manufactured goods to wholesale and retail establishments. *Bookkeeping, accounting, and auditing clerks* and *procurement clerks* keep track of the food products going into and out of the plant. *Janitors and cleaners* keep buildings clean and orderly.

## Training and Advancement

Most production jobs in food manufacturing require little formal education. Graduation from high school is preferred, but not always required. In general, inexperienced workers start as helpers to experienced workers and learn skills on the job. Many of these entry-level jobs can be learned in a few days. Typical jobs include operating a bread-slicing machine, washing fruits and vegetables before processing begins, hauling carcasses, and packing bottles as they come off the production line. Even though it may not take long to learn to operate a piece of equipment, employees may need several years of experience to enable them to keep the equipment running smoothly, efficiently, and safely.

Some food manufacturing workers need specialized training and education. Inspectors and quality control workers, for example, are trained in food safety and usually need a certificate to be employed in a food manufacturing plant. Often, USDA-appointed plant inspectors possess a bachelor's degree in agricultural or food science. Formal educational requirements for managers in food manufacturing plants range from 2-year degrees to master's degrees. Those who hold research positions, such as food scientists, usually need a master's or doctoral degree.

In addition to participating in specialized training, a growing number of workers receive broader training to perform a number of jobs. The need for flexibility in more automated workplaces has meant that many food manufacturing workers are learning new tasks and being trained to work effectively in teams. Some specialized training is provided for bakers and some other positions.

Advancement may come in the form of higher earnings or more responsibility. Helpers usually progress to jobs as machine operators, but the speed of this progression can vary considerably. Some workers who perform exceptionally well on the production line, or those with special training and experience, may advance to supervisory positions. Plant size and the existence of formal promotion tracks may influence advancement opportunities.

Requirements for other jobs are similar to requirements for the same types of jobs in other industries. Employers usually hire high school graduates for secretarial and other clerical work. Graduates of 2-year associate degree or other postsecondary programs often are sought for science technician and related positions. College graduates or highly experienced workers are preferred for middle-management or professional jobs in personnel, accounting, marketing, or sales.

**Table 2. Employment of wage and salary workers in food manufacturing by occupation, 2006 and projected change, 2006-2016.**
(Employment in thousands)

| Occupation | Employment, 2006 | | Percent change, 2006-16 |
|---|---|---|---|
| | Number | Percent | |
| **All occupations** | 1,484 | 100.0 | 0.3 |
| **Management, business, and financial occupations** | 62 | 4.2 | -2.2 |
| Top executives | 16 | 1.1 | -10.1 |
| Industrial production managers | 10 | 0.7 | 0.2 |
| **Professional and related occupations** | 26 | 1.7 | 3.5 |
| Food scientists and technologists | 5 | 0.3 | 5.5 |
| Agricultural and food science technicians | 5 | 0.4 | -1.0 |
| **Service occupations** | 60 | 4.1 | 4.0 |
| Cooks and food preparation workers | 9 | 0.6 | -0.2 |
| Combined food preparation and serving workers, including fast food | 9 | 0.6 | 11.4 |
| Counter attendants, cafeteria, food concession, and coffee shop | 10 | 0.7 | 1.2 |
| Janitors and cleaners, except maids and housekeeping cleaners | 23 | 1.6 | 4.5 |
| **Sales and related occupations** | 54 | 3.6 | -3.1 |
| Retail salespersons | 17 | 1.2 | -2.6 |
| Sales representatives, wholesale and manufacturing, except technical and scientific products | 19 | 1.3 | -0.3 |
| **Office and administrative support occupations** | 105 | 7.1 | -5.9 |
| Bookkeeping, accounting, and auditing clerks | 12 | 0.8 | 0.0 |
| Shipping, receiving, and traffic clerks | 18 | 1.2 | -3.2 |
| Office clerks, general | 12 | 0.8 | -1.0 |
| **Installation, maintenance, and repair occupations** | 86 | 5.8 | 4.9 |
| Industrial machinery mechanics | 24 | 1.6 | 14.2 |
| Maintenance and repair workers, general | 41 | 2.8 | 1.2 |
| **Production occupations** | 799 | 53.8 | 3.7 |
| First-line supervisors/managers of production and operating workers | 48 | 3.2 | 2.0 |
| Team assemblers | 27 | 1.8 | 0.9 |
| Bakers | 49 | 3.3 | 11.1 |
| Butchers and meat cutters | 15 | 1.0 | 13.5 |
| Meat, poultry, and fish cutters and trimmers | 106 | 7.1 | 12.1 |
| Slaughterers and meat packers | 117 | 7.9 | 13.1 |
| Food and tobacco roasting, baking, and drying machine operators and tenders | 14 | 0.9 | 10.4 |
| Food batchmakers | 74 | 5.0 | 8.3 |
| Food cooking machine operators and tenders | 24 | 1.6 | -10.3 |
| Separating, filtering, clarifying, precipitating, and still machine setters, operators, and tenders | 12 | 0.8 | -4.2 |
| Mixing and blending machine setters, operators, and tenders | 24 | 1.6 | -3.2 |
| Cutting and slicing machine setters, operators, and tenders | 11 | 0.7 | 3.6 |
| Inspectors, testers, sorters, samplers, and weighers | 26 | 1.7 | -4.4 |
| Packaging and filling machine operators and tenders | 103 | 7.0 | -11.4 |
| Helpers--Production workers | 74 | 5.0 | 5.5 |

(continued on next column)

(continued from previous column)

**Table 2. Employment of wage and salary workers in food manufacturing by occupation, 2006 and projected change, 2006-2016.**
(Employment in thousands)

| Occupation | Employment, 2006 | | Percent change, 2006-16 |
|---|---|---|---|
| | Number | Percent | |
| **Transportation and material moving occupations** | 267 | 18.0 | -9.1 |
| Driver/sales workers | 15 | 1.0 | -9.2 |
| Truck drivers, heavy and tractor-trailer | 24 | 1.6 | 1.4 |
| Truck drivers, light or delivery services | 12 | 0.8 | 1.8 |
| Industrial truck and tractor operators | 39 | 2.6 | -11.0 |
| Cleaners of vehicles and equipment | 19 | 1.3 | -0.6 |
| Laborers and freight, stock, and material movers, hand | 56 | 3.8 | -8.2 |
| Machine feeders and offbearers | 14 | 1.0 | -8.3 |
| Packers and packagers, hand | 69 | 4.6 | -18.5 |

Note: Columns may not add to totals due to omission of occupations with small employment

## Outlook

*Employment change.* Overall wage and salary employment in food manufacturing is expected to experience little or no change over the 2006-16 period, compared with 11 percent employment growth projected for the entire economy. Despite the rising demand for manufactured food products by a growing population, automation and increasing productivity are limiting employment growth in most industry segments. Nevertheless, numerous job openings will arise within food manufacturing, as experienced workers transfer to other industries or retire or leave the labor force for other reasons.

Fierce competition has led food manufacturing plants to invest in technologically advanced machinery to be more productive. The new machines have been applied to tasks as varied as packaging, inspection, and inventory control. As a result, employment will decrease for some machine operators, such as packaging machine operators, while healthy employment growth is expected for industrial machinery mechanics who repair and maintain the new machinery. Computers also are being widely implemented throughout the industry, reducing employment growth of some mid-level managers and resulting in decreased employment for administrative support workers, but increasing the demand for workers with excellent technical skills. Taken as a whole, automation will continue to have a modest impact on workers in the industry as competition becomes even more intense in coming years.

Food manufacturing firms will be able to use this new automation to better meet the changing demands of a growing and increasingly diverse population. As convenience becomes more important, consumers increasingly demand highly processed foods such as pre-marinated pork loins, peeled and cut carrots, microwaveable soups, or ready-to-cook dinners. Such a shift in consumption will contribute to the demand for food manufacturing workers and will lead to the development of thousands of new processed foods. Domestic producers also will attempt to market these goods abroad as the volume of international trade continues to grow. The increasing size and diversity of the American population has driven demand for a greater variety of foods, including more ethnic foods. The combination of expanding export markets and shifting and increasing domestic consumption will help employment among food manufacturing workers to rise over the next decade and will lead to significant changes throughout the food manufacturing industry.

Job growth will vary by occupation but will be concentrated among food manufacturing workers—the largest group of workers in the industry. Because many of the cutting, chopping, and eviscerating tasks performed by these workers have proven difficult to automate, employment among handworkers will rise along with the growing demand for food products, especially beef. Handworking occupations include slaughterers and meat packers and meat, poultry, and fish cutters and trimmers, whose employment will rise as the consumption of meat, poultry, and fish climbs and as more processing, in the form of case-ready products, takes place at the manufacturing level. Other production workers, such as bakers, food batchmakers, and food and tobacco roasting, baking, and drying machine operators and tenders, also will benefit from the shift in food processing from retail establishments to manufacturing plants.

*Job prospects.* Unlike many other industries, food manufacturing is not highly sensitive to economic conditions. Even during periods of recession, the demand for food is likely to remain relatively stable. While factors such as animal diseases, currency fluctuations, adverse weather, and changing trade agreements often affect short-term demand for various food products, long-term demand will remain mostly stable.

## Earnings

*Industry earnings.* Production workers in food manufacturing averaged $13.13 an hour, compared with $16.76 per hour for all workers in private industry in 2006. (See table 3.) Weekly earnings among food manufacturing workers were lower than

**Table 3. Average earnings of production or nonsupervisory workers in food manufacturing by industry segment, 2006**

| Industry segment | Weekly | Hourly |
|---|---|---|
| Total, private industry | $568 | $16.76 |
| | | |
| Food manufacturing | 526 | 13.13 |
| Grain and oilseed milling | 785 | 18.88 |
| Dairy products | 726 | 16.80 |
| Animal food | 620 | 14.25 |
| Other food products | 561 | 13.88 |
| Fruit and vegetable preserving and specialty | 541 | 13.30 |
| Sugar and confectionery products | 539 | 15.19 |
| Bakeries and tortilla manufacturing | 488 | 12.63 |
| Animal slaughtering and processing | 463 | 11.49 |
| Seafood product preparation and packaging | 408 | 11.74 |

**Table 4. Median hourly earnings of the largest occupations in food manufacturing, May 2006**

| Occupation | Food manufacturing | All industries |
|---|---|---|
| First-line supervisors/managers of production and operating workers | $21.06 | $22.74 |
| Maintenance and repair workers, general | 16.90 | 15.34 |
| Packaging and filling machine operators and tenders | 11.75 | 11.06 |
| Food batchmakers | 11.55 | 11.11 |
| Bakers | 10.84 | 10.59 |
| Laborers and freight, stock, and material movers, hand | 10.56 | 10.20 |
| Slaughterers and meat packers | 10.43 | 10.43 |
| Helpers--production workers | 10.10 | 9.97 |
| Meat, poultry, and fish cutters and trimmers | 9.79 | 9.79 |
| Packers and packagers, hand | 9.35 | 8.48 |

average, $526 compared with $568 for all workers in private industry. Food manufacturing workers averaged about 40.1 hours a week, compared with only 33.9 for all production workers in the private sector. Weekly earnings ranged from $408 in seafood product preparation and packaging plants to $785 in grain and oilseed milling plants. Earnings in selected occupations in food manufacturing appear in table 4.

*Benefits and union membership.* In 2006, 19 percent of workers in the food manufacturing industry belonged to a union or were covered by a union contract, compared with 12 percent of all workers in the private sector. Prominent unions in the industry include the United Food and Commercial Workers; the International Brotherhood of Teamsters; and the Bakery, Confectionery, Tobacco Workers and Grain Millers International Union.

## Sources of Additional Information

For information on job opportunities in food manufacturing, contact individual manufacturers, locals of the unions listed in the section on earnings, and State employment service offices.

Detailed information on many occupations in food manufacturing, including the following, appears in the 2008-09 *Occupational Outlook Handbook*.

- Food processing occupations
- Industrial production managers
- Industrial machinery mechanics and maintenance workers
- Inspectors, testers, sorters, samplers, and weighers
- Material moving occupations
- Truck drivers and driver/sales workers

# Machinery Manufacturing

## SIGNIFICANT POINTS

- High productivity growth is expected to cause employment to decline, but many openings will result from the need to replace workers who retire.

- Production workers, who account for over half of all jobs in the industry, increasingly need training beyond high school.

- Machinery manufacturing has some of the most highly skilled—and highly paid—production jobs in manufacturing.

- Job prospects should be good for high school graduates with strong communication, basic math, and problem solving skills who can be trained for highly skilled production jobs.

## Nature of the Industry

The development and implementation of machinery was responsible for one of the great advances in human history, the industrial revolution. Machinery encompasses a vast range of products, ranging from huge industrial turbines costing millions of dollars to the common lawn mower, but all machinery has one common defining feature: it either reduces or eliminates the amount of human work required to accomplish a task. Machinery is critical to the production of much of the Nation's goods and services because nearly every workplace in every industry uses some form of machinery. From the oil derrick that pumps out oil to the commercial refrigerator in use by your favorite restaurant, machinery is necessary for the way we live today. Thus while people never use or even see most of the machinery that makes their lifestyles possible, they use the products it makes every day.

*Goods and services.* Most machinery is made of metal, which gives the end product strength and durability, but which necessitates specialized procedures in production. Each part needs to be designed to exacting specifications to ensure proper function of the finished product. Techniques such as forging, stamping, bending, forming, and machining are used to create each piece of metal, thousands of which then need to be welded or assembled together in the largest machines. At each stage of production and assembly, extensive testing takes place to maintain quality control standards. Due to the great variety of machinery produced by this industry, firms specialize in designing and producing certain types of equipment for specific applications.

*Industry organization.* The machinery manufacturing industry is comprised of seven more detailed industry segments, as shown in table 1. Three of these make machinery designed for a particular industry—called special purpose machinery: agriculture, construction, and mining machinery manufacturing; industrial machinery manufacturing; and commercial and service machinery manufacturing. The other four segments make machinery used by many different industries—called general purpose machinery: ventilation, heating, air-conditioning, and commercial refrigeration equipment manufacturing; metalworking machinery manufacturing; engine, turbine, and power transmission equipment manufacturing; and other general purpose machinery manufacturing.

The metalworking machinery industry segment makes machinery that forms metal in its molten state and that cuts or shapes metal as a solid. Although the growth in the use of plastics has reduced the prevalence of metals, a wide variety of products have some metal parts, all of which have to be precisely formed from raw metal. The same properties that make metal a desirable component—strength and durability—also make it a difficult material to form. The specialized drills, grinders, molds, presses, and rollers needed to form metal, as well as the accessories used by these machines, are made in this industry. Metalworking machinery manufacturing has a disproportionately large share of the establishments that make up the machinery manufacturing industry because many are small, averaging fewer than 20 workers.

The agriculture, construction, and mining machinery manufacturing industry segment is made up of much larger establishments that produce both large, sophisticated machines and common household equipment. Examples include farm combines, large self-propelled machines that harvest and thresh grains; bulldozers and backhoes, used in construction of roads and buildings; grinders and borers, used for both surface and underground mining; and oil and gas field drilling machinery and derricks, used for extracting these resources. This segment also makes lawnmowers, leaf blowers, and other lawn and garden equipment for residential and commercial use.

The ventilation, heating, air-conditioning, and commercial refrigeration equipment manufacturing industry segment makes climate-control machinery for residential and commercial buildings. In addition to heating and cooling equipment, this industry makes air purification equipment, which is increasingly common in new construction, and commercial refrigeration equipment, which is used primarily for food storage.

The commercial and service machinery manufacturing industry segment produces the machinery that is used by firms that provide services. For example, firms in this segment produce commercial versions of household appliances—such as laundry equipment used in laundromats, coffee makers and microwave ovens used by restaurants, and vacuum cleaners used by cleaning services. Other large components of this industry are manufacturers of automatic vending machines, non-electronic office machinery like typewriters and mail sorters, non-digital cameras, photocopiers, and machinery used to make optical lenses.

The industrial machinery manufacturing industry segment makes machinery used to produce finished goods from raw materials. The materials processed by this segment's machinery include wood, plastics, rubber, paper, textiles, food, glass, and oil. Machinery manufactured in this segment also is used in printing and bookbinding and in making semiconductors and circuit boards.

The engine, turbine, and power transmission equipment manufacturing segment includes a variety of machines that transfer one type of work into another. Turbines use the energy from the motion of steam, gas, water, or wind to create mechanical power by turning a drive shaft. Along with gears, speed changers, clutches, drive chains, and pulleys—all also made in this segment—turbines put assembly lines and other industrial machinery in motion. Attached to a generator, turbines also create electrical power. This industry segment also produces diesel and other internal combustion engines and their components that are used to power portable generators, air compressors, pumps and other equipment. Aircraft and motor vehicle engines are made by the aerospace product and parts manufacturing and motor vehicle and parts manufacturing industries, respectively, which appear elsewhere in the *Guide*.

The last segment—other general purpose machinery manufacturing—produces miscellaneous machines used primarily by manufacturing industries. These include pumps, compressors, welding and soldering equipment, and packaging machinery. This segment also makes a variety of materials handling equipment—such as industrial trucks and tractors, overhead cranes and hoists, conveyors, and many types of hydraulic equipment—used in manufacturing and other industries. Other common machinery produced by this segment includes scales and balances, power-driven handtools, and elevators, escalators, and moving walkways.

The machinery manufacturing industry also includes companies that make parts for larger manufacturers. Some of these parts manufacturers specialize in creating items that require particular skill to make and they sell them to a wide variety of other manufacturers. Companies contract with these parts manufacturers because doing so is often cheaper than if they made the parts themselves. Cost is a primary selling point for these parts manufacturers and many of their parts are generally small and easy to transport, so these companies are particularly threatened by foreign competition.

The wide range of products made in the machinery manufacturing industry means that it includes establishments of all sizes. In general, however, the larger and more complicated the machinery is, the larger the manufacturing facility must be to produce it. Thus, large establishments tend to be a characteristic of the agriculture, construction, and mining machinery and the ventilation, heating, air-conditioning, and commercial refrigeration equipment segments, while the metalworking machinery segment has the smallest ones.

The size of an establishment also contributes to how some machinery is produced. Large firms involved in manufacturing machinery tend to have a multistage production process, with separate teams of individuals responsible for design and testing, manufacture of parts, and for assembly of the finished product. Nonetheless, there is considerable interaction between the various types of workers; for example, design offices are often located near the factory floor to promote interaction with production workers. Small establishments, in contrast, may have a handful of workers responsible for the entire production process.

*Recent developments.* The machinery manufacturing industry, like all U.S. manufacturers, continues to evolve. Domestic and foreign competition has required the industry to adopt new technologies and techniques to lower costs and raise the productivity of its workforce. For example, using high-technology production techniques, including robots, computers, and programmable equipment results in productivity gains and helps to maximize the use of available equipment and workers. Increasing technology and automation also reduces the number of unskilled workers needed in the production process.

Pressures to reduce costs and maximize profits have also caused manufacturers in the industry to adopt new business practices. One example is the practice of contracting out support functions, such as janitorial and security jobs, and increasingly some administrative services and warehouse and shipping jobs. Rather than employ workers directly for these jobs, a manufacturer will often contract with another company that specializes in providing these services. This practice reduces costs by forcing service providers to compete for the work, allows manufacturers to focus on their core design and production activities, and increases manufacturers' flexibility by letting them add and subtract contract workers more easily than they could hire and fire employees.

These changes have had a profound effect on the machinery manufacturing workforce. By automating many of the production processes and outsourcing many of the administrative and support functions, it has reduced the need for many less skilled workers and increased the skill level required for the remaining workers. These changes are allowing the industry to remain competitive and meet the demand for machinery that other industries rely on.

**Table 1. Percent distribution of employment and establishments in machinery manufacturing by detailed industry sector, 2006**

| Industry segment | Employment | Establishments |
|---|---|---|
| **Total** | 100.0 | 100.0 |
| Agriculture, construction, and mining machinery manufacturing | 18.5 | 11.3 |
| Metalworking machinery manufacturing | 16.8 | 34.0 |
| Ventilation, heating, air-conditioning, and commercial refrigeration equipment manufacturing | 13.2 | 6.7 |
| Industrial machinery manufacturing | 10.4 | 13.2 |
| Commercial and service industry manufacturing | 9.2 | 9.3 |
| Engine, turbine, and power transmission equipment manufacturing | 8.5 | 3.4 |
| Other general purpose machinery manufacturing | 23.2 | 22.0 |

## Working Conditions

*Hours.* Most workers in machinery manufacturing work 8 hour shifts, 5 days a week. Overtime can be common, especially during periods of peak demand. As a result, the average production worker worked 42.4 hours per week in 2006, with about 35 percent of all workers in the industry averaging more than 40 hours a week, and 20 percent of workers over 50 hours per week. Opportunities for part time work are rare, as less than 4 percent of workers were employed part time in 2006. Some plants are capable of operating 24 hours a day, but some shifts are able to operate with a reduced workforce because of the automated nature of the production process.

**Work Environment.** Production workers in the machinery manufacturing industry generally encounter conditions that are much improved from the past. New facilities in particular tend to be clean, well lighted, and temperature controlled. Noise can still be a factor, however, especially in larger production facilities. Most of the labor-intensive work is now automated, but some heavy lifting may still be required. Some workers may also have to work with oil and grease or chemicals that require special handling. Certain types of machinery also require special care in their use. Nevertheless, injuries are rare when proper safety procedures are observed. In 2006, the rate of work related injuries and illnesses per 100 workers was 6.2, compared with 6.0 for all manufacturing industries. The rate for the private sector as a whole was 4.4.

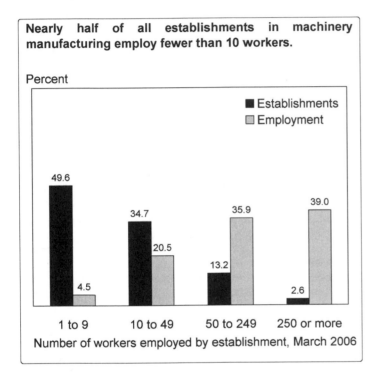

**Nearly half of all establishments in machinery manufacturing employ fewer than 10 workers.**

### Employment
The machinery manufacturing industry provided 1.2 million wage and salary jobs in 2006. Employment was relatively evenly distributed among all segments of the industry (table 1). There were about 31,000 establishments in the industry; about half employed fewer than 10 workers (chart). However, 39 percent of workers were employed in establishments of 250 workers or more.

Although machinery manufacturing jobs are located throughout the country, certain States account for the greatest numbers of jobs. About a third of all jobs were located in the Midwestern States of Illinois, Indiana, Michigan, Ohio, and Wisconsin. Populous states such as California, Texas, New York, and Pennsylvania also had large numbers of jobs.

### Occupations in the Industry
It takes a wide variety of occupations to create and produce a machine, including engineers, technicians, production and assembly workers, supervisors and managers, and support personnel (table 2).

**Professional and related occupations.** Before any work can begin on the production of a particular piece of machinery, an extensive process to create and test the design must be completed. This process can take up to several years, depending on the complexity of the machinery. The work is done primarily by engineers and technicians, although because of the range of tasks involved, different types of these workers are required.

*Engineering managers* oversee the entire design process. Much of the design work is done by *engineers*, who first develop a concept of what a new machine should do or how an existing one could be improved. Starting with this concept, they use computer modeling and simulating software to design the machine. Using software and prototypes, they also test performance, cost, reliability, ease of use, and other factors important to both producers and consumers of the final product.

Most engineers specialize in a particular facet of design. *Mechanical engineers* design the moving parts of the machine, such as the gears, levers, and pistons in engine and hydraulic systems. They also direct the work of *mechanical engineering technicians*, who run tests on materials and parts before they are assembled into the final product. For machines with complicated electric or electronic systems, *electrical and electronics engineers* also assist in the design and testing process. *Industrial engineers* determine how best to allocate the resources of the factory—both workers and equipment—for optimal production.

Once a design is finished and simulation testing complete, *mechanical drafters* create the plans that production workers use in the assembly of the machine. They provide specifications and diagrams for each part required, as well as assembly instructions for the final product.

**Production occupations.** Production workers account for over half of all jobs in the machinery manufacturing industry. *First-line supervisors and managers of production and operating workers* oversee all workers in the production process and ensure that equipment and supplies are available when needed. They usually report to *industrial production managers*, who watch over all activities on the factory floor.

*Metal workers and plastic workers* create all the various parts that are needed in the production and assembly processes. As production becomes more automated, the jobs of most metal and plastic workers are becoming more complex. Fewer workers simply operate machines; most are now also responsible for programming and performing minor repairs on the machine tools.

Among the most skilled metal and plastic workers are *tool and die makers*, and machinery manufacturing has about 28 percent of the Nation's jobs for these workers. Tool and die makers create precision tools and machines, often using computer-aided design software, that are used to cut, shape, and form metal and other materials to exact specifications. Operating computer-controlled machine tools, they produce devices, such as jigs and fixtures, to hold metal while it is being worked on. They also produce gauges and other measuring devices, and dies that are used to shape the metal.

Tools, dies, and jigs are used by *machine tool cutting setters, operators, and tenders, metal and plastic* who set up and operate machines that make parts out of the raw materials. Because most machines now operate automatically, machine tool operators primarily monitor the machine and perform minor repairs as needed.

*Computer control programmers and operators* manage the automatic metalworking machines that can mass produce indi-

**Table 2. Employment of wage and salary workers in machinery manufacturing by occupation, 2006 and projected change, 2006-2016.**
(Employment in thousands)

| Occupation | Employment, 2006 | | Percent change, 2006-16 |
|---|---|---|---|
| | Number | Percent | |
| **All occupations** ................................ | 1,192 | 100.0 | -12.3 |
| **Management, business, and financial occupations**............................. | 110 | 9.2 | -13.7 |
| Top executives ......................................... | 24 | 2.0 | -21.5 |
| Marketing and sales managers ............... | 8 | 0.7 | -11.9 |
| Industrial production managers ............... | 11 | 0.9 | -12.3 |
| Engineering managers ............................. | 10 | 0.8 | -12.3 |
| Purchasing agents, except wholesale, retail, and farm products ........................ | 14 | 1.2 | -14.5 |
| Accountants and auditors ........................ | 10 | 0.8 | -12.0 |
| **Professional and related occupations** .... | 127 | 10.6 | -7.8 |
| Computer specialists ............................... | 19 | 1.6 | -8.0 |
| Electrical and electronics engineers ......... | 12 | 1.0 | -13.3 |
| Industrial engineers ................................ | 15 | 1.3 | 6.6 |
| Mechanical engineers.............................. | 30 | 2.5 | -8.9 |
| Mechanical drafters ................................ | 14 | 1.2 | -11.8 |
| Industrial engineering technicians ............ | 6 | 0.5 | -2.7 |
| Mechanical engineering technicians......... | 8 | 0.7 | -8.1 |
| **Sales and related occupations**................ | 42 | 3.5 | -12.6 |
| Sales representatives, wholesale and manufacturing, technical and scientific products................................................ | 9 | 0.8 | -12.2 |
| Sales representatives, wholesale and manufacturing, except technical and scientific products ................................... | 21 | 1.8 | -11.9 |
| **Office and administrative support occupations** ............................................ | 129 | 10.8 | -15.8 |
| Bookkeeping, accounting, and auditing clerks....................................... | 15 | 1.3 | -12.3 |
| Customer service representatives ............ | 13 | 1.1 | -3.2 |
| Production, planning, and expediting clerks | 12 | 1.0 | -11.1 |
| Shipping, receiving, and traffic clerks ....... | 19 | 1.6 | -15.3 |
| Secretaries and administrative assistants ... | 17 | 1.5 | -17.0 |
| Office clerks, general............................... | 13 | 1.1 | -14.2 |
| **Installation, maintenance, and repair occupations** ............................................ | 48 | 4.1 | -8.1 |
| Industrial machinery installation, repair, and maintenance workers...................... | 32 | 2.6 | -6.9 |
| **Production occupations**........................... | 665 | 55.8 | -12.1 |
| First-line supervisors/managers of production and operating workers .......... | 44 | 3.7 | -12.4 |
| Electrical and electronic equipment assemblers .......................................... | 13 | 1.1 | -29.7 |
| Electromechanical equipment assemblers.. | 10 | 0.9 | -12.0 |
| Engine and other machine assemblers .... | 23 | 1.9 | -11.4 |
| Structural metal fabricators and fitters ...... | 16 | 1.4 | -10.1 |
| Team assemblers.................................... | 120 | 10.1 | -10.4 |
| Computer-controlled machine tool operators, metal and plastic................... | 34 | 2.8 | -4.3 |
| Cutting, punching, and press machine setters, operators, and tenders, metal and plastic............................................ | 29 | 2.4 | -20.4 |
| Drilling and boring machine tool setters, operators, and tenders, metal and plastic . | 9 | 0.7 | -21.4 |
| Grinding, lapping, polishing, and buffing machine tool setters, operators, and tenders, metal and plastic..................... | 16 | 1.4 | -17.2 |
| Lathe and turning machine tool setters, operators, and tenders, metal and plastic.. | 4 | 1.2 | -21.8 |
| Machinists................................................ | 75 | 6.3 | -9.3 |

(continued on next column)

(continued from previous column)

**Table 2. Employment of wage and salary workers in machinery manufacturing by occupation, 2006 and projected change, 2006-2016.**
(Employment in thousands)

| Occupation | Employment, 2006 | | Percent change, 2006-16 |
|---|---|---|---|
| | Number | Percent | |
| **Production occupations (continued)** | | | |
| Molding, coremaking, and casting machine setters, operators, and tenders, metal and plastic.................................... | 12 | 1.0 | -23.6 |
| Multiple machine tool setters, operators, and tenders, metal and plastic................ | 14 | 1.2 | -3.5 |
| Tool and die makers................................ | 28 | 2.4 | -12.4 |
| Welding, soldering, and brazing workers .. | 75 | 6.3 | -3.2 |
| Inspectors, testers, sorters, samplers, and weighers ....................................... | 25 | 2.1 | -17.0 |
| Coating, painting, and spraying machine setters, operators, and tenders ............. | 14 | 1.1 | -14.4 |
| **Transportation and material moving occupations** ......................................... | 46 | 3.8 | -19.1 |
| Industrial truck and tractor operators ........ | 12 | 1.0 | -18.5 |
| Laborers and freight, stock, and material movers, hand......................................... | 18 | 1.5 | -19.6 |

Note: Columns may not add to totals due to omission of occupations with small employment

vidual parts. They also write programs based upon the specifications of the part that defines what operation the machine should perform. *Machinists* produce precision parts that require particular skill or that are needed in quantities too small to require the use of automated machinery. *Welding, soldering, and brazing workers* operate machines that join two or more pieces of metal together; they may also weld manually as well.

Once all of the parts have been made, it is the responsibility of *assemblers and fabricators* to put them all together to finish the product. Some assemblers specialize in one particular stage of the process, while others, such as *team assemblers*, work as a group and may contribute to an entire subassembly process. While there has been increased automation of the assembly process, many parts of the products still have to be put together and fastened by hand. When assembly is complete, *painting workers* apply paint or a protective coating to the exterior of the machine.

While quality control is a responsibility of all production workers, it is the primary focus of *inspectors, testers, samplers, and weighers*. These workers monitor the entire production stage, making sure that individual parts, as well as the finished product, meet the standards set by the company.

***Other occupations.*** Other occupations in the industry provide support to production activities. *Industrial machinery installation, repair, and maintenance workers* are skilled mechanics who make sure that all the machines and other equipment used in the production process are regularly serviced and function properly. *Production, planning, and expediting clerks* produce records and reports related to various aspects of production, such as materials and parts used, products produced, and defects encountered. They also make sure customer orders are completed, deliveries are scheduled, and shipments are made on time. *Purchasing agents* use the data provided by production, planning, and expediting clerks to procure supplies needed in production.

In addition to production-specific occupations, this industry has various managers and administrative support personnel to handle functions such as human relations, accounting, and general management. The sales function for many companies is increasingly important. *Sales representatives* and *sales engineers* often work together to market the company's machines to potential buyers, demonstrating how the machine may reduce costs or increase sales. They also explain how to operate the machine and answer buyer's questions. Sales engineers in particular use their technical background to advise clients on how the machine can best be applied in their individual circumstances and to suggest custom designs or modifications to the equipment as needed.

## Training and Advancement

The composition of employment in machinery manufacturing continues to evolve as automation of labor-intensive tasks raises the skill level required of production workers. Nearly all jobs now require that entry-level workers have at least a high school diploma. Employers also seek people who have good communication and problem solving skills, since new manufacturing processes, such as lean manufacturing, require workers to be able to perform many different tasks depending on where they are most needed. Strong basic mathematical skills are also essential.

*Production occupations.* Skilled production workers, such as tool and die makers and machinists, usually must have previous experience or must have completed a training program at a local college. Some companies also train workers entering the field in apprenticeship programs that can last between 1 and 5 years, depending on the specialty. These programs combine on-the-job training with classroom instruction, either within the company or at local technical schools. Apprenticeship topics include mechanical drawing, tool designing, programming of computer-controlled machines, blueprint reading, mathematics, hydraulics, and electronics. Workers also learn about company policies on quality control, safety, and communications.

Experienced workers may advance into higher skilled positions within their field or into supervisory positions. Because advancement is based on experience and merit, even those workers who enter in low skilled positions can advance to significantly higher skilled jobs by working to improve their skills.

*Management and professional occupations.* Management and professional occupations generally require workers who have a bachelor's degree in the particular field, although some management positions are filled by experienced production workers. Most engineer jobs in the industry require that workers have a degree in mechanical or electrical engineering or one of their specialties. Because engineers usually are familiar with both design and production issues within a company, they may be able to advance into the upper management positions.

## Outlook

Employment in machinery manufacturing is expected to continue its long-term decline as productivity increases allow companies to produce more goods with fewer workers.

*Employment change.* Wage and salary employment in the machinery manufacturing industry is expected to decrease 12 percent over the 2006-16 period compared with an 11 percent increase for all industries combined. As shown in table 3, all segments of the industry are expected to experience some employment declines.

The main factor affecting the level of employment in the machinery manufacturing industry is the high rate of productivity

**Table 3. Employment in machinery manufacturing by industry segment, 2006 and projected change, 2006-16**

(Employment in thousands)

| Industry segment | 2006 Employment | 2006-16 Percent change |
|---|---|---|
| **Machinery manufacturing, total** | **1,192** | **-12.3** |
| Agriculture, construction, and mining machinery manufacturing | 222 | -6.7 |
| Metalworking machinery manufacturing | 203 | -18.2 |
| Ventilation, heating, air-conditioning, and commercial refrigeration equipment manufacturing | 160 | -9.1 |
| Industrial machinery manufacturing | 123 | -18.0 |
| Commercial and service industry machinery manufacturing | 111 | -12.7 |
| Engine, turbine, and power transmission equipment manufacturing | 100 | -16.4 |
| Other general purpose machinery manufacturing | 273 | -10.0 |

growth. Increases in productivity allow companies to produce more goods with the same number of workers. Even though output in machinery manufacturing is expected to increase significantly, firms will be able to meet the increase through higher productivity of existing workers, rather than by creating new jobs.

A second factor expected to cause some employment declines in machinery manufacturing is the growing number of imported parts. This industry is less likely to lose a large part of its output to imports from other countries than some other manufacturing industries. The large size and complexity of many of the types of machinery made by this industry and the relatively skilled workforce it requires is an advantage that many manufacturing industries do not share. However, while most finished machines are made in the United States, it is increasingly common for manufacturers to have some parts of the final product made in other countries and then shipped to U.S. manufacturers for final assembly. While still expected to account for only a small part of the total process, this increased offshore outsourcing of production will have a negative effect on machinery manufacturing employment.

Demand for machinery is expected to remain strong. Machinery is important for all industries because it boosts their productivity, and advances in technology will make machinery even more efficient and thus more desirable. Demand for machinery is highly sensitive to cyclical swings in the economy, however, causing employment in machinery manufacturing to fluctuate. During periods of economic prosperity, companies invest in new equipment, such as machinery, in order to boost production. When economic growth slows, however, many companies are reluctant to purchase new machinery. These changes in demand cause machinery manufacturers to replace fewer workers who leave or even lay off some workers.

Although overall employment in the machinery manufacturing industry is expected to decline, the outlook for occupations will vary; some will experience larger declines than others, while some will even experience growth instead. Increased automation and more efficient production processes will cause employment declines in assembler and fabricator occupations. Office and administrative support workers will also experience declines as a result of increased automation and contracting out. Employment in professional and management occupations will experience smaller declines relative to other occupations in the industry; engineers in particular will experience very good employment opportunities, as they are responsible for increasing innovation and competitiveness in the industry.

*Job prospects.* Despite the decline in employment projected for this sizeable industry, a significant number of job openings will become available because of the need to replace workers who retire or move to jobs outside of the industry. However, not all jobs that are vacated will be filled because attrition is one of the main ways that establishments reduce the number of employees. It is also a way the establishments upgrade the skill mix of their workforce. Machinery manufacturing establishments will continually be seeking to hire more highly skilled workers, especially persons with good basic educational skills that make good candidates to be trained for the high skilled jobs of twenty-first century manufacturing. Workers with these skills are expected to experience excellent job prospects.

**Table 4. Average earnings of production or nonsupervisory workers in machinery manufacturing by industry segment, 2006**

| Industry segment | Weekly | Hourly |
|---|---|---|
| **Total, private industry** | $568 | $16.76 |
| **Machinery manufacturing** | 729 | 17.20 |
| Engine, turbine, and power transmission equipment manufacturing | 897 | 20.20 |
| Commercial and service industry manufacturing. | 810 | 19.87 |
| Metalworking machinery manufacturing | 786 | 18.63 |
| Industrial machinery manufacturing | 782 | 18.64 |
| Other general purpose machinery manufacturing . | 693 | 16.61 |
| Agriculture, construction, and mining machinery manufacturing | 689 | 15.83 |
| Ventilation, heating, air-conditioning, and commercial refrigeration equipment manufacturing | 585 | 13.83 |

## Earnings

*Industry earnings.* The earnings of workers in the machinery manufacturing industry are relatively high, primarily because of the high productivity of workers in this industry. Median weekly earnings in 2006 for production workers in machinery manufacturing were $729, compared with $691 for the manufacturing sector as a whole and $568 for all industries. Earnings vary by detailed industry segment (table 4). They also vary based upon a worker's particular occupation, experience, and the size of the company employing them. Earnings of the largest occupations in machinery manufacturing appear in table 5.

*Benefits and union membership.* In 2006, about 9 percent of workers in machinery manufacturing were union members or were covered by union contracts, slightly less than the proportion for both the manufacturing industry as a whole and all industries combined. Major unions include the International Association of Machinists and Aerospace Workers of America, the

International Brotherhood of Electrical Workers, and the United Automobile, Aerospace, and Agricultural Implement Workers of America.

**Table 5. Median hourly earnings of the largest occupations in machinery manufacturing, May 2006**

| Occupation | Machinery manufacturing | All industries |
|---|---|---|
| Mechanical engineers | $30.38 | $33.58 |
| First-line supervisors/managers of production and operating workers | 24.41 | 22.74 |
| Tool and die makers | 20.15 | 21.29 |
| Machinists | 17.02 | 16.71 |
| Computer-controlled machine tool operators, metal and plastic | 16.58 | 15.23 |
| Inspectors, testers, sorters, samplers, and weighers | 16.01 | 14.14 |
| Welders, cutters, solderers, and brazers | 15.26 | 15.10 |
| Engine and other machine assemblers | 15.19 | 15.99 |
| Cutting, punching, and press machine setters, operators, and tenders, metal and plastic | 13.38 | 12.66 |
| Team assemblers | 12.79 | 11.63 |

## Sources of Additional Information

The Manufacturing Institute of the National Association of Manufacturers sponsors the Dream it, Do it campaign, which provides information on careers in manufacturing. More information is available from:

➤ National Association of Manufacturers, 1331 Pennsylvania Ave., NW., Suite 600, Washington, DC 20004. Internet: **http://www.dreamit-doit.org**

Information on employment and training opportunities in the machinery manufacturing industry is available from State employment service offices, employment offices of machinery manufacturing firms, and locals of the unions listed above.

Detailed information on most occupations in this industry, including the following, appears in the 2008-09 edition of the *Occupational Outlook Handbook:*

- Assemblers and fabricators
- Computer control programmers and operators
- Commercial and industrial designers
- Drafters
- Electricians
- Engineering technicians
- Engineers
- Industrial production managers
- Inspectors, testers, sorters, samplers, and weighers
- Machine setters, operators, and tenders—metal and plastic
- Machinists
- Material moving occupations
- Tool and die makers
- Welding, soldering, and brazing workers

# Motor Vehicle and Parts Manufacturing

(NAICS 3361, 3362, 3363)

## SIGNIFICANT POINTS

- Although approximately 1 out of 5 jobs are located in Michigan, especially the Detroit area, an increasing number are located in other parts of the country, particularly the south.

- Average earnings are very high compared with those in other industries.

- Employment is expected to decline, but retirements will create many job openings.

## Nature of the Industry

Despite news of plant closures and unemployed auto workers, the motor vehicle and parts manufacturing industry continues to be one of the largest employers in the country and a major contributor to our economy's success. Motor vehicle and parts manufacturing is continually evolving to improve efficiency and provide products that consumers want in a highly competitive market, which at times may mean outdated plants are forced to close. It also means companies and workers must adapt more quickly to changes in demand and production practices so that new technologies can be implemented and work can be done on a number of different vehicles at one time. Teamwork and continual retraining are key components to the success of this industry and the ability of the workforce to adapt.

Motor vehicle and parts manufacturers also have a major influence on other industries in the economy as well. Building motor vehicles requires vast quantities of materials from, and creates many jobs in, industries that manufacture steel, rubber, plastics, glass, and other basic materials. It also spurs employment for automobile and other motor vehicle dealers; automotive repair and maintenance shops; gasoline stations; highway construction companies; and automotive parts, accessories, and tire stores.

*Goods and services.* The motor vehicles manufactured in this industry include: automobiles, sport-utility vehicles (SUVs), vans and pickup trucks, heavy duty trucks, buses, truck trailers and motor homes. It also includes the manufacturing of the parts that go into these vehicles, such as the engine, seats, brakes, and electrical systems. According to the Federal Reserve, over 11 million motor vehicles were assembled in the U.S. in 2006. Building and assembling the many different parts of a car or truck requires an amazingly complex design, manufacturing, and assembly process.

*Industry organization.* In 2006, about 9200 establishments manufactured motor vehicles and parts. These ranged from small parts plants with only a few workers to huge assembly plants that employ thousands. By far, the largest sector of this industry is motor vehicle parts manufacturing. It has the most establishments and the most workers. Table 1 shows that about 7 out of 10 establishments in the industry manufactured motor vehicle parts—including electrical and electronic equipment; engines and transmissions; brake systems; seating and interior trim; steering and suspension components; air-conditioners; and motor vehicle stampings, such as fenders, tops, body parts, trim, and molding.

The next largest sector, in terms of number of establishments, is motor vehicle body and trailer manufacturing. In 2006, nearly one-fourth of establishments were engaged in this type of manufacturing. These establishments specialized in manufacturing truck trailers; motor homes; travel trailers; campers; and car, truck, and bus bodies placed on separately purchased chassis.

Automotive and light truck assembly plants make up the third largest sector. In 2006, about 5 percent of establishments that employ 23 percent of all workers in this industry, were engaged in assembling these smaller motor vehicles. A growing number of these assembly plants are owned by foreign automobile makers, known as "domestic internationals." These foreign automobile manufacturers open assembly plants in the United States to be closer to their market, avoid changing exchange rates, and save transportation costs.

A typical automotive assembly plant can be divided into three major sections. In the first section, exterior body panels and interior frame are assembled and welded together. This work is mostly performed by robots, but may also require some manual welding. During this stage, the body is attached to a conveyor system that will move it through the entire assembly process. Throughout the entire process, numerous inspections are performed to ensure the quality of the work.

The painting process comprises the second section of the assembly plant where bodies of cars pass through a series of carefully ventilated, sealed paint rooms. Here, the bodies are dipped into chemicals to prevent rust and seal the metal. Then the bodies are primed, painted, and sealed with a clear coat.

Assembly of the vehicle comprises the third section of the automobile manufacturing process. Here, parts such as seats, dashboard, and the powertrain (engine and transmission) are installed. While machines assist with loading heavy parts, much of the assembly work is still performed by team assemblers working with power tools.

**Table 1. Percent distribution of employment and establishments in motor vehicle and parts manufacturing by detailed industry sector, 2006**

| Industry sector | Employment | Establishments |
|---|---|---|
| **Total** | 100.0 | 100.0 |
| Motor vehicle parts manufacturing | 60.9 | 68.6 |
| Motor vehicle manufacturing | 22.6 | 5.1 |
| Motor vehicle body and trailer manufacturing | 16.5 | 26.3 |

*Recent developments.* The motor vehicle and parts manufacturing industry in the United States is increasingly a global industry. Even "domestic" vehicles are produced using parts manufactured around the world. This healthy competition among both domestic and foreign manufacturers has dramatically increased productivity and improved efficiency.

Competition has also led the U.S. automotive market to be increasingly fragmented. To compete for consumer's attention, automakers have greatly increased the number of models in the market, which has put a strain on the manufacturing process. To adapt, firms have had to be fast and flexible in implementing new production techniques, such as replacing traditional assembly lines with modern systems using computers, robots, and flexible production techniques. Plants designed for production flexibility put resources in the right place at the right time, allowing manufacturers to quickly and efficiently shift from slow-selling models to popular models. Flexible plants allow manufacturers to produce multiple vehicles on the same assembly line.

## Working Conditions

*Hours.* In 2006, about 30 percent of workers in the motor vehicle and parts manufacturing industry worked, on average, more than 40 hours per week. Overtime is especially common during periods of peak demand. Most employees, however, usually work an 8-hour shift: either from 7 a.m. to 3:30 p.m. or from 4 p.m. to 12:30 a.m. A third shift often is reserved for maintenance and cleanup.

*Work Environment.* Although working conditions have improved in recent years, some production workers still are subject to uncomfortable conditions. Heat, fumes, noise, and repetition are not uncommon in this industry. In addition, many workers come into contact with oil and grease and may have to lift and fit heavy objects, although hydraulic lifts and other equipment have eliminated much of the heavy lifting. Employees also may operate powerful, high-speed machines that can be dangerous. Accidents and injuries usually are avoided when protective equipment and clothing are worn and safety practices are observed. Additionally, companies use carefully designed work stations and physical conditioning to reduce injuries from repetitive motions.

Newer plants are more automated and have safer, more comfortable conditions. For example, cars on the assembly line can be raised, lowered, and sometimes even rotated to work on the bottom of the car or to adjust to the worker's height. Workers also typically function as part of a team, doing more than one job and thus reducing the repetitiveness of assembly line work.

Workers in this industry experience higher rates of injury and illness than do workers in most other industries. In 2006, motor vehicle manufacturing, on average, sustained 11.4 cases of work-related injury and illness per 100 full-time workers, 13.2 in motor vehicle body and trailer manufacturing, and 7.7 in motor vehicle parts manufacturing—compared with 6.0 in all manufacturing industries and 4.4 in the entire private sector.

As in other industries, professional and managerial workers normally have clean, comfortable offices and are not subject to the hazards of assembly line work. However, many supervisors and plant managers still need to visit the assembly line and face some of the same hazards as assembly line workers.

## Employment

Motor vehicle and parts manufacturing was among the largest of the manufacturing industries in 2006, providing 1.1 million jobs. The majority of jobs, about 61 percent, were in firms that make motor vehicle parts. About 23 percent of workers in the industry were employed in firms assembling complete motor vehicles,

while about 16 percent worked in firms producing truck trailers; motor homes; travel trailers; campers; and car, truck, and bus bodies placed on separately purchased chassis.

Although motor vehicle and parts manufacturing jobs are scattered throughout the Nation, jobs are concentrated in the Midwest and South. Michigan, which houses the headquarters for the three major domestic manufacturers, accounts for 21 percent of all jobs. Michigan, Ohio, Indiana, Tennessee, and Illinois combined have 54 percent of all the jobs in this industry. Other States that account for significant numbers of jobs include Kentucky, New York, California, Pennsylvania, and North Carolina. Automotive employment is shifting away from its traditional base in the Midwest to southeastern States, such as Alabama, Mississippi, South Carolina, and Tennessee.

Employment is concentrated in a relatively small number of large establishments. More than half of all motor vehicle and parts manufacturing jobs were in establishments employing 500 or more workers (chart). Motor vehicle manufacturing employment, in particular, is concentrated in these large establishments, whereas many motor vehicle parts manufacturing jobs are found in small and medium-sized establishments.

Motor vehicle manufacturing corporations employ many additional workers in establishments that are parts of other industries. Many of these jobs are located in Michigan. Jobs in corporate headquarters often are in separate establishments and so would be classified as part of a different industry. Likewise, workers in research and development (R&D) establishments that are separate from a manufacturing facility are included in a separate industry—research and development in the physical, engineering, and life sciences. (This industry is covered elsewhere in the *Career Guide* in the section on scientific research and development services.) However, given the importance of R&D work to the motor vehicle and parts manufacturing industry, occupations and issues related to R&D are discussed in the following sections even though some of their employment is not included in the motor vehicle manufacturing industry.

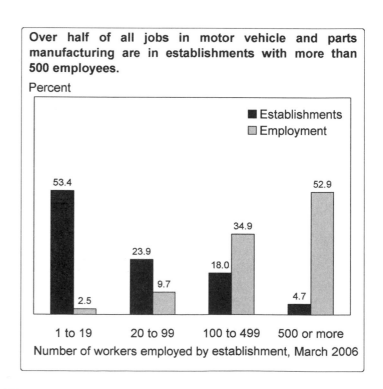

**Over half of all jobs in motor vehicle and parts manufacturing are in establishments with more than 500 employees.**

Percent

■ Establishments
□ Employment

| | 1 to 19 | 20 to 99 | 100 to 499 | 500 or more |
|---|---|---|---|---|
| Establishments | 53.4 | 23.9 | 18.0 | 4.7 |
| Employment | 2.5 | 9.7 | 34.9 | 52.9 |

Number of workers employed by establishment, March 2006

## Occupations in the Industry

As the industry strives to improve the flexibility of its workforce, employees are being asked to perform a greater variety of jobs, particularly in the manufacturing plants. This is causing the number of occupational specialties in this industry to shrink in favor of more generic titles, such as team assembler and maintenance worker. The skill level of workers has also increased to match workers' growing responsibilities.

*Professional and related occupations.* Prior to assembling components in the manufacturing plant, extensive design, engineering, testing, and production planning go into the manufacture of motor vehicles. These tasks often require years to complete and cost millions or even billions of dollars. Professionals are the ones responsible for this aspect of the work. Using artistic talent, computers, and information on product use, marketing, materials, and production methods, *commercial and industrial designers* create designs they hope will make the vehicle competitive in the marketplace. Designers use sketches and computer-aided design techniques to create computer models of proposed vehicles. These computer models eliminate the need for physical body mockups in the design process because they give designers complete information on how each piece of the vehicle will work with others. Workers may repeatedly modify and redesign models until the models meet engineering, production, and marketing specifications. Designers working in parts production increasingly collaborate with manufacturers in the initial design stages to integrate motor vehicle parts into the design specifications for each vehicle.

*Engineers*—who form the largest professional contingent in the industry—play an integral role in all stages of motor vehicle manufacturing. They oversee the building and testing of the engine, transmission, brakes, suspension, and other mechanical and electrical components. Using computers and assorted models, instruments, and tools, engineers simulate various parts of the vehicle to determine whether each part meets cost, safety, performance, and quality specifications. *Mechanical engineers* design improvements for engines, transmissions, and other working parts. *Electrical and electronics engineers* design the vehicle's electrical and electronic systems, as well as industrial robot control systems used to assemble the vehicle. *Industrial engineers* concentrate on designing an efficient plant layout, including the arrangement of assembly line stations, material-moving equipment, work standards, quality control, and other production matters.

Under the direction of engineers, *engineering technicians* prepare specifications for materials, devise and run tests to ensure product quality, and study ways to improve manufacturing efficiency. For example, testing may reveal how metal parts perform under conditions of heat, cold, and stress, and whether emissions-control equipment meets environmental standards. Finally, prototype vehicles incorporating all the components are built and tested on test tracks, on road simulators, and in test chambers that can duplicate almost every driving condition, including crashes.

*Computer systems analysts* work with computer systems to improve manufacturing efficiency. These specialists help put in place the machinery and tools required for assembly line production of the vehicle.

*Management occupations.* Management workers establish guidelines for the design of motor vehicles to provide direction for the teams of experts in engineering, design, marketing, sales, finance, and production. From the earliest stages of planning and design, these specialists help assess whether the vehicle will satisfy consumer demand, meet safety and environmental regulations, and prove economically practical to make. These executives also serve as public representatives for the company.

*Industrial production managers* oversee *first-line supervisors and managers of production and operating workers*. These supervisors oversee inspectors, precision workers, machine setters and operators, assemblers, fabricators, and plant and system operators. They coordinate a variety of manufacturing processes and production activities, including scheduling, staffing, equipment, quality control, and inventory control.

*Production occupations.* These occupations account for about 64 percent of motor vehicle and parts manufacturing jobs (table 2). *Assemblers and fabricators* and *metal workers and plastic workers* put together various parts to form subassemblies, and then put the subassemblies together to build a complete motor vehicle. Most assemblers in this industry are *team assemblers*, who work in teams and perform a variety of tasks. Some may perform other routine tasks such as mounting and inflating tires; adjusting brakes; and adding gas, oil, brake fluid, and coolant. Metal parts are molded or machined, plastic and glass parts are molded and cut, seat cushions are sewn, and many parts are painted. Many manufacturing processes are highly automated; robots, computers, and programmable devices are an integral part of motor vehicle manufacturing.

Throughout the manufacturing process, "statistical process control" (teamwork and quality control) is emphasized. From initial planning and design to final assembly, numerous tests and inspections ensure that vehicles meet quality and safety standards. Modern manufacturing facilities also integrate interchangeable tools on the assembly line so that they can quickly be changed to meet the needs of various models and specifications.

Although robots perform most of the welding, *welding, soldering, and brazing workers* perform welds that are not easily automated and fix mistakes that occur during the manufacturing process. *Machinists* produce precision metal parts that are made in numbers too small to produce with automated machinery. *Tool and die makers* produce, maintain, and repair machine tools, dies, overhead conveyors, and special guiding and holding devices used in machines. *Computer-controlled machine tool operators* use computer-controlled machines or robots programmed to automatically machine and shape parts of different dimensions.

Workers in other production occupations run various machines that produce an array of motor vehicle bodies and parts. These workers set up and operate machines and make adjustments according to their instructions. In computer-controlled systems, they monitor computers controlling the machine processes and may have little interaction with the machinery or materials. Some workers specialize in one type of machine; others operate more than one type.

*Grinding and polishing workers* use handtools or hand-held power tools to sand and polish metal surfaces; *painting workers* paint surfaces of motor vehicles; and *sewing machine operators* sew together pieces of material to form seat covers and other parts.

Throughout the manufacturing process, *inspectors, testers, sorters, samplers, and weighers* and all assembly workers make checks to ensure that motor vehicles and parts meet quality standards. They inspect raw materials, check parts for defects, check the uniformity of subassemblies, and test-drive vehicles. *Help-*

**Table 2. Employment of wage and salary workers in motor vehicle and parts manufacturing by occupation, 2006 and projected change, 2006-2016.**
(Employment in thousands)

| Occupation | Employment, 2006 | | Percent change, 2006-16 |
|---|---|---|---|
| | Number | Percent | |
| All occupations ....................................... | 1,070 | 100.0 | -14.3 |
| **Management, business, and financial occupations**............................ | 63 | 5.9 | -13.8 |
| Top executives ......................................... | 10 | 0.9 | -23.5 |
| Industrial production managers ............... | 9 | 0.8 | -13.5 |
| Purchasing agents, except wholesale, retail, and farm products........................ | 7 | 0.6 | -18.5 |
| **Professional and related occupations**.... | 81 | 7.6 | -9.4 |
| Computer specialists ............................... | 7 | 0.6 | -8.9 |
| Industrial engineers ................................. | 19 | 1.8 | 3.1 |
| Mechanical engineers.............................. | 14 | 1.3 | -14.4 |
| Engineering technicians, except drafters ....................................... | 15 | 1.4 | -14.9 |
| **Office and administrative support occupations** ........................................ | 58 | 5.5 | -18.4 |
| Production, planning, and expediting clerks | 9 | 0.9 | -16.4 |
| Shipping, receiving, and traffic clerks ....... | 12 | 1.1 | -18.9 |
| Secretaries and administrative assistants .. | 7 | 0.7 | -16.6 |
| **Construction and extraction occupations** ........................................... | 28 | 2.6 | -9.8 |
| Electricians ............................................... | 15 | 1.4 | -9.2 |
| **Installation, maintenance, and repair occupations** ........................................... | 68 | 6.4 | -10.5 |
| Industrial machinery mechanics............... | 14 | 1.3 | -2.6 |
| Maintenance and repair workers, general.. | 21 | 1.9 | -14.2 |
| **Production occupations**.......................... | 688 | 64.3 | -14.4 |
| First-line supervisors/managers of production and operating workers ......... | 36 | 3.3 | -13.4 |
| Electrical and electronic equipment assemblers | 10 | 1.0 | -34.8 |
| Engine and other machine assemblers .... | 12 | 1.1 | -13.5 |
| Structural metal fabricators and fitters ...... | 7 | 0.7 | -6.3 |
| Team assemblers.................................... | 201 | 18.8 | -9.5 |
| Assemblers and fabricators, all other........ | 74 | 6.9 | -17.1 |
| Computer-controlled machine tool operators, metal and plastic.................... | 14 | 1.3 | -10.1 |
| Forming machine setters, operators, and tenders, metal and plastic............... | 11 | 1.0 | -29.2 |
| Machine tool cutting setters, operators, and tenders, metal and plastic............... | 62 | 5.8 | -25.1 |
| Machinists.............................................. | 28 | 2.6 | -13.9 |
| Molders and molding machine setters, operators, and tenders, metal and plastic | 13 | 1.2 | -26.8 |
| Multiple machine tool setters, operators, and tenders, metal and plastic............... | 18 | 1.7 | -11.6 |
| Tool and die makers................................ | 21 | 1.9 | -13.2 |
| Welders, cutters, solderers, and brazers... | 36 | 3.4 | -2.6 |
| Welding, soldering, and brazing machine setters, operators, and tenders.. | 13 | 1.2 | -5.9 |
| Inspectors, testers, sorters, samplers, and weighers ......................................... | 33 | 3.1 | -20.0 |
| Painters, transportation equipment........... | 10 | 1.0 | -8.1 |
| **Transportation and material moving occupations** ........................................... | 65 | 6.1 | -22.4 |
| Industrial truck and tractor operators ........ | 23 | 2.2 | -23.9 |
| Laborers and freight, stock, and material movers, hand.......................................... | 21 | 2.0 | -22.8 |

Note: Columns may not add to totals due to omission of occupations with small employment

ers supply or hold materials or tools, and clean work areas and equipment.

*Material moving occupations.* Motor vehicle operators and material moving workers are essential to keeping the plant running smoothly. *Industrial truck and tractor operators* carry components, equipment, and other materials from factory warehouse and outdoor storage areas to assembly areas. *Truck drivers* carry raw materials to plants, components and materials between plants, and finished motor vehicles to dealerships for sale to consumers. *Laborers and hand freight, stock, and material movers* manually move materials to and from storage areas, loading docks, delivery vehicles, and containers. *Machine feeders* and *offbearers* feed materials into, or remove materials from, machines or equipment on the assembly line, and *hand packers and packagers* manually package or wrap materials.

*Installation, maintenance, repair, and construction occupations.* Maintenance workers are some of the most important workers on the floor of the assembly plant. They make sure the assembly line remains in good working order, because any stoppages can greatly reduce the flow of work within the plant and reduce productivity. Workers in these occupations set up, maintain, and repair equipment. Historically, maintenance work has been broken down into a number of specialties. *Electricians* serviced complex electrical equipment. *Machinists* fabricated special parts. *Plumbers and pipefitters* dealt with the hydraulic systems. *Millwrights* installed and moved machinery and heavy equipment according to the factory's layout plans. Factories now are shifting to a different maintenance model. Instead of specializing in a single skill, factory maintenance personnel are skilled in a range of areas: electricity, fluid and hydraulic power, mechanical, welding, and fabrication. These *industrial machinery mechanics and maintenance workers* are expected to fix any equipment problem in their assigned section of the factory.

Motor vehicle manufacturing also employs many *automotive service technicians and mechanics*, who fix bodies, engines, and other parts of motor vehicles, industrial trucks, and other mobile heavy equipment.

**Training and Advancement**
Many jobs in motor vehicle manufacturing have high earnings and good benefits and so are some of the most highly sought after in the country. As a result, standards for entry are high, requiring a strong educational background and the successful completion of tests.

Faced with technological advances and the continued need to cut costs, manufacturers increasingly emphasize continuing education and cross-train many workers in production and maintenance occupations to do more than one job. This has led to a change in the profile of the industry's workers. Standards for new hires are higher now than in the past. Employers increasingly require a strong educational background for assembly jobs, sometimes requiring a community college degree, and most motor vehicle manufacturers administer lengthy examinations to candidates for assembler jobs. Manual dexterity continues to be necessary for many production jobs, but employers also look for employees with good communication and math skills and aptitudes for computers, problem solving, and critical thinking. Many plants now emphasize the team approach and employees interact more with coworkers and supervisors to determine the best way to get the job done. They are expected to work with much less supervision than in the past and take responsibility for ensuring that their work conforms to guidelines.

Opportunities for training and advancement vary considerably by occupation, plant size, and sector. Training programs in larger auto and light truck assembly plants usually are more extensive than those in smaller parts, truck trailer, and motor home factories. Production workers receive most of their training on the job or through more formal apprenticeship programs. Training normally takes from a few days to several months and may combine classroom with on-the-job training under the guidance of more experienced workers. Attaining the highest level of skill in some production jobs requires several years, however. Training often includes courses in health and safety, teamwork, and quality control. With advanced training and experience, production workers can advance to inspector jobs or to more skilled production, craft, operator, or repair jobs.

Skilled production and maintenance workers—such as tool and die makers, industrial machinery mechanics, millwrights, machinists, pipefitters, and electricians—normally are hired on the basis of previous experience, education, and a good score on a competitive examination. Alternatively, the company may train inexperienced workers in apprenticeship programs that combine on-the-job training with classroom instruction. Typical courses include mechanical drawing, tool designing and programming, blueprint reading, shop mathematics, hydraulics, and electronics. Training also includes courses on health and safety, teamwork, quality control, computers, and diagnostic equipment. With training and experience, workers who excel can advance to become supervisors or managers.

Motor vehicle manufacturers provide formal training opportunities to all workers, regardless of educational background. Manufacturers offer some classes themselves and may pay tuition for workers who enroll in colleges, trade schools, or technical institutes. Workers sometimes can get college credit for training received on the job. Subjects of company training courses range from communication skills to computer science. Formal educational opportunities at postsecondary institutions range from courses in English, basic mathematics, electronics, and computer programming languages to work-study programs leading to associate, bachelor's, and graduate degrees in engineering and technician specialties, management, and other fields.

## Outlook

Continued productivity improvements and more foreign outsourcing of parts will cause overall employment to decline over the next decade.

*Employment change.* Overall wage and salary employment in the motor vehicle and parts manufacturing industry is expected to decline by 14 percent over the 2006-16 period, compared with 11 percent growth for all industries combined. Although projections are for more automobiles and light trucks to be manufactured in the U.S. over this period, productivity improvements will enable manufacturers to produce more vehicles and parts with fewer workers. Also, as the foreign-based manufacturers gain market share, employment in the parts industry will be affected because these companies generally import more of their parts than the domestic manufacturers.

The growing intensity of international and domestic competition has increased cost pressures on manufacturers. In response, they have sought to improve productivity and quality with high-technology production techniques, including computer-assisted design, production, and testing. In addition to automation, both domestic and foreign-based manufacturers will reduce costs by shifting some parts and vehicle production to lower-wage countries.

The automotive industry also is increasingly turning to contract employees in an effort to reduce costs. Contract workers are employed by staffing agencies or employment services firms that provide workers to companies on a temporary or as needed basis. Although they work in the manufacturing plants alongside auto manufacturing employees, they are considered workers in the employment services industry and thus are not counted in this industry. Contract workers are less costly to hire and lay off than are permanent employees and they enable plants to expand or reduce production quickly without the need to lay-off or rehire permanent employees. Contract jobs also serve as a screening tool by employers to search for candidates for permanent jobs that are more complex and require more skills.

Expanding factory automation, robotics, efficiency gains, and the need to cut costs will cause nearly all production occupations to decline, but some occupations will decline more than others. Increasing automation will affect more so basic machine operator occupations, but not as much skilled workers to program robots. Assemblers who only perform one or two tasks will be replaced by team assemblers who are interchangeable on a team and can perform multiple functions. Greater automation will boost demand for maintenance workers who service and repair the robots and automated systems essential to a factory. As employers seek more flexible workers in these positions, employment will shift from specialized occupations, such as electricians, to more generalized occupations like industrial machinery mechanics and maintenance workers.

Employment of management, computer, office and administrative support occupations will decline as the number of production workers, who these workers manage, supervise and support, decline. Industrial production engineers are expected to increase as the need to streamline production and reduce costs continues to be important to this industry.

*Job prospects.* Due to the increasingly automated and sophisticated nature of motor vehicle manufacturing and assembly, employers are seeking a better educated workforce. While applicants for assembly jobs may face competition, opportunities will be best for those with a 2-year degree in a technical area. Applicants for maintenance jobs also face competition. As automakers shift to multi-skilled maintenance personnel, opportunities will be best for those with skills across a range of areas, such as hydraulics, electrical, and welding. Employers use screening tests for new applicants and state that both strong math and communications skills are necessary to pass these tests.

Although employment may be declining, there are expected to be a significant number of openings due to the large number of auto workers who are expected to retire in the coming decade. Some of the earlier foreign plants that were built in the 1980s will see much turnover as a large proportion of their workers retire.

## Earnings

*Industry earnings.* Average weekly earnings of production or nonsupervisory workers in the motor vehicle and parts manufacturing industry are relatively high. At $1,213 per week, earnings of production workers in establishments that manufacture complete motor vehicles were among the highest in the Nation in 2006. Workers in establishments that make motor vehicle parts averaged $904 weekly and those in motor vehicle body and trail-

**Table 3. Median hourly earnings of the largest occupations in motor vehicle and parts manufacturing, May 2006**

| Occupation | Motor vehicle manufacturing | Motor vehicle body and trailer manufacturing | Motor vehicle parts manufacturing | All industries |
|---|---|---|---|---|
| First-line supervisors/managers of production and operating workers | $30.98 | $20.26 | $23.52 | $22.74 |
| Inspectors, testers, sorters, samplers, and weighers | 25.45 | 14.40 | 16.74 | 14.14 |
| Assemblers and fabricators, all other | 25.23 | 12.52 | 18.97 | 12.85 |
| Maintenance and repair workers, general | 24.94 | 16.72 | 19.84 | 15.34 |
| Industrial truck and tractor operators | 24.92 | 13.48 | 15.38 | 13.11 |
| Laborers and freight, stock, and material movers, hand | 24.39 | 12.02 | 13.46 | 10.20 |
| Team assemblers | 21.60 | 13.00 | 13.06 | 11.63 |
| Welders, cutters, solderers, and brazers | 20.62 | 13.68 | 15.14 | 15.10 |
| Cutting, punching, and press machine setters, operators, and tenders, metal and plastic | 17.36 | 13.22 | 13.43 | 12.66 |
| Machinists | - | 15.91 | 18.27 | 16.71 |

er manufacturing averaged $683 per week, compared with $690 for workers in all manufacturing industries, and $568 for those in the entire private sector. Earnings in selected occupations in transportation equipment manufacturing, which comprises motor vehicle and parts manufacturing and aerospace product and parts manufacturing, appear in table 3.

These hourly earnings may increase when overtime or special shifts are required. Workers generally are paid 1.5 times their normal wage rate for working more than 8 hours a day or more than 40 hours a week, or for working on Saturdays. They may receive double their normal wage rate for working on Sundays and holidays.

*Benefits and union membership.* The largest manufacturers and suppliers often offer benefits that include paid vacations and holidays; life, accident, and health insurance; education allowances; nonwage cash payment plans, such as performance and profit-sharing bonuses; and pension plans. Some laid-off workers in the motor vehicle and parts manufacturing industry have access to supplemental unemployment benefits, which can provide them with nearly full pay and benefits for up to several years, depending on the worker's seniority.

In 2006, about 1 out of 4 workers in motor vehicle and parts production were union members or were covered by union contracts, more than double the proportion of workers in all manufacturing industries and all workers in the private sector. Workers in motor vehicle production were more likely to be members of unions than were workers in parts production. The primary union in the industry is the United Automobile, Aerospace, and Agricultural Implement Workers of America, also known as the United Auto Workers (UAW). Unionized production workers in motor vehicle assembly plants, and most of those in motor vehicle parts plants, are covered by collective bargaining agree-

ments negotiated by the UAW. Other unions—including the International Association of Machinists and Aerospace Workers of America, the United Steelworkers of America, and the International Brotherhood of Electrical Workers—cover certain plant locations or specified trades in the industry.

## Sources of Additional Information

Information on employment and training opportunities in the motor vehicle and parts manufacturing industry is available from local offices of State employment services, employment offices of motor vehicle and parts manufacturing firms, and locals of the unions mentioned above.

Detailed information on most occupations in this industry, including the following, appears in the 2008-09 edition of the *Occupational Outlook Handbook:*

- Assemblers and fabricators
- Commercial and industrial designers
- Drafters
- Electricians
- Engineers
- Engineering technicians
- Industrial machinery mechanics and maintenance workers
- Industrial production managers
- Inspectors, testers, sorters, samplers, and weighers
- Machine setters, operators, and tenders—metal and plastic
- Machinists
- Material moving occupations
- Millwrights
- Painting and coating workers, except construction and maintenance
- Tool and die makers
- Welding, soldering, and brazing workers

# Pharmaceutical and Medicine Manufacturing

(NAICS 3254)

## SIGNIFICANT POINTS

- This industry ranks among the fastest growing manufacturing industries.

- More than 6 out of 10 workers have a bachelor's, master's, professional, or Ph.D. degree—twice the proportion for all industries combined.

- 43.3 percent of all jobs are in large establishments employing more than 1000 workers.

- Earnings are much higher than in other manufacturing industries.

## Nature of the Industry

The pharmaceutical and medicine manufacturing industry has produced a variety of medicinal and other health-related products undreamed of by even the most imaginative apothecaries of the past. These drugs save the lives of millions of people from various diseases and permit many ill people to recover to lead normal lives.

*Goods and services.* Thousands of medications are available today for diagnostic, preventive, and therapeutic uses. In addition to aiding in the treatment of infectious diseases such as pneumonia, tuberculosis, malaria, influenza, and sexually transmitted diseases, these medicines also help prevent and treat cardiovascular disease, asthma, diabetes, hepatitis, cystic fibrosis, and cancer. For example, antinausea drugs help cancer patients endure chemotherapy; clot-buster drugs help stroke patients avoid brain damage; and psychoactive drugs reduce the severity of mental illness for many people. Antibiotics and vaccines have virtually wiped out such diseases as diphtheria, syphilis, and whooping cough. Discoveries in veterinary drugs have controlled various diseases, some of which are transmissible to humans.

The U.S. pharmaceutical industry has achieved worldwide prominence through research and development (R&D) on new drugs, and spends a relatively high proportion of its funds on R&D compared with other industries. Each year, pharmaceutical industry testing involves tens of thousands of new substances, yet may eventually yield fewer than 100 new prescription medicines.

For the majority of firms in this industry, the actual manufacture of drugs is the last stage in a lengthy process that begins with scientific research to discover new products and to improve or modify existing ones. The R&D departments in pharmaceutical and medicine manufacturing firms start this process by seeking and rapidly testing libraries of thousands to millions of new chemical compounds with the potential to prevent, combat, or alleviate symptoms of diseases or other health problems. Scientists use sophisticated techniques, including computer simulation, combinatorial chemistry, and high-through-put screening (HTS), to hasten and simplify the discovery of potentially useful new compounds.

Most firms devote a substantial portion of their R&D budgets to applied research, using scientific knowledge to develop a drug targeted to a specific use. For example, an R&D unit may focus on developing a compound that will effectively slow the advance of breast cancer. If the discovery phase yields promising compounds, technical teams then attempt to develop a safe and effective product based on the discoveries.

To test new products in development, a research method called "screening" is used. To screen an antibiotic, for example, a sample is first placed in a bacterial culture. If the antibiotic is effective, it is next tested on infected laboratory animals. Laboratory animals also are used to study the safety and efficacy of the new drug. A new drug is selected for testing on humans only if it promises to have therapeutic advantages over drugs already in use, or is safer. Drug screening is an incredibly risky, laborious, and costly process—only 1 in every 5,000 to 10,000 compounds screened eventually becomes an approved drug.

After laboratory screening, firms conduct clinical investigations, or "trials," of the drug on human patients. Human clinical trials normally take place in three phases. First, medical scientists administer the drug to a small group of healthy volunteers to determine and adjust dosage levels, and monitor for side effects. If a drug appears useful and safe, additional tests are conducted in two more phases, each phase using a successively larger group of volunteers or carefully selected patients, sometimes upwards of 10,000 individuals.

After a drug successfully passes animal and clinical tests, the U.S. Food and Drug Administration's (FDA) Center for Drug Evaluation and Research (CDER) must review the drug's performance on human patients before approving the substance for commercial use. The entire process, from the first discovery of a promising new compound to FDA approval, can take over a decade and cost hundreds of millions of dollars.

After FDA approval, problems of production methods and costs must be worked out before manufacturing begins. If the original laboratory process of preparing and compounding the ingredients is complex and too expensive, pharmacists, chemists, chemical engineers, packaging engineers, and production specialists are assigned to develop a manufacturing process economically adaptable to mass production. After the drug is marketed, new production methods may be developed to incorporate new technology or to transfer the manufacturing operation to a new production site.

In many production plants, pharmaceutical manufacturers have developed a high degree of automation. Milling and micronizing machines, which pulverize substances into extremely fine particles, are used to reduce bulk chemicals to the required size. These finished chemicals are combined and processed further in mixing machines. The mixed ingredients may then be mechanically capsulated, pressed into tablets, or made into solutions. One type of machine, for example, automatically fills, seals, and stamps capsules. Other machines fill bottles with capsules, tablets, or liquids, and seal, label, and package the bottles.

Quality control and quality assurance are vital in this industry. Many production workers are assigned full time to quality control and quality assurance functions, whereas other employees may devote part of their time to these functions. For example, although pharmaceutical company sales representatives, often called detailers, work primarily in marketing, they engage in quality control when they assist pharmacists in checking for outdated products.

*Industry organization.* The pharmaceutical and medicine manufacturing industry consists of over 2,500 places of employment, located throughout the country. These include establishments that make pharmaceutical preparations or finished drugs; biological products, such as serums and vaccines; bulk chemicals and botanicals used in making finished drugs; and diagnostic substances such as pregnancy and blood glucose kits.

*Recent developments.* Advances in biotechnology are transforming drug discovery and development. Bioinformatics, a branch of biotechnology using information technologies to work with biological data like DNA, is a particularly dynamic new area of work. Scientists have learned a great deal about human genes, but the real work—translating that knowledge into viable new drugs—has only recently begun. So far, millions of people have benefited from medicines and vaccines developed through biotechnology, and several hundred new biotechnologically-derived medicines are currently in the pipeline. These new medicines, all of which are in human clinical trials or awaiting FDA approval, include drugs for cancer, infectious diseases, autoimmune diseases, neurologic disorders, and HIV/AIDS and related conditions.

Many new drugs are expected to be developed in the coming years. Advances in technology and the knowledge of how cells work will allow pharmaceutical and medicine manufacturing makers to become more efficient in the drug discovery process. New technology allows life scientists to test millions of drug candidates far more rapidly than in the past. Other new technology, such as regenerative therapy using stem cell research, also will allow the natural healing process to work faster, or enable the regrowth of missing or damaged tissue.

There is a direct relationship between gene discovery and identification of new drugs—the more genes identified the more paths available for drug discovery. Data obtained from the mapping of the human genome can be compared with known gene sequences to identify the proteins produced by each gene, and the effect of those proteins on the body. The study of these gene sequences and the varieties of proteins they produce contribute to the development of new medicines, both biotechnological and chemical. Among other uses, new genetic technology is being explored to develop vaccines to prevent or treat diseases that have eluded traditional vaccines, such as AIDS, malaria, tuberculosis, and cervical cancer.

## Working Conditions

*Hours.* In 2006 production workers in pharmaceutical and medicine manufacturing worked an average of 41.8 hours per week, compared with 33.9 for workers in all industries. Some employees work in plants that operate around the clock—three shifts a day, 7 days a week. In most plants, workers receive extra pay

when assigned to the second or third shift. Because drug production is subject to little seasonal variation or fluctuation in economic activity, work is steady.

*Work Environment.* Working conditions in pharmaceutical plants are better than those in most other manufacturing plants. Much emphasis is placed on keeping equipment and work areas clean because of the danger of contamination. Plants usually are air-conditioned, well lighted, and quiet. Ventilation systems protect workers from dust, fumes, and disagreeable odors. Special precautions are taken to protect the relatively small number of employees who work with infectious cultures and poisonous chemicals. With the exception of work performed by material handlers and maintenance workers, most jobs require little physical effort. In 2006, the incidence of work-related injury and illness was 2.4 cases per 100 full-time workers, compared with 6.0 per 100 for all manufacturing industries and 4.4 per 100 for the entire private sector.

## Employment

Pharmaceutical and medicine manufacturing provided 292,000 wage and salary jobs in 2006. Pharmaceutical and medicine manufacturing establishments usually employ many workers. Nearly 90 percent of this industry's jobs in 2006 were in establishments that employed more than 100 workers (chart). Most jobs are in California, Illinois, Texas, Indiana, New Jersey, New York, North Carolina, and Pennsylvania.

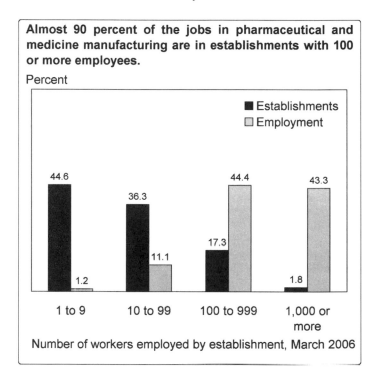

**Almost 90 percent of the jobs in pharmaceutical and medicine manufacturing are in establishments with 100 or more employees.**

Percent

Number of workers employed by establishment, March 2006

Under the North American Industry Classification System (NAICS), workers in research and development (R&D) establishments that are not part of a manufacturing facility are included in a separate industry—research and development in the physical, engineering, and life sciences. However, due to the importance of R&D work to the pharmaceutical and medicine manufacturing industry, drug-related R&D is discussed in this statement even though a large proportion of pharmaceutical industry-related R&D workers are not included in the employment data.

## Occupations in the Industry

About 28 percent of all jobs in the pharmaceutical and medicine manufacturing industry are in professional and related occupations, mostly scientists and science technicians. About 16 percent are in management occupations, another 13 percent are in office and administrative support, and 3 percent are in sales and related occupations. About 3 out of 10 jobs in the industry are in production occupations, including both low skilled and high skilled jobs (table 1).

*Professional and related occupations.* Scientists, engineers, and technicians conduct research to develop new drugs. Others work to streamline production methods and improve environmental and quality control. Life scientists are among the largest scientific occupations in this industry. Most of these scientists are *biological* and *medical scientists* who produce new drugs using biotechnology to recombine the genetic material of animals or plants. Biological scientists normally specialize in a particular area. *Biologists* and *bacteriologists* study the effect of chemical agents on infected animals. *Biochemists* study the action of drugs on body processes by analyzing the chemical combination and reactions involved in metabolism, reproduction, and heredity. *Microbiologists* grow strains of microorganisms that produce antibiotics. *Physiologists* investigate the effect of drugs on body functions and vital processes. *Pharmacologists* and *zoologists* study the effects of drugs on animals. *Virologists* grow viruses, and develop vaccines and test them in animals. *Botanists*, with their special knowledge of plant life, contribute to the discovery of botanical ingredients for drugs. Other biological scientists include *pathologists*, who study normal and abnormal cells or tissues, and *toxicologists*, who are concerned with safety, dosage levels, and the compatibility of different drugs. *Medical scientists*, who also may be physicians, conduct clinical research, test products, and oversee human clinical trials.

The work of physical scientists, particularly *chemists*, also is important in the development of new drugs. *Combinatorial* and *computational chemists* create molecules and test them rapidly for desirable properties. *Organic chemists*, often using combinatorial chemistry, then combine new compounds for biological testing. *Physical chemists* separate and identify substances, determine molecular structure, help create new compounds, and improve manufacturing processes. *Radiochemists* trace the course of drugs through body organs and tissues. *Pharmaceutical chemists* set standards and specifications for the form of products and for storage conditions; they also see that drug labeling and literature meet the requirements of State and Federal laws. *Analytical chemists* test raw and intermediate materials and finished products for quality.

Science technicians, such as *biological* and *chemical technicians*, play an important part in research and development of new medicines. They set up, operate, and maintain laboratory equipment, monitor experiments, analyze data, and record and interpret results. Science technicians usually work under the supervision of scientists or engineers.

Although engineers account for a small fraction of scientific and technical workers, they make significant contributions toward improving quality control and production efficiency. *Chemical engineers* design equipment and devise manufacturing processes. *Bioprocess engineers*, who are similar to chemical engineers, design fermentation vats and various bioreactors for microorganisms that will produce a given product. *Industrial engineers* plan equipment layout and workflow to maintain efficient use of plant facilities.

Table 1. Employment of wage and salary workers in pharmaceutical and medicine manufacturing by occupation, 2006 and projected change, 2006-2016.
(Employment in thousands)

| Occupation | Employment, 2006 Number | Employment, 2006 Percent | Percent change, 2006-16 |
|---|---|---|---|
| **All occupations** | 292 | 100.0 | 23.7 |
| **Management, business, and financial occupations** | 47 | 15.9 | 26.5 |
| Top executives | 6 | 1.9 | 13.4 |
| Marketing and sales managers | 3 | 0.9 | 26.0 |
| Industrial production managers | 4 | 1.3 | 26.0 |
| Natural sciences managers | 3 | 1.1 | 26.0 |
| Managers, all other | 4 | 1.3 | 26.0 |
| Accountants and auditors | 3 | 1.1 | 26.0 |
| **Professional and related occupations** | 81 | 27.8 | 26.4 |
| Computer specialists | 9 | 3.2 | 35.5 |
| Biomedical engineers | 2 | 0.8 | 38.6 |
| Industrial engineers | 2 | 0.8 | 53.1 |
| Engineering technicians, except drafters | 3 | 1.2 | 34.8 |
| Biochemists and biophysicists | 4 | 1.4 | 26.0 |
| Microbiologists | 3 | 1.1 | 26.0 |
| Medical scientists, except epidemiologists | 10 | 3.4 | 26.0 |
| Chemists | 15 | 5.2 | 13.4 |
| Biological technicians | 7 | 2.5 | 26.0 |
| Chemical technicians | 7 | 2.3 | 26.0 |
| **Sales and related occupations** | 9 | 3.0 | 25.5 |
| Sales representatives, wholesale and manufacturing | 8 | 2.6 | 26.0 |
| **Office and administrative support occupations** | 37 | 12.5 | 19.8 |
| Bookkeeping, accounting, and auditing clerks | 3 | 0.9 | 26.0 |
| Customer service representatives | 4 | 1.3 | 38.6 |
| Production, planning, and expediting clerks | 3 | 1.1 | 26.0 |
| Shipping, receiving, and traffic clerks | 4 | 1.4 | 21.3 |
| Secretaries and administrative assistants | 9 | 3.1 | 20.1 |
| Office clerks, general | 3 | 1.2 | 24.2 |
| **Installation, maintenance, and repair occupations** | 14 | 4.8 | 31.0 |
| Industrial machinery mechanics | 3 | 1.1 | 44.9 |
| Maintenance and repair workers, general | 6 | 2.1 | 26.0 |
| **Production occupations** | 84 | 28.6 | 21.9 |
| First-line supervisors/managers of production and operating workers | 8 | 2.6 | 26.0 |
| Team assemblers | 5 | 1.7 | 26.0 |
| Chemical plant and system operators | 2 | 0.8 | 26.0 |
| Chemical equipment operators and tenders | 10 | 3.5 | 26.0 |
| Separating, filtering, clarifying, precipitating, and still machine setters, operators, and tenders | 6 | 1.9 | 26.0 |
| Mixing and blending machine setters, operators, and tenders | 11 | 3.6 | 26.0 |
| Extruding, forming, pressing, and compacting machine setters, operators, and tenders | 2 | 0.8 | 26.0 |
| Inspectors, testers, sorters, samplers, and weighers | 9 | 3.0 | 18.8 |
| Packaging and filling machine operators and tenders | 20 | 7.0 | 13.4 |
| **Transportation and material moving occupations** | 16 | 5.3 | 11.5 |
| Laborers and freight, stock, and material movers, hand | 5 | 1.6 | 13.4 |
| Machine feeders and offbearers | 4 | 1.4 | 13.4 |
| Packers and packagers, hand | 4 | 1.4 | 0.8 |

Note: Columns may not add to totals due to omission of occupations with small employment

*Management, business, and financial occupations.* At the top of the managerial group are executives who make policy decisions concerning matters of finance, marketing, and research. Other managerial workers include *natural sciences managers* and *industrial production managers.*

*Other occupations.* Workers in office and administrative support occupations include *secretaries and administrative assistants, general office clerks,* and others who keep records on personnel, payroll, raw materials, sales, and shipments.

*Sales representatives, wholesale and manufacturing,* describe their company's products to physicians, pharmacists, dentists, and health services administrators. These workers serve as lines of communication between their companies and clients.

Most plant workers fall into one of two occupational groups: Production workers who operate drug-producing equipment, inspect products, and install, maintain, and repair production equipment; and transportation and material moving workers who package and transport the drugs.

Workers among the larger of the production occupations, *assemblers and fabricators,* perform all of the assembly tasks assigned to their teams, rotating through the different tasks rather than specializing in a single task. They also may decide how the work is to be assigned and how different tasks are to be performed.

Other production workers specialize in one part of the production process. *Chemical processing machine setters, operators, and tenders,* such as *pharmaceutical operators,* control machines that produce tablets, capsules, ointments, and medical solutions. Included among these operators are *mixing and blending machine setters, operators, and tenders,* who tend milling and grinding machines that reduce mixtures to particles of designated sizes. *Extruding, forming, pressing, and compacting machine setters, operators, and tenders* tend tanks and kettles in which solutions are mixed and compounded to make up creams, ointments, liquid medications, and powders. *Crushing, grinding, polishing, mixing, and blending workers* operate machines that compress ingredients into tablets. *Coating, painting, and spraying machine setters, operators, and tenders,* often called capsule coaters, control a battery of machines that apply coatings that flavor, color, preserve, or add medication to tablets, or control disintegration time. Throughout the production process, *inspectors, testers, sorters, samplers, and weighers* ensure consistency and quality. For example, *ampoule examiners* inspect ampoules for discoloration, foreign particles, and flaws in the glass. *Tablet testers* inspect tablets for hardness, chipping, and weight to assure conformity with specifications. After the drug is prepared and inspected, it is bottled or otherwise packaged by *packaging and filling machine operators and tenders.*

Plant workers who do not operate or maintain equipment perform a variety of other tasks. Some drive industrial trucks or tractors to move materials around the plant, load and unload trucks and railroad cars, or package products and materials by hand.

## Training and Advancement

Training requirements for jobs in the pharmaceutical and medicine manufacturing industry range from a few hours of on-the-job training to years of formal education plus job experience. More than 6 out of 10 of all workers have a bachelor's, master's, professional, or Ph.D. degree—more than twice the proportion for all industries combined.

*Production occupations.* Manufacturers usually hire inexperienced workers and train them on the job; high school graduates generally are preferred. Beginners in production jobs assist experienced workers and learn to operate processing equipment. With experience, employees may advance to more skilled jobs in their departments.

The industry places a heavy emphasis on continuing education for employees, and many firms provide classroom training in safety, environmental and quality control, and technological advances. Many companies encourage production workers to take courses related to their jobs at local schools and technical institutes or to enroll in correspondence courses. College courses in chemistry and related areas are particularly encouraged for highly skilled production workers who operate sophisticated equipment. Some companies reimburse workers for part, or all, of their tuition. Skilled production workers with leadership ability may advance to supervisory positions.

*Science technician occupations.* To fill these jobs, most companies prefer to hire graduates of technical institutes or community colleges or those who have completed college courses in chemistry, biology, mathematics, or engineering. Some companies, however, require science technicians to hold a bachelor's degree in a biological or chemical science. In many firms, newly hired workers begin as laboratory helpers or aides, performing routine jobs such as cleaning and arranging bottles, test tubes, and other equipment.

The experience required for higher level technician jobs varies from company to company. Usually, employees advance over a number of years from assistant technician, to technician, to senior technician, and then to technical associate, or supervisory technician.

*Scientific and engineering occupations.* A Bachelor of Science degree is typically the minimum requirement for these workers. Scientists involved in research and development usually have a master's or doctoral degree. A doctoral degree is generally the minimum requirement for medical scientists, and those who administer drug or gene therapy to patients in clinical trials must have a medical degree. Because biotechnology is not one discipline, but the interaction of several disciplines, the best preparation for work in biotechnology is training in a traditional biological science, such as genetics, molecular biology, biochemistry, virology, or biochemical engineering. Individuals with a scientific background and several years of industry experience may eventually advance to managerial positions. Some companies offer training programs to help scientists and engineers keep abreast of new developments in their fields and to develop administrative skills. These programs may include meetings and seminars with consultants from various fields. Many companies encourage scientists and engineers to further their education; some companies provide financial assistance or full reimbursement of expenses for this purpose. Publication of scientific papers also is encouraged.

*Sales and related occupations.* Pharmaceutical manufacturing companies prefer to hire college graduates, particularly those with strong scientific backgrounds. In addition to a 4-year degree, most newly employed pharmaceutical sales representatives complete rigorous formal training programs revolving around their company's product lines.

## Outlook

Employment is expected to increase through 2016. Pharmaceutical and medicine manufacturing will be one of the fastest growing manufacturing industries.

*Employment change.* The number of wage and salary jobs in pharmaceutical and medicine manufacturing is expected to increase by 24 percent over the 2006-16 period, compared with the 11 percent projected for all industries combined. Pharmaceutical and medicine manufacturing ranks among the fastest growing manufacturing industries. Demand for this industry's products is expected to remain strong. Even during fluctuating economic conditions, there will be a market for over-the-counter and prescription drugs, including the diagnostics used in hospitals, laboratories, and homes; the vaccines used routinely on infants and children; analgesics and other symptom-easing drugs; antibiotics and other drugs for life-threatening diseases; and "lifestyle" drugs for the treatment of nonlife-threatening conditions.

The use of drugs, particularly antibiotics and vaccines, has helped to eradicate or limit a number of deadly diseases, but many others, such as cancer, Alzheimer's, and heart disease, continue to elude cures. Ongoing research and the manufacture of new products to combat these diseases will continue to contribute to employment growth. Demand also is expected to increase as the population expands because so many of the pharmaceutical and medicine manufacturing industry's products are related to preventive or routine healthcare, rather than just illness. The growing number of older people, who will require more healthcare services, will further stimulate demand—along with the growth of both public and private health insurance programs, which increasingly cover the cost of drugs and medicines.

Another factor propelling demand is the increasing popularity of "lifestyle" drugs. These drugs treat symptoms of chronic nonlife-threatening conditions resulting from aging or genetic predisposition and can enhance one's self-confidence or physical appearance. Other factors expected to increase the demand for drugs include greater personal income and the rising health consciousness and expectations of the general public.

Despite the increasing demand for drugs, drug producers and buyers are expected to place more emphasis on cost effectiveness, due to concerns about the cost of health care, including prescription drugs. Growing competition from the producers of generic drugs also may exert cost pressures on many firms in this industry, particularly as brand-name drug patents expire. In addition, the average time for the FDA to review "nonpriority" drug applications is becoming longer, further delaying the time a drug comes to market. These factors, combined with continuing improvements in manufacturing processes, are expected to result in rapid employment growth over the 2006-16 period, but nevertheless slower than occurred during the previous 10-year period.

Strong demand is anticipated for professional occupations—especially for life and physical scientists engaged in R&D, the backbone of the pharmaceutical and medicine manufacturing industry. Much of the basic biological research done in recent years has resulted in new knowledge, including the successful identification of genes. Life and physical scientists will be needed to take this knowledge to the next stage, which is to understand how certain genes function so that gene therapies can be developed to treat diseases. Computer specialists such as systems analysts, biostatisticians, and computer support specialists also will be in demand as disciplines such as biology, chemistry, and electronics continue to converge and become more interdisciplinary, creating demand in rapidly emerging fields such as bioinformatics and nanotechnology.

Strong demand also is projected for production occupations. Employment of office and administrative support workers is expected to grow more slowly than the industry as a whole, as companies streamline operations and increasingly rely on computers

*Job prospects.* Job opportunities in most occupations should be good, particularly for those employees with science and engineering backgrounds. Unlike many other manufacturing industries, the pharmaceutical and medicine manufacturing industry is not highly sensitive to changes in economic conditions. Even during periods of high unemployment, work is likely to be relatively stable in this industry. Additional openings will arise from the need to replace workers who transfer to other industries, retire, or leave the workforce for other reasons.

## Earnings

*Industry earnings.* Earnings of workers in the pharmaceutical and medicine manufacturing industry are higher than the average for all manufacturing industries. In 2006, production or nonsupervisory workers in this industry averaged $891 a week, while those in all manufacturing industries averaged $695 a week. Earnings in selected occupations in pharmaceutical and medicine manufacturing appear in table 2.

**Table 2. Median hourly earnings of the largest occupations in pharmaceutical and medicine manufacturing, May 2006**

| Occupation | Pharmaceutical and medicine manufacturing | All Industries |
|---|---|---|
| Medical scientists, except epidemiologists | $39.73 | $29.66 |
| Chemists | 27.51 | 28.78 |
| First-line supervisors/managers of production and operating workers | 27.00 | 22.74 |
| Maintenance and repair workers, general | 20.51 | 15.34 |
| Chemical technicians | 19.38 | .87 |
| Biological technicians | 18.93 | 17.17 |
| Chemical equipment operators and tenders | 17.101 | 9.37 |
| Inspectors, testers, sorters, samplers, and weighers | 15.69 | 14.14 |
| Mixing and blending machine setters, operators, and tenders | 14.22 | 14.10 |
| Packaging and filling machine operators and tenders | 11.81 | 11.06 |

*Benefits and union membership.* Workers in the pharmaceutical and medicine manufacturing industry generally receive paid sick and vacation leave and health insurance, and many employers contribute to pension plans and life insurance. Some firms may offer their medicines to employees at a reduced cost.

Only about 5 percent of the workers in the pharmaceutical and medicine manufacturing industry are union members or are covered by a union contract, compared with about 13 percent of workers throughout private industry.

## Sources of Additional Information

For additional information about careers in pharmaceutical and medicine manufacturing, write to the human resources depart-

81

ments of individual pharmaceutical and medicine manufacturing companies.

For information about careers in biotechnology, contact:

➢ Biotechnology Industry Organization, 1625 K St. NW., Suite 1100, Washington, DC 20006. Internet: **http://www.bio.org**

For information on careers in pharmaceutical and medicine manufacturing, contact:

➢ Pharmaceutical Research and Manufacturers of America (PHRMA), 1100 15th St. NW., Washington, DC 20005. Internet: **http://www.phrma.org**

Information on these key pharmaceutical and medicine manufacturing occupations may be found in the 2008-09 edition of the *Occupational Outlook Handbook.*

- Assemblers and fabricators
- Biological scientists
- Computer scientists and database administrators
- Computer support specialists and systems administrators
- Computer systems analysts
- Chemists and material scientists
- Engineers
- Inspectors, testers, sorters, samplers, and weighers
- Medical scientists
- Sales representatives, wholesale and manufacturing
- Science technicians

# Printing

(NAICS 323)

## SIGNIFICANT POINTS

- Employment is expected to decline in the face of increasing computerization, growing imports of some printed materials, and the expanding use of the Internet.

- Computerization has eliminated many prepress and production jobs, but has also provided new job opportunities for digital typesetters, desktop publishers, and other computer-related occupations.

- Though employment is concentrated in establishments that employ 50 or more workers, most establishments are small: 7 out of 10 employ fewer than 10 people.

## Nature of the Industry

The printing industry includes establishments primarily engaged in printing text and images on to paper, metal, glass, and some apparel and other materials. Printing can be divided into three distinct stages: *prepress*, the preparation of materials for printing; *press* or *output*, the actual printing process; and *postpress* or *finishing*, the folding, binding, and trimming of printed sheets into their final form. Companies that provide all three services first prepare the material for printing in the prepress department, then produce the pages on the pressroom floor, and finally trim, bind, or otherwise ready the material for distribution in the postpress department.

*Goods and services.* A wide range of products are produced in the printing industry. In addition to magazines, books, and some small newspapers, other examples of printed products include direct mail, labels, manuals, and marketing material. Less obvious printed goods include memo pads, business order forms, checks, maps, T-shirts, and packaging. The industry also includes establishments that provide the quick printing of documents and support services—such as prepress, embossing, binding, and finishing—to printers.

*Industry organization.* The printing industry is broken into 12 segments that generally reflect the major type of printing method that is used at the establishment or product that is produced. Establishments that use printing plates, or some other form of image carrier, to distribute ink to paper, are broken into five industry segments: lithography, flexography, gravure, screen printing, and letterpress. Lithography, which uses the basic principle that water repels oil, is the most widely used printing process in the industry. Lithography lends itself to computer composition and the economical use of color, which accounts for its dominance. Commercial lithographic printing establishments make up the largest segment of the industry, accounting for about 39 percent of employment and about 30 percent of total establishments. Although most newspapers use the lithographic process, their printing activities are not included in this industry, but rather in the publishing industry. Flexography uses printing plates made of rubber or plastic. It is a high-speed process that uses fast-drying inks and can be used on a variety of materials, qualities valued for labels, shopping bags, milk cartons, and corrugated boxes. Gravure's high-quality reproduction, flexible pagination and formats, and consistent print quality have won it a sig-

nificant share of packaging and product printing and a growing share of periodical printing. Screen printing prints designs on clothes and other fabric items, such as hats and napkins. Where letterpress is still used, it prints images from the raised surfaces on which ink sits. The raised surfaces are generated by means of casting, acid etching, or photoemulsion.

Plateless or nonimpact processes, which are the most technologically advanced methods of printing, are included in the digital printing segment of the industry. These include electronic, electrostatic, or inkjet printing, and are used mainly for copying, duplicating, and specialty printing. Although currently much of the work done using digital printing is low volume and often done by small shops, plateless printing is being used more and more throughout the industry. Digital printing, also known as "variable data printing", offers quick turnaround capabilities and the ability to personalize printed materials. Establishments offering primarily digital printing services constitute one of the smallest segments of the industry—3 percent of total employment.

Quick printing is the industry's third largest segment in terms of the number of jobs and is the industry's second largest segment in terms of number of establishments. Used mostly by small businesses and households, quick printing establishments use a variety of printing and copying methods for projects that have short runs and require quick turnaround. Many of these establishments have expanded into other office-related services, such as shipping and selling office supplies to satisfy the small business user. Other segments of the printing industry include establishments that provide specialty services to the printing industry, such as prepress services and trade binding and related work.

Printing is a large industry composed of many shops that vary in size. More than two-thirds of establishments in printing employ 10 or fewer workers. (See chart.)

*Recent developments.* The printing industry, like many other industries, continues to undergo technological changes, as computers and technology alter the manner in which work is performed. Many of the processes that were once done by hand are becoming more automated, and technology's influence can be seen in all three stages of printing. The most notable changes have occurred in the prepress stage. Instead of cutting and pasting articles by hand, workers now produce entire publications on a computer, complete with artwork and graphics. Columns

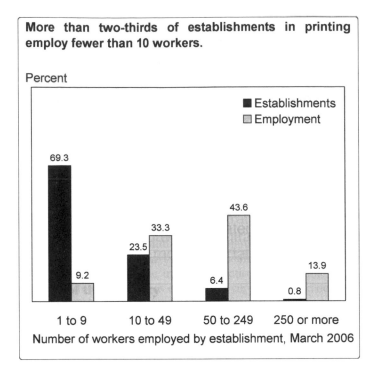

**More than two-thirds of establishments in printing employ fewer than 10 workers.**

Percent

Legend: ■ Establishments ☐ Employment

- 1 to 9: 69.3 / 9.2
- 10 to 49: 23.5 / 33.3
- 50 to 249: 6.4 / 43.6
- 250 or more: 0.8 / 13.9

Number of workers employed by establishment, March 2006

can be displayed and arranged on the computer screen exactly as they will appear in print, and then be printed. Nearly all prepress work is becoming computerized, and prepress workers need considerable training in computer software and graphic communications. Technology has also affected the printing process itself. Press operators increasingly use computers to make adjustments to printing presses in order to complete a job. The same is also true of bindery and other finishing workers.

Although digital printing is currently a small portion of the industry, it is the fastest growing industry segment as printers embrace this technology. Most commercial printers now do some form of digital printing. Printing processes today use scanners and digital cameras to input images and computers to manipulate and format the graphic images prior to printing. Digital printing is transforming prepress operations as well as the printing process. It eliminates much of the lengthy process in manually transferring materials to the printing press by directly transferring digital files to an electronically driven output device.

The printing industry is also taking on new responsibilities that provide further value for clients. This means customers can now have their finished products labeled, packaged, and shipped directly by printing companies. Other ancillary services that printers are adding include database management, warehousing, and prefabricated design work for clients who want to fill out design templates on the Internet rather than creating original design work. Printers feel that these services are increasingly important to their current and potential customers.

## Working Conditions

*Hours.* The average nonsupervisory worker in the printing industry worked 39.2 hours per week in 2006, compared with 41.1 hours per week across all manufacturing industries. Workers in the industry generally put in an 8-hour day, but overtime is often required to meet production deadlines. Larger companies tend to have shift work. Shift schedules and overtime are based largely on seniority, and differ from establishment to establishment.

*Work Environment.* Working conditions vary by occupation. For example, press operators who work with large web presses or pieces of bindery equipment work in a manufacturing plant environment and often need to wear ear protection. On the other hand, prepress technicians and related workers usually work in quiet, clean, air-conditioned offices. In establishments that print confidential data, such as personal credit card statements, employees work in secure areas that are off-limits to other employees.

Most printing work involves dealing with fine detail, which can be tiring both mentally and physically. Fortunately, advanced technology in machinery has reduced eye strain.

In recent years, working conditions have become less hazardous as the industry has become more automated. Also, companies are using fewer chemicals and solutions than in the past and are experiencing fewer equipment-related accidents. Even with more safety-enhanced machinery, however, some workers still are subject to occupational hazards. Press operators, for example, work with rapidly moving machinery that can cause injuries. In 2006, there were 4.2 cases of work-related injury or illness per 100 full-time workers. This was less than the rate of 6.0 per 100 for all manufacturing industries.

## Employment

In 2006, the printing industry had about 636,000 wage and salary jobs, and an additional 26,000 self-employed and unpaid family workers, ranking it among the larger manufacturing industries.

About 39 percent were in the largest segment of the industry—commercial lithographic printing (table 1). Printing plants are widely dispersed throughout the country, but more specialized types of printing tend to be regionally concentrated. For example, the printing of financial documents is concentrated in New York City. Other large printing centers include Chicago, Los Angeles—Long Beach, Minneapolis—St. Paul, and Philadelphia, Boston, and Washington DC.

**Table 1. Percent distribution of employment and establishments in printing by detailed industry sector, 2006**

| Industry segment | Employment | Establishments |
|---|---|---|
| Total | 100.0 | 100.0 |
| Commercial lithographic printing | 38.8 | 30.0 |
| Commercial screen printing | 10.6 | 13.9 |
| Quick printing | 10.6 | 25.9 |
| Other commercial printing | 7.9 | 8.9 |
| Commercial flexographic printing | 6.2 | 3.8 |
| Manifold business forms printing | 5.7 | 2.4 |
| Books printing | 4.9 | 1.6 |
| Prepress services | 4.2 | 4.6 |
| Trade binding and related work | 3.6 | 2.6 |
| Digital printing | 3.4 | 4.7 |
| Commercial gravure printing | 2.6 | 1.0 |
| Blankbook and looseleaf binder manufacturing | 1.4 | 0.5 |

## Occupations in the Industry

Printing occupations range in skill from those found in quick printing to specialized production occupations rarely found in other industries (table 2). Production occupations make up 53 percent of industry employment with printing machine operators accounting for the most employment of any single occupation in the industry at 16 percent.

84

*Production occupations.* *Prepress technicians* prepare print jobs for the presses. They take text or images from clients and ensure that coloring and other issues are resolved before the job goes to press. For those processes that require it, technicians then create the printing plate. Increasingly, prepress technicians receive the material for the pages as electronic computer files, which they upload to their computers, and use digital imaging software to lay out the pages. In very small shops or shops with small format digital equipment, prepress technicians may also design materials for those clients who need it. "Preflight" technicians, a type of prepress worker, examine and edit the pages to ensure that the design, format, settings, quality, and all other aspects of the finished product will be completed according to the client's specifications. Larger printers may add customer service duties to the traditional list of prepress duties in order to streamline business workflow.

When material is ready, *printing machine operators* review the material with the prepress technician, and then install and adjust the printing plate on the press. They must also meter the flow of fountain solution, adjust pressure, ink the printing presses, load paper, and adjust the press to paper size. Operators must correct any problems that might occur during a press run, which means they must monitor the process throughout the run and make minor repairs when necessary. *Job printers,* who usually work in small print shops, perform the prepress work as well as operate the press.

During the binding or finishing stage, the printed sheets are transformed into products such as books, catalogs, magazines, or directories. *Bindery workers* fold and fasten groups of sheets together, often using a machine stapler, to make "signatures". They then feed the signatures into various machines for stitching or gluing—a process that now relies mainly on computers. *Bookbinders* assemble books from large, flat, printed sheets of paper. They cut, saw, and glue parts to bind new books. They also perform other finishing operations, such as decorating and lettering, often using hand tools. A small number of bookbinders work in hand binderies. These highly skilled workers design original or special bindings for publications with limited editions, or restore and rebind rare books.

*Professional and administrative occupations.* *Desktop publishers* and *digital typesetters* perform typesetting and page layout on personal computers. These workers make sure that the files have the correct layout and format, thus taking over some of the work formerly done by prepress workers. *Illustrators* create drawings, charts, graphs, or full-color artwork to complement the text, while *graphic designers* use their creativity and computer skills to layout advertising material, brochures, and other print items that artfully bring together text, photos, and illustrations to create the kind of visual impact desired by clients. One occupation becoming more important is the *customer service representative*, also called a production coordinator. Workers in this job track the various processes of production and act as liaison between clients and technicians.

*Other occupations.* In addition to these specialized printing occupations, managerial, marketing and sales workers, business and financial operations workers, and workers in transportation and material moving occupations are also employed in the printing industry. Common examples of these workers include *sales representatives*, *cost estimators*, and *truck drivers*.

**Table 2. Employment of wage and salary workers in printing by occupation, 2006 and projected change, 2006-2016.**
(Employment in thousands)

| Occupation | Employment, 2006 | | Percent change, 2006-16 |
|---|---|---|---|
| | Number | Percent | |
| **All occupations** | 636 | 100.0 | -21.8 |
| **Management, business, and financial occupations** | 42 | 6.7 | -22.3 |
| Top executives | 13 | 2.0 | -28.7 |
| Industrial production managers | 5 | 0.8 | -20.8 |
| Cost estimators | 6 | 0.9 | -14.4 |
| **Professional and related occupations** | 30 | 4.8 | -20.4 |
| Computer specialists | 7 | 1.1 | -20.5 |
| Graphic designers | 18 | 2.8 | -20.8 |
| **Sales and related occupations** | 39 | 6.2 | -19.4 |
| Sales representatives, wholesale and manufacturing, except technical and scientific products | 25 | 3.9 | -20.8 |
| **Office and administrative support occupations** | 124 | 19.6 | -24.3 |
| Bookkeeping, accounting, and auditing clerks | 10 | 1.6 | -20.8 |
| Customer service representatives | 26 | 4.2 | -12.8 |
| Production, planning, and expediting clerks | 6 | 0.9 | -20.8 |
| Shipping, receiving, and traffic clerks | 13 | 2.0 | -23.8 |
| Secretaries and administrative assistants | 9 | 1.4 | -25.7 |
| Desktop publishers | 8 | 1.2 | -20.8 |
| Mail clerks and mail machine operators, except postal service | 4 | 0.7 | -41.8 |
| Office clerks, general | 10 | 1.5 | -21.9 |
| **Installation, maintenance, and repair occupations** | 11 | 1.7 | -17.3 |
| Industrial machinery installation, repair, and maintenance workers | 8 | 1.3 | -16.9 |
| **Production occupations** | 337 | 53.0 | -20.3 |
| First-line supervisors/managers of production and operating workers | 25 | 4.0 | -20.8 |
| Team assemblers | 7 | 1.1 | -20.8 |
| Bindery workers | 49 | 7.7 | -28.7 |
| Bookbinders | 6 | 1.0 | -20.8 |
| Job printers | 30 | 4.7 | -20.8 |
| Prepress technicians and workers | 41 | 6.5 | -28.7 |
| Printing machine operators | 101 | 15.8 | -10.3 |
| Cutting and slicing machine setters, operators, and tenders | 10 | 1.5 | -20.8 |
| Inspectors, testers, sorters, samplers, and weighers | 7 | 1.1 | -25.3 |
| Paper goods machine setters, operators, and tenders | 9 | 1.5 | -20.8 |
| Helpers--Production workers | 24 | 3.8 | -20.8 |
| **Transportation and material moving occupations** | 48 | 7.5 | -29.1 |
| Truck drivers, light or delivery services | 7 | 1.1 | -20.8 |
| Laborers and freight, stock, and material movers, hand | 9 | 1.4 | -28.7 |
| Machine feeders and offbearers | 12 | 2.0 | -28.7 |
| Packers and packagers, hand | 11 | 1.8 | -36.6 |

Note: Columns may not add to totals due to omission of occupations with small employment

### Training and Advancement
Workers who enter the printing industry are typically trained informally on the job. The length of on-the-job training needed to

learn skills varies by occupation and shop. Through experience and training, workers may then advance to more responsible positions. Workers usually begin as helpers, advance to skilled craft jobs, and eventually may be promoted to supervisor.

Educational backgrounds vary among workers entering the printing industry. Helpers tend to have a high school or vocational school background, while management trainees usually have a college degree. In general, job applicants must be high school graduates with mathematical, verbal, and written communication skills, and be computer literate.

*Production occupations.* Production workers, who comprise the majority of all workers in the printing industry, are trained informally on the job. Learning to operate more complex machinery may take several months. Increasingly, formal education in graphic communications is preferred by employers, particularly for *prepress technicians.* Associate degrees or vocational training are common educational programs, while those looking to advance to management positions usually have a bachelor's degree. Professional certification provides formal recognition for skill acquired on the job and may help workers take on more responsibility or advance within their occupations, but relatively few workers have obtained them.

Production workers need communications skills to work with clients and must be attentive to detail in order to identify and correct printing problems. Workers need a basic familiarity with computers because of the trend toward electronic data and file use. Tight deadlines mean that workers must work under some pressure in order to complete print jobs on time. Employees may undergo background checks if they work with confidential material.

*Professional and administrative occupations.* Most employers prefer a bachelor's or associate degree for entry level administrative and design workers. *Desktop publishers* and *graphic designers* usually complete a 2- or 4-year program in graphic communications or graphic design in addition to completing extensive on-the-job training. These workers may learn new skills for 1 to 3 years before they may be qualified for supervisory positions. They should be comfortable with computers and design software. They also should be creative and demonstrate attention to detail and an ability to meet deadlines in a timely fashion. *Customer service representatives* typically have high school degrees and related experience.

*Other occupations.* While *sales representatives* typically have bachelor's degrees, much of the training for these positions is done on the job. These workers gain valuable experience by attending training seminars and dealing with customers over the phone and at trade shows. In addition to possessing good communication skills, successful sales workers are persuasive and personable. Several credentials for sales representatives are available that may result in increased responsibility, and top sales workers can advance to supervisory positions. Management positions in these occupations are usually filled by those with a bachelor's degree, and who have a proven track record of success in the industry.

## Outlook

Employment in printing is expected to decline rapidly, but the need to replace workers who retire or leave the occupation will create job opportunities, especially for persons with up-to-date printing skills.

*Employment change.* Wage and salary employment in the printing and related support activities industry is projected to decline 22 percent over the 2006-16 period, compared with 11 percent growth projected for the economy as a whole. This decrease reflects the increasing computerization of the printing process, growing imports of some types of printed products, and the expanding use of the Internet, which reduces the need for printed materials. Some small- and medium-size firms are also consolidating in order to afford the investment in new technology, and this development is expected to lead to a drop in employment.

Processes that had been performed manually are now largely automated or done with the help of computers, resulting in a shift from production occupations to computer-related occupations that perform the same function. In some cases, technological advances will shift job duties from printers to the printers' clients. For example, as layout and design are performed and transmitted to the printing press electronically, employment of desktop publishers in client industries should grow. But, demand for workers in the printing industry who perform prepress tasks manually—paste-up workers, photoengravers, camera operators, film strippers, and platemakers—is expected to decrease.

Employment will decline in most segments of the printing industry, but employment in commercial flexographic, digital, and quick printing should increase. Employment in the printing of manifold business forms should continue to decrease as more firms take their customers' orders over the Internet, allowing companies to process orders without printed forms. Declining employment in printing of books, blankbooks and looseleaf binders, and other commercial printing will reflect increased imports of some types of printed products with ample lead times.

Growth in mechanization should result in declines in the employment of bookbinders and bindery workers in the industry, while the increasing sophistication of printing presses is similarly expected to lead to a slight decline in the employment of printing machine operators.

Many printers are expanding the services they offer in response to an increasing number of alternatives to traditional printing services. These secondary customer services include mailing, shipping, and performing inventory and database management. Growth in these services, coupled with increases in digital printing capabilities, will moderate the decline in employment of printing's production occupations and create some new opportunities for workers who are comfortable with customer service and digital printing technology.

*Job prospects.* Despite the projected downturn in overall employment in printing, retirements and turnover will continue to generate job openings, especially for the most skilled. Opportunities should be good for those whose skills are up to date on new technology and equipment, especially in electronic prepress.

## Earnings

*Industry earnings.* In 2006, average weekly earnings for production workers in the printing industry were $619, compared with $695 for all production workers in manufacturing. Average weekly earnings in the printing industry can vary significantly by industry segment and by occupation. The industry segment with the highest earnings is commercial lithography with average weekly earnings of $695. Median hourly earnings of the largest occupations in the industry also vary, as shown in table 3.

*Benefits and union membership.* Workers in larger printing companies generally receive standard benefits. Union membership in this industry is less than average. Just 6 percent of printing industry employees are union members or are covered by a union contract, compared with 12 percent of workers throughout the economy, but this proportion varies greatly from city to city.

**Table 3. Median hourly earnings of the largest occupations in printing, May 2006**

| Occupation | Printing | All industries |
|---|---|---|
| Sales representatives, wholesale and manufacturing, except technical and scientific products | $25.80 | $23.85 |
| First-line supervisors/managers of production and operating workers | 23.84 | 22.74 |
| Prepress technicians and workers | 16.44 | 16.01 |
| Graphic designers | 16.31 | 19.18 |
| Job printers | 15.76 | 15.58 |
| Customer service representatives | 15.71 | 13.62 |
| Printing machine operators | 15.55 | 14.90 |
| Shipping, receiving, and traffic clerks | 13.07 | 12.53 |
| Bindery workers | 12.54 | 12.29 |
| Helpers--production workers | 10.30 | 9.97 |

## Sources of Additional Information

Information on apprenticeships and other training opportunities may be obtained from local employers such as printing shops, local affiliates of Printing Industries of America/Graphics Arts Technical Foundation, or local offices of the State employment service.

For general information on careers and training programs in printing, contact:

➤ NPES The Association for Suppliers of Printing, Publishing, and Converting Technologies, 1899 Preston White Dr., Reston, VA 20191-4367. Internet: **http://www.teched.vt.edu/gcc/**

➤ Printing Industries of America/Graphic Arts Technical Foundation, 200 Deer Run Rd., Sewickley, PA 15143-2600. Internet: **http://www.gain.net**

➤ Graphic Arts Education and Research Foundation, 1899 Preston White Dr., Reston, VA 20191-5468. Internet: **http://www.makeyourmark.org**

➤ National Association for Printing Leadership, 75 W. Century Rd., Paramus, NJ 07652-1408. Internet: **http://www.napl.org**

Information on most occupations in the printing and publishing industry, including the following, may be found in the 2008-09 *Occupational Outlook Handbook*:

• Artists and related workers
• Bookbinders and bindery workers
• Desktop publishers
• Graphic designers
• Prepress technicians and workers
• Printing machine operators

# Steel Manufacturing

(NAICS 3311, 3312)

## SIGNIFICANT POINTS

- Employment is expected to continue to decline due to consolidation and further automation of the steelmaking process.

- Employers staffing production and maintenance jobs increasingly prefer individuals with 2-year degrees in mechanical or electrical technology.

- Opportunities will be best for engineers, computer scientists, business majors, and skilled production and maintenance workers.

## Nature of the Industry

Steel is one of the basic building blocks of the modern world. Automobiles, appliances, bridges, oil pipelines, and buildings, are all made with steel. While steel manufacturing has existed for centuries, the process for making steel continues to evolve.

*Goods and services.* Establishments in this industry produce steel by melting iron ore, scrap metal, and other additives in furnaces. The molten metal output is then solidified into semi-finished shapes before it is rolled, drawn, cast, and extruded to make sheet, rod, bar, tubing, beams, and wire. Other establishments in the industry make finished steel products directly from purchased steel.

The least costly method of making steel uses scrap metal as its base. Steel scrap from many sources—such as old bridges, refrigerators, and automobiles—and other additives are placed in an electric arc furnace, where the intense heat produced by carbon electrodes and chemical reactions melts the scrap, converting it into molten steel. Establishments that use this method of producing steel are called electric arc furnace (EAF) mills, or minimills. While EAFs are sometimes small, some are large enough to produce 400 tons of steel at a time. The growth of EAFs has been driven by the technology's smaller initial capital investment and lower operating costs. Moreover, scrap metal is found in all parts of the country, so EAFs are not tied as closely to raw material deposits as are integrated mills and can be placed closer to consumers. EAFs now account for well over half of American steel production and their share is expected to continue to grow in coming years as they move to produce more higher end products by adding virgin iron ore to the mix of steel scrap and other additives.

The growth of EAFs comes partly at the expense of integrated mills. Integrated mills reduce iron ore to molten pig iron in blast furnaces. The iron is then sent to the oxygen furnace, where it is combined with scrap to make molten steel. The steel produced by integrated mills generally is considered to be of higher quality than steel from EAFs but, because the production process is more complicated and consumes more energy, it is more costly.

*Industry organization.* The steel industry consists of EAFs and integrated mills that produce iron and steel from scrap or molten metal. Most of these mills also have finishing mills on site that convert iron and steel into both finished and unfinished prod-

ucts. Some of the goods produced in finishing mills are steel wire, pipe, bars, rods, and sheets. While wire, steel reinforcing bars, and pipes are considered finished products, rolled steel is unfinished, meaning it is normally shipped to companies, such as automotive plants, that stamp, shape, and machine the rolled steel into car parts. In these finishing mills, products also may be coated with chemicals, paints, or other metals that give the steel desired characteristics for various industries and consumers.

Finished products also are manufactured by other companies in this industry that make pipe and tubing, plate, strip, rod, bar, and wire from purchased steel. Competition from all these mills has resulted in increasing specialization of steel production, as various mills attempt to capture different niches in the market.

Also included in the steel manufacturing industry are firms that produce alloys by adding materials such as silicon and manganese to the steel. Varying the amounts of carbon and other elements contained in the final product can yield thousands of different types of steel, each with specific properties suited for a particular use.

*Recent developments.* Steel manufacturing is an intensely competitive global industry. By continually improving its manufacturing processes and consolidating businesses, the U.S. steel industry has increased productivity sufficiently to remain competitive in the global market for steel. Investment in modern equipment and worker training has transformed the industry from one of the Nation's most moribund to one of the world's leaders in worker productivity and the lowest cost producer for some types of steel. Over the past 25-30 years, steel producers have, in some cases, reduced the number of work-hours required to produce a ton of steel by 90 percent.

To achieve these productivity improvements as well as product improvements, steel mills employ some of the most sophisticated technology available. Computers have been essential to many of these advancements, from production scheduling and machine control to metallurgical analysis. For workers, modernization of integrated, EAF, and finishing mills often has meant learning new skills to operate sophisticated equipment.

With these changes has come a growing emphasis on flexibility and adaptability for both workers and production technology. As strong international and domestic competition continue for U.S. steel producers, the nature of the industry and the jobs of its workers are expected to continue to change.

## Working Conditions

*Hours.* The expense of plant and machinery and significant production startup costs force most mills to operate around the clock, 7 days a week. Workers averaged 44.6 hours per week in 2006 in iron and steel mills and 43.7 hours in steel product manufacturing; only about 2 percent of workers are employed part time. Workers usually work varying shifts, switching between working days one week and nights the next. Some mills operate two 12-hour shifts, while others operate three 8-hour shifts. Overtime work during peak production periods is common.

*Work Environment.* Steel mills evoke images of strenuous, hot, and potentially dangerous work. While many dangerous and difficult jobs remain in the steel industry, modern equipment and facilities have helped to change this. The most strenuous tasks were among the first to be automated. For example, computer-controlled machinery helps to monitor and move iron and steel through the production processes, reducing the need for heavy labor. Many key tasks are now performed by machines that are controlled by workers sitting in air-conditioned pulpits supervising the production process through windows and by monitoring banks of computer screens.

Nevertheless, large machinery and molten metal can be hazardous unless safety procedures are observed. Hardhats, safety shoes, protective glasses, earplugs, and protective clothing are required in most production areas.

The rates of occupational injury and illness per 100 full-time workers in 2006 were 5.4 in iron and steel mills and 8.8 in steel product manufacturing, higher than the rate of 4.4 per 100 workers for the entire private sector. The rate for all of manufacturing was 6.0 per 100.

## Employment

The steel industry provided about 154,000 wage and salary jobs in 2006. Employment in the steel industry is broken into two major sectors: iron and steel mills and ferroalloy production, which employed 94,000 workers; and steel products from purchased steel, which employed 60,000 workers. The steel industry traditionally has been located in the eastern and midwestern regions of the country, where iron ore, coal, or one of the other natural resources required for steel are found. Even today, about 43 percent of steelworkers are employed in Pennsylvania, Ohio, and Indiana. The growth of EAFs has allowed steelmaking to spread to virtually all parts of the country, although many firms find lower cost rural areas the most attractive. Although most steel mills are small, about 80 percent of the jobs in 2006 were in establishments employing at least 100 workers (chart).

## Occupations in the Industry

Although the steel making process varies with the type of furnace used, the jobs associated with the various processes are similar. By a large margin, production occupations, transportation and material moving occupations, and installation, maintenance and repair occupations make up the majority of jobs in steel mills. In addition, significant numbers of engineers and managers are needed to assist in the production process and repair of equipment. Workers generally are assigned to work in a particular sector of the production line, such as the blast furnace or rolling mill areas, and their titles reflect the types of machines they work on.

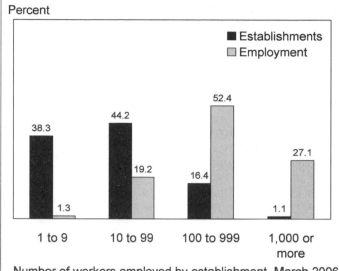

**Almost 80 percent of the jobs in the steel manufacturing industry are in establishments with 100 or more employees.**

Percent

Number of workers employed by establishment, March 2006

*Material-moving and production occupations.* At integrated mills, production begins when *material-moving workers* use robots and cranes to load iron ore, coke, and limestone into the top of a blast furnace. As the materials are heated, a chemical reaction frees the iron from other elements in the ore. *Metal-refining furnace operators and tenders*, also known as blowers and melters, use automated and computer controls to manage the overall operation of the furnace to melt and refine metal before casting or to produce specific types of steel. They gather information on the characteristics of the raw materials they will use and the type and quality of steel they are expected to produce. They oversee the loading of the furnace with raw materials and supervise the taking of samples, to ensure that the steel has the desired qualities. They may also coordinate the loading and melting of raw materials with the steel molding or casting operation to avoid delays in production.

Generally, either a basic oxygen or an electric arc furnace is used to make steel. Operators and tenders use controls to tilt the furnace to receive the raw materials. Once they have righted the furnace, they use levers and buttons to control the flow of oxygen and other materials into the furnace. During the production process, *testers* routinely take samples to be analyzed. Based on this analysis, operators determine how much longer they must process the steel or what materials they must add to meet specifications. Operators also pay close attention to conditions within the furnace and correct any problems that arise during the production process.

*Metal pourers and casters* tend machines that release the molten steel from the ladle at a controlled rate into water-cooled molds, where it solidifies into semifinished shapes. This process is called "continuous casting." These shapes are then cut to desired lengths as they emerge from the caster. During this process, operators monitor the flow of raw steel and the supply of water to the mold.

The "rolling" method is used to shape most steel processed in steel mills. In this method, hot steel is squeezed between two cylinders, or "rollers," which flatten or shape the steel. This process is repeated through a series of rollers until the steel reaches the desired thickness. *Rolling machine operators* operate the rolling mills that produce the finished product; the quality of the product and the speed at which the work is completed depend on the operator's skills. Placing the steel and positioning the rollers are very important, for they control the product's final shape. Improperly adjusted equipment may damage the rolling mill or gears.

*Extruding and drawing machine operators* control equipment that extrudes, or draws, metal materials into tubes, rods, hoses, wire, bars, or structural shapes. *Cutting, punching, and press machine operators* run machines that saw, cut, shear, slit, punch, crimp, notch, bend, or straighten metal. *Welding, soldering, and brazing workers* join metal components or fill holes, indentations, or seams of fabricated metal products. *Multiple machine tool operators* are skilled in the operation of more than one type of cutting or forming machine tool or robot.

*Other occupations.* *Millwrights* and *industrial machinery mechanics* are employed to install and maintain much of the sophisticated machinery in steel mills. They are expected to have a range of skills, including welding and machining. As the technology becomes more advanced, they work more closely with electricians, who help repair and install electrical equipment such as computer controls for machine tools.

*Engineers*, *chemists*, and *computer specialists* are playing an increasing role at steel mills, helping to address a variety of issues. *Metallurgical engineers* work with the metals and ores that go into steel in order to change or improve its properties or to find new applications for steel. They make adjustments to the steel-making process in response to quality control issues. *Industrial engineers* work in process control and use computer models to design production processes to maximize efficient production of each job. They also work with engineers from other specialties to make plants more productive and energy efficient by designing and installing the latest technology. *Mechanical engineers* often are found in supervisory or management jobs, helping to solve mechanical problems on the production line. *Environmental engineers* design environmental control systems to maintain water and air quality standards or to clean up old sites.

Additionally, as with most companies, there are accountants, sales agents, various managers, and administrative and clerical workers who perform company administrative tasks and market the product.

## Training and Advancement

As the technology that runs many of the steel and finishing mills becomes more complicated, the skill levels needed to operate these plants has grown. While some entry-level workers need only a high school diploma, further education is usually required to obtain the more skilled maintenance and production jobs.

*Material moving, production, and maintenance and repair occupations.* Many workers enter the steel manufacturing industry as material moving workers. Material moving workers usually need to have a high school diploma and a driver's license, and pass a drug test. While they are expected to show some mechanical aptitude, experience is not normally required. After workers are hired, they receive on-the-job training. After a year, the best workers may be promoted to lesser skilled machine operator positions.

Workers entering the production process as lower skilled operators and maintenance personnel generally assist more experienced workers, beginning with relatively simple tasks. As

**Table 1. Employment of wage and salary workers in steel manufacturing by occupation, 2006 and projected change, 2006-2016.**

(Employment in thousands)

| Occupation | Employment, 2006 Number | Employment, 2006 Percent | Percent change, 2006-16 |
|---|---|---|---|
| **All occupations** | 154 | 100.0 | -25.1 |
| **Management, business, and financial occupations** | 8 | 5.1 | -24.5 |
| Top executives | 2 | 1.1 | -28.2 |
| Industrial production managers | 1 | 0.9 | -23.1 |
| **Professional and related occupations** | 6 | 4.1 | -24.1 |
| Computer specialists | 1 | 0.5 | -24.3 |
| Engineers | 3 | 2.2 | -22.6 |
| **Sales and related occupations** | 3 | 2.1 | -20.7 |
| Sales representatives, wholesale and manufacturing | 3 | 1.9 | -20.2 |
| **Office and administrative support occupations** | 11 | 7.3 | -25.9 |
| Bookkeeping, accounting, and auditing clerks | 1 | 0.7 | -23.6 |
| Production, planning, and expediting clerks | 2 | 1.0 | -24.3 |
| Shipping, receiving, and traffic clerks | 2 | 1.3 | -22.8 |
| Secretaries and administrative assistants | 1 | 0.7 | -28.1 |
| Office clerks, general | 1 | 0.8 | -24.8 |
| **Construction and extraction occupations** | 7 | 4.3 | -27.8 |
| Electricians | 4 | 2.6 | -25.9 |
| **Installation, maintenance, and repair occupations** | 18 | 11.7 | -25.1 |
| First-line supervisors/managers of mechanics, installers, and repairers | 2 | 1.3 | -28.5 |
| Industrial machinery mechanics | 3 | 2.0 | -14.4 |
| Maintenance and repair workers, general | 7 | 4.8 | -27.0 |
| Millwrights | 3 | 1.7 | -24.5 |
| **Production occupations** | 78 | 50.8 | -23.8 |
| First-line supervisors/managers of production and operating workers | 7 | 4.4 | -24.0 |
| Team assemblers | 3 | 2.2 | -16.3 |
| Computer-controlled machine tool operators, metal and plastic | 1 | 0.6 | -17.6 |
| Extruding and drawing machine setters, operators, and tenders, metal and plastic | 5 | 3.5 | -15.7 |
| Forging machine setters, operators, and tenders, metal and plastic | 1 | 0.8 | -35.8 |
| Rolling machine setters, operators, and tenders, metal and plastic | 8 | 5.3 | -20.6 |
| Cutting, punching, and press machine setters, operators, and tenders, metal and plastic | 7 | 4.9 | -27.0 |
| Grinding, lapping, polishing, and buffing machine tool setters, operators, and tenders, metal and plastic | 2 | 1.2 | -24.9 |
| Lathe and turning machine tool setters, operators, and tenders, metal and plastic | 2 | 1.2 | -32.5 |
| Milling and planing machine setters, operators, and tenders, metal and plastic | 1 | 0.8 | -31.5 |
| Machinists | 3 | 1.7 | -22.3 |
| Metal-refining furnace operators and tenders | 4 | 2.7 | -24.9 |
| Pourers and casters, metal | 2 | 1.6 | -26.0 |
| Molding, coremaking, and casting machine setters, operators, and tenders, metal and plastic | 1 | 0.8 | -38.3 |
| Welders, cutters, solderers, and brazers | 4 | 2.6 | -17.9 |
| Heat treating equipment setters, operators, and tenders, metal and plastic | 3 | 1.8 | -22.6 |
| Inspectors, testers, sorters, samplers, and weighers | 4 | 2.6 | -28.0 |
| Helpers--Production workers | 6 | 4.1 | -23.0 |

(continued on next column)

(continued from previous column)

**Table 1. Employment of wage and salary workers in steel manufacturing by occupation, 2006 and projected change, 2006-2016.**
(Employment in thousands)

| Occupation | Employment, 2006 | | Percent change, 2006-16 |
|---|---|---|---|
| | Number | Percent | |
| **Transportation and material moving occupations** ............................................. | 21 | 13.8 | -30.1 |
| Crane and tower operators .......................... | 5 | 3.3 | -27.3 |
| Industrial truck and tractor operators .......... | 4 | 2.5 | -30.8 |
| Laborers and freight, stock, and material movers, hand........................................... | 6 | 3.7 | -32.2 |
| Machine feeders and offbearers ................. | 2 | 1.4 | -29.8 |
| Packers and packagers, hand...................... | 1 | 0.7 | -37.1 |

Note: Columns may not add to totals due to omission of occupations with small employment

workers acquire experience, they specialize in a particular process and acquire greater skill in that area. The time required to become a skilled worker depends upon individual abilities, acquired skills, and available job openings. It generally takes at least 2 to 5 years, and sometimes longer, to advance to a skilled position. Increasingly, workers are trained to perform a variety of tasks to provide more flexibility to the firm as company needs change. As computers have become more important, workers must learn to operate computers and other advanced equipment to get ahead.

As just stated, an employee can work his way up from an entry-level position to become a skilled operator and repairer through a mixture of on-the-job training and some classroom instruction. However, as machinery continues to become more complex, and as growing numbers of operating and maintenance positions are highly skilled, employers increasingly prefer to hire graduates from formal postsecondary technical and trade schools. Two-year degrees in mechanical or electrical technology, similar military experience, or 2- to 4-year apprenticeships will make a worker more competitive when seeking the best production and maintenance jobs.

***Professional and managerial occupations.*** To work as an engineer or scientist, or in some other technical occupations in the steel industry, a college education is necessary and some positions require an advanced degree. Many workers in administrative and managerial occupations have degrees in business or possess a combination of technical and business degrees. A master's degree may give an applicant an advantage in getting hired or help an employee advance. Managers need strong problem-solving, planning, and supervisory skills.

## Outlook

Job opportunities should be very good for engineers and skilled production and maintenance workers despite a projected decline in employment over the 2006-2016 period.

***Employment change.*** Employment in the steel industry is expected to decline 25 percent over the 2006-16 period, primarily due to increasing consolidation, improvements in productivity, and strong foreign competition. Automation, computerization, and changes in business practices that have led to a leaner workforce have reduced the number of work-hours needed to produce

a ton of steel and raised productivity substantially in the last few decades. These productivity improvements, which were a leading cause of employment declines in the past, are not expected to be as powerful a factor in the future, as some companies have automated the process as much as they can. Technological improvements, however, will continue to be made, affecting the number and type of workers hired. Low-skilled jobs will continue to be automated and the jobs that remain will require more education and training.

EAF mills, with their leaner workforce and lower cost structure, are expected to benefit from the industry's transformation and will continue to gain market share. They now produce more than 50 percent of the country's steel, up from 25 percent two decades ago. They are improving the quality of the steel they make by melting pig iron along with the scrap. In this way, they can more effectively compete with integrated mills in markets that demand higher quality steel. Thus, as EAFs continue to grow in relation to integrated mills, job opportunities will be better at these mills.

Employment in the steel industry varies with overall economic conditions and the demand for goods produced with steel. Much of the demand for steel is derived from the demand for products that consume large amounts of steel. Industries that are significant users of steel include manufacturers of structural metal products used in construction, motor vehicle parts and equipment—a typical car uses about a ton of steel—and household appliances. Many of these goods are expensive so the consuming public is less likely to purchase them during economic downturns.

Currently, strong economic growth in some developing countries is driving up both the global demand for and price of steel. These developing countries use large amounts of steel in the construction of buildings, bridges, and other infrastructure. In addition, as these countries grow wealthier, their citizens are purchasing more automobiles, appliances, and other steel products. If the economic growth of developing countries continues, they will greatly affect the worldwide demand and production of steel.

***Job prospects.*** Despite the projected decline in the number of jobs in the industry, job opportunities are expected to be very good for a number of occupations. Demand is expected to be excellent for all types of engineers, including mechanical, metallurgical, industrial, electrical, and civil. Companies report great difficulty in hiring these highly skilled professionals. Also, computer scientists and business majors should be in great demand.

For skilled production and maintenance jobs, workers with associate degrees in technology or equivalent training will also have very good job opportunities as there is a great need for people to operate computer-controlled machines and to repair equipment. Among persons without postsecondary training, those who have good math and computer skills will have better opportunities to be hired and trained for skilled production jobs. Those without a degree must be flexible and willing to go through extensive classroom and on-the-job training.

Keen competition can be expected for low-skilled material handling and machine operator jobs, for which employment is expected to decline. Despite the declines in employment, many workers will need to be hired to replace those who leave the industry or retire. A large number of workers are expected to retire over the next decade.

**Table 2. Median hourly earnings of the largest occupations in steel manufacturing, May 2006**

| Occupation | Iron and steel mills and ferroalloy manufacturing | Steel product manufacturing from purchased steel | All Industries |
|---|---|---|---|
| First-line supervisors/managers of production and operating workers..... | $26.75 | $23.58 | $22.74 |
| Maintenance and repair workers, general............ | 19.11 | 18.16 | 15.34 |
| Rolling machine setters, operators, and tenders, metal and plastic........ | 18.41 | 15.38 | 14.93 |
| Metal-refining furnace operators and tenders............ | 17.97 | 16.36 | 15.69 |
| Inspectors, testers, sorters, samplers, and weighers.................. | 17.38 | 15.02 | 14.14 |
| Crane and tower operators .............. | 17.18 | 16.36 | 18.77 |
| Laborers and freight, stock, and material movers, hand .................... | 15.51 | 10.32 | 10.20 |
| Extruding and drawing machine setters, operators, and tenders, metal and plastic........................... | 15.28 | 15.04 | 13.58 |
| Cutting, punching, and press machine setters, operators, and tenders, metal and plastic.............. | 15.00 | 13.84 | 12.66 |
| Helpers--production workers............ | 12.22 | 12.15 | 9.97 |

# Earnings

*Industry earnings.* Earnings in the steel industry vary by type of production and occupation but are higher than average earnings in private industry as a whole. Average weekly earnings of non-supervisory production workers in 2006 were $1091 in iron and steel mills, and $775 in establishments making steel products from purchased steel, compared with $691 in all manufacturing and $568 throughout private industry. Earnings in selected occupations in steel manufacturing appear in table 2.

*Benefits and union membership.* Union membership, geographic location, and plant size affect earnings and benefits of workers. In most firms, earnings or bonuses are linked to output. Workers generally receive standard benefits, including health insurance, paid vacation and sick leave, and pension plans.

The iron and steel industry traditionally has been highly unionized, but that has changed. In 2006, only 26 percent of the workers in steel manufacturing were members of unions or covered by union contracts, compared with 12 percent in all manufacturing and in all industries. In some instances, companies are closed shops—that is, workers must belong to the union in order to work there. EAFs are less frequently unionized than integrated mills. The overall decline in employment in traditional integrated steel mills, together with the growth of EAFs, has caused union membership to decline in recent years.

## Sources of Additional Information

For additional information about employers and training in the steel industry, contact:

➢ American Iron and Steel Institute, 1140 Connecticut Ave. NW., Suite 705, Washington, DC 20036. Internet: **http://www.steel.org**
➢ Steel Manufacturers Association, 1150 Connecticut Ave., NW., Suite 715, Washington, DC 20036. Internet: **http://www.steelnet.org**

Information on the following occupations may be found in the 2008-09 *Occupational Outlook Handbook*:

- Electricians
- Engineers
- Industrial machinery mechanics and maintenance workers
- Inspectors, testers, sorters, samplers, and weighers
- Machine setters, operators, and tenders—metal and plastic
- Machinists
- Material moving occupations
- Millwrights

# Textile, Textile Product, and Apparel Manufacturing

(NAICS 313, 314, 315)

## SIGNIFICANT POINTS

- Employment is expected to decline because of technological advances and imports of apparel and textiles from lower-wage countries.

- Extensive on-the-job training is required to operate new high-technology machinery.

- Production workers account for almost 2 out of 3 jobs.

- About 4 out of 10 jobs are in three States—California, North Carolina, and Georgia.

## Nature of the Industry

The textile, textile product, and apparel manufacturing industries include establishments that turn fiber into fabric and fabric into clothing and other textile products. While some factories are highly automated, others still rely mostly on people to cut and sew pieces of fabric together. The apparel industry has moved mainly to other countries with cheaper labor costs, while the textile industry has been able to automate much of its production to effectively compete with foreign suppliers. This industry is evolving and its need for a more highly skilled workforce is growing.

*Goods and services.* The establishments in these industries produce a variety of goods, some of which are sold to the consumer, while others are sold as inputs to the manufacture of other products. Natural and synthetic fibers are used to produce threads and yarns—which may be woven, knitted, or pressed or otherwise bonded into fabrics—as well as rope, cordage, and twine. Coatings and finishes are applied to the fabrics to enhance the decorative patterns woven into the fabric, or to make the fabric more durable, stain-resistant, or have other properties. Fabrics are used to make many products, including awnings, tents, carpets and rugs, as well as a variety of linens—curtains, tablecloths, towels, and sheets. However, the principal use of fabrics is to make apparel. Establishments in the apparel manufacturing industry produce many knitted clothing products, such as hosiery and socks, shirts, sweaters, and underwear. They also produce many cut-and-sew clothing items like dresses, suits, shirts, and trousers.

*Industry organization.* The three individual industries—textile mills, textile product mills, and apparel manufacturing—have many unique characteristics. Textile mills provide the raw material to make apparel and textile products. They take natural and synthetic fibers, such as cotton and polyester, and transform them into fiber, yarn, and thread. Yarns are strands of fibers in a form ready for weaving, knitting, or otherwise intertwining to form a textile fabric. They form the basis for most textile production and commonly are made of cotton, wool, or a synthetic fiber such as polyester. Yarns also can be made of thin strips of plastic, paper, or metal. To produce spun yarn, natural fibers such as cotton and wool must first be processed to remove impurities and give products the desired texture and durability, as well as other characteristics. After this initial cleaning stage, the fibers are spun into yarn.

Textile mills then go on to produce fabric by means of weaving and knitting. Workers in weaving mills use complex, automated looms to transform yarns into cloth. Looms weave or interlace two yarns, so they cross each other at right angles to form fabric. Knitting mills use automated machines to produce fabric of interlocking loops of one or more yarns

At any time during the production process, a number of processes, called finishing, may be performed on the fabric. These processes—which include dyeing, bleaching, and stonewashing, among others—may be performed by the textile mill or at a separate finishing mill. Finishing encompasses chemical or mechanical treatments performed on fiber, yarn, or fabric to improve appearance, texture, or performance.

Textile mills that also make the end products in the same factory are included in this sector; otherwise, if the fabric is purchased the product made is considered a product of the textile mills products sector or apparel manufacturing sector. The textile product mills sector comprises establishments that produce a wide variety of textile products for use by individuals and businesses, but not including apparel. Some of the items made in this sector include household items, such as carpets and rugs; towels, curtains, and sheets; cord and twine; furniture and automotive upholstery; and industrial belts and fire hoses. Because the process of converting raw fibers into finished textile products is complex, most textile mills specialize.

The apparel manufacturing industry transforms fabrics produced by textile manufacturers into clothing and accessories. By cutting and sewing fabrics or other materials, such as leather, rubberized fabrics, plastics, and furs, workers in this industry help to keep consumers warm, dry, and fashionable.

The apparel industry traditionally has consisted mostly of production workers who performed the cutting and sewing functions in an assembly line. This industry remains labor-intensive, despite advances in technology and workplace practices. Although many workers still perform this work in the United States, the industry increasingly contracts out its production work to foreign suppliers to take advantage of lower labor costs in other countries. In its place, a growing number of apparel manufacturers perform only the entrepreneurial functions involved in apparel manufacturing—buying raw materials, designing clothes and accessories and preparing samples, arranging for the production and distribution of the apparel, and marketing the finished product.

Many of the remaining production workers work in teams. For example, sewing machine operators are organized into pro-

93

duction "modules." Each operator in a module is trained to perform nearly all of the functions required to assemble a garment. Each module is responsible for its own performance, and individuals usually receive compensation based on the team's performance.

*Recent developments.* The textile and apparel manufacturing industries are rapidly modernizing, as new investments in automation and information technology have been made necessary by growing international competition. Firms also have responded to competition by developing new products and services. For example, some manufacturers are producing textiles developed from fibers made from recycled materials. These innovations have had a wide effect across the industry. Advanced machinery is boosting productivity levels in textiles, costing some workers their jobs while fundamentally changing the nature of work for others. New technology also has led to increasingly technical training for workers throughout the industry. Computers and computer-controlled equipment aid in many functions, such as design, patternmaking, and cutting. Wider looms, more computerized equipment, and the increasing use of robotics to move material within the plant are other technologies recently designed to make the production plant more efficient. Despite these changes, however, the apparel industry—especially its sewing function—has remained significantly less automated than many other manufacturing industries.

One advantage the domestic industry has is its closeness to the market and its ability to react to changes in fashion more quickly than can its foreign competitors. Also, as retailers consolidate and become more cost conscious, they require more apparel manufacturers to move toward a just-in-time delivery system, in which purchased apparel items are quickly replaced by new items directly from the manufacturer, rather than from a large inventory kept by the retailer. Through electronic data interchange—mainly using barcodes—information is quickly communicated to the manufacturers, providing information not only on inventory, but also about the desires of the public for fashion items.

Some apparel firms have responded to growing competition by merging with other apparel firms and by moving into the retail market. In addition to the production of garments they also are contracting out functions—for example, warehousing and order fulfillment—to concentrate on their strengths: design and marketing. Computer aided design systems have led to the development of "product life cycle management, under which potential new fashions can now be transmitted around the planet over the Internet. Such changes may help the apparel manufacturing industry meet the growing competition and continue to supply the Nation's consumers with garments at an acceptable cost.

## Working Conditions

*Hours.* Some factories run 24 hours a day causing production workers to work evenings and weekends. Many operators work on rotating schedules, which can cause sleep disorders and other stress from constant changes in work hours. Overtime is common for these workers during periods of peak production. Managerial and administrative support personnel typically work a 5-day, 40-hour week in an office setting, although some of these employees also may work significant overtime. Travel is an important part of the job for many managers and designers, who oversee the design and production of apparel. As more production moves abroad, foreign travel is becoming more common.

Quality-control inspectors and other workers also may need to travel to other production sites, especially if working for large companies.

*Work Environment.* Working conditions vary greatly. Production workers, including frontline managers and supervisors, spend most of their shift on or near the production floor. Some factories are noisy and can have airborne fibers and odors, but most modern facilities are relatively clean, well lit, and ventilated.

In 2006, work-related injuries and illnesses in textile mills averaged 4.4 per 100 full-time workers, compared with 6.0 percent for all manufacturing and 4.4 percent for the entire private sector. Work-related injuries and illnesses in textile product mills averaged 4.5 per 100 full-time workers, and in apparel manufacturing, the rate was 2.9 per 100 full-time workers.

When appropriate, the use of protective shoes, clothing, facemasks, and earplugs is required. Also, new machinery is designed with additional protection, such as noise shields. Still, many workers in textile production occupations must stand for long periods while bending over machinery, and noise and dust still are a problem in some plants. Apparel manufacturing operators often sit for long periods and lean over machines. New ergonomically designed chairs and machines that allow workers to stand during their operation are some of the means that firms use to minimize discomfort for production workers. Another concern for workers is injuries caused by repetitive motions. The implementation of modular units and specially designed equipment reduces potential health problems by lessening the stress of repetitive motions. Workers sometimes are exposed to hazardous situations that could produce cuts or minor burns if proper safety practices are not observed.

The movement away from traditional piecework systems in apparel manufacturing often results in a significant change in working conditions. Modular manufacturing involves teamwork, increased responsibility, and greater interaction among coworkers than on traditional assembly lines.

**Over 70 percent of the jobs in the textile, textile products, and apparel manufacturing industry are in establishments that employ 50 or more workers.**

Percent

Number of workers employed by establishment, March 2006

## Employment

In 2006, approximately 595,000 wage and salary workers were employed by the textile, textile product, and apparel manufacturing industries. The apparel manufacturing segment, particularly cut and sew apparel manufacturing, was the largest of the three employing 238,000 workers. In addition, there were also about 39,000 self-employed workers in this industry.

Most of the wage and salary workers employed in the textile mills, textile product, and apparel manufacturing industries in 2006 were found in California and in the southeastern States. California, Georgia, and North Carolina, together accounted for over 40 percent of all workers. The Northeast and South Carolina also have significant employment in this industry. While most apparel and textile establishments are small, employment is concentrated in mills employing 50 or more persons. These establishments accounted for more than 70 percent of all apparel and textile workers (chart).

**Table 1. Percent distribution of employment and establishments in textile, textile product, and apparel manufacturing by detailed industry sector, 2006**

| Industry segment | Employment | Establishments |
|---|---|---|
| **Total** | 100.0 | 100.0 |
| **Textile mills** | 32.7 | 18.1 |
| Fabric mills | 15.0 | 7.0 |
| Textile and fabric finishing and fabric coating mills | 9.7 | 8.8 |
| Fiber, yarn, and thread mills | 8.0 | 2.2 |
| **Textile product mills** | 27.1 | 33.0 |
| Textile furnishings mills | 15.2 | 12.7 |
| Other textile product mills | 11.9 | 20.3 |
| **Apparel manufacturing** | 40.3 | 48.9 |
| Cut and sew apparel manufacturing | 31.3 | 43.1 |
| Apparel knitting mills | 5.6 | 2.5 |
| Apparel accessories and other apparel manufacturing | 3.3 | 3.4 |

## Occupations in the Industry

The textile and apparel industries offer employment opportunities in a variety of occupations, but production occupations accounted for 65 percent of all jobs; some of which are unique to the industry (table 2). Additional jobs may be found at the headquarters of some of these textile and apparel companies that are generally classified in a separate industry.

*Production occupations.* Many workers enter these industries as *machine setters and operators.* They are responsible for setting each machine and monitoring its operation. They also determine if they need repairs or adjustments, and if so, they may clean and oil the machines and repair or replace worn parts. If the machine breaks down, machine setters and operators must be able to diagnose problems quickly and get it restarted as soon as possible to reduce costly machine idle time. Textile machine setters and operators also install, level, and align components such as gears, chains, dies, cutters, and needles.

Textile machine setters and operators thread yarn, thread, or fabric through guides, needles, or rollers. They adjust the controls for proper tension, speed, and heat; for electronically controlled equipment, they program controls or key in instructions using a computer keyboard. Operators then start the machines and monitor their operation, observing control panels and gauges to detect problems.

Skilled production occupations also include quality-control inspectors, who use precision measuring instruments and complex testing equipment to detect product defects, wear, or deviations from specifications.

The apparel manufacturing industry also has a large number of production occupations that help transform the fabric into clothing and accessories. Before sewing can begin, pattern pieces must be made, layouts determined, and fabric cut. *Fabric and apparel patternmakers* create the "blueprint" or pattern pieces for a particular apparel design. This often involves "grading," or adjusting the pieces for different-sized garments. Grading once was a time-consuming job, but now it is quickly completed with the aid of a computer. *Markers* determine the best arrangement of pattern pieces to minimize wasted fabric. Traditionally, markers judged the best arrangement of pieces by eye; today, computers quickly help determine the best layout.

The layout arrangement is then given to *cutters*. In less automated companies, cutters may use electric knives or cutting machines to cut pattern pieces. In more automated facilities, markers electronically send the layout to a computer-controlled cutting machine, and *textile cutting machine setters, operators, and tenders* monitor the machine's work.

*Sewing machine operators* assemble or finish clothes. Most sewing functions are specialized and require the operator to receive specific training. Although operators specialize in one function, the trend toward cross-training requires them to broaden their skills. *Team assemblers* perform all of the assembly tasks assigned to their team, rotating through the different tasks, rather than specializing in a single task. They also may decide how the work is to be assigned and how tasks are to be performed.

*Pressers* receive a garment after it has been assembled. Pressers eliminate wrinkles and give shape to finished products. Most pressers use specially formed, foot-controlled pressing machines to perform their duties. Some pressing machines now have the steam and pressure controlled by computers. *Inspectors, testers, sorters, samplers, and weighers* inspect the finished product to ensure consistency and quality.

*Other occupations.* *Industrial machinery mechanics* account for about 2 percent of industry group employment. They inspect machines to make sure they are working properly. They clean, oil, and grease parts and tighten belts on a regular basis. When necessary, they make adjustments or replace worn parts and put the equipment back together. Mechanics are under pressure to fix equipment quickly because breakdowns usually stop or slow production. In addition to making repairs, mechanics help install new machines. They may enter instructions for computer-controlled machinery and demonstrate the equipment to machine operators.

Plant workers who do not operate or maintain equipment mostly perform a variety of other material-moving tasks. Some drive industrial trucks or tractors to move materials around the plant, load and unload trucks, or package products and materials by hand.

*Engineers and engineering technicians*, although a vital part of the textile and apparel industries, account for less than 1 percent of employment in these industries. Some engineers are *textile engineers*, who specialize in the design of textile machinery or new textile production methods, or the study of fibers. The industries also employ other types of engineers, particularly *in-*

*dustrial* and *mechanical engineers*.

*Fashion designers* are the artists of the apparel industry. They create ideas for a range of products including coats, suits, dresses, hats, and underwear. Fashion designers begin the process by making rough sketches of garments or accessories, often using computer-assisted design (CAD) software. This software prints detailed designs from a computer drawing. It can also store fashion styles and colors that can be accessed and easily changed. Designers then create the pattern pieces that will be used to construct the finished garment. They measure and draw pattern pieces to actual size on paper. Then, they use these pieces to measure and cut pattern pieces in a sample fabric. Designers sew the pieces together and fit them on a model. They examine the sample garment and make changes until they get the effect they want. Some designers use assistants to cut and sew pattern pieces to their specifications.

## Training and Advancement

As the production of textiles and apparel items becomes more technologically advanced, education and training is playing a larger role in the workplace. While a high school diploma or GED may be sufficient for some entry-level positions and for some machine operators, familiarity with computers and some postsecondary training is needed for more technical jobs and to operate more sophisticated machinery. Additionally, as more of the production of apparel is moved offshore, the workers who remain in apparel manufacturing are more likely to be administrative and professional workers who often require more formal postsecondary education or a Bachelor's degree.

*Production occupations.* Most production workers in textile and apparel manufacturing are trained on the job. Although a high school diploma is not required, some employers prefer it. Extensive on-the-job training has become an integral part of working in today's textile mills. This training is designed to help workers understand complex automated machinery, recognize problems, and restart machinery when the problem is solved. Some of this training may be obtained at technical schools and community colleges. Basic math and computer skills are important for computer-controlled machine operators so some job applicants are screened through the use of tests, to ensure that they have the necessary skills.

Increasingly, training is offered to enable people to work well in a team-oriented environment. Many firms have established training centers or host seminars that encourage employee self direction and responsibility and the development of interpersonal skills. Because of the emphasis on teamwork and the small number of management levels in modern textile mills, firms place a premium on workers who show initiative and communicate effectively.

Cutters and pressers are trained on the job, while patternmakers and markers usually have technical or trade school training. All of these workers must understand textile characteristics and have a good sense of three-dimensional space. Traditional cutters need exceptional hand-eye coordination. Computers are becoming a standard tool for these occupations because patternmakers and markers increasingly design pattern pieces and layouts on a computer screen. New entrants seeking these jobs should learn basic computer skills. Those running automatic cutting machines could need technical training, which is available from vocational schools.

Sewing machine operators must have good hand-eye coordination and dexterity, as well as an understanding of textile fabrics. They normally are trained on the job for a period of several

Table 2. Employment of wage and salary workers in textile, textile product, and apparel manufacturing by occupation, 2006 and projected change, 2006-2016.
(Employment in thousands)

| Occupation | Employment, 2006 | | Percent change, 2006-16 |
|---|---|---|---|
| | Number | Percent | |
| **All occupations** | 595 | 100.0 | -35.4 |
| **Management, business, and financial occupations** | 27 | 4.5 | -35.8 |
| Top executives | 9 | 1.6 | -40.4 |
| Industrial production managers | 5 | 0.8 | -32.2 |
| **Professional and related occupations** | 15 | 2.5 | -33.3 |
| Fashion designers | 4 | 0.6 | -47.8 |
| **Sales and related occupations** | 17 | 2.8 | -35.0 |
| Sales representatives, wholesale and manufacturing | 12 | 2.0 | -33.8 |
| **Office and administrative support occupations** | 64 | 10.8 | -38.5 |
| Bookkeeping, accounting, and auditing clerks | 6 | 1.0 | -34.9 |
| Customer service representatives | 6 | 1.1 | -28.3 |
| Production, planning, and expediting clerks | 5 | 0.9 | -36.0 |
| Shipping, receiving, and traffic clerks | 12 | 2.0 | -39.7 |
| Stock clerks and order fillers | 6 | 1.0 | -44.0 |
| Secretaries and administrative assistants | 6 | 0.9 | -37.2 |
| Office clerks, general | 8 | 1.4 | -36.0 |
| **Installation, maintenance, and repair occupations** | 28 | 4.7 | -20.9 |
| Industrial machinery mechanics | 10 | 1.7 | -13.3 |
| Maintenance and repair workers, general | 9 | 1.5 | -26.3 |
| Maintenance workers, machinery | 3 | 0.5 | -26.1 |
| **Production occupations** | 389 | 65.3 | -35.8 |
| First-line supervisors/managers of production and operating workers | 22 | 3.7 | -32.0 |
| Team assemblers | 11 | 1.9 | -20.5 |
| Printing machine operators | 7 | 1.1 | -35.4 |
| Pressers, textile, garment, and related materials | 7 | 1.2 | -46.2 |
| Sewing machine operators | 142 | 23.9 | -42.5 |
| Sewers, hand | 3 | 0.5 | -42.8 |
| Tailors, dressmakers, and custom sewers | 5 | 0.8 | -42.4 |
| Textile bleaching and dyeing machine operators and tenders | 17 | 2.9 | -32.7 |
| Textile cutting machine setters, operators, and tenders | 13 | 2.2 | -35.6 |
| Textile knitting and weaving machine setters, operators, and tenders | 36 | 6.1 | -33.0 |
| Textile winding, twisting, and drawing out machine setters, operators, and tenders | 40 | 6.7 | -24.7 |
| Extruding and forming machine setters, operators, and tenders, synthetic and glass fibers | 4 | 0.7 | -30.9 |
| Fabric and apparel patternmakers | 5 | 0.9 | -47.0 |
| Cutting workers | 8 | 1.3 | -35.5 |
| Inspectors, testers, sorters, samplers, and weighers | 20 | 3.4 | -37.6 |
| Packaging and filling machine operators and tenders | 5 | 0.8 | -31.9 |
| Helpers--Production workers | 15 | 2.6 | -29.1 |
| **Transportation and material moving occupations** | 49 | 8.2 | -38.3 |
| Industrial truck and tractor operators | 8 | 1.3 | -30.3 |
| Laborers and freight, stock, and material movers, hand | 15 | 2.5 | -38.4 |
| Packers and packagers, hand | 16 | 2.7 | -46.4 |

Note: Columns may not add to totals due to omission of occupations with small employment

weeks to several months, depending on their previous experience and the function for which they are training. Operators usually begin by performing simple tasks, working their way up to more difficult assemblies and fabrics as they gain experience.

Advancement for sewing machine operators, however, is limited. Advancement often takes the form of higher wages as workers become more experienced, although operators who have good people and organizational skills may become supervisors. Operators with a high school diploma and some vocational school training have more chances for advancement.

***Professional and related occupations.*** Above all else, fashion designers need a good sense of color, texture, and style. In addition, they must know how to use computer-assisted design and understand the characteristics of specific fabrics, such as durability and stiffness, and anticipate construction problems. Obtaining a 4-year degree in art or fashion design is preferred, although a 2-year degree may suffice. This specialized training usually is obtained through a university or design school that offers 4-year or 2-year degrees in art, fine art, or fashion design. Many schools do not allow entry into a bachelor's degree program until a student has completed a year of basic art and design courses. Applicants may be required to submit drawings and other examples of their artistic ability. Formal training also is available in 2- and 3-year fashion design schools that award certificates or associate degrees. Graduates of 2-year programs generally qualify as assistants to designers.

Beginning designers usually receive on-the-job training. They normally need 1 to 3 years of training before they advance to higher level positions, such as assistant technical designer, pattern designer, or head designer. Sometimes fashion designers advance by moving to bigger firms. Some designers choose to move into positions in business or merchandising.

Engineering applicants generally need a bachelor's or advanced degree in a field of engineering or production management. Degrees in mechanical or industrial engineering are common, but concentrations in textile-specific areas of engineering are especially useful. For example, many applicants take classes in textile engineering, textile technology, textile materials, and design. These specialized programs usually are found in engineering and design schools in the South and Northeast. As in other industries, a technical degree with an advanced degree in business can lead to opportunities in management.

## Outlook

Jobs in textile, textile product, and apparel manufacturing will continue to become fewer as advances in manufacturing technology allow fewer workers to produce greater output, and because growing imports compete with domestically made textile and apparel products.

***Employment change.*** Wage and salary employment in the textile, textile product, and apparel manufacturing industries is expected to decline by 35 percent through 2016, compared with a projected increase of 11 percent for all industries combined. Nevertheless, some job openings will arise as experienced workers transfer to other industries or retire or leave the workforce for other reasons.

Increasing investment in technology by textile mills, and the resulting increase in labor productivity, is the major reason for the projected decline in employment in the textile mills sector. Wider looms, robotics, new methods for making textiles that do not require spinning or weaving, and the application of comput-ers to various processes result in fewer workers being needed to produce the same amount of textile products. Companies are also continuing to open new, more modern plants, which use fewer workers, while closing inefficient ones. As this happens, overall demand for textile machine operators and material handlers will continue to decline, but demand for those who have the skills to operate the more high-technology machines will grow.

Changing trade regulations are the single most important factor influencing future employment patterns. Because the apparel manufacturing sector is labor intensive, it is especially vulnerable to import competition from nations in which workers receive lower wages. In 2005, quotas for apparel and textile products were lifted among members of the World Trade Organization, including most U.S. trading partners and, in particular, China. Although some bilateral quotas have been re-imposed between the United States and China, the expiration of quotas in 2005 has allowed more apparel and textile products to be imported into the United States. Because many U.S. firms will continue to move their assembly operations to low-wage countries, this trend is likely to affect the jobs of lower skilled machine operators most severely. It does not, however, have as adverse an effect on the demand for some of the pre-sewing functions, such as designing, because much of the apparel will still be designed by American workers.

Continuing changes in the market for apparel goods will exert cost-cutting pressures that affect all workers in the textile and apparel industries. Consumers are becoming more price conscious, retailers are gaining bargaining power over apparel producers, and increasing competition is limiting the ability of producers to pass on costs to consumers. Apparel firms are likely to respond by relying more on foreign production and boosting productivity through investments in technology and new work structures.

Apparel firms also continue to merge or consolidate to remain competitive. This trend continues to drive down the number of firms in this industry. In the future, the apparel manufacturing sector will be dominated by highly efficient, profitable organizations that have developed their dominance through strategies that enable them to be among the lowest cost producers of apparel. Consolidation and mergers are likely to result in layoffs of some workers.

Some segments of the textile mill products sector, like industrial fabrics, carpets, and specialty yarns, are highly automated, innovative, and competitive on a global scale, so they will be able to expand exports as a result of more open trade. Other sectors, such as fabric for apparel, will be negatively affected, as a number of apparel manufacturers relocate production to other countries. Textile mills are likely to lose employment as a result. The expected increase in apparel imports will adversely affect demand for domestically produced textiles.

New technology will increase the apparel manufacturing sector's productivity, although it is likely to remain labor-intensive. The variability of cloth and the intricacy of the cuts and seams of the assembly process have been difficult to automate. Machine operators, therefore, will continue to perform most sewing tasks, and automated sewing will be limited to simple functions. In some cases, however, computerized sewing machines will increase the productivity of operators and reduce required training time.

Technology also is increasing the productivity of workers who perform other functions, such as designing, marking, cutting, and pressing. Computers and automated machinery will continue to raise productivity and reduce the demand for workers in these areas, but the decline will be moderated by growth in demand for the services of these workers generated by offshore assembly sites. The rapid rate at which fashions change also will boost demand for workers employed in U.S.-based firms that have quick-response capabilities.

*Job prospects.* Despite the overall decline in employment, job prospects for skilled production workers, engineers, merchandisers, and designers should be fair as the industry evolves into one that primarily requires people with good communication skills, creativity, and who are skilled enough to operate today's high technology computer-operated machines. The United States is leading the world in discovering new fibers and finding new uses for high-technology textiles. For example, biotechnology research is expected to lead to new sources of fibers, such as corn and other plants, and result in improvements in existing fibers. Some fibers currently being introduced have built-in memories of color and shape, and some have antibacterial qualities. Nanotechnology will also contribute to development of original fibers and garments for specialty uses. As these technologies and engineering advancements in textile production are implemented, the need will grow for more highly skilled workers who can work in an increasingly high-technology environment.

## Earnings

*Industry earnings.* Average weekly earnings of nonsupervisory production workers were $509 in textile mills, $478 in textile product mills, and $387 in apparel manufacturing establishments in 2006, compared with $691 for production workers in all manufacturing and $568 for production workers throughout private industry. Wages within the textile industry depend upon skill level and type of mill. In addition to typical benefits, employees often are eligible for discounts in factory merchandise stores.

Earnings in selected occupations in textile and apparel manufacturing appear in table 3. Traditionally, sewing machine operators are paid on a piecework basis determined by the quantity of goods they produce. Many companies are changing to incentive systems based on group performance that considers both the quantity and the quality of the goods produced. A few companies pay production workers a salary.

*Benefits and union membership.* Relatively few workers in the textile and apparel industries belong to unions. Only 3 percent

Table 3. Median hourly earnings of the largest occupations in textile, textile product, and apparel manufacturing, May 2006

| Occupation | Textile mills | Textile product mills | Apparel manu-facturing | All Industries |
|---|---|---|---|---|
| First-line supervisors/managers of production and operating workers.. | $20.44 | $19.71 | $16.84 | $22.74 |
| Textile knitting and weaving machine setters, operators, and tenders | 11.96 | 12.36 | 10.22 | 11.68 |
| Inspectors, testers, sorters, samplers, and weighers | 11.37 | 11.01 | 9.33 | 14.14 |
| Textile bleaching and dyeing machine operators and tenders | 11.17 | 12.53 | 10.22 | 11.20 |
| Textile winding, twisting, and drawing out machine setters, operators, and tenders | 10.78 | 11.98 | 10.19 | 11.08 |
| Textile cutting machine setters, operators, and tenders | 10.41 | 10.52 | 9.71 | 10.39 |
| Helpers--production workers | 10.29 | 9.66 | 8.40 | 9.97 |
| Laborers and freight, stock, and material movers, hand | 10.11 | 9.86 | 8.81 | 10.20 |
| Sewing machine operators | 9.53 | 9.63 | 8.45 | 9.04 |
| Packers and packagers, hand | 9.24 | 8.91 | 8.44 | 8.48 |

of apparel and textile workers were union members or were covered by a union contract in 2006, compared with 12 percent for the economy as a whole.

## Sources of Additional Information
Information about job opportunities in textile, apparel, and furnishings occupations is available from local employers and local offices of the State employment service. Information about job opportunities in technical and design occupations in the apparel industry can be obtained from colleges offering programs in textile and apparel engineering, production, and design.

Information on the following occupations employed in the textile, textile product, and apparel manufacturing industries can be found in the 2008-09 edition of the *Occupational Outlook Handbook*.
- Fashion designers
- Engineers
- Engineering technicians
- Industrial machinery mechanics and maintenance workers
- Inspectors, testers, sorters, samplers, and weighers
- Machinists
- Material moving occupations
- Textile, apparel, and furnishings occupations

# Trade

# Automobile Dealers

## SIGNIFICANT POINTS

- Employment is expected to grow, but will remain sensitive to downturns in the economy.

- Opportunities should be very favorable for automotive service technicians who complete formal training programs.

- Average weekly earnings in this industry are relatively high.

## Nature of the Industry

Automobile dealers are the link between the manufacturer of the automobile and the U.S. consumer. With their large inventories of cars, dealers provide consumers with a wide array of vehicles to meet their needs at different price points.

*Goods and services.* The automobile dealer industry sells most of the automobiles, light trucks, and vans that operate on the road today. Sales of these vehicles are subject to changing consumer tastes, the popularity of the manufacturer's vehicle models, and the intensity of competition with other dealers. Along with the sale of the car, most dealers also sell additional automobile-related services to potential buyers. These services include extended warranties, undercoating, insurance, and financing. Aftermarket sales departments sell these services and other merchandise after vehicle salespersons have closed a deal. Sales of these packages greatly increase the revenue generated for each vehicle sold. Because sales of automobiles fluctuate significantly, automotive dealers offer generous incentives, rebates, and financing deals during slow periods to maintain high sales volumes and to reduce inventories.

Leasing a car or truck is an alternative to purchasing a vehicle and an additional service provided primarily by new car dealers. Leasing services have grown in recent years to accommodate changing consumer purchasing habits. As vehicles have become more costly, growing numbers of consumers are unable or reluctant to make a long-term investment in a new car or truck purchase. Leasing provides an escape from high initial investment costs and typically yields lower monthly payments than purchasing options.

Performing repair work on vehicles is another profitable service provided by dealers. Service departments at motor vehicle dealers provide repair services and sell accessories and replacement parts. While most service departments perform repairs only, some dealers also have body shops to do collision repair, refinishing, and painting. The work of the service department has a major influence on customers' satisfaction and willingness to purchase future vehicles from the dealer.

*Industry organization.* The automobile dealer industry is comprised of two segments. *New car dealers*, often called franchised dealers, primarily sell new cars, sport utility vehicles (SUVs), and passenger and cargo vans. These franchised dealers sell and lease vehicles manufactured by a particular company—which may include several brands. *Used car dealers* comprise the other segment of the industry, and are sometimes referred to as independent dealers. These dealers sell a variety of vehicles that have been previously owned or formerly rented and leased. Im-

provements in technology have increased the durability and longevity of new cars, raising the number of high-quality used cars that are available for sale. While used car dealers by definition do not sell new cars, most new car dealers also sell used cars.

According to the National Automobile Dealers Association, new vehicle sales account for more than half of total sales revenue at franchised new car and new truck dealers. But more importantly, these sales generate additional revenue in other departments of new car dealers, which are more profitable to the dealer. By putting new vehicles on the road, dealers can count on new repair and service customers and future trade-ins of used vehicles.

Independent used car dealers usually have smaller staffs than their franchised counterparts. Most are stand-alone dealers, but increasingly nationwide companies are opening large superstores across the country. These large used car and truck dealers typically contract out warranty and other service-related work to other dealers or to satellite service facilities.

*Recent developments.* In recent years, the sale of used cars has become a major source of profits for many new car dealers in the wake of shrinking margins on new cars. And to make them acceptable to more customers, some dealers promote "certified pre-owned" vehicles to customers who want a warranty on their used vehicle. This often raises the price, but in return provides customers with peace of mind. In economic downturns, the relative demand for these and other used cars often increases as sales of new cars decline.

Nationwide used automotive dealer chains have increased in popularity over the last decade. Like the used car departments of new car dealers, they capitalize on the relatively large profits on sales of previously owned cars, trucks, and vans. Some of the larger dealers offer low-hassle sales on large inventories of these used vehicles. Growth in leasing agreements and rental company inventory will continue to provide quality vehicles to these large independent dealers, thus providing for future employment growth in the used car market.

In an effort to achieve greater financial and operational efficiency and flexibility, greater emphasis will be placed on aftermarket services, such as financing and vehicle maintenance and repair, at both new and used car dealers. These services typically provide large profit margins for dealers, and remain less susceptible to business cycle downturns. They are also part of an effort to enhance customer loyalty and overall customer service.

Perhaps the most significant recent development for automotive dealers has been increasing use of the Internet to market new and used cars and light trucks. Through websites, consumers can easily access vehicle reviews; view pictures of vehicles;

and compare models, features, and prices. Many Websites also allow consumers to research insurance, financing, leasing, and warranty options. As a result, consumers are generally better informed and spend less time meeting with salespersons.

## Working Conditions

*Hours.* Employees with automobile dealers work longer hours than do those in most other industries. Eighty-four percent of automobile dealer employees worked full time in 2006, and 37 percent worked more than 40 hours a week. To satisfy customer service needs, many dealers provide evening and weekend service. The 5-day, 40-hour week is the exception, rather than the rule, in this industry.

*Work Environment.* Most automobile salespersons and administrative workers spend their time at shared desks or nearby offices in dealer showrooms. The competitive nature of selling is stressful to automotive salespersons, as they try to meet company sales quotas and personal earnings goals. Compared with that for all occupations, the proportion of workers who transfer from automotive sales jobs to other occupations is relatively high.

Service technicians and automotive body repairers generally work indoors in well-ventilated and well-lighted repair shops. However, some shops are drafty and noisy. Technicians and repairers frequently work with dirty and greasy parts, and in awkward positions. They often lift heavy parts and tools, and minor cuts, burns, and bruises are common. Despite hazards, precautions taken by dealers to prevent injuries have kept the workplace relatively safe. In 2006, there were 4.1 cases of work-related injuries and illnesses per 100 full-time workers in the automobile dealers industry, close to the national average of 4.4 cases per 100.

## Employment

Automobile dealers provided about 1.2 million wage and salary jobs in 2006. In addition, there were 58,000 self-employed workers in this industry. New car dealers employed 1.1 million wage and salary workers while used car dealers employed about 127,000 workers.

Since 1950, the trend for new car dealers has been toward consolidation. Franchised dealers have decreased in number, while their sales volume has increased. Larger dealers can offer more services, typically at lower costs to themselves and the customer. The number of used car dealers, however, has recently been increasing. Almost 2 out of 3 workers in the automobile dealer industry work in establishments with 50 or more employees (chart).

## Occupations in the Industry

The number of workers employed by automobile dealers varies significantly depending on dealer size, location, makes of vehicles handled, and distribution of sales among departments. Table 1 indicates that the majority of workers in this industry were in sales occupations; installation, maintenance, and repair occupations; and office and administrative support occupations.

*Sales and related occupations.* These occupations are among the most important in automobile dealerships and account for 37 percent of industry employment. Sales workers' success in selling vehicles and services determines the success of the dealer. Automotive *retail salespersons* usually are the first to greet customers and determine their interests through a series of

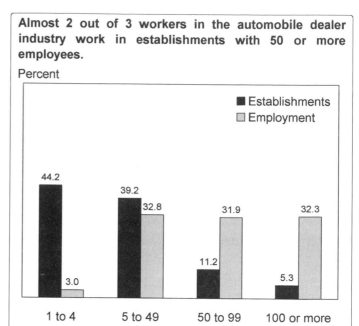

**Almost 2 out of 3 workers in the automobile dealer industry work in establishments with 50 or more employees.**

Number of workers employed by establishment, March 2006

questions. Salespersons then explain and demonstrate vehicles' features in the showroom and on the road. Working closely with automotive *sales worker supervisors* and the customers, salespersons negotiate the final terms and price of the sale. Automotive salespersons must be tactful, well groomed, and able to express themselves: their success depends on winning the respect and trust of prospective customers.

In support of the service and repair department, *parts salespersons* supply vehicle parts to technicians and repairers. They also sell replacement parts and accessories to the public. *Parts managers* run the parts department and keep the automotive parts inventory. They display and promote sales of parts and accessories and deal with garages and other repair shops seeking to purchase parts.

*Installation, maintenance, and repair-related occupations.* Workers in automotive maintenance and repair are another integral part of automobile dealers, constituting 26 percent of industry employment. *Automotive service technicians and mechanics* service, diagnose, adjust, and repair automobiles such as cars, vans, pickups, and sport utility vehicles (SUVs). These workers are the largest repair occupation at 18 percent of industry employment. Closely related to service technicians, *automotive body and related repairers* repair and finish vehicle bodies, straighten bent body parts, remove dents, and replace crumpled parts that are beyond repair.

*Supervisors of installation, maintenance and repair workers,* usually called *shop managers* are among the most experienced service technicians. They supervise and train other technicians to make sure that service work is performed properly. *Service managers* oversee the entire service department and are responsible for the department's reputation, efficiency, and profitability. Increasingly, service departments use computers to increase productivity and improve service workflow by scheduling customer appointments, troubleshooting technical problems, and locating service information and parts.

*Service advisors* cover service departments' administrative and customer relations duties. They greet customers, listen to their description of problems or service desired, write repair orders, and estimate the cost and time needed to do the repair. They also contact customers when technicians discover new problems with their vehicles and explain to customers the work performed and the charges associated with the repairs.

*Other occupations. Office and administrative support workers* organize and maintain the paperwork of automobile dealers and make up about 15 percent of employment in the industry. *Bookkeeping, accounting, and auditing clerks; general office clerks;* and *secretaries and administrative assistants* prepare reports on daily operations, inventory, and accounts receivable. *Office supervisors* organize, supervise, and coordinate administrative operations. Some perform managerial duties as well.

Management positions are often filled by promoting workers with years of related experience. *Sales managers* hire, train, and supervise the dealer's sales force. They are the final executors in all transactions between sales workers and customers. They also review market analyses to determine customer needs, estimate volume potential for various models, and develop sales campaigns.

*General and operations managers* are in charge of all dealer operations. They need extensive business and management skills, usually acquired through experience as a manager in one or more of the dealer departments. Dealer performance and profitability ultimately are up to them.

*Transportation and material moving occupations* account for about 13 percent of jobs in automobile dealers. *Cleaners of vehicles and equipment* prepare new and used cars for display in the showroom or parking lot and for delivery to customers. *Truck drivers* typically operate light delivery trucks to pick up and deliver automotive parts, while some drive tow trucks that bring damaged vehicles to the dealer for repair.

## Training and Advancement

In today's competitive job market nearly all dealers require at least a high school diploma for most sales and service-related jobs; about half of all workers in the industry had some formal education beyond the high school level in 2006. Courses in automotive technology, electronics, and computers are important for maintenance and repair jobs, as is certification by the National Institute for Automotive Service Excellence. For managerial occupations, a basic background in business, marketing, or sales is usually required.

*Sales and related occupations.* Sales workers require strong communication and customer service skills to deal with the public. Most new *retail salespersons* receive extensive on-the-job training, beginning with mentoring from sales managers and experienced sales workers. In large dealers, beginners receive several days of classroom training to learn about vehicle features, methods for approaching prospective customers, negotiation techniques, and ways to close sales. Some manufacturers furnish training manuals and other informational materials to sales workers. Managers continually guide and train sales workers, both on the job and at periodic sales meetings. Successful retail sales persons can become office supervisors, sales managers, or operations managers.

*Installation, maintenance, and repair-related occupations.* Automotive technology is rapidly increasing in sophistication, and dealers prefer to hire graduates of postsecondary automotive training programs for entry-level *automotive service technician* or *automotive body repairer* positions. Graduates of such

**Table 1. Employment of wage and salary workers in automobile dealers by occupation, 2006 and projected change, 2006-2016.**
(Employment in thousands)

| Occupation | Employment, 2006 | | Percent change, 2006-16 |
|---|---|---|---|
| | Number | Percent | |
| **All occupations** | 1,247 | 100.0 | 11.3 |
| **Management, business, and financial occupations** | 91 | 7.3 | 8.9 |
| Top executives | 28 | 2.2 | 2.1 |
| Sales managers | 22 | 1.8 | 13.4 |
| Financial managers | 8 | 0.7 | 13.4 |
| Accountants and auditors | 8 | 0.7 | 13.4 |
| Credit analysts | 7 | 0.6 | 2.1 |
| **Sales and related occupations** | 461 | 36.9 | 11.9 |
| First-line supervisors/managers of retail sales workers | 47 | 3.8 | 10.2 |
| Cashiers | 23 | 1.8 | 2.1 |
| Counter and rental clerks | 33 | 2.7 | 24.8 |
| Parts salespersons | 62 | 5.0 | 2.1 |
| Retail salespersons | 280 | 22.5 | 13.4 |
| **Office and administrative support occupations** | 190 | 15.2 | 6.7 |
| First-line supervisors/managers of office and administrative support workers | 13 | 1.0 | 5.6 |
| Switchboard operators, including answering service | 14 | 1.1 | -9.2 |
| Bill and account collectors | 5 | 0.4 | 13.4 |
| Billing and posting clerks and machine operators | 8 | 0.7 | 2.1 |
| Bookkeeping, accounting, and auditing clerks | 32 | 2.6 | 13.4 |
| Customer service representatives | 16 | 1.3 | 24.8 |
| Receptionists and information clerks | 13 | 1.0 | 12.9 |
| Secretaries and administrative assistants | 15 | 1.2 | 5.2 |
| Office clerks, general | 37 | 2.9 | 11.8 |
| **Installation, maintenance, and repair occupations** | 321 | 25.7 | 16.4 |
| Supervisors of installation, maintenance, and repair workers | 32 | 2.6 | 13.4 |
| Automotive body and related repairers | 36 | 2.9 | 2.1 |
| Automotive service technicians and mechanics | 221 | 17.7 | 19.7 |
| Helpers--Installation, maintenance, and repair workers | 15 | 1.2 | 13.4 |
| **Transportation and material moving occupations** | 159 | 12.8 | 6.1 |
| Driver/sales workers | 7 | 0.5 | 2.1 |
| Truck drivers, light or delivery services | 17 | 1.4 | 13.4 |
| Taxi drivers and chauffeurs | 12 | 1.0 | 11.7 |
| Motor vehicle operators, all other | 11 | 0.9 | 13.4 |
| Parking lot attendants | 9 | 0.7 | 2.1 |
| Cleaners of vehicles and equipment | 81 | 6.5 | 3.2 |
| Laborers and freight, stock, and material movers, hand | 12 | 0.9 | 2.1 |

Note: Columns may not add to totals due to omission of occupations with small employment

programs often earn promotion to the journey level after a few months on the job. Most community and junior colleges and vocational and technical schools offer postsecondary automotive training programs leading to an associate degree in automotive technology or auto body repair. They generally provide intense career preparation through a combination of classroom instruction and hands-on practice. In addition, dealers increasingly send experienced technicians to factory training centers to receive special training in the repair of components, such as electronic fuel injection or air-conditioning. Factory representatives also often visit shops to conduct short training sessions.

Applicants for automotive service jobs should have good reading ability and basic math skills to understand technical manuals, keep abreast of new technology, and learn new service and repair techniques. Some service technicians and mechanics may begin as apprentices or trainees, helpers, or *lubrication workers*. They work under close supervision of experienced technicians, repairers, and service managers, and require several years of experience to advance to journey level positions.

Certification through the National Institute for Automotive Service Excellence (ASE) provides recognized credentials in automotive service and repair. Though not mandatory—currently ASE estimates around 50 percent of workers in automotive service positions are certified—certification increases technicians' chances of finding employment and advancing within the occupation once employed.

*Other occupations.* Dealers require years of related experience in sales, service, or administration for workers to advance to management positions such as *sales manager* or *operations manager*. Employers increasingly prefer persons with 4-year college degrees in business administration and marketing for these positions. This is especially true of the larger, more competitive dealers. In addition, some motor vehicle manufacturers offer management training classes and seminars.

Workers in *transportation and material moving occupations* usually need a high school diploma or equivalent, or experience in a related field.

## Outlook

Employment growth will result from an increased focus on sales of automotive-related services at both new and used dealers. Finance and insurance services, automotive repair, and sales of used cars at new car dealerships will be responsible for many of the new jobs in this industry. Opportunities will be good for salespersons and customer service representatives with related experience and computer skills, and for automotive service technicians who have several years of experience or are ASE certified.

*Employment change.* Wage and salary jobs at automobile dealers are projected to grow 11 percent over the 2006-2016 period, the same as the 11 percent growth for all industries combined. Job growth in automobile dealers typically is a reflection of consumer confidence and purchasing habits. The long-term strength of the Nation's economy and trends in consumer transportation preferences heavily influence the employment outlook for this industry.

Through 2016, growth in the driving-age population will increase demand for passenger vehicles and boost employment in automobile dealers. However, the trend for the public to keep vehicles longer than in the past may have a dampening effect on motor vehicle sales. New and used car dealers may also face increasing competition from online electronic auctions that enable new and used goods, including vehicles, to be traded consumer-to-consumer and business-to-consumer.

Any future dealer consolidation should have a minimal effect on the industry because of continued demand for vehicles and related services. Dealers will continue to seek greater financial and operational efficiency and flexibility, resulting in greater emphasis on aftermarket services, such as financing and vehicle service and repair. This focus will require additional workers—for example, loan officers and service technicians—to help with the larger workload.

Independent used car dealers will continue to experience employment growth as increases in vehicle leasing and rental company fleets continue to provide quality vehicles to the used car market. Increasingly, these dealers also provide repair services for their vehicles and will demand more service technicians, although some used car dealers still prefer to contract out their warranty and service-related work to other dealers or perform them at satellite service facilities.

Employment growth among sales occupations will be limited somewhat by consumers' increasing use of the Internet to research automobile purchases. As consumers become more knowledgeable, salespersons will need less time to inform customers of vehicle features and options, making these workers more productive.

*Job prospects.* In the future, dealers will seek more highly educated salespersons, and those who have a college degree and previous sales experience will have the best job opportunities.

Opportunities in vehicle maintenance and repair should be very good for persons who complete formal automotive service technician training. The growing complexity of automotive technology increasingly requires highly trained automotive service technicians and mechanics to service vehicles. Automotive service technicians in this industry may expect steady work because changes in economic conditions have little effect on this part of the dealer's business.

Opportunities in management occupations will be best for persons with college degrees and those with considerable industry experience. However, consolidation of new car dealers will slow the growth of managerial jobs. Competition for managerial positions will remain relatively keen.

The need to replace workers who retire or transfer to other occupations will result in many additional job openings for workers in automobile dealers—retail salespersons in particular. Some dealers are trying to reduce turnover among salespersons by using alternative sales techniques and compensation systems, such as paying salaries rather than commissions. This may lead to more income stability and less turnover in the sales department.

## Earnings

*Industry earnings.* Average weekly earnings of nonsupervisory workers in automobile dealers were $636 in 2006, substantially higher than the $383 average for retail trade, as well as the $568 average for all private industry. Earnings vary depending on occupation, experience, and the dealer's geographic location and size. Earnings in selected occupations in automobile dealers appear in table 2.

Most automobile sales workers are paid on commission. Commission systems vary, but dealers often guarantee new salespersons a modest salary for the first few months until they learn how to sell vehicles. Many dealers also pay experienced, commissioned sales workers a modest weekly or monthly salary to compensate for the unstable nature of sales. Dealers, especially larger ones, also pay bonuses and have special incentive programs for exceeding sales quotas. With increasing customer service requirements, small numbers of dealers have adopted a sales force paid entirely by salary.

Most automotive service technicians and mechanics also receive a commission related to the labor cost charged to the customer. Their earnings depend on the amount of work available and completed. Like new salespersons, entry-level technicians may be paid a modest salary until they are able to perform repairs on their own.

***Benefits and union membership.*** Managers and some salespersons may enjoy the use of dealership vehicles for official business use. It is also common for dealership owners to drive vehicles owned by the dealership for limited personal use, such as driving to and from work.

In 2006, relatively few workers in automobile dealers, 3 percent, were union members or were covered by union contracts, compared with 12 percent of workers in all industries.

**Table 2. Median hourly earnings of the largest occupations in automobile dealers, May 2006**

| Occupation | Automobile dealers | All industries |
|---|---|---|
| First-line supervisors/managers of retail workers | $32.98 | $16.33 |
| First-line supervisors/managers of mechanics, installers, and repairers | 27.55 | 25.91 |
| Counter and rental clerks | 19.15 | 9.41 |
| Automotive service technicians and mechanics | 18.85 | 16.24 |
| Retail salespersons | 18.70 | 9.50 |
| Automotive body and related repairers | 17.85 | 16.92 |
| Parts salespersons | 16.19 | 13.19 |
| Bookkeeping, accounting, and auditing clerks | 13.81 | 14.69 |
| Office clerks, general | 11.00 | 11.40 |
| Cleaners of vehicles and equipment | 9.28 | 8.68 |

## Sources of Additional Information

For more information about work opportunities, contact local automobile dealers or the local offices of the State employment service. The latter also may have information about training programs.

For additional information about new car dealers, including information on careers and training, contact:
➢ National Automobile Dealers Association, 8400 Westpark Dr., McLean, VA 22102. Internet: **http://www.nada.org**

For additional information about independent used care dealers, including information on careers and training, see the following Website, sponsored by State Independent Dealers Associations: **http://www.piada.org/Used_Car_Dealer_Info.htm**

For additional information about automotive service and repair careers and training in the automotive dealer industry, contact:
➢ Automotive Youth Educational Systems (AYES), 100 W. Big Beaver, Suite 300, Troy, MI 48084. Internet: **http://www.ayes.org**

More information on the following occupations may be found in the 2008-2009 edition of the *Occupational Outlook Handbook*:
- Advertising, marketing, promotions, public relations, and sales managers
- Automotive body and related repairers
- Automotive service technicians and mechanics
- Retail salespersons
- Sales worker supervisors

# Clothing, Accessory, and General Merchandise Stores

(NAICS 448, 452)

## SIGNIFICANT POINTS

- Sales and administrative support jobs account for 84 percent of employment in the industry.

- Most jobs do not require formal education; many people get their first jobs in this industry.

- Clothing, accessory, and general merchandise stores offer many part-time jobs, but earnings are relatively low.

- Many workers in this large industry transfer to other occupations or leave the labor force, so there will be numerous job openings.

## Nature of the Industry

*Goods and services.* Clothing, accessory, and general merchandise stores are some of the most visited retail establishments in the country. Whether shopping for an item of clothing, a piece of jewelry, a household appliance, or even food, you will likely go to one of these stores to make your purchase or compare selections with other retail outlets.

*Industry organization.* General merchandise stores sell a large assortment of items. Stores include department stores—including discount department stores—supercenters, and warehouse club stores, as well as "dollar stores" that sell a wide variety of inexpensive merchandise.

Department stores sell an extensive selection of merchandise, with no one line predominating. As the name suggests, these stores generally are arranged into departments, each headed by a manager. The various departments can sell apparel, furniture, appliances, home furnishings, cosmetics, jewelry, paint and hardware, electronics, and sporting goods. They also may sell services such as optical, photography, and pharmacy services. Discount department stores typically rely more on self-service features, and have centrally located cashiers. Department stores that sell large items, like major appliances, usually provide delivery and installation services. Upscale department stores may offer tailoring for their clothing lines and more personal service.

Warehouse club stores and supercenters, the fastest growing segment of this industry, sell an even more eclectic mix of products and services at the retail level and at low prices. These stores typically include an assortment of food items, often sold in bulk, along with an array of household and automotive goods, clothing, and services that may vary over time. Often, such stores require that shoppers purchase a membership that entitles them to shop there. They offer very little service and usually require the customer to take home the item.

Compared with department stores, clothing and accessory stores sell a much narrower group of items that include apparel for all members of the family, as well as shoes, luggage, leather goods, lingerie, jewelry, uniforms, and bridal gowns. Stores in this sector may sell a relatively broad range of these items or concentrate on a few. They often are staffed with knowledgeable salespersons who can help in the selection of sizes, styles, and accessories. Many of these stores are located in shopping malls across the country and have significantly fewer workers than department stores.

*Recent developments.* Over the past few years, many department stores in this industry have consolidated, seeking more efficient operations in order to stay competitive. Some clothing, accessory, and general merchandise stores are also moving toward obtaining goods directly from the manufacturer, bypassing the wholesale level completely. Additionally, many large retailers try to reach as many different consumers as possible, and so have added online stores, discount outlets, and sometimes high-end boutiques, since more apparel and accessories shoppers enjoy designer and other high-society items. E-commerce also continues to be a popular way for consumers to shop and for stores to showcase all of their items for sale.

Some larger national retailers, such as superstores, have begun to institute radio-frequency identification technology (RFID) into their logistics and inventory systems. They have many different goods to keep track of, making RFID a cost effective investment.

## Working Conditions

*Hours.* About 29 percent of the workers were employed part time. Most employees work during peak selling times, including nights, weekends, and holidays. Weekends are busy days in retailing, so almost all employees work at least one of these days and have a weekday off. Longer than normal hours may be scheduled during busy periods, such as holidays and the back-to-school season, when vacation time is limited for most workers, including buyers and managers.

*Work Environment.* Most employees in clothing, accessory, and general merchandise stores work in clean, well-lit conditions. Retail salespersons and cashiers often stand for long periods, and stock clerks may perform strenuous tasks, such as moving heavy, cumbersome boxes. Sales representatives and buyers often travel to visit clients and may be away from home for several days or weeks at a time. Those who work for large manufacturers and retailers may travel outside of the country.

The incidence of work-related illnesses and injuries varies greatly among segments of the industry. In 2006, workers in clothing and accessory stores had 2.7 cases of injury and illness per 100 full-time workers, while those in general merchandise stores had 6.7 cases per 100 full-time workers. These figures compare with an average of 4.4 throughout private industry.

## Employment

Clothing, accessory, and general merchandise stores—one of the largest employers in the Nation—had about 4.4 million wage and salary jobs in 2006. In contrast to many industries, this industry employs workers in all sections of the country, from the largest cities to the smallest towns. Many of the industry's workers are young—31 percent were under 24 years old in 2006, compared with about 14 percent for all industries (table 1).

**Table 1. Percent distribution of employment, by age group, 2006**

| Age group | Clothing, accessory, and general merchandise stores | All industries |
|---|---|---|
| Total .......................................... | 100.0% | 100.0% |
| 16-19................................... | 12.3 | 4.3 |
| 20-24 ..................................... | 18.8 | 9.6 |
| 25-34 ..................................... | 19.5 | 21.5 |
| 35-44 ..................................... | 17.6 | 23.9 |
| 45-54 ..................................... | 16.1 | 23.6 |
| 55-64 ..................................... | 11.2 | 13.4 |
| 65 and older............................ | 4.6 | 3.7 |

Department stores accounted for about 36 percent of jobs in the industry, but for only about 7 percent of establishments. In 2006, about 7 out of 10 workers were employed in clothing, accessory, and general merchandise stores having more than 50 workers (chart).

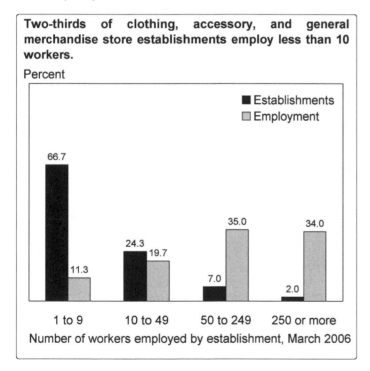

**Two-thirds of clothing, accessory, and general merchandise store establishments employ less than 10 workers.**

Percent

Legend:
- ■ Establishments
- ▨ Employment

| Number of workers employed by establishment, March 2006 | Establishments | Employment |
|---|---|---|
| 1 to 9 | 66.7 | 11.3 |
| 10 to 49 | 24.3 | 19.7 |
| 50 to 249 | 7.0 | 35.0 |
| 250 or more | 2.0 | 34.0 |

## Occupations in the Industry

Sales and related occupations accounted for 65 percent of workers in this industry in 2006. Office and administrative support occupations make up the next largest group of employees, accounting for 19 percent of total industry employment (table 2).

*Sales and related occupations.* *Retail salespersons*, who make up 41 percent of employment in the industry, help customers select and purchase merchandise. Their primary job is to interest customers in the merchandise and to answer any questions the customers may have. In order to do this, they may describe the product's various models, styles, and colors or demonstrate its use. To sell expensive and complex items, workers need extensive knowledge of the products.

In addition to selling, most retail salespersons register the sale electronically on a cash register or terminal; receive cash, checks, and charge payments; and give change and receipts. Depending on the hours they work, they may open or close their cash registers or terminals. Either of these operations may include counting the money in the cash register; separating charge slips, coupons, and exchange vouchers; and making deposits at the cash office. Salespersons are held responsible for the contents of their register, and repeated shortages often are cause for dismissal.

Salespersons may be responsible for handling returns and exchanges of merchandise, wrapping gifts, and keeping their work areas neat. In addition, they may help stock shelves or racks, arrange for mailing or delivery of a purchase, mark price tags, take inventory, and prepare displays. They also must be familiar with the store's security practices to help prevent theft of merchandise. *Cashiers* total bills, receive money, make change, fill out charge forms, and give receipts. Retail salespersons and cashiers often have similar duties.

*Office and administrative support occupations.* *Stock clerks and order fillers* bring merchandise to the sales floor and stock shelves and racks. They also may mark items with identifying codes or prices so that they can be recognized quickly and easily, although many items today arrive preticketed. *Customer service representatives* investigate and resolve customers' complaints about merchandise, service, billing, or credit ratings. The industry also employs administrative occupations found in most industries, such as general office clerks and bookkeepers.

*Management, business, and financial operations occupations.* Management and business and financial operations occupations accounted for 2 percent of industry employment in 2006. *Buyers* purchase merchandise for resale from wholesalers or manufacturers. Using historical records, market analysis, and their sense of consumer demand, they buy merchandise, keeping in mind their customer's demand for style, quality, and price range. Wrong decisions mean that the store will mark down slow-selling merchandise, thus losing profits. Buyers for larger stores or chains usually buy one classification of merchandise, such as casual menswear or home furnishings; those working for smaller stores may buy all the merchandise sold in the store. They also plan and implement sales promotion plans for their merchandise, such as arranging for advertising and ensuring that the merchandise is displayed properly.

*Department managers* oversee sales workers in a department or section of the store. They set the work schedule, supervise employee performance, and are responsible for the overall sales and profitability of their departments. They also may be called upon to settle a dispute between a customer and a salesperson.

*Merchandise managers* are in charge of a group of buyers and department managers; they plan and supervise the purchase and marketing of merchandise in a broad area, such as women's apparel or appliances. In department store chains, with numerous stores, many of the buying and merchandising functions are centralized in one location. Some local managers might decide which merchandise, among that bought centrally, would be best for their own stores.

*Department store managers* direct and coordinate the activities in these stores. They may set pricing policies to maintain profitability and notify senior management of concerns or problems. Department store managers usually directly supervise department managers and indirectly oversee other department store workers.

*Clothing and accessory store managers*—often the only managers in smaller stores—combine many of the duties of department managers, department store managers, and buyers. They are almost always employed at the specific retail establishment.

**Table 2. Employment of wage and salary workers in clothing, accessory, and general merchandise stores by occupation, 2006 and projected change, 2006-2016.**
(Employment in thousands)

| Occupation | Employment, 2006 | | Percent change, 2006-16 |
|---|---|---|---|
| | Number | Percent | |
| **All occupations** | 4,352 | 100.0 | 7.5 |
| **Management, business, and financial occupations** | 99 | 2.3 | 5.8 |
| General and operations managers | 40 | 0.9 | -1.7 |
| **Professional and related occupations** | 88 | 2.0 | 25.3 |
| Merchandise displayers and window trimmers | 18 | 0.4 | 7.3 |
| Pharmacists | 23 | 0.5 | 26.2 |
| Pharmacy technicians | 26 | 0.6 | 41.0 |
| **Service occupations** | 211 | 4.9 | 14.1 |
| Security guards | 29 | 0.7 | -6.9 |
| Fast food and counter workers | 31 | 0.7 | 26.1 |
| Janitors and cleaners, except maids and housekeeping cleaners | 52 | 1.2 | 20.2 |
| Hairdressers, hairstylists, and cosmetologists | 19 | 0.4 | 0.5 |
| **Sales and related occupations** | 2,834 | 65.1 | 9.3 |
| First-line supervisors/managers of retail sales workers | 324 | 7.4 | 7.3 |
| Cashiers | 689 | 15.8 | 5.0 |
| Retail salespersons | 1,789 | 41.1 | 11.2 |
| **Office and administrative support occupations** | 815 | 18.7 | -1.6 |
| First-line supervisors/managers of office and administrative support workers | 72 | 1.6 | 6.0 |
| Bookkeeping, accounting, and auditing clerks | 29 | 0.7 | 10.4 |
| Customer service representatives | 60 | 1.4 | 28.8 |
| Shipping, receiving, and traffic clerks | 55 | 1.3 | 3.5 |
| Stock clerks and order fillers | 486 | 11.2 | -7.4 |
| Office clerks, general | 26 | 0.6 | 7.0 |
| **Transportation and material moving occupations** | 163 | 3.7 | 5.5 |
| Laborers and freight, stock, and material movers, hand | 127 | 2.9 | 5.3 |

Note: Columns may not add to totals due to omission of occupations with small employment

## Training and Advancement

Many jobs in the clothing, accessory, and general merchandise store industry do not require more than a high school diploma. Most of the skills needed for these jobs can be learned through on-the-job training from an experienced employee.

*Sales and related occupations.* Generally, no formal education is required to become a retail salesperson or cashier; in fact, many people get their first jobs in this industry. A high school diploma or less is sufficient for most people in retail sales, since most of their tasks can be learned through on-the-job training. However, almost all managers of retail sales workers require some retail experience or education beyond high school.

In most small stores, an experienced employee or the manager instructs newly hired sales personnel on how to make out sales checks and operate the cash register. In larger stores, training programs are more formal and usually are conducted over several days. Some stores provide periodic training seminars to refresh and improve the customer service and selling skills of their sales workers. Initially, trainees are taught how to make cash, check, and charge sales; eventually, they are instructed on how to deal with returns and special orders. Other topics usually covered are customer service, security, and store policies and procedures. Depending on the type of product they are selling, sales workers may be given specialized training in their area. For example, those working in cosmetic sales receive instruction on the types of products that are available and the types of customers most likely to purchase those products.

Salespersons should enjoy working with people. Among other desirable characteristics are a pleasant personality, a neat appearance, and the ability to communicate clearly. Because of the trend toward providing more service, it is becoming increasingly important for salespersons to be knowledgeable about the products and merchandise that are available. Some employers may conduct a background check of applicants, especially of those seeking work selling high-priced items.

Some salespersons are hired for a particular department, whereas others are placed after they have completed training. Placement usually is based on where positions are available. Salespersons called "floaters" are not assigned to a particular department; instead, they work where they are needed.

Advancement opportunities for salespersons vary. As those who work full time gain experience and seniority, they usually move to positions of greater responsibility or to positions with potentially higher commissions. In larger companies, having several years of experience or some postsecondary education may help a salesperson move quickly into a first level managerial position. Salespersons who are paid on a commission basis—that is, they earn a percentage of the value of what they sell—may advance to selling more expensive items. The most experienced and highest paid salespersons sell big-ticket items. This work requires the most knowledge of the product and the greatest talent for persuasion. In some establishments, advancement opportunities are limited because one person, often the owner, is the only manager, but sales experience may be useful in finding a higher level job elsewhere. Retail selling experience is an asset when one is applying for sales positions with larger retailers or in other kinds of sales of, for example, motor vehicles, financial services, or wholesale merchandise.

The National Retail Federation offers the National Professional Certification in Customer Service for customer service and sales-related occupations. Certification is voluntary and is earned by passing an exam and applying for certification.

*Office and administrative support occupations.* There are no formal educational requirements for most office and administrative support jobs in retail trade. A high school education is preferred, especially by larger employers. Many of the workers who seek to enter jobs in this industry are recent immigrants, so employers may require proficiency in English and may even offer language training to employees. Advancement opportunities from these jobs may be limited, but in larger companies may include moving into a supervisory position.

***Management, business, and financial operations occupations.*** Traditionally, capable salespersons with good leadership skills, but without a college degree, could advance to management positions. However, a college education is becoming increasingly important for obtaining higher level managerial positions such as department manager, store manager, or buyer. Many retailers prefer to hire persons with an associate or bachelor's degree in marketing, merchandising, or business as management trainees or assistant managers. Many colleges and universities offer educational programs in retail management, retail merchandising, retail marketing, retail sales, and fashion and apparel merchandising. Additionally, computer skills have become extremely important in all parts of this industry in areas such as inventory control, human resources, sales forecasting, and electronic commerce, and especially for business and financial operations occupations.

## Outlook

Clothing, accessory, and general merchandise stores will have many job openings over the 2006-16 period, fueled by the large number of workers who transfer to jobs in other industries and must be replaced. Employment growth will be steady and determined mostly by consumer behavior and preferences.

***Employment change.*** Overall, the number of wage and salary jobs in clothing, accessory, and general merchandise stores is expected to increase 7 percent over the 2006-16 period, compared with the 11 percent increase projected for all industries combined. Growth of this industry is extremely dependent on consumers' spending habits and the health of the economy. Growth will be the result of continued increases in spending on clothing, accessories, and general merchandise, together with an increasing number of consumers, and will keep in line with the overall growth of the economy. Many wholesale clubs and superstores will expand and create many jobs in this industry, especially in sales and related occupations. Job growth will also stem from the continued growth and popularity of family clothing stores, where the store is not catering to a specific age or gender. Employment in full-service department stores will slowly decline as more people buy from warehouse clubs and superstores.

Alternative retail outlets such as mail-order companies, home shopping, and the Internet will continue to take some business away from traditional retail stores. However, this trend will be minimized as traditional retailers increase their presence in these outlets. Although online sales are expected to grow rapidly, sales at traditional retail stores are projected to continue to account for a major portion of total retail sales. Also, although electronic commerce is expected to limit the growth of some retail jobs, it will increase job opportunities for other occupations, such as Internet sales managers, webmasters, technical support workers, and other related workers.

Many stores in this industry, particularly clothing and accessory stores, are highly sensitive to changes in the economy and to changing tastes of consumers. Guessing wrong on upcoming trends, especially several years in a row, or being unable to weather a recession can cause even large, well-established stores to go bankrupt or out of business. As a result, changes in employment can be volatile and may include periods of rapid increases and decreases in the number of jobs.

Worker productivity is increasing because of technological

advances, particularly among clerks, managers, and buyers. For example, computerized systems allow companies to streamline purchasing and obtain customer information and preferences, reducing the need for buyers. However, employment of sales workers such as retail salespersons who interact personally with customers will be less negatively affected by technological advances because direct customer contact will remain important.

***Job prospects.*** Numerous job openings will result from the need to replace workers who leave jobs in this large industry. Jobs will be available for young workers, first-time jobseekers, persons with limited job experience, senior citizens, and people seeking part-time work, such as those with young children or those who wish to supplement their income from other jobs. Persons with a college degree or computer skills will be sought for managerial positions.

## Earnings

***Industry earnings.*** Hourly earnings of nonsupervisory workers in clothing, accessory, and general merchandise stores are well below the average for all workers in private industry. This reality reflects both the high proportion of part-time and less experienced workers in these stores and the fact that even experienced workers receive relatively low pay compared with experienced workers in many other industries (table 3). Earnings in selected occupations in clothing, accessory, and general merchandise stores appear in table 4.

**Table 3. Average earnings of nonsupervisory workers in clothing, accessory, and general merchandise stores, 2006.**

| Industry segment | Weekly | Hourly |
|---|---|---|
| **Total, private industry** | $568 | $16.76 |
| **General merchandise stores** | 314 | 10.61 |
| **Clothing and clothing accessory stores** | 265 | 11.31 |
| Jewelry, luggage, and leather goods stores | 482 | 15.35 |
| Shoe stores | 263 | 10.58 |
| Clothing stores | 234 | 10.61 |

**Table 4. Median hourly earnings of the largest occupations in clothing, accessory, and general merchandise stores, May 2006**

| Occupation | Clothing and clothing accessories stores | General merchandise stores | All Industries |
|---|---|---|---|
| General and operations managers | $27.16 | $31.89 | $40.97 |
| First-line supervisors/managers of retail sales workers | 16.05 | 14.08 | 16.33 |
| Bookkeeping, accounting, and auditing clerks | 13.11 | 13.38 | 14.69 |
| Security guards | 11.76 | 10.54 | 10.35 |
| Customer service representatives | 10.68 | 10.05 | 13.62 |
| Shipping, receiving, and traffic clerks | 10.42 | 9.98 | 12.53 |
| Laborers and freight, stock, and material movers, hand | 8.94 | 8.67 | 10.20 |
| Retail salespersons | 8.63 | 8.74 | 9.50 |
| Stock clerks and order fillers | 8.58 | 8.97 | 9.83 |
| Cashiers | 7.86 | 8.10 | 8.08 |

**Benefits and union membership.** Many employers permit workers to buy merchandise at a discount. Smaller stores usually offer limited employee benefits. In larger stores, benefits are more comparable with those offered by employers in other industries and can include vacation and sick leave, health and life insurance, profit sharing, and pension plans.

Unionization in this industry is limited. Only about 2 percent of workers were union members or covered by union contracts, compared with 12 percent in all industries.

## Sources of Additional Information

General information on careers in retail establishments is available from the following organizations:

➢ National Retail Federation, 325 7th St. NW., Suite 1100, Washington, DC 20004.

➢ International Council of Shopping Centers, 665 5th Ave., New York, NY 10022. Internet: **http://www.icsc.org**

The 2008–09 *Occupational Outlook Handbook* has information on many occupations in clothing, accessory, and general merchandise stores, including the following:

- Advertising, marketing, promotions, public relations, and sales managers
- Cashiers
- Customer service representatives
- Fashion designers
- Purchasing managers, buyers, and purchasing agents
- Retail salespersons
- Sales worker supervisors
- Security guards and gaming surveillance officers
- Stock clerks and order fillers

# Grocery Stores

## SIGNIFICANT POINTS

- Numerous job openings—many of them part time—should be available due to the industry's large size and high replacement needs.

- Young workers age 16 to 24 hold one-third of grocery store jobs.

- Cashiers and stock clerks account for one-half of all jobs.

## Nature of the Industry

Grocery stores are familiar to most people and located throughout the country, although their size and range of goods and services they sell varies. The grocery store industry is made up of supermarkets and convenience stores that do not sell gas. Stores in the grocery store industry sell primarily food items, including perishable foods, and may sell some nonfood items, but they do not specialize in selling certain types of foods, such as just meat, seafood, or health food. Stores that sell a mixture of food and more general merchandise, such as supercenters or warehouse club stores, are not in this industry.

*Goods and services.* Traditional supermarkets sold mostly fresh meats and produce, canned or packaged goods, and dry goods such as flour and sugar to people who lived in the neighborhood. They also usually stocked a few nonfood items used in preparing home-cooked meals, such as aluminum foil and paper napkins. These days supermarkets sell a wide range of traditional grocery items, general merchandise, and health and beauty products, plus a wide assortment of prepared foods, such as hot entrees, salads, and deli sandwiches for takeout. Most supermarkets have several specialty departments that may include seafood, meat, bakery, deli, produce, and floral. Nonfood items that can be found at larger supermarkets include household goods, health and beauty care items, pet products, and greeting cards. Some of the largest supermarkets may have concession counters, hot food and beverage bars or food courts, plus seating areas where patrons can eat while on the premises. In addition, many grocery stores offer catering services, automated teller machines, a pharmacy, postal services, and drop-off locations for film processing, drycleaning, and video rentals. Some grocery stores may lease space to banks, coffee shops, and other service providers, but these services are usually not performed by the grocery store.

Convenience stores typically sell a limited line of high-convenience items and food basics, such as milk, bread, beverages, and snacks. Some also offer readymade sandwiches and other prepared foods for immediate consumption along with an assortment of nonfood items, such as magazines. Most are also open longer hours than a typical supermarket.

*Industry organization.* In 2006, there were approximately 34,000 traditional supermarkets, each with sales of over $2 million, offering a full line of groceries, meat, and produce. Of these, 75 percent were operated by a chain of supermarkets that owned 11 or more grocery stores. The rest were operated by independent owners that operate fewer than 11 grocery stores. In addition, there were approximately 13,000 small grocery stores

with limited selections that generated sales of under $2 million each. There are many more convenience stores than grocery stores, but they employ only a few workers per store. Many convenience stores are independently owned and are often franchises of convenience store chains.

Traditionally, grocery store chains have been based in a particular region of the country. Recently, however, many of these regional chains have been bought out by other chains, and although the names of the chains often remain the same, their administrative offices have been consolidated, resulting in fewer workers in management jobs.

*Recent developments.* Over the last couple decades, grocery store supermarkets have been facing growing competition for the food dollar. More and more time-pressed people are eating out on a regular basis or buying takeout meals. Also, a greater variety of stores are selling groceries, with warehouse club stores and supercenters becoming some of the biggest food sellers. To compete with restaurants, fast food outlets, and club and supercenter stores, grocery stores have been selling more general merchandise items and providing a greater variety of services to cater to the one-stop shopper. They are also selling more prepared foods, deli items, and food to go. Some provide tables for eating in the store.

While some supermarkets have grown and added more floor space and more nonfood items, others have opened that sell more limited lines of groceries and often cater to particular groups of people. Ethnic grocery stores are some of the fastest-growing stores in the country. Also, there is an increase in the number of grocery stores that cater to upscale clientele and those that sell mostly organic foods. Providing specialized services and products unique to a particular neighborhood and its shoppers helps these grocers build loyalty and contribute to a sense of community among local residents.

Specialization is also occurring within the stores. Grocery store inventory tracking systems can now quickly let managers know what is selling in their store and what is not. This allows them to adjust their merchandise regularly and focus on the big sellers. They also do not need to keep as large an inventory of items in the store because cash registers linked to the inventory systems can automatically tell managers when something needs to be reordered. New scanning technology is also making it easier for stores to provide self-service checkout, although cashiers will always remain. Some stores have begun providing customers with hand-held bar code readers that they use to scan items when they place them in their cart and which automatically tallies their total spending as they add each item. As they compete for food sales, grocery stores are attempting to get better at offering items for sale that people want and become more efficient at providing them.

## Working Conditions

*Hours.* Grocery stores are open more hours and days than most work establishments, so employees are needed for early morning, late night, weekend, and holiday shifts. With the average workweek for nonsupervisory workers being 29.8 hours and nearly 32 percent of employees working a part-time schedule, these jobs are particularly attractive to those looking for work with flexible hours. Part-time schedules predominate for most cashiers and counter service workers, but most managers work full-time schedules and often work longer hours. Typically managers are needed to oversee and train staff on all shifts and may be needed at additional times to fill in during unanticipated busy periods.

*Work Environment.* Most grocery store employees work in a clean, well-lighted, and climate-controlled environment. However, work at times can become hectic, and dealing with some customers can be stressful.

Most grocery store workers wear some sort of uniform, such as a jacket, shirt, or apron that identifies them as store employees and keeps their personal clothing clean. Health and safety regulations require employees who handle fresh food items—such as those who work in the prepared foods, delicatessen, or meat departments—to wear head coverings, safety glasses, or gloves. Some States require health certification for employees who handle food.

In 2006, cases of work-related injury and illness averaged 6.2 per 100 full-time workers in grocery stores, compared with 4.4 per 100 full-time workers in the entire private sector. Some injuries occur while workers transport or stock goods. Persons in food-processing occupations, such as butchers and meatcutters, may sustain cuts and cashiers and others working with computer scanners or traditional cash registers may be vulnerable to cumulative trauma and other repetitive motion injuries.

Table 1. Percent distribution of employment, by age group, 2006

| Age group | Grocery stores | All industries |
|---|---|---|
| Total | 100.0% | 100.0% |
| 16-19 | 17.9 | 4.3 |
| 20-24 | 14.6 | 9.6 |
| 25-34 | 17.0 | 21.5 |
| 35-44 | 18.7 | 23.9 |
| 45-54 | 17.6 | 23.6 |
| 55-64 | 10.4 | 13.4 |
| 65 and older | 3.8 | 3.7 |

## Employment

Grocery stores ranked among the largest industries in 2006, providing 2.5 million wage-and-salary jobs. There were also 59,000 self-employed workers in this industry, mainly operating very small grocery or convenience stores.

Most grocery stores are small, with 80 percent employing fewer than 50 workers. Most jobs, however, are found in the largest stores. Seventy-five percent of workers were employed in grocery stores having more than 50 workers (chart).

Young workers between the ages of 16 and 24 held 33 per-

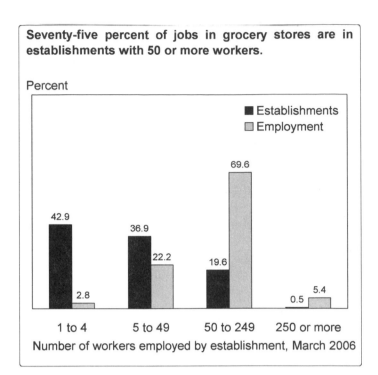

Seventy-five percent of jobs in grocery stores are in establishments with 50 or more workers.

Percent

- Establishments
- Employment

Number of workers employed by establishment, March 2006

cent of grocery store jobs (table 1). This reflects the large number of jobs in this industry open to young workers who have little or no work experience.

## Occupations in the Industry

Fifty percent of all grocery store employees are cashiers or stock clerks and order fillers. Others in the industry prepare food, assist customers, dispense medications, and provide management and support services to the establishment.

*Sales and related workers.* Cashiers make up the largest occupation in grocery stores, accounting for 33 percent of all workers (table 2). They scan the items being purchased by customers into the cash register or read hand-stamped prices and total the amount due. They accept payment consisting of cash, credit cards, and checks and make change or fill out charge forms. They then produce a cash register receipt that shows the quantity and price of the items purchased. Cashiers usually place items in bags or give them to "baggers" to load. When cashiers are not needed to check out customers, they sometimes assist other workers. In grocery stores with separate self-checkout lanes, cashiers verify that the items have been paid for before the customer leaves the store, and if needed, assist the customer in completing the transaction.

*First-line managers of retail sales workers* supervise the employees in the different specialty departments, such as produce, meat, and bakery. These managers train employees and schedule their hours; oversee ordering, inspection, pricing, and inventory of goods; monitor sales activity; and make reports to store managers. *Demonstrators and product promoters* offer samples of various products to entice customers to purchase them.

*Office and administrative support occupations.* Stock clerks and order fillers are the second largest occupation in grocery stores, comprising 17 percent of workers. They fill the shelves with merchandise and arrange displays to attract customers. In stores without computer-scanning equipment, stock clerks and order fillers may have to manually mark prices on individual items and count stock for inventory control.

**Table 2. Employment of wage and salary workers in grocery stores by occupation, 2006 and projected change, 2006-2016**
(Employment in thousands)

| Occupation | Employment, 2006 | | Percent change, 2006-16 |
|---|---|---|---|
| | Number | Percent | |
| **All occupations** | 2,463 | 100.0 | 0.7 |
| **Management, business, and financial occupations** | 53 | 2.1 | 1.9 |
| General and operations managers | 28 | 1.1 | -1.8 |
| Professional and related occupations | 51 | 2.1 | 21.5 |
| Floral designers | 8 | 0.3 | 9.1 |
| Pharmacists | 20 | 0.8 | 20.0 |
| Pharmacy technicians | 19 | 0.8 | 30.9 |
| **Service occupations** | 313 | 12.7 | 13.9 |
| First-line supervisors/managers of food preparation and serving workers | 21 | 0.9 | 20.9 |
| Cooks | 16 | 0.7 | 12.9 |
| Food preparation workers | 119 | 4.8 | 20.1 |
| Combined food preparation and serving workers, including fast food | 91 | 3.7 | 9.1 |
| Counter attendants, cafeteria, food concession, and coffee shop | 24 | 1.0 | 9.1 |
| Janitors and cleaners, except maids and housekeeping cleaners | 16 | 0.7 | 11.5 |
| **Sales and related occupations** | 1,013 | 41.1 | 0.0 |
| First-line supervisors/managers of retail sales workers | 121 | 4.9 | 6.0 |
| Cashiers, except gaming | 823 | 33.4 | -1.8 |
| Retail salespersons | 48 | 1.9 | 9.1 |
| **Office and administrative support occupations** | 574 | 23.3 | -3.8 |
| First-line supervisors/managers of office and administrative support workers | 26 | 1.1 | 1.6 |
| Bookkeeping, accounting, and auditing clerks | 21 | 0.9 | 9.1 |
| Customer service representatives | 57 | 2.3 | 20.0 |
| Shipping, receiving, and traffic clerks | 15 | 0.6 | 5.0 |
| Stock clerks and order fillers | 406 | 16.5 | -8.7 |
| Office clerks, general | 19 | 0.8 | 7.5 |
| **Production occupations** | 194 | 7.9 | 3.2 |
| First-line supervisors/managers of production and operating workers | 17 | 0.7 | 9.1 |
| Bakers | 41 | 1.6 | 8.6 |
| Butchers and meat cutters | 89 | 3.6 | -1.8 |
| Meat, poultry, and fish cutters and trimmers | 22 | 0.9 | 9.1 |
| Food cooking machine operators and tenders | 9 | 0.4 | -1.8 |
| **Transportation and material moving occupations** | 256 | 10.4 | -9.5 |
| Laborers and freight, stock, and material movers, hand | 44 | 1.8 | -1.8 |
| Packers and packagers, hand | 195 | 7.9 | -12.7 |

Note: Columns may not add to totals due to omission of occupations with small employment

Many office clerical workers—such as *general office clerks* and *bookkeeping, accounting, and auditing clerks*—prepare and maintain the records necessary to keep grocery stores running smoothly.

***Food preparation and production occupations.*** *Butchers and other meat-, poultry-, and fish-processing workers* prepare meat, poultry, and fish for purchase by cutting up and trimming carcasses and large sections into smaller pieces, which they pack-age, weigh, price, and place on display. They also prepare ground meat from other cuts and fill customers' special orders. These workers also may prepare ready-to-heat and ready-to-cook foods by filleting or cutting meat, poultry, or fish into bite-sized pieces, preparing and adding vegetables, and applying sauces, marinades, or breading. While most butchers and other meat-, poultry-, and fish-processing workers work in the meat or seafood sections of grocery stores, many others are employed at central processing facilities, from which smaller packages are sent to area stores.

Some specialty workers prepare food for sale in grocery stores but others work in kitchens located in other facilities. Many newer stores, however, are incorporating kitchens into store designs and devoting more floor space to display prepared foods and employing a bigger variety of workers. *Bakers* produce breads, rolls, cakes, cookies, and other baked goods. *Cooks and food preparation workers* make salads and entrees. They also may prepare ready-to-heat foods for sale in the delicatessen, gourmet food or prepared food departments. Other food preparation workers arrange party platters or prepare various vegetables and fruits that are sold at the salad bar.

In supermarkets that serve food and beverages for consumption on the premises, *food and beverage serving workers*, including *fast food* and *counter workers*, take orders and serve customers. They may prepare short-order items, such as salads or sandwiches, to be taken out and consumed elsewhere or eaten on the premises in a designated seating area.

***Transportation and material moving occupations.*** In the warehouses and stockrooms of large supermarkets, *hand laborers and freight, stock, and material movers* move stock and goods in storage and deliver them to the sales floor; they also help load and unload delivery trucks. *Hand packers and packagers*, also known as courtesy clerks or baggers, perform a variety of simple tasks, such as bagging groceries, loading parcels in customers' cars, and returning merchandise to shelves.

***Management occupations.*** *General and operations managers* are responsible for the efficient and profitable operation of grocery stores. Often called store managers or department managers, they set store policy, hire and train employees, develop merchandising plans, maintain good customer and community relations, address customer complaints, and monitor the store's profits or losses. A new type of manager in grocery stores is the "category manager." Similar to a purchasing manager, they specialize in a particular category of goods, such as snack food. These managers must thoroughly understand consumer preferences for the specific category of items, package sizes, and marketing strategies, and are responsible for ordering the correct amount in the correct package. Category managers evaluate their store's sales and inventory reports to determine product demand, sales trends, and profitability. They also consider comments from department managers and customers to adjust future orders, change product displays, and plan budgets. *Marketing and sales managers* forecast sales and develop a marketing plan based on demographic trends, sales data, community needs, and consumer feedback.

***Other occupations.*** Grocery stores employ a number of workers in other occupations to help meet customer service needs. For example, *pharmacists* fill customers' drug prescriptions and advise them on over-the-counter medicines. *Pharmacy technicians* assist pharmacists in filling orders. *Human resources, training,* and *labor relations specialists* recruit and screen prospective employees and are responsible for making sure that employees maintain and, if necessary, improve their skill levels. *Building cleaning workers* keep the stores clean and orderly.

## Training and Advancement
Grocery stores provide many young people with their first work experience. Training for the most numerous occupations—cashiers, stock clerks and order fillers, and food preparation workers—usually is short term and provided on the job. Longer-term training or related work experience is required for management positions and many specialty occupations, such as butcher.

*Cashiers and stock clerks and order fillers.* A high school diploma is generally all that is needed to become a *cashier*. In large supermarket chains, prospective employees are matched with available jobs, hours, and locations and are usually trained in the store. Cashiers are often trained in a few days, and many larger retailers offer formal web-based or computer-based classroom training to familiarize workers with company guidelines and the equipment with which they will work. Some cashiers may receive additional in-house training to supervise multiple self-checkout stations and oversee their smooth operation and provide customer service.

Stock clerks and order fillers generally learn the store layout and inventory system while on the job. They must become knowledgeable of the store's stock and the proper storage location and temperature conditions for each item. Stock clerks and order fillers also are trained to read purchase orders and temperature gauges and to maintain inventory records to reflect the movement of items from the delivery trucks to back-room storage to the sales floor. They also are responsible for replenishing the stock of items on the store shelves as they empty.

Courtesy clerks or baggers also receive short-term on-the-job training to learn store layout, product locations, and company procedures. They also are provided guidance on how to bag groceries securely to avoid damaging goods. Courtesy clerks and baggers may learn to run a register and help out at the customer service desk answering questions from customers.

Grocery store jobs require that workers be in good physical condition and have a neat appearance and a pleasant, businesslike manner because most workers are on the sales floor constantly dealing with the public. Cashiers, stock clerks, and order fillers must be able to do repetitive work swiftly and accurately. Cashiers need basic arithmetic skills, good hand-eye coordination, and manual dexterity. Stock clerks and order fillers must especially be in good physical condition because they do a lot of lifting, crouching, and climbing.

*Food preparation and processing occupations.* Butchers and other meat-, poultry-, and fish-processing workers, bakers, and food preparation workers must receive training in sanitation and safe food handling practices before they are allowed to handle food for resale. Many States require workers to obtain certification for completing training on State health code requirements for safely handling food. Food preparation workers generally learn simple knife skills, proper food storage and serving procedures, and how to follow straightforward recipes while on the job. More complex food processing and preparation skills may be acquired through training courses provided by trade schools and industry associations. As workers acquire more skills, they may advance to performing more difficult tasks, such as preparing custom cuts of meat or preparing more complex dishes, or to training and supervising lesser skilled employees.

*Management occupations.* Grocery store management has become increasingly complex and technical. Managers of some large supermarkets are responsible for millions of dollars in yearly revenue and for hundreds of employees. They use sophisticated software to manage budgets, schedule work, track and order products, set prices, control inventory, manage shelf space, and assess product profitability. While experience in retail sales, particularly at a grocery store, is the primary attribute sought for management jobs, companies are hiring more workers with a bachelor's degree or some college training for new management positions. Employers increasingly seek graduates of college and university, junior and community college, and technical institute programs in food marketing, food management, and supermarket management or design, as well as graduates of bachelor's or master's degree programs in business administration. Many supermarket chains start these graduates in management training programs working various professional positions in areas such as logistics, supply chain management, marketing, inventory management and stock replenishment, food safety, human resources, and strategic planning. Management trainees often start as assistant or department managers and, depending on experience and performance, may advance to positions of greater responsibility. It is not unusual for managers to supervise a large number of employees early in their careers.

Entry-level workers may advance to management positions, depending on experience and performance. Stores that promote from within have established tracks by which employees move from department to department, gaining broad experience, until they are considered ready for entry-level management positions. Opportunities for advancement to management jobs exist in both large supermarket chains and in small, independent grocery stores. For managers, good communication skills, initiative, leadership ability, and attention to detail are important, as well as the ability to solve problems quickly and to perform well under pressure. Managers also need good business, marketing, and inventory management skills.

## Outlook
Wage and salary jobs in grocery stores are expected to increase by 1 percent over the 2006-16 period, compared to 11 percent growth projected for wage and salary employment in all industries combined. Despite the lack of new jobs, numerous job opportunities will be available for people with limited job skills, first-time job seekers, and those seeking part-time or alternative work schedules due to the relatively high turnover in this industry. Specialty occupations and managers will require higher skill levels and more training or experience.

*Employment change.* Competition for the consumer food dollar from restaurants and other eating places, and from supercenters and warehouse club stores, will cause some grocery stores to close and others to get bigger or specialize in order to compete. Consumer demand for more diversified food tastes and shopping convenience—including one-stop shopping—is driving grocery stores to increase product variety and expand the number of sales departments and consumer services. This restructuring of the retail food business requires a broader range of workers to staff newer and larger departments, such as prepared food and fresh fish and deli counters that make sandwiches to go. Conversely, many smaller grocery stores are choosing to sell a narrower range of grocery products, often specializing in products or services to fit a specific clientele or particular store category, like organic foods. As stores develop a niche for being a source for particular items and gain a competitive selling edge for them, they become grocery destinations for shoppers. Staffing patterns within the store will adjust as a result to reflect consumer buying habits and the changing product focus.

Employment of those in specialty food processing, preparation, and serving occupations—bakers, food preparation workers, and fast food and counter workers—is expected to grow faster than the industry average because of the growing popularity of purchasing freshly baked breads and pastries and other prepared meals for both re-heating at home and for consumption on the premises.

Little change is expected in employment of cashiers and other front-end occupations. Online grocery shopping, implementation of RFID technology to speed up register check out, and use of self-checkout registers will cause some lessening in demand for cashiers. But shoppers continue to want the personal service provided by cashiers, baggers, and courtesy clerks and to be able to judge the quality of fresh grocery items for themselves.

*Job prospects.* Job opportunities in grocery stores should be plentiful because of the relatively short tenure of the many young and part-time employees in the workforce. Many will need to be replaced when they leave to find new jobs, seek full-time employment, return to school, or stop working. The greatest numbers of job openings will be in the largest occupations: cashiers and stock clerks and order fillers. These jobs generally have high replacement needs.

## Earnings

*Industry earnings.* Average weekly earnings in grocery stores are considerably lower than the average for all industries, reflecting the large proportion of entry-level, part-time jobs. In 2006, nonsupervisory workers in grocery stores averaged $328.26 a week, compared with $567.87 a week for all workers in the private sector. Earnings in selected occupations in grocery stores appear in table 3.

Managers receive a salary and often a bonus based on store or department performance. Managers in highly profitable stores generally earn more than those in less profitable stores.

*Benefits and union membership.* Full-time workers generally receive typical benefits, such as paid vacations, sick leave, and health and life insurance. Part-time workers who are not unionized may receive few benefits. Unionized part-time workers sometimes receive partial benefits. Grocery store employees may receive a discount on purchases.

Twenty percent of all employees in grocery stores belong to a union or are covered by union contracts, compared with 13 percent in all industries. The United Food and Commercial Workers International Union is the primary union representing grocery store workers. Workers in chain stores are more likely to be unionized or covered by contracts than workers in independent grocery stores. In independent stores, wages often are determined by job title, and increases are tied to length of job service and to job performance.

## Sources of Additional Information

For information on job opportunities in grocery stores, contact individual stores or the local office of the State employment service.

General information on careers in grocery stores is available from:

➢ United Food and Commercial Workers International Union, 1775 K St. NW., Washington, DC 20006-1502. Internet: **http://www.ufcw.org**
➢ Food Marketing Institute, 2345 Crystal Drive, Suite 800, Arlington, VA 22202-4801. Internet: **http://www.fmi.org**
➢ National Association of Convenience Stores, 1600 Duke St., Alexandria, VA 22314.

Information on most occupations in grocery stores, including the following, appears in the 2008-09 *Occupational Outlook Handbook*:

- Building cleaning workers
- Cashiers
- Chefs, cooks, and food preparation workers
- Demonstrators, product promoters, and models
- Food and beverage serving and related workers
- Food-processing occupations
- Food service managers
- Material moving occupations
- Pharmacists
- Pharmacy aides
- Pharmacy technicians
- Retail salespersons
- Sales worker supervisors
- Stock clerks and order fillers

**Table 3. Median hourly earnings of the largest occupations in grocery stores, May 2006**

| Occupation | Grocery stores | All industries |
|---|---|---|
| First-line supervisors/managers of retail sales workers | $16.05 | $16.33 |
| Butchers and meat cutters | 13.38 | 12.95 |
| Retail salespersons | 9.62 | 9.50 |
| Customer service representatives | 9.22 | 13.62 |
| Stock clerks and order fillers | 9.10 | 9.83 |
| Food preparation workers | 9.10 | 8.37 |
| Combined food preparation and serving workers, including fast food | 8.80 | 7.24 |
| Laborers and freight, stock, and material movers, hand | 8.68 | 10.20 |
| Cashiers | 8.20 | 8.08 |
| Packers and packagers, hand | 7.33 | 8.48 |

# Wholesale Trade

## SIGNIFICANT POINTS

- Most workplaces are small, employing fewer than 20 workers.

- About 7 in 10 work in office and administrative support, sales, or transportation and material-moving occupations.

- While some jobs require a college degree, a high school education is sufficient for many jobs.

- Consolidation and new technology should slow employment growth in some occupations, but many new jobs will be created in other occupations.

## Nature of the Industry

When consumers purchase goods, they usually buy them from a retail establishment, such as a supermarket, department store, gas station, or Internet site. When businesses, government agencies, or institutions, such as universities or hospitals, need to purchase goods, they normally buy them from wholesale trade establishments. Retail establishments purchase goods for resale to consumers, but other establishments purchase equipment, motor vehicles, office supplies, or any other items for their own use.

*Goods and services.* The size and scope of firms in the wholesale trade industry vary greatly. Wholesale trade firms sell any and every type of good. Customers of wholesale trade firms buy goods for use in making other products, as in the case of a bicycle manufacturer that purchases steel tubing, wire cables, and paint. Customers also may purchase items for use in the course of daily operations, as when a corporation buys office furniture, paper clips, or computers. Other customers purchase a wide variety of goods for resale to the public, as does a department store that purchases socks, flatware, or televisions. Wholesalers may offer only a few items for sale, perhaps all made by one manufacturer, or only a narrow range of goods, such as very specialized machine tools. Others may offer thousands of items produced by hundreds of different manufacturers, such as all the supplies necessary to open a new store, including shelving, light fixtures, wallpaper, floor coverings, signs, cash registers, accounting ledgers, and perhaps even some merchandise for resale.

Wholesale trade firms are essential to the economy. They simplify flows of products, payments, and information by acting as intermediaries between the manufacturer and the final customer. They may store goods that neither manufacturers nor retailers can store until consumers require them. In so doing, they fill several roles in the economy. They provide businesses, institutions, and governments a convenient nearby source of goods made by many different manufacturers that allows them to devote minimal time and resources to transactions. For manufacturers, wholesalers provide a national network of a manageable number of distributors of their goods that allow their products to reach a large number of users. In addition, wholesalers help manufacturers by taking on some marketing, new customer sales contact, order processing, customer service, and technical support—work manufacturers otherwise would have to perform.

Besides selling and moving goods to their customers, some wholesalers may provide them other services. These include the financing of purchases, customer service and technical support,

product marketing services such as advertising and promotion, technical or logistical advice, and installation and repair services. After customers buy equipment, such as cash registers, copiers, computer workstations, or various types of industrial machinery, they may need assistance to integrate the products into the customer's workplace. Wholesale trade firms often employ workers to visit customers, install or repair equipment, train users, troubleshoot problems, or provide expertise on how to use the equipment most efficiently.

*Industry organization.* There are two main types of wholesalers: Merchant wholesalers and wholesale electronic markets, agents, and brokers. *Merchant wholesalers* generally take title to the goods that they sell; in other words, they buy and sell goods on their own account. The merchant wholesale segment also includes the individual sales offices and sales branches (but not retail stores) of manufacturing and mining enterprises that are specifically set up to perform the sales and marketing of their products.

Merchant wholesalers deal in either durable or non-durable goods. Durable goods are new or used items that generally have a normal life expectancy of 3 years or more. Establishments in this part of wholesale trade are engaged in wholesaling goods, such as motor vehicles, furniture, construction materials, machinery and equipment (including household appliances), metals and minerals (except petroleum), sporting goods, toys and hobby goods, recyclable materials, and parts. Nondurable goods are items that generally have a normal life expectancy of less than 3 years. Establishments in this part of wholesale trade are engaged in wholesaling goods, such as paper and paper products, chemicals and chemical products, drugs, textiles and textile products, apparel, footwear, groceries, farm products, petroleum and petroleum products, alcoholic beverages, books, magazines, newspapers, flowers and nursery stock, and tobacco products.

Firms in the *wholesale electronic markets, and agents, and brokers* segment arrange for the sale of goods owned by others, generally on a fee or commission basis. They act on behalf of the buyers and sellers of goods, but generally do not take ownership of the goods. This sector includes agents and brokers as well as business-to-business electronic markets that use electronic means, such as the Internet or Electronic Data Interchange (EDI), to facilitate wholesale trade.

Only firms that sell their wares to businesses, institutions, and governments are considered part of wholesale trade. As a marketing ploy, many retailers that sell mostly to the general public present themselves as wholesalers. For example, "wholesale" price clubs, factory outlets, and other organizations are retail establishments, even though they sell their goods to the public at "wholesale" prices.

***Recent developments.*** Recent consolidation of smaller wholesale distributors has led to more companies serving their customers regionally, nationally, and internationally. This has resulted in companies offering more lines of related products from a larger variety of manufacturers.

Additionally, radio frequency identification (RFID) technology is becoming used more frequently by larger wholesale distributors with warehouses. RFID tags coupled with a satellite and receiver system allow wholesalers to keep track of the goods they have in stock and through transit to ensure delivery. Although this technology is highly promising, many smaller companies do not use it because it has not yet become cost effective in those situations.

Many larger independent wholesale distribution companies have also started "private-labeling" their goods—contracting with the manufacturer to put their name on the label instead of the manufacturers.

## Working Conditions

***Hours.*** Most workers in wholesale trade worked at least 40 hours a week in 2006, and about 21 percent worked 50 or more hours a week. Many put in long shifts, particularly during peak times. Other workers, such as produce wholesalers, work unusual hours. Produce wholesalers must be on the job before dawn to receive shipments of vegetables and fruits, and they must be ready to begin delivering goods to local grocers in the early morning.

***Work Environment.*** Working conditions and physical demands of wholesale trade jobs vary greatly. Moving stock and heavy equipment can be strenuous, but freight, stock, and material movers may make use of forklifts in large warehouses. Workers in some automated warehouses use computer-controlled storage and retrieval systems that further reduce labor requirements. Employees in refrigerated meat warehouses work in a cold environment and those in chemical warehouses often wear protective clothing to avoid harm from toxic chemicals. Outside sales workers are away from the office for much of the workday and may spend a considerable amount of time traveling. On the other hand, most management, administrative support, and marketing staff work in offices.

Overall, work in wholesale trade is relatively safe. In 2006 there were 4.1 work-related injuries or illnesses per 100 full-time workers, comparable with the rate of 4.4 per 100 for the entire private sector. Not all parts of wholesale trade are equally safe, however. Occupational injury and illness rates were considerably higher than the national average for wholesale trade workers who dealt with lumber and construction materials (6.3 per 100 workers); groceries (7.0 per 100 workers); and beer, wine, and distilled beverages (8.4 per 100 workers).

## Employment

Wholesale trade had about 5.9 million wage and salary jobs in 2006. About 90 percent of the establishments in the industry are small, employing fewer than 20 workers, and they have about 35 percent of the industry's jobs (chart 1). Although some large firms employ many workers, wholesale trade is characterized by a large number of relatively small establishments when compared

with other industries. Wholesale trade jobs are spread throughout the country. Few workers in wholesale trade are members of unions.

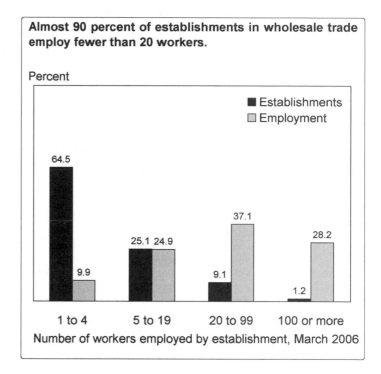

**Almost 90 percent of establishments in wholesale trade employ fewer than 20 workers.**

Percent

- ■ Establishments
- ▢ Employment

Number of workers employed by establishment, March 2006

## Occupations in the Industry

Many occupations are involved in wholesale trade, but not all are represented in every type of wholesale trade firm. Merchant wholesalers are by far the largest segment of the industry. The activities of these wholesale trade firms commonly center on storing, selling, and transporting goods. As a result, the three largest occupational groups in the industry are office and administrative support workers, many of whom work in inventory management; sales and related workers; and workers in transportation and material moving occupations, most of whom are truck drivers and material movers. In 2006, 71 percent of wholesale trade workers were concentrated in these three groups (table 1).

***Office and administrative support occupations.*** Many *secretaries and administrative assistants; bookkeeping, accounting and auditing clerks;* and *general office clerks* are employed in wholesale trade, as in most industries. Most of the other administrative support workers are needed to control inventory. *Shipping, receiving, and traffic clerks* check the contents of all shipments, verifying condition, quantity, and sometimes shipping costs. They may use computer terminals or barcode scanners and, in small firms, may pack and unpack goods. *Order clerks* handle order requests from customers, or from the firm's regional branch offices in the case of a large, decentralized wholesaler. These workers take and process orders, and route them to the warehouse for packing and shipment. Often, they must be able to answer customer inquiries about products and monitor inventory levels or record sales for the accounting department. *Stock clerks and order fillers* code or price goods and store them in the appropriate warehouse sections. When they receive a customer order, they retrieve from the warehouse the appropriate type and quantity of goods. In some cases, they also may perform tasks similar to those performed by shipping and receiving clerks.

*Sales and related occupations.* Generally, workers in sales and related occupations try to interest customers in purchasing a wholesale firm's goods and assist them in buying the goods. There are three primary types of sales people in wholesale firms: Inside sales workers, outside sales workers, and sales worker supervisors.

*Sales representatives* may work in either inside sales or outside sales. Inside sales workers generally work in sales offices taking sales orders from customers. They also increasingly perform duties such as problem solving, solicitation of new and existing customers, and handling complaints. Outside sales workers are the more highly skilled workers and one of the largest occupations in the wholesale trade industry. They travel to places of business—whether manufacturers, retailers, or institutions—to maintain contact with current customers or to attract new ones. They make presentations to buyers and management or may demonstrate items to production supervisors. *Sales engineers* have similar job functions as sales representatives, except that these workers tend to specialize in selling technologically advanced products. Because of the complex nature of these products, sales engineers often need a great deal of highly technical knowledge, usually obtained through postsecondary training. As more customers gather information and complete orders through the Internet, outside sales workers devote more time to developing prospective clients and offering services to existing clients such as installation, maintenance, and advising on the most efficient use of purchases. Sales representatives and sales engineers also may be known as manufacturers' representatives or agents in some wholesale trade firms.

*Sales worker supervisors* monitor and coordinate the work of the sales staff and often do outside sales work themselves. *Counter clerks* wait on customers who come to the firm to make a purchase.

*Transportation and material moving occupations.* Transportation and material-moving workers move goods around the warehouse, pack and load goods for shipment, and transport goods to buyers. *Laborers and freight, stock, and material movers* manually move goods to or from storage and help to load delivery trucks. *Hand packers and packagers* also prepare items for shipment. *Industrial truck and tractor operators* use forklifts and tractors with trailers to transport goods within the warehouse, to outdoor storage facilities, or to trucks for loading. *Truck drivers* transport goods between the wholesaler and the purchaser or between distant warehouses. *Driver/sales workers* deliver goods to customers, unload goods, set up retail displays, and take orders for future deliveries. They are responsible for maintaining customer confidence and keeping clients well-stocked. Sometimes these workers visit prospective clients, in hopes of generating new business.

*Management, business, and financial operations occupations.* Management and business and financial operations workers direct the operations of wholesale trade firms. *General and operations managers* and *chief executives* supervise workers and ensure that operations meet standards and goals set by top management. Managers with ownership interest in smaller firms often also have some sales responsibilities. *First-line supervisors* oversee warehouse workers—such as clerks, material movers, and truck drivers—and see that standards of efficiency are maintained.

In order to provide manufactured goods to businesses, governments, or institutional customers, merchant wholesalers employ large numbers of *wholesale buyers* and *purchasing managers.* Wholesale buyers purchase goods from manufacturers for resale, based on price and what they think customers want. Purchasing managers coordinate the activities of buyers and determine when to purchase what types and quantities of goods.

*Installation, maintenance, and repair occupations.* Many wholesalers do not just sell goods to other businesses; they may also install and service these goods. *Installation, maintenance, and repair* workers set up, service, and repair these goods. Others maintain vehicles and other equipment.

**Training and Advancement**

Although many jobs in wholesale trade require only a high school diploma, employers increasingly prefer at least some postsecondary education for their sales team and management positions. All entry-level workers usually receive on-the-job training—for example, in the operation of inventory management databases, online purchasing systems, or electronic data interchange systems. Workers must keep abreast of new selling techniques, management methodologies, and information systems because the industry is constantly being changed by technological advances and market forces. In addition, technological advances are affecting the skill requirements for occupations across the entire industry—from warehouse workers to truck drivers to managers. As a result, numerous firms devote significant resources to worker training.

Advancement opportunities may depend on the occupation. As the wholesale trade industry continues to evolve in the coming years, advancement opportunities will be more limited. Increasing use of the Internet and other electronic means of communication, as well as changing sales techniques place increased demands on managers, making it more difficult to promote less educated workers from within the firm. However, consolidation among wholesale trade firms has resulted in larger companies with more advancement opportunities for those with the appropriate skills.

*Office and administrative support occupations.* Many office and administrative positions currently do not require education beyond a high school degree. However, any additional education or previous experience is considered an asset by many employers. Advancement opportunities for these occupations may be more limited. Workers may eventually become an office or administrative supervisor or perform different tasks within the office. Some workers may move into an inside sales or customer service position after spending some time with the company.

*Sales and related occupations.* Many sales and related workers enter the industry with some form of postsecondary training, although some have only a high school diploma. Employers prefer candidates with an associate's or bachelor's degree in business, marketing, industrial distribution, or a related field. Additionally, many employers seek applicants with prior sales experience. Depending on the type of product being sold or distributed, some technical expertise may also be an asset.

There are a growing number of industrial distribution programs at community colleges and universities, providing students with the business and technical training that employers find desirable. All sales workers should expect to periodically take classes and seminars to learn new skills as the industry adapts to new technology and business practices.

Some sales personnel may advance inside the company,

118

**Table 1. Employment of wage and salary workers in wholesale trade by occupation, 2006 and projected change, 2006-2016.**
(Employment in thousands)

| Occupation | Employment, 2006 | | Percent change, 2006-16 |
|---|---|---|---|
| | Number | Percent | |
| **All occupations** | 5,898 | 100.0 | 7.3 |
| **Management, business, and financial occupations** | 553 | 9.4 | 7.7 |
| Top executives | 155 | 2.6 | -0.7 |
| Sales managers | 62 | 1.1 | 11.5 |
| Wholesale and retail buyers, except farm products | 57 | 1.0 | 0.2 |
| Accountants and auditors | 59 | 1.0 | 10.5 |
| **Professional and related occupations** | 23 | 5.5 | 17.0 |
| Computer specialists | 157 | 2.7 | 19.7 |
| Engineers | 40 | 0.7 | 17.7 |
| Designers | 39 | 0.7 | 11.5 |
| **Sales and related occupations** | 1,551 | 26.3 | 10.2 |
| First-line supervisors/managers of non-retail sales workers | 100 | 1.7 | 6.2 |
| Parts salespersons | 63 | 1.1 | -1.8 |
| Retail salespersons | 68 | 1.1 | 8.4 |
| Sales representatives, wholesale and manu-facturing, technical and scientific products | 229 | 3.9 | 14.4 |
| Sales representatives, wholesale and manufacturing, except technical and scientific products | 922 | 15.6 | 10.9 |
| **Office and administrative support occupations** | 1,398 | 23.7 | 4.0 |
| First-line supervisors/managers of office and administrative support workers | 73 | 1.2 | 3.4 |
| Billing and posting clerks and machine operators | 42 | 0.7 | -1.0 |
| Bookkeeping, accounting, and auditing clerks | 151 | 2.6 | 9.3 |
| Customer service representatives | 183 | 3.1 | 23.0 |
| Order clerks | 80 | 1.4 | -27.8 |
| Receptionists and information clerks | 39 | 0.7 | 10.1 |
| Production, planning, and expediting clerks | 8 | 0.5 | 10.8 |
| Shipping, receiving, and traffic clerks | 171 | 2.9 | 7.0 |
| Stock clerks and order fillers | 191 | 3.2 | -6.9 |
| Secretaries and administrative assistants | 143 | 2.4 | 3.9 |
| Office clerks, general | 174 | 3.0 | 8.5 |
| **Installation, maintenance, and repair occupations** | 390 | 6.6 | 12.7 |
| Computer, automated teller, and office machine repairers | 54 | 0.9 | 13.1 |
| Automotive technicians and repairers | 19 | 0.3 | 12.2 |
| Bus and truck mechanics and diesel engine specialists | 40 | 0.7 | 9.7 |
| Farm equipment mechanics | 23 | 0.4 | 4.9 |
| Mobile heavy equipment mechanics, except engines | 36 | 0.6 | 26.5 |
| Industrial machinery installation, repair, and maintenance workers | 87 | 1.5 | 12.2 |
| **Production occupations** | 329 | 5.6 | 8.7 |
| Team assemblers | 80 | 1.4 | 12.1 |
| **Transportation and material moving occupations** | 1,236 | 21.0 | 2.2 |
| Supervisors, transportation and material moving workers | 70 | 1.2 | 9.5 |
| Driver/sales workers | 111 | 1.9 | -1.4 |
| Truck drivers, heavy and tractor-trailer | 208 | 3.5 | 5.9 |
| Truck drivers, light or delivery services | 197 | 3.3 | 10.3 |
| Industrial truck and tractor operators | 106 | 1.8 | -0.4 |
| Laborers and freight, stock, and material movers, hand | 413 | 7.0 | -0.8 |
| Packers and packagers, hand | 75 | 1.3 | -11.2 |

Note: Columns may not add to totals due to omission of occupations with small employment

through promotion to supervisor or to outside sales. *Sales representatives* may also decide to advance by starting their own sales company, commonly called a manufacturers' representative company. The owners of these companies, along with their sales personnel may obtain certifications such as the Certified Professional Manufacturers' Representative certification (CPMR) or the Certified Sales Professional (CSP) certification.

*Transportation and material moving occupations.* Workers involved in transportation or material moving do not necessarily need education beyond a high school diploma. For some occupations, such as *truck drivers* and d*river/sales workers*, having a driver's license or a State Commercial Driver's License (CDL) may be essential. Drivers of medium and heavy trucks need a CDL.

Those starting in warehouses may also have some room for advancement. For example, they may be trained for jobs as *industrial truck and tractor operators*. Others become familiar with the products and procedures of the firm while working in the warehouse or stock room and may be promoted to counter sales or even to inside sales positions. Some may be trained to install, service, and repair the products sold by the firm. Eventually, some workers may advance to outside sales positions or possibly to managerial positions, though this is less frequent than in the past.

*Management, business, and financial operations occupations.* Due to technological advances and changing job responsibilities, wholesale employers are increasingly hiring candidates with some postsecondary education for many management, business and financial operations occupations. For upper-level and senior management positions, many employers look for candidates with a bachelor's degree or higher, along with some previous managerial experience.

Depending on what level an employee enters a company, there are various advancement opportunities. For example, *first-line supervisors* may move up to senior level management or receive more responsibilities. Currently, several large firms in the industry have formal management training programs that train college graduates for management positions, and the number of these programs will probably grow.

*Installation, maintenance, and repair occupations.* Although there are no formal education requirements for these occupations, firms usually hire workers with maintenance and repair experience or mechanically inclined individuals who can be trained on the job.

Like transportation and material moving workers, installation, maintenance, and repair occupations may have some room for advancement. This may include promotion to a sales position or to becoming a first-line supervisor. Many firms also have opportunities for on-the-job or offsite training for workers to acquire more skills in their profession.

## Outlook

Employment in wholesale trade will increase slowly as consolidation into fewer and larger firms occurs eliminating the jobs of redundant workers, while new technology allows operations to become more efficient. Employment will decline in some occupations but new jobs will be created in others.

*Employment change.* Over the 2006-2016 period, wage and salary employment in wholesale trade is projected to grow by 7 percent, compared to 11 percent growth for all industries combined. Consolidation and the spread of new technology are the main reasons for slow employment growth. Employment in the industry still depends primarily on overall levels of consumption of goods, which should grow with the economy. Growth will vary, however, depending on the products and sectors of the economy with which individual wholesale trade firms are involved. For example, due to the Nation's aging population, growth is expected to be higher than average for wholesale trade firms that distribute pharmaceuticals and medical devices.

Consolidation of wholesale trade firms into fewer and larger companies is a trend that is likely to continue. There is strong competition among wholesale distribution companies, manufacturers' representative companies, and logistics companies for business from manufacturers. Globalization and cost pressures are likely to continue to force wholesale distributors to merge with other firms or to acquire smaller firms. As retail firms operate growing numbers of stores across the country, demand will increase for large, national wholesale distributors to supply them. The differences between large and small firms will become more pronounced as they compete less for the same customers, and instead emphasize their area of expertise. The consolidation of wholesale trade into fewer, larger firms will make some staff redundant and reduce demand for some workers, especially office and administrative support workers.

New technologies are constantly changing the shape and scope of the workforce in wholesale trade. The internet, e-commerce, and Electronic Data Interchange (EDI) have allowed wholesalers and their customers to better gather price data, track deliveries, obtain product information, and market products. This technology will increasingly allow customers of wholesale firms to purchase goods and track deliveries electronically, limiting the growth of sales and customer service workers who would normally perform these functions. Further automation of recordkeeping, ordering, and processing will result in slower growth for office and administrative support occupations. Customers frequently order and pay for goods electronically so fewer billing and posting clerks will be needed as to process fewer paper transactions.

New radio frequency identification (RFID) technology has the potential to streamline the inventory and ordering process further, replace the need for manual barcode scans, and eliminate most counting and packing errors. As RFID spreads it may lessen demand for administrative workers, particularly order clerks, file clerks, and stock clerks and order fillers. Not all wholesalers will implement this technology because specially trained workers will be needed to maintain the new systems and it may not be cost effective for some firms.

With these new technologies making it easier for firms to bypass the wholesaler and order directly from the manufacturer or supplier, wholesale firms are putting greater emphasis on customer service to differentiate themselves from these other suppliers. Wholesale firms are offering more services such as installation, maintenance, assembly, and repair work and creating many jobs for workers to perform these functions. Sales workers will also be in demand to more aggressively develop prospective clients, including demonstrating new products, and offering improved customer service to clients. Additionally, the passing of the Sarbanes-Oxley Act in 2002, officially implemented in 2004, may also stimulate some growth in sales and other business occupations because of the new requirements for full transparency and accountability when dealing with public companies.

*Job prospects.* Job growth in wholesale trade will be slow, but a large number of job openings will arise as people retire or leave the occupation for other reasons. Job prospects are still expected to be good for some occupations.

This 21st Century supply chain will create favorable job prospects for computer specialists in the wholesale trade industry. Wholesalers' presence in e-commerce and the uses of electronic data interchanges (EDI) will require more computer specialists to develop, maintain, and update these systems. Computer specialists will also be needed to install and develop radio frequency identification systems for those firms that adopt it, and to troubleshoot any problems these systems encounter.

There will also some opportunities for self-employment, with some managers and sales workers starting their own manufacturers' representative company. For example, brokers match buyers with sellers and never actually own goods, so individuals with the proper connections can establish their own agency with only a small investment—perhaps even working out of their home.

## Earnings

*Industry earnings.* Nonsupervisory wage and salary workers in wholesale trade averaged $718 a week in 2006, higher than the average of $568 a week for the entire workforce. Earnings varied greatly among specialties in wholesale trade. For example, in the area with the highest earnings—commercial equipment—workers averaged $922 a week; but in the area with the lowest earnings—farm-product raw materials—workers made $509 a week. Earnings in selected occupations in wholesale trade appear in table 2.

Part of the earnings of some workers is based on perfor-

Table 2. Median hourly earnings of the largest occupations in wholesale trade, May 2006

| Occupation | Merchant wholesalers, durable goods | Merchant wholesalers, nondurable goods | Wholesale electronic markets and agents and brokers | All industries |
|---|---|---|---|---|
| Sales representatives, wholesale and manufacturing, technical and scientific products | $29.68 | $31.06 | $33.42 | $30.98 |
| Sales representatives, wholesale and manufacturing, except technical and scientific products | 23.14 | 22.38 | 26.40 | 23.85 |
| Truck drivers, heavy and tractor-trailer | 15.37 | 16.97 | 16.03 | 16.85 |
| Customer service representatives | 15.35 | 14.41 | 15.16 | 13.62 |
| Bookkeeping, accounting, and auditing clerks | 15.14 | 14.52 | 15.10 | 14.69 |
| Shipping, receiving, and traffic clerks | 12.69 | 12.70 | 12.32 | 12.53 |
| Office clerks, general | 11.79 | 11.12 | 10.73 | 11.40 |
| Truck drivers, light or delivery services | 11.48 | 12.34 | 11.64 | 12.17 |
| Stock clerks and order fillers | 11.41 | 11.19 | 11.44 | 9.83 |
| Laborers and freight, stock, and material movers, hand | 10.69 | 10.42 | 10.29 | 10.20 |

mance, especially in the case of outside sales workers, who frequently receive commissions on their sales. Although many sales workers receive a base salary in addition to a commission, some receive compensation based solely on sales revenue. Performance-based compensation may become more common among other occupations as wholesaling firms attempt to offer more competitive compensation packages.

***Benefits and union membership.*** Like earnings, benefits vary widely from firm to firm. Some small firms offer few benefits. Larger firms may offer common benefits such as life insurance, health insurance, and a pension. Senior level management may receive additional benefits, such as bonuses and a company car. Only about 5 percent of workers in the wholesale trade industry were union members or were covered by union contracts in 2006, compared with about 12 percent of the entire workforce.

## Sources of Additional Information

For information about job opportunities in wholesale trade, contact local firms.

For general information on the wholesale trade industry, contact:

➢ National Association of Wholesaler-Distributors, 1725 K St. NW, Washington, DC 20006. Internet: **http://www.naw.org**

Information on careers for manufacturers' representatives and agents is available from:
➢ Manufacturers' Agents National Association, 1 Spectrum Pointe, Suite 150, Lake Forest, CA 92360. Internet: **http://www.manaonline.org**
➢ Manufacturers' Representatives Educational Research Foundation, 8329 Cole Street, Arvada, CO 80005 Internet: **http://www.mrerf.org**

Information on many key occupations in wholesale trade may be found in the 2008-09 *Occupational Outlook Handbook*:
* Bookkeeping, accounting, and auditing clerks
* Computer, automated teller, and office-machine repairers
* Order clerks
* Purchasing managers, buyers, and purchasing agents
* Sales engineers
* Sales representatives, wholesale and manufacturing
* Shipping, receiving, and traffic clerks
* Stock clerks and order fillers
* Truck drivers and driver/sales workers

Career Guide to Industries 2008-09 Edition

# Transportation and Warehousing

# Air Transportation

## SIGNIFICANT POINTS

- Although flight crews—pilots and flight attendants—are the most visible occupations, the vast majority of the industry's employees work in ground occupations.

- Senior pilots for major airlines are among the highest paid workers in the Nation.

- A bachelor's degree is increasingly required or preferred for most pilot and flight attendant jobs.

- Job prospects generally are better in regional and low-cost carriers than in major airlines, where competition for many jobs is keen; a unique benefit—free or reduced-fare transportation for airline employees and their immediate families—attracts many jobseekers.

## Nature of the Industry

*Goods and services.* From 2001 to 2004, a series of major global and economic events resulted in air transportation industry employment remaining below its 2001 level. During this period, the industry endured a recession, terror attacks, and concerns about pandemics. The impact of these events was especially devastating to the major airlines. However, air travel remains one of the most popular modes of transportation, expanding from 172 million passengers in 1970 to 741 million in 2006, an average growth of 4 percent per year.

*Industry organization.* Airlines transport passengers and freight over regularly scheduled routes or on routes, called "charters," specifically designed for a group of travelers or a particular cargo. Several classes of airlines function in the United States. As of 2006, there were 33 mainline air carriers that use large passenger jets (more than 90 seats); 81 regional carriers that use smaller piston, turboprop, and regional aircraft (up to 90 seats); and 25 all-cargo carriers.

Seven of the mainline carriers are known as network carriers, which have a "hub" and also fly internationally. A hub is a centrally located airport designated by an airline to receive a large number of its flights from many locations, and where passengers can transfer to flights destined for points served by the airline's system. In this way, the airline serves the greatest number of passengers, from as many locations as possible, in the most efficient manner.

The mainline group also includes seven low-cost carriers. These carriers generally don't have a hub and only offer flights between a limited numbers of cities. In the past, low-cost carriers focused primarily on transporting leisure passengers on routes less than 400 miles and had a reputation for "no frills" service. At present, low-cost carriers are expanding their routes to include longer transcontinental and nonstop flights with in-flight service that parallels their competition. These moves have helped low-cost carriers expand their customer base to include more business travelers. Low-cost carriers are the fastest growing segment of commercial aviation, flying one out of every four domestic passengers.

Another type of passenger airline carrier is the regional carrier. In 2006, there were approximately 81 of these carriers. Regional airlines operate short-haul and medium-haul scheduled airline service with an emphasis on connecting smaller communities with larger cities and hubs. Some of the largest regional carriers are subsidiaries of the major airlines, but most are independently owned, often contracting their services to the majors.

Air cargo is another segment of the airline industry. As of 2006, there were 25 of these carriers. Cargo can be carried in cargo holds of passenger airlines or on aircraft designed exclusively to carry freight. Cargo carriers in the air transportation industry do not provide door-to-door service. Instead, they provide only air transport from an airport near the cargo's origin to an airport near the cargo's destination. Companies that provide door-to-door delivery of parcels, either across town or across the continent, are classified in the couriers and messengers industry.

*Recent developments.* After the tragic events of September 11, 2001, passenger traffic dropped sharply, causing airlines to slash flights, lay off employees, and park surplus aircraft. During the ensuing years, most of the network carriers restructured operations, with four out of seven seeking bankruptcy protection. At the end of 2006, only two of the network carriers remained in bankruptcy. Since 2000, network carriers have reduced domestic capacity by 21 percent, while low-cost and regional carriers have increased capacity by 57 and 141 percent, respectively. While the industry as a whole was on track to post an operating profit in 2006, record-high fuel prices made this target elusive for the sixth consecutive year.

Demand for air travel is expected to continue into the future. Growth in the more mature domestic markets is expected to be moderate, while travel between the U.S. and foreign points is expected to be moderate to strong. International travel will be spurred by the emerging economies in and around Asia, and by liberal regulations that allow U.S. carriers to fly to more foreign destinations.

The airline industry faces many challenges in the future. Airlines must focus on cost control, cash preservation, and cautious growth. In the long run, a strong national economy, inexpensive tickets, and increasing demand for seats aboard aircraft should bode well for the industry and consumers.

## Working Conditions

*Hours.* Airlines operate flights at all hours of the day and night. As a result, many workers have irregular hours or variable work schedules. Flight and ground personnel, including mechanics and reservation and transportation ticket agents, may have to work at night or on weekends or holidays. Flight personnel may be away from their home bases frequently. When they are away from home, the airlines provide them with hotel accommodations, transportation between the hotel and airport, and an allowance for meals and expenses. Flight attendants typically fly from 65 to 85 hours a month. In addition to flight time, they have about 50 hours a month of duty time between flights.

## Work Environment

Working conditions in air transportation vary widely, depending on the occupation. Most employees work in fairly comfortable surroundings, such as offices, terminals, or airplanes. However, mechanics and others who service aircraft are subject to excessive noise, dirt, and grease and sometimes work outside in bad weather.

In 2006, the air transportation industry had 9.9 injuries and illnesses per 100 full-time workers, compared with 4.4 throughout private industry. Virtually all work-related fatalities resulted from transportation accidents.

Flight crews, especially those on international routes, often suffer jet lag—disorientation and fatigue caused by flying into different time zones. Because employees must report for duty well rested, they must allow ample time to rest during their layovers.

## Employment

The air transportation industry provided 487,000 wage and salary jobs in 2006. Most employment is found in larger establishments—nearly 2 out of 3 jobs are in establishments with 1,000 or more workers. However, 93 percent of all establishments in the industry employ fewer than 100 workers (chart 1).

Most air transportation jobs are at large airports that are located close to cities and that serve as hubs for major airlines.

**Employment in air transportation is heavily concentrated in establishments with 1,000 or more employees, which provide nearly two-thirds of all jobs.**

Percent

Number of workers employed by establishment, March 2006

## Occupations in the Industry

*Office and administrative support occupations and installation, maintenance, and repair occupations.* Although pilots and flight attendants are the most visible occupations in this in-

dustry, nearly 44 percent of all employees in air transportation work in office and administrative support occupations and installation, maintenance, and repair occupations (table 1). The two largest occupations in these occupational groups are *reservation and transportation ticket agents and travel clerks* and *aircraft mechanics and service technicians.*

*Aircraft mechanics and service technicians* service, inspect, and repair planes. They may work on several different types of aircraft, such as jet transports, small propeller-driven airplanes, or helicopters. Many mechanics and technicians specialize, working on the airframe (the body of the aircraft) or the powerplant (the engines) or avionics (the parts of an aircraft that depend on electronics, such as navigation and communication equipment). In small, independent repair shops, they usually inspect and repair many different types of aircraft.

Some mechanics and technicians specialize in scheduled maintenance required by the Federal Aviation Administration (FAA). Following a schedule based on the number of hours flown, calendar days, cycles of operation, or a combination of these factors, mechanics inspect the engines, landing gear, instruments, and other parts of aircraft and perform necessary maintenance and repairs.

A *reservation and transportation ticket agent* is most often the first employee that passengers meet after entering the airport. Ticket agents work at airport ticket counters and boarding gates and use computers to provide customer service to incoming passengers. They make and confirm reservations, sell tickets, and issue boarding passes. They also may work in call centers, answering phone inquiries about flight schedules and fares, verifying reservations, issuing tickets, and handling payments. *Customer service representatives* assist passengers, check tickets when passengers board or disembark from an airplane, and check luggage at the reception area and ensure that it is placed on the proper carrier. They assist elderly or handicapped persons and unaccompanied children in claiming personal belongings and baggage, and in getting on and off the plane. They also may provide assistance to passengers who become ill or injured.

Other ground occupations include *airplane cargo agents, baggage handlers,* and *aircraft cleaners. Airplane cargo agents* take orders from shippers and arrange for transportation of their goods. *Baggage handlers,* classified under *laborers and freight, stock, and material movers, hand,* are responsible for loading and unloading passengers' baggage. They stack baggage on specified carts or conveyors to see that it gets to the proper destination and also return baggage to passengers at airline terminals. *Aircraft cleaners* clean aircraft interiors after each flight.

*Transportation and material moving occupations and service occupations.* Flight crewmembers make up 36 percent of air transportation employment, and include pilots and flight attendants. *Airline pilots, copilots, and flight engineers* are highly trained professionals who fly and navigate jet and turboprop airplanes. Generally, the most experienced pilot, or captain, is in command and supervises all other crewmembers. The pilot and copilot split flying and other duties, such as communicating with air traffic controllers and monitoring the instruments. Some aircraft have a third pilot in the cockpit—the *flight engineer* or second officer—who assists the other pilots by monitoring and operating many of the instruments and systems and watching for other aircraft. Most new aircraft are designed to be flown without a flight engineer. Small aircraft and helicopters that transport passengers and cargo and perform activities such as cropdusting, monitoring traffic, firefighting, and rescue missions are flown and navigated by *commercial pilots.*

**Table 1. Employment of wage and salary workers in air transportation by occupation, 2006 and projected change, 2006-2016.**
(Employment in thousands)

| Occupation | Employment, 2006 Number | Employment, 2006 Percent | Percent change, 2006-16 |
|---|---|---|---|
| All occupations | 487 | 100.0 | 7.3 |
| **Management, business, and financial occupations** | 24 | 5.0 | 12.8 |
| Top executives | 3 | 0.6 | 0.3 |
| Transportation, storage, and distribution managers | 2 | 0.4 | 10.8 |
| Human resources, training, and labor relations specialists | 3 | 0.7 | 14.6 |
| **Professional and related occupations** | 10 | 2.0 | 13.7 |
| Computer specialists | 4 | 0.9 | 14.8 |
| **Service occupations** | 111 | 22.9 | 9.7 |
| Baggage porters and bellhops | 9 | 1.8 | -0.1 |
| Flight attendants | 96 | 19.8 | 10.5 |
| Transportation attendants, except flight attendants and baggage porters | 3 | 0.6 | 10.6 |
| **Office and administrative support occupations** | 162 | 33.3 | 2.4 |
| First-line supervisors/managers of office and administrative support workers | 11 | 2.3 | 2.9 |
| Customer service representatives | 9 | 1.9 | 21.9 |
| Reservation and transportation ticket agents and travel clerks | 98 | 20.1 | -0.6 |
| Cargo and freight agents | 20 | 4.0 | 8.4 |
| Stock clerks and order fillers | 5 | 0.9 | -7.5 |
| Secretaries and administrative assistants | 4 | 0.7 | 7.0 |
| Office clerks, general | 3 | 0.7 | 9.5 |
| **Installation, maintenance, and repair occupations** | 52 | 10.6 | 2.5 |
| First-line supervisors/managers of mechanics, installers, and repairers | 5 | 1.0 | 10.8 |
| Avionics technicians | 2 | 0.4 | 1.8 |
| Aircraft mechanics and service technicians | 38 | 7.7 | -0.2 |
| Maintenance and repair workers, general | 5 | 1.1 | 10.5 |
| **Transportation and material moving occupations** | 121 | 24.9 | 11.4 |
| Aircraft cargo handling supervisors | 2 | 0.3 | 21.9 |
| Airline pilots, copilots, and flight engineers | 69 | 14.2 | 13.7 |
| Commercial pilots | 9 | 1.9 | 12.8 |
| Air traffic controllers and airfield operations specialists | 2 | 0.4 | 11.4 |
| Cleaners of vehicles and equipment | 4 | 0.8 | 10.8 |
| Laborers and freight, stock, and material movers, hand | 10 | 2.1 | -0.2 |

Note: Columns may not add to totals due to omission of occupations with small employment

Airline flights must have one or more *flight attendants* on board, depending on the number of passengers. The attendants' most important function is assisting passengers in the event of an emergency. This may range from reassuring passengers during occasional encounters with strong turbulence to opening emergency exits and inflating escape chutes. More routinely, flight attendants instruct passengers in the use of safety and emergency equipment. Once in the air, they serve meals and snacks, answer questions about the flight, distribute magazines and pillows, and help care for small children and elderly and disabled persons. They also may administer first aid to passengers who become ill.

*Other occupations.* The airline industry also relies on many management, professional, and administrative support workers to keep operations running smoothly.

## Training and Advancement

The skills and experience needed by workers in the air transportation industry differ by occupation. Some jobs may be entered directly from high school, while others require specialized training. Most positions in the airline industry involve extensive customer service contact, requiring strong interpersonal and communication skills. Mechanics and pilots require specialized formal training and must be certified by the FAA. A bachelor's degree is increasingly required or preferred for most pilot and flight attendant jobs. Skills for many other air transportation occupations can be learned on the job or through company-sponsored training.

*Office and administrative support occupations and installation, maintenance, and repair occupations.* When hiring aircraft mechanics, employers prefer graduates of aircraft mechanic trade schools, particularly those who gained experience in the military and are certified. Additionally, employers prefer mechanics who are in good physical condition and able to perform a variety of tasks. After being hired, aircraft mechanics must keep up to date on the latest technical changes and improvements in aircraft and associated systems. Most mechanics remain in the maintenance field, but they may advance to lead mechanic and, sometimes, to crew chief or shop supervisor.

A good speaking voice and a pleasant personality are essential for reservation and transportation ticket agents and customer service representatives. Airlines prefer applicants with experience in sales or in dealing with the public, and most require a high school education, although some college is preferred. Formal company training is required to learn how to operate airline computer systems, issue tickets, and plan trips. Agents and service representatives usually are promoted through the ranks. For example, an experienced ticket agent may advance to lead worker on the shift. Agents who obtain additional skills, experience, and training improve their chances for advancement, although a college degree may be required for some administrative positions.

Some entry-level jobs in this industry, such as baggage handler and aircraft cleaner, require little or no previous training. The basic tasks associated with many of these jobs are learned in less than a week, and most newly hired workers are trained on the job under the guidance of an experienced employee or a manager. However, advancement opportunities for many ground occupations are limited because of the narrow scope of duties and specialized skills necessary for other occupations. Some may advance to supervisor or to another administrative position.

*Transportation and material moving occupations and service occupations.* Pilots must have a commercial pilot's license with an instrument rating, a medical certificate, and certification to fly the types of aircraft that their employer operates. For example, helicopter pilots must hold a commercial pilot's certificate with a helicopter rating. Pilots receive their flight training from the military or from civilian flying schools. Physical requirements are strict. A medical exam, from an FAA-designated physician, must be taken to get a medical certificate. With or without glasses, pilots must have 20/20 vision and good hearing and be in excellent health. In addition, airlines generally require 2 years of college and increasingly prefer or require a college degree.

Pilots who work for smaller airlines may advance to flying for larger companies. They also can advance from flight engineer to copilot to captain and, by becoming certified, to flying larger planes.

Applicants for flight attendant jobs must be in excellent health. Employers increasingly prefer applicants who have a college degree and experience in dealing with the public. Speaking a foreign language also is an asset. Airlines operate flight attendant training programs on a continuing basis. Training usually lasts from 4 to 8 weeks, depending on the size and the type of carrier, and may include crew resource management, which emphasizes teamwork and safety. Courses also are provided in personal grooming and weight control. After completing initial training, flight attendants must go through additional training, where they obtain certification, and pass an FAA safety exam each year in order to continue flying. Advancement opportunities are limited, although some attendants become customer service directors, instructors, or recruiting representatives.

## Outlook

Job prospects generally are better in regional and low-cost carriers than in major airlines, where competition for many jobs is keen; a unique benefit—free or reduced-fare transportation for airline employees and their immediate families—attracts many jobseekers.

*Employment change.* Wage and salary jobs in the air transportation industry are projected to increase by 7 percent over the 2006-16 period, compared with 11 percent for all industries combined. However, the number of job openings may vary from year to year, because the demand for air travel—particularly pleasure travel, a discretionary expense—fluctuates with ups and downs in the economy. In the long run, passenger and cargo traffic is expected to continue expanding in response to increases in population, income, and business activity. Job prospects will continue to be better in regional and low-cost carriers than in major airlines, where competition for many jobs is keen.

Demographic and income trends indicate favorable conditions for leisure travel in the United States and abroad over the next decade. The aging of the population, in combination with growth of disposable income among older people, should continue to increase the demand for air transportation services. Also, business travel has and will continue to improve as the U.S. economy and world trade expand, companies continue to go global, and the economies in many foreign countries become more robust. However, as businesses also try to reduce costs, they are resorting to cheaper alternatives to flying and finding new ways to communicate. Many business travelers are using other means of transportation—for example, automobile or train—and are conducting more business by phone, e-mail, and better and lower-cost videoconferencing technologies.

International cargo traffic is expected to continue to increase with the economy and growing world trade. It also should be stimulated by the development of global electronic commerce and manufacturing trends such as just-in-time delivery, which requires materials to be shipped rapidly. Other factors contributing to growth include the increase in international trade from open skies agreements—which set ground rules for international aviation markets and minimize government intervention—and the expanded use of all-cargo carriers by the U.S. Postal Service to transport mail. Growth of domestic air cargo traffic is not expected to increase as much as international cargo, primarily because of the increased use of mail and the rise of time-definite

trucking. Increasingly, shipments will be sent via trucks, as opposed to aircraft, because trucks are reliable, can be monitored through Global Positioning System (GPS) technology, and are more cost-effective.

Employment growth will differ among the various occupations in the air transportation industry. Employment of aircraft pilots and flight engineers will continue to grow primarily because of increasing demand for leisure and business air travel, population growth, and an expanding economy.

Employment of flight attendants is expected to grow as an improving economy and population growth boost the number of airline passengers, and as airlines expand their capacity to meet rising demand by increasing the number and size of planes in operation.

Similar to other air transportation occupations, aircraft and avionics equipment mechanics and service technicians should have their best chance for landing a job at smaller commuter and regional airlines, primarily because of the relatively lower wages. However, advances in technology are increasing productivity of mechanics, limiting job growth. Employment growth also will be sporadic and follow closely with changes in the economy. When the economy is slow, airlines reduce the number of flights, resulting in less demand for aircraft maintenance and, thus, less demand for mechanics.

The number of reservation and transportation ticket agents will grow more slowly than the overall industry as airlines outsource jobs to lower-wage countries, such as India, in order to cut costs, and as more airlines phase out paper tickets and allow passengers to purchase electronic tickets over the Internet. However, the safety and security responsibilities of these jobs will continue to increase, thereby preventing job declines.

*Job prospects.* Job opportunities in the air transportation industry are expected to vary depending on the occupation. Opportunities for aircraft pilots and flight engineers are expected to be best with the faster growing regional and low-cost carriers. College graduates and former military pilots can expect to have the best job prospects. Opportunities will continue to exist for those pilots who choose to work for air-cargo carriers because of the increase in global freight demand.

Job opportunities for flight attendants will vary by setting. Competition for job opportunities at major airlines is expected to be keen because of the few jobs that are available. Opportunities are expected to be best with the faster growing regional and commuter, low-cost, and charter airlines. Job opportunities for flight attendants also will arise in the corporate jet sector, where flight attendants cater to a high-end clientele. Finally, turnover among flight attendants will produce additional job opportunities as many workers leave for occupations that offer more stable work schedules or better salaries.

Opportunities should be excellent for aircraft and avionics equipment mechanics and service technicians, reflecting the likelihood of fewer entrants from the military and a large number of retirements. Job opportunities at smaller airports are expected to be best as experienced mechanics transfer to positions at major airlines. Meanwhile, competition for mechanic jobs is expected to be keen at major airlines because of their relatively higher wages and travel benefits. Applicants who have experience and who keep abreast of the latest technological advances in electronics and composite materials should have the best opportunities.

Competition for reservation and transportation ticket agent jobs will continue to be keen as the number of applicants continues to exceed the number of job openings. Entry requirements are few, and many people seeking to enter the travel business start in these types of jobs. Also, people are attracted to this occupation because it provides excellent travel benefits. Some job opportunities will occur as agents transfer to other occupations or retire.

Opportunities also are expected to be good for those seeking lesser skilled, entry-level positions, such as baggage handler and aircraft cleaner, because many workers leave these jobs and need to be replaced.

## Earnings

*Industry earnings.* Senior pilots for major airlines are among the highest paid workers in the Nation. Earnings in selected occupations in air transportation appear in table 2.

*Benefits and union membership.* Most employees in the air transportation industry receive standard benefits, such as paid vacation and sick leave; life and health insurance; and often profit-sharing and retirement plans. Some airlines provide allowances to employees for purchasing and cleaning their company

uniforms. A unique benefit—free or reduced-fare transportation for airline employees and their immediate families—attracts many jobseekers.

In 2006, more than half of all workers in the air transportation industry were union members or were covered by union contracts, compared with 13 percent of workers throughout the economy.

## Sources of Additional Information

Information about specific job opportunities and qualifications required by a particular airline may be obtained by writing to personnel managers of the airlines.

For further information on how to apply for a job in the air transportation industry, contact:

➤ Federal Aviation Administration, 800 Independence Ave. SW., Washington, DC 20591. Internet: **http://www.faa.gov**

For information on airline careers, contact:

➤ Air Transport Association of America, Inc., 1301 Pennsylvania Ave. NW., Suite 1100, Washington, DC 20004.

For information on airline pilots, contact:

➤ Air Line Pilots Association, International, 1625 Massachusetts Ave. NW., Washington, DC 20036.

For information on helicopter pilots, contact:

➤ Helicopter Association International, 1635 Prince St., Alexandria, VA 22314.

For information on job opportunities with regional airlines, contact:

➤ Regional Airline Association, 2025 M St. NW., Suite 800, Washington, DC 20036.

Information on these key air transportation occupations may be found in the 2008-09 *Occupational Outlook Handbook*:

- Aircraft and avionics equipment mechanics and service technicians
- Aircraft pilots and flight engineers
- Flight attendants
- Reservation and transportation ticket agents and travel clerks

**Table 2. Mean annual earnings of the largest occupations in air air transportation, May 2006**

| Occupation | Air Transportation | All industries |
|---|---|---|
| Airline pilots, copilots, and flight engineers | $145,900 | $140,380 |
| Commercial pilots | 67,640 | 66,720 |
| Aircraft mechanics and service technicians | 56,630 | 49,300 |
| Flight attendants | 56,200 | 56,150 |
| First-line supervisors/managers of office and administrative support workers | 49,660 | 46,530 |
| Transportation workers, all other | 37,170 | 32,350 |
| Cargo and freight agents | 35,680 | 38,560 |
| Reservation and transportation ticket agents and travel clerks | 33,010 | 30,120 |
| Customer service representatives | 30,280 | 30,400 |
| Laborers and freight, stock, and material movers, hand | 24,980 | 23,050 |

# Truck Transportation and Warehousing

(NAICS 484, 493)

## SIGNIFICANT POINTS

- Truck drivers and driver/sales workers hold 45 percent of all jobs in the industry.

- Job opportunities are expected to be favorable for truck drivers and diesel service technicians.

- Growth in the industry reflects ups and downs in the national economy.

- Many jobs require only a high school education.

## Nature of the Industry

*Goods and services.* Firms in the truck transportation and warehousing industry provide a link between manufacturers and consumers. Businesses, and occasionally individuals, contract with trucking and warehousing companies to pick up, transport, store, and deliver a variety of goods. The industry includes general freight trucking, specialized freight trucking, and warehousing and storage.

*Industry organization.* *General freight trucking* uses motor vehicles, such as trucks and tractor-trailers, to provide over-the-road transportation of general commodities. This industry segment is further subdivided based on distance traveled. Local trucking establishments carry goods primarily within a single metropolitan area and its adjacent non-urban areas. Long-distance trucking establishments carry goods between distant areas.

*Local trucking* comprised 28,000 trucking establishments in 2006. The work of local trucking firms varies with the products transported. Produce truckers usually pick up loaded trucks early in the morning and spend the rest of the day delivering produce to many different grocery stores. Lumber truck drivers, on the other hand, make several trips from the lumberyard to one or more construction sites. Some local truck transportation firms also take on sales and customer relations responsibilities, in addition to delivering the firm's products. Some local trucking firms specialize in garbage collection and trash removal or hauling dirt and debris.

*Long-distance trucking* comprises establishments engaged primarily in providing trucking between distant areas and sometimes between the United States and Canada or Mexico. Numbering 41,000 establishments, these firms handle every kind of commodity.

*Specialized freight trucking* provides over-the-road transportation of freight, which, because of size, weight, shape, or other inherent characteristics, requires specialized equipment, such as flatbeds, tankers, or refrigerated trailers. This industry sector also includes the moving industry—that is, the transportation of used household, institutional, and commercial furniture. Like general freight trucking, specialized freight trucking is subdivided into local and long-distance components. The specialized freight trucking sector contained 48,000 establishments in 2006.

Some goods are carried cross country using intermodal transportation to save time and money. Intermodal transportation encompasses any combination of transportation by truck, train, plane, or ship. Typically, trucks perform at least one leg of the trip. For example, a shipment of cars from an assembly plant begins its journey when they are loaded onto rail cars. Next, trains haul the cars across country to a depot, where the shipments are broken into smaller lots and loaded onto tractor-trailers, which drive them to dealerships. Each of these steps is carefully orchestrated and timed so that the cars arrive just in time to be shipped on their next leg of their journey. Goods can be transported at lower cost this way, but they cannot be highly perishable—like fresh produce—or have strict delivery schedules. Trucking dominates the transportation of perishable and time-sensitive goods.

*Warehousing and storage* facilities comprised 14,000 establishments in 2006. These firms are engaged primarily in operating warehousing and storage facilities for general merchandise and refrigerated goods. They provide facilities to store goods; self-storage mini-warehouses that rent to the general public also are included in this segment of the industry.

*Recent developments.* The deregulation of interstate trucking in 1980 encouraged many firms to add a wide range of customer-oriented services to complement trucking and warehousing services and led to innovations in the distribution process. Increasingly, trucking and warehousing firms provide logistical services encompassing the entire transportation process. Firms that offer these services are called third-party logistics providers. Logistical services manage all aspects of the movement of goods between producers and consumers. Among their value-added services are sorting bulk goods into customized lots, packaging and repackaging goods, controlling and managing inventory, order entering and fulfillment, labeling, performing light assembly, and marking prices. Some full-service companies even perform warranty repair work and serve as local parts distributors for manufacturers. Some of these services, such as maintaining and retrieving computerized inventory information on the location, age, and quantity of goods available, have helped to improve the efficiency of relationships between manufacturers and customers.

Many firms rely on new technologies and the coordination of processes to expedite the distribution of goods. The use of computers to analyze work routines in order to optimize the use of available labor has led to increases in productivity. Voice control software allows a computer to coordinate workers through audible commands—telling workers what items to pack for which orders—helping to reduce errors and increase efficiency. Voice control software also can be used to perform inventory checks and reordering. Some firms use Radio Frequency Identification Devices (RFID) to track and manage incoming and outgoing shipments. RFID simplifies the receiving process by allowing entire shipments to be scanned without unpacking a load to manually compare it against a bill of lading. Just-in-time shipping is a process whereby goods arrive just before they are needed, saving recipients money by reducing their need to carry large inventories. These technologies and processes reflect two major trends in warehousing: supply chain integration, whereby firms involved in production, transportation, and storage all move in concert so as to act with the greatest possible efficiency; and ongoing attempts to reduce inventory levels and increase inventory accuracy.

## Working Conditions

*Hours.* In 2006, workers in the truck transportation industry averaged 40.9 hours a week, compared with an average of 37.9 hours in warehousing and storage and 33.9 in all private industries. The U.S. Department of Transportation governs work hours and many other working conditions of truck drivers engaged in interstate commerce. Long-distance drivers are not permitted to drive after having worked for 60 hours in the past 7 days or 70 hours in the past 8 days, unless they have taken at least 34 consecutive hours off duty. Drivers are required to document their time in logbooks. Many drivers, particularly on long runs, work close to the maximum time permitted because employers usually compensate them on the basis of the number of miles or hours they drive. Drivers frequently travel at night, on holidays, and on weekends to avoid traffic delays so that they can deliver their cargo on time.

*Work environment.* Truck drivers must cope with a variety of working conditions, including variable weather and traffic conditions, boredom, and fatigue. Many truck drivers enjoy the independence and working without direct supervision found in long-distance driving. Local truck drivers often have regular routes or assignments that allow them to return home in the evening.

Improvements in roads and trucks reduce stress and increase the efficiency of long-distance drivers. Many advanced trucks are equipped with refrigerators, televisions, and beds for their drivers' convenience. Included in some of these state-of-the-art vehicles are satellite links with their company's headquarters, so that drivers can get directions, weather and traffic reports, and other important communications in a matter of seconds. In the event of bad weather or mechanical problems, truckers can communicate with dispatchers to discuss delivery schedules and courses of action. Satellite links allow dispatchers to track the location of the truck and monitor fuel consumption and engine performance.

Vehicle and mobile equipment mechanics, installers, and repairers usually work indoors, although they occasionally make repairs on the road. Minor cuts, burns, and bruises are common, but serious accidents typically can be avoided if the shop is kept clean and orderly and if safety practices are observed. Service technicians and mechanics handle greasy and dirty parts and may stand or lie in awkward positions to repair vehicles and equipment. They usually work in well-lighted, heated, and ventilated areas, but some shops are drafty and noisy.

Laborers, and hand freight, stock, and material movers usually work indoors, although they may do occasional work on trucks and fork lifts outside. These occupations often require a great deal of physical labor, including heavy lifting.

Safety is a major concern for the truck transportation and warehousing industry. The operation of trucks, fork lifts, and other technically advanced equipment can be dangerous without proper training and supervision. Truck drivers must adhere to federally mandated certifications and regulations requiring them to submit to drug and alcohol tests as a condition of employment. Employers are required to perform random on-the-job checks for drugs and alcohol.

In 2006, work-related injuries and illnesses per 100 full-time workers averaged 5.8 in the truck transportation industry and 8.0 in warehousing and storage, compared with a rate of 4.4 for the entire private sector. More than 8 out of 10 on-the-job fatalities in the truck transportation industry resulted from transportation related incidents.

## Employment

The truck transportation and warehousing industry provided 2.1 million wage and salary jobs in 2006.

Most employees in the truck transportation and warehousing industry work in small establishments. About 60 percent of trucking and warehousing establishments employ fewer than 5 workers (chart). Consolidation in the industry has reduced the number of small, specialized firms. Trucking and warehousing establishments are found throughout the United States.

Truck drivers held about 45 percent of all salaried jobs, 924,000, in the industry. Other transportation and material moving jobs accounted for 25 percent of industry employment, while various office and administrative support occupations employed another 17 percent. Management, business, and financial occupations held 4 percent of all jobs in the industry; vehicle and mobile equipment mechanics, installers, and repairers accounted for 3 percent; and sales and related workers held 2 percent. In addition to the wage and salary workers, there were an estimated 292,000 self-employed and unpaid family workers in the industry.

## Occupations in the Industry

Transportation and material moving occupations account for 69 percent of all jobs in the industry (table 1). *Truck drivers and driver/sales workers,* who hold 45 percent of all trucking and

**Over half of all jobs in truck transportation and warehousing were in establishments with fewer than 100 employees.**

Percent

Number of workers employed by establishment, March 2006

131

warehousing jobs, transport goods from one location to another. They ensure the safe delivery of cargo to a specific destination, often by a designated time. Drivers also perform some minor maintenance work on their vehicles and make routine safety checks.

The length of trips varies with the type of merchandise and its final destination. Local drivers provide regular service while other drivers make intercity and interstate deliveries that take longer and may vary from job to job. The driver's responsibilities and assignments change according to the time spent on the road and the type of payloads transported.

Local drivers typically have regular schedules and return home at the end of the day. They may deliver goods to stores or homes or haul away dirt and debris from excavation sites. Many local drivers cover the same routes daily or weekly. Long-distance truck drivers often are on the road for long stretches of time. Their trips vary from an overnight stay to a week or more. On longer trips, drivers sometimes sleep in bunks in their cabs or share the driving with another driver.

*Laborers, and hand freight, stock, and material movers* help load and unload freight and move it around warehouses and terminals. Often, these unskilled employees work together in groups of three or four. They may use conveyor belts, handtrucks, pallet jacks, or fork lifts to move freight. They may place heavy or bulky items on wooden skids or pallets to be moved by industrial trucks.

Office and administrative support workers perform the daily recordkeeping operations for the truck transportation and warehousing industry. *Dispatchers* coordinate the movement of freight and trucks, and provide the main communication link that informs the truck drivers of their assignments, schedules, and routes. Dispatchers frequently receive new shipping orders on short notice and must juggle drivers' assignments and schedules to accommodate a client. *Shipping, receiving, and traffic clerks* keep records of shipments arriving and leaving. They verify the contents of trucks' cargo against shipping records. They also may pack and move stock. *Billing and posting clerks and machine operators* maintain company records of the shipping rates negotiated with customers and shipping charges incurred; they also prepare customer invoices.

Workers in installation, maintenance, and repair occupations generally enter these jobs only after acquiring experience in related jobs or after receiving specialized training. Many *vehicle and mobile equipment mechanics, installers, and repairers* require special vocational training. Service technicians and mechanics in trucking and warehousing firms perform preventive safety checks as well as routine service and repairs. Service technicians and mechanics sometimes advance to parts manager positions. *Parts managers* maintain the supply of replacement parts needed to repair vehicles. Parts managers monitor the parts inventory using a computerized system and purchase new parts to replenish supplies. These employees need mechanical knowledge and must be familiar with computers and purchasing procedures.

*Sales and related workers* sell trucking and warehousing services to shippers of goods. They meet with prospective buyers, discuss the customers' needs, and suggest appropriate services. Travel may be required, and many analyze sales statistics, prepare reports, and handle some administrative duties.

Managerial staff provides general direction to the firm. They staff, supervise, and provide safety and other training to workers in the various occupations. They also resolve logistical problems such as forecasting the demand for transportation; mapping out the most efficient traffic routes; ordering parts and equipment service support; and scheduling the transportation of goods.

## Training and Advancement

Many jobs in the truck transportation and warehousing industry require only a high school education, although an increasing number of workers have at least some college education. College education is most important for those seeking positions in management. Increasing emphasis on formal education stems

**Table 1. Employment of wage and salary workers in truck transportation and warehousing by occupation, 2006 and projected change, 2006-2016.**
(Employment in thousands)

| Occupation | Employment, 2006 | | Percent change, 2006-16 |
|---|---|---|---|
| | Number | Percent | |
| **All occupations** | 2,074 | 100.0 | 14.8 |
| **Management, business, and financial occupations** | 80 | 3.9 | 17.9 |
| Top executives | 26 | 1.3 | 6.7 |
| Transportation, storage, and distribution managers | 15 | 0.7 | 20.7 |
| Business operations specialists | 20 | 1.0 | 27.2 |
| **Sales and related occupations** | 42 | 2.0 | 25.3 |
| Retail sales workers | 11 | 0.5 | 27.0 |
| Sales representatives, services | 15 | 0.7 | 27.1 |
| Sales representatives, wholesale and manufacturing | 11 | 0.5 | 24.2 |
| **Office and administrative support occupations** | 353 | 17.0 | 13.9 |
| First-line supervisors/managers of office and administrative support workers | 18 | 0.9 | 13.7 |
| Billing and posting clerks and machine operators | 13 | 0.6 | 4.5 |
| Bookkeeping, accounting, and auditing clerks | 21 | 1.0 | 17.4 |
| Customer service representatives | 27 | 1.3 | 32.8 |
| Cargo and freight agents | 9 | 0.4 | 18.1 |
| Dispatchers | 38 | 1.8 | 2.5 |
| Shipping, receiving, and traffic clerks | 45 | 2.2 | 25.8 |
| Stock clerks and order fillers | 61 | 2.9 | 11.1 |
| Secretaries and administrative assistants | 24 | 1.1 | 9.3 |
| Office clerks, general | 46 | 2.2 | 16.1 |
| **Installation, maintenance, and repair occupations** | 91 | 4.4 | 17.7 |
| Bus and truck mechanics and diesel engine specialists | 47 | 2.3 | 13.7 |
| Maintenance and repair workers, general | 18 | 0.9 | 25.7 |
| Miscellaneous installation, maintenance, and repair workers | 6 | 0.3 | 14.6 |
| **Production occupations** | 35 | 1.7 | 27.1 |
| Other production occupations | 20 | 1.0 | 24.6 |
| **Transportation and material moving occupations** | 1,440 | 69.4 | 13.8 |
| Supervisors, transportation and material moving workers | 68 | 3.3 | 20.5 |
| Truck drivers, heavy and tractor-trailer | 843 | 40.6 | 13.7 |
| Truck drivers, light or delivery services | 82 | 3.9 | 16.7 |
| Industrial truck and tractor operators | 105 | 5.1 | 15.7 |
| Laborers and freight, stock, and material movers, hand | 253 | 12.2 | 12.1 |
| Packers and packagers, hand | 48 | 2.3 | 3.5 |

Note: Columns may not add to totals due to omission of occupations with small employment

132

from the increasing use of technology in the industry. Nearly all operations involve computers and information management systems. Many occupations—especially those involved in scheduling, ordering, and receiving—require detail-oriented people with computer skills. A growing number of employers recommend some form of formal training. Some companies provide such training in-house. Other sources of training include trade associations, unions, and vocational schools. Many companies have specific curricula on safety and procedural issues, as well as on occupational duties.

Whereas many States allow those who are 18 years old to drive trucks within their borders, the U.S. Department of Transportation establishes minimum qualifications for truck drivers engaged in interstate commerce. Federal Motor Carrier Safety Regulations require truck drivers to be at least 21 years old, have at least 20/40 vision and good hearing, and be able to read and speak English. They also must have good driving records and a commercial driver's license, which they obtain by passing a written examination and a skills test in which they operate the type of vehicle they will be driving. Commercial driver's licenses are issued by the individual States. Companies often have additional requirements that applicants must meet.

Some enter the occupation by attending training schools for truck drivers. Many large trucking companies have formal training programs that prospective drivers attend. Other companies assign experienced drivers to teach and mentor newer drivers. Schools vary greatly in the quality of training they provide, but they are becoming more standardized. Local trucking firms often start drivers as truck driver helpers.

Experienced and reliable truck drivers with good driving records receive better pay as well as more desirable routes, schedules, or loads. Because of increased competition for experienced drivers, some larger companies are luring these drivers with higher wages, signing bonuses, and preferred assignments. Some trucking firms hire only experienced drivers.

Some long-distance truck drivers purchase trucks and go into business for themselves. Although many of these owner-operators are successful, some fail to cover expenses and eventually go out of business. Owner-operators should have good business sense as well as truck-driving experience. Courses in accounting, business, and business mathematics are helpful, and knowledge of truck mechanics can enable owner-operators to perform their own routine maintenance and minor repairs. Some trucking companies engage in franchising, providing drivers with the means to purchase a truck while also lining up loads for them to haul.

Unskilled employees may work as helpers, laborers, and material movers in their first jobs. They must be in good physical condition because the work often involves a great deal of physical labor and heavy lifting. They acquire skills on the job and can advance to more skilled jobs, such as industrial truck operator, truck driver, shipping and receiving clerk, or supervisor.

Office and administrative support jobs in the truck transportation and warehousing industry require familiarity with computers. Shipping and receiving clerks watch and learn the skills of the trade from more experienced workers while on the job. Stock clerks may advance to dispatcher positions after becoming familiar with company operations and procedures.

While some vehicle and mobile equipment mechanics, installers, and repairers learn the trade on the job, most employers prefer to hire graduates of programs in diesel mechanics offered by community and junior colleges or vocational and technical schools. Those with no training often start as helpers to mechanics, doing basic errands and chores, such as washing trucks or moving them to different locations. Experience as an automotive service technician is helpful because many of the skills relate to diesel technology. Experienced technicians may advance to shop supervisor or parts manager positions.

For managerial jobs in the truck transportation and warehousing industry, employers prefer persons with bachelor's degrees in business, marketing, accounting, industrial relations, or economics. Good communication, problem-solving, and analytical skills are valuable in entry-level jobs. Since trucking and warehousing firms may rely heavily on computer technology to aid in the distribution of goods, knowledge of information systems also is helpful for advancement. Although most managers must learn logistics through extensive training on the job, several universities offer undergraduate and graduate programs in logistics. These programs emphasize the tools necessary to manage the distribution of goods and may be associated with the business departments of schools. Managers hired for entry-level positions sometimes advance to top-level managerial jobs.

Marketing and sales workers must be familiar with their firm's products and services and have strong communication skills.

## Outlook

Growth in the truck transportation and warehousing industry reflects ups and downs in the national economy. Job opportunities are expected to be favorable for truck drivers and diesel service technicians.

*Employment change.* The number of wage and salary jobs in the truck transportation and warehousing industry is expected to grow 15 percent from 2006 through 2016, compared with projected growth of 11 percent for all industries combined. Growth will result in many job openings because the industry is so large. There also will be openings due to replacement needs for the large number of workers who will transfer to other industries or retire.

One of the main factors influencing the growth of the truck transportation and warehousing industry is the state of the national economy. Growth in the industry reflects ups and downs in the national economy. As the national economy grows and the production and sales of goods increases, there is an increase in the demand for transportation services to move goods from their producers to consumers. During economic downturns, the truck transportation and warehousing industry is one of the first to slow down as orders for goods and shipments decline. Competition in truck transportation is intense, both among trucking companies and, in some long-haul truckload segments, with the railroad industry. Nevertheless, trucking accounts for the bulk of freight transportation. Warehousing is expected to grow faster than the rest of the industry.

Additional employment growth will result from manufacturers' willingness to concentrate more on their core competencies—producing goods—while outsourcing their distribution functions to trucking and warehousing companies which can perform these tasks with greater efficiency. As firms in other industries increasingly employ the industry's logistical services, such as inventory management and just-in-time shipping, many new jobs will be created. Also, as more consumers and businesses make purchases over the Internet, the expansion of electronic commerce will continue to increase demand for the transportation, logistical, and value-added services offered by the truck transportation and warehousing industry.

*Job prospects.* Opportunities for truck drivers are expected to be favorable. Many people leave the career because of the lengthy periods away from home, the long hours of driving, and the negative public image that drivers face. Employment opportunities should be better among truckload carriers than among less-than-truckload (LTL) carriers because many workers prefer the working conditions of LTL carriers. Stricter requirements for obtaining—and keeping—a commercial driver's license also make truck driving a less attractive career. New restrictions on who can obtain or renew their hazardous-material endorsement should increase opportunities for those able to pass the criminal background checks now required. Opportunities for diesel service technicians and mechanics also are expected to be favorable, especially for applicants with formal postsecondary training.

Growth in the truck transportation and warehousing industry should prompt an increase in office and administrative support employment. More dispatchers, stock clerks, and shipping, receiving, and traffic clerks will be needed to support expanded logistical services across the country. Opportunities for those with information technology skills should be excellent.

## Earnings

*Industry earnings.* In 2006, average earnings in the truck transportation portion of the industry were higher than the average for all private industry, as shown in table 2, while average weekly earnings in the warehousing portion were about the same as the average in all private industry. Earnings in selected occupations in truck transportation and warehousing appear in table 3.

Most employers compensate truck drivers with an hourly rate, a rate per mile, or a percentage of their load's revenue.

*Benefits and union membership.* Benefits, including performance-related bonuses, health insurance, and sick and vacation leave, are common in the trucking industry.

The major union in the truck transportation and warehousing industry is the International Brotherhood of Teamsters. About

**Table 2. Average earnings of nonsupervisory workers in truck transportation and warehousing, 2006**

| Industry segment | Weekly | Hourly |
|---|---|---|
| **All private industry** | $568 | $16.76 |
| **Truck transportation** | 706 | 17.24 |
| General freight trucking | 722 | 17.54 |
| Specialized freight trucking | 667 | 16.52 |
| **Warehousing and storage** | 570 | 15.04 |
| Refrigerated warehousing and storage | 605 | 14.76 |
| General warehousing and storage | 568 | 15.24 |
| Miscellaneous warehousing and storage | 553 | 13.40 |

**Table 3. Median hourly earnings of the largest occupations in truck transportation and warehousing, May 2006**

| Occupation | Truck transportation | Warehousing and storage | All Industries |
|---|---|---|---|
| First-line supervisors/managers of transportation and material-moving machine and vehicle operators | $23.96 | $23.02 | $23.24 |
| Truck drivers, heavy and tractor-trailer.. | 17.83 | 18.41 | 16.85 |
| Bus and truck mechanics and diesel engine specialists | 16.84 | 18.41 | 18.11 |
| Industrial truck and tractor operators.... | 14.48 | 13.04 | 13.11 |
| Truck drivers, light or delivery services.. | 14.43 | 13.64 | 12.17 |
| Shipping, receiving, and traffic clerks .... | 13.48 | 13.56 | 12.53 |
| Laborers and freight, stock, and material movers, hand | 12.20 | 11.81 | 10.20 |
| Stock clerks and order fillers | 12.06 | 13.27 | 9.83 |
| Office clerks, general | 11.12 | 12.71 | 11.40 |
| Packers and packagers, hand | 9.90 | 10.29 | 8.48 |

12 percent of trucking and warehousing workers are union members or are covered by union contracts, compared with approximately 13 percent of workers in all industries combined. Since union drivers tend to make more than nonunion drivers, some trucking companies use "double breasting"—employing union as well as nonunion operating divisions in an attempt to lower labor costs. Other companies use graduated pay scales and pay lower wages for new hires. Many give pay increases after predetermined periods to those with safe driving records. Some deal exclusively with owner-operators in order to offset the cost of owning and maintaining a fleet of vehicles.

## Sources of Additional Information

For additional information about careers and training in the truck transportation and warehousing industry, write to any of the following organizations:

➤ American Trucking Associations, 2200 Mill Rd., Alexandria, VA 22314-4677.
➤ International Association of Refrigerated Warehouses, 1500 King St., Suite 201, Alexandria, VA 22314.
➤ International Brotherhood of Teamsters, 25 Louisiana Ave, NW., Washington, DC 20001.
➤ Professional Truck Driver Institute, 2200 Mill Rd., Alexandria, VA 22314. Internet: **http://www.ptdi.org**
➤ Warehousing Education and Research Council, 1100 Jorie Blvd., Suite. 170, Oak Brook, IL 60523-4413. Internet: **http://werc.org**

Detailed information on the following occupations can be found in the 2008–09 *Occupational Outlook Handbook*:

• Diesel service technicians and mechanics
• Dispatchers
• Material moving occupations
• Shipping, receiving, and traffic clerks
• Truck drivers and driver/sales workers

# Information

# Broadcasting

## SIGNIFICANT POINTS

- Keen competition is expected for many jobs, particularly in large metropolitan areas, because of the large number of jobseekers attracted by the glamour of this industry.

- Job prospects will be best for applicants with a college degree in broadcasting, journalism, or a related field, and relevant experience, such as work at college radio and television stations or internships at professional stations.

- In this highly competitive industry, broadcasters are less willing to provide on-the-job training, and instead seek candidates who can perform the job immediately.

- Many entry-level positions are at smaller broadcast stations; consequently, workers often must change employers, and sometimes relocate, in order to advance.

## Nature of the Industry

*Goods and services.* The broadcasting industry consists of radio and television stations and networks that create content or acquire the right to broadcast pre-recorded television and radio programs. Networks transmit their signals from broadcasting studios via satellite signals to local stations or cable distributors. Broadcast signals then travel over cable television lines, satellite distribution systems, or the airwaves from a station's transmission tower to the antennas of televisions and radios. Anyone in the signal area with a radio or television can receive the programming. Cable and other pay television distributors provide television broadcasts to most Americans. Although cable television stations and networks are included in this statement, cable and other pay television distributors are classified in the telecommunications industry. (See the statement on telecommunications elsewhere in the *Career Guide*.)

*Industry organization.* Radio and television stations and networks broadcast a variety of programs, such as national and local news, talk shows, music programs, movies, other entertainment, and advertisements. Stations produce some of these programs, most notably news programs, in their own studios; however, much of the programming is produced outside the broadcasting industry. Revenue for commercial radio and television stations and networks comes from the sale of advertising time. The rates paid by advertisers depend on the size and characteristics (age, gender, and median income, among others) of a program's audience. Educational and noncommercial stations generate revenue primarily from donations by individuals, foundations, government, and corporations. These stations generally are owned and managed by public broadcasting organizations, religious institutions, or school systems.

Establishments that produce filmed or taped programming for radio and television stations and networks—but do not broadcast the programming—are in the motion picture industry. Many television networks own production companies that produce their many shows. (A statement on the motion picture and video industry appears elsewhere in the *Career Guide*.)

Seventy-three percent of workers within the broadcasting industry work in television and radio broadcasting, with 34 percent employed in radio and 39 percent in television.

Cable and other program distributors compensate local television stations and cable networks for rebroadcast rights. For popular cable networks and local television stations, distributors pay a fee per subscriber and/or agree to broadcast a less popular channel owned by the same network. Only 27 percent of workers within the industry work in cable broadcasting.

*Recent developments.* Changes in Federal Government regulation and communication technology have affected the broadcast industry. The Telecommunications Act of 1996 relaxed ownership restrictions, an action that has had a tremendous impact on the industry. Instead of owning only one radio station per market, companies can now purchase up to eight radio stations in a single large market. These changes have led to a large-scale consolidation of radio stations. In some areas, five FM and three AM radio stations are owned by the same company and share the same offices. The ownership of commercial radio stations is increasingly concentrated. In television, owners are permitted two stations in larger markets and are restricted in the total number of stations nationwide (in terms of percent of all viewers).

The U.S. Federal Communications Commission (FCC) is a proponent of digital television (DTV), a technology that uses digital signals to transmit television programs. Digital signals consist of pieces of simple electronic code that can carry more information than conventional analog signals. This code allows for the transmission of better quality sound and higher resolution pictures, often referred to as high-definition television (HDTV). FCC regulations require all stations to broadcast digital signals as well as conventional analog signals. The current goal of the FCC is to have all stations stop broadcasting analog signals by February of 2009. After the switch is complete, any viewers using an analog TV and over-the-air signals will need a converter box to change the signal from digital to analog. Most television stations are currently broadcasting digital signals in response to FCC regulations. Many digital cable systems and satellite television providers already broadcast all their channels digitally, with some channels in high definition.

The transition to HDTV broadcasting has also accelerated the conversion of other aspects of television production from analog to digital. Many stations have replaced specialized hardware with less specialized computers equipped with software that performs the same functions. Stations are beginning to switch away from tapes and instead use digital recording devices. This way footage can be more easily transferred to a computer for editing and storage. Many major network shows now use HDTV cameras and editing equipment as well.

The transition to digital broadcasting also is occurring in radio. Most stations already store music, edit clips, and broadcast their analog signals with digital equipment. Satellite radio services, which offer over 100 channels of digital sound, operate on a subscription basis, like pay television services. To compete, some radio stations are embedding a digital signal into their analog signals. With a specially equipped radio, these digital services offer better quality sound and display some limited text, such as the title of the song and the artist.

## Working Conditions

*Hours.* Many broadcast employees have erratic work schedules, sometimes having to work early in the morning or late at night. In 2006 an employee in broadcasting worked an average of 36 hours a week, with workers in television working more than those in radio. Only 9 percent of employees are part-time compared with 15 percent for all industries.

*Work Environment.* Most employees in this industry work in clean, comfortable surroundings in broadcast stations and studios. Some employees work in the production of shows and broadcasting while other employees work in advertising, sales, promotions, and marketing.

Television news teams made up of reporters, camera operators, and technicians travel in electronic news-gathering vehicles to various locations to cover news stories. Although such location work is exciting, some assignments, such as reporting on military conflicts or natural disasters, may be dangerous. These assignments may also require outdoor work under adverse weather conditions.

Camera operators working on such news teams must have the physical stamina to carry and set up their equipment. Broadcast technicians on electronic news-gathering trucks must ensure that the mobile unit's antenna is correctly positioned for optimal transmission quality and to prevent electrocution from power lines. Field service engineers work on outdoor transmitting equipment and may have to climb poles or antenna towers; their work can take place under a variety of weather conditions. Broadcast technicians who maintain and set up equipment may have to do heavy lifting. Technological changes have enabled camera operators also to fulfill the tasks of broadcast technicians, operating the transmission and editing equipment on a remote broadcasting truck. News operations, programming, and engineering employees work under a great deal of pressure in order to meet deadlines. As a result, these workers are likely to experience varied or erratic work schedules, often working on early morning or late evening news programs.

Sales workers may face stress meeting sales goals. Aside from sometimes erratic work schedules, management and administrative workers typically find themselves in an environment similar to any other office.

For many people, the excitement of working in broadcasting compensates for the demanding nature of the work. Although this industry is noted for its high pressure and long hours, the work is generally not hazardous.

## Employment

Broadcasting provided about 331,000 wage and salary jobs in 2006.

Although 36 percent of all establishments employed fewer than 5 people, most jobs were in large establishments; about 74 percent of all jobs were in establishments with at least 50 employees (chart). Broadcasting establishments are found throughout the country, but jobs in larger stations are concentrated in large cities.

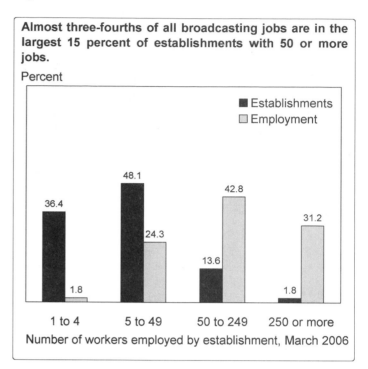

**Almost three-fourths of all broadcasting jobs are in the largest 15 percent of establishments with 50 or more jobs.**

Percent

- ■ Establishments
- □ Employment

Number of workers employed by establishment, March 2006

## Occupations in the Industry

Occupations at large broadcast stations and networks fall into five general categories: Program production, news-related, and technical, all of which fall under professional and related occupations; sales; and management. At small stations, jobs are less specialized, and employees often perform several functions. Although on-camera or on-air positions are the most familiar occupations in broadcasting, the majority of employment opportunities are behind the scenes (table 1).

*Program production occupations.* Most television programs are produced by the motion picture and video industry; actors, directors, and producers working on these prerecorded programs are not employed by the broadcasting industry. Employees in program production occupations at television and radio stations create programs such as news, talk, and music shows.

*Assistant producers* provide clerical support and background research; assist with the preparation of musical, written, and visual materials; and time productions to make sure that they do not run over schedule. Assistant producers also may operate cameras and other audio and video equipment.

*Video editors* select and assemble pre-recorded video to create a finished program, applying sound and special effects as necessary. Conventional editing requires assembling pieces of videotape in a linear fashion to create a finished product. The editor first assembles the beginning of the program and then works sequentially towards the end. Newer computerized editing allows an editor to electronically cut and paste video segments. This electronic technique is known as nonlinear editing because the editor is no longer restricted to working sequentially. A segment may be moved at any time to any location in the program.

*Producers* plan and develop live or taped productions, determining how the show will look and sound. They select the script, talent, sets, props, lighting, and other production elements. Producers also coordinate the activities of on-air personalities, production staff, and other personnel. *Web site* or *Internet producers*, a relatively new occupation in the broadcasting industry, plan and develop Internet sites that provide news updates, program schedules, and information about popular shows. These producers decide what will appear on the Internet sites, and design and maintain them.

*Announcers* read news items and provide other information, such as program schedules and station breaks for commercials or public service information. Many radio announcers, referred to as disc jockeys, play recorded music on radio stations. Disc jockeys may take requests from listeners; interview guests; and comment on the music, weather, or traffic. Most stations now have placed all of their advertisements, sound bites, and music on a computer, which is used to select and play or edit the items. Technological advances have simplified the monitoring and adjusting of the transmitter, leaving disc jockeys responsible for most of the tasks associated with keeping a station on the air. Traditional tapes and CDs are used only as backups in case of a computer failure. Announcers and disc jockeys need a good speaking voice; the latter also need a significant knowledge of music.

*Program directors* are in charge of on-air programming in radio stations. Program directors decide what type of music will be played, supervise on-air personnel, and often select the specific songs and the order in which they will be played. Considerable experience, usually as a disc jockey, is required, as well as a thorough knowledge of music.

*News-related occupations.* News, weather, and sports reports are important to many television stations because these reports attract a large audience and account for a large proportion of revenue. Many radio stations depend on up-to-the-minute news for a major share of their programming. Program production staffs, such as producers and announcers, also work on the production of news programs.

*Reporters* gather information from various sources, analyze and prepare news stories, and present information on the air. *Correspondents* report on news occurring in U.S. and foreign cities in which they are stationed. *Newswriters* write and edit news stories from information collected by reporters and correspondents. Newswriters may advance to positions as reporters or correspondents.

*Broadcast news analysts*, also known as news anchors, analyze, interpret, and broadcast news received from various sources. News anchors present news stories and introduce videotaped news or live transmissions from on-the-scene reporters. Newscasters at large stations may specialize in a particular field. Weathercasters, also called weather reporters, report current and forecasted weather conditions. They gather information from national satellite weather services, wire services, and local and regional weather bureaus. Some weathercasters are trained *atmospheric scientists* and can develop their own weather forecasts. Sportscasters, who are responsible for reporting sporting events, usually select, write, and deliver the sports news for each newscast.

*Assistant news directors* supervise the newsroom. They coordinate wire service reports, tape or film inserts, and stories from individual newswriters and reporters. *Assignment editors* assign stories to news teams, sending the teams on location if necessary.

*News directors* have overall responsibility for the news team made up of reporters, writers, editors, and newscasters as well as studio and mobile unit production crews. This senior administrative position entails responsibilities that include determining what events to cover, and how and when they will be presented in a news broadcast.

*Technical occupations.* Employees in these occupations operate and maintain the electronic equipment that records and transmits radio or television programs. The titles of some of these occupations use the terms "engineer," "technician," and "operator" interchangeably.

*Radio operators* manage equipment that regulates the signal strength, clarity, and range of sounds and colors of broadcasts. They also monitor and log outgoing signals and operate transmitters. *Audio and video equipment technicians* operate equipment to regulate the volume, sound quality, brightness, contrast, and visual quality of a broadcast. *Broadcast technicians* set up and maintain electronic broadcasting equipment. Their work can extend outside the studio, as when they set up portable transmitting equipment or maintain stationary towers.

*Television and video camera operators* set up and operate studio cameras, which are used in the television studio, and electronic news gathering cameras, which are mobile and used outside the studio when a news team is pursuing a story at another location. In both cases cameras are evolving from tape to disc-based formats. Camera operators need training in video production as well as some experience in television production.

*Master control engineers* ensure that all of the radio or television station's scheduled program elements, such as on-location feeds, prerecorded segments, and commercials, are smoothly transmitted. They also are responsible for ensuring that transmissions meet FCC requirements.

*Technical directors* direct the studio and control room technical staff during the production of a program. They need a thorough understanding of both the production and technical aspects of broadcasting. This knowledge often is acquired by working as a lighting director or camera operator, or as another type of broadcast worker.

*Network and computer systems administrators* and *network systems and data communications analysts* design, set up, and maintain systems of computer servers. These servers store recorded programs, advertisements, and news clips.

*Assistant chief engineers* oversee the day-to-day technical operations of the station. *Chief engineers* or *directors of engineering* are responsible for all of the station's technical facilities and services. These workers need a bachelors' degree in electrical engineering, technical training in broadcast engineering, and years of broadcast engineering experience.

*Sales and related occupations.* Most workers in this category are *advertising sales agents*, sometimes known as *account executives*. They sell advertising time to sponsors, advertising agencies, and other buyers. Sales representatives must have a thorough knowledge of the size and characteristics of their network's or station's audience, including income levels, gender, age, and consumption patterns.

Sales work has expanded beyond the traditional role of simply selling advertising to a wide range of marketing efforts. For instance, stations earn additional revenue by broadcasting from a business, such as a dance club. Businesses also sponsor concerts

**Table 1. Employment of wage and salary workers in broadcasting by occupation, 2006 and projected change, 2006-2016.**
(Employment in thousands)

| Occupation | Employment, 2006 | | Percent change, 2006-16 |
|---|---|---|---|
| | Number | Percent | |
| **All occupations** | 331 | 100.0 | 9.4 |
| | | | |
| **Management, business, and financial occupations** | 30 | 9.2 | 5.7 |
| Top executives | 9 | 2.7 | -3.6 |
| Marketing and sales managers | 5 | 1.4 | 7.5 |
| Administrative services managers | 1 | 0.3 | 8.2 |
| Financial managers | 1 | 0.4 | 8.8 |
| Engineering managers | 1 | 0.3 | 9.3 |
| Human resources, training, and labor relations specialists | 1 | 0.4 | 17.7 |
| Accountants and auditors | 3 | 0.9 | 8.5 |
| | | | |
| **Professional and related occupations** | 166 | 50.2 | 5.6 |
| Computer specialists | 9 | 2.8 | 24.4 |
| Engineers | 3 | 0.9 | 14.0 |
| Market research analysts | 2 | 0.6 | 10.3 |
| Multi-media artists and animators | 1 | 0.4 | 24.0 |
| Graphic designers | 2 | 0.7 | 9.9 |
| Actors, producers, and directors | 26 | 7.7 | 8.3 |
| Radio and television announcers | 38 | 11.5 | -9.7 |
| Broadcast news analysts | 6 | 1.8 | 6.1 |
| Reporters and correspondents | 10 | 2.9 | 9.0 |
| Public relations specialists | 4 | 1.3 | 5.8 |
| Editors | 4 | 1.2 | 8.2 |
| Writers and authors | 3 | 0.9 | 5.9 |
| Miscellaneous media and communications workers | 3 | 0.8 | 7.7 |
| Audio and video equipment technicians | 4 | 1.3 | 13.3 |
| Broadcast technicians | 25 | 7.4 | 12.2 |
| Sound engineering technicians | 3 | 0.8 | 6.2 |
| Camera operators, television, video, and motion picture | 8 | 2.5 | 6.6 |
| Film and video editors | 4 | 1.1 | 1.0 |
| | | | |
| **Sales and related occupations** | 46 | 13.9 | 20.9 |
| Advertising sales agents | 33 | 9.8 | 24.7 |
| Sales representatives, services, all other | 4 | 1.3 | 28.7 |
| Telemarketers | 2 | 0.6 | -6.8 |
| | | | |
| **Office and administrative support occupations** | 59 | 17.8 | 8.9 |
| First-line supervisors/managers of office and administrative support workers | 4 | 1.2 | 3.9 |
| Bookkeeping, accounting, and auditing clerks | 4 | 1.2 | 7.2 |
| Customer service representatives | 13 | 3.9 | 30.4 |
| Receptionists and information clerks | 4 | 1.1 | 5.8 |
| Dispatchers | 2 | 0.7 | 8.0 |
| Executive secretaries and administrative assistants | 7 | 2.0 | 9.9 |
| Secretaries, except legal, medical, and executive | 4 | 1.1 | -5.4 |
| Office clerks, general | 10 | 2.9 | 6.5 |
| | | | |
| **Installation, maintenance, and repair occupations** | 26 | 8.0 | 19.0 |
| Telecommunications equipment installers and repairers, except line installers | 5 | 1.6 | 19.9 |
| Telecommunications line installers and repairers | 14 | 4.2 | 20.2 |

Note: Columns may not add to totals due to omission of occupations with small employment

or other promotions that are organized by a station. In return for sponsorship, the businesses are usually allowed to set up a booth or post large signs at the event.

*Continuity directors* schedule and produce commercials. Continuity directors carefully schedule commercials, taking into account both the timeslot in which a commercial is to be played, as well as competing advertisements. For example, two car dealership advertisements should not be played during the same commercial break. Continuity directors also create and produce advertisements for clients who do not produce their own.

Large stations and networks generally have several workers who spend all of their time handling sales. *Sales worker supervisors*, who may handle a few large accounts personally, supervise these workers. In small stations, part-time sales personnel or announcers often handle sales responsibilities during hours when they are not on the air.

***Management occupations.*** *General managers* or *station managers* coordinate all radio and television station activities. In very small stations, the manager and a bookkeeper may handle all of the accounting, purchasing, hiring, and other routine office work. In larger stations, the general administrative staff includes business managers, accountants, lawyers, personnel workers, public relations workers, and others. These professionals are assisted by office and administrative support workers, such as secretaries, word processors, typists, and financial clerks.

## Training and Advancement
Professional, management, and sales occupations generally require a college degree; technical occupations often do not. It is easier to obtain employment and gain promotions with a degree, especially in larger, more competitive markets. Advanced schooling generally is required for supervisory positions—including technical occupations—having greater responsibility and higher salaries.

Employees in the radio and television broadcasting industry often find their first job in broadcast stations that serve smaller markets. Competition for positions in large metropolitan areas is stronger, and stations in these areas usually seek highly experienced personnel. Because many radio and television stations are small, workers in this industry often must change employers to advance. Relocation to other parts of the country frequently is necessary for advancement.

***News-related and program production occupations.*** Entry-level jobs in news or program production increasingly require a college degree and some broadcast experience. More than 1,500 institutions offer programs in communications, journalism, and related programs. As of 2006, there were 109 schools accredited by the Accrediting Council on Education in Journalism and Mass Communications. Some community colleges offer 2-year programs in broadcasting. Broadcast trade schools offer courses that last 6 months to a year and teach radio and television announcing, writing, and production.

Individuals pursuing a career in broadcasting often gain initial experience through work at college radio and television stations or through internships at professional stations. Although these positions usually are unpaid, they sometimes provide college credit or tuition. More importantly, they provide hands-on experience and a competitive edge when applying for jobs. In this highly competitive industry, broadcasters are less willing to provide on-the-job training, and instead seek candidates who can perform the job immediately.

***Technical occupations.*** Some technical positions require only a high school diploma. However, many broadcast stations seek individuals with training in broadcast technology, electronics, or engineering from a technical school, community college, or 4-year college. Due to the increase in the use of digital technology, an understanding of computer networks and software is especially important for potential employees. Supervisory technical positions and jobs in large stations generally require a college degree.

The Society of Broadcast Engineers (SBE) issues certification to technicians who pass a written examination. Several classes of certification are available, requiring increasing levels of experience and knowledge for eligibility. The Telecommunications Act of 1996 mandated that the FCC drop its licensing requirements for transmitter maintenance; SBE certification has filled the void left by the elimination of this license.

*Sales and related occupations.* These positions generally require a 4-year degree. As with the rest of the industry, it is easier to begin work in a small station or market and move on to a larger one as experience is acquired.

*Management occupations.* Station managers should have a 4-year degree and significant experience working at a television or radio station. The administrative staff is extremely varied and will require different amounts of education and training depending on the job.

## Outlook

Keen competition is expected for many jobs, particularly in large metropolitan areas, because of the large number of jobseekers attracted by the glamour of this industry.

*Employment change.* Employment in broadcasting is expected to increase about 9 percent over the 2006-16 period, more slowly than the 11 percent increase projected for all industries combined. Factors contributing to the relatively slow rate of growth include industry consolidation, introduction of new technologies, and competition from other media outlets. This will be tempered, however, by growth in the cable and subscription division of broadcasting.

Consolidation of individual broadcast stations into large networks, especially in radio, has increased as the result of relaxed ownership regulations. This trend will continue to limit employment growth as networks use workers more efficiently. For example, a network can run eight radio stations from one office, producing news programming at one station and then using the programming for broadcast from other stations, thus eliminating the need for multiple news staffs. Similarly, technical workers, upper level management, and marketing and advertising sales workers are pooled to work for several stations simultaneously. In the consolidation of the radio industry, several major companies have purchased numerous stations nationwide. These companies plan to achieve cost savings through consolidation and economies of scale, limiting employment growth.

The introduction of new technology also is slowing employment growth. Conventional broadcast equipment used to be relatively specialized; each piece of equipment served a separate function and required an operator with specialized knowledge. Newer computerized equipment often combines the functions of several older pieces of equipment and does not require specialized knowledge for operation. This reduces the need for certain types of workers, including those responsible for editing, recording, and creating graphics. However, the mandated switch to digital TV will create a need for other types of technical workers, such as broadcast technicians, in order for many stations to meet the FCC deadline.

Job growth also is being constrained by the increased use of radio and television programming created by services outside the broadcasting industry. These establishments provide prepared programming, including music, news, weather, sports, and professional announcer services. The services can easily be accessed through satellite connections and the Internet, reducing the need for program production and news staff at radio and television stations.

Radio broadcasters expect continued growth in revenues as national media companies that own multiple cable stations, network television stations, and/or radio stations use their combined marketing power to include radio advertising packages with other marketing deals. However, employment in this segment of the broadcast industry is not expected to grow. The new national scope of radio networks allows radio to more effectively sell advertising to large national advertisers to better compete with television networks. The major threats to the radio industry, especially smaller, marginal stations, are from car CD and MP3 players and from satellite radio, which functions like cable television with subscribers paying a monthly fee.

*Job prospects.* Keen competition is expected for many jobs, particularly in large metropolitan areas, because of the large number of jobseekers attracted by the glamour of this industry. Job prospects will be best for applicants with a college degree in broadcasting, journalism, or a related field as well as relevant work experience, such as work at college radio and television stations or internships at professional stations.

Technology in the broadcasting industry is rapidly changing and forcing workers to continually update their skills. Those with more computer training will increasingly have an advantage over others in the production and news-related occupations as well as in technical occupations. Workers with little job experience will find it easier to gain employment in smaller markets or at small stations in large markets. Large stations usually only hire people with more experience.

## Earnings

*Industry earnings.* Weekly earnings of nonsupervisory workers in broadcasting averaged $827 in 2006, higher than the average of $568 for all private industry. Earnings of broadcast personnel typically are highest in large metropolitan areas. Earnings in selected occupations in broadcasting for May 2006 appear in table 2.

*Benefits and union membership.* Workers in broadcasting generally receive standard benefits, including health insurance, paid vacation and sick leave, and pension plans, although often few benefits are available to part time workers and those who work for small employers.

About 8 percent of workers in broadcasting were union members or covered by union contracts, compared with 13 percent in all industries. The principal unions representing employees in broadcasting are the National Association of Broadcast Employees and Technicians (NABET), the International Brotherhood of Electrical Workers (IBEW), the International Alliance of Theatrical Stage Employees (IATSE), and the American Federation of Television and Radio Artists (AFTRA).

141

**Table 2. Median hourly earnings of the largest occupations in broadcasting, May 2006**

| Occupation | Broadcasting except internet | All industries |
|---|---|---|
| General and operations managers | $44.65 | $40.97 |
| Producers and directors | 23.78 | 27.07 |
| Advertising sales agents | 20.08 | 20.55 |
| Reporters and correspondents | 18.27 | 16.09 |
| Telecommunications line installers and repairers | 17.72 | 22.25 |
| Camera operators, television, video, and motion picture | 16.18 | 19.26 |
| Customer service representatives | 14.29 | 13.62 |
| Broadcast technicians | 13.44 | 14.75 |
| Office clerks, general | 12.11 | 11.40 |
| Radio and television announcers | 11.55 | 11.69 |

## Sources of Additional Information

For a list of schools with accredited programs in broadcast journalism, send a request to:

➤ Accrediting Council on Education in Journalism and Mass Communications, University of Kansas, School of Journalism, Stauffer-Flint Hall, Lawrence, KS 66045-7575. Internet: **http://www.ku.edu/~acejmc**

For career information and links to employment resources, contact:

➤ National Association of Broadcast Employees and Technicians, Communications Workers of America, 501 Third St. NW., Washington, DC 20001. Internet: **http://www.nabetcwa.org**

For information on broadcasting education and scholarship resources, contact:

➤ National Association of Broadcasters, Career Center, 1771 N St. NW., Washington, DC 20036. Internet: **http://www.nab.org**
➤ Society of Broadcast Engineers, 9102 N. Meridian Street, Suite 150, Indianapolis, IN 46260. Internet: **http://www.sbe.org**

Information on many occupations employed by the broadcasting industry, including the following, appears in the 2008-09 *Occupational Outlook Handbook*:

• Actors, producers, and directors
• Advertising, marketing, promotions, public relations, and sales managers
• Announcers
• Broadcast and sound engineering technicians and radio operators
• News analysts, reporters, and correspondents
• Television, video, and motion picture camera operators and editors
• Writers and editors

# Internet Service Providers, Web Search Portals, and Data Processing Services

(NAICS 518)

## SIGNIFICANT POINTS

- Rapid employment growth is expected in web search portals and data processing, hosting, and related services, while employment in internet service providers is expected to decline.

- About a third of all jobs are in computer occupations; another third are in office and administrative support occupations.

- About 46 percent of jobs are in California, Texas, Florida, Virginia, New York, and Georgia.

## Nature of the Industry

The ability to quickly transmit information over long distances has become an important part of modern life. The Internet has changed the way people find and use information to communicate, work, shop, learn, and live.

*Goods and service.* Internet service providers, Web search portals, and data processing services are the backbone of the Internet and provide the infrastructure for it to operate smoothly. By processing and storing data, and allowing people to access and sort these data, they facilitate the flow of information that has become vital to the economy.

*Industry organization.* Internet service providers (ISPs) directly connect people, businesses, and organizations to the Internet by routing data from one location to another. ISPs develop and maintain the physical, technical, and contractual connections and agreements needed for the internet to function. In order to maintain the necessary flow of data, ISPs use peering points—physical connections to the computer equipment of other ISPs—to share networks. These connections provide a nearly unlimited number of potential pathways through which information can travel.

In addition to forming the infrastructure of the Internet, service providers must also connect with clients. These clients may range from individual homes to large office buildings. To allow end users to access their networks, establishments in the industry may provide them with proprietary software, user identification names, e-mail addresses, or equipment. Like telephone or electric service, ISPs offer access to customers on a subscription basis. They may also provide related services beyond Internet access, such as Web hosting, Web page design, and consulting services related to networking software and hardware.

While ISPs connect clients to the Internet by routing data, the physical connections that carry the information to end users are often the wires or cables of telecommunications establishments (the telecommunications industry is covered in a separate section of the *Career Guide*).

Web search portals canvas the Web to create databases of web pages and their corresponding Internet addresses. These databases can then be searched by typing key words into a prompt on the search portal's Web site. These sites, commonly called "search engines," enable users to sort through the huge amount of information on the Internet quickly. In order to find as much information as possible, search engines automatically follow every link on a Web page, catalogue each new page found, and store their location along with text that can be searched at a later point. Because the Internet offers such a vast array of sites, advanced algorithms must be developed to rank the results of a search according to their relevance. Some Web search portals also offer additional services, such as news, e-mail, maps, and local business directories. The key distinction of Web search portals is that the information is gathered automatically from across the Web, rather than manually edited and entered into a predetermined directory.

Data processing, hosting, and related services are involved primarily in handling large amounts of data for businesses, organizations, and individuals. Data hosting often takes the form of Web hosting, in which Web site content is placed on a server that allows it to be accessed by users over the Internet. While establishments in this industry host Web sites, the content is typically produced by someone else and then made accessible through the Web hosting service. Other data hosting services allow clients to place electronic data, such as streaming music and video or company databases, onto servers that can be accessed directly through specialized computer programs. An additional service provided by this industry is to store old data for archival purposes with no Internet access to it.

Data processing covers a broad range of data services, including data entry, conversion, and analysis. Organizations with large quantities of data on paper may turn to data processing services to enter the data, either by hand or with optical scanners, into a computer database. Similarly, clients may want old data files or several databases converted to a single, more easily accessible format. Aside from converting data to another format, data processing services also produce reports that summarize the data for better analysis by their clients. While most data hosting companies sell subscription services, data processing services companies often work on projects of defined scope.

*Recent developments.* The Internet is constantly expanding and evolving, and so are the industries associated with it. Many firms in the telecommunications and broadcasting industries now provide internet service (the telecommunications and broadcasting industries are covered in separate sections of the *Career Guide*). Technology is constantly changing and companies also are frequently upgrading their existing services, since most new services involve relatively low additional cost, and offering new services can attract or retain customers.

## Working Conditions

*Hours.* In 2006, workers in Internet service providers, Web search portals, and data processing services averaged 37.3 hours per week, compared with 33.9 for all industries combined. While most worked a standard 40-hour workweek, about 20 percent worked 50 hours or more. About 8 percent worked part time, compared with 15 percent for all industries combined.

Jobs in many occupations in this industry have "non-traditional" schedules. Customer service representatives may work weekends, evenings, or holidays, and as a result, the occupation is well suited for flexible work schedules. At times, some computer specialists may be required to work unusual or long hours to fix problems or perform routine maintenance. In order to minimize the disruptive impact of scheduled maintenance and updates, many Internet service providers and data hosting services perform major work at night or on the weekends.

*Work Environment.* Most workers in this industry work in clean, quiet offices, and spend the majority of their time sitting at computer monitors. Even though major projects typically are tested before implementation, there may be periods of stress and long work hours before and after implementation deadlines. Similarly, long hours and intense work may be required to fix unexpected problems arising from system upgrades, viruses, or malicious attacks by computer hackers. The popularity of Web search portals has made them particularly attractive targets for hackers.

## Employment

In 2006, there were 383,000 wage and salary jobs in Internet service providers, Web search portals, and data processing services. Data processing, hosting, and related services accounted for about 68 percent of the jobs, with the other 32 percent in ISPs and Web search portals.

Due to the relatively low capital costs of equipment for data hosting services, and to the geographic distribution of ISPs, about 94 percent of establishments have fewer than 50 workers, and about 65 percent have fewer than 5 workers (chart). While this industry can be found in every State, employment is concentrated in a few areas. Just six States—California, Texas, Florida, Virginia, New York, and Georgia—account for about 46 percent of industry employment.

Compared to the rest of the economy, this industry has a relatively young work force. Rapid employment growth in the 1990's created job opportunities for young workers with the latest technical skills, and as a result, a large portion of the industry's workers are in the 25-to-44 age range (table 1).

**Table 1. Percent distribution of employment, by age group, 2006**

| Age group | Internet services providers, web search portals, and data processing services | All industries |
|---|---|---|
| Total | 100.0% | 100.0% |
| 16-19 | 1.1 | 4.3 |
| 20-24 | 10.1 | 9.6 |
| 25-34 | 26.8 | 21.5 |
| 35-44 | 31.8 | 23.9 |
| 45-54 | 19.6 | 23.6 |
| 55-64 | 7.8 | 13.4 |
| 65 and older | 2.2 | 3.7 |

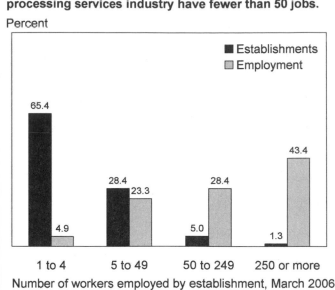

**Over 90 percent of establishments in the internet service providers, web search portals, and data processing services industry have fewer than 50 jobs.**

Percent

- Establishments
- Employment

1 to 4: 65.4 / 4.9
5 to 49: 28.4 / 23.3
50 to 249: 5.0 / 28.4
250 or more: 1.3 / 43.4

Number of workers employed by establishment, March 2006

## Occupations in the Industry

This industry employs a wide range of occupations. Professional and related occupations is the largest group and accounts for approximately 41 percent of wage and salary employment. The second largest group, office and administrative support occupations, makes up about 32 percent of jobs. An additional 17 percent of workers are in management, business, and financial occupations (table 2).

*Professional and related occupation.* Computer specialists develop and maintain the computer equipment and software programs that form the basis of the Internet. They make up the majority of professional and related occupations, and account for about 34 percent of the industry as a whole. *Computer programmers* write, test, and customize the detailed instructions, called programs or software, that computers follow to perform various functions such as connecting to the Internet or displaying a Web page. Using programming languages such as C++ or Java, they break down tasks into a logical series of simple commands for the computer to implement.

*Computer software engineers* analyze user needs to formulate software specifications, and then design, develop, test, and evaluate programs to meet these requirements. While computer software engineers must possess strong programming skills, they generally focus on developing programs, which are then coded by computer programmers.

*Computer systems analysts* develop customized computer systems and networks for clients. They work with organizations to solve problems by designing or tailoring systems to meet unique requirements and then implementing these systems. By customizing systems to specific tasks, they help their clients maximize the benefit from investment in hardware, software, and other resources.

*Computer support specialists* provide technical assistance to users who experience computer problems. They may provide support either to customers or to other employees within their own organization. Using automated diagnostic programs and their own technical knowledge, they analyze and solve problems with hardware, software, and systems. In this industry, they connect with users primarily through telephone calls and e-mail messages.

*Office and administrative support occupations.* Office and administrative support occupations are involved primarily with business process operations such as billing, recordkeeping, and customer service. Financial clerks, information and record clerks, and data entry keyers account for about 17 percent of industry employment. *Financial clerks* keep track of money, recording all amounts coming into or leaving a company. They perform a wide variety of financial recordkeeping duties, from preparing bills and invoices to computing wages for payroll records.

*Information and record clerks* process a variety of records, ranging from payrolls to information on the receipt of goods. *Customer service representatives*, which are included in information and record clerks, respond to customer inquiries and complaints. Some customer service representatives handle general questions and complaints, whereas others specialize in a particular area. In ISPs they help customers set up or discontinue Internet service, but their primary function is not sales. They generally connect with customers by telephone or e-mail.

*Data entry keyers* input lists of items, numbers, or other data into computers using keyboards or scanners. They also may manipulate existing data, edit current information, or proofread new entries to a database for accuracy. Nearly all data entry keyers in this industry are employed in data processing, hosting, and related services; relatively few work for ISPs or Web search portals.

*Management, business, and financial occupations.* Computer and information systems managers plan, coordinate, and direct the activities of computer specialists to ensure that the internal and external computer systems meet the needs of users or clients. Because the industry is primarily engaged in facilitating data transmission over the Internet, these managers work closely with top executives or clients to set schedules for implementing Web sites, performing system maintenance, or installing new hardware and software.

## Training and Advancement
The occupations in Internet service providers, Web search portals, and data processing services require a variety of educational levels and specialized training. About 61 percent of workers held college degrees in 2006, while 20 percent had some college education and another 18 percent held high school diplomas. Entry-level computer and management positions in the industry, however, often require a bachelor's degree in a computer-related field.

*Professional and related occupations.* Educational requirements have been less rigid for computer specialists than for most other occupations. In the early days of the Internet and Web, many employers struggled to meet ballooning demand for technical workers. However, the growing number of qualified workers and the reduction of demand for computer specialists in recent years have led employers to look for more education and experience when hiring. While employers may seek workers with high-demand skills regardless of formal training in the short term, such conditions, if they do arise, are unlikely to last long. The general trend has been toward greater demand for

**Table 2. Employment of wage and salary workers in internet services providers, web search portals, and data processing services by occupation, 2006 and projected change, 2006-2016.**
(Employment in thousands)

| Occupation | Employment, 2006 | | Percent change, 2006-16 |
|---|---|---|---|
| | Number | Percent | |
| **All occupations** | 383 | 100.0 | 14.0 |
| **Management, business, and financial occupations** | 65 | 17.1 | 15.2 |
| Top executives | 9 | 2.4 | 2.5 |
| Marketing and sales managers | 5 | 1.3 | 12.2 |
| Computer and information systems managers | 12 | 3.2 | 15.5 |
| Financial managers | 3 | 0.8 | 18.5 |
| Human resources, training, and labor relations specialists | 4 | 1.0 | 17.5 |
| Management analysts | 7 | 1.8 | 23.8 |
| Accountants and auditors | 5 | 1.4 | 15.6 |
| Financial analysts | 2 | 0.6 | 27.5 |
| **Professional and related occupations** | 156 | 40.8 | 20.1 |
| Computer programmers | 15 | 3.9 | -7.4 |
| Computer software engineers, applications | 20 | 5.2 | 35.6 |
| Computer software engineers, systems software | 24 | 6.2 | 26.8 |
| Computer support specialists | 20 | 5.3 | 0.4 |
| Computer systems analysts | 20 | 5.2 | 36.3 |
| Database administrators | 4 | 1.1 | 27.1 |
| Network and computer systems administrators | 13 | 3.4 | 21.2 |
| Network systems and data communications analysts | 10 | 2.6 | 39.7 |
| Computer specialists, all other | 4 | 1.1 | 18.2 |
| Operations research analysts | 3 | 0.8 | 12.8 |
| Engineers | 4 | 0.9 | 14.1 |
| Industrial engineering technicians | 3 | 0.8 | 45.4 |
| Market and survey researchers | 4 | 1.0 | -9.4 |
| Writers and editors | 3 | 0.7 | -2.2 |
| **Sales and related occupations** | 26 | 6.9 | 0.1 |
| Sales representatives, services | 13 | 3.4 | 8.7 |
| Sales representatives, wholesale and manufacturing | 7 | 1.7 | 7.2 |
| **Office and administrative support occupations** | 121 | 31.5 | 9.2 |
| First-line supervisors/managers of office and administrative support workers | 7 | 1.9 | 12.0 |
| Bookkeeping, accounting, and auditing clerks | 7 | 1.8 | 15.3 |
| Customer service representatives | 24 | 6.3 | 17.0 |
| Secretaries and administrative assistants | 8 | 2.1 | 12.0 |
| Computer operators | 8 | 2.0 | -15.4 |
| Data entry keyers | 19 | 5.0 | 5.6 |
| Mail clerks and mail machine operators, except postal service | 6 | 1.5 | -1.8 |
| Office clerks, general | 12 | 3.0 | 21.7 |
| Office machine operators, except computer | 8 | 2.1 | 7.2 |
| **Installation, maintenance, and repair occupations** | 7 | 2.0 | 3.2 |
| Computer, automated teller, and office machine repairers | 2 | 0.5 | 19.3 |
| Telecommunications equipment installers and repairers, except line installers | 3 | 0.7 | -7.3 |

Note: Columns may not add to totals due to omission of occupations with small employment

145

workers with computer-related college degrees and more experience. Those with bachelor's degrees in computer-related fields also enjoy greater opportunities for advancement to managerial positions.

Computer programmers typically hold a bachelor's degree in computer science, mathematics, or information systems. Those without bachelor's degrees or degrees in other fields generally take additional courses in computer programming methods and languages. The needs of employers vary extensively and change over time, so a 2-year degree or certificate, coupled with the right programming knowledge, may be sufficient for some positions. Entry-level programmers usually start by updating existing code, then advance to more difficult programming. Computer programmers with general business experience may become systems analysts.

Computer software engineers usually have at least a bachelor's degree in computer science, software engineering, or computer information systems. Educational requirements vary, however, with some workers holding advanced degrees in technical fields, and others simply earning certifications offered by systems software vendors. Experience working with a broad range of computer systems is valued highly by employers. Because computer software engineers often work closely with computer programmers, communications skills are important in this occupation.

Computer systems analysts and database administrators typically hold a bachelor's degree in computer science, information science, or management information systems (MIS). Many computer systems analysts hold advanced degrees in business administration or technical fields, and becoming certified in various types of systems software may provide a competitive advantage. Relevant work experience also is very important and can be obtained by participating in internship or co-op programs, or by working in related occupations. Systems analysts may begin working on one aspect of a system, and with experience advance to more complex systems.

Computer support specialists usually need only an associate degree in a computer-related field and experience with computers. They also must possess strong problem-solving, analytical, and communication skills, as troubleshooting and helping others are their main job functions. Computer support specialists may advance by developing expertise in a particular area, with job promotions typically depending more on performance than on formal education. Some become applications developers, using their troubleshooting experience to design products to be more reliable and user-friendly.

As advances in the computer field continue, all computer specialists must keep abreast of developing technologies to remain competitive. Obtaining technical certification is a way in which workers can demonstrate their competency to employers. Certification can be obtained voluntarily through many organizations, and many vendors now offer certification to professionals who work with their products.

*Office and administrative support occupations.* Office and administrative support occupations generally require only a high school diploma, but this may vary by occupation and firm. Although some positions may require previous experience in the occupation or industry, many of these jobs are entry level. Some workers in these occupations are college graduates who accept entry-level clerical positions to get into the industry or into a particular company. Most companies fill office and administrative support supervisory and managerial positions by promoting

individuals within their organization, so those who acquire additional skills, experience, and training improve their opportunities for advancement. However, a college degree often is required for advancement to management ranks.

Customer service representatives typically need only a high school diploma or its equivalent. Because they constantly interact with customers, good interpersonal skills are essential for success in this occupation. Both verbal and written communications skills are important, as these workers may address inquiries by telephone, in person, through e-mail, or by letter. Customer service representatives represent the companies for which they work, so employers place great emphasis on a friendly and professional demeanor, as well as the ability to remain patient when dealing with difficult or angry customers. Nearly all employers provide training in basic customer service skills and company-specific services, policies, and systems. Strong problem-solving abilities and basic computer knowledge also are important.

Data entry keyers typically hold a high school diploma or its equivalent and usually are hired based on their typing speed. Familiarity with basic computer operations and with word processing, spreadsheet, and database software is highly desirable. The skills required by data entry keyers can be developed by taking high school, community college, or business school courses; by working for temporary help agencies; and by making use of self-teaching aids. Attention to detail is important in this occupation, as are spelling, punctuation, and grammar skills.

Financial, information and record, and general office clerks commonly need at least a high school diploma. For financial clerks, particularly those working in bookkeeping and accounting, an associate degree often is required. While basic computer knowledge and general office skills are required for all clerks, good interpersonal skills are particularly important for those whose work involves frequent interaction with the public. Nearly all financial, information and record, and general office clerks receive some on-the-job training, and learn company procedures under the guidance of a supervisor or other senior worker. With experience and training, clerks may be promoted to supervisory or specialist positions.

*Management, business, and financial occupations.* Computer and information systems managers typically have a bachelor's degree and several years of experience in computer occupations, particularly as computer systems analysts. However, many employers prefer those with advanced degrees in business administration (MBA) or information systems management. In addition to technical knowledge, they must possess strong business and communication skills.

## Outlook

While growth rates will vary by sector, employment is projected to increase by 14 percent for the industry as a whole. Job growth will lead to excellent opportunities in data processing, hosting, and related services and in web search portals, but declines will create competition for positions in Internet service providers.

*Employment change.* Wage and salary employment in Internet service providers, Web search portals, and data processing services is expected to increase by 14 percent between 2006 and 2016, faster than the 11 percent projected for all industries combined. This growth will vary by industry sector, with data processing, hosting, and related services growing at 33 percent, and Internet service providers and Web search portals declining by 27 percent.

146

As the information revolution advances, the amount of data in use continues to grow. Companies will turn to data processing, hosting, and related services firms to organize, store, analyze, and interpret this data. In addition, the number of Web sites in operation will grow as the number of Internet users continues to increase. Many businesses and individuals wish to establish web sites, but do not have the necessary hardware, so they will use the services of data hosting firms. The need for increased information security also will require advanced technical solutions, resulting in further job growth within the industry.

Employment in Internet services providers will decline despite growth in the number of web sites online and an increase in the number of internet users. As the industry continues to consolidate, and a small number of national providers begin to service a larger portion of Internet users, fewer workers will be needed to meet the needs of the industry. In addition, telephone and cable companies offer broadband services to an increasing number of consumers, so more of the workers associated with providing internet access will be classified in either the telecommunications or broadcasting industries (see sections on theses industries elsewhere in the *Career Guide*).

Employment of Web search portals, conversely, should increase rapidly. Growth will result from consumers demand for more efficient search functions, and the expanding array of services continued to be offered by Web search portals. This growth will have little impact on the industry as a whole, however, as Web search portals represent only a small portion of employment.

***Job prospects.*** Job prospects should be excellent in data processing, hosting, and related services and in web search portals. Job openings will result from rapid employment growth, and from the need to replace workers who leave the industry. Prospects will be best for computer specialists such as computer software engineers, computer systems analysts, and network and computer system administrators. Applicants for jobs in Internet service providers should face competition as employment declines will limit the number of openings.

## Earnings

***Industry earnings.*** In 2006, nonsupervisory workers in Internet service providers, Web search portals, and data processing services earned $809 per week on average, compared with an average of $568 for all industries combined. Workers in Internet service providers and Web search portals averaged $914, the highest earnings in this industry. Those in data processing, hosting, and related services earned less, an average of $763 per week.

Like those of the entire workforce, earnings also varied considerably by occupation, with workers in professional occupations earning more than those in office and administrative support occupations. For example, customer service representatives and computer software engineers, systems software—the two largest occupations in the industry—had median hourly earnings of $14.15 and $39.88, respectively. As in other industries, managers had higher earnings because they have greater responsibilities and are more experienced than their staffs. Median

**Table 3. Median hourly earnings of the largest occupations in internet services providers, web search portals, and data processing services, May 2006**

| Occupation | Internet services providers, web search portals, and data processing services | All industries |
|---|---|---|
| Computer and information systems managers | $51.28 | $48.84 |
| Computer software engineers, systems software | 39.88 | 41.04 |
| Computer software engineers, applications | 37.86 | 38.36 |
| Computer systems analysts | 34.43 | 33.54 |
| Computer programmers | 30.74 | 31.50 |
| Network and computer systems administrators | 30.25 | 29.87 |
| Sales representatives, services, all other | 29.00 | 23.12 |
| Computer support specialists | 18.74 | 19.94 |
| Customer service representatives | 14.15 | 13.62 |
| Data entry keyers | 10.92 | 11.87 |

hourly earnings for specific occupations within the industry are shown in table 3.

***Benefits and union membership.*** Workers in the Internet service providers, Web search portals, and data processing services industry generally receive paid sick and vacation leave and health insurance, and many employers contribute to pension plans and life insurance.

Unionization is rare in the industry. In 2006 virtually no workers were union members or covered by union contracts, compared with 13 percent of workers throughout private industry.

## Sources of Additional Information

Further information about computer careers is available from:
> Association for Computing Machinery, 2 Penn Plaza, Suite 701, New York, NY 10121-0701. Internet: **http://www.acm.org**
> National Workforce Center for Emerging Technologies, 3000 Landerholm Circle S.E., Bellevue, WA 98007. Internet: **http://www.nwcet.org**
> Institute of Electrical and Electronics Engineers Computer Society, Headquarters Office, 1730 Massachusetts Ave. NW., Washington, DC 20036-1992. Internet: **http://www.computer.org**
> University of Washington Computer Science and Engineering Department, AC101 Paul G. Allen Center, Box 352350, 185 Stevens Way, Seattle, WA 98195-2350. Internet: **http://www.cs.washington.edu/WhyCSE/**

Information on the following occupations can be found in the 2008-09 edition of the *Occupational Outlook Handbook*:
- Computer and information systems managers
- Computer programmers
- Computer software engineers
- Computer support specialists and systems administrators
- Computer systems analysts
- Customer service representatives
- Data entry and information processing workers
- Office clerks, general

# Motion Picture and Video Industries

(NAICS 5121)

## SIGNIFICANT POINTS

- Keen competition is expected for the more glamorous, high-paying jobs—writers, actors, producers, and directors—but better job prospects are expected for multimedia artists and animators, film and video editors, and others skilled in digital filming and computer-generated imaging.

- Although many films are shot on location, employment is centered in several major cities, particularly New York and Los Angeles.

- Many workers have formal training, but experience, talent, creativity, and professionalism are the factors that are most important in getting many jobs in this industry.

## Nature of the Industry

*Goods and services.* The U.S. motion picture industry produces much of the world's feature films and most of its recorded television programs. The industry is dominated by several large studios, based mostly in Hollywood. However, with the increasing popularity and worldwide availability of cable television, digital video recorders, computer graphics and editing software, and the Internet, many small and medium-sized independent filmmaking companies have sprung up to fill the growing demand.

*Industry organization.* In addition to producing feature films and filmed television programs, the industry produces made-for-television movies, music videos, and commercials. Establishments engaged primarily in operating motion picture theaters and exhibiting motion pictures or videos at film festivals also are included in this industry. Other establishments provide postproduction services to the motion picture industry, such as editing, film and tape transfers, titling and subtitling, credits, closed captioning, computer-produced graphics, and animation and special effects.

Some motion picture and video companies produce films for limited, or specialized, audiences. Among these films are documentaries, which use film clips and interviews to chronicle actual events with real people, and educational films ranging from "do-it-yourself" projects to exercise films. In addition, the industry produces business, industrial, and government films that promote an organization's image, provide information on its activities or products, or aid in fundraising or worker training. Some of these films are short enough to release to the public through the Internet; many offer an excellent training ground for beginning filmmakers.

*Recent developments.* Making a movie can be a difficult, yet rewarding, experience. However, it is also a very risky one. Although thousands of movies are produced each year, only a small number of them account for most box office receipts. Indeed, most films do not make a full return on their investment from domestic box office revenues, so filmmakers rely on profits from other markets, such as broadcast and cable television, DVD sales and rentals, and foreign distribution. In fact, major film companies are receiving a growing portion of their revenue from abroad. These cost pressures have reduced the number of film production companies to the current six major studios, which produce most of the filmed television programs, as well as the movies released nationally. Smaller, independent filmmakers often find it difficult to finance new productions and pay for a film's distribution, because they must compete with large motion picture production companies for talent and available movie screens. However, digital technology is lowering production costs for some small-budget films, enabling more independents to succeed in getting their films released nationally.

Although studios and other production companies are responsible for financing, producing, publicizing, and distributing a film or program, the actual making of the film often is done by hundreds of small businesses and independent contractors hired by the studios on an as-needed basis. These companies provide a wide range of services, such as equipment rental, lighting, special effects, set construction, and costume design, as well as much of the creative and technical talent that go into producing a film. The industry also contracts with a large number of workers in other industries that supply support services to the crews while they are filming, such as truck drivers, caterers, electricians, and makeup artists. Many of these workers, particularly those in Los Angeles, depend on the motion picture industry for their livelihood.

Most motion pictures are still made on film. However, digital technology and computer-generated imaging are rapidly making inroads and are expected to transform the industry. Making changes to a picture is much easier using digital techniques. Backgrounds can be inserted after the actors perform on a sound stage, or locations can be digitally modified to reflect the script. Even actors can be created digitally. Independent filmmakers will continue to benefit from this technology, as reduced costs improve their ability to compete with the major studios.

Digital technology also makes it possible to distribute movies to theaters through the use of satellites or fiber-optic cable. Bulky metal film canisters can be replaced by easy-to-transport hard-drives, although relatively few theaters are capable of receiving and screening movies in that manner now. In the future, however, more theaters will be capable of projecting films digitally and the costly process of producing and distributing films will be sharply reduced.

## Working Conditions

*Hours.* Unusual hours are normal in this industry, with 42 percent of workers having part-time or variable schedules. In 2006, workers averaged 29 hours per week.

*Work Environment.* Most individuals in this industry work in clean, comfortable surroundings. Filming outside the studio or on location, however, may require working in adverse weather, and under unpleasant and sometimes dangerous conditions. Actors, producers, directors, cinematographers, and camera operators also need stamina to withstand the heat of studio and stage lights, long and irregular hours, and travel.

Directors and producers often work under stress as they try to meet schedules, stay within budget, and resolve personnel and production problems. Actors, producers, directors, cinematographers, and camera operators face the anxiety of rejection and intermittent employment. Writers and editors must deal with criticism and demands to restructure and rewrite their work many times until the producer and director are finally satisfied. All writers must be able to withstand such criticism and disappointment, but freelance writers work under the added pressure of always looking for new jobs. In spite of these difficulties, many people find that the glamour and excitement of filmmaking more than compensate for the frequently demanding and uncertain nature of careers in motion pictures.

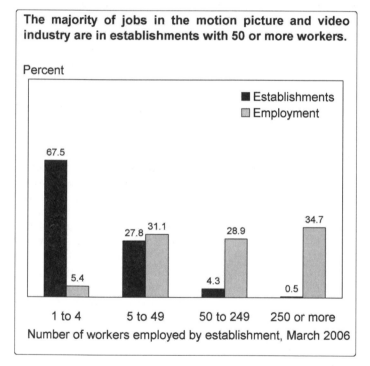

**The majority of jobs in the motion picture and video industry are in establishments with 50 or more workers.**

Percent

Number of workers employed by establishment, March 2006

## Employment

In 2006, there were about 357,000 wage and salary jobs in the motion picture and video industries. Most of the workers were in motion picture and video production. They are involved in casting, acting, directing, editing, film processing, and motion picture and videotape reproduction. Ten percent of people in the film industry were self-employed, selling their services to anyone who needs them and often working on productions for many different companies during the year.

Although six major studios produce most of the motion pictures released in the United States, many small companies are used as contractors throughout the process. Most motion picture and video establishments employ fewer than 5 workers (chart 1).

Many additional individuals work in the motion picture and video industries on a freelance, contract, or part-time basis, but accurate statistics on their numbers are not available. Competition for these jobs is intense, and many people are unable to earn a living solely from freelance work.

The workforce of this industry is much younger than most, with 57 percent of employees being 34 or younger. In addition 19 percent of employees are aged 16 to 20 compared with only 4 percent of employees in that age group in all industries (table 1).

Employment in the production of motion pictures and other films for television is centered in Los Angeles and New York City. In addition, many films are shot on location throughout the United States and abroad.

**Table 1. Percent distribution of employment, by age group, 2006**

| Age group | Motion picture and video industries | All industries |
|---|---|---|
| **Total** | 100.0% | 100.0% |
| 16-19 | 19.0 | 4.3 |
| 20-24 | 12.5 | 9.6 |
| 25-34 | 25.5 | 21.5 |
| 35-44 | 19.2 | 23.9 |
| 45-54 | 5.5 | 23.6 |
| 55-64 | 6.5 | 13.4 |
| 65 and older | 1.9 | 3.7 |

## Occupations in the Industry

The length of the credits at the end of most feature films and television programs gives an idea of the variety of workers involved in producing and distributing films. The motion picture industry employs workers in every major occupational group. Professional and related occupations account for about 4 in 10 salaried jobs in the industry. Approximately 3 in 10 salaried workers hold jobs in service occupations (table 2).

Jobs in the industry can be broadly classified according to the three phases of filmmaking: Preproduction, production, and postproduction. Preproduction is the planning phase, which includes budgeting, casting, finding the right location, set and costume design and construction, and scheduling. Production is the actual making of the film. The number of people involved in the production phase can vary from a few, for a documentary film, to hundreds, for a feature film. It is during this phase that the actual filming is done. Postproduction activities take place in editing rooms and recording studios, where the film is shaped into its final form.

Some individuals work in all three phases. *Producers,* for example, are involved in every phase, from beginning to end. These workers look for ideas that they believe can be turned into lucrative film projects or television shows. They may see many films, read hundreds of manuscripts, and maintain numerous contacts with literary agents and publishers. Producers are also responsible for all of the financial aspects of a film, including finding financing for its production. The producer works closely with the director on the selection of the script, the principal members of the cast, and the filming locations, because these decisions greatly affect the cost of a film. Once financing is obtained, the producer works out a detailed budget and sees to it that the production costs stay within that budget. In a large production, the producer also works closely with *production managers,* who are

**Table 2. Employment of wage and salary workers in motion picture and video industries by occupation, 2006 and projected change, 2006-2016.**

(Employment in thousands)

| Occupation | Employment, 2006 Number | Employment, 2006 Percent | Percent change, 2006-16 |
|---|---|---|---|
| **All occupations** | 357 | 100.0 | 10.9 |
| **Management, business, and financial occupations** | 20 | 5.5 | 13.0 |
| Top executives | 6 | 1.8 | 1.5 |
| Advertising, marketing, promotions, public relations, and sales managers | 2 | 0.7 | 15.2 |
| Financial managers | 1 | 0.3 | 18.1 |
| Accountants and auditors | 3 | 0.8 | 17.9 |
| **Professional and related occupations** | 148 | 41.4 | 19.4 |
| Computer specialists | 5 | 1.4 | 22.8 |
| Art directors | 1 | 0.4 | 18.4 |
| Multi-media artists and animators | 7 | 1.8 | 47.4 |
| Graphic designers | 3 | 0.9 | 18.3 |
| Actors | 19 | 5.4 | 15.3 |
| Producers and directors | 18 | 5.0 | 18.3 |
| Entertainers and performers, sports and related workers, all other | 44 | 12.2 | 18.4 |
| Editors | 4 | 1.0 | 18.4 |
| Writers and authors | 2 | 0.5 | 16.3 |
| Audio and video equipment technicians | 7 | 2.1 | 18.3 |
| Broadcast technicians | 2 | 0.5 | 18.4 |
| Sound engineering technicians | 5 | 1.3 | 18.4 |
| Camera operators, television, video, and motion picture | 9 | 2.6 | 18.3 |
| Film and video editors | 11 | 3.0 | 18.4 |
| **Service occupations** | 106 | 29.7 | 1.6 |
| Combined food preparation and serving workers, including fast food | 7 | 1.9 | 13.3 |
| Counter attendants, cafeteria, food concession, and coffee shop | 34 | 9.4 | 2.8 |
| Janitors and cleaners, except maids and housekeeping cleaners | 5 | 1.3 | 9.4 |
| First-line supervisors/managers of personal service workers | 5 | 1.4 | 2.8 |
| Motion picture projectionists | 10 | 2.8 | -9.4 |
| Ushers, lobby attendants, and ticket takers | 37 | 10.3 | -0.9 |
| **Sales and related occupations** | 35 | 9.9 | 3.4 |
| Cashiers, except gaming | 22 | 6.3 | -7.4 |
| Advertising sales agents | 4 | 1.1 | 42.0 |
| **Office and administrative support occupations** | 34 | 9.6 | 11.4 |
| Bookkeeping, accounting, and auditing clerks | 3 | 1.0 | 15.6 |
| Customer service representatives | 5 | 1.5 | 29.7 |
| File clerks | 2 | 0.6 | -40.8 |
| Receptionists and information clerks | 2 | 0.6 | 17.0 |
| Production, planning, and expediting clerks | 2 | 0.7 | 18.4 |
| Shipping, receiving, and traffic clerks | 2 | 0.6 | 13.9 |
| Secretaries and administrative assistants | 7 | 1.9 | 13.3 |
| Office clerks, general | 5 | 1.3 | 14.2 |
| **Production occupations** | 3 | 1.0 | -6.1 |
| Photographic process workers and processing machine operators | 1 | 0.4 | -43.1 |
| **Transportation and material moving occupations** | 8 | 2.2 | 7.0 |
| Laborers and freight, stock, and material movers, hand | 6 | 1.6 | 6.6 |

Note: Columns may not add to totals due to omission of occupations with small employment

in charge of crews, travel, casting, and equipment. For television shows, much of this process requires adhering to especially tight recording deadlines.

*Directors* interpret the script and develop its thematic and visual images for the film. They also are involved in every stage of production. They may supervise hundreds of people, from screenwriters to costume, lighting, and set designers. Directors are in charge of all technical and artistic aspects of the film or television show. They conduct auditions and rehearsals and approve the location, scenery, costumes, choreography, and music. In short, they direct the entire cast and crew during shooting. *Assistant directors* (or *first and second assistants*) help them with such details as handling the transportation of equipment, arranging for food and accommodations, and hiring performers who appear in the film, but have no lines. Some directors assume multiple roles, such as *director-producer* or *writer-producer-director*. Successful directors must know how to hire the right people and create effective teams.

***Preproduction occupations.*** Before a film or a television program moves into the production phase, it begins with an idea. Anyone can pitch an idea to a studio executive or an independent producer, but usually an agent representing an actor, writer, or director will have the best opportunity—the best access—to someone who can approve a project.

Once a project is approved, whether developed from an original idea or taken from an existing literary work, *screenwriters* will be brought in to turn that idea into a screenplay or a script for a television pilot (a sample episode of a proposed television series). Screenwriters work closely with producers and directors. Sometimes they prepare a treatment, a synopsis of the story and how a few scenes will play out, but no dialogue. Before filming or taping can begin, screenwriters will prepare a "shooting script," which has instructions pertaining to shots, camera angles, and lighting. Frequently, screenwriters make changes to reflect the directors' and producers' ideas and desires. The work, therefore, requires not only creativity, but also an ability to collaborate with others, and to write and rewrite many versions of a script under pressure. Although the work of feature film screenwriters generally ends when shooting begins, writing for a television series usually continues throughout the television season with a new script required for each episode.

*Art directors* design the physical environment of the film or television set to create the mood called for by the script. Television art directors may design elaborate sets for use in situation comedies or commercials. They supervise many different people, including *illustrators*, *scenic designers*, *model makers*, *carpenters*, *painters*, *electricians*, *laborers*, *set decorators*, *costume designers*, and *makeup and hairstyling artists*. These positions can provide an entry into the motion picture industry. Many people begin their careers in such jobs in live theater productions and then move back and forth between the stage, film, and television.

***Production occupations.*** *Actors* entertain and communicate with the audience through their interpretation of dramatic or comedic roles. Only a small number achieve recognition in motion pictures or television. Many are cast in supporting roles or as walk-ons. Some start as background performers with no lines to deliver. Also called "extras," these are the people in the background—crowds on the street, workers in offices, or dancers at a ball. Others perform stunts, such as driving cars in chase scenes or falling from high places. Although a few actors find parts in feature films straight out of drama school, most support themselves by working for many years outside of the industry. Most acting jobs are found through an agent, who finds auditions that may lead to acting assignments.

Cinematographers, camera operators, and gaffers work together to capture the scenes in the script on film. *Cinematographers* compose the film shots to reflect the mood the director wishes to create. They do not usually operate the camera; instead, they plan and coordinate the actual filming. *Camera operators* handle all camera movements and perform the actual shooting. *Assistant camera operators* check the equipment, load and position cameras, run the film to a lab or darkroom, and take care of the equipment. *Commercial camera operators* specialize in shooting commercials. This experience translates easily into filming documentaries or working on smaller-budget independent films. *Gaffers*, or lighting technicians, set up the different kinds of lighting needed for filming. They work for the *director of photography*, who plans all lighting needs.

*Sound engineering technicians, film recordists,* and *boom operators* record dialogue, sounds, music, and special effects during the filming. Sound engineering technicians are the "ears" of the film, supervising all sound generated during filming. They select microphones and the level of sound from mixers and synthesizers to assure the best sound quality. Recordists help to set up the equipment and are in charge of the individual tape recorders. Boom operators handle long booms with microphones that are moved from one area of the set to another. One person often performs many of these functions because more and more filming is done on location and the equipment has become compact, lighter, and simpler to operate.

*Multimedia artists and animators* create the movie "magic." Through their imagination, creativity, and skill, they can create anything required by the script, from talking animals to flaming office buildings and earthquakes. They not only need a good imagination, but also must be equal parts carpenter, plumber, electrician, and electronics expert. These workers must be familiar with many ways of achieving a desired special effect, because each job requires different skills. Computer skills are very important in this field, as many areas of television and film production, including animation and visual effects, now rely heavily on computer technology. Although there was a time when elaborate computer animation was restricted to blockbuster movies, much of the three-dimensional work being generated today occurs in small to mid-size companies. Some specialists create "synthespians"—realistic digital characters. These digital images are often used when a stunt or scene is too dangerous for an actor.

Many individuals get their start in the industry by running errands, moving objects on the set, controlling traffic, and helping with props. *Production assistants* and *grips* (stagehands) often work in this way.

***Postproduction occupations.*** One of the most important tasks in filmmaking and television production is editing. After a film is shot and processed, *film and video editors* study footage, select the best shots, and assemble them in the most effective way. Their goal is to create dramatic continuity and the right pace for the desired mood. They must have a good eye and understand the subject of the film and the director's intentions. The ability to work with digital media also is becoming increasingly important since most editing now takes place on a computer. However, few industry-wide standards exist, so companies often look for people with skills in the hardware or software they are currently using.

*Assistant editors* or *dubbing editors* select the soundtrack and special sound effects to produce the final combination of sight and sound as it appears on the screen. *Editing-room assistants* help with splicing, patching, rewinding, coding, and storing film. Some television networks have *film librarians*, who are responsible for organizing, filing, cataloging, and selecting footage for the film editors. There is no one way of entering the occupation of editor; but experience as a film librarian, camera operator, sound editor, or assistant editor—plus talent and perseverance—usually help.

*Sound effects editors* or *audio recording engineers* perform one of the final jobs in postproduction: Adding prerecorded and live sound effects and background music by manipulating various elements of music, dialogue, and background sound to fit the picture. Their work is becoming increasingly computer driven, as electronic equipment replaces conventional tape-recording devices. The best way to gain experience in sound editing is through work in radio stations, with music groups, in music videos, or by adding audio to Internet sites.

Even before the film or television show starts production, *marketing managers* develop the marketing strategy for the release. They estimate the demand for the film or show and the audience to whom it will appeal, develop an advertising plan, and decide where and when to release the work. They also may follow the filming or review film while in production, looking for images to use in movie trailers and advertising. *Advertising and promotion managers*, or "unit publicists," write press releases and short biographies of actors and directors for newspapers and magazines. They may also set up interviews or television appearances for the stars or director to promote a film or television series. *Sales representatives* sell the finished product. Many production companies hire staff to distribute, lease, and sell their films and made-for-television programs to theater owners and television networks. The best way to enter sales is to start by selling advertising time for television stations.

Large film and television studios are headed by a *chief executive officer* (CEO), who is responsible to a board of directors and stockholders. Various managers, such as *financial managers* and *business managers*, as well as *accountants* and *lawyers*, report to the CEO. Small film companies and those in business and educational film production cannot afford to have so many different people managing only one aspect of the business. As a result, they usually are headed by an *owner-producer*, who originates, develops, produces, and distributes films with just a small staff and some freelance workers. These companies offer good training opportunities to beginners, exposing them to many phases of film and television production.

## Training and Advancement

Formal training can be a great asset to workers in filmmaking and television production, but experience, talent, creativity, and professionalism usually are the most important factors in getting a job. Many entry-level workers start out by working on documentary, business, educational, industrial, or government films or in the music video industry. This kind of experience can lead to more advanced jobs.

In addition to colleges and technical schools, many independent centers offer training programs on various aspects of filmmaking, such as screenwriting, film editing, directing, and acting. For example, the American Film Institute offers training in directing, production, cinematography, screenwriting, editing, and production design.

Promotion opportunities for many jobs are extremely limited because of the narrow scope of the duties and skills of the occupations. Thousands of jobs are also temporary, intermittent, part time, or on a contract basis, making advancement difficult. Individual initiative is very important for advancement in the motion picture industry.

*Preproduction occupations.* There are no specific training requirements for producers and directors. Talent, experience, and business acumen are very important. An ability to deal with many different kinds of people while under stress also is essential. Producers and directors come from varied backgrounds. Many start as assistant directors; others gain industry experience first as actors, writers, film editors, or business managers. Formal training in directing and producing is available at some colleges and universities. Individuals interested in production management who have a bachelor's or associate degree or 2 years of work experience may qualify for the Assistant Directors Training Program offered jointly by the Directors Guild of America and the Alliance of Motion Picture and Television Producers. Training is given in Los Angeles with the possibility of travel to other locations. To enroll in this highly competitive program, individuals must take a written exam and go through a series of assessments.

Screenwriters usually have had writing experience as freelance writers or editors or in other employment settings. As they build a reputation in their career, demand for their screenplays or teleplays increases, and their earnings grow. Some become directors or producers. Although many screenwriters have college degrees, talent and creativity are even more important determinants of success in the industry. Screenwriters need to develop creative writing skills, a mastery of film language, and a basic understanding of filmmaking. Self-motivation, perseverance, and an ability to take criticism also are valuable. Feature-film writers usually have many years of experience and work on a freelance basis. Many start as copywriters in advertising agencies and as writers for educational film companies, government audiovisual departments, or in-house corporate film divisions. These jobs not only serve as a good training ground for beginners, but also have greater job security than freelancing.

*Production occupations.* Actors usually are required to have formal dramatic training or acting experience. Training can be obtained in acting conservatories, university programs, theatre-sponsored training programs, and independent dramatic arts schools. The National Association of Schools of Theatre accredits 150 colleges and universities that offer bachelor's or higher degrees in dramatic and theater arts. However, many reputable studio programs offer training on a course-by-course basis or that do not lead to a formal degree. Many professional actors who are between acting jobs obtain additional advanced training through private sessions with an acting coach or by participating in a master class to focus on a particular challenge or to broaden their skills.

Training in singing, dancing, or stage combat, or experience in modeling, stand-up comedy, or acting in commercials is especially useful, and helps an actor stand out among the many resumes being considered. But actual performance credits, even those for performing in local and regional theater productions, can be the most useful in getting into an audition. Many actors begin their career by performing in smaller markets and commercials and working as extras. Most professional actors rely on agents or managers to find auditions for them.

Film and video editors often begin as camera operators or editing-room assistants, cinematographers usually start as assis-

tant camera operators, and sound recordists often start as boom operators and gradually progress to become sound engineers. Computer courses in digital sound and electronic mixing often are important for upward mobility. Cinematographers, camera operators, and sound engineers usually have either a college or technical school education, or they go through a formal training program. Computer skills are required for many editing, special-effects, and cinematography positions.

*Postproduction occupations.* The educational background of managers and top executives varies widely, depending on their responsibilities. Most managers have a bachelor's degree in liberal arts or business administration. Their majors often are related to the departments they direct. For example, a degree in accounting or finance, or in business administration with an emphasis on accounting or finance, is suitable academic preparation for financial managers.

For top-level positions in marketing, promotions, or general or human resources management, employers prefer individuals with an undergraduate degree in a field related to the department in which they will work, such as degrees in marketing, advertising, or business administration. Experience in retail and print advertising also is helpful. A high school diploma and retail or telephone sales experience are beneficial for sales jobs.

General managers may advance to top executive positions, such as executive or administrative vice president, either in their own firm or to similar positions in a larger firm. Top-level managers may advance to chief operating officer and chief executive officer. Financial, marketing, and other managers may be promoted to top management positions or may transfer to closely related positions in other industries. Some may start their own businesses.

## Outlook

Keen competition is expected for the more glamorous, high-paying jobs—writers, actors, producers, and directors—but better job prospects are expected for multimedia artists and animators and others skilled in digital filming and computer-generated imaging. Small or independent filmmakers may provide the best job prospects for beginners.

*Employment change.* Wage and salary employment in the motion picture and video industries is projected to grow 11 percent between 2006 and 2016, about as fast as growth projected for wage and salary employment in all industries combined. Job growth will result from the explosive increase in demand for programming needed to fill the rising number of cable and satellite television channels, both in the United States and abroad. Also, more films will be needed to meet in-home demand for videos, DVDs, and films over the Internet. Responding to an increasingly fragmented audience will create many opportunities to develop films. The international market for U.S.-made films is expected to continue growing as more countries and foreign individuals acquire the ability to view our movies. As the industry registers employment growth, many more job openings will arise through people leaving the industry, mainly for more stable employment.

There is concern in the motion picture industry over the number of films that are being made abroad. Tax breaks offered chiefly by English-speaking countries, especially Canada, have induced U.S. filmmakers to increasingly move the production of films to other countries. Production of many lower budget films, such as made-for-television movies, and commercials has been moved abroad to reduce production costs. In addition, more feature films are being made abroad, but mostly for artistic reasons. When a film's production crew leaves, it takes with it large numbers of jobs that are filled at the site of the filming—most of the noncritical supporting actors and behind-the-scenes workers, caterers, drivers, and production assistants. To address this issue, several cities and States have initiated tax breaks and other incentives to encourage filmmakers to make movies in their locales. Also, the U.S. Congress has considered legislation that offers tax incentives for filmmakers to stay in the United States.

The motion picture industry is also concerned about piracy of its work, which can occur in several ways. For example, as the power and speed of the Internet grows, more movies are being downloaded directly into homes, causing declines in theater attendance and losses in revenue from ticket sales. The industry estimates that it loses billions of dollars annually due to piracy which could, potentially, have an adverse affect on employment. The Motion Picture Association of America has enacted a number of measures to combat this trend, including lawsuits, lobbying Congress for legislation, and new in-theater security measures. Digital transmission of motion pictures from studios directly to movie houses for exhibition will also work to prevent some piracy problems, but it also has high start-up costs—expensive digital projectors and the added costs to install transmission and distribution technology and security software.

*Job prospects.* Opportunities will be better in some occupations than in others. Computer specialists, multimedia artists and animators, film and video editors, and others skilled in digital filming, editing, and computer-generated imaging should have the best job prospects. There also will be opportunities for broadcast and sound engineering technicians and other specialists, such as gaffers and set construction workers. In contrast, keen competition can be expected for the more glamorous, high-paying jobs in the industry—writers, actors, producers, and directors—as many more people seek a fewer number of these jobs. Small or independent filmmakers may provide the best job prospects for beginners, because they are likely to grow more quickly as digital technology cuts production costs.

**Table 3. Median hourly earnings of the largest occupations in motion picture and video industries, May 2006**

| Occupation | Motion picture and video industries | All industries |
|---|---|---|
| Producers and directors | $34.01 | $27.07 |
| Film and video editors | 25.76 | 22.44 |
| Camera operators, television, video, and motion picture | 21.16 | 19.26 |
| Audio and video equipment technicians | 16.60 | 16.75 |
| Entertainers and performers, sports and related workers, all other | 15.58 | 15.11 |
| Actors | 10.69 | 11.61 |
| Motion picture projectionists | 8.33 | 8.39 |
| Cashiers | 7.39 | 8.08 |
| Ushers, lobby attendants, and ticket takers | 7.00 | 7.64 |
| Counter attendants, cafeteria, food concession, and coffee shop | 6.96 | 7.76 |

# Earnings

*Industry earnings.* Earnings of workers in the motion picture and video industries vary, depending on education and experi-

ence, type of work, union affiliation, and duration of employment. In 2006, median weekly earnings of wage and salary workers in the motion picture and video industries were $593, compared with $568 for wage and salary workers in all industries combined.

On the basis of a union contract negotiated in July 2005, motion picture and television actors who are members of the Screen Actors Guild earn a minimum daily rate of $759, or $2,634 for a 5-day week. They also receive additional compensation for reruns. Annual earnings for many actors are low, however, because employment is intermittent. Many actors supplement their incomes from acting with earnings from other jobs outside the industry. Some established actors get salaries well above the minimums, and earnings of the few top stars are astronomical.

Salaries for directors vary widely. Producers seldom have a set salary, because they get a percentage of a show's earnings or ticket sales. Earnings in selected occupations in the motion picture and video industries appear in table 3.

*Benefits and union membership.* Smaller employers usually offer limited employee benefits. Larger employers offer benefits are more comparable with those offered by employers in other industries and can include vacation and sick leave, health and life insurance, profit sharing, and pension plans.

Unions are very important in this industry. Virtually all film production companies and television networks sign contracts with union locals that require the employment of workers according to union contracts. Nonunion workers may be hired because of a special talent, to fill a specific need, or for a short period. Although union membership is not mandated, nonunion workers risk eligibility for future work assignments. Actors who appear in filmed entertainment—including television, commercials, and movies—belong to the Screen Actors Guild (SAG), while those in broadcast television generally belong to the American Federation of Television and Radio Artists (AFTRA). SAG and AFTRA, however, share jurisdiction over several types of film work, including industrial/educational film work not for broadcast, interactive media (computer games), and freelance television commercial work. Actors from either union may qualify for this work; and many actors belong to more than one union. Film and television directors are members of the Directors Guild of America. Art directors, cartoonists, editors, costumers, scenic artists, set designers, camera operators, sound technicians, projectionists, and shipping, booking, and other distribution employees belong to the International Alliance of Theatrical Stage Employees, Moving Picture Technicians, Artists and Allied Crafts (I.A.T.S.E.), or the United Scenic Artists Association.

## Sources of Additional Information

For general information on employment as an actor, contact either of the following organizations:

➤ Screen Actors Guild, 5757 Wilshire Blvd., Los Angeles, CA 90036-3600. Internet: **http://www.sag.org**
➤ American Federation of Television and Radio Artists—Screen Actors Guild, Suite 204, 4340 East-West Hwy., Bethesda, MD 20814. Internet: **http://www.aftra.org**

For general information about arts education and a list of accredited college-level programs, contact

➤ National Office for Arts Accreditation in Higher Education, 11250 Roger Bacon Dr., Suite 21, Reston, VA 22091. Internet: **http://www.arts-accredit.org**

Information on many motion picture and video occupations, including the following, may be found in the 2008–09 *Occupational Outlook Handbook*:

- Actors, producers, and directors
- Artists and related workers

- Broadcast and sound engineering technicians and radio operators
- Television, video, and motion picture camera operators and editors
- Writers and editors

# Publishing, Except Software

(NAICS 5111)

SIGNIFICANT POINTS

- Strong communication skills and the ability to meet tight deadlines are crucial for many jobs in this industry.

- Mergers and computerization will make firms more productive and limit employment growth.

- Writers and editors face keen competition for jobs, as this industry attracts a large number of applicants, especially at nationally known publications.

- Technological advances will result in a decline in employment of some workers, such as prepress technicians.

## Nature of the Industry

*Goods and services.* The publishing industry produces a variety of publications, including magazines, books, newspapers, and directories. It also produces greeting cards, databases, calendars, and other published material, excluding software. Although mostly producing printed materials, the publishing industry is increasingly producing its material in other formats, such as audio or video discs (e.g., CD-ROM), or other electronic media.

Although the content and formats may vary, most companies follow similar steps when publishing material. First, editorial departments must acquire the content, or material, to be published. Some publishers have a staff of writers, reporters, and editors who research and write articles, stories, and other text for the publication. Photographers and artists are also brought in to supplement the written material with photos and illustrations as needed. Other publishers purchase their written and graphic material from outside sources, mainly independent "freelance" writers, photographers, or artists. When this is done, the publishers obtain the legal right to publish the material from the content providers prior to publication. After the story or article is written, the manuscript is reviewed to check that the information it contains is accurate and then it is edited to ensure that it uses correct grammar and a writing style that is clear and interesting. Editors and publishers develop captions and headlines and design the pages and the covers.

The sale of advertisements, including classified advertising, is the major source of revenue for magazines, newspapers, and directories, such as the telephone Yellow Pages. Advertising sales agents work with clients and advertising agencies to sell space in the publication. While most commercial advertisements are produced by advertising agencies, small advertisers may require the help of copywriters and graphic artists in the publisher's advertising department to create an advertisement.

When complete, all of the content—manuscript, photos and captions, illustrations, and any other artwork, including advertisements—is collected at one location and, with the help of desktop publishing software, the pages are laid out. Most newspapers and many magazines have art and design staffs that perform this "prepress" operation. Other publishers contract out their prepress work to commercial printers, along with the physical production of the publication.

Publishers' publicity, marketing, and circulation departments are responsible for promoting a publication and increasing sales and circulation. Book publishers, in particular, promote new books by creating elaborate publicity campaigns involving book signings and public appearances by the author.

Getting the publication to the readers is a function of the distribution department. Major book publishers often have large warehouse operations, where books are stored and from which they are delivered as needed. Newspapers and magazines, however, distribute each issue only once. Immediately after they are printed, newspapers are folded, filled with inserts, bundled, and wrapped. The newspapers are then transported to distributors, who deliver the newspapers to newsstands and individual carriers. Another major function of newspaper distribution is making sure that newspapers are delivered on time at readers' doorsteps. Magazines are mailed to subscribers after printing or shipped to retail distributors. Many magazines and some newspapers contract out their distribution.

*Industry organization.* Newspapers employ the largest number of workers in the publishing industry. (See table 1.) With a staff of reporters and correspondents, newspapers report on events taking place locally and around the world. Despite the local nature of most newspaper reporting, the newspaper industry is dominated by several large corporations that own most of the newspapers in the country. It also is becoming common for companies to buy several newspapers in a single region so that they can be produced more efficiently. This is known as "clustering." Under this arrangement, multiple newspapers share the same printing plant, and advertising sales agents can sell advertising space as a bundle in all of the papers.

Newspaper publishers usually own the printing plants that print their newspapers. Over the years, this type of printing operation has become highly automated and the skills needed to produce a newspaper are changing with the technology. The dominant printing process used to produce newspapers is lithography. The process involves putting the pages of the newspaper on film, and then "burning" the images from the film onto a thin aluminum plate, which is then installed on a press. In the plant, rolls of paper are brought in from the warehouse, the plates are treated with chemicals, ink is mixed, and presses move the paper along the rotating inked plates at very high rates of speed.

Book publishing is also dominated by a few very large companies, primarily based in New York City. However, some mid-size and small publishers across the country are thriving, particularly those that specialize in certain subjects. Textbooks and technical, scientific, and professional books provide nearly

155

half of the revenues of the book publishing industry. The other half consists of adult trade—that which is typically found in a bookstore—and juvenile, religious, paperback, mail-order, book club, and reference books.

Magazine, or periodical, publishers run the gamut from small one- or two-person shops to large media conglomerates that may publish dozens of magazines. There are two types of magazines—business-to-business, called "trade," and consumer magazines. Trade magazines serve a particular industry, profession, or service, while consumer magazines are written for general audiences.

Directory and mailing list publishers produce collections and compilations of data and information for residential and business customers. The most common directories are the telephone directories known as the white pages and yellow pages. These directories are designed to help calling parties locate residential telephone numbers and addresses and to allow people to search for businesses by category.

*Recent developments.* Much of the publishing industry is venturing online. Newspapers, in particular, and some magazines have extensive Web sites that are updated around the clock as news breaks. These Web sites may have their own writers and editors to supply content, but, for the most part, they reformat material developed by the print publication's regular staff. Books are also beginning to be reproduced electronically, so that they can be read on computers or on hand-held "readers."

Computerization, especially digital technology, is having a significant impact on the publishing industry. Digital photography eliminates the need for film processing and allows for easy manipulation of images. Electronic mail also allows advertisers to send their ads directly to the publisher's production department for insertion. In the latest print technologies, computers use lasers to burn images and text onto the printing plate, eliminating the need to produce a film negative of each page.

**Table 1. Percent distribution of employment and establishments in publishing, except software, by detailed industry sector, 2006**

| Industry segment | Employment | Percent |
|---|---|---|
| Total ................................................................. | 100.0 | 100.0 |
| Newspapers.......................................................... | 55.0 | 36.5 |
| Periodicals .......................................................... | 21.8 | 34.8 |
| Book publishing .................................................. | 12.3 | 15.1 |
| Directory and mailing lists................................ | 6.8 | 7.9 |
| Other publishers ................................................ | 4.1 | 5.8 |

## Working Conditions

*Hours.* Working nights, weekends, and holidays is common, especially for those working on newspapers. The average non-supervisory production worker in newspaper publishing worked 33.6 hours per week in 2006, compared with 33.9 hours per week across all industries. Nonsupervisory production workers worked an average of 34.7 hours per week in periodical publishing, and 36.2 hours per week in book publishing. Part-time employment is significant in this industry, with 19 percent working part time. Newspaper distributors and drivers usually work five to six hours a day, often in the middle of the night. Although the hours are long and often irregular, most advertising sales agents have the freedom to determine their own schedule. Some tele-

phone advertising and classified sales representatives also work part time.

*Work Environment.* Meeting deadlines is one of the primary conditions of employment in this industry. Magazines and newspapers, in particular, are published on a very tight schedule and workers must be prepared to meet these deadlines. This can often make for a very chaotic and stressful environment, and employees frequently may be required to work overtime.

Writers, editors, reporters, and correspondents have the most varied working conditions. Many work from home, particularly in book publishing, sending manuscripts back and forth using e-mail. For most writers and reporters, travel is required to perform research and conduct interviews. News correspondents for large metropolitan newspapers or national news publications may be stationed in cities around the world, reporting on events in their territory.

Many advertising sales agents also travel in order to meet with potential customers, although some sell over the telephone. Rejection by clients and the need to meet quotas can be stressful for some agents.

At headquarters, many in publishing work in comfortable, private offices, while others—particularly at newspapers—work in large, noisy, cubicle-filled rooms. Classified advertising clerks and customer service representatives increasingly work in call-center environments, manning telephones much of the day. Newspaper pressrooms are manufacturing plants that can be noisy and dangerous if safety procedures are not followed, but computerization of the machines has reduced injuries. In 2006, occurrences of work-related injury and illness in the publishing industry ranged from an average of 1.6 per 100 full-time workers in periodical publishing to 3.7 per 100 full-time workers in newspaper publishing, lower than the average of 4.4 per 100 full-time workers for all private industry.

## Employment

The publishing industry provided 660,000 wage and salary jobs in 2006. In addition, there were 32,000 self-employed workers. The industry does not include independent, or "freelance," writers, artists, journalists, or photographers, whose jobs are included in the arts, entertainment, and recreation industry, but who contribute a significant amount of content material to this industry.

Newspaper publishing companies employ the largest number of workers in this industry, because they write much of their own material and typically print, and sometimes distribute, their newspapers. While newspaper publishing is done throughout the country, magazine and book publishers are based mostly in large cities. The largest concentration of publishers is in New York City. Half of the establishments in the publishing industry have less than 5 employees, but 2 out of 5 jobs are in establishments with over 250 employees (chart).

## Occupations in the Industry

Most occupations in the publishing industry fall into 1 of 4 categories: Writing and editing; production; advertising sales and marketing; and general administration (table 2). However, variations in the number and type of workers employed occur by type of publication. For example, most book publishing companies employ few writers because most of their content is acquired from freelance writers and photographers. In contrast, newspapers employ a large number of writers and reporters, who supply the content for the paper. Also, newspapers generally perform

**Half of the establishments in the publishing industry have less than 5 employees, but over 40 percent of jobs are in establishments with 250 or more.**

Percent

- Establishments
- Employment

| | 1 to 4 | 5 to 49 | 50 to 249 | 250 or more |
|---|---|---|---|---|
| Establishments | 50.6 | 40.0 | 7.6 | 1.8 |
| Employment | 3.2 | 23.9 | 30.8 | 42.1 |

Number of workers employed by establishment, March 2006

their own printing, whereas most books and magazines are printed by companies in the printing industry. Differences also exist depending on the size of the company and the variety of media in which the company publishes.

***Writing and editing occupations.*** Everything that is published in this industry must first be written. *Writers and authors* and *reporters and correspondents,* who comprise the majority of publishing's professional and related occupations, write the articles, stories, and other text that end up in publications. Writers are assigned stories to write by *editors.* At newspapers and news magazines, reporters usually specialize in certain categories, or "beats," such as education, crime, sports, or world news. Writers and reporters gather information on their topic by performing Internet and library research and by interviewing people in person, by telephone, or by email. They must then organize their material and write it down in a coherent manner that will interest and entertain readers. *Copywriters,* who write advertising copy, also are common in this industry.

*Editors* assign, review, rewrite, and correct the work of writers. They may also do original writing, such as producing editorials for newspapers or columns for magazines. In book publishing, they oversee the acquisition and selection of material, often working directly with the authors to achieve the final product. Most publishing companies employ several types of editors. The executive editor generally has the final say about what will be published and how it will be covered and presented. Managing editors are responsible for the day-to-day operation of the editorial department. They make sure that materials conform to guidelines, and that deadlines are met. Associate and assistant editors give assignments to writers and reporters, oversee projects, and do much of the editing of text. Copy editors review manuscripts or reporters' copy for accuracy, content, grammar, and style. Editors also are performing more layout design and prepress functions as computerization moves these jobs from the production department to the editorial department.

Other occupations that work closely with the editorial department are *art and design workers* and *photographers,* whose work often complements the written material. They illustrate

children's books, photograph news events, design book jackets and magazine covers, and lay out every page of publications. The *art director* determines the overall look of the publication, overseeing placement of text, artwork and photographs, and any advertising on the page, and selecting type sizes and styles, or fonts.

***Production and related occupations.*** *Industrial production managers,* with the help of *production and planning clerks,* oversee the production of the publication. They set up production schedules and see that deadlines are met. They also try to keep printing costs low while maintaining product integrity. The production manager also determines how much it will cost to produce, for example, a 300-page textbook or an advertising insert in a magazine. In newspaper publishing, the production manager oversees and controls the entire production operation.

Other production occupations found mainly in newspaper printing plants are *prepress technicians* and *printing machine operators.* Prepress technicians scan images and do page layout and camera work. They then produce the printing plates containing the text and images that will be printed. Printing machine operators set up and run the printing presses to produce the printed materials. *Driver/sales workers* and *truck drivers, light and delivery* deliver the newspapers to newsstands and residential customers.

***Sales, promotion, and marketing occupations.*** Magazines, newspapers, and directories, in particular, employ many *advertising sales agents,* who generate most of the revenue for these publications. Using demographic data produced by the market research department, they make presentations to potential clients promoting the use of their publication for advertising purposes. Increasingly, advertising agents sell integrated packages that include advertisements to be placed online or with a broadcast subsidiary, along with additional promotional tie-ins. This job can require substantial travel for some, while others may sell advertising over the telephone. Classified advertising sales are handled by *telemarketers* or *customer service representatives,* depending on the origin of the call. *Advertising and promotions managers,* called circulation directors at some magazines and newspapers, study trends and devise promotion campaigns to generate new readers. They also work with the driver/sales workers to ensure that the publications are delivered on time.

Because books do not have advertising, book publishers generate sales through the use of publicity campaigns and a sales force. *Public relations specialists* promote books by setting up media interviews with authors and book signings, and by placing advertisements in relevant publications. *Sales representatives* go to places, such as libraries, schools, and bookstores to promote the sale of their books. They also are responsible for finding additional sources of profit for a title, including book clubs, paperback editions, audio, e-books, and foreign rights for publishing the title in other languages.

***General administration occupations.*** The publishing industry, as with most industries, has a variety of *general managers, accountants,* and administrative support staff who help to run the company. There are also *computer specialists* to keep the computer systems running and to implement new technologies. Others work as Internet site developers, who work with the design, editorial, and production departments in order to implement content changes and redesigns of Web sites operated by the publication.

157

Other occupations that are unique or important to operations include publishers, or *chief executives,* of a company. Publishers are in charge of the business side of the organization and are responsible for implementing company policies. Subsidiary rights and permissions personnel are *business operations specialists,* who negotiate the copyrights for material and also license to others the right to reproduce or reprint copyrighted material. *Stock clerks and order fillers* and *customer service representatives* keep track of books in publisher's warehouses and respond to customer inquiries. As publications, particularly books, are published in more than one format, workers are needed to develop the new formats. Audio books, for example, require *sound engineering technicians* to transfer the books to tape or CD.

## Training and Advancement

The ability to communicate well is one of the most important skills needed to enter the publishing industry. Although it is especially critical for those in the editorial and sales departments, it is also required for those in production, who may be called upon to compose text. Computer literacy also is becoming a requirement for almost everyone seeking work in this industry, and the ability to meet tight deadlines is a must for most workers.

Most nonentry-level jobs in this industry require experience, especially if one wants to work for a top newspaper, magazine, or book publishing company. Experience can be obtained by working for a school newspaper or by performing an internship with a publishing company. However, most people start by working for small publishing companies or newspapers in smaller cities and towns and work their way up to better paying jobs with larger newspapers or publishers. Others break into the field by doing freelance work.

*Writing and editing occupations. Writers, reporters, and editors* generally need a bachelor's degree. Most people in these occupations majored in English, communication, or journalism. Some publishers, however, prefer graduates with liberal arts degrees or specific subject knowledge if the person will be writing about a complex topic or doing technical writing. For the most part, writers and editors need to be able to express ideas clearly and logically and to write under pressure. Familiarity with desktop publishing software is helpful.

Writers and editors often start as assistants, performing fact-checking, doing research, or copy editing along with clerical tasks. News reporters often start by covering local community events or criminal cases and advance to reporting regional or national news. Writers and reporters can advance to editorial positions, but some choose to continue writing and advance by becoming nationally known experts in their field.

*Sales, promotion, and marketing occupations.* A college degree is preferred for most advertising, sales, and marketing positions that require meetings with clients. Courses in marketing, communication, business, and advertising are helpful. For those who sell over the telephone, a high school degree may be sufficient. However, more important for success are excellent communication and interpersonal skills. Those in advertising and sales must be able to get along with others, as well as be self-motivated, well-organized, persistent, independent, and able to handle rejection. Enthusiasm and a sense of humor also help. One advances in these fields by taking on bigger, more important clients or by going into management.

**Table 2. Employment of wage and salary workers in publishing, except software by occupation, 2006 and projected change, 2006-2016.**
(Employment in thousands)

| Occupation | Employment, 2006 | | Percent change, 2006-16 |
|---|---|---|---|
| | Number | Percent | |
| **All occupations** | 660 | 100.0 | -7.5 |
| **Management, business, and financial occupations** | 64 | 9.7 | -4.1 |
| General and operations managers | 11 | 1.7 | -13.5 |
| Advertising and promotions managers | 3 | 0.4 | -14.3 |
| Marketing and sales managers | 8 | 1.3 | -3.6 |
| Computer and information systems managers | 3 | 0.4 | -2.5 |
| Financial managers | 3 | 0.4 | -3.0 |
| Accountants and auditors | 6 | 0.9 | -3.2 |
| **Professional and related occupations** | 192 | 29.1 | -4.4 |
| Computer programmers | 3 | 0.5 | -20.9 |
| Computer software engineers | 6 | 1.0 | 18.0 |
| Computer support specialists | 4 | 0.6 | -3.3 |
| Computer systems analysts | 3 | 0.5 | 6.7 |
| Market research analysts | 6 | 0.8 | -0.8 |
| Art directors | 5 | 0.8 | -2.8 |
| Graphic designers | 27 | 4.0 | -1.7 |
| Reporters and correspondents | 39 | 5.9 | -3.0 |
| Public relations specialists | 3 | 0.4 | -2.0 |
| Editors | 59 | 9.0 | -11.1 |
| Writers and authors | 8 | 1.2 | -7.9 |
| Photographers | 6 | 0.9 | -12.8 |
| **Sales and related occupations** | 100 | 15.1 | 1.7 |
| First-line supervisors/managers of non-retail sales workers | 8 | 1.1 | -11.4 |
| Advertising sales agents | 54 | 8.1 | 10.9 |
| Sales representatives, services, all other | 7 | 1.0 | 9.5 |
| Sales representatives, wholesale and manufacturing, except technical and scientific products | 12 | 1.8 | -2.4 |
| Telemarketers | 12 | 1.8 | -24.6 |
| Door-to-door sales workers, news and street vendors, and related workers | 3 | 0.4 | -13.2 |
| **Office and administrative support occupations** | 156 | 23.6 | -11.8 |
| First-line supervisors/managers of office and administrative support workers | 10 | 1.5 | -11.6 |
| Bookkeeping, accounting, and auditing clerks | 11 | 1.7 | -6.2 |
| Customer service representatives | 20 | 3.0 | 4.7 |
| Order clerks | 8 | 1.2 | -39.1 |
| Receptionists and information clerks | 5 | 0.7 | -8.4 |
| Production, planning, and expediting clerks | 5 | 0.7 | -2.4 |
| Shipping, receiving, and traffic clerks | 4 | 0.6 | -5.6 |
| Executive secretaries and administrative assistants | 11 | 1.6 | -3.9 |
| Secretaries, except legal, medical, and executive | 7 | 1.0 | -15.5 |
| Desktop publishers | 11 | 1.7 | -3.0 |
| Mail clerks and mail machine operators, except postal service | 11 | 1.7 | -33.6 |
| Office clerks, general | 20 | 3.1 | -8.0 |
| Proofreaders and copy markers | 4 | 0.7 | -4.4 |
| **Production occupations** | 76 | 11.4 | -12.5 |
| First-line supervisors/managers of production and operating workers | 7 | 1.0 | -8.5 |
| Bindery workers | 6 | 0.9 | -10.3 |
| Job printers | 7 | 1.0 | -8.9 |
| Prepress technicians and workers | 16 | 2.4 | -17.7 |
| Printing machine operators | 20 | 3.1 | -9.8 |
| Packaging and filling machine operators and tenders | 4 | 0.6 | -21.7 |

**(continued on next column)**

(continued from previous column)

**Table 2. Employment of wage and salary workers in publishing, except software by occupation, 2006 and projected change, 2006-2016.**
(Employment in thousands)

| Occupation | Employment, 2006 | | Percent change, 2006-16 |
|---|---|---|---|
| | Number | Percent | |
| **Production occupations**............................. | 76 | 11.4 | -12.5 |
| First-line supervisors/managers of production and operating workers................................. | 7 | 1.0 | -8.5 |
| Bindery workers........................................... | 6 | 0.9 | -10.3 |
| Job printers................................................. | 7 | 1.0 | -8.9 |
| Prepress technicians and workers .............. | 16 | 2.4 | -17.7 |
| Printing machine operators......................... | 20 | 3.1 | -9.8 |
| Packaging and filling machine operators and tenders.............................................. | 4 | 0.6 | -21.7 |
| **Transportation and material moving occupations** ............................................... | 62 | 9.4 | -18.2 |
| Driver/sales workers ................................... | 9 | 1.3 | -22.0 |
| Truck drivers, light or delivery services ....... | 11 | 1.7 | -11.9 |
| Laborers and freight, stock, and material movers, hand.......................................... | 14 | 2.1 | -17.1 |
| Machine feeders and offbearers ................. | 12 | 1.8 | -20.4 |
| Packers and packagers, hand.................... | 9 | 1.3 | -27.9 |

Note: Columns may not add to totals due to omission of occupations with small employment

*Production occupations.* Most *prepress technicians* and *printing machine operators* learn through a combination of formal education and by working alongside experienced workers. Although a high school education is sufficient for entry-level printing machine operator jobs, taking classes in printing techniques or getting an associate degree at a postsecondary institution will enhance one's credentials and make it easier to find a job. This is particularly true for those interested in prepress work. Computer skills and familiarity with publishing software packages are important because prepress work and printing are increasingly computerized. Training on new machines will be needed throughout one's career. Advancement usually comes by working on more complex printing jobs or by becoming a supervisor.

## Outlook

Employment in publishing is expected to see a moderate decline as newspapers continue to lose subscribers and jobs, but book, periodical and directory publishing remaining stable. Additionally, keen competition is expected for most job openings for writers and editors.

*Employment change.* Over the period 2006–16, wage and salary employment in publishing, except software, is projected to decline 7 percent, compared with 11 percent growth for all industries combined. Whether published in print or using electronic media, books, newspapers, and magazines will continue to be needed to keep people informed and entertained. However, efficiencies in production and a trend towards using more freelance workers will cause overall employment to decline, predominantly in the newspaper publishing segment.

Newspaper subscriptions have been declining for many years as more people turn to television and the Internet for their news. Also, mergers in the industry that make newspapers more efficient, allow reporters and advertising sales agents to write stories or sell advertising for several newspapers, or even several media outlets, at once. Those working in company administration also are more productive. Efficiencies will be particularly apparent in the printing plants. In addition to multiple newspapers being printed at one location due to clustering, computerization of the printing process has become widespread. With increasing regularity, printing plates will be made directly from electronic images of publications' pages, which have been developed, stored, and transmitted by computer. As a result, employment of prepress technicians and printing machine operators is expected to decline because fewer will be needed to operate the new computerized equipment. Newspapers will increasingly use temporary workers, instead of full-time employees, to fill open positions in postpress.

As lines between information mediums begin to blur, workers may be required to work in broadcasting, print, and online. Many newspapers feel that this is the best way to provide information to readers who increasingly seek an interactive approach to news media. Photographers, for example, will also have to learn to use video cameras, and print reporters may need to provide news stories for broadcast, host online discussions, or maintain a series of online journal entries known as a "blog."

Over the next decade, employment in periodical and book publishing, along with miscellaneous publishing, will be relatively flat. Magazine turnover will dull the need for additional workers in this publishing segment. However, other segments of publishing are expected to exhibit increased demand for new workers. The segment of the industry producing textbooks is expected to benefit from a growing number of high school and college students over the next decade and the need to implement new learning standards in classrooms. Technical and scientific books and journals also will be needed to relay new discoveries to the public. Custom publishing is a new type of publishing in which a specialized firm or magazine publisher produces customized newsletters and magazines for clients. Custom publishing also is expected to grow as more businesses and organizations use this format to directly market new products to clients and to retain customer loyalty.

*Job prospects.* The need for workers in the publishing industry usually varies with the economy. When the economy is depressed, advertising declines and publishers look to cut costs and personnel. In addition, when the economy is down, State and local governments cut back on spending on books for libraries and, to a lesser extent, for schools.

The best job opportunities in the future will be for those who have good computer skills and can work in multiple mediums. Most newspapers and magazines, in particular, now have Web sites that must be regularly updated and the content on the sites continues to expand. Some publishers will require additional writers, reporters, and editors to update content on a Web site, but most of the work will be done by the writers and reporters themselves. The sites also need webmasters, designers, and other computer experts to maintain the sites. In addition, production of e-books is likely to expand and grow in popularity over the next decade, requiring workers skilled in incorporating graphics and other digital inputs.

Job opportunities vary among occupations. However, one can expect keen competition for most writing and editing jobs in this industry, which attracts a large number of applicants, especially at nationally known publications. Writers with specialized knowledge and those who can write on subjects appealing to minority and ethnic readers will have better job prospects.

Job openings for advertising sales agents are expected to be good, because turnover in this occupation is generally high, and new workers are always in demand for these jobs. Advertising sales agents who have a bachelor's degree and direct sales experience will have the best opportunities.

## Earnings

*Industry earnings.* Average weekly earnings for workers in the publishing industry varied by type of publication. In 2006, average weekly earnings were $759 in periodical publishing, $674 in book publishing, and $598 in newspaper publishing, compared with $568 for all private sector industries. Writers, editors, and reporters working on major metropolitan newspapers, or those with technical expertise writing for specialized magazines, usually have the highest salaries. Advertising sales representatives usually earn a base salary plus an amount based on sales. Earnings for selected occupations in publishing appear in table 3.

*Benefits and union membership.* Writers, reporters, and editors who cover foreign affairs or other international news may enjoy extensive paid travel or reassignment to other cities in order to better acquaint themselves with their subject matter. Photographers also find it necessary to travel in order to capture their assignments.

**Table 3. Median hourly earnings of the largest occupations in publishing, except software, May 2006**

| Occupation | Publishing, except software | All industries |
|---|---|---|
| Editors | $22.10 | $22.59 |
| Advertising sales agents | 17.73 | 20.55 |
| Printing machine operators | 17.27 | 14.90 |
| Graphic designers | 16.49 | 19.18 |
| Reporters and correspondents | 15.24 | 16.09 |
| Prepress technicians and workers | 15.17 | 16.01 |
| Customer service representatives | 13.42 | 13.62 |
| Office clerks, general | 11.40 | 11.40 |
| Telemarketers | 10.79 | 10.09 |
| Laborers and freight, stock, and material movers, hand | 9.78 | 10.20 |

Those in publishing who choose to freelance are not provided with medical insurance or retirement benefits by those who buy their work. Twelve percent of workers in the newspaper industry are union members or are covered by a contract as compared to 13 percent for all industries combined. The Newspaper Guild-CWA is the major union representing most nonsupervisory employees in the newspaper industry.

## Sources of Additional Information

For information about careers in book publishing, contact:
➢ Association of American Publishers, 71 Fifth Ave., 2nd Floor, New York, NY 10003. Internet: **http://www.publishers.org**

For information about careers in newspaper publishing, contact:
➢ Newspaper Association of America, 4401 Wilson Blvd., Suite 900, Arlington, VA 22203. **Internet: http://www.naa.org**
➢ American Society of Newspaper Editors, 11690 B Sunrise Valley Dr., Reston, VA 20191. **Internet: http://www.asne.org**

For information about careers in periodical or magazine publishing, contact:
➢ Magazine Publishers of America, 810 Seventh Ave., 24th Floor, New York, NY 10019 **Internet: http://www.magazine.org**

Information on most occupations in the publishing industry may be found in the 2008–09 *Occupational Outlook Handbook.* Among those occupations are:
- Advertising, marketing, promotions, public relations, and sales managers
- Advertising sales agents
- Artists and related workers
- Graphic designers
- Desktop publishers
- News analysts, reporters, and correspondents
- Photographers
- Prepress technicians and workers
- Printing machine operators
- Writers and editors

# Software Publishers

- Employment is projected to increase by 32 percent between 2006 and 2016.

- Computer specialists account for 52 percent of all workers.

- Job opportunities will be excellent for most workers, but professional workers should enjoy the best prospects, reflecting continuing demand for higher level skills needed to keep up with changes in technology.

## Nature of the Industry

*Goods and services.* All organizations today rely on computer and information technology to conduct business and operate more efficiently. Computer software is needed to run and protect computer systems and networks. Software publishing establishments are involved in all aspects of producing and distributing computer software, such as designing, providing documentation, assisting in installation, and providing support services to customers. The term "publishing" often implies the production and distribution of information in printed form. The software publishing industry also produces and distributes information, but usually it does so by other methods, such as CD-ROMs, the sale of new computers already preloaded with software, or through distribution over the Internet. Establishments in this industry may design, develop, and publish software, or publish only. Establishments that provide access to software for clients from a central host site, design custom software to meet the needs of specific users, or are involved in the mass duplication of software are classified elsewhere. (For more information, see the section on computer systems design and related services found elsewhere in the *Career Guide.*)

*Industry organization.* Software is often divided into two main categories—applications software and systems software. Applications software includes individual programs for computer users—such as word processing and spreadsheet packages, games and graphics packages, data storage programs, and Web browsing programs. Systems software, on the other hand, includes operating systems and all of the related programs that enable computers to function. Establishments that design and publish prepackaged software may specialize in one of these areas, or may be involved in both. Some establishments also may install software on a customer's system and provide user support. In 2006, there were approximately 10,000 establishments that were engaged primarily in computer software publishing, or in publishing and reproduction.

*Recent developments.* The Internet has vastly altered the complexion of the software industry over the last decade. Much of the applications and system software that is now developed is intended for use on the Internet, and for connections to the Internet.

Organizations are constantly seeking to implement technologies that will improve efficiency. Enterprise resource planning (ERP) software is such an example. ERP, which is typically implemented by large organizations with vast computer networks, consists of cross-industry applications that automate a firm's business processes. Common ERP applications include human resources, manufacturing, and financial management software. Recently developed ERP applications also manage a firm's customer relations and supply-chain.

Electronic business (e-business) is any process that a business organization conducts over a computer network. Electronic commerce (e-commerce) is the part of e-business that involves the buying and selling of goods and services. With the growth of the Internet and the expansion of e-commerce, there is significant demand for e-commerce software that enables businesses to become as efficient as possible.

This widespread use of the Internet and intranets also has led to greater focus on the need for computer security. Security threats range from damaging computer viruses to online credit card fraud. The robust growth of e-commerce increases this concern, as firms use the internet to exchange sensitive information with an increasing number of clients. As a result, organizations and individual computer users are demanding software, such as firewalls and antivirus software, that secures their computer networks or individual computer environments.

## Working Conditions

*Hours.* In 2006, workers in the software publishing industry averaged 37.6 hours per week, compared with 33.9 for all industries combined. Many workers in this industry worked more than the standard 40-hour workweek—about 26 percent worked 50 or more. For some professionals, evening or weekend work may be necessary to meet deadlines or solve problems. Professionals working for large establishments may have less freedom in planning their schedule than do consultants for very small firms, whose work may be more varied. Only about 3 percent of the workers in the software publishing industry worked part time, compared with 15 percent of workers throughout all industries.

*Work Environment.* Most workers in this industry work in clean, quiet offices. Given the technology available today, however, more work can be done from remote locations using fax machines, e-mail, and especially the Internet. Employees who work at video terminals for extended periods may experience musculoskeletal strain, eye problems, stress, or repetitive motion illnesses, such as carpal tunnel syndrome.

## Employment

In 2006, there were about 243,000 wage and salary jobs in the software publishing industry. While the industry has both large and small firms, the average establishment in software publishing is relatively small; more than half of the establishments employed fewer than 5 workers. Many of these small establishments are startup firms that hope to capitalize on a market niche. About 76 percent of jobs, however, are found in establishments that employ 50 or more workers (chart 1).

Relative to the rest of the economy, there are significantly fewer workers 45 years of age and older in software publishing establishments. This industry's workforce remains younger than most, with large proportions of workers in the 25-to-44 age range (table 1). This reflects the industry's explosive growth in employment in the 1980s and 1990s, which afforded opportunities to thousands of young workers who possessed the latest technical skills.

## Occupations in the Industry

Providing a wide array of information services to clients requires a diverse and well-educated workforce. The majority of workers in the software publishing industry are professional and related workers, such as computer software engineers and computer programmers (table 2). This major occupational group accounts for about 61 percent of the jobs in the industry, reflecting the emphasis on high-level technical skills and creativity. By 2016, the employment share of professional and related occupations is expected to be even greater, while the employment share of office and administrative support jobs, currently accounting for about 11 percent of industry employment, is projected to fall.

*Professional and related occupations.* Computer specialists make up the vast majority of professional and related occupations among software publishers, and account for about 52 percent of the industry as a whole. Their duties vary substantially, and include such tasks as developing software applications, designing information networks, and assisting computer users.

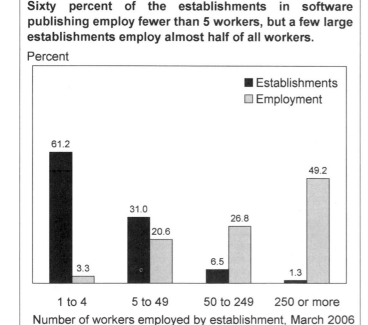

**Sixty percent of the establishments in software publishing employ fewer than 5 workers, but a few large establishments employ almost half of all workers.**

Percent

- Establishments
- Employment

61.2 / 3.3 — 1 to 4
31.0 / 20.6 — 5 to 49
6.5 / 26.8 — 50 to 249
1.3 / 49.2 — 250 or more

Number of workers employed by establishment, March 2006

**Table 1. Percent distribution of employment, by age group, 2006**

| Age group | Software publishers | All industries |
|---|---|---|
| Total | 100.0% | 100.0% |
| 16-19 | 0.7 | 4.3 |
| 20-24 | 4.4 | 9.6 |
| 25-34 | 28.7 | 21.5 |
| 35-44 | 36.8 | 23.9 |
| 45-54 | 19.1 | 23.6 |
| 55-64 | 8.1 | 13.4 |
| 65 and older | 2.2 | 3.7 |

*Programmers* write, test, and maintain the detailed instructions, called programs or software, that computers must follow to perform their functions. These programs tell the computer what to do—which information to identify and access, how to process it, and what equipment to use. Programmers write these commands by breaking down each operation into a logical sequence of steps, and converting the instructions for those steps into a language that the computer understands. While some still work with traditional programming languages like COBOL, most programmers today work with more sophisticated tools. Object-oriented programming languages, such as C++ and Java, computer-aided software engineering (CASE) tools, and artificial intelligence tools are now widely used to create and maintain programs. These languages and tools allow portions of code to be reused in programs that require similar routines. Many programmers also customize purchased software or create better software to meet a client's specific needs.

*Computer software engineers* design, develop, test, and evaluate software programs and systems. Although programmers write and support programs in new languages, much of the design and development now is the responsibility of *software engineers* or *software developers*. Software engineers must possess strong programming skills, but are more concerned with developing algorithms and analyzing and solving programming problems than with actually writing code. These professionals develop many types of software, including operating systems software, network distribution software, and a variety of applications software. *Computer systems software engineers* coordinate the construction and maintenance of a company's computer systems, and plan their future growth. They develop software systems for control and automation in manufacturing, business, and other areas. They research, design, and test operating system software, compilers—software that converts programs for faster processing—and network distribution software. *Computer applications software engineers* analyze users' needs and design, create, and modify general computer applications software or specialized utility programs. For example, video game programmers are software engineers who plan and write video game software.

*Computer support specialists* provide technical assistance, support, and advice to customers and users. This group of occupations includes workers with a variety of titles, such as *technical support specialists* and *help-desk technicians*. These troubleshooters interpret problems and provide technical support for software and systems. They answer telephone calls, analyze problems using automated diagnostic programs, and resolve difficulties encountered by users. Support specialists may work either within a company or other organization that uses computer software, or directly for a computer software vendor.

Other computer specialists include a wide range of professionals who specialize in operation, analysis, education, application, or design for a particular piece of the system. Many are involved in the design, testing, and evaluation of network systems such as local area networks (LAN), wide area networks (WAN), the Internet, and other data communications systems. Specialty occupations reflect an emphasis on client-server applications and end-user support; however, occupational titles shift rapidly to reflect new developments in technology.

*Sales and related occupations.* A growing number of marketing and sales workers also are employed in this industry. In order to compete successfully in the online world, the presentation and features of software and other content related to information technology becomes increasingly important. For example, publishers of software that provides connections to the Internet must be able to differentiate their products from those of their competitors. Marketing and sales workers are responsible for promoting and selling the products and services produced by the industry.

## Training and Advancement

Occupations in the software publishing industry require varying levels of education, but in 2006, more than 8 in 10 workers held college degrees. The level of education and type of training required depend on the employer's needs, which often are affected by such things as local demand for workers, project timelines, and changes in technology and business conditions.

*Professional and related occupations.* Although there are no universal educational requirements for computer programmers, workers in this occupation commonly hold a bachelor's degree. Some hold a degree in computer science, mathematics, or information systems. Others have taken special courses in computer programming to supplement their study in fields such as accounting, inventory control, or other areas of business. Because employers' needs are varied, a 2-year degree or certificate may be sufficient for some positions so long as applicants possess the right technical skills. In addition, some employers seek applicants with technical or professional certification. Certification can be obtained independently through a number of organizations, although many vendors now assist employees in becoming certified.

Entry-level computer programmers usually start working with an experienced programmer to update existing code, generate lines of one portion of a larger program, or write relatively simple programs. They then advance to more difficult programming assignments, and may become project supervisors. With continued experience, they may move into management positions within their organizations. Many programmers who work closely with systems analysts advance to systems analyst positions.

Most computer software engineers have at least a bachelor's degree, in addition to broad knowledge and experience with computer systems and technologies. Common degree concentrations for applications software engineers include computer science and software engineering, and common degree concentrations for systems software engineers include computer science and computer information systems. Graduate degrees are preferred for some of the more complex software engineering jobs. Some employers also are seeking workers with additional knowledge and experience. For example, a computer software engineer interested in developing e-commerce applications should have some expertise in sales or finance. In addition, some employers are seeking applicants with technical or professional certification.

**Table 2. Employment of wage and salary workers in software publishers by occupation, 2006 and projected change, 2006-2016.** (Employment in thousands)

| Occupation | Employment, 2006 | | Percent change, 2006-16 |
|---|---|---|---|
| | Number | Percent | |
| **All occupations** | 243 | 100.0 | 32.0 |
| **Management, business, and financial occupations** | 45 | 18.6 | 28.6 |
| General and operations managers | 5 | 2.1 | 15.9 |
| Marketing managers | 4 | 1.5 | 28.8 |
| Sales managers | 3 | 1.1 | 28.8 |
| Computer and information systems managers | 8 | 3.2 | 28.8 |
| Financial managers | 2 | 0.8 | 28.8 |
| Human resources, training, and labor relations specialists | 3 | 1.1 | 33.9 |
| Management analysts | 4 | 1.7 | 28.8 |
| Accountants and auditors | 4 | 1.6 | 28.8 |
| **Professional and related occupations** | 148 | 60.8 | 35.2 |
| Computer and information scientists, research | 3 | 1.2 | 41.6 |
| Computer programmers | 19 | 7.6 | 3.0 |
| Computer software engineers, applications | 37 | 15.2 | 54.5 |
| Computer software engineers, systems software | 21 | 8.8 | 41.6 |
| Computer support specialists | 21 | 8.6 | 15.9 |
| Computer systems analysts | 12 | 5.0 | 41.6 |
| Database administrators | 2 | 1.0 | 41.3 |
| Network and computer systems administrators | 5 | 2.1 | 41.6 |
| Network systems and data communications analysts | 3 | 1.2 | 73.8 |
| Engineers | 2 | 0.8 | 35.1 |
| Market research analysts | 5 | 2.2 | 28.8 |
| Multi-media artists and animators | 2 | 0.9 | 45.7 |
| Graphic designers | 1 | 0.5 | 28.8 |
| Public relations specialists | 1 | 0.5 | 28.8 |
| Technical writers | 3 | 1.3 | 28.8 |
| **Sales and related occupations** | 21 | 8.5 | 28.4 |
| Sales representatives, services | 3 | 1.2 | 42.1 |
| Sales representatives, wholesale and manufacturing, technical and scientific products | 9 | 3.7 | 28.8 |
| Sales representatives, wholesale and manufacturing, except technical and scientific products | 4 | 1.7 | 28.8 |
| Sales engineers | 1 | 0.4 | 28.8 |
| Telemarketers | 1 | 0.6 | 3.0 |
| **Office and administrative support occupations** | 26 | 10.6 | 24.2 |
| Bookkeeping, accounting, and auditing clerks | 3 | 1.2 | 28.8 |
| Customer service representatives | 5 | 1.9 | 41.6 |
| Executive secretaries and administrative assistants | 4 | 1.6 | 28.8 |
| Office clerks, general | 3 | 1.3 | 26.8 |

Note: Columns may not add to totals due to omission of occupations with small employment

Computer software engineers who show leadership ability can become project managers or advance into management positions, such as manager of information systems or even chief information officer.

Persons interested in becoming a computer support specialist generally need only an associate's degree in a computer-related field, as well as significant hands-on experience with computers. They also must possess strong problem-solving, analytical, and communication skills, because troubleshooting and helping

163

others are their main job functions. As technology continues to improve, computer support specialists must constantly strive to stay up to date and acquire new skills if they wish to remain in the field. One way to achieve this is through technical or professional certification.

Computer support specialists who develop expertise in a particular program or type of software can advance to a position as a programmer or software engineer.

*Sales and related occupations.* Many marketing and sales workers are able to secure entry-level jobs with little technical experience, and acquire knowledge of their company's products and services through on-the-job training. Computer specialists also have opportunities to move into sales positions as they gain knowledge of specific products and services. Computer programmers who write accounting software, for example, may use their specialized knowledge to sell such products to similar firms. Also, computer support specialists providing technical support for an operating system may eventually market that product, based on their experience and knowledge of the system.

## Outlook

Employment in the software publishing industry has more than doubled since 1990. As firms continue to invest heavily in information technology, and as the demand for specialized software rises, employment in software publishing is projected to increase by 32 percent from 2006 to 2016.

*Employment change.* Wage and salary jobs in software publishing are expected to increase by 32 percent between 2006 and 2016, nearly three times as fast as the 11 percent growth projected for all industries combined. Growth will not be as rapid as it was during the technology boom of the 1990s, however, as the software industry begins to mature and as routine work is increasingly outsourced to workers in other countries.

Demand for software publishing services will grow as a result of an increasing reliance on information technology, combined with falling prices of computers and related hardware. Individuals and organizations will continue to invest in applications and systems software to maximize the return on their investments in equipment, and to fulfill their growing computing needs. Also, such investments usually continue even during economic downturns, because improved software boosts productivity, increases efficiency, and, in some cases, reduces the need for workers.

The growing reliance on the Internet will be a major driver of job growth. The way the Internet is used is constantly changing, and so is the software required to run the new and emerging computer applications. Electronic commerce, for example, has changed the way companies transact business. E-commerce is automating many steps in the transaction of business between companies, allowing firms to operate more efficiently. Businesses also are moving their supply networks online and developing online marketplaces. The sustained growth of electronic commerce, as well as the growing uses of intranets and extranets, will drive demand for increasingly sophisticated software tools geared towards these technologies. And, as the amount of electronic information stored and accessed continues to grow, new applications and security needs will increase demand for database software.

The proliferation of "mobile" technologies also has created demand for a wide variety of new products and services. For example, the expansion of the wireless Internet, known as WiFi, brings a new aspect of mobility to information technology by allowing people to stay connected to the Internet anywhere, anytime. As businesses and individuals become more dependent on this new technology, there will be an increased need for new software applications in order to maximize the potential of wireless products.

Another significant factor contributing to growth in software is computer security. Organizations invest heavily in software to protect their information and secure their systems from attack. And, as more individuals and organizations are conducting business electronically, the importance of maintaining computer system and network security will increase, leading to greater demand for security software.

Given the increasingly widespread use of information technology and the overall rate of growth expected for the industry, most occupations should grow very rapidly, although some faster than others. The most rapid job growth will occur among computer specialists—especially computer software engineers—as organizations continue to rely on software to maximize the return on their investments in equipment, and as individuals continue to use new and increasing amounts of software applications. Employment of computer programmers should continue to expand, but more slowly than that of other occupations, as more routine programming functions are automated, and as more programming services are outsourced offshore.

*Job prospects.* Job opportunities in software publishing should be excellent for most workers, given the rate at which the industry is expected to grow, and the increasing integration and application of software in all sectors of the economy. Professional workers should enjoy the best opportunities, reflecting employers' continuing demand for higher level skills to keep up with changes in technology. In addition, as individuals and organizations continue to conduct business electronically, the importance of maintaining system and network security will increase. Employment opportunities should be excellent for individuals involved in the development of security software

## Earnings

*Industry earnings.* Employees in the software publishing industry generally command higher earnings than the national average. All production or nonsupervisory workers in the industry averaged $1,444 a week in 2006, significantly higher than the average of $568 for all industries. This reflects the concentration of professionals and specialists who often are highly compensated for their skills or expertise. Given the pace at which technology advances in this industry, earnings can be driven by demand for specific skills or experience. Earnings in the occupations with the largest employment in software publishing appear in table 3.

As one might expect, education and experience influence earnings as well. For example, hourly earnings of computer software engineers, applications ranged from less than $25.17 for the lowest 10 percent to more than $59.78 for the highest 10 percent in May 2006. Managers usually earn more because they have been on the job longer and are more experienced than their staffs, but their salaries also can vary by level and experience. For example, hourly earnings of computer and information systems managers ranged from less than $35.30 for the lowest 10 percent to more than $70.00 for the highest 10 percent in May 2006. Earnings also may be affected by size, location, and type of establishment, hours and responsibilities of the employee, and level of sales.

**Table 3. Median hourly earnings of the largest occupations in software publishers, May 2006**

| Occupation | Software publishers | All industries |
|---|---|---|
| General and operations managers......... | $61.09 | $40.97 |
| Computer and information systems managers................................. | 54.26 | 48.84 |
| Market research analysts........................ | 43.08 | 28.28 |
| Computer software engineers, systems software ................................. | 42.04 | 41.04 |
| Computer software engineers, applications............................................ | 40.66 | 38.36 |
| Computer programmers........................ | 38.11 | 31.50 |
| Computer systems analysts.................... | 35.45 | 33.54 |
| Sales representatives, wholesale and manufacturing, technical and scientific products ............................... | 34.39 | 30.98 |
| Network and computer systems administrators ....................................... | 33.05 | 29.87 |
| Computer support specialists ................. | 22.24 | 19.94 |

***Benefits and union membership.*** Workers generally receive standard benefits, including health insurance, paid vacation and sick leave, and pension plans. Unionization is rare in the software publishing industry. In 2006, virtually no workers were union members or covered by union contracts, compared with 13 percent of workers throughout private industry.

## Sources of Additional Information

Further information about computer careers is available from:
> Association for Computing Machinery, 2 Penn Plaza, Suite 701, New York, NY 10121-0701. Internet: **http://www.acm.org**
> National Workforce Center for Emerging Technologies, 3000 Landerholm Circle SE., Bellevue, WA 98007. Internet: **http://www.nwcet.org**

Information on the certified software development professional program can be found at:
> Institute of Electrical and Electronics Engineers Computer Society, Headquarters Office, 1730 Massachusetts Ave. NW., Washington, DC 20036-1992. Internet: **http://www.computer.org/certification**
> University of Washington Computer Science and Engineering Department, AC101 Paul G. Allen Center, Box 352350, 185 Stevens Way, Seattle, WA 98195-2350. Internet: **http://www.cs.washington.edu/WhyCSE/**

Information on the following occupations can be found in the 2008–09 *Occupational Outlook Handbook*:
* Computer and information systems managers
* Computer programmers
* Computer scientists and database administrators
* Computer software engineers
* Computer support specialists and systems administrators
* Computer systems analysts

# Telecommunications

## SIGNIFICANT POINTS

- Telecommunications includes voice, video, and Internet communications services.

- Employment will grow because technological advances will expand the range of services offered.

- With rapid technological changes in telecommunications, those with up-to-date technical skills will have the best job opportunities.

- Average earnings in telecommunications greatly exceed average earnings throughout private industry.

## Nature of the Industry

*Goods and services.* The telecommunications industry delivers voice communications, data, graphics, television, and video at ever increasing speeds and in an increasing number of ways. Whereas wireline telephone communication was once the primary service of the industry, wireless communication services, Internet service, and cable and satellite program distribution make up an increasing share of the industry.

*Industry organization.* The largest sector of the telecommunications industry continues to be made up of wired telecommunications carriers. Establishments in this sector mainly provide telecommunications services via wires and cables that connect customers' premises to central offices maintained by telecommunications companies. The central offices contain switching equipment that routes content to its final destination or to another switching center that determines the most efficient route for the content to take. These companies also maintain the cable network that connects different regions of the country as well as foreign countries, and forms the backbone of the industry. While voice used to be the main type of data transmitted over the wires, wired telecommunications service now includes the transmission of all types of graphic, video, and electronic data mainly over the Internet.

These new services are made possible through the use of digital technologies that provide much more efficient use of the telecommunications networks. One major technology breaks digital signals into packets during transmission. Networks of computerized switching equipment route the packets. Packets may take separate paths to their destination and may share the paths with packets from other users. At the destination, the packets are reassembled, and the transmission is completed. Because packet switching considers alternate routes, and allows multiple transmissions to share the same route, it results in a more efficient use of telecommunications capacity as packets are routed along less congested routes.

The transmission of voice signals requires relatively small amounts of capacity on telecommunications networks. By contrast, the transmission of data, video, and graphics requires much higher capacity. This transmission capacity is referred to as "bandwidth." As the demand increases for high-capacity transmissions—especially with the rising volume of Internet data—telecommunications companies have been expanding and upgrading their networks to increase the amount of available bandwidth.

Cable and other program distribution is another sector of the telecommunications industry. Establishments in this sector provide television and other services on a subscription or fee basis. These establishments do not include cable networks. (Information on cable networks is included in the section on broadcasting, which appears elsewhere in the *Career Guide.*) Distributors of pay television services transmit programming through two basic types of systems. Cable systems transmit programs over fiber optic and coaxial cables. Direct broadcasting satellite (DBS) operators constitute a growing segment of the pay television industry. DBS operators transmit programming from orbiting satellites to customers' receivers, known as minidishes. Establishments in the cable and other program distribution industry generate revenue through subscriptions, providing Internet access, providing phone service, and advertising sales. They also charge fees for pay-per-view or video-on-demand programs.

Wireless telecommunications carriers, many of which are subsidiaries of the wired carriers, transmit voice, graphics, data, and Internet access through the transmission of signals over networks of radio towers. The signal is transmitted through an antenna into the wireline network. Increasing numbers of consumers are choosing to replace their home landline phones with wireless phones. Other wireless services include beeper and paging services.

Resellers of telecommunications services are another sector of the telecommunications industry. These resellers lease transmission facilities, such as telephone lines or space on a satellite, from existing telecommunications networks, and then resell the service to other customers. Other sectors in the industry include message communications services such as e-mail and facsimile services, satellite telecommunications, and operators of other communication services ranging from radar stations to radio networks used by taxicab companies.

*Recent developments.* Telecommunications carriers are expanding their bandwidth by replacing copper wires with fiber optic cable. Fiber optic cable, which transmits light signals along glass strands, permits faster, higher capacity transmissions than traditional copper wirelines. In some areas, carriers are extending fiber optic cable to residential customers, enabling them to offer cable television, video-on-demand, very high-speed Internet, and conventional telephone communications over a single line. However, the high cost of extending fiber to homes has slowed deployment. In most areas, wired carriers are instead leveraging existing copper lines that connect most residential customers with a central office, to provide digital subscriber lines (DSL)

Internet service. Technologies in development will further boost the speeds and services available through a DSL connection.

Changes in technology and regulation now allow cable television providers to compete directly with telephone companies. An important change has been the rapid increase in two-way communications capacity. Conventional pay television services provided communications only from the distributor to the customer. These services could not provide effective communications from the customer back to other points in the system due to signal interference and the limited capacity of conventional cable systems. Cable operators are implementing new technologies to reduce signal interference and increase the capacity of their distribution systems by installing fiber optic cables and improving data compression. This allows some pay television systems to offer two-way telecommunications services, such as video-on-demand and high-speed Internet access.

Cable companies are increasing their share of the telephone communications market by using high-speed Internet access to provide VoIP (voice over Internet protocol). VoIP is sometimes called Internet telephony, because it uses the Internet to transmit phone calls. While conventional phone networks use packet switching to break up a call onto multiple shared lines between central offices, VoIP extends this process to the phone. A VoIP phone will break the conversation into digital packets and transmit those packets over a high-speed Internet connection. Cable companies use the technology to offer phone services without building a conventional phone network. Wireline providers' high-speed Internet connections also can be used for VoIP and cellular phones are being developed that use VoIP to make calls using local wireless Internet connections. All of the major sectors of the telecommunications industry are or will increasingly use VoIP.

Wireless telecommunications carriers are deploying several new technologies to allow faster data transmission and better Internet access that should make them more competitive with wireline carriers. With faster Internet connections speeds, wireless carriers are selling music, videos, and other exclusive content that can be downloaded and played on cellular phones. Wireless equipment companies are developing the next generation of technologies that will allow even faster data transmission. The replacement of landlines with cellular service should become increasingly common because advances in wireless systems will provide ever faster data transmission speeds.

## Working Conditions

***Hours.*** The telecommunications industry offers steady, year-round employment. Workers in this industry are sometimes required to work overtime, especially during emergencies such as floods or hurricanes when employees may need to report to work with little notice.

***Work Environment.*** Installation, maintenance, and repair occupations account for 1 in 4 telecommunications jobs. One of the largest occupations is telecommunications line installers and repairers, who work in a variety of places, both indoors and outdoors, and in all kinds of weather. Their work involves lifting, climbing, reaching, stooping, crouching, and crawling. They must work in high places such as rooftops and telephone poles, or below ground when working with buried lines. Their jobs bring them into proximity with electrical wires and circuits, so they must take precautions to avoid shocks. These workers must wear safety equipment when entering manholes, and test for the presence of gas before going underground.

Telecommunications equipment installers and repairers, except line installers, generally work indoors—most often in a telecommunication company's central office or a customer's home or place of business. They may have to stand for long periods; climb ladders; and do some reaching, stooping, and light lifting. Following safety procedures is essential to guard against work injuries such as minor burns and electrical shock.

Most communications equipment operators, such as telephone operators, work at video display terminals in pleasant, well-lighted, air-conditioned surroundings. The rapid pace of the job and close supervision may cause stress. Some workplaces have introduced innovative practices among their operators to reduce job-related stress.

Most other telecommunications managers, administrative workers, and professionals work 40-hour weeks in comfortable offices. Customer service representatives may work in call centers where they answer customer service calls—many during evening and weekend hours.

In past years the number of disabling injuries in telephone communications, the principal sector of the telecommunications industry, has been well below the average for all industries.

## Employment

The telecommunications industry provided 973,000 wage and salary jobs in 2006. Wired telecommunications carriers accounted for 49 percent of all telecommunications jobs in 2006, while 21 percent of jobs were with the wireless telecommunications carriers, and 15 percent were with cable and other program distributors. The remaining jobs were mostly with satellite telecommunications and telecommunications resellers.

More than half of telecommunications employees work in small to medium size establishments employing between 5 and 249 workers (chart). With continuing deregulation, the number of small contractors has been increasing. Telecommunications jobs are found in almost every community, but most employees work in cities that have large concentrations of industrial and business establishments.

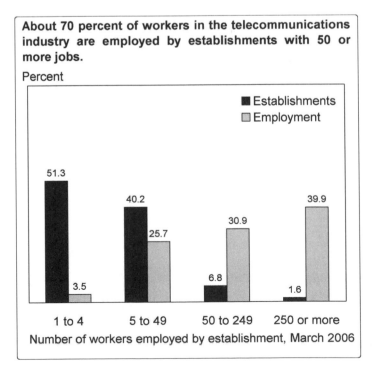

**About 70 percent of workers in the telecommunications industry are employed by establishments with 50 or more jobs.**

Percent

- ■ Establishments
- □ Employment

| | 1 to 4 | 5 to 49 | 50 to 249 | 250 or more |
|---|---|---|---|---|
| Establishments | 51.3 | 40.2 | 6.8 | 1.6 |
| Employment | 3.5 | 25.7 | 30.9 | 39.9 |

Number of workers employed by establishment, March 2006

## Occupations in the Industry

Although the telecommunications industry employs workers in many different occupations, 56 percent of all workers are employed in either installation, maintenance, and repair occupations or office and administrative support occupations (table 1).

*Installation, maintenance, and repair occupations.* Telecommunications craft workers install, repair, and maintain telephone equipment, cables and access lines, and telecommunications systems. These workers can be grouped by the type of work they perform. *Line installers and repairers* connect central offices to customers' buildings. They install poles and terminals, and place wires and cables that lead to a consumer's premises. Some may install lines or equipment inside a customer's business or residence. They use power-driven equipment to dig holes and set telephone poles. Line installers climb the poles or work in truck-mounted buckets (aerial work platforms) that lift them up to lines and attach the cables using various handtools. After line installers place cables on poles or towers or in underground conduits and trenches, they complete the line connections. Some line installers, called *cable splicers,* specialize in splicing together two telecommunication lines.

*Telecommunications equipment installers and repairers, except line installers,* install, repair, and maintain the array of increasingly complex and sophisticated communications equipment and cables. Their work includes setting up, rearranging, and removing the complex switching and dialing equipment used in central offices. They may also solve network-related problems and program equipment to provide special features.

Some telecommunications equipment installers are referred to as telephone station installers and repairers. They install, service, and repair telephone systems and other communications equipment on customers' property. When customers move or request new types of service, such as a high-speed Internet connection, a fax, or an additional line, installers relocate telephones or make changes in existing equipment. They assemble equipment and install wiring. They also connect telephones to outside service wires and sometimes must climb poles or ladders to make these connections.

Cable installers travel to customers' premises to set up pay television service so that customers can receive programming. Cable service installers connect a customer's television set to the cable serving the entire neighborhood. Wireless and satellite service installers attach antennas or satellite dishes to the sides of customers' houses. These devices must be positioned to provide clear lines of sight to satellite locations. (Satellite installation may be handled by employees of retail stores that sell satellite dishes. Such workers are not employed by the telecommunications industry.) Installers check the strength and clarity of the television signal before completing the installation. They also may need to explain to the subscriber how pay television services operate. As these services expand to include telephone and high-speed Internet access, it is increasingly important that they have an understanding of these services' basic technology and computer software and be able to communicate that knowledge to customers.

*Office and administrative support occupations.* Telephone operators make telephone connections, assist customers with specialized services such as reverse-charge calls, and provide telephone numbers. They also may provide emergency assistance.

*Customer service representatives* help customers understand the new and varied types of services offered by telecommunica-

**Table 1. Employment of wage and salary workers in telecommunications by occupation, 2006 and projected change, 2006-2016.**
(Employment in thousands)

| Occupation | Employment, 2006 | | Percent change, 2006-16 |
|---|---|---|---|
| | Number | Percent | |
| **All occupations** | 973 | 100.0 | 5.0 |
| **Management, business, and financial occupations** | 102 | 10.5 | 3.6 |
| General and operations managers | 9 | 0.9 | -3.0 |
| Marketing and sales managers | 8 | 0.8 | 8.9 |
| Computer and information systems managers | 5 | 0.6 | 3.6 |
| Purchasing agents, except wholesale, retail, and farm products | 5 | 0.5 | 0.9 |
| Human resources, training, and labor relations specialists | 9 | 1.0 | 10.2 |
| Management analysts | 6 | 0.7 | -5.7 |
| Accountants and auditors | 8 | 0.8 | 1.3 |
| Financial analysts | 5 | 0.5 | 13.6 |
| **Professional and related occupations** | 160 | 16.5 | 6.8 |
| Computer software engineers | 26 | 2.7 | 9.0 |
| Computer support specialists | 13 | 1.4 | 10.4 |
| Computer systems analysts | 9 | 1.0 | 12.4 |
| Network and computer systems administrators | 15 | 1.5 | 2.6 |
| Network systems and data communications analysts | 21 | 2.2 | 26.1 |
| Electrical and electronics engineers | 26 | 2.7 | 2.2 |
| Electrical and electronic engineering technicians | 13 | 1.4 | -6.2 |
| Market research analysts | 6 | 0.6 | 3.8 |
| **Sales and related occupations** | 162 | 16.7 | 10.7 |
| Supervisors, sales workers | 16 | 1.7 | 10.9 |
| Retail salespersons | 37 | 3.8 | 24.4 |
| Sales representatives, services | 66 | 6.7 | 14.1 |
| Sales representatives, wholesale and manufacturing | 15 | 1.6 | 8.4 |
| Sales engineers | 5 | 0.5 | -9.9 |
| Telemarketers | 19 | 2.0 | -21.3 |
| **Office and administrative support occupations** | 283 | 29.0 | 8.9 |
| First-line supervisors/managers of office and administrative support workers | 21 | 2.1 | -0.9 |
| Telephone operators | 18 | 1.8 | -45.0 |
| Bill and account collectors | 8 | 0.8 | 15.1 |
| Bookkeeping, accounting, and auditing clerks | 10 | 1.1 | 2.1 |
| Customer service representatives | 137 | 14.1 | 28.3 |
| Order clerks | 12 | 1.2 | -37.0 |
| Dispatchers, except police, fire, and ambulance | 5 | 0.5 | 9.4 |
| Secretaries and administrative assistants | 16 | 1.6 | 0.9 |
| Office clerks, general | 17 | 1.8 | 2.2 |
| **Installation, maintenance, and repair occupations** | 258 | 26.6 | -3.3 |
| First-line supervisors/managers of mechanics, installers, and repairers | 19 | 1.9 | -1.9 |
| Telecommunications equipment installers and repairers, except line installers | 126 | 13.0 | -8.5 |
| Electrical and electronics repairers, commercial and industrial equipment | 3 | 0.3 | 30.6 |
| Electronic home entertainment equipment installers and repairers | 4 | 0.4 | 29.3 |
| Telecommunications line installers and repairers | 90 | 9.2 | -0.4 |

Note: Columns may not add to totals due to omission of occupations with small employment

tions providers. Some customer service representatives also are expected to sell services and may work on a commission basis. Other administrative support workers include *financial, information, and records clerks*; *secretaries and administrative assistants*; and *first-line supervisors/managers of office and administrative support workers*. These workers keep service records, compile and send bills to customers, and prepare statistical and other company reports, among other duties.

*Professional and sales occupations.* Seventeen percent of the industry's employees are professional workers. (Many additional workers in these occupations are employed at the headquarters or research facilities of the companies, establishments included in other industries, not the telecommunications industry.) Many of these are scientific and technical personnel such as engineers and computer specialists. *Engineers* plan cable and microwave routes, central office and PBX equipment installations, and the expansion of existing structures, and solve other engineering problems. Some engineers also engage in research and development of new equipment. Many specialize in telecommunications design or voice, video, or data communications systems, and integrate communications equipment with computer networks. Others research, design, and develop gas lasers and related equipment needed to send messages through fiber optic cables. They study the limitations and uses of lasers and fiber optics; find new applications for them; and oversee the building, testing, and operations of the new applications. They work closely with clients, who may not understand sophisticated communications systems, and design systems that meet their customers' needs.

*Computer software engineers* and *network systems and data communications analysts* design, develop, test, and debug software products. These include computer-assisted engineering programs for schematic cabling projects; modeling programs for cellular and satellite systems; and programs for telephone options, such as voice mail, e-mail, and call waiting. Telecommunications specialists coordinate the installation of these systems and may provide follow-up maintenance and training. In addition, the industry employs many other managerial, business and financial, professional, and technical workers, such as *accountants and auditors*; *human resources, training, and labor relations managers; engineering technicians*; and *computer programmers*.

Seventeen percent of the industry's employees are in sales and related occupations. In addition to selling telecommunications and related services to businesses and residential customers, the industry employs a large number of advertising sales workers that sell advertising on their cable or satellite systems or for their telephone directories.

## Training and Advancement
Training is a key component in the careers of most who work in the telecommunications industry. Due to the rapid introduction of new technologies and services, the telecommunications industry is among the most rapidly changing in the economy. This means workers must keep their job skills up to date. From managers to communications equipment operators, increased knowledge of both computer hardware and software is of paramount importance. Telecommunications industry employers now look for workers with knowledge of and skills in computer programming and software design; voice telephone technology, known as telephony; laser and fiber optic technology; wireless technology; and data compression. Several major companies and the telecommunications unions have created a Web site that provides free training for employees, enabling them to keep their knowledge current and helping them to advance.

The telecommunications industry offers employment in jobs requiring a variety of skills and training. Many jobs require at least a high school diploma or an associate degree in addition to on-the-job training. Other jobs require particular skills that may take several years of experience to learn completely. For some managerial, professional, and maintenance and repair jobs, employers require a college education.

*Installation, maintenance, and repair occupations.* Telecommunications line installers and repairers often are hired initially as helpers, grounds workers, or tree trimmers who clear branches from lines. Because the work entails a lot of climbing, applicants should have physical stamina and be unafraid of heights. The ability to distinguish colors is important because wires and cables are coded by color. Although many line installers and repairers do not complete a formal apprenticeship, they generally receive several years of on-the-job training, which may also include some classroom or online training. Line installers may transfer to other highly skilled jobs, such as telecommunications equipment installer and repairer, or may move into other kinds of work, such as sales. Promotion to crew supervisor, technical staff, or instructor of new employees also is possible.

Most companies prefer to hire telecommunications equipment installers and repairers with postsecondary training in electronics; some choose to hire persons with experience as line installers. Training sources include 2- and 4-year college programs in electronics or communications, trade schools, and training provided by telecommunications companies and equipment and software manufacturers. Employers often provide training to help equipment installers and repairers to keep up-to-date with advances current technology and improve their skills. The National Coalition For Telecommunications Education and Learning (NACTEL) is one of several organizations that work with companies and unions to offer such training. Telecommunications equipment installers and repairers may advance to jobs maintaining more sophisticated equipment or to engineering technician positions.

*Office and administrative occupations.* Communications equipment operators should have clear speech and good hearing; computer literacy and keyboarding skills also are important. New operators learn equipment operation and procedures for maximizing efficiency. Instructors monitor both the time and quality of trainees' responses to customer requests. Formal classroom instruction and on-the-job training may last several weeks.

*Professional and sales occupations.* A bachelor's degree in engineering usually is required for entry-level jobs as electrical and electronics engineers. Continuing education is important for these engineers; those who fail to keep up with the rapid changes in technology risk technological obsolescence, which makes them more susceptible to layoffs or, at a minimum, more likely to be passed over for advancement.

While there is no universally accepted way to prepare for a job as a computer professional, most employers place a premium on some formal college education. Computer software engineers usually hold a degree in computer science or in software engineering. For systems analyst, computer scientist, or database administrator positions, many employers seek applicants who have a bachelor's degree in computer science, information science, or management information systems.

For sales jobs, individuals are sought with sales ability enhanced by interpersonal skills and knowledge of telecommunications terminology.

## Outlook

Greater demand for an increasing number of telecommunications services will cause overall employment in the telecommunications industry to increase. In addition, many job opportunities will result from the need to replace a large number of workers who are expected to retire in the coming decade.

*Employment change.* Employment in the telecommunications industry is expected to increase by 5 percent over the 2006-16 period, compared with 11 percent growth for all industries combined. The building of more advanced communications networks, such as fiber optic lines, faster wireless networks, and advanced switching equipment, will increase employment, particularly in the near term. In the long-term, employment gains will be partially offset by the improved reliability of these advanced networks which is expected to reduce maintenance requirements.

These improvements in the telecommunications networks are expected to result in greater demand by people and businesses for ever wider ranges of telecommunications services. Residences will demand more services such as high-speed Internet, video-on-demand, and wireless and Internet-based telephone services. Businesses will demand faster and improved telecommunications systems to conduct electronic commerce, ordering, record keeping, and video conferencing. These services are being supplied increasingly by all the competing sectors of the industry, as the lines become blurred between cable and satellite TV, wireless, and wireline telecommunications systems. However, employment is projected to vary by sector. Wireless companies will continue to expand their networks and increase the density of their towers to provide higher speed services, which will cause employment to grow in this sector. Cable distribution companies also will grow as they upgrade their networks to expand the array of channels and other services they offer. Wired telecommunications carriers are expected to employ fewer people as a result of increased competition from wireless and cable distribution companies. The growth of these services will lead to continued upgrades of telecommunications networks and the continuing need for workers to install and repair the communications network. Demand for high-speed global bandwidth by businesses and consumers will drive growth in the construction of undersea cables and orbiting satellites.

Employment is projected to differ among the various occupations in the telecommunications industry. As more residences and businesses become wired and the networks become more reliable, the need for installation and repair workers will show little change or decline, but as the number of services offered increases and competition between companies grows, sales and customer service workers will grow and make up a larger portion of the workforce.

Employment of line installers and repairers is expected to show little change as increasing installations are offset by newer more reliable networks and greater use of wireless technology. Employment of telecommunications equipment installers and repairers is expected to decline because newer, more reliable technologies will reduce the need for equipment maintenance. Employment of these workers also will be limited by the tendency of many companies to contract out maintenance and installation work to specialized contractors that are part of the construction

or retail industries.

Sales occupations and customer service representatives will have the largest increases in employment. These people are needed to sell the wider array of services being offered and to answer customer's questions about these increasingly complex services and to help solve problems when they arise.

Employment of electrical and electronics engineers and computer professionals also are expected to grow. The expansion of communications networks and the need for telecommunications providers to invest in research and development will create job opportunities for these workers.

Employment of telephone operators is expected to decline due to increasing automation. Computer voice recognition technology lessens the need for central office operators, as customers can obtain help with long-distance calls from automated systems. This technology, which also enables callers to request numbers from a computer instead of a person, is expected to reduce the number of directory assistance operators. The numbers of these workers will drop further as more customers use automated directory assistance resources on the Internet.

*Job prospects.* With a growing number of retirements and the continuing need for skilled workers, good job opportunities will be available for individuals with up-to-date technical skills. Jobs prospects will be best for those with 2 or 4-year degrees.

## Earnings

*Industry earnings.* Average weekly earnings of nonsupervisory workers in the telecommunications industry were $963 in 2006, significantly higher than average earnings of $579 in private industry. Table 2 presents earnings in selected occupations in telecommunications in 2006.

*Benefits and union membership.* Most full-time workers in the utilities industry receive substantial benefits in addition to their salaries or hourly wages. This is particularly true for those workers covered by a collective bargaining agreement. Twenty-two percent of employees in the industry are union members or covered by union contracts, compared with about 13 percent for all industries. Most telecommunications employees belong to the Communications Workers of America or the International Brotherhood of Electrical Workers.

**Table 2. Median hourly earnings of the largest occupations in telecommunications, May 2006**

| Occupation | Telecommunications | All industries |
|---|---|---|
| Electronics engineers, except computer .. | $35.28 | $38.97 |
| Network systems and data communications analysts...................... | 34.11 | 31.06 |
| Business operations specialists, all other.............. | 32.28 | 26.76 |
| First-line supervisors/managers of office and administrative support workers....... | 26.37 | 20.92 |
| Telecommunications equipment installers and repairers, except line installers........ | 26.07 | 25.21 |
| Telecommunications line installers and repairers............. | 25.43 | 22.25 |
| Sales representatives, services, all other .. | 23.13 | 23.12 |
| Telemarketers ......................... | 16.16 | 10.09 |
| Customer service representatives ........... | 15.62 | 13.62 |
| Retail salespersons ............... | 11.10 | 9.50 |

170

## Sources of Additional Information

For information about employment opportunities, contact your local telecommunications company, or:

➤ International Brotherhood of Electrical Workers, Telecommunications Department, 900 Seventh St. NW., Washington, DC 20001.
➤ Communications Workers of America, 501 3rd St. NW., Washington, DC 20001.

For information about certifications and courses in telecommunications, particularly for those already in the telecommunications industry, contact:

➤ NACTEL National Coalition For Telecommunications Education and Learning, CAEL, 6021 South Syracuse Way, Suite 213 Greenwood Village, CO 80111. Internet: **http://www.nactel.org**

For information about certifications and courses on cable and telecommunications technology, contact:

➤ Society of Cable and Telecommunications Engineers (SCTE), 140 Phillips Rd., Exton, PA 19341-1318. Internet: **http://www.scte.org**

More information about the following occupations in the telecommunications industry appears in the 2008-09 edition of the *Occupational Outlook Handbook*.

• Communications equipment operators
• Customer service representatives
• Engineers
• Line installers and repairers
• Radio and telecommunications equipment installers and repairers

# Financial Activities

# Banking

(NAICS 521, 5221)

## SIGNIFICANT POINTS

- Office and administrative support workers constitute 2 out of 3 jobs; tellers account for about 3 out of 10 jobs.

- Many job opportunities are expected for tellers and other office and administrative support workers, because these occupations are large and have high turnover.

- Many management positions are filled by promoting experienced, technically skilled professional personnel.

## Nature of the Industry

Banks safeguard money and valuables and provide loans, credit, and payment services, such as checking accounts, money orders, and cashier's checks. Banks also may offer investment and insurance products, which they were once prohibited from selling. As a variety of models for cooperation and integration among finance industries have emerged, some of the traditional distinctions between banks, insurance companies, and securities firms have diminished. In spite of these changes, banks continue to maintain and perform their primary role—accepting deposits and lending funds from these deposits.

*Goods and services.* Banking is comprised of two parts: Monetary Authorities—Central Bank, and Credit Intermediation and Related Activities. The former includes the bank establishments of the U.S. Federal Reserve System that manage the Nation's money supply and international reserves, hold reserve deposits of other domestic banks and the central banks of other countries, and issue the currency we use. The establishments in the credit intermediation and related services industry provide banking services to the general public. They securely save the money of depositors, provide checking services, and lend the funds raised from depositors to consumers and businesses for mortgages, investment loans, and lines of credit.

*Industry organization.* There are several types of banks, which differ in the number of services they provide and the clientele they serve. Although some of the differences between these types of banks have lessened as they have begun to expand the range of products and services they offer, there are still key distinguishing traits. *Commercial banks*, which dominate this industry, offer a full range of services for individuals, businesses, and governments. These banks come in a wide range of sizes, from large global banks to regional and community banks. Global banks are involved in international lending and foreign currency trading, in addition to the more typical banking services. Regional banks have numerous branches and automated teller machine (ATM) locations throughout a multi-state area that provide banking services to individuals. Banks have become more oriented toward marketing and sales. As a result, employees need to know about all types of products and services offered by banks. Community banks are based locally and offer more personal attention, which many individuals and small businesses prefer. In recent years, online banks—which provide all services entirely over the Internet—have entered the market, with some

success. However, many traditional banks have also expanded to offer online banking, and some formerly Internet-only banks are opting to open branches.

*Savings banks* and *savings and loan associations*, sometimes called thrift institutions, are the second largest group of depository institutions. They were first established as community-based institutions to finance mortgages for people to buy homes and still cater mostly to the savings and lending needs of individuals.

*Credit unions* are another kind of depository institution. Most credit unions are formed by people with a common bond, such as those who work for the same company or belong to the same labor union or church. Members pool their savings and, when they need money, they may borrow from the credit union, often at a lower interest rate than that demanded by other financial institutions.

*Federal Reserve banks* are Government agencies that perform many financial services for the Government. Their chief responsibilities are to regulate the banking industry and to help implement our Nation's monetary policy so our economy can run more efficiently by controlling the Nation's money supply—the total quantity of money in the country, including cash and bank deposits. For example, during slower periods of economic activity, the Federal Reserve may purchase government securities from commercial banks, giving them more money to lend, thus expanding the economy. Federal Reserve banks also perform a variety of services for other banks. For example, they may make emergency loans to banks that are short of cash, and clear checks that are drawn and paid out by different banks.

Interest on loans is the principal source of revenue for most banks, making their various lending departments critical to their success. The commercial lending department loans money to companies to start or expand their business or to purchase inventory and capital equipment. The consumer lending department handles student loans, credit cards, and loans for home improvements, debt consolidation, and automobile purchases. Finally, the mortgage lending department loans money to individuals and businesses to purchase real estate.

The money banks lend comes primarily from deposits in checking and savings accounts, certificates of deposit, money market accounts, and other deposit accounts that consumers and businesses set up with the bank. These deposits often earn interest for their owners, and accounts that offer checking provide owners with an easy method for making payments safely without using cash. Deposits in many banks are insured by the

Federal Deposit Insurance Corporation, which guarantees that depositors will get their money back, up to a stated limit, if a bank should fail.

***Recent developments.*** Technology is having a major impact on the banking industry. Direct deposit allows companies and governments to electronically transfer payments into various accounts. Debit cards, which may also be used as ATM cards, instantaneously deduct money from an account when the card is swiped across a machine at a store's cash register. Electronic banking by phone or computer allows customers to access information such as account balances and statement history, pay bills, and transfer money from one account to another. Some banks also have begun offering online account aggregation, which makes available in one place detailed and up-to date information on a customer's accounts held at various institutions.

Advancements in technology have also led to improvements in the ways in which banks process information. The use of check imaging allows banks to store photographed checks on the computer instead of paper files. Also, the availability and growing use of credit scoring software allows lending departments to approve loans in minutes, rather than days.

Other fundamental changes are occurring in the industry as banks diversify their services to become more competitive. Many banks now offer their customers financial planning and asset management services, as well as brokerage and insurance services, often through a subsidiary or third party. Others are beginning to provide investment banking services—usually through a subsidiary—that help companies and governments raise money through the issuance of stocks and bonds. As banks respond to deregulation and as competition in this sector grows, the nature of the banking industry will continue to undergo significant change.

## Working Conditions

***Hours.*** The average workweek for nonsupervisory workers in depository credit intermediation was 35.7 hours in 2006. Supervisory and managerial employees, however, usually work substantially longer hours. About 1 out of 10 employees in 2006, mostly tellers, worked part-time.

Employees in a typical branch work weekdays, some evenings if the bank is open late, and Saturday mornings. However, banks are increasingly expanding the hours that their branches are open and opening branches in nontraditional locations. For example, hours may be longer for workers in bank branches located in grocery stores and shopping malls, which are open most evenings and weekends. To improve customer service and provide greater access to bank personnel, banks are establishing centralized phone centers, staffed mainly by customer service representatives. Employees of phone centers spend most of their time answering phone calls from customers and must be available to work evening and weekend shifts.

Administrative support employees may work in large processing facilities, in the banks' headquarters, or in other administrative offices. Most support staff work a standard 40-hour week; some may work overtime. Those support staff located in the processing facilities may work evening shifts.

***Work Environment.*** Branch office jobs, particularly teller positions, require continual communication with customers, repetitive tasks, and a high level of attention to security. Tellers also work for long periods in a confined space.

Commercial and mortgage loan officers often work out of the office, visiting clients, checking loan applications, and soliciting new business. Loan officers may travel to meet out-of-town clients, or work evenings if that is the only time at which a client can meet. Financial service-sales representatives also may visit clients in the evenings and on weekends to go over the client's financial needs.

The remaining employees located primarily at the headquarters or other administrative offices usually work in comfortable surroundings and put in a standard workweek. In general, banks are relatively safe places to work. In 2006, the rate of work-related injury and illness per 100 full-time workers was 1.1 in central banks (monetary authorities) and 2.7 in other banking establishments (depository credit intermediation), both lower than the overall rate of 4.4 per 100 employees in the private sector.

## Employment

The banking industry employed about 1.8 million wage and salary workers in 2006.

About 7 out of 10 jobs were in commercial banks; the remainder were concentrated in savings institutions and credit unions (table 1).

In 2006, about 84 percent of establishments in banking employed fewer than 20 workers (chart). However, these small establishments, mostly bank branch offices, employed 36 percent of all employees. About 64 percent of the jobs were in establishments with 20 or more workers. Banks are found everywhere in the United States, but most bank employees work in heavily populated States such as New York, California, Illinois, Pennsylvania, and Texas.

## Occupations in the Industry

Banks employ various types of financial and customer service occupations. Tellers make up the largest number of workers, and overall office and administrative support occupations make up the largest portion of jobs in the industry. Management, business, and financial occupations also employ a significant number of employees in the banking industry.

***Office and administrative support occupations.*** These occupations account for 2 out of 3 jobs in the banking industry (table 2). *Bank tellers*, the largest number of workers in banking, provide routine financial services to the public. They handle customers' deposits and withdrawals, change money, sell money orders and traveler's checks, and accept payment for loans and utility bills. Increasingly, tellers also are selling bank services to customers. *New accounts clerks* and *customer service representatives* answer questions from customers, and help them open and close accounts and fill out forms to apply for banking services. They are knowledgeable about a broad array of bank services and must

**Table 1. Percent distribution of employment and establishments in banking by detailed industry sector, 2006**

| Industry Segment | Employment | Establishments |
|---|---|---|
| **Total** | 100.0% | 100.0% |
| **Monetary authorities - central bank** | 1.2 | 0.3 |
| **Depository credit intermediation** | 98.8 | 99.7 |
| Commercial banking | 72.5 | 69.7 |
| Savings institutions | 13.1 | 14.7 |
| Credit unions | 12.1 | 14.2 |
| Other depository credit intermediation | 1.2 | 1.1 |

176

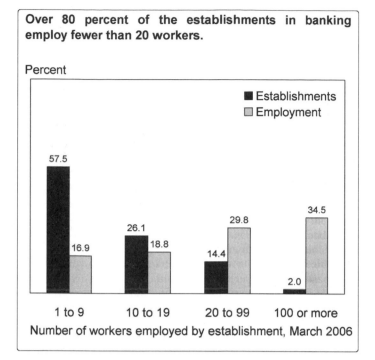

**Over 80 percent of the establishments in banking employ fewer than 20 workers.**

Percent

Legend:
■ Establishments
□ Employment

- 1 to 9: 57.5 (Establishments), 16.9 (Employment)
- 10 to 19: 26.1 (Establishments), 18.8 (Employment)
- 20 to 99: 14.4 (Establishments), 29.8 (Employment)
- 100 or more: 2.0 (Establishments), 34.5 (Employment)

Number of workers employed by establishment, March 2006

be able to sell those services to potential clients. Some customer service representatives work in a call or customer contact center environment, taking phone calls and answering emails from customers. In addition to responding to inquiries, these workers also help customers over the phone with routine banking transactions, and handle and resolve problems or complaints.

*Loan* and *credit clerks* assemble and prepare paperwork, process applications, and complete the documentation after a loan or line of credit has been approved. They also verify applications for completeness. *Bill and account collectors* attempt to collect payments on overdue loans. Many *general office clerks* and *bookkeeping, accounting, and auditing clerks* are employed to maintain financial records, enter data, and process the thousands of deposit slips, checks, and other documents that banks handle daily. Banks also employ many *secretaries*, *data entry and information processing workers*, *receptionists*, and other office and administrative support workers. *Office and administrative support worker supervisors and managers* oversee the activities and training of workers in the various administrative support occupations.

*Management, business, and financial occupations.* These occupations account for about 25 percent of employment in the banking industry. *Financial managers* direct bank branches and departments, resolve customers' problems, ensure that standards of service are maintained, and administer the institutions' operations and investments. *Loan officers* evaluate loan applications, determine an applicant's ability to repay a loan, and recommend approval of loans. They usually specialize in commercial, consumer, or mortgage lending. When loans become delinquent, loan officers, or *loan counselors*, may advise borrowers on the management of their finances or take action to collect outstanding amounts. Loan officers also play a major role in bringing in new business and spend much of their time developing relationships with potential customers. *Trust officers* manage a variety of assets that were placed in trust with the bank for other people or organizations; these assets can include pension funds, school endowments, or a company's profit-sharing plan. Sometimes,

trust officers act as executors of estates upon a person's death. They also may work as accountants, lawyers, and investment managers.

*Securities, commodities, and financial services sales agents*, who make up the majority of sales positions in banks, sell complex banking services. They contact potential customers to explain their services and to ascertain the customer's banking and other financial needs. They also may discuss services, such as deposit accounts, lines of credit, sales or inventory financing, certificates of deposit, cash management, or investment services. These sales agents also solicit businesses to participate in consumer credit card programs. At most small and medium-size banks, however, branch managers and commercial loan officers are responsible for marketing the bank's financial services. This has become a more important task in recent years.

***Other occupations.*** Occupations used widely by banks to maintain financial records and ensure the bank's compliance with Federal and State regulations are *accountants and auditors*, and *lawyers*. In addition, *computer specialists* maintain and upgrade the bank's computer systems and implement the bank's entry into the world of electronic banking and paperless transactions.

## Training and Advancement

A high school education is usually all that is needed for most office and administrative occupations, while management, business and financial occupations usually employ workers with at least a college degree. Good communication and customer service skills are necessary for all occupations in the banking industry.

***Office and administrative support occupations.*** Bank tellers and other clerks usually need only a high school education. Most banks seek people who have good basic math and communication skills, enjoy public contact, and feel comfortable handling large amounts of money. Through a combination of formal classroom instruction and on-the-job training under the guidance of an experienced worker, tellers learn the procedures, rules, and regulations that govern their jobs. Banks are offering more products and spending more on reaching out to their customers. As a result, they will need more creative and talented people to compete in the market place. Banks encourage upward mobility by providing access to higher education and other sources of additional training.

Some banks have their own training programs which result in teller certification. Experienced tellers qualify for certification by taking required courses and passing examinations. Experienced tellers and clerks may advance to head teller, new accounts clerk, or customer service representative. Outstanding tellers who have had some college or specialized training are sometimes promoted to managerial positions.

***Management, business, and financial occupations.*** Workers in management, business, and financial occupations usually have at least a college degree. A bachelor's degree in business administration or a liberal arts degree with business administration courses is suitable preparation, as is a bachelor's degree in any field followed by a master's degree in business administration (MBA). Many management positions are filled by promoting experienced, technically skilled professional personnel—for example, accountants, auditors, budget analysts, credit analysts, or financial analysts—or accounting or related department supervisors in large banks.

**Table 2. Employment of wage and salary workers in banking by occupation, 2006 and projected change, 2006-2016.**
(Employment in thousands)

| Occupation | Employment, 2006 Number | Percent | Percent change, 2006-16 |
|---|---|---|---|
| All occupations ......................................... | 1,825 | 100.0 | 4.0 |
| **Management, business, and financial occupations**................................ | 449 | 24.6 | 5.4 |
| General and operations managers ............. | 34 | 1.8 | -8.4 |
| Marketing and sales managers .................. | 11 | 0.6 | 1.9 |
| Financial managers .................................... | 73 | 4.0 | 1.9 |
| Human resources, training, and labor relations specialists .................................. | 15 | 0.8 | 5.3 |
| Management analysts .................................. | 8 | 0.5 | 1.4 |
| Accountants and auditors .......................... | 27 | 1.5 | 1.7 |
| Credit analysts........................................... | 15 | 0.8 | -8.3 |
| Financial analysts ...................................... | 18 | 1.0 | 11.4 |
| Personal financial advisors ........................ | 24 | 1.3 | 22.3 |
| Loan officers .............................................. | 133 | 7.3 | 12.1 |
| **Professional and related occupations**...... | 72 | 4.0 | 6.9 |
| Computer specialists ................................. | 56 | 3.0 | 8.8 |
| **Sales and related occupations**................. | 82 | 4.5 | 11.8 |
| Securities, commodities, and financial services sales agents ............................... | 50 | 2.7 | 17.2 |
| **Office and administrative support occupations** ............................................. | 1,202 | 65.9 | 2.9 |
| First-line supervisors/managers of office and administrative support workers .......... | 111 | 6.1 | -5.2 |
| Bookkeeping, accounting, and auditing clerks........................................................ | 63 | 3.5 | 1.7 |
| Tellers ........................................................ | 546 | 29.9 | 12.1 |
| Brokerage clerks........................................ | 9 | 0.5 | -1.0 |
| Customer service representatives .............. | 106 | 5.8 | 12.0 |
| New accounts clerks................................... | 73 | 4.0 | -18.4 |
| Receptionists and information clerks.......... | 9 | 0.5 | 1.5 |
| Couriers and messengers.......................... | 6 | 0.3 | -8.3 |
| Executive secretaries and administrative assistants................................................. | 36 | 2.0 | 1.9 |
| Secretaries, except legal, medical, and executive......................................... | 15 | 0.8 | -9.6 |
| Data entry keyers....................................... | 8 | 0.5 | -18.6 |
| Office clerks, general................................. | 40 | 2.2 | 0.2 |
| Office machine operators, except computer.. | 12 | 0.6 | -14.9 |

Note: Columns may not add to totals due to omission of occupations with small employment

There are currently no specific licensing requirements for loan counselors and officers working in banks or credit unions. Training and licensing requirements for loan counselors and officers who work in mortgage banks or brokerages vary by State, depending on whether they are employed by a mortgage bank or mortgage brokerage.

Various banking-related associations and private schools offer courses and programs for students interested in lending, as well as for experienced loan officers who want to keep their skills current. Completion of these courses and programs generally enhances the individual's employment and advancement opportunities. The Banking Administration Institute offers the Loan Review Certificate program for persons who review and approve loans. The Mortgage Bankers Association (MBA) offers the Certified Mortgage Banker (CMB) program. A candidate who earns the CMB exhibits a deep understanding of the mortgage business. To obtain the CMB, one must have at least 3 years of experience, earn educational credits, and pass an exam.

Financial services sales agents usually need a college degree; a major or courses in finance, accounting, economics, marketing, or related fields serve as excellent preparation. Experience in sales also is very helpful. These workers learn on the job under the supervision of bank officers. Sales agents selling securities need to be licensed by the National Association of Securities Dealers, and agents selling insurance also must obtain an appropriate license.

Advancement to higher level executive, administrative, managerial, and professional positions may be accelerated by taking additional training. Banks often provide opportunities and encourage employees to take classes offered by banking and financial management affiliated organizations or other educational institutions. Classes often deal with one of the different phases of financial management and banking, such as accounting management, budget management, corporate cash management, financial analysis, international banking, and data processing systems procedures and management. Employers also sponsor seminars and conferences, and provide textbooks and other educational materials. Many employers pay all or part of the costs for those who successfully complete courses.

In recent years, the banking field has been revolutionized by technological advancements in computer and data processing equipment. Learning how to apply this technology can greatly improve one's skills and advancement opportunities in the banking industry.

## Outlook

The number of local branches and offices in the United States has been steadily increasing, and this trend is expected to continue to result in moderate growth in employment in banking.

*Employment change.* Wage and salary employment in banking is projected to increase by about 4 percent between 2006 and 2016, compared with the 11 percent growth projected for wage and salary employment across all industries. Growth will result from banks refocusing on the local branch as a critical means of servicing customers, because branch location is often the most important factor for customers in selecting a bank. New branches also will be appearing more frequently in nontraditional locations, such as inside local grocery stores or shopping malls. Growth will likely be greatest in areas where the population is growing.

The combined effects of deregulation, technology, demographic changes, and mergers will continue to affect total employment growth and the mix of occupations in the banking industry. Deregulation of the banking industry allows banks to offer a variety of financial and insurance products that they were once prohibited from selling. The need to develop, analyze, and sell these new services will spur demand for securities and financial services sales representatives, financial analysts, and personal financial advisors. Demand for "personal bankers" to advise and manage the assets of wealthy clients, as well as the aging baby-boom generation, also will grow. However, banks will continue to face considerable competition—particularly in lending—from nonbank establishments, such as consumer credit companies and mortgage brokers. Companies and individuals now are able to obtain loans and credit and raise money through a variety of means other than bank loans. Therefore, some loan officers may be replaced by financial services sales representatives, who sell loans along with other bank services.

Advances in technology should continue to have a significant effect on employment in the banking industry. Demand for computer specialists will grow, as more banks make their services available electronically and eliminate much of the paperwork involved in many banking transactions. On the other hand, these changes in technology will reduce the need for some office and administrative support occupations. Employment growth among tellers will be limited as customers increasingly use ATMs, direct deposit, debit cards, and telephone and Internet banking to perform routine transactions. The number of electronic payments has increased and checks now account for less than half of consumers' monthly bill payments. In addition, technological improvements, such as digital imaging and computer networking, are likely to lead to a decrease or change in the nature of employment of the "back-office" clerical workers who process checks and other bank statements. Employment of customer service representatives, however, is expected to increase as banks hire more of these workers to staff phone centers and respond to e-mails.

The increasing number of retired baby boomers should have a beneficial effect on total employment in the banking industry. They are more likely than younger age groups to hold bank deposits and visit branches to do their banking. Many also may need help in retirement planning and investing wealth inherited from their parents and so may seek the services of the various financial professionals in banking, such as financial managers, and securities, commodities, and financial services sales agents.

In the past, consolidation within the banking industry contributed significantly to employment declines, but the effect of mergers on employment within the industry is expected to be minimal in the years ahead. Merger activity has slowed recently, and a balance is beginning to develop between the numbers of new banks established and existing banks lost due to mergers and acquisitions.

*Job prospects.* Job opportunities should be favorable for tellers and other administrative support workers because they make up a large proportion of bank employees and many individuals leave these positions for other jobs that offer higher pay or greater responsibilities. The need for skilled workers will create good job opportunities for individuals with up-to-date computer skills and financial services backgrounds.

## Earnings

*Industry earnings.* Earnings of nonsupervisory bank employees involved in depository credit intermediation averaged $535 a week in 2006, compared with $738 for all workers in finance and insurance industries, and $568 for workers throughout the private sector. Relatively low pay in the banking industry reflects the high proportion of low-paying administrative support jobs.

Greater responsibilities generally result in a higher salary. Experience, length of service, and, especially, the location and size of the bank also are important. Earnings in the banking industry also vary significantly by occupation. Earnings in the largest occupations in banking appear in table 3.

*Benefits and union membership.* In addition to common benefits offered by many industries, equity sharing and performance-based pay increasingly are part of compensation packages for

**Table 3. Median hourly earnings of the largest occupations in depository credit intermediation, May 2006**

| Occupation | Depository credit intermediation | All industries |
|---|---|---|
| General and operations managers | $40.89 | $40.97 |
| Financial managers | 34.89 | 43.74 |
| Loan officers | 23.51 | 24.89 |
| First-line supervisors/managers of office and administrative support workers | 19.66 | 20.92 |
| Executive secretaries and administrative assistants | 18.05 | 17.90 |
| Loan interviewers and clerks | 14.35 | 14.89 |
| Customer service representatives | 13.68 | 13.62 |
| New accounts clerks | 13.60 | 13.65 |
| Office clerks, general | 11.82 | 11.40 |
| Tellers | 10.63 | 10.64 |

some bank employees. As banks encourage employees to become more sales-oriented, incentives are increasingly tied to meeting sales goals, and some workers may even receive commissions for sales or referrals. As in other industries, part-time workers do not enjoy the same benefits that full-time workers do.

Very few workers in the banking industry are unionized—only 2 percent are union members or are covered by union contracts, compared with 13 percent of workers throughout private industry.

## Sources of Additional Information

State bankers' associations can furnish specific information about job opportunities in their State. Individual banks can provide detailed information about job openings and the activities, responsibilities, and preferred qualifications of banking personnel.

Information on banking careers is also available from:
➢ Bank Administration Institute, 1 North Franklin St., Chicago, Il 60606. Internet: **www.bai.org**

Information about careers with the Federal Reserve System is available from the Web site or human resources department of the various regional Federal Reserve Banks. Internet: www.federalreserve.gov

Information on many of the occupations in banking, including the following, may be found in the 2008–09 edition of the *Occupational Outlook Handbook*:
• Accountants and auditors
• Bill and account collectors
• Bookkeeping, accounting, and auditing clerks
• Computer scientists and database administrators
• Computer support specialists and systems administrators
• Computer systems analysts
• Credit authorizers, checkers, and clerks
• Customer service representatives
• Financial analysts and personal financial advisors
• Financial managers
• Loan officers
• Securities, commodities, and financial services sales agents
• Tellers

# Insurance

## SIGNIFICANT POINTS

- Job growth in this large industry will be limited by corporate downsizing, new technology, and increasing direct mail, telephone, and Internet sales, but numerous job openings will arise from the need to replace workers who leave or retire.

- Growing areas of the insurance industry are medical services and health insurance, and its expansion into other financial services, such as securities and mutual funds.

- Jobs in office and administrative occupations usually may be entered with a high school diploma, but employers prefer college graduates for sales, managerial, and professional jobs.

## Nature of the Industry

*Goods and services.* The insurance industry provides protection against financial losses resulting from a variety of perils. By purchasing insurance policies, individuals and businesses can receive reimbursement for losses due to car accidents, theft of property, and fire and storm damage; medical expenses; and loss of income due to disability or death.

*Industry organization.* The insurance industry consists mainly of insurance carriers (or insurers) and insurance agencies and brokerages. In general, insurance carriers are large companies that provide insurance and assume the risks covered by the policy. Insurance agencies and brokerages sell insurance policies for the carriers. While some of these establishments are directly affiliated with a particular insurer and sell only that carrier's policies, many are independent and are thus free to market the policies of a variety of insurance carriers. In addition to supporting these two primary components, the insurance industry includes establishments that provide other insurance-related services, such as claims adjustment or third-party administration of insurance and pension funds.

These other insurance industry establishments also include a number of independent organizations that provide a wide array of insurance-related services to carriers and their clients. One such service is the processing of claims forms for medical practitioners. Other services include loss prevention and risk management. Also, insurance companies sometimes hire independent claims adjusters to investigate accidents and claims for property damage and to assign a dollar estimate to the claim.

Insurance carriers assume the risk associated with annuities and insurance policies and assign premiums to be paid for the policies. In the policy, the carrier states the length and conditions of the agreement, exactly which losses it will provide compensation for, and how much will be awarded. The premium charged for the policy is based primarily on the amount to be awarded in case of loss, as well as the likelihood that the insurance carrier will actually have to pay. In order to be able to compensate policyholders for their losses, insurance companies invest the money they receive in premiums, building up a portfolio of financial assets and income-producing real estate which can then be used to pay off any future claims that may be brought. There are two basic types of insurance carriers: primary and reinsurance. Primary carriers are responsible for the initial underwriting of insurance policies and annuities, while reinsurance carriers assume all or part of the risk associated with the existing insurance policies originally underwritten by other insurance carriers.

Primary insurance carriers offer a variety of insurance policies. Life insurance provides financial protection to beneficiaries—usually spouses and dependent children—upon the death of the insured. Disability insurance supplies a preset income to an insured person who is unable to work due to injury or illness, and health insurance pays the expenses resulting from accidents and illness. An annuity (a contract or a group of contracts that furnishes a periodic income at regular intervals for a specified period) provides a steady income during retirement for the remainder of one's life. Property-casualty insurance protects against loss or damage to property resulting from hazards such as fire, theft, and natural disasters. Liability insurance shields policyholders from financial responsibility for injuries to others or for damage to other people's property. Most policies, such as automobile and homeowner's insurance, combine both property-casualty and liability coverage. Companies that underwrite this kind of insurance are called property-casualty carriers.

Some insurance policies cover groups of people, ranging from a few to thousands of individuals. These policies usually are issued to employers for the benefit of their employees or to unions, professional associations, or other membership organizations for the benefit of their members. Among the most common policies of this nature are group life and health plans. Insurance carriers also underwrite a variety of specialized types of insurance, such as real-estate title insurance, employee surety and fidelity bonding, and medical malpractice insurance.

Other organizations in the industry are formed by groups of insurance companies, to perform functions that would result in a duplication of effort if each company carried them out individually. For example, service organizations are supported by insurance companies to provide loss statistics, which the companies use to set their rates.

*Recent developments.* Congressional legislation now allows insurance carriers and other financial institutions, such as banks and securities firms, to sell one another's products. More insurance carriers now sell financial products such as securities, mutual funds, and various retirement plans. This approach is most common in life insurance companies that already sold annuities, but property and casualty companies also are increasingly selling a wider range of financial products. In order to expand into one another's markets, insurance carriers, banks, and securities firms have engaged in numerous mergers, allowing the merging companies access to each other's client base and geographical markets.

Insurance carriers have discovered that the Internet can be a powerful tool for reaching potential and existing customers. Most carriers use the Internet simply to post company information, such as sales brochures and product information, financial statements, and a list of local agents. However, an increasing number of carriers are starting to expand their Web sites to enable customers to access online account and billing information, and some carriers even allow claims to be submitted online. Many carriers also provide insurance quotes online based on the information submitted by customers on their Internet sites. In fact, some carriers will allow customers to purchase policies through the Internet without ever speaking to a live agent.

In addition to individual carrier-sponsored Internet sites, several "lead-generating" sites have emerged. These sites allow potential customers to input information about their insurance policy needs. For a fee, the sites forward customer information to a number of insurance companies, which review the information and, if they decide to take on the policy, contact the customer with an offer. This practice gives consumers the freedom to accept the best rate.

## Working Conditions

*Hours.* Many workers in the insurance industry—especially those in administrative support positions—work a 5-day, 40-hour week. Those in executive and managerial occupations often put in more than 40 hours. There are several occupations in the insurance industry where workers may work irregular hours outside of office settings. Those working in sales jobs need to be available for their clients at all times. This accommodation may result in these individuals working 50 to 60 hours per week. Also, call centers operate 24 hours a day, 7 days a week, so some of their employees must work evening and weekend shifts. The irregular business hours in the insurance industry provide some workers with the opportunity for part-time work. Part-time employees make up 8 percent of the workforce.

*Work Environment.* Insurance employees working in sales jobs often visit prospective and existing customers' homes and places of business to market new products and provide services. Others working in the industry may need to frequently leave the office to inspect damaged property, and at times can be away from home for days, traveling to the scene of a disaster—such as a tornado, flood, or hurricane—to work with affected policyholders and government officials.

A small, but increasing, number of insurance employees spend most of their time on the telephone working in call centers, answering questions and providing information to prospective clients or current policyholders. These jobs may include selling insurance, taking claims information, or answering medical questions.

As would be expected in an industry dominated by office and sales employees, the incidence of occupational injuries and illnesses among insurance workers is low. In 2006, only 1.3 cases per 100 full-time workers were reported among insurance carriers, while just 0.7 cases per 100 full-time workers were reported among agents and brokers. These figures compare with an average of 4.4 for all private industry.

## Employment

The insurance industry had about 2.3 million wage and salary jobs in 2006. Insurance carriers accounted for 62 percent of jobs, while insurance agencies, brokerages, and providers of other insurance-related services accounted for 38 percent of jobs.

The majority of establishments in the insurance industry were small; however, a few large establishments accounted for many of the jobs in this industry. Insurance carriers tend to be large establishments, often employing 250 or more workers, whereas agencies and brokerages tend to be much smaller, frequently employing fewer than 20 workers (chart).

Many insurance carriers' home and regional offices are situated near large urban centers. Insurance workers who deal directly with the public are located throughout the country. Almost all of those working in sales work out of local company offices or independent agencies. Many others in the industry work for independent firms in small cities and towns throughout the country.

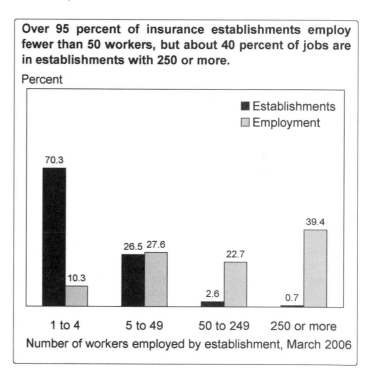

Over 95 percent of insurance establishments employ fewer than 50 workers, but about 40 percent of jobs are in establishments with 250 or more.

Percent

■ Establishments
□ Employment

70.3

26.5  27.6
10.3

39.4

22.7

2.6

0.7

1 to 4    5 to 49    50 to 249    250 or more

Number of workers employed by establishment, March 2006

## Occupations in the Industry

About 44 percent of insurance workers are in office and administrative support jobs such as those found in every industry (table 1). Many office and administrative support positions in the insurance industry, however, require skills and knowledge unique to the industry. About 29 percent of insurance workers are in management or business and financial operations occupations. About 16 percent of wage and salary employees in the industry are sales workers, selling policies to individuals and businesses. Several others are employed in computer and mathematical science occupations.

*Office and administrative support occupations.* Office and administrative support occupations in this industry include *secretaries, typists, word processors, bookkeepers,* and other clerical workers. *Secretaries and administrative assistants* perform routine clerical and administrative functions such as drafting correspondence, scheduling appointments, organizing and maintaining paper and electronic files, or providing information to callers.

*Bookkeeping, accounting, and auditing clerks* handle all financial transactions and recordkeeping for an insurance company. They compute, classify, update, and record numerical data to keep financial records complete and accurate. *Insurance claims and policy processing clerks* process new policies, modifications to existing policies, and claims forms. They review applications for completeness, compile data on policy changes, and verify the accuracy of insurance company records. *Customer service representatives* have duties similar to insurance claims and policy processing clerks, except they work directly with customers by processing insurance policy applications, changes, and cancellations over the phone. They may also process claims and sell new policies to existing clients. These workers recently are taking on increased responsibilities in insurance offices, such as handling most of the continuing contact with clients. A growing number of customer service representatives work in call centers that are open 24 hours a day, 7 days a week, where they answer clients' questions, update policy information, and provide potential clients with information regarding the types of policies the company issues.

## Management, business, and financial operations occupations.

*Top executives* direct the operations of an independent insurance agency, brokerage, or a large insurance carrier. *Marketing managers* direct carriers' development of new types of policies that might appeal to the public and strategies for selling them to customers. *Sales managers* direct the activities of the sales workers in local sales offices of insurance carriers and independent agencies. They sell insurance products, work with clients, and supervise staff. Other managers who work in their companies' home offices are in charge of functions such as actuarial calculations, policy issuance, accounting, and investments.

*Claims adjusters, appraisers, examiners, and investigators* decide whether claims are covered by the customer's policy, estimate and confirm payment, and, when necessary, investigate the circumstances surrounding a claim. *Claims adjusters* work for property and liability insurance carriers or for independent adjusting firms. They inspect property damage, estimate how much it will cost to repair, and determine the extent of the insurance company's liability; in some cases, they may help the claimant receive assistance quickly in order to prevent further damage and begin repairs. Adjusters plan and schedule the work required to process claims, which may include interviewing the claimant and witnesses and consulting police and hospital records. In some property-casualty companies, claims adjusters are called claims examiners, but in other companies, a claims examiner's primary job is to review claims to ensure that proper guidelines have been followed. Only occasionally—especially when disasters suddenly increase the volume of claims—do these examiners aid adjusters with complicated claims.

In the offices of life and health insurance carriers, *claims examiners* are the counterparts of the claims adjuster who works in a property and casualty insurance firm. Examiners in the health insurance carriers review health-related claims to see whether the costs are reasonable based on the diagnosis. Examiners check claim applications for completeness and accuracy, interview medical specialists, and consult policy files to verify information on a claim. Claims examiners in the life insurance carriers review causes of death and also may review new applications for life insurance to make sure that the applicants have no serious illnesses that would prevent them from qualifying for insurance.

*Insurance investigators* handle claims in which companies suspect fraudulent or criminal activity, such as suspicious fires, questionable workers' disability claims, difficult-to-explain accidents, and dubious medical treatment. Investigators usually perform database searches on suspects to determine whether they have a history of attempted or successful insurance fraud. Then, the investigators may visit claimants and witnesses to obtain a recorded statement, take photographs, inspect facilities, and conduct surveillance on suspects. Investigators often consult with legal counsel and are sometimes called to testify as expert witnesses in court cases.

*Auto damage appraisers* usually are hired by insurance companies and independent adjusting firms to inspect the damage to a motor vehicle after an accident and to provide unbiased estimates of repair cost. Claims adjusters and auto damage appraisers can work for insurance companies, or they can be independent or public adjusters. Insurance companies hire independent adjusters to represent their interests while assisting the insured, whereas public adjusters are hired to represent the insured's interests against insurance carriers.

*Management analysts*, often called *loss control representatives* in the insurance industry, assess various risks faced by insurance companies. These workers inspect the business operations of insurance applicants, analyze historical data regarding workplace injuries and automobile accidents, and assess the potential for natural hazards, dangerous business practices, and unsafe workplace conditions that may result in injuries or catastrophic physical and financial loss. They might then recommend, for example, that a factory add safety equipment, that a house be reinforced to withstand environmental catastrophes, or that incentives be implemented to encourage automobile owners to install air bags in their cars or take more effective measures to prevent theft. Because the changes they recommend can greatly reduce the probability of loss, loss control representatives are increasingly important to both insurance companies and the insured.

Underwriting is another important management and business and financial occupation in insurance. *Underwriters* evaluate insurance applications to determine the risk involved in issuing a policy. They decide whether to accept or reject an application, and they determine the appropriate premium for each policy.

## Sales and related occupations.

*Insurance sales agents,* also referred to as *producers,* may work as exclusive agents, or captive agents, selling for one company, or as independent agents selling for several companies. Through regular contact with clients, agents are able to update coverage, assist with claims, ensure customer satisfaction, and obtain referrals. Insurance sales agents may sell many types of insurance, including life, annuities, property-casualty, health, and disability insurance. Many insurance sales agents are involved in "cross-selling" or "total account development," which means that, besides offering insurance, they have become licensed to sell mutual funds, annuities, and other securities. These agents usually find their own customers and ensure that the policies sold meet the specific needs of their policyholders.

## Professional and related occupations.

The insurance industry employs relatively few people in professional and related occupations, but they are essential to company operations. For example, insurance companies' lawyers defend clients who are sued, especially when large claims may be involved. These lawyers also review regulations and policy contracts. Nurses and other medical professionals advise clients on wellness issues and on medical procedures covered by the company's managed-care plan. *Computer systems analysts, computer programmers,* and *computer support specialists* are needed to analyze, design, develop, and program the systems that support the day-to-day operations of the insurance company.

*Actuaries* represent a relatively small proportion of employment in the insurance industry, but they are vital to the industry's profitability. Actuaries study the probability of an insured loss and determine premium rates. They must set the rates so that there is a high probability that premiums paid by customers will cover claims, but not so high that their company loses business to competitors.

## Training and Advancement

A few jobs in the insurance industry, especially in office and administrative support occupations, require no more than a high school diploma. However, employers prefer to hire workers with a college education for most jobs, including sales, managerial, and professional jobs. When specialized training is required, it usually is obtained on the job or through independent study during work or after-work hours. Many insurance companies expect their employees to take continuing education courses to improve their people skills and their knowledge of the industry. Opportunities for advancement are relatively good in the insurance industry.

*Office and administrative support occupations.* Graduation from high school or a 2-year postsecondary business program is adequate preparation for most beginning office and administrative support jobs. Courses in word processing and business math are assets, and the ability to operate computers is essential. On-the-job training usually is provided for clerical jobs such as customer service representatives. Because representatives in call centers must be knowledgeable about insurance products in order to provide advice to clients, more States are requiring customer service representatives to become licensed. Several years of experience and training can help beginners advance to higher paying positions. Office and administrative support workers may also advance to higher paying claims adjusting positions and entry-level underwriting jobs.

*Management, business, and financial operations occupations.* Management, business, and financial jobs require the same college training as similar jobs in other industries. Managerial positions usually are filled by promoting college-educated employees from within the company. However, some companies prefer to hire liberal arts graduates at a lower cost, and many insurers send them to company schools or enroll them in outside institutes for professional training. A master's degree, particularly in business administration or a related field, is an asset for advancement into higher levels of management.

For beginning underwriting jobs, many insurance companies prefer college graduates who have a degree in business administration or a related field. As an underwriter's career develops, it becomes beneficial to earn one of the voluntary professional certifications in underwriting. For example, the National Association of Health Underwriters offers two certification programs: the Registered Health Underwriter (RHU) designation and the Registered Employee Benefits Consultant (REBC) designation.

The American Institute for Chartered Property-Casualty Underwriters (AICPU) offers the CPCU program, which includes courses covering a broad range of insurance, risk management,

**Table 1. Employment of wage and salary workers in insurance by occupation, 2006 and projected change, 2006-2016.**
(Employment in thousands)

| Occupation | Employment, 2006 | | Percent change, 2006-16 |
|---|---|---|---|
| | Number | Percent | |
| **All occupations** | 2,316 | 100.0 | 7.4 |
| **Management, business, and financial occupations** | 661 | 28.6 | 8.3 |
| General and operations managers | 41 | 1.8 | -1.9 |
| Marketing and sales managers | 20 | 0.9 | 7.2 |
| Computer and information systems managers | 14 | 0.6 | 5.9 |
| Financial managers | 24 | 1.0 | 6.6 |
| Claims adjusters, examiners, and investigators | 218 | 9.4 | 10.8 |
| Insurance appraisers, auto damage | 12 | 0.5 | 12.0 |
| Human resources, training, and labor relations specialists | 28 | 1.2 | 10.9 |
| Management analysts | 29 | 1.2 | 5.4 |
| Accountants and auditors | 40 | 1.7 | 7.8 |
| Financial analysts | 16 | 0.7 | 16.9 |
| Insurance underwriters | 91 | 3.9 | 5.6 |
| **Professional and related occupations** | 258 | 11.2 | 8.6 |
| Computer programmers | 21 | 0.9 | -15.1 |
| Computer software engineers | 28 | 1.2 | 24.7 |
| Computer support specialists | 19 | 0.8 | 6.8 |
| Computer systems analysts | 33 | 1.4 | 15.5 |
| Actuaries | 11 | 0.5 | 5.4 |
| Market research analysts | 12 | 0.5 | 6.5 |
| Lawyers | 12 | 0.5 | 5.6 |
| Title examiners, abstractors, and searchers | 23 | 1.0 | -5.5 |
| Registered nurses | 25 | 1.1 | 6.2 |
| **Sales and related occupations** | 367 | 15.8 | 14.4 |
| First-line supervisors/managers of non-retail sales workers | 18 | 0.8 | 3.8 |
| Insurance sales agents | 313 | 13.5 | 15.7 |
| **Office and administrative support occupations** | 1,009 | 43.6 | 4.0 |
| First-line supervisors/managers of office and administrative support workers | 62 | 2.7 | -6.1 |
| Billing and posting clerks and machine operators | 18 | 0.8 | -2.5 |
| Bookkeeping, accounting, and auditing clerks | 47 | 2.1 | 8.9 |
| Customer service representatives | 266 | 11.5 | 19.2 |
| File clerks | 15 | 0.7 | -45.3 |
| Receptionists and information clerks | 24 | 1.0 | 10.0 |
| Executive secretaries and administrative assistants | 57 | 2.4 | 8.2 |
| Secretaries, except legal, medical, and executive | 62 | 2.7 | -1.5 |
| Data entry keyers | 22 | 0.9 | -13.5 |
| Insurance claims and policy processing clerks | 222 | 9.6 | -2.6 |
| Mail clerks and mail machine operators, except postal service | 14 | 0.6 | -21.0 |
| Office clerks, general | 106 | 4.6 | 7.8 |

Note: Columns may not add to totals due to omission of occupations with small employment

and general business topics involving both personal and commercial loss exposures. Earning the CPCU designation requires passing 8 exams, meeting a requirement of at least three years of insurance experience, and abiding by the AICPU's and CPCU Society's code of professional ethics. In conjunction with the Insurance Institute of America, the AICPCU offers 22 insurance-related educational programs, including claims, underwriting, risk management, and reinsurance.

In almost every State, those working as a claims examiner or adjuster must obtain a license. Licensing requirements for these workers vary by State and can include prelicensing education or passing a licensing exam. In some cases, professional designations may be substituted for the exam requirement. Separate or additional requirements may apply to public adjusters. For example, some States may require public adjusters to file a surety bond. Often, claims adjusters working for companies can work under the company license and not need to become licensed themselves. Most companies prefer to hire college graduates and those with previous experience or who have obtained licensure for claims adjuster and examiner positions. No specific college major is required, although most workers in these positions have a business, accounting, engineering, legal, or medical background. In addition, many adjusters and examiners choose to pursue certain certifications and designations to distinguish themselves. Many State licenses and professional designations require continuing education for renewal. Continuing education is important because adjusters and examiners must be knowledgeable about changes in the laws, recent court decisions, and new medical procedures.

Auto damage appraisers typically begin as auto body repairers and then are hired by insurance companies or independent adjusting firms. Most companies prefer auto damage appraisers to have formal training, and many vocational colleges offer 2-year programs on how to estimate and repair damaged vehicles. Some States require them to be licensed, and certification may be required or preferred. Computer skills also are an important qualification for many auto damage appraiser positions. As with adjusters and examiners, continuing education is important for appraisers, because many new car models and repair techniques are introduced each year.

Licensing requirements to become an insurance investigator may vary among States. Most insurance companies prefer to hire former law enforcement detectives or private investigators as insurance investigators. Many experienced claims adjusters or examiners also can become investigators. Most employers look for individuals with ingenuity and who are persistent and assertive. Investigators must not be afraid of confrontation, should communicate well, and should be able to think on their feet. Good interviewing and interrogation skills also are important and usually are developed in earlier careers in law enforcement.

*Sales and related occupations.* Although some employers hire high school graduates with potential or proven sales ability for entry-level sales positions, most prefer to hire college graduates.

All insurance sales agents must obtain licenses in the States in which they plan to sell insurance. In most States, licenses are issued only to applicants who complete specified courses and pass written examinations covering insurance fundamentals and State insurance laws. New agents receive training from their employer, either at work or at the insurance company's home office. Sometimes, entry-level employees attend company-sponsored classes to prepare for examinations. The National Alliance for Insurance Education and Research offers a wide variety of courses in health, life, and property and casualty insurance for independent insurance agents. Others study on their own and, as on-the-job training, accompany experienced agents when they meet with prospective clients. After obtaining a license, agents must earn continuing education credits throughout their careers

in order to remain licensed insurance sales agents.

Insurance sales agents wishing to sell securities and other financial products must meet State licensing requirements in these areas. Specifically, they must pass an additional examination—either the Series 6 or Series 7 licensing exam, both of which are administered by the Financial Industry Regulatory Authority (FINRA). The Series 6 exam is for individuals who wish to sell only mutual funds and variable annuities; the Series 7 exam is the main FINRA series license and qualifies agents as general securities representatives. To demonstrate further competency in financial planning, many agents also find it worthwhile to obtain a certified financial planner (CFP) or chartered financial consultant (ChFC) designation.

Sales workers may advance by handling greater numbers of accounts and more complex commercial insurance policies. They may also choose to start an independent insurance agency. Many also obtain related designations such as the CPCU underwriting designation, offered by the AICPCU.

*Professional and related occupations.* For actuarial jobs, companies prefer candidates to have degrees in actuarial science, mathematics, or statistics. However, candidates with degrees in business, finance, or economics are becoming more common. Actuaries must pass a series of national examinations to become fully qualified. Completion of all the exams takes from 5 to 10 years. Some of the exams may be taken while an individual is in college, but most require extensive home study. Many companies grant study time to their actuarial students to prepare for the exams.

## Outlook

Demand for insurance will increase, but employment in the insurance industry will increase more slowly than employment growth across all industries.

*Employment change.* Wage and salary employment in the insurance industry is projected to grow about 7 percent between 2006 and 2016, compared to the 11 percent growth projected for wage and salary employment in all industries combined. While demand for insurance is expected to rise, job growth will be limited by corporate downsizing, productivity increases due to new technology, and increasing use of direct mail, telephone, and Internet sales. However, some job growth will result from the industry's expansion into the broader financial services field, new types of insurance entering the market, and growth in demand for medical service and health insurance.

Medical service and health insurance is the fastest growing segment of the insurance industry. Significant growth is expected over the long term, even though increasing health insurance premiums have recently become difficult for some people to afford. As the members of the baby boom generation grow older and a growing share of the Nation's population moves into the older age groups, more people are expected to buy health insurance and long-term-care insurance, as well as annuities and other types of pension products sold by insurance sales agents. If legislation is enacted that makes health insurance affordable to more people, even greater increases in demand for this type of insurance should result.

Population growth also will stimulate demand for auto insurance and homeowners insurance. Also, population growth will create additional demand for businesses to service the needs of more people, and these businesses will need insurance as well. In addition, growing numbers of individuals and businesses are purchasing liability policies to protect against possible large liability awards from lawsuits brought by people claiming injury or damage from a product.

Many successful insurance companies will recognize the Internet's potential as a powerful marketing tool, increasing employment growth of some occupations while slowing growth of others. Growing use of the Internet might reduce costs for insurance companies, but it also could enable many clients to turn first to the Internet to get information on their policies, obtain price quotes on possible new policies, or submit claims. As insurance companies begin to offer more information and services on the Internet, employment in some occupations, such as insurance sales agents, could be adversely affected.

Productivity gains caused by the greater use of computer software will continue to limit the growth of certain jobs within the insurance industry. For example, the use of underwriting software that automatically analyzes and rates insurance applications will limit the employment growth of underwriters. Workers in claims now may not have to visit the site of customers' damage; they may use satellite imagery to inspect the damage from their computers. In addition, the Internet allows insurance investigators to handle an increasing number of cases by drastically reducing the amount of time it takes them to perform background checks, limiting the additional investigators that must be hired to handle a growing workload. Also, computers have made communications easier among sales agents, adjusters, and insurance carriers—making all much more productive—by linking them directly to the databases of insurance carriers and other organizations. Furthermore, insurance carriers contain costs by increasing using customer service representatives to deal with the day-to-day processing of policies and claims.

*Job prospects.* Workers in property and casualty insurance, particularly in auto insurance, will be most affected by increasing reliance on the Internet. Auto policies are relatively straightforward and can be issued more easily without the involvement of a live agent. Also, auto premiums tend to cost more per year than do other types of policies, so people are more likely to shop around for the best price—and the Internet makes it easier to compare rates among companies.

Insurance companies will continue to face increased competition from banks and securities firms entering the insurance markets. As more of these firms begin to sell insurance policies, they will employ increasing numbers of insurance sales agents. In order to stay competitive, more insurance companies are expanding the range of financial products and services they offer, or are establishing partnerships with banks or brokerage firms.

Although employment in the insurance industry is expected to grow slowly, thousands of openings are expected to arise in this large industry to replace workers who leave the industry, retire, or stop working for other reasons. Despite the fact that the internet allows many people to buy policies online, many sales agents still will be needed to meet face-to-face with clients; some customers prefer to talk directly with an agent, especially regarding complicated policies. Opportunities will be best for sales agents who sell more than one type of insurance or financial service. Opportunities should be good for adjusters because they will still be needed to inspect damage and interview witnesses as the insurance industry, the Nation's population, and the number of claims all grow. Opportunities likewise should be good for actuaries, even though the number of available jobs will small, because many people are discouraged from following this career path due to the stringent qualifying requirements of the examination system.

Table 2. Median hourly earnings of the largest occupations in insurance, May 2006

| Occupation | Insurance | All industries |
|---|---|---|
| General and operations managers | $53.02 | $40.97 |
| Insurance underwriters | 25.29 | 25.17 |
| First-line supervisors/managers of office and administrative support workers | 24.36 | 20.92 |
| Claims adjusters, examiners, and investigators | 23.42 | 24.36 |
| Executive secretaries and administrative assistants | 18.70 | 17.90 |
| Bookkeeping, accounting, and auditing clerks | 15.55 | 14.69 |
| Insurance claims and policy processing clerks | 14.97 | 14.96 |
| Customer service representatives | 14.79 | 13.62 |
| Secretaries, except legal, medical, and executive | 12.65 | 13.20 |
| Office clerks, general | 11.38 | 11.40 |

## Earnings

*Industry earnings.* Weekly earnings of nonsupervisory workers in the insurance industry averaged $798 in May 2006, considerably higher than the average of $568 for all private industry. Earnings of the largest occupations in insurance in May 2006, appear in table 2.

The method by which insurance sales agents are paid varies greatly. Most independent sales agents own their own businesses and are paid a commission only. Sales agents who are employees of an agency may be paid a salary only, a salary plus commission, or a salary plus a bonus. An agent's earnings usually increase rapidly with experience. Many agencies also pay an agent's expenses for automobiles and transportation, travel to conventions, and continuing education.

*Benefits and union membership.* Insurance carriers offer attractive benefits packages, as is frequently the case with large companies. Yearly bonuses, retirement investment plans, insurance, and paid vacation often are standard. Insurance agencies, which generally are smaller, offer less extensive benefits.

Unionization is not widespread in the insurance industry. In 2006, 3 percent of all insurance workers were union members or were covered by union contracts, compared with 12 percent of workers throughout private industry.

## Sources of Additional Information

General information on employment opportunities in the insurance industry may be obtained from the human resources departments of major insurance companies or from insurance agencies in local communities. Information about licensing requirements for insurance sales agents and claim adjusters may be obtained from the department of insurance in each State.

For information on the property and casualty segment of the insurance industry, contact:

➤ Insurance Information Institute, 110 William St., New York, NY 10038. Internet: **http://www.iii.org**
➤ Property Casualty Insurers Association of America, 2500 River Rd., Des Plaines, IL 60018. **http://www.pciaa.net**

For information about the health insurance segment of the insurance industry, contact:

➤ National Association of Health Underwriters, 2000 North 14th St., Suite 450, Arlington, VA 22201. Internet: **http://www.nahu.org**

For information about the reinsurance segment of the insurance industry, contact:

➤ Reinsurance Association of America, 1301 Pennsylvania Avenue, NW, Suite 900, Washington DC 20004. Internet: **http://www.reinsurance.org**

For information about insurance sales careers and training, contact:

➤ The American Institute for Chartered Property Casualty Underwriters (AICPCU) and Insurance Institute of America, 720 South Providence Rd., Malvern, PA 19355-0716. Internet: **http://www.aicpcu.org**

➤ Independent Insurance Agents of America, 127 South Peyton St., Alexandria, VA 22314. Internet: **http://www.iiaa.org**

➤ Insurance Vocational Education Student Training (InVEST), 127 South Peyton St., Alexandria, VA 22314. Internet: **http://www.investprogram.org**

➤ National Association of Professional Insurance Agents, 400 North Washington St., Alexandria, VA 22314. Internet: **www.pianet.org**

For information on insurance education and training, contact:

➤ The American College, 270 Bryn Mawr Ave., Bryn Mawr, PA 19010. Internet: http://www.theamericancollege.edu

➤ LOMA (Life Office Management Association), 2300 Windy Ridge Pkwy., Suite 600, Atlanta, GA 30339-8443 Internet: **http://www.loma.org**

➤ Insurance Education Institute, 3601 Vincennes Road, Indianapolis, IN 46268. Internet: **http://www.theiei.org**

➤ The National Alliance for Insurance Education and Research, P.O. Box 27027, Austin, TX 78755.

Information on the following insurance occupations may be found in the 2008–09 *Occupational Outlook Handbook*:

• Actuaries
• Claims adjusters, appraisers, examiners, and investigators
• Customer service representatives
• Insurance sales agents
• Insurance underwriters

# Securities, Commodities, and Other Investments

(NAICS 523)

## SIGNIFICANT POINTS

- Most workers in this industry hold associate or bachelor's degrees.

- Employment is expected to grow as a result of increasing investment in securities and commodities, along with a growing need for investment advice.

- The high earnings of successful securities sales agents and investment bankers will result in keen competition for these positions.

## Nature of the Industry

The securities, commodities, and other investments industry comprises a diverse group of companies and organizations that manage the issuance, purchase, and sale of financial instruments. These instruments—often called securities—are contracts which give their owner the right to an asset or the right to purchase an asset in the future. Companies sell these financial instruments to raise money from investors to finance new business operations or to improve or expand existing ones. Investors purchase these instruments with the goal of earning money by earning dividends, interest, executing the agreement, or selling the security at a higher price.

*Goods and services.* The securities industry is made up of a variety of firms and organizations that structure investments, bring together buyers and sellers of securities and commodities, manage investments, and offer financial advice. The products provided by the industry are called securities. The most basic types of security are stocks and bonds, which provide capital to finance corporations. Stocks entitle their holders to partial ownership of a company, whereas bonds are a form of debt that a company pays back with interest. Investors purchase stocks and bonds in order to earn money in the form of dividends or interest, or to sell the issues to other investors at a higher price.

Another type of security is called a derivative, which is a contract to purchase an asset at a specified future date. There are two basic types of derivatives: options and futures. An investor who holds an option has a contractual right to purchase an asset at a set price on a specified date, but is not required to do so. A futures contract is an agreement to purchase an asset at a set price and date with no option to decline. Commodities, for example, corn, wheat, and pork bellies, are often bought and sold in this way, and are among the best-known derivatives. Other goods sold on the derivatives market include foreign currencies, precious metals, oil and natural gas, and electricity. Buyers purchase derivatives with the hope that the price of the asset involved will be higher than the agreed price when the contract matures.

Mutual funds and exchange traded funds (ETFs) are also common investments. In both cases, the issuing firm owns a large portfolio of other securities which, on average, are expected to increase in value. In the case of mutual funds, this portfolio is typically managed by a team of financial analysts who determine which stocks to buy and sell; however, some mutual funds are not actively managed and are instead designed to track a benchmark index, such as the Standard and Poor's 500 or Dow Jones Industrial Average. Exchange traded funds are almost always de-signed to replicate a stock index. ETFs can be traded like stocks, unlike mutual funds. Because both of these types of securities require management, the companies who issue them charge a fee. Investors are willing to pay this fee because mutual funds and ETFs have a lower level of risk than other securities.

Besides selling securities, segments of the securities industry also sell advisory services. Investment banks, for example, help companies to plan stock or bond issues and sell them to investors. Securities and commodities exchanges, on the other hand, provide forums for buyers and sellers to trade securities. Private banks and investment advisories help individual investors to determine how to invest their money.

*Industry organization.* The securities industry is organized by the types of products and services they produce. *Investment banks* help corporations to finance their operations by underwriting—or purchasing and reselling—new stock and bond issues. They also provide advisory services to companies who are issuing securities or undergoing a merger or acquisition. The typical investment bank has several departments, each of which specializes in a specific part of the process. Corporate finance specializes in structuring stock and bond issues. They are often involved in initial public offerings (IPOs) of the stock of companies that are selling to the public for the first time. Mergers and acquisitions departments help companies plan and manage the purchase of other companies. Sales and trading departments work together to sell underwritten securities to investors. Research and quantitative analytics departments specialize in studying company financial reports to help the bank and its customers make informed decisions about stock purchases.

*Securities and commodities exchanges* offer a central location where buyers and sellers of securities meet to trade securities and commodities. All of the major exchanges have been at least partially computerized, but the trading floors are still very active. While a small number of workers at the exchanges are actually employed by the exchanges themselves, most of the people who work there are actually employed by other firms. These include investment banking and brokerage firms, as well as specialist firms that manage the sale of securities for listed companies.

*Brokerage firms* trade securities for those who cannot directly trade on exchanges. Investors place their buy and sell orders by telephone, online, or through a broker. Since most brokerage firms are fairly large, many orders are filled by other buyers and sellers who use the same brokerage. If the stock or commodity is sold on an exchange, the firm may send the order electronically to the company's floor broker at the exchange. The floor broker then posts the order and executes the trade by finding a seller or buyer who offers the best price for the client. Alternatively, the broker can access an electronic market that lists the prices for which dealers in that particular security are willing to buy or sell it. If the broker finds an acceptable price, then a purchase or sale is made. Firms can also buy and sell securities and commodities on electronic communications networks (ECNs), which are powerful computer systems that automatically list, match, and execute trades, eliminating the floor broker.

Brokerage firms are usually classified as full-service or discount. Investors who do not have time to research investments on their own will likely rely on full-service brokers to help them construct investment portfolios, manage their investments, and make recommendations regarding which investments to buy. Full-service brokers have access to a wide range of reports and analyses developed by financial analysts who research companies and recommend investments to people with different financial needs. People who prefer to select their own investments often use discount or online brokerages and pay lower fees and commission charges. Discount firms, also known as wire houses, usually do not offer advice about specific securities, although they may still provide access to reports. Most brokerage firms now have call centers staffed with both licensed sales agents and customer service representatives who take orders and answer questions at all hours of the day.

*Investment advisory firms* are also included in this industry. Much like full-service brokerages, these firms provide advice to their investors on how to best manage their investments. However, they also provide advice on other matters, such as life insurance, estate planning and tax preparation. In exchange, advisors act as brokers and receive fees and commissions for investments and insurance purchases. They may also charge fees for consultations.

*Portfolio management* firms, such as mutual funds, hedge funds, and private banks manage a pool of money for investors in exchange for fees. This frees individual investors from having to manage their own portfolios and puts their money in the hands of experienced professionals. In a mutual fund, this pool of money comes from investors who purchase shares of the mutual fund. Hedge funds are similar, although their shares are only available to certain experienced investors—called accredited investors—as they are considered very risky. In private banks, the pool of money comes from a wealthy individual. Portfolio management companies have teams of financial analysts who determine which securities should be bought and sold.

*Recent developments.* The securities industry is continuously changing because of improvements in technology, regulatory changes, the globalization of the marketplace, and demographics. The Internet and private high-speed networks have dramatically altered the way in which securities and commodities are bought and sold, almost completely automating the transaction process. At the same time, the number of financial services being offered is rising as firms look for new ways to attract the business of an increasingly wealthy and investment-savvy public.

New technology has greatly changed the way securities are traded. The growth of online trading in particular has produced a number of online trading firms. In order to compete, many full-service brokerage firms offer online trading to their customers. This explosion in technology is changing the nature of many of the jobs and the mix of people employed by securities firms. Some companies are more likely to resemble information technology companies than securities firms, with most of the employees working in computer-related occupations. Across the

industry, computer professionals account for a greater proportion of the workforce. Moreover, with so much business now being conducted online and through call centers, traditional sales agents are spending less time processing orders and more time seeking out new clients and offering detailed advice.

Regulatory changes also are a major development for the industry. The Securities and Exchange Commission (SEC) and major stock exchanges have instituted accounting and corporate reforms to increase public confidence in investment markets, but they have meant more paperwork and compliance issues for securities firms. These new rules address conflicts-of-interest raised by Federal, State, and industry investigations of companies that later failed, or whose stock declined dramatically in value, costing investors billions of dollars. The SEC now requires corporate chief executive officers to certify the reliability of their companies' financial reports. All of these new regulations have meant more paperwork and compliance issues for securities firms. On the other hand, the recent merger of the New York Stock Exchange Regulation with the National Association of Securities Dealers should ease some of the licensing and regulations burden for firms.

## Working Conditions

*Hours.* Long working hours, including evenings and weekends, are common in the securities industry. About 1 in 4 employees worked 50 or more hours per week in 2006. Even when not working, professionals in the industry must keep abreast of events that may affect the markets in which they specialize. Opportunities for part-time work are limited—only about 9 percent worked part time, compared to 15 percent of workers in all industries combined.

Hours vary greatly among the different parts of the industry. Investment banks, for instance, are known for requiring extremely long hours from their entry-level workers. Portfolio management companies also require long hours for their workers. In contrast, workers in many brokerages work standard 40 hour workweeks or less. Workers in jobs that are closely attached to the market do most of their work while the major exchanges are open between 9:30 am and 4 pm, but this is changing as after hours and international trading are becoming more important.

*Work Environment.* Most workers in the securities industry enjoy comfortable office environments. Investment banks are known for their exceptionally long hours and the stressful work environment. They are often under great pressure to meet deadlines and generate new business. This is often balanced, however, by large salaries. Some jobs require extensive travel, especially in corporate finance and mergers and acquisitions departments. Most investment banks strongly emphasize teamwork, and as such they often promote socialization among staff members. Because customer relationships are so important, investment bankers often get to take their clients to exclusive restaurants, sporting events, and other exclusive places

Brokerage jobs vary greatly depending on the type of brokerage. Those working in full-service brokerages tend to have comfortable office environments where they meet with clients and make sales calls. They may travel for training, conventions, or to meet with important clients.

During the day, sales agents spend most of their time on the phone soliciting business or with customers. They may spend time after hours and during lunch meeting with top clients. Sales agents at brokerage and mutual fund companies increasingly work in call centers, opening accounts for individuals, entering trades, and providing advice over the phone on different investment products. This is almost exclusively true in discount brokerages. Although many simply respond to inquiries and do not actively solicit customers, others may be required to contact potential clients. Call centers also employ customer service representatives, who answer questions for current clients about their accounts and make any needed changes or transfers. All workers in call centers must maintain a professional and courteous attitude, work well under pressure, and be able to speak for long periods of time. Many call centers operate 24 hours a day, 7 days a week, and employees may be required to work evenings and weekends.

Traders, whether on the floor of an investment bank, brokerage firm, or at the exchanges, work in very loud and stressful environments. They not only take orders from clients and try to get the best price for them, but also must constantly keep an eye on market activity and stay in touch with other traders and brokers to know what prices are being offered. Trading jobs are very stressful because a mistake could potentially cost the firm or the client thousands or even millions of dollars.

Personal financial advisors work in professional office environments. Most work between 40 and 50 hours per week, but many accommodate clients by visiting them at their homes in the evenings or on weekends. Office and administrative support workers usually work a 40-hour week, but overtime may be necessary during times of heavy trading.

Portfolio management companies, like investment banks, are often very high-stress, high pressure places to work. As with most parts of the securities industry, timing is critical and opportunities can be missed quickly. Compensation and job security are tied directly to performance.

## Employment
The securities, commodities, and other investments industry employed 816,000 wage and salary workers in 2006. With their extensive networks of retail sales representatives located in branch offices throughout the country, the large nationally known brokerage companies have the greatest share of jobs in the industry (table 1) where they operate the majority of establishments. About three-fourths of the establishments in the industry employ fewer than 5 workers. However, many of the industry's jobs are in the headquarters of major firms. About 1 in 4 workers in the securities industry is located in the New York metropolitan area.

## Occupations in the Industry
Securities industry employees are concentrated in a variety of financial and sales occupations that analyze and sell financial instruments. Other employees support these roles, mainly as clerks, administrative support workers, and computer specialists (table 2).

*Sales and related occupations.* Workers in sales and related occupations account for 1 in 5 wage and salary jobs in this industry. These include investment bankers, sales agents, traders, exchange workers, stock brokers, and investment advisors, among others.

Investment bankers are among the most prestigious workers in the industry. Those in corporate finance work directly with companies who are issuing stock or bonds to help them structure those offerings. This includes everything from determining the value of the company to deciding how many shares should be released. Workers in mergers and acquisitions assist firms plan

**Table 1. Percent distribution of employment and establishments in securities, commodities and other investments by detailed industry sector, 2006**

| Industry Segment | Employment | Establishments |
|---|---|---|
| **Total** | 100.0% | 100.0% |
| **Contracts intermediation and brokerage...** | 61.0 | 41.0 |
| Securities brokerage | 36.4 | 25.0 |
| Investment banking and securities dealing .. | 21.6 | 12.2 |
| Commodity contracts brokerage | 1.6 | 2.0 |
| Commodity contracts dealing | 1.3 | 1.7 |
| **Security and commodity exchanges** | 1.1 | 0.3 |
| **Other financial investment activities** | 37.9 | 58.7 |
| Investment advice | 14.9 | 32.1 |
| Portfolio management | 14.7 | 15.7 |
| All other financial investment activities | 5.4 | 3.9 |
| Miscellaneous intermediation | 3.0 | 7.0 |
| Other depository credit intermediation | 1.2 | 1.1 |

mergers with other companies. This includes analysis of which target companies to consider, how to fund acquisitions, and how to structure the resulting company's stock. Those in sales departments call investors to offer stocks and bonds that the bank has underwritten, while traders execute the transactions.

A very small number of people work directly on the floor of stock and commodities exchanges. Floor brokers execute trades as directed by their firms' trading departments. Independent brokers represent themselves, rather than a firm, and are often on hand to perform trades when floor brokers are too busy. Specialists, or market makers, are the auctioneers who work as a bridge between buyers and sellers. Each stock listed on the exchange has one of these workers on hand to assure fair trading. They also provide liquidity by buying stock when demand is low or selling stock when demand is too high.

Brokers are the people who sell stocks to individuals. They take buy and sell orders from customers and execute those trades through their firms' trading departments. This position can vary greatly depending on the type of brokerage. In a discount brokerage or wire house, brokers may work in a call center environment, where they answer calls as they come in. In full-service brokerages, another type of broker often called an investment advisor is more typical. Investment advisors go beyond just buying and selling to give advice to their customers. They may also meet with their clients in person to discuss their needs and desire to avoid risk.

*Office and administrative support occupations.* Keeping track of transactions and paperwork constitutes a large portion of the work in this industry, which is why its largest major occupational group is office and administrative support workers. *Brokerage clerks*, the largest occupation in this category, handle much of the day-to-day operations within a brokerage firm. A type of brokerage clerk, called a sales assistant, takes calls from brokers' clients, writes up order tickets and enters them into the computer. They also handle the paperwork for new accounts, inform clients of stock prices, and perform other tasks as needed. Most sales assistants obtain licenses to sell securities, allowing them to call brokers' clients with recommendations from the broker regarding specific investments.

Because more clients are choosing to trade without the use of sales agents or brokers, *customer service representatives* now play a larger role in securities firms. While some may have licenses to sell securities or other financial products, most are not in the business of sales or offering advice, but rather they mainly take questions from current customers. Customer service representatives usually work in central call centers, where they handle account transfers, redemptions, and address changes; answer tax questions; and help clients navigate the Web, among other services.

*Management, business, and financial occupations.* This category includes a wide range of jobs that require expertise in finance and investment policy, including *accountants and auditors*, who prepare the firms' financial statements, and *general and operations managers*, who manage the businesses. The largest occupations in this area, however, are *financial analysts* and *personal financial advisors.*

*Financial analysts* generally work in the research departments of securities firms. They are especially common in investment banks and portfolio management firms, but also may work in brokerages. They review financial statements of companies, evaluate economic and market trends, and make recommendations concerning the potential profits from investments in specific companies. Financial analysts examine company financial reports, such as balance sheets and income statements, to determine fair market value. Those in large firms usually specialize in a certain industry sector, such as transportation; in a product type, such as bonds; or in a region, such as Latin America.

*Personal financial advisors*, also called financial planners, provide advice to both individuals and businesses on a broad range of financial subjects, such as investments, retirement planning, tax management, estate planning, and employee benefits. They may take a comprehensive approach to the client's financial needs or specialize in a particular area, such as retirement planning. Advisors also may buy and sell financial products on behalf of their clients, such as stocks, bonds, mutual funds, and insurance. Private bankers and wealth managers are personal financial advisors who work with wealthy clients. These specialists may take a very active role in their clients' finances, authorizing payments and trades, and writing checks on behalf of the client's account.

*Financial managers* are employed throughout the industry. They prepare financial documents for the regulatory authorities and direct firms' investment policies. In many departments, managers act as senior advisors and oversee teams of junior analysts or brokers while continuing to be actively involved in working out deals with clients.

The increasingly computerized environment in this industry also requires the expertise of *computer software engineers, computer programmers,* and other computer specialists to develop and operate the communications networks that provide online trading.

## Training and Advancement

The securities, commodities, and other investments industry has one of the most highly educated and skilled workforces of any industry. About 2 out of 3 workers have bachelors' or higher degrees. The requirements for entry are high—even brokerage clerks often have college degrees. The most successful workers at all levels have an aptitude for working with numbers and a keen interest in investing.

*Licensure.* Many people in the industry must be licensed by the Financial Industry Regulatory Authority (FINRA) before they can legally sell securities or recommend specific investments. To be licensed, brokers and assistants must pass an examination that tests their knowledge of investments. Various licenses are available for different investment products. The most common is the Series 7 license, which allows agents to act as registered representatives of a firm. The Series 63 and 66 licenses, which allow their holders to legally give financial advice, are also very common.

*Investment banking and securities dealing.* Investment bankers are expected to have very strong educational backgrounds, including courses in finance, accounting, and economics. A competitive candidate will combine strong quantitative skills with good interpersonal skills and the ability to work in teams. Success in a competitive internship can also be very helpful.

Most investment banks have a standardized system of advancement. Recent college graduates start out as analysts. Assignments to these positions usually last 2 to 3 years and involve a great deal of training. Analysts do the routine work of the investment bank, and generally spend much of their time working in teams. Those who succeed are promoted to similar jobs at the associate level, where they have more responsibilities and may even act as team leaders. Recent business school graduates often start at the associate level.

Successful associates are generally promoted to the title of vice president. At this stage, employees are much more trusted by the investment bank, and begin to spend more of their time dealing directly with customers. Top vice presidents may become directors or executive directors after a few years. Because there are fewer of these, many vice presidents move to different firms to get to this level. At the very top of the structure is the managing director, a highly coveted and well paid position, with a great deal of authority.

*Securities brokerage and investment advice.* There are many paths of entry into brokerages. Many professionals in this industry begin their careers as sales assistants. Others transfer from sales or financial careers in a different industry. This path is often more successful, as people who have had other careers generally know more people and can find clients quickly. A third group enters directly into a broker training program. The Series 7 and 63 or 66 licenses are required for most brokers. Generally new workers are given a fair amount of training, which helps them to better understand the various products, as well as to learn how to properly execute trades and analyze financial statements.

For securities, commodities, and financial services sales agent jobs, a college education is increasingly important, although not essential, because it helps the sales agent to understand economic conditions and trends. The overwhelming majority of entrants to this occupation are college graduates but many employers consider personal qualities and skills, such as self-motivation and the ability to handle rejection, to be more important than academic training.

Brokers earn a significant portion of their salaries through commissions and many successful brokers build and maintain a large client base. The larger and wealthier the client base, the more money the broker earns. On the other hand, many brokers opt to open their own branches of securities firms or become personal financial advisors. While this generally carries more risks, it can also be very lucrative.

Although there are no specific licensure requirements for personal financial advisors, most must be knowledgeable about economic trends, finance, budgeting, and accounting. Therefore, a college education is important. Personal financial advisors must possess excellent communication and interpersonal skills to be

**Table 2. Employment of wage and salary workers in securities, commodities, and other investments by occupation, 2006 and projected change, 2006-2016.**
(Employment in thousands)

| Occupation | Employment, 2006 | | Percent change, 2006-16 |
|---|---|---|---|
| | Number | Percent | |
| **All occupations** | 816 | 100.0 | 46.1 |
| | | | |
| **Management, business, and financial occupations** | 268 | 32.8 | 57.9 |
| General and operations managers | 15 | 1.8 | 30.2 |
| Marketing and sales managers | 10 | 1.2 | 45.6 |
| Computer and information systems managers | 8 | 1.0 | 45.5 |
| Financial managers | 33 | 4.1 | 45.6 |
| Compliance officers, except agriculture, construction, health and safety, and transportation | 6 | 0.7 | 43.6 |
| Human resources, training, and labor relations specialists | 6 | 0.7 | 49.9 |
| Management analysts | 6 | 0.8 | 44.8 |
| Accountants and auditors | 21 | 2.6 | 52.2 |
| Financial analysts | 48 | 5.9 | 68.9 |
| Personal financial advisors | 72 | 8.8 | 78.8 |
| | | | |
| **Professional and related occupations** | 84 | 10.3 | 55.7 |
| Computer programmers | 6 | 0.8 | 15.8 |
| Computer software engineers | 21 | 2.6 | 72.4 |
| Computer support specialists | 8 | 1.0 | 42.8 |
| Computer systems analysts | 10 | 1.2 | 58.4 |
| Network and computer systems administrators | 6 | 0.8 | 58.2 |
| Market research analysts | 7 | 0.9 | 45.1 |
| Lawyers | 4 | 0.5 | 43.8 |
| | | | |
| **Sales and related occupations** | 184 | 22.5 | 35.6 |
| Securities, commodities, and financial services sales agents | 166 | 20.4 | 35.2 |
| | | | |
| **Office and administrative support occupations** | 273 | 33.4 | 38.7 |
| First-line supervisors/managers of office and administrative support workers | 18 | 2.2 | 35.1 |
| Bookkeeping, accounting, and auditing clerks | 18 | 2.2 | 43.7 |
| Brokerage clerks | 55 | 6.8 | 25.7 |
| Customer service representatives | 34 | 4.1 | 68.9 |
| Receptionists and information clerks | 7 | 0.8 | 44.1 |
| Executive secretaries and administrative assistants | 43 | 5.3 | 44.5 |
| Secretaries, except legal, medical, and executive | 20 | 2.5 | 28.0 |
| Office clerks, general | 44 | 5.4 | 44.1 |

Note: Columns may not add to totals due to omission of occupations with small employment

able to explain complicated issues to their clients. Many advisors entering the field earn a Certified Financial Planner credential. To receive this designation, a person must pass an exam on insurance, investments, tax planning, employee benefits, and retirement and estate planning. They also must have 3 years of experience in a related field and an accredited college degree and must agree to abide by the rules and regulations issued by the Board of Standards. Like brokers, personal financial advisors advance by increasing their client base or opening branch offices.

*Portfolio management.* Entry-level portfolio management positions are filled by college graduates, most of whom have majored in business administration, marketing, economics, accounting,

industrial relations, or finance. Analysts usually start with a training program that helps them to understand the complexities of securities analysis. After this training period, they join a team which specializes in a specific product, industry, or region. Successful analysts are given more responsibilities and greater influence. They may be put in charge of more important specialties, or become team leaders. Those who are not successful may be asked to leave the firm. Top analysts are often promoted to portfolio manager or fund manager and take on responsibility for the mix of products in the portfolio and have ultimate say in its composition.

Those working as financial analysts are encouraged to obtain the Chartered Financial Analyst (CFA) designation sponsored by the CFA Institute. To qualify, applicants must have at least 4 years of applicable experience and pass a series of 3 rigorous essay exams requiring an extensive knowledge of many fields, including accounting, economics, and security valuation, risk management, and portfolio management.

## Outlook

The securities, commodities, and other investments industry should experience employment growth between 2006 and 2016, but competition for jobs in the industry will be quite keen.

*Employment change.* Wage and salary employment in the securities, commodities, and other investments industry is projected to rise 46 percent from 2006 to 2016, compared to the 11 percent increase across all industries. Employment growth will be driven by increasing levels of investment in securities and commodities in the global marketplace, as well as the growing need for investment advice.

Over the projections decade, the baby boom generation will move from their peak saving years to their first years of retirement. More retirement savings will be managed by the retirees themselves because most companies have moved from defined benefit plans—such as traditional pensions—to defined contribution plans—such as 401(k) programs and Roth IRAs. This will continue to boost the stock and bond markets, as well as mutual funds and investment advisory as retirees look for reliable investments.

Another factor contributing to projected employment growth is the globalization of securities and commodities markets—the extension of traditional exchange and trading boundaries into new markets in foreign countries. Recent developments, from the rapid growth of Asian economies to the recent merger of the New York Stock Exchange and Euronext, will continue to make Americans more eager to invest abroad and at the same time encourage investors in other nations to purchase U.S securities.

Online trading will grow and reduce the need for direct contact with actual brokers, but the number of investment advisors is nevertheless expected to increase as many people remain willing to pay for the guidance that a full-service representative can offer. Employment of personal financial advisors is also expected to increase rapidly. As the complexity of financial planning grows, individuals will continue to look to experts to help them manage their money.

Financial analyst positions are also expected to grow modestly. Globalization and the growth of developing countries will provide a multitude of investment opportunities, and financial analysts with knowledge of foreign accounting standards and economies will be needed to examine these investments. Furthermore, the growth of mutual funds, hedge funds, and other large-scale investments will continue to create jobs in this occupation.

Advances in telecommunications and computer technology will continue to shape the industry as companies look for faster and more secure ways to perform tasks. Computer programmers and information systems managers will continue to have important roles in this industry as trading and the recordkeeping that supports trading become more automated, while the jobs of brokerage clerks will become less clerical and have more high-level tasks. More clerks will be licensed and expected to work more independently.

Compliance is a rising concern for companies, as various scandals have rocked the industry over the past several years. While the merger of NASD with NYSE Regulation creating FINRA should provide some relief for companies, the amount of oversight from both private regulators and the Securities and Exchange Commission (SEC) continues to increase. This will continue to lead to greater employment of lawyers and compliance specialists, as well as recordkeeping clerks.

*Job prospects.* Despite continued growth in the securities industry, keen competition is expected for most jobs. This will be especially true for jobs in the upper echelons of the industry that have extremely high earnings. Jobs in investment banks, exchanges, and fund management companies will be especially difficult to enter. Positions at regional securities firms and brokerages will be somewhat more accessible.

Prospects will be best for graduates from 4-year degree programs from nationally recognized universities and colleges. Companies value a background in accounting, finance, and economics. Successful completion of a recognized internship program may also be very helpful to beginners. Earning a Master's of Business Administration degree or one of the professional certifications recognized in the industry are important assets for advancement.

## Earnings

*Industry earnings.* In May 2006, the average weekly earnings of nonsupervisory workers in the industry were $1055 compared with $568 in all industries combined. Median earnings for the largest occupations in the securities, commodities, and other investments industry in May 2006 are shown in table 3.

Earnings of many securities industry employees—especially those working in sales positions—depend on commissions from the sale or purchase of securities. Commissions are likely to be lower during recessionary periods or when there is a slump in market activity. Earnings can also be based on the amount of assets that a broker or portfolio manager has under his or her management, with the broker or portfolio manager receiving a small percentage of the value of the assets.

In other positions, a large part of annual earnings are paid in the form of an annual bonus based on the success of the firm or the individual's team. This is particularly common in investment banks and portfolio management companies. Profit sharing and stock options are also common.

*Benefits and union membership.* Most workers in the industry receive substantial benefits packages, including health insurance, retirement programs, and reimbursement of expenses associated with company travel or entertainment of clients. Additionally, top employees often receive perks, such as opportunities to eat at expensive restaurants and attend sporting events. Those who travel receive frequent flyer miles and hotel points which can be redeemed for personal use. Most of these opportunities come as a result of the need to connect with clients and make sales, however many workers consider them to be a significant benefit of the job.

Union membership is very low in this industry, and does not affect the salaries or benefits of workers.

**Table 3. Median hourly earnings of the largest occupations in securities, commodities, and other investments, May 2006**

| Occupation | Securities commodities, and other investments | All industries |
|---|---|---|
| Financial managers | $63.52 | $43.74 |
| Securities, commodities, and financial services sales agents | 40.24 | 32.93 |
| Financial analysts | 38.97 | 32.02 |
| Personal financial advisors | 34.89 | 31.79 |
| Accountants and auditors | 29.65 | 26.26 |
| Executive secretaries and administrative assistants | 20.92 | 17.90 |
| Brokerage clerks | 17.90 | 17.50 |
| Customer service representatives | 16.65 | 13.62 |
| Secretaries, except legal, medical, and executive | 14.60 | 13.20 |
| Office clerks, general | 11.48 | 11.40 |

## Sources of Additional Information

For more information about jobs in the securities industry, contact:
➤ Securities Industry and Financial Markets Association, 120 Broadway, 35th Floor, New York, NY 10271. **http://www.sifma.org.**
➤ Financial Planning Association, 4100 E. Mississippi Ave., Suite 400, Denver, CO 80246-3053. Internet: **http://www.fpanet.org**

For information on licensing, contact:
➤ Financial Industry Regulatory Authority (FINRA). 1735 K St., NW. Washington, DC 20006. Internet: **http://www.finra.org**

For information on professional certifications, contact:
➤ American Academy of Financial Management, 2 Canal St., Suite 2317, New Orleans, LA 70130. Internet: **http://www.aafm.org**
➤ Certified Financial Planner Board of Standards, Inc., 1670 Broadway, Suite 600, Denver, CO 80202. Internet: **http://www.cfp.net/**
➤ CFA Institute, P.O. Box 3668, 560 Ray C. Hunt Dr., Charlottesville, VA 22903. Internet: **http://www.cfainstitute.org**

Information on the following occupations can be found in the 2008–09 *Occupational Outlook Handbook*:
• Accountants and auditors
• Brokerage clerks
• Customer service representatives
• Financial managers
• Financial analysts and personal financial advisors
• Securities, commodities, and financial services sales agents

# Professional and Business Services

# Advertising and Public Relations Services

(NAICS 5418)

## SIGNIFICANT POINTS

- Competition for many jobs will be keen because the glamour of the industry traditionally attracts many more jobseekers than there are job openings.

- California and New York together account for about 1 in 5 firms and more than 1 in 4 workers in the industry.

- Layoffs are common when accounts are lost, major clients cut budgets, or agencies merge.

## Nature of the Industry

*Goods and services.* Firms in the advertising and public relations services industry prepare advertisements for other companies and organizations and design campaigns to promote the interests and image of their clients. This industry also includes media representatives—firms that sell advertising space for publications, radio, television, and the Internet; display advertisers—businesses engaged in creating and designing public display ads for use in shopping malls, on billboards, or in similar media; and direct mail advertisers. A firm that purchases advertising time (or space) from media outlets, thereafter reselling it to advertising agencies or individual companies directly, is considered a media buying agency. Divisions of companies that produce and place their own advertising are not considered part of this industry.

*Industry organization.* In 2006, there were about 48,000 advertising and public relations services establishments in the United States. About 4 out of 10 write copy and prepare artwork, graphics, and other creative work, and then place the resulting ads on television, radio, or the Internet or in periodicals, newspapers, or other advertising media. Within the industry, only these full-service establishments are known as *advertising agencies.* About 1 in 6 were public relations firms. Many of the largest agencies are international, with a substantial proportion of their revenue coming from abroad.

Most advertising firms specialize in a particular market niche. Some companies produce and solicit outdoor advertising, such as billboards and electric displays. Others place ads in buses, subways, taxis, airports, and bus terminals. A small number of firms produce aerial advertising, while others distribute circulars, handbills, and free samples.

Many agencies have created units to serve their clients' electronic advertising needs on the Internet. Online advertisements link users to a company's or product's Web site, where information such as new product announcements, contests, and product catalogs appears, and from which purchases may be made.

Some firms are not involved in the creation of ads at all; instead, they sell advertising time or space on radio and television stations or in publications. Because these firms do not produce advertising, their staffs are mostly sales workers.

Companies often look to advertising as a way of boosting sales by increasing the public's exposure to a product or service. Most companies do not have the staff with the necessary skills or experience to create effective advertisements; furthermore, many advertising campaigns are temporary, so employers would

have difficulty maintaining their own advertising staff. Instead, companies commonly solicit bids from ad agencies to develop advertising for them; the ad agencies offering their services to the company often make presentations. After winning an account, various departments within an agency—such as creative, production, media, and research—work together to meet the client's goal of increasing sales.

Widespread public relations services firms can influence how businesses, governments, and institutions make decisions. Often working behind the scenes, these firms have a variety of functions. In general, firms in public relations services advise and implement public exposure strategies. For example, a public relations firm might issue a press release that is printed in newspapers across the country. Firms in public relations services offer one or more resources that clients cannot provide themselves. Usually this resource is expertise in the form of knowledge, experience, special skills, or creativity; but sometimes the resource is time or personnel that the client cannot spare. Clients of public relations firms include all types of businesses, institutions, trades, and public interest groups, and even high-profile individuals. Clients are large and small for-profit firms in the private sector; State, local, or Federal Governments; hospitals, universities, unions, and trade groups; and foreign governments or businesses.

Public relations firms help secure favorable public exposure for their clients, advise them in the case of a sudden public crisis, and design strategies to help them attain a certain public image. Toward these ends, public relations firms analyze public or internal sentiment about clients; establish relationships with the media; write speeches and coach clients for interviews; issue press releases; and organize client-sponsored publicity events, such as contests, concerts, exhibits, symposia, and sporting and charity events.

Lobbying firms, a special type of public relations firm, differ somewhat. Instead of attempting to secure favorable public opinion about their clients, they attempt to influence legislators in favor of their clients' special interests. Lobbyists often work for large businesses, industry trade organizations, unions, or public interest groups.

*Recent developments.* In an effort to attract and maintain clients, advertising and public relations services agencies are diversifying their services, offering advertising as well as public relations, sales, marketing, and interactive media services. Advertising and public relations services firms have found that highly creative work is particularly suitable for their services, resulting in a better product and increasing their clients' profitability.

## Working Conditions

*Work environment.* Most employees in advertising and public relations services work in comfortable offices operating in a teamwork environment; however, long hours, including evenings and weekends, are common. There are fewer opportunities for part-time work than in many other industries; in 2006, 12 percent of advertising and public relations employees worked part time, compared with 15 percent of all workers.

Work in advertising and public relations is fast-paced and exciting, but it also can be stressful. Being creative on a tight schedule can be emotionally draining. Some workers, such as lobbyists, consultants, and public relations writers, frequently must meet deadlines and consequently may work long hours at times. Workers, whose services are billed hourly, such as advertising consultants and public relations specialists, are often under pressure to manage their time carefully. In addition, frequent meetings with clients and media representatives may involve substantial travel.

Most firms encourage employees to attend employer-paid time-management classes, which help reduce the stress sometimes associated with working under strict time constraints. Also, with today's hectic lifestyle, many firms in this industry offer or provide health facilities or clubs to help employees maintain good health.

*Hours.* In 2006, workers in the industry averaged 34.7 hours per week, slightly higher than the national average of 33.9.

## Employment

The advertising and public relations services industry employed 458,000 wage and salary workers in 2006; an additional 46,800 workers were self-employed.

Although advertising and public relations services firms are located throughout the country, they are concentrated in the largest States and cities. California and New York together account for about 1 in 5 firms and more than 1 in 4 workers in the industry. Firms vary in size, ranging from one-person shops to international agencies employing thousands of workers. However, 68 percent of all advertising and public relations establishments employ fewer than 5 employees (chart).

The small size of the average advertising and public relations services firm demonstrates the opportunities for self-employment. It is relatively easy to open a small agency; in fact, many successful agencies began as one-person or two-person operations.

About 74 percent of advertising and public relations employees are 25 to 54 years of age. Very few advertising and public relations services workers are below the age of 20, which reflects the need for postsecondary training or work experience.

## Occupations in the Industry

Management, business, and financial occupations; professionals and related occupations; and sales and related occupations account for about 63 percent of all jobs in the industry (table 1). An additional 27 percent of jobs are in office and administrative support occupations. Employees have varied responsibilities in agencies with only a few workers, and the specific job duties of each worker often are difficult to distinguish. Workers in relatively large firms specialize more, so the distinctions among occupations are more apparent.

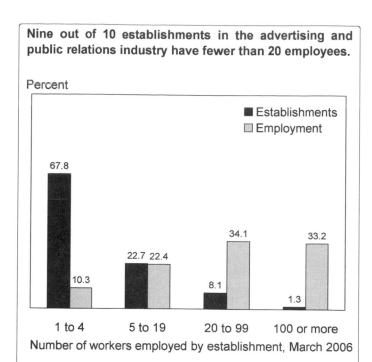

**Nine out of 10 establishments in the advertising and public relations industry have fewer than 20 employees.**

Percent

- Establishments
- Employment

67.8 / 10.3 — 1 to 4
22.7 / 22.4 — 5 to 19
8.1 / 34.1 — 20 to 99
1.3 / 33.2 — 100 or more

Number of workers employed by establishment, March 2006

*Management and professional and related occupations.* Within advertising and public relations, the account management department links the agency and the client—it represents the agency to the client, as well as the client to the agency. Account management brings business to the agency and ultimately is responsible for the quality of the advertisement or public relations campaign. Account management workers carefully monitor the activities of the other areas to ensure that everything runs smoothly. Account managers, or *advertising and promotions managers,* and their assistants analyze competitive activity and consumer trends, report client billing, forecast agency income, and combine the talents of the creative, media, and research areas. The creative director oversees the *copy writer* and *art director* and their respective staffs. The media director oversees planning groups that select the communication media—for example, radio, television, newspapers, magazines, Internet, or outdoor signs—to be used to promote the organization, issue, product, or service.

In public relations firms, *public relations managers* direct publicity programs to a targeted public. They often specialize in a specific area, such as crisis management—or in a specific industry, such as health care. They use every available communication medium in their effort to maintain the support of the specific group upon whom their organization's success depends, such as consumers, stockholders, or the general public. For example, public relations managers may clarify or justify the firm's point of view on health or environmental issues to community or special interest groups. *Public relations specialists* handle organizational functions such as media, community, consumer, and governmental relations; political campaigns; interest-group representation; conflict mediation; or employee and investor relations. They prepare press releases and contact people in the media who might print or broadcast their material. Many radio or television special reports, newspaper stories, and magazine articles start on the desks of public relations specialists.

Working with an idea that account management obtains from the client, the creative department brings the idea to life. For example, an ad agency's staff works together to transform a blank piece of paper into an advertisement. As the idea takes shape, *copy writers* and their assistants write the words of ads—both the written part of print ads as well as the scripts of radio and television spots. *Art directors* and their assistants develop the visual concepts and designs of advertisements. They prepare pasteups and layouts for print ads and television storyboards, cartoon-style summaries of how an advertisement will appear. They also oversee the filming of television commercials and photo sessions. *Graphic designers* use a variety of print, electronic, and film media to create designs that meet clients' commercial needs. Using computer software, they develop the overall layout and design of print ads for magazines, newspapers, journals, corporate reports, and other publications. They also may produce promotional displays and marketing brochures for products and services, design distinctive company logos for products and businesses, and develop signs and environmental graphics—aesthetically pleasing signs that deliver a message, such as a sunset to advertise a beach resort. An increasing number of graphic designers develop material to appear on the Internet.

Workers in the research department try to understand the desires, motivations, and ideals of consumers, in order to produce and place the most effective advertising or public relations campaign in the most effective media. Research executives compile data, monitor the progress of internal and external research, develop research tools, and interpret and provide explanations of the data gathered. Research executives often specialize in specific research areas and perform supervisory duties. *Market research analysts* are concerned with the potential sales of a product or service. They analyze statistical data on past sales to predict future sales. They provide a company's management with information needed to make decisions on the promotion, distribution, design, and pricing of products or services.

*Sales and related occupations.* Media planners gather information on the public's viewing and reading habits, and evaluate editorial content and programming to determine the potential use of media such as newspapers, magazines, radio, television, or the Internet. The media staff calculates the numbers and types of people reached by different media, and how often they are reached. Media buyers track the media space and times available for purchase, negotiate and purchase time and space for ads, and make sure ads appear exactly as scheduled. Additionally, they calculate rates, usage, and budgets. *Advertising sales agents* sell air time on radio and television, and page space in print media. They generally work in firms representing radio stations, television stations, and publications. *Demonstrators* promote sales of a product to consumers, while *product promoters* try to induce retail stores to sell particular products and market them effectively. Product demonstration is an effective technique used by both to introduce new products or promote sales of old products because it allows face-to-face interaction with potential customers.

*Office and administrative support occupations.* Office and administrative support occupations accounted for 27 percent of jobs in 2006. Positions ranged from secretaries and administrative assistants to financial clerks. The occupational composition of this group varies widely among agencies. The remaining jobs in the industry were in service, construction and extraction, production, transportation, and installation, maintenance, and repair occupations.

## Training and Advancement

Most entry-level professional and managerial positions in advertising and public relations services require a bachelor's degree,

**Table 1. Employment of wage and salary workers in advertising and public relations services by occupation, 2006 and projected change, 2006-2016**
(Employment in thousands)

| Occupation | Employment, 2006 Number | Employment, 2006 Percent | Percent change, 2006-16 |
|---|---|---|---|
| All occupations | 458 | 100.0 | 13.6 |
| **Management, business, and financial occupations** | 65 | 14.3 | 12.0 |
| General and operations managers | 13 | 2.9 | 1.5 |
| Advertising and promotions managers | 7 | 1.5 | 15.2 |
| Marketing and sales managers | 7 | 1.5 | 12.8 |
| Public relations managers | 4 | 1.0 | 24.1 |
| Purchasing agents, except wholesale, retail, and farm products | 5 | 1.0 | 12.8 |
| Accountants and auditors | 7 | 1.5 | 12.8 |
| **Professional and related occupations** | 116 | 25.3 | 20.1 |
| Computer programmers | 5 | 1.0 | -9.7 |
| Network and computer systems administrators | 3 | 0.7 | 24.1 |
| Market research analysts | 7 | 1.6 | 24.1 |
| Art directors | 10 | 2.3 | 12.8 |
| Multi-media artists and animators | 4 | 0.9 | 40.4 |
| Graphic designers | 23 | 5.0 | 24.1 |
| Merchandise displayers and window trimmers | 4 | 0.9 | 12.8 |
| Producers and directors | 3 | 0.6 | 12.8 |
| Public relations specialists | 29 | 6.4 | 24.1 |
| Writers and authors | 8 | 1.8 | 10.9 |
| **Sales and related occupations** | 109 | 23.8 | 14.5 |
| First-line supervisors/managers of non-retail sales workers | 7 | 1.5 | 7.7 |
| Advertising sales agents | 53 | 11.7 | 16.5 |
| Sales representatives, wholesale and manufacturing | 9 | 1.9 | 12.8 |
| Demonstrators and product promoters | 17 | 3.7 | 12.8 |
| Telemarketers | 5 | 1.1 | -9.7 |
| **Office and administrative support occupations** | 124 | 27.0 | 8.8 |
| First-line supervisors/managers of office and administrative support workers | 7 | 1.6 | 5.1 |
| Bookkeeping, accounting, and auditing clerks | 12 | 2.5 | 12.8 |
| Customer service representatives | 15 | 3.4 | 24.1 |
| Receptionists and information clerks | 6 | 1.2 | 12.3 |
| Production, planning, and expediting clerks | 6 | 1.3 | 12.8 |
| Shipping, receiving, and traffic clerks | 5 | 1.0 | 8.6 |
| Stock clerks and order fillers | 3 | 0.7 | -5.6 |
| Executive secretaries and administrative assistants | 12 | 2.7 | 12.8 |
| Secretaries, except legal, medical, and executive | 8 | 1.8 | 0.4 |
| Mail clerks and mail machine operators, except postal service | 20 | 4.3 | 3.4 |
| Office clerks, general | 18 | 3.8 | 11.2 |
| **Production occupations** | 22 | 4.8 | 12.7 |
| Printers | 10 | 2.1 | 18.0 |
| **Transportation and material moving occupations** | 13 | 2.8 | 2.8 |
| Truck drivers, light or delivery services | 3 | 0.6 | 12.8 |
| Laborers and material movers, hand | 8 | 1.7 | -1.5 |

Note: Columns may not add to totals due to omission of occupations with small employment

preferably with broad liberal arts exposure.

Beginners in advertising usually enter the industry in the account management or media department. Occasionally, entry-level positions are available in the market research or creative departments of an agency, but these positions usually require some experience. Completing an advertising-related internship while in school provides an advantage when applying for an entry-level position; in fact, internships are becoming a necessary step to obtaining permanent employment. In addition to an internship, courses in marketing, psychology, accounting, statistics, and creative design can help prepare potential entrants for careers in this field.

Assistant account executive positions—the entry-level account management occupation in most firms—require a bachelor's degree in marketing or advertising, although some firms require a master's degree in business administration.

Bachelor's degrees are not required for entry-level positions in the creative department. Assistant art directors usually need at least a 2-year degree from an art or design school. Although assistant copywriters do not need a degree, obtaining one helps to develop the superior communication skills and abilities required for this job.

Assistant media planner or assistant media buyer also are good entry-level positions, but almost always require a bachelor's degree, preferably with a major in marketing or advertising. Experienced applicants who possess at least a master's degree usually fill research positions. Often, they have a background in marketing or statistics and years of experience. Requirements for support services and administrative positions depend on the job and vary from firm to firm.

In public relations, employers prefer applicants with degrees in communications, journalism, English, or business. Some 4-year colleges and universities have begun to offer a concentration in public relations. Because there is keen competition for entry-level public relations jobs, workers are encouraged to gain experience through internships, co-op programs, or one of the formal public relations programs offered across the country. However, these programs are not available everywhere, so most public relations workers get the bulk of their training on the job. At some firms, this training consists of formal classroom education but, in most cases, workers train under the guidance of senior account executives or other experienced workers, gradually familiarizing themselves with public relations work. Entry-level workers often start as research or account assistants and may be promoted to account executive, account supervisor, vice president, and executive vice president.

A voluntary accreditation program for public relations specialists is offered by the Public Relations Society of America. The program is a recognized mark of competency in the profession and requires that workers have been employed in the field for several years.

Employees in advertising and public relations services should have good people skills, common sense, creativity, communication skills, and problem-solving ability. Foreign language skills have always been important for those wanting to work abroad for domestic firms or to represent foreign firms domestically. However, these skills are increasingly vital to reach minorities not fluent in English in U.S. cities, such as Los Angeles, New York, Miami, Houston, and Phoenix. New media, such as the Internet, are creating opportunities to market products, but also are increasing the need for additional training for those already employed. Keeping pace with technology is fundamental to suc-

cess in the industry. In addition, advertisers must keep in tune with the changing values, cultures, and fashions of the Nation.

Success in increasingly responsible staff assignments usually leads to advancement to supervisory positions. As workers advance on the job, broad vision and planning skills become extremely important. Another way to get to the top in this industry is to open one's own firm. In spite of the difficulty and high failure rate, many find starting their own business to be personally and financially rewarding. Advancement among the self-employed takes the form of increasing the size and strength of their own company.

## Outlook

Competition for many jobs will be keen because the glamour of the industry traditionally attracts many more jobseekers than there are job openings.

*Employment change.* Employment in the advertising and public relations services industry is projected to grow 14 percent over the 2006-16 period, compared with 11 percent for all industries combined. New jobs will be created as the economy expands and generates more products and services to advertise.

*Job prospects.* Competition for many jobs will be keen because the glamour of the advertising and public relations services industry traditionally attracts many more job seekers than there are job openings. Employment also may be adversely affected if legislation, aimed at protecting public health and safety, further restricts advertising for specific products such as alcoholic beverages and tobacco. The best job opportunities will be for job seekers skilled in employing the increasing number and types of media outlets used to reach an increasingly diverse customer base.

In addition to new jobs created over the 2006-16 period, job opportunities also will arise from the need to replace workers who transfer to other industries or leave the workforce.

Layoffs are common in advertising and public relations services firms when accounts are lost, major clients cut budgets, or agencies merge.

## Earnings

*Industry earnings.* In 2006, nonsupervisory workers in advertising and public relations services averaged $724 a week—significantly higher than the $568 a week for all nonsupervisory workers in private industry.

**Table 2. Median hourly earnings of the largest occupations in advertising and public relations services, May 2006**

| Occupation | Advertising and public relations services | All industries |
|---|---|---|
| General and operations managers | $58.15 | $40.97 |
| Sales representatives, services, all other | 24.05 | 23.12 |
| Public relations specialists | 24.03 | 22.76 |
| Advertising sales agents | 22.91 | 20.55 |
| Graphic designers | 20.00 | 19.18 |
| Executive secretaries and administrative assistants | 18.75 | 17.90 |
| Customer service representatives | 15.01 | 13.62 |
| Office clerks, general | 11.27 | 11.40 |
| Mail clerks and mail machine operators, except postal service | 10.34 | 11.45 |
| Demonstrators and product promoters | 9.57 | 10.65 |

Earnings of workers in selected occupations in advertising and public relations services appear in table 2.

***Benefits and union membership.*** In addition to a straight salary, many workers receive additional compensation, such as profit sharing, stock ownership, or performance-based bonuses.

Only 2 percent of workers in advertising and public relations services belong to unions or are covered by union contracts, compared with about 13 percent of workers in all industries combined.

## Sources of Additional Information

For information about careers or training, contact:
➤ American Association of Advertising Agencies, 405 Lexington Ave., New York, NY 10174.  Internet: **http://www.aaaa.org**
➤ American Advertising Federation, 1101 Vermont Ave. NW., Suite 500, Washington, DC 20005.  Internet: **http://www.aaf.org**

For more information on accreditation for public relations professionals, contact:
➤ Public Relations Society of America, Inc., 33 Maiden Lane, New York, NY 10038-5150.  Internet: **http://www.prsa.org**

Information on these occupations can be found in the 2008-09 edition of the *Occupational Outlook Handbook*:
* Advertising, marketing, promotions, public relations, and sales managers
* Artists and related workers
* Demonstrators, product promoters, and models
* Market and survey researchers
* Public relations specialists
* Television, video, and motion picture camera operators and editors
* Writers and editors

# Computer Systems Design and Related Services

## SIGNIFICANT POINTS

- The computer systems design and related services industry is expected to experience rapid growth, adding 489,000 jobs between 2006 and 2016.

- Professional and related workers will enjoy the best job prospects, reflecting continuing demand for higher level skills needed to keep up with changes in technology.

- Computer specialists accounted for 54 percent of all employees in this industry in 2006.

## Nature of the Industry

All organizations today rely on computer and information technology to conduct business and operate more efficiently. Often, however, these institutions do not have the internal resources to effectively implement new technologies or satisfy their changing needs. When faced with such limitations, organizations turn to the computer systems design and related services industry to meet their specialized needs.

*Goods and services.* Firms enlist the services of an establishment in the computer systems design and related services industry on a contract or customer basis for help with a particular project or problem, such as setting up a secure Web site or establishing a marketplace online. Alternatively, firms may choose to contract out to a computer services firm one or more activities, such as the management of their onsite data center or help-desk support.

Services provided by this industry include custom computer programming services; computer systems design services; computer facilities management services, including computer systems or data processing facilities support services; and other computer-related services such as disaster recovery and software installation. Computer training contractors, however, are included in the *Career Guide* in the section on educational services, and establishments that manufacture computer equipment are included in the *Career Guide* in the section on computer and electronic product manufacturing. Establishments primarily engaged in providing computer data processing services at their own facility for others are discussed in the *Career Guide* in the section on Internet services providers, Web search portals, and data processing services. Producers of packaged software and Internet-based software are covered in the *Career Guide* in the section on the software publishers industry. Telecommunications services, including cable Internet providers, are covered in the *Career Guide* in the section on the telecommunications industry.

*Industry organization.* In 2006, there were 159,000 establishments in the computer systems design and related services industry. Custom programming establishments write, modify, test, and support software to meet the needs of a particular customer. These service firms may be hired to code large programs, or to install a software package on a user's system and customize it to the user's specific needs. Programming service firms also may update or reengineer existing systems.

Systems design services firms plan and design computer systems that integrate computer hardware, software, and communications technologies. In addition, they often install these

systems and train and support the people who use them. The systems' hardware and software components may be provided by the design firm as part of integrated services, or may be provided by third parties or vendors.

Computer facilities management services usually are offered at the customer's site. Establishments offering these services provide onsite management and operation of clients' computer systems and facilities, as well as facilities support services.

Electronic business, referred to as e-business, is any process that a business organization conducts over a computer-mediated network. Electronic commerce, referred to as e-commerce, is the part of e-business that involves the buying and selling of goods and services online. With the growth of the Internet and the expansion of e-commerce, some service firms specialize in developing and maintaining sites on the World Wide Web (see below) for client companies. Others create and maintain corporate intranets or self-contained internal networks that link multiple users within an organization by means of the Internet or, more recently, wireless technology. These firms design sophisticated computer networks, assist with upgrades or conversions, design programming features for clients, and engage in continual maintenance. They help clients select the right hardware and software products for a particular project, and then develop, install, and implement the system, as well as train the client's users. Service firms also offer consulting services for any stage of development throughout the entire process, from design and content development to administration and maintenance of site security.

*Recent developments.* The widespread use of the Internet and intranets also has resulted in an increased focus on security. Security threats range from damaging computer viruses to online credit card fraud and identity theft. The robust growth of e-commerce highlights this concern, as firms use the Internet to exchange sensitive information with an increasing number of clients. In order to mitigate this threat, many organizations are employing the services of security consulting firms, which specialize in all aspects of information technology (IT) security. These firms assess computer systems for areas of vulnerability, manage firewalls, and provide protection against intrusion and software "viruses." They also play a vital role in homeland security by keeping track of people and information.

## Working Conditions

*Hours.* In 2006, workers in the computer systems design and related services industry averaged 38.3 hours per week, compared with 33.9 for all industries combined. Many workers in this

200

industry worked more than the standard 40-hour workweek—about 19 percent work 50 or more hours a week. For many professionals and technical specialists, evening or weekend work is commonly necessary to meet deadlines or solve problems. Professionals working for large establishments may have less freedom in planning their schedule than do consultants for very small firms, whose work may be more varied. Only about 7 percent of the workers in the computer systems design and related services industry work part time, compared with 15 percent of workers throughout all industries.

*Work Environment.* Most workers in the computer systems design and related services industry work in clean, quiet offices. Those in facilities management and maintenance may work in computer operations centers. Given the technology available today, however, more work can be done from remote locations using fax machines, e-mail, and especially the Internet. For example, systems analysts may work from home with their computers linked directly to computers at their employer or a client. Computer support specialists, likewise, can tap into a customer's computer remotely in order to identify and fix problems. Even programmers and consultants, who often relocate to a customer's place of business while working on a project, may perform work from offsite locations.

Those who work with personal computers for extended periods may experience musculoskeletal strain, eye problems, stress, or repetitive motion illnesses, such as carpal tunnel syndrome.

## Employment

In 2006, there were about 1.3 million wage and salary jobs in the computer systems design and related services industry. While the industry has both large and small firms, the average establishment in computer systems design and related services is relatively small; about 78 percent of establishments employed fewer than 5 workers in 2006. Many of these small establishments are startup firms that hope to capitalize on a market niche. The majority of jobs, however, are found in establishments that employ 50 or more workers (chart).

Compared with the rest of the economy, there are significantly fewer workers 45 years of age and older in the computer systems design and related services industry. This industry's workforce remains younger than most, with large proportions of workers in the 25-to-44 age range (table 1). This reflects the industry's explosive growth in employment in the 1980s and 1990s that provided opportunities to thousands of young workers who possessed the latest technological skills.

## Occupations in the Industry

Providing a wide array of information services to clients requires a diverse and well-educated workforce. The majority of workers in the computer systems design and related services industry are professional and related workers—overwhelmingly computer specialists such as computer systems analysts, computer software engineers, and computer programmers (table 2). This occupational group accounts for about 62 percent of the jobs in the industry, reflecting the emphasis on high-level technical skills and creativity. By 2016, the share of professional and related occupations is expected to be even greater, while the share of office and administrative support occupations, currently accounting for 13 percent of industry employment, is expected to fall.

*Professional and related occupations,* Computer specialists make up the vast majority of professional and related occupa-

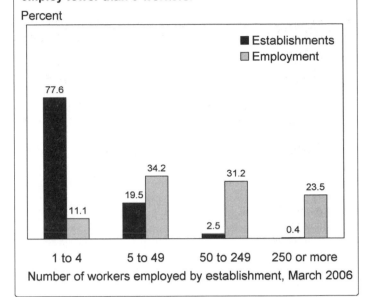

**More than three-fourths of the establishments in the computer systems design and related services industry employ fewer than 5 workers.**

Percent

Number of workers employed by establishment, March 2006

Table 1. Percent distribution of employment, by age group, 2006

| Age group | Computer systems design and publishers | All industries |
|---|---|---|
| **Total** | 100.0% | 100.0% |
| 16-19 | 0.4 | 4.3 |
| 20-24 | 4.8 | 9.6 |
| 25-34 | 31.0 | 21.5 |
| 35-44 | 31.8 | 23.9 |
| 45-54 | 21.5 | 23.6 |
| 55-64 | 8.8 | 13.4 |
| 65 and older | 1.7 | 3.7 |

tions, and account for more than 54 percent of the industry as a whole. Their duties vary by occupation, and include such tasks as developing computer software, designing information systems, and maintaining network security.

*Programmers* write, test, and maintain the detailed instructions, called programs or software, that computers must follow to perform their functions. These specialized programs tell the computer what to do—for example, which information to identify and access, how to process it, and what equipment to use. *Custom programmers* write these commands by breaking down each step into a logical series, converting specifications into a language that the computer understands. While some still work with traditional programming languages, such as COBOL, most programmers today use more sophisticated tools. Object-oriented programming languages, such as C++ and Java, computer-aided software engineering (CASE) tools, and artificial intelligence shells are widely used to create and maintain programs, because they allow portions of code to be reused in programs that require similar routines. Many programmers also customize a package to clients' specific needs or create better packages.

*Computer engineers* design, develop, test, and evaluate computer software programs, systems, and hardware and related equipment. Although programmers write and support programs in new languages, much of the design and development now is the responsibility of *software engineers* or *software developers*. (See the section in the Career Guide on software publishers.) Software engineers in the systems design and related services industry must possess strong programming skills but are more concerned with developing algorithms, and analyzing and solving programming problems for specific network systems than with actually writing code. *Computer systems software engineers* primarily write, modify, test, and develop software to meet the needs of a particular customer. They develop software systems for control and automation in manufacturing, business, and other areas.

*Computer and information scientists* work as theorists, researchers, or inventors. They apply a higher level of theoretical expertise and innovation and develop solutions to complex problems relating to computer hardware and software. Computer and information scientists with advanced backgrounds in security may be employed as *cyberspace security specialists* in disaster recovery situations or in custom security software installation.

*Systems analysts* integrate hardware and software to make computer systems more efficient. By implementing new software applications, or even designing entirely new systems, they help organizations maximize their investments in machines, personnel, and business processes. To perform their jobs they use data modeling, structured analysis, information engineering, and other methods. They prepare charts for programmers to follow for proper coding and perform cost-benefit analyses to help management evaluate systems. They also ensure that systems perform to their specifications by testing them thoroughly.

*Network systems and data communications analysts* design and evaluate network systems, such as local area networks (LANs), wide area networks (WANs), and Internet systems. They perform network modeling, analysis, and planning, and may deal with the interfacing of computer and communications equipment. With the explosive growth of the Internet, this worker group has come to include a variety of occupations related to design, development, and maintenance of Web sites and their servers. *Web developers* are responsible for day-to-day site design and creation. *Webmasters* are responsible for the technical aspects of the Web site, including performance issues, and for approving site content.

*Network or computer systems administrators* install, configure, and support an organization's LAN, WAN, network segment, or Internet functions. They maintain network hardware and software, analyze problems, and monitor the network to ensure availability to system users. Administrators also may plan, coordinate, and implement network security measures.

*Database administrators* determine ways to organize and store data. They set up computer databases and test and coordinate changes to them. Because they also may be responsible for the design and implementation of system security, database administrators often plan and coordinate security measures. In some organizations, *computer security specialists* are responsible for the organization's information security.

*Computer support specialists* provide technical assistance, support, and advice to customers and users. This group of occupations includes workers with a variety of titles, such as *technical support specialists* and *help-desk technicians*. These troubleshooters interpret problems and provide technical support for hardware, software, and systems. They answer telephone calls, analyze problems using automated diagnostic programs, and resolve recurrent difficulties encountered by users. Support specialists may work within a company or other organization that uses computers and computer systems, or directly for a computer hardware or software vendor.

*Management, business, and financial occupations. Computer and information systems managers* direct the work of systems analysts, computer programmers, and other computer-related workers. They analyze the computer and information needs of their organization and determine personnel and equipment requirements. These managers plan and coordinate activities such as the installation and upgrading of hardware and software; programming and systems design; the development of computer networks; and the construction of Internet and intranet sites.

*Sales and related occupations.* Due in part to the robust growth in e-commerce, a growing number of workers in this industry are employed in sales and related occupations. In order to compete successfully in the online world, firms employ marketing and sales workers to improve the presentation and features of Web sites and other Web-related content. These workers are vital for the successful promotion and sales of the products and services offered by the industry.

## Training and Advancement

Occupations in the computer systems design and related services industry require varying levels of education, but in 2006, about 75 percent of workers had college degrees. The level of education and type of training required depend on employers' needs, which often are affected by such aspects as local demand for workers, project timelines, and changes in technology and business conditions. For example, the recent emphasis on cyberspace security has increased the demand for workers with expertise in security services. Employers also are demanding workers with skill and expertise in other fields. Computer software engineers who develop e-commerce applications, for example, should have some expertise in sales or finance.

With more formal education, employees may advance to completely different jobs within the industry. For those wishing to advance to management positions, business skills are becoming increasingly important. Education or training in a specialty area can also lead to advancement opportunities.

*Professional and related occupations.* Although there are no universal educational requirements for computer programmers, workers in this occupation commonly hold a bachelor's degree. Some hold a degree in computer science, mathematics, or information systems. Others have taken special courses in computer programming to supplement their study in fields such as accounting, inventory control, or other areas of business. Because employers' needs are varied, a 2-year degree or certificate may be sufficient for some positions, so long as applicants possess the right technical skills. Some employers seek applicants with technical or professional certification. Certification can be obtained independently, although many organizations now assist employees in becoming certified.

Entry-level computer programmers usually start working with an experienced programmer to update existing code, generate lines of one portion of a larger program, or write relatively simple programs. They then advance to more difficult programming assignments, and may become project supervisors. With continued experience, they may move into management positions within their organizations. Many programmers who work closely with systems analysts advance to systems analyst positions.

**Table 2. Employment of wage and salary workers in computer systems design and related services by occupation, 2006 and projected change, 2006-2016.**

(Employment in thousands)

| Occupation | Employment, 2006 | | Percent change, 2006-16 |
|---|---|---|---|
| | Number | Percent | |
| **All occupations** | 1,278 | 100.0 | 38.3 |
| **Management, business, and financial occupations** | 214 | 16.7 | 35.0 |
| General and operations managers | 30 | 2.4 | 21.5 |
| Marketing and sales managers | 15 | 1.2 | 35.0 |
| Computer and information systems managers | 39 | 3.1 | 35.0 |
| Financial managers | 7 | 0.6 | 35.0 |
| Engineering managers | 6 | 0.5 | 35.0 |
| Human resources, training, and labor relations specialists | 18 | 1.4 | 38.5 |
| Management analysts | 28 | 2.2 | 35.0 |
| Accountants and auditors | 15 | 1.2 | 48.5 |
| **Professional and related occupations** | 787 | 61.5 | 41.1 |
| Computer and information scientists, research | 7 | 0.5 | 35.0 |
| Computer programmers | 133 | 10.4 | 8.0 |
| Computer software engineers, applications | 159 | 12.4 | 62.0 |
| Computer software engineers, systems software | 93 | 7.3 | 48.5 |
| Computer support specialists | 86 | 6.7 | 21.5 |
| Computer systems analysts | 100 | 7.8 | 48.5 |
| Database administrators | 16 | 1.3 | 48.1 |
| Network and computer systems administrators | 46 | 3.6 | 48.5 |
| Network systems and data communications analysts | 34 | 2.7 | 82.3 |
| Computer hardware engineers | 15 | 1.2 | 35.0 |
| Electrical and electronics engineers | 7 | 0.6 | 35.0 |
| Engineering technicians, except drafters | 8 | 0.6 | 40.2 |
| Market research analysts | 9 | 0.7 | 35.0 |
| Graphic designers | 7 | 0.6 | 35.0 |
| Technical writers | 8 | 0.6 | 35.0 |
| **Sales and related occupations** | 81 | 6.3 | 38.6 |
| Sales representatives, services | 28 | 2.2 | 48.3 |
| Sales representatives, wholesale and manufacturing, technical and scientific products | 25 | 1.9 | 35.0 |
| Sales engineers | 9 | 0.7 | 35.0 |
| **Office and administrative support occupations** | 166 | 13.0 | 30.4 |
| Bookkeeping, accounting, and auditing clerks | 16 | 1.2 | 35.0 |
| Customer service representatives | 33 | 2.6 | 48.5 |
| Secretaries and administrative assistants | 32 | 2.5 | 30.1 |
| Office clerks, general | 28 | 2.2 | 33.0 |
| **Installation, maintenance, and repair occupations** | 19 | 1.5 | 33.6 |
| Computer, automated teller, and office machine repairers | 8 | 0.7 | 31.5 |

Note: Columns may not add to totals due to omission of occupations with small employment

Most computer engineers and scientists have a bachelor's or higher degree and work experience. For computer and information scientists, a doctoral degree generally is required due to the highly technical nature of the work. Employers of some occupations, such as software engineers, may seek applicants with technical or professional certification.

Computer engineers and scientists who show leadership abil-ity can become project managers or advance into management positions, such as manager of information systems or chief information officer.

For systems analyst, programmer-analyst, and database administrator positions, many employers seek applicants who have a bachelor's degree in computer science, information science, or management information systems (MIS). Many of these workers hold an advanced degree in a technical field, and some hold a master's degree in business administration (MBA) with a concentration in information systems, and are specialists in their fields. An associate's degree or certificate generally is sufficient for some positions as network systems and data communication analysts positions, such as Webmaster, although more advanced positions might require a computer-related bachelor's degree. Government, academic institutions, and other employers increasingly are seeking workers with certifications in information security, reflecting the importance of keeping complex computer networks and vital electronic infrastructure safe from intruders.

Systems analysts generally begin with limited responsibilities. They may begin working with experienced analysts, or may deal only with small systems or one aspect of a system. As they gain further education or work experience, they may move into supervisory positions. Systems analysts who work with one type of system, or one aspect or application of a system, can become specialty consultants or move into management positions.

Persons interested in becoming a computer support specialist generally need an associate degree's in a computer-related field, as well as significant hands-on experience with computers. They also must possess strong problem-solving, analytical, and communication skills, because troubleshooting and helping others are their main job functions. As technology continues to improve, computer support specialists must constantly strive to acquire new skills if they wish to remain competitive in the field. One way to achieve this is through technical or professional certification.

Computer support specialists may advance by developing expertise in an area that leads to other opportunities. For example, those responsible for network support may advance into network administration or network security positions.

Consulting is an attractive option for experienced workers who do not wish to advance to management positions, or who would rather continue to work with hands-on applications or in a particular specialty. These workers may market their services on their own, under contract as specialized consultants, or with an organization that provides consulting services to outside clients. Many of the largest firms today have subsidiaries that offer specialized consulting services to other departments within the organization, and to outside clients. Large consulting and computer firms often hire inexperienced college graduates and put them through intensive, company-based programs that train them to provide such services.

***Sales and related occupations.*** Many experienced workers move into sales positions, as they gain knowledge of specific products. The emergence of e-commerce has created opportunities for professionals who specialize in Web marketing and sales. For example, computer programmers who adapt prepackaged software for accounting organizations may use their specialized knowledge to sell such products to similar firms.

***Management, business, and financial occupations.*** Computer and information systems managers usually are required to have a bachelor's degree in a computer-related field and work experience, but employers often prefer a graduate degree. An MBA with technology as a core component is especially preferred, as business skills are becoming increasingly important.

## Outlook

The computer systems design and related services industry grew dramatically throughout the 1990s, as employment more than doubled. And despite recent job losses in certain sectors, this remains one of the 20 fastest growing industries in the Nation. However, due to increasing productivity and the offshore outsourcing of some services to lower wage foreign countries, employment growth will not be as robust as it was during the last decade. Job opportunities should be favorable for most workers, but the best opportunities will be in professional and related occupations.

*Employment change.* Wage-and-salary employment is expected to grow 38 percent by the year 2016, compared with only 11 percent growth projected for the entire economy. In addition, this industry will add more than 489,000 jobs over the decade, placing it among the 10 industries with the largest job growth. An increasing reliance on information technology, combined with the falling prices of computers and related hardware, will spur demand for computer systems design and related services. Individuals and organizations will continue to turn to firms in this industry to maximize their return on investments in equipment, and to help them satisfy their growing computing needs. Such needs include a growing reliance on the Internet, faster and more efficient internal and external communication, and the implementation of new technologies and applications.

The computer systems design and related services industry also has seen an increase in the offshore outsourcing of some of the more routine services to lower wage foreign countries as companies strive to remain competitive. For example, firms have been able to cut costs by shifting some support services operations to countries with highly educated workers who have strong technical skills. This trend, however, will adversely affect employment of only certain types of workers, such as programmers and computer support specialists. Other tasks, such as integrating and designing systems, will be insulated from the effects of offshoring.

Given the overall rate of growth expected for the entire industry, most occupations should continue to grow rapidly, although some will grow faster than others. The most rapid growth will occur among network systems and data communications analysts. The growing use of sophisticated computer networks and Internet and intranet sites will increase the demand for their services. Other rapidly growing occupations include computer software engineers, computer systems analysts, and network and computer systems administrators. Employment of programmers should continue to expand, but more slowly than that of other occupations, as more routine programming functions are automated, and as more programming services are offshored.

The demand for networking and the need to integrate new hardware, software, and communications technologies will drive demand for consulting and integration. A need for more customized applications development, and for support and services to assist users, will drive demand for applications development and facilities support services.

Recent events have made society more conscious of the vulnerability of technology and the Internet, and the increasing need for security will spur employment growth in cyberspace security services. Security specialists will be employed more often to asses a system's vulnerability, and custom programmers and designers will be needed to develop new antivirus software, programs, and procedures. Therefore, employment of analysts and of consultants in areas such as disaster recovery services, custom security programming, and security software installation services should rise rapidly.

The expansion of the Internet and the proliferation "mobile" technologies have also created demand for a wide variety of new products and services. For example, the expansion of the wireless Internet, known as WiFi, brings a new aspect of mobility to information technology by allowing people to stay connected to the Internet anywhere, anytime. As businesses and individuals become more dependent on this new technology, there will be an increased need for "mobility consultants," or service firms that can design and integrate computer systems, so that they will be compatible with mobile technologies.

The ways in which the Internet is used are constantly changing, along with the products, services, and personnel required to support new applications. E-commerce changed the nature of business transactions, enabling markets to expand and an increasing array of services to be provided. And, as the amount of computer-stored information grows, organizations will continue to look for ways to tap the full potential of their vast stores of data. Demand for an even wider array of services should increase as companies continue to expand their capabilities, integrate new technologies, and develop new applications.

*Job prospects.* Given the rate at which the computer systems design and related services industry is expected to grow, and the increasing complexity of technology, job opportunities should be favorable for most workers. The best opportunities will be in professional and related occupations, reflecting their growth and the continuing demand for higher level skills to keep up with changes in technology. In addition, as individuals and organizations continue to conduct business electronically, the importance of maintaining system and network security will increase. Employment opportunities should be excellent for individuals involved in cyberspace security services, such as disaster recovery services, custom security programming, and security software installation services.

## Earnings

*Industry earnings.* Workers in the computer systems design and related services industry generally command higher earnings than the national average. All production or nonsupervisory workers in the industry averaged $1,265 a week in 2006, significantly higher than the average of $568 for all industries. This reflects the concentration of professionals and specialists, who often are highly compensated for their specialized skills or expertise. Given the pace at which technology advances in this industry, earnings can be driven by demand for specific skills or experience. Workers in segments of the industry that offer only professional services have even higher average earnings because they employ fewer low-skilled, lower paid workers. Earnings in selected occupations in computer systems design and related services appear in table 3.

As one might expect, education and experience influence earnings as well. For example, in May 2006, hourly earnings of computer software engineers, applications ranged from less than $2250 for the lowest paid 10 percent to more than $58.59 for the highest paid 10 percent. Managers usually earn more because they have been on the job longer and are more experienced than their staffs, but their salaries, too, can vary by level and experience. Accordingly, hourly earnings of computer and information systems managers in May 2006, ranged from less than $31.36 for the lowest paid 10 percent to more than $70.00 for the highest paid 10 percent. Earnings also are affected by other factors, such as the size, location, and type of establishment, hours and responsibilities of the employee, and level of sales.

**Table 3. Median hourly earnings of the largest occupations in computer systems design and related services, May 2006**

| Occupation | Computer systems design and related services | All industries |
|---|---|---|
| General and operations managers | $59.39 | $40.97 |
| Computer and information systems managers | 52.47 | 48.84 |
| Computer software engineers, systems software | 40.70 | 41.04 |
| Computer software engineers, applications | 37.91 | 38.36 |
| Computer systems analysts | 34.46 | 33.54 |
| Computer programmers | 32.64 | 31.50 |
| Network systems and data communications analysts | 32.25 | 31.06 |
| Network and computer systems administrators | 32.06 | 29.87 |
| Computer support specialists | 20.44 | 19.94 |
| Customer service representatives | 14.41 | 13.62 |

***Benefits and union membership.*** Workers generally receive standard benefits, including health insurance, paid vacation and sick leave, and pension plans. Unionization is rare in the computer systems design and related services industry. In 2006, only 1 percent of all workers were union members or covered by union contracts, compared with 13 percent of workers throughout private industry.

## Sources of Additional Information

Further information about computer careers is available from:
➤ Association for Computing Machinery, 2 Penn Plaza, Suite 701, New York, NY 10121-0701. Internet: **http://www.acm.org**
➤ National Workforce Center for Emerging Technologies, 3000 Landerholm Circle SE., Bellevue, WA 98007. Internet: **http://www.nwcet.org**
➤ University of Washington Computer Science and Engineering Department, AC101 Paul G. Allen Center, Box 352350, 185 Stevens Way, Seattle, WA 98195-2350. Internet: **http://www.cs.washington.edu/WhyCSE/**

Information on the following occupations can be found in the 2008–09 *Occupational Outlook Handbook*:
• Computer and information systems managers
• Computer programmers
• Computer scientists and database administrators
• Computer software engineers
• Computer support specialists and systems administrators
• Computer systems analysts

# Employment Services

(NAICS 5613)

## SIGNIFICANT POINTS

- Although future job growth in the employment services industry expected to continue at a faster-than-average pace, this growth will represent a slowdown from the very rapid growth of the 1990s.

- Most temporary jobs in this industry require only graduation from high school, while some permanent jobs may require a bachelor's or higher degree.

- Temporary jobs provide an entry into the workforce, supplemental income, and a bridge to full-time employment for many workers.

## Nature of the Industry

*Goods and services.* The employment services industry provides a variety of human resources services to businesses. These services include providing temporary workers to other businesses, helping employers locate suitable employees, and providing human resources services to clients.

*Industry organization.* The employment services industry has three distinct segments. *Employment placement agencies* list employment vacancies and place permanent employees. *Temporary help services*, also referred to as temporary staffing agencies, provide employees to other organizations, on a contract basis and for a limited period, to supplement the workforce of the client. *Professional employer organizations* are engaged in providing human resources and human resources management services to staff client businesses. They also may share responsibility as a co-employer of workers in order to provide a cost-effective approach to the management and administration of the human resources functions of their clients.

The typical employment placement agency has a relatively small permanent staff, usually fewer than 10 workers, who interview jobseekers and try to match their qualifications and skills to those being sought by employers for specific job openings (chart 1).

In contrast to the smaller employment placement agencies, temporary help agencies typically employ many more workers. Temporary help services firms provide temporary employees to other businesses to support or supplement their workforce in special situations, such as employee absences, temporary skill shortages, and varying seasonal workloads. Temporary workers are employed and paid by the temporary help services firm but are contracted out to a client for either a prearranged fee or an agreed hourly wage. Some companies choose to use temporary workers full time on an ongoing basis, rather than employ permanent staff, who typically would receive greater salaries and benefits. As a result, the overwhelming majority of workers in the temporary help services segment of the employment services industry are temporary workers; relatively few are permanent staff.

Professional employer organizations specialize in performing a wide range of human resource and personnel management duties for their client businesses, including payroll processing, accounting, benefits administration, recruiting, and labor relations. Employee leasing establishments, which are a type of professional employer organization, typically acquire and lease back some or all of the employees of their clients and serve as the employer of the leased employees for payroll, benefits, and related purposes.

## Working Conditions

*Hours.* The average annual work week in the employment services industry was about 33 hours in 2006, compared with the average of 34 hours across all industries. The low average work week reflects the fact that a temporary employee could work 40 or more hours a week on a contract for an extended period and then take a few weeks off from work. Most full-time temporary workers put in 35 to 40 hours a week, while some work longer hours. Permanent employees in employment agencies usually work a standard 40-hour week, unless seasonal fluctuations require more or fewer hours.

Workers employed as permanent staff of employment agencies, temporary help services firms, or professional employer organizations usually work in offices and may meet numerous people daily. Temporary employees work in a variety of envi-

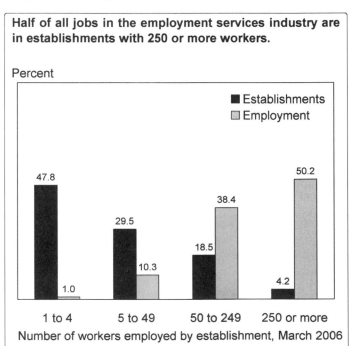

**Half of all jobs in the employment services industry are in establishments with 250 or more workers.**

Percent

- ■ Establishments
- ▨ Employment

| 1 to 4 | 5 to 49 | 50 to 249 | 250 or more |

47.8  1.0  29.5  10.3  18.5  38.4  4.2  50.2

Number of workers employed by establishment, March 2006

ronments and often do not stay in any one place long enough to settle into a personal workspace or establish close relationships with coworkers. Most assignments are of short duration because temporary workers may be called to replace a worker who is ill or on vacation or to help with a short-term surge of work. However, assignments of several weeks or longer occasionally may be offered. On each assignment, temporary employees may work for a new supervisor.

Employment as a temporary is attractive to some. The opportunity for a short-term source of income while enjoying flexible schedules and an ability to take extended leaves of absence is well-suited to students, persons juggling job and family responsibilities, those exploring various careers, and those seeking permanent positions in a chosen career. Firms try to accommodate workers' preferences for particular days or hours of work and for frequency or duration of assignments. Temporary work assignments provide an opportunity to experience a variety of work settings and employers, to sharpen skills through practice, and to learn new skills. Nevertheless, many workers in temporary assignments would prefer the stability and greater benefits associated with full-time work.

*Work Environment.* Since temporary and leased workers are used by a variety of different businesses, the work environments faced can vary greatly, depending on the type of work done. For example, temporary or leased clerical workers typically work in offices while production workers work in manufacturing plants. Permanent employees who are responsible for the day-to-day activities of firms within the industry tend to work in offices.

The annual injury and illness rate for the employment services industry as a whole was 3.3 cases for every 100 full-time workers in 2006, lower than the rate of 4.4 for the entire private sector. Temporary workers in industrial occupations often perform work that is more strenuous and potentially more dangerous, and may have a higher rate of injury and illness.

## Employment

The employment services industry provided 3.7 million jobs in 2006, about 2.6 million of them in temporary help services firms. Professional employer organizations employed about 729,000, and employment placement agencies employed another 296,000. About 40,000 of the 68,000 establishments in the industry are temporary help services firms which employ 7 out of 10 industry workers.

Employment in the employment services industry is distributed throughout the United States. Workers are somewhat younger than those in other industries—42 percent of employment services workers are under 35, compared with 35 percent of all workers, reflecting the large number of clerical and other entry-level positions in the industry that require little formal education.

## Occupations in the Industry

The employment services industry encompasses many occupations, from office and administrative support occupations to professional and production occupations (table 1). In general, occupations in the industry include the permanent staff of employment services firms, and the variety of occupations supplied through the temporary help services segment of the industry and the professional employer organizations.

*Management, business, financial, and sales occupations.* The staff of employment service agencies is responsible for the daily operation of the firm. Many of these workers are in management, business, financial, and sales occupations, which together account for about 9 percent of jobs in this industry. *Managers* ensure that the agency is run effectively, and they often conduct interviews of potential clients and jobseekers. *Employment, recruitment, and placement specialists* recruit and evaluate applicants and attempt to match them with client firms. *Sales workers* actively pursue new client firms and recruit qualified workers. Because of fierce competition among agencies, marketing and sales work at times can be quite stressful.

*Office and administrative support occupations.* About 24 percent of workers in this industry are in office and administrative support jobs. These positions may be either temporary or permanent. Experience in office and administrative support occupations usually is preferred for these jobs, although some persons take special training to learn skills such as bookkeeping. *Receptionists* greet visitors, field telephone calls, and perform assorted office functions. *Secretaries* perform a range of tasks, such as keyboarding, producing reports, and answering the telephone, depending on the type of firm in which they work. *Medical secretaries* make appointments and need a familiarity with common medical terms and procedures; *legal secretaries* must be familiar with the format of common legal documents. *General office clerks* file documents, type reports, and enter computer data. *File clerks* classify and store office information and records. *Data entry keyers* enter information into a computer data base. *Word processors and typists* enter and format drafts of documents using computers. *Bookkeeping clerks* compute, classify, and record transaction data for financial records and reports.

*Production, transportation, and material moving occupations.* Production occupations and transportation and material moving occupations together account for 40 percent of employment in the employment services industry. Few of these jobs require education beyond high school, although in many of them related work experience is an asset. Others require significant experience and on-the-job training. Highly skilled *assemblers and fabricators* may assemble and connect parts of electronic devices, while other less skilled workers perform simpler, more repetitive tasks on production lines. *Laborers and freight, stock, and material movers* transport goods to and from storage areas in either factories, warehouses, or other businesses. *Hand packers and packagers* wrap, package, inspect, and label materials manually, often keeping records of what has been packed and shipped.

*Professional and related occupations.* A growing number of temporary workers are specialized professional and related workers, who currently account for another 11 percent of employment. Professional and related occupations include a variety of specialists and practitioners, some of whom require many years of postsecondary education to qualify for their positions. For example, *engineers* require at least a bachelor's degree. Other professionals requiring some postsecondary education include *registered nurses*, who administer medication, tend to patients, and advise patients and family members about procedures and proper care. They usually work in hospitals, but they may be assigned to private duty in patients' homes. *Licensed practical nurses* provide basic bedside care to patients. *Computer programmers* write, test, and maintain computer software, the programs that computers follow to perform functions. While computer programmers are not required to have postsecondary education, formal training is an asset.

*Service occupations.* Service workers employed on a temporary basis also include a number of health care support occupations. *Home health aides* usually work in the home of an elderly or ill patient, allowing the patient to stay at home instead of being institutionalized. Becoming a home health aide generally does not require education beyond high school. *Nursing aides* and *orderlies* also seldom need education beyond high school, but employers do prefer previous experience. These workers assist nurses with patient care in hospitals and nursing homes.

The remainder of the workers in this industry includes those in farming, fishing, and forestry as well as installation, maintenance, and repair occupations.

## Training and Advancement

The employment services industry offers opportunities in many occupations for workers with a variety of skill levels and experience. The majority of temporary jobs still require only graduation from high school or the equivalent, while some permanent jobs, such as those in management, may require a bachelor's or higher degree. In general, the training requirements of temporary workers mirror those for permanent employees in the economy as a whole. As the industry expands to include various professional and managerial occupations, therefore, a growing number of jobs will require a bachelor's or advanced degree.

Some temporary help services firms offer skills training to newly hired employees to make them more marketable. This training often is provided free to the temporary worker and is an economical way to acquire training in important skills such as word processing. Agency training policies vary, so persons considering temporary work should ask firms what training they offer and at what cost.

Advancement as a temporary employee usually takes the form of pay increases or greater choice of jobs. More often, temporary workers transfer to full-time jobs with other employers. Turnover among temporary workers within help supply firms usually is very high; many accept offers to work full time for clients for whom they worked as temporary workers. Some experienced temporary workers may be offered permanent jobs with help firms, such as training others for temporary jobs.

Staff of employment placement agencies and permanent staff of temporary help services firms typically comprise employment interviewers, administrative support workers, and managers. The qualifications required of employment interviewers depend partly on the occupations that the employment placement agency or temporary help services firm specializes in placing. For example, agencies that place professionals, such as accountants or nurses, usually employ interviewers with college degrees in similar fields. Agencies specializing in placing administrative support workers, such as secretaries or data entry keyers, are more likely to hire interviewers with less education, but who have experience in those occupations. Staffs of professional employer organizations include professionals in human resources management, payroll, risk management, legal services, financial management, employment compliance, and administration.

Although administrative support occupations, such as receptionists, usually do not require formal education beyond high school, related work experience may be needed. Sometimes, staff experienced in administrative support occupations advance to employment interviewer positions. Most managers have college degrees; an undergraduate degree in personnel management or a related field is the best preparation for these jobs. Employment, recruitment, and placement specialists often advance to managerial positions, but seldom without a bachelor's degree.

**Table 1. Employment of wage and salary workers in employment services by occupation, 2006 and projected change, 2006-2016.**
(Employment in thousands)

| Occupation | Employment, 2006 Number | Employment, 2006 Percent | Percent change, 2006-16 |
|---|---|---|---|
| **All occupations** | 3,657 | 100.0 | 18.9 |
| **Management, business, and financial occupations** | 205 | 5.6 | 21.9 |
| Top executives | 28 | 0.8 | 13.9 |
| Employment, recruitment, and placement specialists | 70 | 1.9 | 11.6 |
| **Professional and related occupations** | 392 | 10.7 | 27.7 |
| Computer specialists | 70 | 1.9 | 31.6 |
| Engineers | 25 | 0.7 | 30.4 |
| Engineering technicians, except drafters | 18 | 0.5 | 27.7 |
| Primary, secondary, and special education teachers | 18 | 0.5 | 26.6 |
| Registered nurses | 95 | 2.6 | 26.6 |
| Licensed practical and licensed vocational nurses | 54 | 1.5 | 26.6 |
| **Service occupations** | 376 | 10.3 | 25.8 |
| Nursing aides, orderlies, and attendants | 52 | 1.4 | 26.6 |
| Fast food and counter workers | 21 | 0.6 | 37.7 |
| Waiters and waitresses | 47 | 1.3 | 26.6 |
| Janitors and cleaners, except maids and housekeeping cleaners | 49 | 1.3 | 29.4 |
| Maids and housekeeping cleaners | 20 | 0.6 | 26.6 |
| Landscaping and groundskeeping workers | 28 | 0.8 | 11.1 |
| **Sales and related occupations** | 110 | 3.0 | 19.6 |
| Retail sales workers | 26 | 0.7 | 21.5 |
| Telemarketers | 30 | 0.8 | 1.3 |
| **Office and administrative support occupations** | 872 | 23.8 | 12.8 |
| Bookkeeping, accounting, and auditing clerks | 40 | 1.1 | 26.6 |
| Customer service representatives | 106 | 2.9 | 39.2 |
| Receptionists and information clerks | 61 | 1.7 | 7.0 |
| Shipping, receiving, and traffic clerks | 44 | 1.2 | 21.8 |
| Stock clerks and order fillers | 44 | 1.2 | 5.9 |
| Secretaries and administrative assistants | 129 | 3.5 | 11.7 |
| Data entry keyers | 54 | 1.5 | 1.3 |
| Office clerks, general | 183 | 5.0 | 12.2 |
| **Construction and extraction occupations** | 178 | 4.9 | 22.6 |
| Carpenters | 29 | 0.8 | 26.6 |
| Construction laborers | 91 | 2.5 | 26.6 |
| **Installation, maintenance, and repair occupations** | 58 | 1.6 | 26.5 |
| Maintenance and repair workers, general | 32 | 0.9 | 26.6 |
| **Production occupations** | 697 | 19.1 | 21.2 |
| Team assemblers | 200 | 5.5 | 26.6 |
| Machine tool cutting setters, operators, and tenders, metal and plastic | 32 | 0.9 | 22.2 |
| Machinists | 24 | 0.7 | 32.9 |
| Inspectors, testers, sorters, samplers, and weighers | 37 | 1.0 | 19.3 |
| Packaging and filling machine operators and tenders | 61 | 1.7 | 13.9 |
| Helpers--Production workers | 120 | 3.3 | 18.9 |
| **Transportation and material moving occupations** | 752 | 20.6 | 13.0 |
| Truck drivers, heavy and tractor-trailer | 42 | 1.1 | 26.6 |
| Truck drivers, light or delivery services | 26 | 0.7 | 26.6 |
| Industrial truck and tractor operators | 38 | 1.1 | 13.9 |
| Laborers and freight, stock, and material movers, hand | 469 | 12.8 | 13.9 |
| Packers and packagers, hand | 139 | 3.8 | 1.3 |

Note: Columns may not add to totals due to omission of occupations with small employment

## Outlook

*Employment change.* Employment services has been one of the fastest growing industries in the Nation. Although future job growth is expected to continue at a faster-than-average pace, this growth will represent a slowdown from the very rapid growth of the 1990s. The industry is expected to gain about 692,000 new jobs over the 2006–16 projection period. Wage and salary employment in the employment services industry is expected to grow 19 percent over this period, compared to the 11 percent growth projected for all industries combined.

Temporary help agencies, the largest sector within employment services, should continue to generate the most new jobs in this industry. This growth will be spurred by businesses in need of workers to manage seasonal and other temporary increases in their workloads, demand for specialized workers, and those businesses seeking to expand without incurring the initial costs associated with permanent employees.

Employment in professional employer organizations is expected to grow in response to demands by businesses for changes in human resources management. The increasing complexity of employee-related laws and regulations and a desire to control costs, reduce risks, and provide more integrated services will spur more businesses to contract with professional employer organizations to handle their personnel management, health benefits, workers' compensation claims, payroll, tax compliance, and unemployment insurance claims. Businesses are expected to increasingly enter into relationships with professional employer organizations and shift these responsibilities to specialists.

Employment placement agencies are expected to continue growing, but not as fast as temporary help services or professional employer organizations. Growth in these agencies stems from employers' increasing willingness to allow outside agencies to perform the preliminary screening of candidates and the growing acceptance of executive recruitment services. However, online employment placement agencies operate without employment counselors and need fewer administrative support workers. Job postings on employer Web sites; online newspaper classified ads; and job matching Internet sites operated by educational institutions and professional associations compete with this industry, thereby limiting employment growth.

*Job prospects.* Increasing demand for flexible work arrangements and schedules, coupled with significant turnover in these positions, should create plentiful job opportunities for persons who seek jobs as temporary or contract workers through 2016. In particular, suppliers of medical personnel to hospitals and other medical facilities should continue to fare well, as demand for temporary health care staffing grows to meet the needs of aging baby boomers and to supplement demand for more health care services throughout the country. Also, businesses are expected to continue to seek new ways to make their staffing patterns more responsive to changes in demand. As a result, firms increasingly may hire temporary employees with specialized skills to reduce costs and to provide the necessary knowledge or experience in certain types of work.

Most new jobs will arise in the largest occupational groups in this industry—office and administrative support, production, and transportation and material moving occupations. However, the continuing trend toward specialization also will spur growth among professional workers, including engineers and health care practitioners such as registered nurses. Managers also will see an increase in new jobs, as government increasingly contracts out man-

agement functions. In addition, growth of temporary help firms and professional employer organizations—which provide human resource management, risk management, accounting, and information technology services—will provide more opportunities for professional workers within those fields. Marketing and sales representative jobs in temporary staffing firms also are expected to increase along with competition among these firms for the most qualified workers and the best clients.

## Earnings

*Industry earnings.* In 2006, earnings among nonsupervisory workers in employment services firms were $13.76 per hour and $453 per week, lower than the $16.76 an hour and $568 a week for all private industry.

Earnings vary as widely as the range of skills and formal education among workers in employment services. As in other industries, managers and professionals earn more than clerks and laborers. Also, temporary workers usually earn less than workers employed as permanent staff, but some experienced temporary workers make as much as or more than workers in similar occupations in other industries. Earnings in the largest occupations in employment services appear in table 2.

*Benefits and union membership.* Most permanent workers receive basic benefits; temporary workers usually do not receive such benefits unless they work a minimum number of hours or days per week to qualify for benefit plans. Only 2 percent of workers in employment services are union members or are covered by union contracts, compared with about 13 percent of workers in all industries combined.

## Sources of Additional Information

For information concerning employment in temporary help services, contact:

➤ American Staffing Association, 277 S. Washington St., Suite 200, Alexandria, VA 22314. Internet: **http://www.staffingtoday.net**

For information about professional employer organizations, contact:

➤ National Association of Professional Employer Organizations. Internet: **http://www.napeo.org**

For information about employment placement agencies, contact:

➤ National Association of Personnel Services, P.O. Box 2128, The Village At Banner Elk, Suite 108, Banner Elk, NC 28604.

**Table 2. Median hourly earnings of the largest occupations in employment services, May 2006**

| Occupation | Employment services | All industries |
|---|---|---|
| Registered nurses | $30.89 | $27.54 |
| Employment, recruitment, and placement specialists | 19.10 | 20.40 |
| Customer service representatives | 11.74 | 13.62 |
| Office clerks, general | 10.53 | 11.40 |
| Construction laborers | 9.90 | 12.66 |
| Production workers, all other | 9.38 | 11.97 |
| Team assemblers | 9.20 | 11.63 |
| Laborers and freight, stock, and material movers, hand | 8.69 | 10.20 |
| Helpers--production workers | 8.63 | 9.97 |
| Packers and packagers, hand | 8.04 | 8.48 |

More information about many occupations in this industry, including the following, appears in the 2008-09 *Occupational Outlook Handbook*:

- Computer programmers
- Construction laborers
- Data entry and information processing workers
- Engineers
- Human resources assistants, except payroll and timekeeping
- Human resources, training, and labor relations managers and specialists
- Interviewers
- Licensed practical and licensed vocational nurses
- Office and administrative support worker supervisors and managers
- Office clerks, general
- Personal and home care aides
- Receptionists and information clerks
- Registered nurses
- Secretaries and administrative assistants

# Management, Scientific, and Technical Consulting Services

## SIGNIFICANT POINTS

- This industry is the fastest growing and one of the highest paying.

- Job competition will be keen; the most educated and experienced workers will have the best job prospects.

- About 21 percent of all workers are self-employed.

- About 74 percent of workers have a bachelor's or higher degree; 60 percent of all jobs are in managerial, business, financial, and professional occupations.

## Nature of the Industry

Management, scientific, and technical consulting firms influence how businesses, governments, and institutions make decisions. Often working behind the scenes, these firms offer technical expertise, information, contacts, and tools that clients cannot provide themselves. They then work with their clients to provide a service or solve a problem.

*Goods and services.* Usually, one of the resources that consulting firms provide to clients is expertise—in the form of knowledge, experience, special skills, or creativity; another resource is time or personnel that the client cannot spare. Clients include large and small companies in the private sector; Federal, State, and local government agencies; institutions, such as hospitals, universities, unions, and nonprofit organizations; and foreign governments or businesses.

The management, scientific, and technical consulting services industry is diverse. Almost anyone with expertise in a given area can enter consulting. Management consulting firms advise on almost every aspect of corporate operations. This includes marketing, finance, corporate strategy and organization, manufacturing processes, information systems and data processing, electronic commerce (e-commerce) or business, and human resources including benefits and compensation. Scientific and technical consulting firms provide technical advice relating to almost all nonmanagement organizational activities, including compliance with environmental and workplace safety and health regulations, the application of technology, and knowledge of sciences such as biology, chemistry, and physics.

*Industry organization.* Larger consulting firms usually provide expertise in a variety of areas, whereas smaller consulting firms generally specialize in one area of consulting. *Administrative management and general management consulting services* firms, for example, offer advice on an organization's day-to-day operations, such as budgeting, asset management, strategic and financial planning, records management, and tax strategy. A manufacturing firm building a new factory might seek the help of management consultants to determine in which geographic location it would incur the lowest startup costs. A family opening a new restaurant might hire a management consulting firm to help develop a business plan and provide tax advice. Management consulting firms also might advise clients in the implementation

and use of the latest office technology or computer programs that could increase office productivity. (For information on consulting firms that are engaged primarily in developing computer systems and computer software, see the statements on computer systems design and related services, and software publishing, elsewhere in the *Career Guide.*) Some clients might turn to management consulting firms to manage the financial aspects of their business. Management consultants also may provide insight into why a division of the company is not profitable or may recommend an investment strategy that meets the client's needs. (For information on firms that engage in buying and selling financial assets, see the statement on securities, commodities, and other investments, elsewhere in the *Career Guide.*)

Effective management of a client's human capital is the primary work of consulting firms that offer *human resources consulting services.* Firms that focus on this area advise clients on effective personnel policies, employee salaries and benefits, employee recruitment and training, and employee assessment. A client with high employee turnover might seek the help of a human resources consulting firm in improving its retention rate. Human resources consulting firms also might be asked to help determine the appropriate level of employer and employee contributions to health care and retirement plans. Increasingly, firms are outsourcing, or contracting out, the administrative functions of their human resources division to human resources consulting firms that manage timekeeping and payroll systems and administer employee benefits.

One human resources consulting specialty is *executive search consulting* or *executive recruiting.* Firms in this industry often are referred to as "*headhunters.*" Executive search consulting firms are involved in locating the best candidates for top-level management and executive positions. Clients hire executive recruiters in order to save time and preserve confidentiality. Executive search firms keep a large database of executives' resumes and search this database for clients in order to identify candidates who would likely complement the client's corporate culture and strategic plan. Information on these candidates is then submitted to the clients for their selection. Executive search consulting firms also might conduct prescreening interviews and reference and background checks. Some executive search consulting firms specialize in recruiting for a particular industry or geographic area, while others conduct general searches. (For information on firms that provide employment services to jobseekers at all employment levels, see the statement on employment services, elsewhere in the *Career Guide*.)

*Marketing consulting services* firms provide assistance to firms in areas ranging from product development to customer service. They may advise on new product marketability, new and existing product pricing (to maximize sales and profit), forecasting sales, planning and implementing a marketing strategy, and improving customer service to help the firm's overall image. A pharmaceutical firm, for example, might seek advice as to whether it should remove a drug from the market, or a retail clothing chain might seek advice regarding the most effective way to market and sell its clothes—in a direct-mail or online catalog or over the telephone. Clients also might seek the help of a marketing consultant to set up business franchises or license their products.

Another specialty within management consulting is *process, physical distribution, and logistics consulting services*. Firms in this industry specialize in the production and distribution of goods, from the first stages of securing suppliers to the delivery of finished goods to consumers. Such firms give advice on improvements in the manufacturing process and productivity, product quality control, inventory management, packaging, order processing, the transportation of goods, and materials management and handling. A domestic manufacturing firm might hire a logistics consulting firm to calculate shipping rates and import duties for goods being exported or to determine the most cost-effective method of shipping products. Consulting firms in this segment of the industry also advise on the latest technology that links suppliers, producers, and customers together to streamline the manufacturing process. Finally, these consulting firms might suggest improvements to the manufacturing process in order to use inputs better, increase productivity, or decrease the amount of excess inventory.

While some management consulting firms specialize in a particular business process, others provide a range of business services specific to one industry, such as health care. Many professionals—for example, doctors—are highly skilled in the technical aspects of their job, but lack the business expertise to manage their practice effectively. Management consultants advise these clients regarding issues such as staff recruitment, compensation and benefits, asset management, marketing, and other business operations. Some management consultants offer advice on matters pertaining directly to the industry in question. For instance, management consultants for the health care industry may advise on compliance with biohazard removal and patient confidentiality regulations, avoidance of malpractice suits, and methods of dealing with managed care and health insurance companies. Industries such as legal services, telecommunication, and utilities also have consulting firms that specialize in industry-specific issues.

Scientific and technical consulting services firms provide services similar to those offered by management consulting firms, but the information is not management-related. One of the largest specialties in scientific and technical consulting services is *environmental consulting services*. Environmental consulting firms identify and evaluate environmental problems, such as inspecting sites for water contaminants, and offer solutions. Some firms in this segment of the industry advise clients about controlling the emissions of environmental pollutants, cleaning up contaminated sites, establishing a recycling program, and complying with government environmental laws and regulations. A real estate developer, for example, might hire an environmental consulting firm to help design and develop property without damaging natural habitats, such as wetlands. A manufacturing or utilities firm might hire environmental consultants to assess whether the firm is meeting government emissions standards, in order to avoid penalties before government regulators inspect the property in question. Finally, many government agencies contract work out to environmental consulting firms to assess environmental contamination in a particular geographic area or to evaluate the costs and benefits of new regulations.

*Occupational safety consulting services* firms provide services similar to those offered by government agencies and private businesses, identifying workplace safety hazards and ensuring that employers are in compliance with government worker safety regulations. Safety consulting firms might help plan a safe and healthy environment for workers, identify hazardous materials or systems that may cause illness or injury, assess safety risks associated with machinery, investigate accidents, and assess the likelihood of lawsuits resulting from safety code violations. For example, a manufacturing firm building a new plant may seek the advice of a safety consulting firm about how to build equipment and design the building layout in order to increase workplace safety and reduce human error. A restaurant may look to a safety consultant to develop occupational safety and health systems for employees, such as slip-resistant floors and shoes. Some safety consulting firms might specialize in a particular type of hazardous material, while others might specialize in a particular industry, such as construction, mining, manufacturing, health care, or food processing. As with environmental consulting firms, many government agencies contract out work to safety consulting firms for help with safety engineering, technical projects, and various kinds of assessment.

*Security consulting*, by contrast, seeks to ensure the safety and security of an organization's physical and human assets that may be threatened by natural or human-made disasters. Clients might hire security consulting firms to assess a building's security needs. The firms may then protect the building against theft and vandalism by installing security cameras, hiring security guards, and providing employee background checks. Other security consultants study a building's design and recommend measures to protect it from damage from fires, tornadoes, floods, earthquakes, or acts of terrorism. Security consultants also may recommend emergency evacuation procedures in the event that these disasters occur. Increasingly, clients are hiring security consulting firms to protect their confidential computer records against hackers and viruses. Recently, government agencies have hired security consulting firms to advise them on how to protect national monuments and the national transportation, utility, and defense infrastructure—airports, bridges, nuclear reactor plants, water treatment plants, and military barracks—against terrorism.

Scientific and technical consulting firms also advise on a diverse range of issues relating to the physical and social sciences—issues having to with agriculture, biology, chemistry, economics, energy, and physics. Agricultural consulting firms might advise on different farming techniques or machinery that increases agricultural production. Economic consultants might develop forecasting models and advise clients about the potential for a recession or an increase in interest rates that could affect business decisions. Energy consultants might advise clients on how to reduce costs by implementing energy-saving machinery. Finally, biological, chemical, and physics consultants might give theoretical or applied expertise in their chosen field.

212

*Recent developments.* Management, scientific, and technical consulting has grown rapidly over the past several decades, with businesses increasingly using consulting services. Hiring consultants is advantageous because these experts are experienced, are well trained, and keep abreast of the latest technologies, government regulations, and management and production techniques. In addition, consultants are cost effective, because they can be hired temporarily and can perform their duties objectively, free of the influence of company politics.

## Working Conditions

*Hours.* In 2006, production workers in the industry averaged 35.9 hours per week, slightly higher than the national average of 33.9. However, many consultants must meet hurried deadlines, which frequently requires working long hours in stressful environments. Consultants whose services are billed hourly often are under pressure to manage their time very carefully. Occasionally, weekend work also is necessary, depending upon the job that is being performed.

*Work Environment.* Working conditions in management, scientific, and technical consulting services are generally similar to those of most office workers operating in a team environment. The work is rarely hazardous, with a few exceptions—for example, environmental or safety consultants who inspect sites for contamination from hazardous materials. In 2006, the industry had only 0.6 injuries and illnesses per 100 full-time workers, compared with an average of 4.4 throughout private industry.

In addition, some projects might require many executives and consultants to travel extensively or to live away from home for extended periods of time. However, new technology—such as laptop computers with remote access to the firm's computer server and videoconferencing machines—allow some consultants to work from home or conduct meetings with clients in different locations, reducing some of the need for business travel.

Most firms encourage employees to attend employer-paid time-management classes. The classes teach participants to reduce the stress sometimes associated with working under strict time constraints. Also, with today's hectic lifestyle, many firms in this industry offer or provide health facilities or clubs that employees may use to maintain good health.

## Employment

The management, scientific, and technical consulting services industry had about 921,000 wage and salary workers in 2006; an additional 250,000 workers were self-employed and unpaid family workers, comprising 21 percent of all jobs in this industry.

Table 1 details how employment is distributed among the different segments of the industry.

The vast majority of establishments in the industry were fairly small, employing fewer than five workers (chart). Self-employed individuals operated many of these small firms. Despite the prevalence of small firms and self-employed workers, large firms tend to dominate the industry. Approximately 58 percent of jobs are found in the 4 percent of establishments with 20 or more employees, and some of the largest firms in the industry employ several thousand people.

Many individuals move into consulting after gaining experience in their field by working in another industry. As a result, the average age in the consulting industry is higher than in all industries. Table 2 shows that the consulting industry has higher proportions of older workers and lower proportions of younger

**Table 1. Percent distribution of employment and establishments in management, scientific, and technical consulting services by detailed industry sector, 2006**

| Industry Segment | Employment | Establishments |
|---|---|---|
| **Total** .............................................. | 100.0 | 100.0 |
| | | |
| Administrative management and general management consulting ........................... | 35.9 | 37.9 |
| Marketing consulting..................................... | 13.9 | 14.9 |
| Human resources and executive search consulting....................................... | 12.4 | 8.7 |
| Other scientific and technical consulting .... | 12.2 | 17.8 |
| Other management consulting ................... | 9.3 | 9.6 |
| Process, physical distribution, and logistics consulting................................ | 8.4 | 5.7 |
| Environmental consulting............................ | 7.9 | 5.4 |

workers than are present across all industries.

Although employees in this industry work in all parts of the country, many workers are concentrated near large urban centers.

## Occupations in the Industry

Most management, scientific, and technical consulting services are fairly specialized; still, the industry comprises a variety of occupations (table 3). Some, such as *environmental engineers,* are specific to only one segment of the industry, whereas others, such as *secretaries and administrative assistants,* can be found throughout the industry.

Compared with other industries, the management, scientific, and technical consulting services industry has a relatively high proportion of highly educated workers. About 42 percent have a bachelor's degree, compared with 20 percent of workers throughout the economy. Around 32 percent have a master's or higher degree, compared with 10 percent of workers throughout the economy. Certain jobs may have stringent entry requirements. For example, some management consulting firms prefer to hire only workers who have a master's degree in business administration (MBA). Other positions can be attained only after many years of related experience.

In management, scientific, and technical consulting services, 60 percent of employment consists of workers in management, business and financial operations occupations, and in professional and related occupations. These same occupational groups account for about 30 percent of workers across the entire economy. These groups of workers comprise a disproportionate share of jobs in the industry, because workers with education and experience in business management and workers with scientific, engineering, and other technical backgrounds conduct most of the consulting work in this industry.

**Table 2. Percent distribution of employment, by age group, 2006**

| Age group | Management, scientific and technical consulting services | All industries |
|---|---|---|
| **Total** ................................................. | 100.0% | 100.0% |
| | | |
| 16-19................................................... | 0.2 | 4.3 |
| 20-24 .................................................. | 4.4 | 9.6 |
| 25-34 .................................................. | 19.8 | 21.5 |
| 35-44 .................................................. | 24.7 | 23.9 |
| 45-54 .................................................. | 24.7 | 23.6 |
| 55-64 .................................................. | 18.9 | 13.4 |
| 65 and older.......................................... | 7.1 | 3.7 |

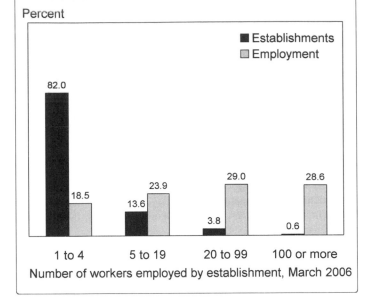

Percent

Number of workers employed by establishment, March 2006

*Management, business, and financial operations occupations.*
*Top executives,* the largest managerial occupation in the industry, includes both the highest-level managers—such as chief executive officers and vice presidents—and many top managers with diverse duties. In consulting firms, top executives with partial ownership and profit-sharing privileges might be referred to as partners. Top-level managers or partners shape company policy, often with the help of other executives or a board of directors. They oversee all activities of the firm, coordinate the duties of subordinate executives and managers, and often bear ultimate responsibility for a firm's performance. Mid-level managers or partners may oversee all the activities of one department or all the activities of one or more clients.

*Management analysts,* also called *management consultants,* is the largest occupation in the management consulting industry. Their work is quite varied, depending on the nature of the project and the client's needs. In general, management consultants study and analyze business-related problems, synthesizing information from many sources, and recommend solutions. The solutions can include overhauling a client's computer systems, offering early retirement incentives to middle managers, recommending a switch in health plans, improving just-in-time inventory systems, hiring public relations firms, or selling troublesome parts of businesses. Because of the varied nature of these jobs, firms hire workers with diverse backgrounds, such as backgrounds in engineering, finance, actuarial science, chemistry, or business. Many firms require consultants to have an MBA, whereas others hire workers who have only a bachelor's degree. Many workers have experience in other industries prior to entering management consulting work.

Other management and business and financial operations occupations include *administrative services managers,* who typically administer a consulting firm's support services. These managers oversee secretaries, data entry keyers, bookkeepers, and other clerical staff. In the management consulting services industry, they also often supervise a client's clerical and support staff and do consulting work in that area. *Advertising, marketing, promotions, public relations, and sales managers* oversee the consulting firm's marketing and sales departments, researching

Table 3. Employment of wage and salary workers in management, scientific, and technical consulting services by occupation, 2006 and projected change, 2006-2016.
(Employment in thousands)

| Occupation | Employment, 2006 | | Percent change, 2006-16 |
|---|---|---|---|
| | Number | Percent | |
| **All occupations** | 921 | 100.0 | 77.9 |
| **Management, business, and financial occupations** | 311 | 33.7 | 79.8 |
| Top executives | 32 | 3.5 | 60.7 |
| Marketing and sales managers | 9 | 1.0 | 78.5 |
| Computer and information systems managers | 7 | 0.7 | 78.5 |
| Financial managers | 6 | 0.6 | 78.5 |
| Employment, recruitment, and placement specialists | 20 | 2.2 | 75.0 |
| Logisticians | 4 | 0.4 | 96.4 |
| Management analysts | 125 | 13.5 | 78.5 |
| Accountants and auditors | 19 | 2.0 | 96.4 |
| Financial analysts | 7 | 0.8 | 96.4 |
| **Professional and related occupations** | 245 | 26.6 | 85.8 |
| Computer programmers | 8 | 0.9 | 42.8 |
| Computer software engineers | 27 | 2.9 | 107.1 |
| Computer support specialists | 10 | 1.1 | 78.5 |
| Computer systems analysts | 16 | 1.7 | 96.4 |
| Network and computer systems administrators | 8 | 0.8 | 96.4 |
| Network systems and data communications analysts | 7 | 0.8 | 141.0 |
| Actuaries | 4 | 0.4 | 78.5 |
| Operations research analysts | 5 | 0.6 | 70.6 |
| Engineers | 28 | 3.0 | 84.6 |
| Engineering technicians, except drafters | 5 | 0.6 | 79.5 |
| Environmental scientists and specialists, including health | 18 | 1.9 | 78.5 |
| Market research analysts | 19 | 2.1 | 96.4 |
| Environmental science and protection technicians, including health | 8 | 0.8 | 78.5 |
| Graphic designers | 5 | 0.6 | 78.5 |
| Public relations specialists | 6 | 0.7 | 78.5 |
| Writers and editors | 5 | 0.6 | 77.8 |
| **Sales and related occupations** | 66 | 7.2 | 77.9 |
| Sales representatives, services | 24 | 2.6 | 95.8 |
| Sales representatives, wholesale and manufacturing | 12 | 1.3 | 78.5 |
| Demonstrators and product promoters | 7 | 0.7 | 78.5 |
| Telemarketers | 12 | 1.3 | 42.8 |
| **Office and administrative support occupations** | 236 | 25.6 | 68.5 |
| First-line supervisors/managers of office and administrative support workers | 15 | 1.6 | 66.2 |
| Bookkeeping, accounting, and auditing clerks | 20 | 2.2 | 78.5 |
| Customer service representatives | 33 | 3.6 | 96.4 |
| Interviewers, except eligibility and loan | 5 | 0.6 | 78.5 |
| Receptionists and information clerks | 8 | 0.9 | 77.8 |
| Executive secretaries and administrative assistants | 36 | 3.9 | 78.5 |
| Secretaries, except legal, medical, and executive | 26 | 2.8 | 58.8 |
| Data entry keyers | 9 | 0.9 | 42.8 |
| Office clerks, general | 37 | 4.1 | 58.3 |
| **Transportation and material moving occupations** | 19 | 2.1 | 64.2 |
| Laborers and freight, stock, and material movers, hand | 11 | 1.2 | 60.7 |

Note: Columns may not add to totals due to omission of occupations with small employment

214

and targeting new clients and also helping on consulting projects having to do with marketing. *Computer and information systems managers* ensure that the consulting firm's computer and network systems are fully operational and oversee other computer and technical workers, such as computer support specialists. These managers might also supervise certain consulting projects involving computer and information technology. *Financial managers* prepare financial statements and assess the financial health of firms. Often, they must have at least a bachelor's degree in accounting or finance. *Human resources, training, and labor relations managers and specialists* supervise the activities of a consulting firm's human resources department, managing personnel records, payroll, benefits, and employee recruitment and training. These managers might also supervise projects for clients in the human resources consulting industry. In scientific and technical consulting firms, *engineering and natural sciences managers* oversee the engineers and scientists working for their consulting firms. *Accountants* and *auditors* monitor firms' financial transactions and often report to financial managers. More recently, accountants and auditors have been involved in consulting projects for clients involving the preparation of financial statements, tax strategy, budget or retirement planning, and the implementation of accounting software.

*Professional and related occupations.* Workers in professional and related occupations are employed mainly in the scientific and technical consulting portion of the industry. Many of these workers are engineers and scientists who use their expertise through consulting. For example, *environmental engineers* and *environmental scientists and geoscientists* are employed by environmental consulting firms to evaluate environmental damage or assess compliance with environmental laws and regulations. Other engineers, such as *agricultural, biomedical, chemical, mining and geological, nuclear,* and *petroleum engineers*; and physical and life scientists, such as *agricultural and food scientists, biological scientists, chemists, materials scientists,* and *physicists and astronomers*, are employed by consulting firms specializing in their scientific disciplines. *Architects* and *civil and industrial engineers* are sometimes employed by safety and security consulting firms to assess the construction of buildings and other structures, such as bridges, and to make recommendations regarding reinforcing these structures against damage.

The rapid spread of computers and information technology has generated a need for highly trained computer specialists to design and develop new hardware and software systems and to incorporate new technologies. *Systems analysts* design new computer systems or redesign old systems for new applications. They solve computer problems and enable computer technology to meet their organization's particular needs. For example, a systems analyst from a management consulting firm might be hired by a wholesale firm to implement an online inventory database. *Computer software engineers*, by contrast, can be involved in the design and development of software systems for the control and automation of manufacturing, business, and management processes. Other computer specialists include *computer support specialists*, who provide technical assistance, support, and advice to customers and users, and *database administrators*, who work with database management systems software and determine ways to organize and store data. Computer specialists such as systems analysts, computer scientists, and computer engineers sometimes are referred to simply as "consultants."

Technical workers also include *computer programmers*, who write programs and create software, often in close conjunction with systems analysts. Like systems analysts, these workers are found primarily in the business and management consulting segments of the industry.

Designers in this industry are mostly *graphic designers* who use a variety of print, electronic, and film media to create designs that meet clients' commercial needs. Using computer software, these workers develop the overall layout and design of magazines, newspapers, journals, corporate reports, and other publications. They also may produce promotional displays and marketing brochures for products and services and may design distinctive company logos for products and businesses. An increasing number of graphic designers develop material to appear on Internet homepages.

Other professional and related workers include *economists, market and survey researchers, lawyers,* and *engineering technicians*. Economists are employed by economic consulting firms to conduct economic research and advise clients on economic trends. Market and survey researchers are mainly employed by marketing consulting firms to conduct surveys and research on various topics. *Lawyers* are employed in virtually all management, scientific, and technical consulting industries to represent their consulting firms in case of a lawsuit and to advise the firms, as well as clients, on changes in laws and regulations pertaining to their areas of expertise. *Engineering technicians* aid engineers in research and development. Like engineers, these workers are found primarily in the business and management consulting segments of the industry.

*Office and administrative support occupations.* Office and administrative support positions in management, scientific, and technical consulting services resemble those in other industries, and account for 26 percent of industry employment. Particularly numerous are *secretaries* and *administrative assistants* and *bookkeeping, accounting, and auditing clerks*, who record and classify financial data. The industry also employs many *supervisors* and *managers of office and administrative support workers*, who oversee the support staff, often reporting to administrative services managers.

*Other occupations.* Management, scientific, and technical consulting services firms do not produce any goods and, as a result, employ relatively few services, sales, and production workers, who, together with the remaining occupational groups, make up only about 14 percent of industry employment.

### Training and Advancement

Training and advancement opportunities vary widely within management, scientific, and technical consulting services, but most jobs in the industry are similar in three respects. First, clients usually hire consulting firms on the basis of the expertise of their staffs, so proper training of employees is vital to the success of firms. Second, although employers generally prefer a bachelor's or higher degree, most jobs also require extensive on-the-job training or related experience. Third, advancement opportunities are best for workers with the highest levels of education.

Most consulting specialties provide a variety of different ways to enter the profession. Whereas very few universities or colleges offer formal programs of study in management consulting, many fields provide a suitable background. These fields include most areas of business and management, such as marketing and accounting, as well as economics, computer and information sciences, and engineering. Also, many business schools

215

have consulting clubs that offer exposure to consulting firms or opportunities to provide consulting services to businesses. Some schools offer programs in logistics and safety that relate directly to consulting jobs in those areas. Some college graduates with a bachelor's or master's degree and no previous work experience are hired right out of school by consulting firms and go through extensive on-the-job training. The method and extent of training can vary with the type of consulting involved and the nature of the firm. Some college students might have an advantage over other candidates if they complete an internship with a consulting firm during their studies. Other workers with related experience are hired as consultants later in their careers. For example, former military or law enforcement workers often work for security consulting firms. Similarly, some government workers with experience in enforcing regulations might join an environmental or safety consulting firm. Consultants in scientific fields often have a master's or doctoral degree, and some previously have taught at colleges and universities.

Most consulting firms require their employees to possess a variety of skills in addition to technical skills or industry knowledge. To a large extent, a college degree is only one desired qualification; workers also must possess proven analytical and problem-solving abilities, excellent written and verbal communications skills, experience in a particular specialty, assertiveness and motivation, strong attention to detail, and a willingness to work long hours if necessary. Many consultants undergo training to learn these and related skills, such as project management and building relationships with clients. Consultants also must possess high ethical standards, because most consulting firms and clients will contact references and former clients to make sure that the quality of their work was of the highest standard.

Management and leadership classes and seminars are available throughout the United States. Some classes and seminars are hosted by volunteer senior executives and management experts representing a variety of businesses and industries. A number of large firms invest a great deal of time and money in training programs, educating new hires in formal classroom settings over several weeks or even months, and some even have separate training facilities. Small firms often combine formal and on-the-job training.

The Institute of Management Consultants USA, Inc. (IMC USA), offers a wide range of professional development programs and resources, such as meetings, workshops, interest groups, and national conferences that can be helpful for management consultants. The IMC USA also offers the certified management consultant (CMC) designation to those who meet education and experience requirements as well as pass an interview and oral and written examinations. Management consultants with a CMC designation must be recertified every 3 years.

Other areas of specialization, such as logistics and safety, also offer certification programs for professionals, but these programs are not necessarily designed for consultants. Still, consultants might find it beneficial to receive designations from these programs as well. Although certification is not mandatory for management consultants, it may give a jobseeker a competitive advantage.

It can be difficult to sustain a business as an independent management consultant without consulting experience. As a result, most entry-level positions are in relatively large firms, and often involve very little responsibility at the beginning. Striving for and displaying quality work results in more responsibility. Most management consulting firms have two entry-level positions—workers who hold bachelor's degrees usually start as research associates; those with graduate degrees generally begin as consultants. Successful workers progress through the ranks from research associate to consultant, management consultant, senior consultant, junior partner, and, after many years, senior partner. In some firms, however, it is very difficult for research associates to progress to the next level without further education or certification. As a result, many management consulting firms offer tuition assistance, grants, or reimbursement plans so that workers can attain an MBA or some other degree.

Almost all workers in management consulting services receive on-the-job training; some have prior work experience in a related field. Most managerial and supervisory workers gain experience informally, overseeing a few workers or part of a project under the close supervision of a senior manager. Workers who advance to high-level managerial or supervisory jobs in management services firms usually have an extensive educational background. Less commonly, some large firms offer formal management training.

The management, scientific, and technical consulting services industry offers excellent opportunities for self-employment. Because capital requirements are low, highly experienced workers can start their own businesses fairly easily and cheaply; indeed, every year, thousands of workers in this industry go into business for themselves. Some of these workers come from established management, scientific, and technical consulting services firms, whereas others leave industry, government, or academic jobs to start their own businesses. Still others remain employed in their primary organizations, but have their own consulting jobs on the side.

## Outlook

Management, scientific, and technical consulting services is projected to be one of the fastest growing industries over the next decade. However, because of the number of people looking to work in this industry, competition for jobs is expected to be keen.

*Employment change.* Between 2006 and 2016, wage and salary employment in the management, scientific, and technical consulting services industry is expected to grow by 78 percent, much faster than the 11 percent growth projected for all industries, ranking the industry as the fastest growing industry in the economy. All areas of consulting should experience strong growth.

Projected job growth can be attributed primarily to economic growth and to the continuing complexity of business. A growing number of businesses means increased demand for advice in all areas of business planning. Firms will look to management consultants to draft business plans and budgets, develop strategy, and determine appropriate salaries and benefits for employees. The expansion of franchised restaurants and retail stores will spur demand for marketing consultants to determine the best locations and develop marketing plans. The expansion of business also will create opportunities for logistics consulting firms in order to link new suppliers with producers and to get the finished goods to consumers. Finally, businesses will continue to need advice on compliance with government workplace safety and environmental laws. Clients need consultants to keep them up to date on the latest changes in legislation affecting their businesses, including changes to tax laws, environmental regulations, and policies affecting employee benefits and health care and workplace safety. As a result, firms specializing in human resources, environmental, and safety consulting should be in strong demand.

The increasing use of new technology and computer software is another major factor contributing to growth in all areas of consulting. Management consulting firms help clients implement new accounting and payroll software, whereas environmental and safety consulting firms advise clients on the use of computer technology in monitoring harmful substances in the environment or workplace. Consulting firms also might help design new computer systems or online distribution systems. One of the biggest areas upon which technology has had an impact is logistics consulting. The Internet has greatly increased the ability of businesses to link to and communicate with their suppliers and customers, increasing productivity and decreasing costs. Technology-related consulting projects have become so important that many traditional consulting firms are now merging with or setting up joint ventures with technology companies so that each firm has access to the other's resources in order to better serve clients.

The trend toward outsourcing and mergers also will create opportunities for consulting firms. In order to cut costs, many firms are outsourcing administrative and human resources functions to consultants specializing in these services. This should provide opportunities in human resources consulting for firms that manage their clients' payroll systems and benefits programs. At the same time, increasing competition has led to more business mergers, providing opportunities for consulting firms to assist in the process. Also, as increasing numbers of older business owners retire, consultants will be used to assist in liquidation, acquisition, or restructuring of those businesses.

Globalization, too, will continue to provide numerous opportunities for consulting firms wishing to expand their services, or help their clients expand, into foreign markets. Consulting firms can advise clients on strategy, as well as foreign laws, regarding taxes, employment, worker safety, and the environment. The growth of international businesses will create numerous opportunities for logistics consulting firms as businesses seek to improve coordination in the expanding network of suppliers and consumers.

An increasing emphasis on protecting a firm's employees, facilities, and information against deliberate acts of sabotage will continue to create numerous opportunities for security consultants. These consultants provide assistance on every aspect of security, from protecting against computer viruses to reinforcing buildings against bomb blasts. Logistics consulting firms also are finding opportunities helping clients secure their supply chain against interruptions that might arise from terrorist acts, such as the disruption of shipping or railroad facilities. Growing security concerns, rising insurance costs, and the increasing threat of lawsuits provide added incentives for businesses to protect the welfare of their employees.

Growth in management, scientific, and technical consulting services might be hampered by increasing competition from nontraditional consulting firms, such as investment banks, accounting firms, technology firms, and law firms. As consulting firms continue to expand their services, they will be forced to compete with a more diverse group of firms that provide similar services.

Economic downturns also can have an adverse effect on employment growth in consulting. As businesses are forced to cut costs, consultants may be among the first expenses that businesses eliminate. Furthermore, growth in some consulting specialties, such as executive search consulting, is directly tied to the health of the industries in which they operate. However, some consulting firms might experience growth during recessions; as

**Table 4. Median hourly earnings of the largest occupations in management, scientific, and technical consulting services, May 2006**

| Occupation | Management, scientific and technical consulting services | All industries |
|---|---|---|
| General and operations managers | $58.97 | $40.97 |
| Management analysts | 36.83 | 32.72 |
| Business operations specialists, all other | 26.42 | 26.76 |
| Sales representatives, services, all other | 25.86 | 23.12 |
| Employment, recruitment, and placement specialists | 25.51 | 20.40 |
| Executive secretaries and administrative assistants | 19.41 | 17.90 |
| Bookkeeping, accounting, and auditing clerks | 15.67 | 14.69 |
| Customer service representatives | 14.91 | 13.62 |
| Secretaries, except legal, medical, and executive | 13.07 | 13.20 |
| Office clerks, general | 11.14 | 11.40 |

firms look to cut costs and remain competitive, they might seek the advice of consultants on the best way to do so.

*Job prospects.* Despite the projected growth in the industry, there will be keen competition for jobs because the prestigious and independent nature of the work and the generous salary and benefits generally attract more jobseekers than openings every year. Individuals with the most education and job experience will likely have the best job prospects.

## Earnings

*Industry earnings.* Management, scientific, and technical consulting services is one of the highest paying industries. Non-supervisory wage and salary workers in the industry averaged $899 a week in 2006, compared with $579 for workers throughout private industry. Median hourly earnings in the largest occupations in management, scientific, and technical consulting appear in table 4. The data in the table do not reflect earnings for self-employed workers, who often have high earnings.

Both managerial workers and high-level professionals can make considerably more than the industry average. According to a 2006 survey conducted by Abbot, Langer, and Associates, the median annual total cash compensation for research associates was $38,600; for junior consultants, $46,010; for consultants, $58,240; for senior consultants, $80,500; for principal consultants, $82,618; for vice presidents, $140,005; and for senior or executive vice presidents, $155,000.

*Benefits and union membership.* Besides earning a straight salary, many workers receive additional compensation, such as profit sharing, stock ownership, or performance-based bonuses. In some firms, bonuses can constitute one-third, or more, of annual pay.

Only about 2 percent of workers in management, scientific, and technical consulting services belong to unions or are covered by union contracts, compared with 12 percent of workers in all industries combined.

## Sources of Additional Information

For more information about career opportunities in general management consulting, contact:

➤ Association of Management Consulting Firms, 3580 Lexington Ave., New York, NY 10168. Internet: **http://www.amcf.org**

For more information about career opportunities in executive search consulting, contact:

➤ Association of Executive Search Consultants, 500 Fifth Ave., Suite 930, New York, NY 10110. Internet: **http://www.aesc.org**

For more information about career opportunities in safety consulting, contact:

➤ American Society of Safety Engineers, 1800 E. Oakton St., Des Plaines, IL 60018. Internet: **http://www.asse.org**

For more information about the Certified Management Consultant designation, contact:

➤ Institute of Management Consultants USA, 2025 M St., Suite 800, Washington, DC 20036. Internet: **http://www.imcusa.org**

For more information about the Certified Investment Management Analyst designation, contact:

➤ Investment Management Consultants Association, 5619 DTC Parkway, Suite 500, Greenwood Village, CO 80111. Internet: **http://www.imca.org**

In addition, information on the following occupations found in the management, scientific, and technical consulting services industry appears in the 2008-09 *Occupational Outlook Handbook*:

- Accountants and auditors
- Administrative services managers
- Advertising, marketing, promotions, public relations, and sales managers
- Architects, except landscape and naval
- Bookkeeping, accounting, and auditing clerks
- Commercial and industrial designers
- Computer and information systems managers
- Computer programmers
- Computer scientists and database administrators
- Computer software engineers
- Computer support specialists and systems administrators
- Computer systems analysts
- Economists
- Engineering and natural sciences managers
- Engineers
- Environmental scientists and hydrologists
- Financial managers
- Graphic designers
- Human resources, training, and labor relations managers and specialists
- Lawyers
- Management analysts
- Office and administrative support worker supervisors and managers
- Secretaries and administrative assistants
- Top executives

# Scientific Research and Development Services

(NAICS 5417)

## SIGNIFICANT POINTS

- Professional and related occupations account for 59 percent of all jobs.

- Workers must continually update their knowledge to retain marketable skills in this industry, which is on the cutting edge of scientific knowledge and technology.

- Biotechnology and nanotechnology will continue to attract research funding and generate employment growth, but increases in productivity and international competition should dampen growth.

- Opportunities for scientists and engineers should be best for those who have doctoral degrees; competition for basic and applied research funding is expected to be keen.

## Nature of the Industry

*Goods and services.* From carbon nanotubes to vaccines, workers in the scientific research and development services industry create today the technologies that will change the way people live and work in the future. The importance of this industry is demonstrated by the considerable attention paid to it by the press, business associations, politicians, and financial markets. Major discoveries are heralded in both the technical and the popular media, and many studies monitor the pace of research and development. New technologies can quickly revolutionize business and leisure, as the Internet has.

*Industry organization.* Research and development (R&D) comprises three types of activities. Basic research is conducted to further scientific knowledge without any direct application. This sort of research typically involves a high level of theory and is very risky; many projects fail to produce conclusive or novel results. Due to this risk and the broad applicability of the results, most basic research is funded by government, universities, or nonprofit organizations. Applied research is the bridge between science and business. It is directed toward solving some general problem, but may produce several viable options that all achieve some aspect of the goal. Development, which accounts for more than half of all R&D spending, according to the National Science Board, then refines the technologies or processes of applied research into immediately usable products. Most development is done by private industry and is generally oriented toward manufacturing. Nearly everything consumers use, from antibiotics to zoom lenses, is a product of basic research, applied research, and development.

This industry includes diverse fields. The most fundamental division of the scientific research and development services industry is that between R&D in the physical, engineering, and life sciences and R&D in the social sciences and humanities. Important areas of research and development in the physical, engineering, and life sciences fields include biotechnology; nanotechnology; pharmaceutical; chemical and materials science; electronics; aerospace; and automotive. Important fields of research and development in the social sciences and humanities include economics, sociology, anthropology, and psychology.

Biotechnology is among the most active field of research. Work in this area seeks to understand and use the fundamental processes of cellular life to develop more effective medicines, consumer products, and industrial processes. Advances in biotechnology have led to new drugs and vaccines, disease-resistant crops, more efficient enzymatic manufacturing processes, and novel methods of dealing with hazardous materials. Bioinformatics, a branch of biotechnology using information technologies to work with biological data like DNA, is a particularly vibrant new area of work. Much of the interest in biotechnology has derived from the medical applications of its basic and applied research.

Nanotechnology is perhaps even more of an emerging field than biotechnology, and they often overlap in their work on the molecular level, such as with DNA tagging. Nanotechnology is the study of new structures roughly on the same scale as individual atoms, or one millionth of a millimeter. At this size, materials behave differently and can be made into new structures such as quantum dots, which are small devices that behave like artificial atoms and can be used to tag sequences of DNA. These materials can also be used to make nanoscopic switches for electronics, or produce extremely small lasers for communications equipment. Because basic and applied research comprises the bulk of work, immediate applications of nanotechnology are still relatively few. The National Nanotechnology Initiative coordinates research funding from Federal Government agencies and facilitates the development of new technologies resulting from this research.

Pharmaceutical R&D involves the discovery of new drugs, antibiotics, and vaccines to treat or prevent a wide range of health problems. This field also has benefited greatly from advances in biotechnology, nanotechnology, and chemistry, allowing better models of biochemical processes and more efficient testing. Because a great deal of time is required to develop a new treatment, most companies have several major programs running concurrently, in what is sometimes referred to as the development "pipeline." Because many projects incorporate all aspects of R&D, the pharmaceuticals field tends to do more basic research than other established fields.

Chemical and materials science R&D focuses on the design and creation of new molecules or materials with useful properties. By researching and modeling the properties of molecules under various conditions, scientists in this field can develop new chemical structures that are stable or volatile, rigid or flexible, insulating or conductive. Since chemical R&D is important to many technologies, it can include work on computer chip manufacturing, composite materials development, or pollution reduction through chemical treatment. Research on petroleum derivatives and substitutes continues to be an important part of this field. Chemical R&D also plays a large role in both biotechnology and nanotechnology R&D.

Electronics R&D incorporates a broad range of technologies, including computer hardware, telecommunications, consumer electronics, automated control systems, medical equipment, and electronic sensing. R&D in this field leads to advances that make electronic systems faster, and more reliable, compact, useful, powerful, and accessible. The development of new technologies, such as polymorphic processors for more powerful computers, and the integration of these technologies into new systems account for much of the R&D in this field. Basic research in areas like electromagnetics and photonics also is a significant part of the work.

Aerospace R&D relates to aircraft, spacecraft, missiles, and component parts and systems. About half of the R&D in aerospace is federally funded, with the Department of Defense and the National Aeronautics and Space Administration supporting most of the work. Civil aerospace R&D ranges from developing more efficient passenger aircraft to designing private spacecraft to launch satellites or transport humans into space, but most is devoted to making air transportation safer and more efficient.

Automotive R&D creates new vehicles and systems that are more efficient, powerful, and reliable. While automotive R&D may be directed toward the integration of new technologies into vehicles, much research also is done on improving the individual components such as LED headlights or fuel injectors. As electronic technology has advanced, so have automotive designs. The incorporation of computer systems both for monitoring performance and as separate additional features has added a new dimension to R&D in this field. With the demand for more efficient vehicles that provide more power while using less fuel, a good deal of time and many resources are devoted to powertrain and car body R&D.

R&D in the social sciences and humanities is more closely aligned with specific occupations than it is in the physical, engineering, and life sciences. Economic research typically involves monitoring and forecasting economic trends relating to issues such as business cycles, competitiveness of markets, or international trade. Sociological research analyzes the institutions and patterns of social behavior in society, and the results are used mainly by administrators to formulate policies. Anthropological research focuses on the influence of evolution and culture on all aspects of human behavior. Psychological research studies human thought, learning, motivation, and abnormal behavior.

***Recent developments.*** Since the scientific research and development services industry is continuously on the cutting edge of knowledge, it is constantly evolving. New technologies and research methods, such as nanotechnology and biotechnology in recent years, have opened new avenues of research. Similarly, recent advances in fundamental understanding of genetics, chemistry, and physics have led to the development of new technologies.

## Working Conditions

***Hours.*** In 2006, workers in scientific research and development services averaged 38.5 hours per week, compared with 33.9 for workers in all industries. The average for research and development in the physical, engineering, and life sciences was 39.0, while the average for research and development in the social sciences and humanities was only 34.6.

***Work Environment.*** Most workers in this industry work in offices or laboratories; the location and hours of work vary greatly, however, depending on the requirements of each project. Experiments may run at odd hours, require constant observation, or depend on external conditions such as the weather. In some fields, research or testing must be done in harsh environments to ensure the usefulness of the final product in a wide range of environments. Other research, particularly biomedical research, is conducted in hospitals. Workers in product development may spend much time building prototypes in workshops or laboratories, while research design typically takes place in offices.

Although there generally is little risk of injury or illness due to the working conditions, certain fields require working with potentially dangerous materials. In such cases, comprehensive safety procedures are strictly enforced.

## Employment

Scientific research and development services provided 593,000 jobs in 2006. Research and development in the physical, engineering, and life sciences accounted for about 89 percent of the jobs; the rest were in research and development in the social sciences and humanities.

Workers in this industry conduct much, but not all, of the scientific research and R&D in the economy. Under the North American Industrial Classification System (NAICS), each establishment is categorized by the activity in which it is primarily engaged; an establishment is defined as a single physical location where business is conducted or services are performed. This means that much of the R&D conducted by companies in a wide range of industries—such as pharmaceuticals, chemicals, motor vehicles, and aerospace products—is conducted within the scientific research and development services industry, because many companies maintain laboratories and other R&D facilities that are located apart from production plants and other establishments characteristic of these industries. While workers in separate R&D establishments are classified in the scientific research and development services industry, some R&D occurs in establishments that mainly engage in other activities, such as manufacturing or educational services. The latter type of R&D is not included within the scientific research and development services industry.

Although scientific research and development services can be found in many places, the industry is concentrated in a few areas. Just seven states—California, New York, Massachusetts, Illinois, Maryland, Pennsylvania, and New Jersey—account for over half of all employment in the industry. Michigan also has a sizable amount of R&D, particularly in the automotive field. Although 92 percent of establishments have fewer than 50 workers, 53 percent of employment in the industry is in establishments with more than 250 workers (chart).

## Occupations in the Industry

Professional and related occupations account for 59 percent of employment in this industry. About 38 percent of jobs are in computer and mathematical sciences, engineering occupations, and life and physical science occupations, and 3 percent of jobs are in social sciences and related occupations (table 1).

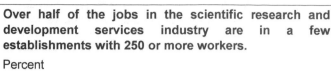

**Over half of the jobs in the scientific research and development services industry are in a few establishments with 250 or more workers.**

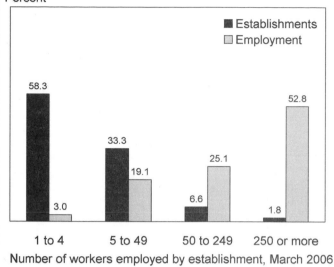

Percent

■ Establishments
□ Employment

58.3
3.0
33.3
19.1
6.6
25.1
1.8
52.8

1 to 4    5 to 49    50 to 249    250 or more

Number of workers employed by establishment, March 2006

*Life, physical, and social science occupations.* These workers form the core of the research operations in the industry. *Biological scientists* conduct research to understand biological systems, develop new drugs, and work with genetic material. Many work for pharmaceutical or biotechnology companies; others perform their research in Federal or academic laboratories. *Medical scientists* research the causes of health problems and diseases, and then use this information to develop medical treatments and preventive measures. Their work is similar to that of biological scientists, but with a specific emphasis on disease prevention and treatment. *Chemists and materials scientists* research the nature of chemical systems and reactions, investigate the properties of materials, and develop new products or processes using this knowledge. They perform research used by a broad array of industries to develop new products. Along with *physicists*, chemists and materials scientists conduct basic and applied research on nanotechnology. Social scientists, such as *economists*, *market and survey researchers*, *sociologists*, and *anthropologists*, perform research on human behavior and social interaction. *Science technicians*, sometimes called research assistants, assist scientists in their research and typically specialize in an area of research. They may set up and maintain lab equipment, monitor experiments, record results, or interpret collected data.

*Engineers and computer specialists.* Engineers and computer specialists usually are involved in applied research or in development. *Engineers* design, produce, and evaluate solutions to problems, either by creating new products or refining existing ones. They apply the most current research findings to develop more efficient products or processes of manufacture. *Engineering technicians* assist engineers in preparing equipment for experiments, recording and calculating results, or building prototypes. Their work is similar to that of the engineers with whom they work, but is more limited in scope. Computer specialists, such as *computer scientists*, *computer programmers*, and *computer software engineers*, develop new computer technologies, programming languages, operating systems, and programs to increase the usefulness of computers. Their work may include integrating advances in computing theory into more efficient processing techniques.

*Management, business, and financial operations occupations.* These occupations account for another 19 percent of the industry. *Engineering and natural science managers* accounted for a larger portion of the employment than in most industries. These managers plan, coordinate, and direct the activities of engineers, natural scientists, technicians, and support personnel to conduct research or develop new products. As with engineers and natural scientists, engineering managers tend to be involved in development, while natural science managers tend to be involved in basic research. Both use their technical expertise and business acumen to bridge the gap between goals set by top executives and the incremental work done by engineers and scientists.

*Office and administrative support occupations.* These workers comprise 14 percent of the industry's jobs and primarily handle general business administration and clerical work. *Interviewers, except eligibility and loan,* are particularly prevalent in research and development in the social sciences and humanities. They may be involved in soliciting and verifying information from individuals or groups for sociological, psychological, or market survey research, either in person or by phone. In the life sciences, they may collect and verify participant information for medical research.

Since the scientific research and development services industry deals mainly in innovation and design, there are relatively few jobs in production, installation, maintenance, repair, transportation, sales, or service occupations, which account for 9 percent of employment.

*Training and Advancement.* Scientific research and development services rely heavily on workers with extensive postsecondary education. Those with bachelor's or higher degrees held 72 percent of jobs in the industry, compared with only 30 percent in all industries. The difference is particularly great for those with graduate degrees, who account for 37 percent of workers in scientific research and development services but only 10 percent of workers in all industries.

Science and engineering technicians may enter the industry with a high school diploma, some college, or an associate degree, but some bachelor's degree holders begin as technicians before advancing to become researchers or pursuing additional education. Technicians usually begin working directly under a scientist, engineer, or more senior technician and advance to working with less supervision. Continuing on-the-job training is important in order to learn to use the newest equipment and methods. Some technicians become supervisors responsible for a laboratory or workshop.

For other science and engineering occupations, a bachelor's degree is generally the minimum level of education, and a master's or Ph.D. degree is typically necessary for senior researchers. Some fields require a Ph.D. even for entry-level research positions, particularly in the physical and life sciences. A bachelor's degree is sufficient for many types of work in development outside of the life sciences, but a master's degree is also common. Continuing training is necessary for workers to keep pace with current developments in their fields. It may take the form of on-the-job training or formal training, or it may consist of attending conferences or meetings of professional societies. Workers who fail to remain current in their field and related disciplines may face unfavorable job prospects if interest in their specific area declines.

For those with a Ph.D., a period of academic research immediately after obtaining the degree—known as a "postdoc"—is increasingly preferred by employers. These postdocs may last several years with low salaries and little independence, effectively increasing the cost of doctoral degrees in time and forgone income. Once in the industry, workers with doctorates typically begin as researchers, conducting and designing research projects in their field of expertise with a fair degree of autonomy. With their research training and specialized expertise, scientists or engineers with doctoral degrees design, conduct, and analyze experiments or studies. To keep current in their fields, researchers often attend conferences, read specialized journals, and confer with colleagues in industry and academia.

As scientists or engineers gain expertise in a particular field of R&D, they may advance to more senior research positions or become managers. Those who remain in technical positions may undertake more creative work, designing research or developing new technologies at a higher level. Those in science and engineering management usually coordinate work in several disciplines or components of a project. As their careers progress, they manage larger projects and ensure the work aligns with the strategic goals of their organization. Nearly all managers are responsible for some aspect of funding and for meeting deadlines.

Self-employment is uncommon in scientific research and development services because of the high cost of equipment, but opportunities to start small companies do exist. These opportunities are particularly prevalent in rapidly growing fields, partly due to the availability of investment capital. Self-employed workers in scientific R&D typically have advanced degrees and have worked in academia or other research facilities and form companies to develop commercial products resulting from prior basic or applied research.

## Outlook

*Employment change.* Wage and salary employment in scientific research and development services is projected to increase 9 percent between 2006 and 2016, compared with 11 percent employment growth for the economy as a whole. Biotechnology and nanotechnology will continue to attract research funding and generate employment growth. Increased demand for medical and pharmaceutical advances also will lead to growth in these areas as the population ages. While demand for new R&D is expected to continue to grow across all major fields, this industry will continue to experience rapid productivity growth as a result of advances in computer and communications systems, reducing employment opportunities. Increasing international competition should also dampen employment growth.

Some of this slower job growth rate is attributable to the stagnation of the office and administrative support occupations, which are expected to see only modest employment growth as technology leads to greater efficiency in general office functions. Similarly slow growth is expected in other major occupational groups within the industry, but many new jobs will be created in professional occupations.

Significant job growth is expected among computer specialists, scientists, and engineers—particularly those in the life and medical sciences. With the aging of the population, the demand for lifesaving new drugs and procedures to cure and prevent disease will drive this demand. Biological scientists, for example,

may be employed in biotechnology or pharmaceuticals, both growing areas. Many other scientists and engineers will be employed in defense and security R&D, also a growing field. As information technology continues to be an integral component of R&D, employment of computer specialists is expected to grow rapidly, particularly for those with some biological science background working in bioinformatics.

**Table 1. Employment of wage and salary workers in scientific research and development services by occupation, 2006 and projected change, 2006-2016.**
(Employment in thousands)

| Occupation | Employment, 2006 | | Percent change, 2006-16 |
|---|---|---|---|
| | Number | Percent | |
| **All occupations** | 593 | 100.0 | 9.4 |
| **Management, business, and financial occupations** | 110 | 18.6 | 7.9 |
| Top executives | 17 | 2.9 | -4.1 |
| Marketing and sales managers | 4 | 0.7 | 6.7 |
| Computer and information systems managers | 6 | 0.9 | 6.7 |
| Financial managers | 4 | 0.7 | 6.6 |
| Engineering managers | 7 | 1.2 | 6.7 |
| Natural sciences managers | 10 | 1.8 | 17.1 |
| Purchasing agents, except wholesale, retail, and farm products | 5 | 0.8 | 6.7 |
| Human resources, training, and labor relations specialists | 6 | 1.0 | 11.5 |
| Management analysts | 6 | 1.0 | 6.5 |
| Accountants and auditors | 7 | 1.3 | 6.6 |
| **Professional and related occupations** | 349 | 58.9 | 12.0 |
| Computer and information scientists, research | 4 | 0.6 | 6.7 |
| Computer programmers | 6 | 1.0 | -14.7 |
| Computer software engineers | 28 | 4.8 | 22.0 |
| Computer support specialists | 5 | 0.8 | 6.5 |
| Computer systems analysts | 9 | 1.6 | 17.3 |
| Network and computer systems administrators | 5 | 0.8 | 17.3 |
| Network systems and data communications analysts | 4 | 0.7 | 43.9 |
| Statisticians | 3 | 0.5 | 6.6 |
| Engineers | 70 | 11.8 | 10.8 |
| Engineering technicians, except drafters | 18 | 3.1 | 7.5 |
| Life scientists | 51 | 8.7 | 16.5 |
| Physical scientists | 34 | 5.8 | 11.9 |
| Market and survey researchers | 7 | 1.2 | 6.3 |
| Biological technicians | 20 | 3.4 | 17.2 |
| Chemical technicians | 7 | 1.2 | 6.7 |
| Social science research assistants | 7 | 1.1 | 6.3 |
| **Sales and related occupations** | 9 | 1.5 | 7.8 |
| **Office and administrative support occupations** | 81 | 13.6 | 2.1 |
| Bookkeeping, accounting, and auditing clerks | 5 | 0.9 | 6.6 |
| Interviewers, except eligibility and loan | 5 | 0.8 | 6.1 |
| Secretaries and administrative assistants | 33 | 5.5 | 2.7 |
| Office clerks, general | 13 | 2.1 | 4.9 |
| **Installation, maintenance, and repair occupations** | 10 | 1.7 | 8.2 |
| Maintenance and repair workers, general | 6 | 1.0 | 6.7 |
| **Production occupations** | 14 | 2.3 | 4.3 |

Note: Columns may not add to totals due to omission of occupations with small employment

*Job prospects.* Opportunities for both scientists and engineers are expected to be best for those who have doctoral degrees, which prepare graduates for research. However, competition for basic and applied research funding is expected to be keen in all fields. Creativity is crucial, because scientists and engineers engaged in R&D are expected to propose new research or designs. For experienced scientists and engineers, it also is important to remain current and adapt to changes in technologies that may shift interest—and employment—from one area of research to another.

Most R&D programs have long project cycles that continue during economic downturns. However, funding of R&D, particularly by private industry, is closely scrutinized during these periods. Since the Federal Government provides a significant portion of all R&D funding, shifts in policy also could have a marked impact on employment opportunities, particularly in basic research and aerospace.

## Earnings

*Industry earnings.* In 2006, nonsupervisory workers in scientific research and development services earned $1,136 per week on average, substantially higher than the $568 average for all industries. The earnings of those engaged in research and development in the physical, engineering, and life sciences differ markedly from the earnings of those in research and development in the social sciences and humanities, with respective averages of $1,175 and $818.

Earnings also varied considerably by occupation, with workers in management and professional occupations earning more. This was similar to other industries. Occupations in the industry with higher earnings typically require higher levels of education and experience. Hourly wages for specific occupations in the industry are shown in table 2.

*Benefits and union membership.* Workers in scientific research and development services generally receive standard benefits, including health insurance, paid vacation and sick leave, and pension plans.

In 2006, only 4 percent of all workers in the scientific research and development industry were union members or covered by union contracts, compared with about 13 percent of all workers throughout private industry.

## Sources of Additional Information

For additional information on careers in biotechnology R&D, contact:
➢ Biotechnology Institute, 1840 Wilson Blvd., Suite 202, Arlington, VA 22201.
 Internet: **http://www.biotechinstitute.org**
➢ Biotechnology Industry Organization, 1225 Eye St. NW., Suite 400, Washington, DC 20005. Internet: **http://www.bio.org**

For additional information on careers in nanotechnology R&D, contact:
➢ National Nanotechnology Coordination Office, 4201 Wilson Blvd., Stafford II Room 405, Arlington, VA 22230. Internet: **http://www.nano.gov**

For additional information on careers in pharmaceutical R&D, contact:
➢ Pharmaceutical Research and Manufacturers of America, 1100 15th St. NW., Washington, DC 20005. Internet: **http://www.phrma.org**

For additional information on careers in chemical and materials science R&D, contact:
➢ American Chemical Society, 1155 16th St. NW., Washington, DC 20036. Internet: **http://www.chemistry.org**

For additional information on careers in electronics R&D, contact:
➢ Institute of Electrical and Electronics Engineers–USA, 1828 L St. NW., Suite 1202, Washington, DC 20036. Internet: **http://www.ieeeusa.org**

For additional information on careers in aerospace R&D, contact:
➢ American Institute of Aeronautics and Astronautics, 1801 Alexander Bell Dr., Suite 500, Reston, VA 20191. Internet: **http://www.aiaa.org**
➢ Aerospace Industries Association, 1000 Wilson Blvd., Suite 1700, Arlington, VA 22209. Internet: **http://www.aia-aerospace.org**

For additional information on careers in automotive R&D, contact:
➢ SAE International, 400 Commonwealth Dr., Warrendale, PA 15096. Internet: **http://www.sae.org**

Information on the following occupations may be found in the 2008-09 edition of the *Occupational Outlook Handbook.*
• Biological scientists
• Chemists and materials scientists
• Economists
• Engineering and natural sciences managers
• Engineering technicians
• Engineers
• Market and survey researchers
• Medical scientists
• Physicists and astronomers
• Science technicians
• Social scientists, other

**Table 2. Median hourly earnings of the largest occupations in scientific research and development services, May 2006**

| Occupation | Scientific research and development services | All industries |
|---|---|---|
| General and operations managers | $59.80 | $40.97 |
| Computer software engineers, systems software | 46.72 | 41.04 |
| Computer software engineers, applications | 41.97 | 38.36 |
| Medical scientists, except epidemiologists | 34.32 | 29.66 |
| Business operations specialists, all other | 33.25 | 26.76 |
| Chemists | 33.06 | 28.78 |
| Executive secretaries and administrative assistants | 20.66 | 17.90 |
| Biological technicians | 19.14 | 17.17 |
| Secretaries, except legal, medical, and executive | 16.20 | 13.20 |
| Office clerks, general | 13.70 | 11.40 |

# Education, Health Care, and Social Services

# Child Day Care Services

## SIGNIFICANT POINTS

- Preschool teachers, teacher assistants, and child care workers account for almost 8 out of 10 wage and salary jobs.

- About 42 percent of all child care workers have a high school degree or less, reflecting the minimal training requirements for most jobs.

- More than a quarter of all employees work part time, and nearly 18 percent of full-time employees in the industry work more than 40 hours per week

- Job openings should be numerous because dissatisfaction with benefits, pay, and stressful working conditions causes many to leave the industry.

## Nature of the Industry

Obtaining affordable, quality child day care, especially for children under age 5, is a major concern for many parents, particularly in recent years with the rise in families with two working parents. As the need for child day care has increased in the last decade, the child day care services industry began to fill the need of non-relative child care.

*Goods and services.* Child day care needs are met in different ways. Care in a child's home, care in an organized child care center, and care in a provider's home—known as family child care—are all common arrangements for preschool-aged children. Older children also may receive child day care services when they are not in school, generally through before- and after-school programs or private summer school programs. With the increasing number of households in which both parents work full time, this industry has been one of the fastest growing in the U.S. economy.

The industry consists of establishments that provide paid care for infants, toddlers, preschool children, or older children in before- and after-school programs. (For information on other social assistance services for children and youths, see the *Career Guide* section on social assistance, except child day care.)

*Industry organization.* Two main types of child care make up the child day care services industry: center-based care and family child care. Formal child day care centers include preschools, child care centers, and Head Start centers. Family child care providers care for children in their home for a fee and are the majority of self-employed workers in this industry. This does not include persons who provide unpaid care in their homes for the children of relatives or friends or occasional babysitters. Also, child care workers who work in the child's home, such as nannies, are included primarily in the private household industry, not this industry.

The for-profit part of this industry includes centers that operate independently or as part of a local or national company. The number of for-profit establishments has grown rapidly in response to demand for child care services. Nonprofit child day care organizations may provide services in religious institutions, YMCAs and other social and recreation centers, colleges, public schools, social service agencies, and worksites ranging from

factories to office complexes. Within the nonprofit sector, there has been strong growth in Head Start, the federally funded child care program designed to provide disadvantaged children with social, educational, and health services.

Some employers offer child care benefits to their employees, recognizing that the unavailability of child care is a barrier to the employment of many parents, especially qualified women, and that the cost of the benefits is offset by increased employee morale and productivity and reduced absenteeism. Some employers sponsor child care centers in or near the workplace, while others provide direct financial assistance, vouchers, or discounts for child care or after-school or sick-child care services. Still others offer a dependent-care option in a flexible benefits plan.

## Working Conditions

*Hours.* The hours of child day care workers vary. Many centers are open 12 or more hours a day and cannot close until all of the children are picked up by their parents or guardians. Unscheduled overtime, traffic jams, and other types of emergencies can cause parents or guardians to be late. Nearly 18 percent of full-time employees in the child day care services industry work more than 40 hours per week. Self-employed workers tend to work longer hours than do their salaried counterparts. The industry also offers many opportunities for part-time work: more than 26 percent of all employees worked part time in 2006.

*Work Environment.* Helping children grow, learn, and gain new skills can be very rewarding. Preschool teachers and child care workers often improve their own communication, learning, and other personal skills by working with children. The work is sometimes routine; however, new activities and challenges mark each day. Child care can be physically and emotionally taxing, as workers constantly stand, walk, bend, stoop, and lift to attend to each child's needs, interests, and problems. Child care workers must be constantly alert, anticipate and prevent trouble, deal effectively with disruptive children, and provide fair, but firm, discipline.

Many child day care workers become dissatisfied with their jobs' stressful conditions, low pay, and lack of benefits and eventually leave.

## Employment

Child day care services provided about 807,000 wage and salary jobs in 2006. There were an additional 467,000 self-employed and unpaid family workers in the industry, most of whom were family child care providers, although some were self-employed managers of child care centers.

Jobs in child day care are found across the country, mirroring the distribution of the population. However, day care centers are less common in rural areas, where there are fewer children to support a separate facility. Child day care operations vary in size, from the self-employed person caring for a few children in a private home to the large corporate-sponsored center employing a sizable staff. Almost half of all wage and salary jobs in 2006 were located in establishments with fewer than 20 employees. Nearly all establishments have fewer than 50 workers (chart 1).

Opportunities for self-employment in this industry are among the best in the economy. About 37 percent of all workers in the industry are self-employed or unpaid family workers, compared with only 8 percent in all industries. This disparity reflects the ease of entering the child day care business.

The median age of child day care providers is 38, compared with 44 for all workers. About 21 percent of all care providers are 24 years or younger as opposed to about 14 percent for all industries (table 1). About 6 percent of these workers are below the age of 20, reflecting the minimal training requirements for many child day care positions.

## Occupations in the Industry

Jobs in the child day care services industry are concentrated in a smaller number of occupations than in most other industries. Three occupations—*preschool teachers, teacher assistants,* and *child care workers*—account for 77 percent of all wage and salary jobs (table 2).

*Professional and related occupations. Preschool teachers* make up the largest occupation in the child day care industry, accounting for about 32 percent of wage and salary jobs. They teach pupils basic physical, intellectual, and social skills needed to enter primary school. *Teacher assistants* account for about 14 percent

Table 1.  Percent distribution of employment, by age group, 2006

| Age group | Child day care services | All industries |
|---|---|---|
| Total | 100.0% | 100.0% |
| 16-19 | 5.6 | 4.3 |
| 20-24 | 14.9 | 9.6 |
| 25-34 | 23.1 | 21.5 |
| 35-44 | 21.8 | 23.9 |
| 45-54 | 20.5 | 23.6 |
| 55-64 | 10.8 | 13.4 |
| 65 and older | 3.4 | 3.7 |

of industry employment; they give teachers more time for teaching by assuming a variety of tasks. For example, they may set up and dismantle equipment or prepare instructional materials.

*Service occupations. Child care workers* account for about 31 percent of wage and salary jobs, as well as a large proportion of the self-employed who care for children in their homes, also known as *family child care providers*. Regardless of the setting, these workers feed, diaper, comfort, and play with infants. When dealing with older children, they attend to the children's basic needs and organize activities that stimulate physical, emotional, intellectual, and social development.

*Management, business, and financial occupations.* About 4 percent of the industry's wage and salary workers are *education administrators, preschool and child care center/program.* They establish overall objectives and standards for their centers, provide day-to-day supervision of their staffs, and bear overall responsibility for program development, as well as for marketing, budgeting, staffing, and all other administrative tasks.

Child day care centers also employ a variety of *office and administrative support workers, building cleaning workers, cooks,* and *busdrivers.*

## Training and Advancement

Most States do not regulate family child care providers who care for just a few children, typically between ages 2 and 5. Providers who care for more children are required to be licensed and, in a few States, have some minimal training. Once a provider joins the industry, most States require the worker to complete a number of hours of training per year. In nearly all States, licensing regulations require criminal record checks for all child day care staff. This screening requirement protects children from abuse and reduces liability risks, making insurance more available and affordable.

Many local governments regulate family child care providers who are not covered by State regulations. Home safety inspections and criminal background checks are usually required of an applicant.

Child care centers have staffing requirements that are imposed by States and by insurers. Although requirements vary, in most cases a minimum age of 18 years is required for teachers, and directors or officers must be at least 21. In some States, assistants may work at age 16—in several, at age 14. Most States have established minimum educational or training requirements. Training requirements are most stringent for directors, less so for teachers, and minimal for child care workers and teacher assistants. In many centers, directors must have a college degree, often with experience in child day care and specific training in early childhood development. Teachers must have a high school

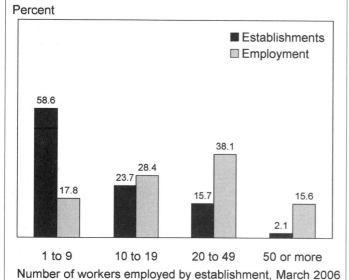

**More than 80 percent of child day care services establishments employ fewer than 20 workers, accounting for nearly half of the industry's jobs.**

Percent

- ■ Establishments
- ☐ Employment

| | 1 to 9 | 10 to 19 | 20 to 49 | 50 or more |
|---|---|---|---|---|
| Establishments | 58.6 | 23.7 | 15.7 | 2.1 |
| Employment | 17.8 | 28.4 | 38.1 | 15.6 |

Number of workers employed by establishment, March 2006

diploma and, in many cases, a combination of college education and experience. Assistants and child care workers usually need a high school diploma, but that is not always a requirement. Many States also mandate other types of training for staff members, such as on health and first aid, fire safety, and child abuse detection and prevention. Some employers prefer to hire workers who have received credentials from a nationally recognized child day care organization.

State governments also have established requirements for workers who provide services associated with child care—those involved in food preparation, the transportation of children, the provision of medical services, and other services. Most States have defined minimum ratios of the number of staff-to-children, which vary both by State and the age of the children involved.

## Outlook

Employment in child day care services is projected to increase rapidly, and an unusually large number of job openings will result each year from that growth and the need to replace the large numbers of experienced workers who leave the industry for other jobs.

*Employment change.* Wage and salary jobs in the child day care

Table 2. Employment of wage and salary workers in child day care services by occupation, 2006 and projected change, 2006-2016. (Employment in thousands)

| Occupation | Employment, 2006 | | Percent change, 2006-16 |
|---|---|---|---|
| | Number | Percent | |
| **All occupations** | 807 | 100.0 | 33.7 |
| **Management, business, and financial occupations** | 44 | 5.5 | 25.0 |
| Top executives | 5 | 0.6 | 9.5 |
| Education administrators, preschool and child care center/program | 32 | 4.0 | 27.8 |
| **Professional and related occupations** | 415 | 51.4 | 30.1 |
| Child, family, and school social workers | 8 | 0.9 | 21.6 |
| Preschool teachers, except special education | 259 | 32.1 | 30.2 |
| Kindergarten teachers, except special education | 7 | 0.8 | 21.6 |
| Special education teachers, preschool, kindergarten, and elementary school | 5 | 0.6 | 21.6 |
| Teacher assistants | 110 | 13.7 | 33.8 |
| **Service occupations** | 308 | 38.1 | 41.7 |
| Cooks, institution and cafeteria | 17 | 2.1 | 21.6 |
| Janitors and cleaners, except maids and housekeeping cleaners | 8 | 0.9 | 24.3 |
| First-line supervisors/managers of personal service workers | 12 | 1.5 | 21.6 |
| Child care workers | 253 | 31.4 | 46.0 |
| **Office and administrative support occupations** | 30 | 3.7 | 17.6 |
| Bookkeeping, accounting, and auditing clerks | 5 | 0.7 | 21.6 |
| Secretaries and administrative assistants | 8 | 1.1 | 14.8 |
| Office clerks, general | 10 | 1.2 | 19.8 |
| **Transportation and material moving occupations** | 8 | 1.0 | 21.3 |
| Bus drivers, school | 7 | 0.9 | 21.6 |

Note: Columns may not add to totals due to omission of occupations with small employment

services industry are projected to grow about 34 percent over the 2006-16 period, compared with the 11 percent employment growth projected for all industries combined. The rising demand for child day care services driving industry growth reflects in part demographic trends. Over the same period, the number of children under age 5 is expected to increase at a faster rate than in previous years and many of them will continue to be raised in households with two working parents or a single working parent. Furthermore, growing numbers of parents will hold jobs that require work during weekends, evenings, and late nights. As a result, demand will grow significantly for child care programs that can provide care during not only traditional weekday hours, but nontraditional hours as well. In addition, school-aged children, who generally require child care only before and after school, increasingly are being cared for in centers.

Center-based day care should continue to expand its share of the industry because an increasing number of parents prefer its more formal setting and believe that it provides a better foundation for children before they begin traditional schooling. However, family child care providers will continue to remain an important source of care for many young children because some parents prefer the more personal attention that such a setting can provide. Demand for child care centers and preschool teachers to staff them could increase even further if more States implement preschool programs for 3- and 4-year-old children, which some States have begun and others are planning to start. In addition, subsidies for children from low-income families attending child day care programs also could result in more children being served in centers, as could the increasing involvement of employers in funding and operating day care centers. Legislation requiring more welfare recipients to work also could contribute to growing demand for child day care services.

*Job prospects.* Opportunities within this industry are expected to be excellent because of the need to replace workers who choose to leave the industry to return to school or enter a new occupation or industry. Replacement needs are substantial, reflecting the low wages and relatively meager benefits provided to most workers. The substantial replacement needs, coupled with faster-than-average employment growth, should create numerous employment opportunities.

## Earnings

*Industry earnings.* In 2006, hourly earnings of nonsupervisory workers in the child day care services industry averaged $10.53, much less than the average of $16.76 throughout private industry. On a weekly basis, earnings in child day care services averaged only $316 in 2006, compared with the average of $568 in private industry. Weekly earnings reflect, in part, the large number of part-time jobs in the industry. Earnings in selected occupations in child day care services in May 2006 appear in table 3.

*Benefits and union membership.* Employee benefits in child day care services often are minimal. A substantial number of child day care centers offer no healthcare benefits to any teaching staff. Reduced day care fees for workers' children, however, are a common benefit. Wage levels and employee benefits depend in part on the type of center. Nonprofit and religiously affiliated centers generally pay higher wages and offer more generous benefits than do for-profit establishments.

In 2006, about 3 percent of all workers in child day care ser-

**Table 3. Median annual earnings of the largest occupations in child day care services, May 2006**

| Occupation | Child day care services | All industries |
|---|---|---|
| Education administrators, preschool and child care center/program | $35,380 | $37,740 |
| Child, family, and school social workers ... | 29,480 | 37,480 |
| First-line supervisors/managers of personal service workers | 26,640 | 32,800 |
| Preschool teachers, except special education | 20,920 | 22,680 |
| Office clerks, general | 20,680 | 23,710 |
| Bus drivers, school | 19,750 | 24,820 |
| Janitors and cleaners, except maids and housekeeping cleaners | 19,030 | 19,930 |
| Teacher assistants | 18,020 | 20,740 |
| Cooks, institution and cafeteria | 17,420 | 20,410 |
| Child care workers | 16,320 | 17,630 |

vices were union members or were covered by a union contract, compared with about 12 percent of workers in all industries.

## Sources of Additional Information

For additional information about careers in early childhood education, contact:

➢ National Association for the Education of Young Children, 1509 16th St. N.W., Washington, DC 20036. Internet: **http://www.naeyc.org**

For more information about the child care workforce, contact:

➢ Center for the Child Care Workforce, 555 New Jersey Ave., N.W., Washington, DC 20001. Internet: **http://www.ccw.org**

For an electronic question-and-answer service on child care, information on becoming a child care provider, and other child care resources, contact:

➢ National Child Care Information Center, 10530 Rosehaven St, Suite 400, Fairfax, VA 22030. Internet: **http://www.nccic.org**

For a database on licensing requirements of child care settings by State, contact:

➢ National Resource Center for Health and Safety in Child Care and Early Education, University of Colorado Health and Sciences Center at Fitzsimons, Campus Mail Stop F541, P.O. Box 6508, Aurora, CO 80045-0508. Telephone (toll free): 800-598-5437. Internet: **http://nrc.uchsc.edu**

For a list of colleges offering courses in early childhood education, contact:

➢ Council for Professional Recognition, 2460 16th St. N.W., Washington, DC 20009-3575. Internet: **http://www.cdacouncil.org**

State Departments of Human Services or Social Services can supply State regulations concerning child day care programs, child care workers, teacher assistants, and preschool teachers.

Detailed information on the following key occupations in the child day care services industry appears in the 2008–09 *Occupational Outlook Handbook*:

• Education administrators
• Child care workers
• Teacher assistants
• Teachers—preschool, kindergarten, elementary, middle, and secondary

# Educational Services

## SIGNIFICANT POINTS

- With about 1 in 4 Americans enrolled in educational institutions, educational services is the second largest industry, accounting for about 13.3 million jobs.

- Most teaching positions, which constitute almost half of all educational services jobs, require at least a bachelor's degree, and some require a master's or doctoral degree.

- Retirements in a number of education professions will create many job openings.

## Nature of the Industry

*Goods and services.* Education is an important part of life. The amount and type of education that individuals receive are a major influence on both the types of jobs they are able to hold and their earnings. Lifelong learning is important in acquiring new knowledge and upgrading one's skills, particularly in this age of rapid technological and economic changes. The educational services industry includes a variety of institutions that offer academic education, vocational or career and technical instruction, and other education and training to millions of students each year.

*Industry organization.* Because school attendance is compulsory until at least age 16 in all 50 States and the District of Columbia, elementary, middle, and secondary schools are the most numerous of all educational establishments. They provide academic instruction to students in kindergarten through grade 12 in a variety of settings, including public schools, parochial schools, boarding and other private schools, and military academies. Some secondary schools offer a mixture of academic and career and technical instruction.

Postsecondary institutions—universities, colleges, professional schools, community or junior colleges, and career and technical institutes—provide education and training in both academic and technical subjects for high school graduates and other adults. Universities offer bachelor's, master's, and doctoral degrees, while colleges generally offer only the bachelor's degree. Professional schools offer graduate degrees in fields such as law, medicine, business administration, and engineering. The undergraduate bachelor's degree typically requires 4 years of study, while graduate degrees require additional years of study. Community and junior colleges and technical institutes offer associate degrees, certificates, or other diplomas, usually involving 2 years of study or less. Career and technical schools provide specialized training and services primarily related to a specific job. They include computer and cosmetology training institutions, business and secretarial schools, correspondence schools, and establishments that offer certificates in commercial art and practical nursing.

This industry also includes institutions that provide training, consulting, and other support services to schools and students, such as curriculum development, student exchanges, and tutoring. Also included are schools or programs that offer nonacademic or self-enrichment classes, such as automobile driving and cooking instruction, among others.

*Recent developments.* In recent decades, the Nation has focused attention on the educational system because of the growing importance of producing a trained and educated workforce. Many institutions, including government, private industry, and research organizations, are involved in improving the quality of education. The passage of the No Child Left Behind Act of 2001 established Federal guidelines to ensure that all students in public elementary through secondary schools receive a high-quality education. Through this act, individual States are given more flexibility on how to spend the educational funds they are allocated. In return, the Act requires standardized testing of all students in core subject areas. In this manner, students, teachers, and all staff involved in education are held accountable for the results of testing, and teachers and teacher assistants must demonstrate that they are sufficiently qualified in the subjects or areas in which they teach. States are responsible for following these guidelines and can lose Federal funding if the standards are not met. Despite the increased Federal role, State and local governments are still the most important regulators of public education. Many States had already begun to introduce performance standards individually prior to passage of the Act, and the Act still allows States a considerable amount of discretion in how they implement many of its provisions.

In an effort to promote innovation in public education, many local and State governments have authorized the creation of public charter schools, in the belief that, by presenting students and their parents with a greater range of instructional options, schools and students will be encouraged to strive for excellence. Charter schools, which usually are run by teachers and parents or, increasingly, by private firms, operate independently of the school system, set their own standards, and practice a variety of innovative teaching methods. Businesses strive to improve education by donating instructional equipment, lending personnel for teaching and mentoring, hosting visits to the workplace, and providing job-shadowing and internship opportunities. Businesses also collaborate with educators to develop curricula that will provide students with the skills they need to cope with new technology in the workplace.

Quality improvements also are being made to career and technical education at secondary and postsecondary schools. Academics are playing a more important role in career and technical curricula, and programs are being made more relevant to the local job market. Often, students must meet rigorous standards, set in consultation with private industry, before receiving a certificate or degree. Career and technical students in secondary school programs must pass the same standardized tests in core subject areas as students who are enrolled in academic programs of study. A growing number of career and technical programs emphasize general workplace skills, such as problem solving, teamwork, and customer service. Many high schools now offer technical preparatory ("tech-prep") programs, which are developed jointly by high schools and community colleges to provide a continuous course of study leading to an associate degree or other postsecondary credential.

Computer technology continues to affect the education industry. Computers simplify administrative tasks and make it easier to track student performance. Teachers use the Internet in classrooms as well as to communicate with colleagues around the country; students use the Internet for research projects. Distance learning continues to expand as more postsecondary institutions use Internet-based technology to conduct lessons and coursework electronically, allowing students in distant locations access to educational opportunities formerly available only on campus.

Despite these improvements in quality, problems remain. High school completion rates remain low, particularly for minority students, and employers contend that numerous high school graduates still lack many of the math and communication skills needed in today's workplace. School budgets often are not sufficient to meet the institution's various goals, particularly in the inner cities, where aging facilities and chronic teacher shortages make educating children more difficult.

## Working Conditions

*Hours.* Elementary and secondary schools generally operate 10 months a year, but summer sessions for special education or remedial students are common. In addition, education administrators, office and administrative support workers, and janitors and cleaners often work the entire year. Postsecondary institutions operate year-round, but may have reduced offerings during summer months. Institutions that cater to adult students, and those that offer educational support services such as tutoring, generally operate year-round as well. Night and weekend work is common for teachers of adult literacy and remedial and self-enrichment education, for postsecondary teachers, and for library workers in postsecondary institutions. Part-time work is common for this same group of teachers, as well as for teacher assistants and school bus drivers. The latter often work a split shift, driving one or two routes in the morning and afternoon; drivers who are assigned to drive students on field trips, to athletic and other extracurricular activities, or to midday kindergarten programs work additional hours during or after school. Many teachers spend significant time outside of school preparing for class, doing administrative tasks, conducting research, writing articles and books, and pursuing advanced degrees.

*Work Environment.* Elementary and secondary school conditions often vary from town to town. Some schools in poorer neighborhoods may be rundown, have few supplies and equipment, and lack air conditioning. Other schools may be new and well equipped and maintained. Conditions at postsecondary institutions are generally very good. Regardless of the type of conditions facing elementary and secondary schools, seeing students develop and enjoy learning can be rewarding for teachers and other education workers. However, dealing with unmotivated students or those with social or behavioral problems can be stressful and require patience and understanding.

Despite occurrences of violence in some schools, the educational services industry is relatively safe. There were 2.3 cases

**Table 1. Distribution of wage and salary employment in educational services by industry, 2006**
(Employment in thousands)

| Industry | Employment | Percent |
|---|---|---|
| **Educational services, public and private, total** | 13,152 | 100.0 |
| **Elementary and secondary schools** | 8,346 | 63.5 |
| **Junior colleges, colleges, universities, and professional schools** | 4,215 | 32.1 |
| Colleges, universities, and professional schools | 3,434 | 26.1 |
| Junior colleges | 781 | 5.9 |
| **Other educational services** | 591 | 4.5 |
| Other schools and instruction | 285 | 2.2 |
| Technical and trade schools | 134 | 1.0 |
| Educational support services | 91 | 0.7 |
| Business schools and computer and management training | 80 | 0.6 |

of occupational injury and illness per 100 full-time workers in private educational establishments in 2005, compared with 4.4 in all industries combined.

## Employment

The educational services industry was the second largest industry in the economy in 2006, providing jobs for about 13.3 million workers—about 13.2 million wage and salary workers, and 195,000 self-employed and unpaid family workers. Most jobs are found in elementary and secondary schools, either public or private, as shown in table 1. Public schools employ more workers than private schools because most students attend public educational institutions. According to the latest data from the Department of Education's National Center for Education Statistics, close to 90 percent of students attend public primary and secondary schools, and about 75 percent attend public postsecondary institutions.

## Occupations in the Industry

Workers in the educational services industry take part in all aspects of education, from teaching and counseling students to driving school buses and serving cafeteria lunches. Although 2 out of 3 workers in educational services are employed in professional and related occupations, the industry also employs many administrative support, managerial, service, and other workers. (See table 2.)

*Teaching occupations.* Teachers account for almost half of all workers in the industry. Their duties depend on the age group and subject they teach, as well as on the type of institution in which they work. Teachers should have a sincere interest in helping students and should also have the ability to inspire respect, trust, and confidence. Strong speaking and writing skills, inquiring and analytical minds, and a desire to pursue and disseminate knowledge are vital prerequisites for teachers.

*Preschool, kindergarten,* and *elementary school teachers* play a critical role in the early development of children. They usually instruct one class in a variety of subjects, introducing the children to mathematics, language, science, and social studies. Often, they use games, artwork, music, computers, and other tools to teach basic skills.

*Middle* and *secondary school teachers* help students delve

**Table 2. Employment of wage and salary workers in educational services by occupation, 2006 and projected change, 2006-2016.**
(Employment in thousands)

| Occupation | Employment, 2006 | | Percent change, 2006-16 |
|---|---|---|---|
| | Number | Percent | |
| All occupations | 13,152 | 100.0 | 10.7 |
| **Management, business, and financial occupations** | 822 | 6.3 | 11.3 |
| Education administrators, elementary and secondary school | 213 | 1.6 | 7.5 |
| Education administrators, postsecondary | 125 | 1.0 | 14.4 |
| **Professional and related occupations** | 8,870 | 67.4 | 12.7 |
| Computer specialists | 199 | 1.5 | 15.7 |
| Clinical, counseling, and school psychologists | 46 | 0.4 | 6.9 |
| Educational, vocational, and school counselors | 190 | 1.4 | 10.3 |
| Child, family, and school social workers | 40 | 0.3 | 7.4 |
| Postsecondary teachers | 1,627 | 12.4 | 22.9 |
| Preschool teachers, except special education | 70 | 0.5 | 16.0 |
| Kindergarten teachers, except special education | 158 | 1.2 | 15.9 |
| Elementary school teachers, except special education | 1,499 | 11.4 | 13.4 |
| Middle school teachers, except special and vocational education | 650 | 4.9 | 11.1 |
| Secondary school teachers, except special and vocational education | 1,027 | 7.8 | 5.5 |
| Vocational education teachers, secondary school | 94 | 0.7 | -4.9 |
| Special education teachers, preschool, kindergarten, and elementary school | 205 | 1.6 | 18.9 |
| Special education teachers, middle school | 100 | 0.8 | 16.0 |
| Special education teachers, secondary school | 133 | 1.0 | 8.1 |
| Adult literacy, remedial education, and GED teachers and instructors | 61 | 0.5 | 11.7 |
| Self-enrichment education teachers | 99 | 0.8 | 23.1 |
| Librarians | 95 | 0.7 | 3.9 |
| Instructional coordinators | 90 | 0.7 | 22.8 |
| Teacher assistants | 1,086 | 8.3 | 6.5 |
| Coaches and scouts | 117 | 0.9 | 15.0 |
| Registered nurses | 86 | 0.7 | 13.2 |
| Speech-language pathologists | 53 | 0.4 | 6.2 |
| **Service occupations** | 1,402 | 10.7 | 7.3 |
| Security guards | 63 | 0.5 | 8.7 |
| Cooks, institution and cafeteria | 138 | 1.1 | -3.7 |
| Fast food and counter workers | 172 | 1.3 | 8.2 |
| Janitors and cleaners, except maids and housekeeping cleaners | 469 | 3.6 | 7.2 |
| Child care workers | 135 | 1.0 | 17.6 |
| **Office and administrative support occupations** | 1,480 | 11.3 | 3.0 |
| Bookkeeping, accounting, and auditing clerks | 95 | 0.7 | 9.9 |
| Library assistants, clerical | 43 | 0.3 | 2.9 |
| Secretaries and administrative assistants | 580 | 4.4 | 1.6 |
| Office clerks, general | 369 | 2.8 | 8.8 |
| **Installation, maintenance, and repair occupations** | 165 | 1.3 | 8.7 |
| Maintenance and repair workers, general | 105 | 0.8 | 8.6 |
| **Transportation and material moving occupations** | 295 | 2.2 | 5.5 |
| Bus drivers, school | 251 | 1.9 | 5.5 |

Note: Columns may not add to totals due to omission of occupations with small employment

more deeply into subjects introduced in elementary school. Middle and secondary school teachers specialize in a specific academic subject, such as English, mathematics, or history, or a career and technical area, such as automobile mechanics, business education, or computer repair. Some supervise after-school extracurricular activities, and some help students deal with academic problems, such as choosing courses, colleges, and careers.

*Special education teachers* work with students—from toddlers to those in their early twenties—who have a variety of learning and physical disabilities. While most work in traditional schools and assist those students who require extra support, some work in schools specifically designed to serve students with the most severe disabilities. With all but the most severe cases, special education teachers modify the instruction of the general education curriculum and, when necessary, develop alternative assessment methods to accommodate a student's special needs. They also help special education students develop emotionally, feel comfortable in social situations, and be aware of socially acceptable behavior.

*Postsecondary teachers*, or *faculty*, as they are usually called, generally are organized into departments or divisions, based on their subject or field. They teach and advise college students and perform a significant part of our Nation's research. They prepare lectures, exercises, and laboratory experiments; grade exams and papers; and advise and work with students individually. Postsecondary teachers keep abreast of developments in their field by reading current literature, talking with colleagues and businesses, and participating in professional conferences. They also consult with government, business, nonprofit, and community organizations. In addition, they do their own research to expand knowledge in their field, often publishing their findings in scholarly journals, books, and electronic media.

*Adult literacy and remedial education teachers* teach English to speakers of other languages (ESOL), prepare sessions for the General Educational Development (GED) exam, and give basic instruction to out-of-school youths and adults. *Self-enrichment teachers* teach classes that students take for personal enrichment, such as cooking or dancing.

***Other professional occupations.*** *Education administrators* provide vision, direction, leadership, and day-to-day management of educational activities in schools, colleges and universities, businesses, correctional institutions, museums, and job training and community service organizations. They set educational standards and goals and aid in establishing the policies and procedures to carry them out. They develop academic programs; monitor students' educational progress; hire, train, motivate, and evaluate teachers and other staff; manage counseling and other student services; administer recordkeeping; prepare budgets; and handle relations with staff, parents, current and prospective students, employers, and the community.

*Instructional coordinators* evaluate school curricula and recommend changes to them. They research the latest teaching methods, textbooks, and other instructional materials and coordinate and provide training to teachers. They also coordinate equipment purchases and assist in the use of new technology in schools.

*Educational, vocational, and school counselors* work at the elementary, middle, secondary, and postsecondary school levels and help students evaluate their abilities, talents, and interests so that the students can develop realistic academic and career options. Using interviews, counseling sessions, tests, and other methods, secondary school counselors also help students understand and deal with their social, behavioral, and personal problems. They advise on college majors, admission requirements, and entrance exams and on trade, technical school, and apprenticeship programs. Elementary school counselors do more social and personal counseling and less career and academic counseling than do secondary school counselors. School counselors may work with students individually or in small groups, or they may work with entire classes.

*Librarians* help people find information and learn how to use it effectively in their scholastic, personal, and professional pursuits. Librarians manage library staff and develop and direct information programs and systems for the public, as well as oversee the selection and organization of library materials. *Library technicians* help librarians acquire, prepare, and organize material; direct library users to standard references; and retrieve information from computer databases. *Clerical library assistants* check out and receive library materials, collect overdue fines, and shelve materials.

*Teacher assistants*, also called *teacher aides* or *instructional aides*, provide instructional and clerical support for classroom teachers, allowing the teachers more time to plan lessons and to teach. Using the teacher's lesson plans, they provide students with individualized attention, tutoring and assisting children—particularly special education and non-English speaking students—in learning class material. Assistants also aid and supervise students in the cafeteria, in the schoolyard, in hallways, or on field trips. They record grades, set up equipment, and prepare materials for instruction.

**Other occupations.** The educational services industry employs many other workers who are found in a wide range of occupations. This industry employs many office and administrative support workers such as *secretaries, administrative assistants,* and *general office clerks.* They also employ many *school bus drivers,* who transport students to and from schools and related activities.

## Training and Advancement

The educational services industry employs some of the most highly educated workers in the labor force. Almost 2 in 3 employees have at least a bachelor's degree, which is required for nearly all professional occupations. Many professional occupations also require a master's degree or doctorate, particularly for jobs at postsecondary institutions or in administration.

*Teaching occupations.* Kindergarten, elementary, middle, and secondary school teachers in public schools must have a bachelor's degree and complete an approved teacher training program, with a prescribed number of subject and education credits, as well as supervised practice teaching. All States require public school teachers to be licensed; however, licensure requirements vary by State. Many States offer alternative licensure programs for people who have bachelor's degrees in the subject they will teach, but lack the education courses required for a regular license. Certain teacher occupations require additional specific training: special education teachers need either a master's degree in special education or some other form of specialized training in the subject, while vocational education teachers often need work experience in their field.

Teachers in private elementary, middle, and secondary schools do not have to meet State licensing standards; however,

schools prefer candidates who have a bachelor's degree in the subject they intend to teach for secondary school teachers, or in childhood education for elementary school teachers. They seek candidates among recent college graduates as well as from those who have established careers in other fields. Private schools affiliated with religious institutions also desire candidates who share the values that are important to the institution.

With additional education or certification, teachers may become school librarians, reading specialists, curriculum specialists, or guidance counselors. Some teachers advance to administrative or supervisory positions—such as instructional coordinator, assistant principal, or principal—but the number of these jobs is limited. In some school systems, highly qualified, experienced elementary and secondary school teachers can become senior or mentor teachers, with higher pay and additional responsibilities.

Postsecondary teachers who teach at 4-year colleges and universities generally must have a doctoral or other terminal degree for full-time, tenure-track employment, and usually also for part-time teaching at these institutions as well, though a master's degree is sometimes sufficient. At 2-year colleges, however, most positions are held by teachers with a master's degree. Most faculty members are hired as instructors or assistant professors and may advance to associate professor and full professor. Some faculty may also advance to administrative and managerial positions, such as department chairperson, dean, or president. At some institutions, these positions are temporary, with the holder returning to the faculty of their department after a set term.

*Other professional occupations.* School counselors are required to hold State school counseling certification; however, certification procedures vary from State to State. A master's degree is generally required, and some States also require public school counselors to have teaching certificates and a number of years of teaching experience in addition to a counseling certificate. Experienced school counselors may advance to a larger school; become directors or supervisors of counseling, guidance, or student personnel services; or, with further graduate education, become counseling psychologists or school administrators.

Training requirements for education administrators depend on where they work. Principals, assistant principals, and other school administrators in school districts usually have held a teaching or related job before entering administration, and they generally need a master's or doctoral degree in education administration or educational supervision, as well as State teacher certification. At postsecondary institutions, academic deans usually have a doctorate in their specialty. Other administrators can begin with a bachelor's degree, but generally will need a master's or doctorate to advance to top positions. In addition to climbing up the administrative ladder, advancement is also possible by transferring to larger schools or school systems.

Training requirements for teacher assistants range from a high school diploma to an associate degree. The No Child Left Behind Act mandates that all teacher assistants working in schools that receive Title I funds either have a minimum of 2 years of postsecondary education or an associate degree, or pass a State approved examination. Districts that assign teaching responsibilities to teacher assistants usually have higher training requirements than those that do not. Teacher assistants who obtain a bachelor's degree, usually in education, may become certified teachers.

Librarians normally need a master's degree in library science. Many States require school librarians to be licensed as teachers and to have taken courses in library science. Experienced librarians may advance to administrative positions, such as department head, library director, or chief information officer. Training requirements for library technicians range from a high school diploma to specialized postsecondary training; a high school diploma is sufficient for library assistants. Library workers can advance—from assistant, to technician, to librarian—with experience and the required formal education. School bus drivers need a commercial driver's license and have limited opportunities for advancement; some become supervisors or dispatchers.

## Outlook

Greater numbers of children and adults enrolled in all types of schools will generate employment growth in this industry. A large number of retirements will add additional job openings and create good job prospects for many of those seeking work in educational services.

*Employment change.* Wage and salary employment growth of 11 percent is expected in the educational services industry over the 2006-16 period, comparable to the 11 percent increase projected for all industries combined. Over the long-term, the overall demand for workers in educational services will increase as a result of a growing emphasis on improving education and making it available not only to more children and young adults, but also to those currently employed and in need of improving their skills. Much of the demand for educational services is driven by growth in the population of students at each level. Low enrollment growth projections at the elementary, middle, and secondary school level are likely to limit growth somewhat, resulting in average growth for these teachers. However, reforms, such as universal preschool and all-day kindergarten, will require more preschool and kindergarten teachers.

Among other workers in primary and secondary education, the number of special education teachers is projected to experience faster than average growth through 2016 due to continued emphasis on the inclusion of disabled students in general education classrooms and an effort to reach students with problems

Table 3. Median annual earnings of the largest occupations in educational services, May 2006

| Occupation | Educational services | All industries |
|---|---|---|
| Education administrators, elementary and secondary school | $77,790 | $77,740 |
| Secondary school teachers, except vocational and special education | 47,780 | 47,740 |
| Special education teachers, preschool, kindergarten, and elementary school | 46,900 | 46,360 |
| Middle school teachers, except vocational and special education | 46,340 | 46,300 |
| Elementary school teachers, except special education | 45,610 | 45,570 |
| Secretaries, except legal, medical, and executive | 28,130 | 27,450 |
| Bus drivers, school | 24,100 | 24,820 |
| Janitors and cleaners, except maids and housekeeping cleaners | 23,760 | 19,930 |
| Office clerks, general | 23,750 | 23,710 |
| Teacher assistants | 21,110 | 20,740 |

at younger ages. Employment of teacher assistants will grow about as fast as the average. School reforms calling for more individual attention to students will require additional teacher assistants, particularly to work with special education and English-as-a-second-language students.

Enrollments are expected to grow at a faster rate in postsecondary institutions as more high school graduates attend college and as more working adults return to school to enhance or update their skills. As a result, employment of postsecondary teachers is expected to experience much faster than average growth.

Despite expected increases in education expenditures over the next decade, budget constraints at all levels of government may place restrictions on educational services, particularly in light of the rapidly escalating costs associated with increased college enrollments, special education, construction of new schools, and other services. Funding constraints generally affect student services (such as school busing, library and educational materials, and extracurricular activities) before employment of administrative, instructional, and support staff, though supplementary programs, such as music and foreign language instruction, also often face cuts when budgets become tight. Even if no reductions are required, budget considerations also may affect attempts to expand school programs, such as increasing the number of counselors and teacher assistants in elementary schools.

*Job prospects.* In addition to job openings due to employment growth, retirements will create large numbers of job openings as a greater-than-average number of workers are over the age of 45 in nearly all the major occupations that make up the industry—from janitors to education administrators. (See chart)

School districts, particularly those in urban and rural areas, continue to report difficulties in recruiting qualified teachers, administrators, and support personnel. Fast-growing areas of the country—including several States and cities in the South and West—also report difficulty recruiting education workers, especially teachers. Retirements are expected to remain high over the 2006-16 period, so the number of students graduating with education degrees may not be sufficient to meet this industry's growing needs, making job opportunities for graduates in many education fields good to excellent. Currently, alternative licensing programs are helping to attract more people into teaching, especially those from other career paths, but opportunities should continue to be very good for highly qualified teachers,

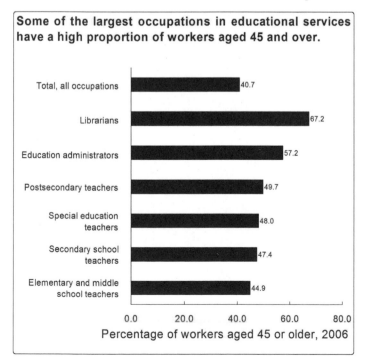

**Some of the largest occupations in educational services have a high proportion of workers aged 45 and over.**

| Occupation | Percentage |
|---|---|
| Total, all occupations | 40.7 |
| Librarians | 67.2 |
| Education administrators | 57.2 |
| Postsecondary teachers | 49.7 |
| Special education teachers | 48.0 |
| Secondary school teachers | 47.4 |
| Elementary and middle school teachers | 44.9 |

Percentage of workers aged 45 or older, 2006

especially those in subject areas with the highest needs, such as math, science, and special education.

At the postsecondary level, increases in student enrollments and projected retirements of current faculty should contribute to a favorable job market for postsecondary teachers. However, candidates applying for tenured positions will continue to face keen competition as many colleges and universities rely on adjunct or part-time faculty and graduate students to make up a larger share of the total instructional staff than in the past.

## Earnings

*Industry earnings.* Earnings of occupations concentrated in the educational services industry—education administrators, teachers, counselors, and librarians—are significantly higher than the average for all occupations because the workers tend to be older and have higher levels of educational attainment. Among teachers, earnings increase with higher educational attainment and more years of service. Full-time postsecondary teachers earn the most, followed by elementary, middle, and secondary school teachers. Most teachers are paid a salary, but part-time instructors in postsecondary institutions usually are paid a fixed amount per course. Educational services employees who work the traditional school year can earn additional money during the summer in jobs related to, or outside of, education. Benefits generally are good, but, as in other industries, part-time workers often do not receive the same benefits that full-time workers do. Earnings for selected occupations within the education industry appear in table 3.

*Benefits and union membership.* About 38 percent of workers in the educational services industry are union members or are covered by union contracts, compared with only 13 percent of workers in all industries combined. Unionization is more common in public elementary, middle, and secondary schools than in other school settings. The American Federation of Teachers and the National Education Association are the largest unions representing teachers and other school personnel.

## Sources of Additional Information

Information on unions and education-related issues can be obtained from the following organizations:

➢ American Federation of Teachers, 555 New Jersey Ave. NW, Washington, DC 20001.
➢ National Education Association, 1201 16th St. NW, Washington, DC 20036.

Information on most occupations in the educational services industry, including the following, appears in the 2008-09 edition of the *Occupational Outlook Handbook*:

- Bus drivers
- Counselors
- Education administrators
- Instructional coordinators
- Librarians
- Library assistants, clerical
- Library technicians
- Teacher assistants
- Teachers—adult literacy and remedial education
- Teachers—self-enrichment education
- Teachers—postsecondary
- Teachers—preschool, kindergarten, elementary, middle, and secondary
- Teachers—special education

# Health Care

## SIGNIFICANT POINTS

- As the largest industry in 2006, health care provided 14 million jobs—13.6 million jobs for wage and salary workers and about 438,000 jobs for the self-employed.

- 7 of the 20 fastest growing occupations are health care related.

- Health care will generate 3 million new wage and salary jobs between 2006 and 2016, more than any other industry.

- Most workers have jobs that require less than 4 years of college education, but health diagnosing and treating practitioners are among the most educated workers.

## Nature of the Industry

Combining medical technology and the human touch, the health care industry administers care around the clock, responding to the needs of millions of people—from newborns to the critically ill.

*Industry organization.* About 580,000 establishments make up the health care industry; they vary greatly in terms of size, staffing patterns, and organizational structures. Nearly 77 percent of health care establishments are offices of physicians, dentists, or other health practitioners. Although hospitals constitute only 1 percent of all health care establishments, they employ 35 percent of all workers (table 1).

The health care industry includes establishments ranging from small-town private practices of physicians who employ only one medical assistant to busy inner-city hospitals that provide thousands of diverse jobs. In 2006, almost half of non-hospital health care establishments employed fewer than five workers (chart 1). By contrast, 7 out of 10 hospital employees were in establishments with more than 1,000 workers (chart 2).

The health care industry consists of the following nine segments:

**Table 1. Percent distribution of employment and establishments in health services by detailed industry sector, 2006**

| Industry segment | Employment | Establishment |
|---|---|---|
| **Total** | 100.0 | 100.0 |
| | | |
| **Ambulatory health care services** | 42.2 | 87.1 |
| Offices of physicians | 17.1 | 36.7 |
| Home health care services | 6.9 | 3.3 |
| Offices of dentists | 6.3 | 20.7 |
| Offices of other health practitioners | 4.6 | 19.3 |
| Outpatient care centers | 3.9 | 3.4 |
| Other ambulatory health care services | 1.7 | 1.4 |
| Medical and diagnostic laboratories | 1.6 | 2.3 |
| | | |
| **Hospitals** | 34.8 | 1.3 |
| General medical and surgical hospitals | 32.8 | 1.0 |
| Other hospitals | 1.3 | 0.2 |
| Psychiatric and substance abuse hospitals | 0.8 | 0.1 |
| | | |
| **Nursing and residential care facilities** | 23.0 | 11.5 |
| Nursing care facilities | 12.6 | 2.8 |
| Community care facilities for the elderly | 5.1 | 3.4 |
| Residential mental health facilities | 4.0 | 4.1 |
| Other residential care facilities | 1.3 | 1.1 |

*Hospitals.* Hospitals provide complete medical care, ranging from diagnostic services, to surgery, to continuous nursing care. Some hospitals specialize in treatment of the mentally ill, cancer patients, or children. Hospital-based care may be on an inpatient (overnight) or outpatient basis. The mix of workers needed varies, depending on the size, geographic location, goals, philosophy, funding, organization, and management style of the institution. As hospitals work to improve efficiency, care continues to shift from an inpatient to outpatient basis whenever possible. Many hospitals have expanded into long-term and home health care services, providing a wide range of care for the communities they serve.

*Nursing and residential care facilities.* Nursing care facilities provide inpatient nursing, rehabilitation, and health-related personal care to those who need continuous nursing care, but do not require hospital services. Nursing aides provide the vast majority of direct care. Other facilities, such as convalescent homes, help patients who need less assistance. Residential care facilities provide around-the-clock social and personal care to children, the elderly, and others who have limited ability to care for themselves. Workers care for residents of assisted-living facilities, alcohol and drug rehabilitation centers, group homes, and halfway houses. Nursing and medical care, however, are not the main functions of establishments providing residential care, as they are in nursing care facilities.

*Offices of physicians.* About 37 percent of all health care establishments fall into this industry segment. Physicians and surgeons practice privately or in groups of practitioners who have the same or different specialties. Many physicians and surgeons prefer to join group practices because they afford backup coverage, reduce overhead expenses, and facilitate consultation with peers. Physicians and surgeons are increasingly working as salaried employees of group medical practices, clinics, or integrated health systems.

*Offices of dentists.* About 1 out of every 5 health care establishments is a dentist's office. Most employ only a few workers, who provide preventative, cosmetic, or emergency care. Some offices specialize in a single field of dentistry such as orthodontics or periodontics.

*Home health care services.* Skilled nursing or medical care is sometimes provided in the home, under a physician's supervision. Home health care services are provided mainly to the elderly. The development of in-home medical technologies, substantial cost savings, and patients' preference for care in the

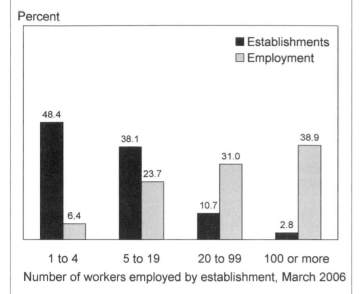

Chart 1. **Over 85 percent of nonhospital health services establishments employ fewer than 20 workers.**

Percent

- ■ Establishments
- □ Employment

48.4 · 6.4 · 38.1 · 23.7 · 10.7 · 31.0 · 2.8 · 38.9

| 1 to 4 | 5 to 19 | 20 to 99 | 100 or more |

Number of workers employed by establishment, March 2006

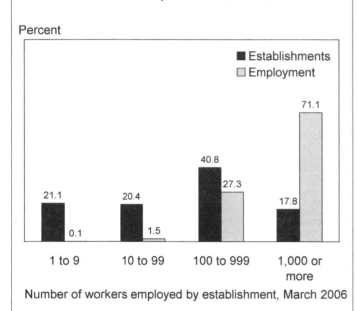

Chart 2. **More than 70 percent of jobs in hospitals are in establishments with 1,000 or more workers.**

Percent

- ■ Establishments
- □ Employment

21.1 · 0.1 · 20.4 · 1.5 · 40.8 · 27.3 · 17.8 · 71.1

| 1 to 9 | 10 to 99 | 100 to 999 | 1,000 or more |

Number of workers employed by establishment, March 2006

home have helped change this once-small segment of the industry into one of the fastest growing parts of the economy.

*Offices of other health practitioners.* This segment of the industry includes the offices of chiropractors, optometrists, podiatrists, occupational and physical therapists, psychologists, audiologists, speech-language pathologists, dietitians, and other health practitioners. Demand for the services of this segment is related to the ability of patients to pay, either directly or through health insurance. Hospitals and nursing facilities may contract out for these services. This segment also includes the offices of practitioners of alternative medicine, such as acupuncturists, homeopaths, hypnotherapists, and naturopaths.

*Outpatient care centers.* The diverse establishments in this group include kidney dialysis centers, outpatient mental health

and substance abuse centers, health maintenance organization medical centers, and freestanding ambulatory surgical and emergency centers.

*Other ambulatory health care services.* This relatively small industry segment includes ambulance and helicopter transport services, blood and organ banks, and other ambulatory health care services, such as pacemaker monitoring services and smoking cessation programs.

*Medical and diagnostic laboratories.* Medical and diagnostic laboratories provide analytic or diagnostic services to the medical profession or directly to patients following a physician's prescription. Workers may analyze blood, take x rays and computerized tomography scans, or perform other clinical tests. Medical and diagnostic laboratories provide the fewest number of jobs in the health care industry.

***Recent developments.*** In the rapidly changing health care industry, technological advances have made many new procedures and methods of diagnosis and treatment possible. Clinical developments, such as infection control, less invasive surgical techniques, advances in reproductive technology, and gene therapy for cancer treatment, continue to increase the longevity and improve the quality of life of many Americans. Advances in medical technology also have improved the survival rates of trauma victims and the severely ill, who need extensive care from therapists and social workers as well as other support personnel.

In addition, advances in information technology continue to improve patient care and worker efficiency with devices such as hand-held computers that record notes on each patient. Information on vital signs and orders for tests are transferred electronically to a main database; this process eliminates the need for paper and reduces recordkeeping errors.

Cost containment also is shaping the health care industry, as shown by the growing emphasis on providing services on an outpatient, ambulatory basis; limiting unnecessary or low-priority services; and stressing preventive care, which reduces the potential cost of undiagnosed, untreated medical conditions. Enrollment in managed care programs—predominantly preferred provider organizations, health maintenance organizations, and hybrid plans such as point-of-service programs—continues to grow. These prepaid plans provide comprehensive coverage to members and control health insurance costs by emphasizing preventive care. Cost effectiveness also is improved with the increased use of integrated delivery systems, which combine two or more segments of the industry to increase efficiency through the streamlining of functions, primarily financial and managerial. These changes will continue to reshape not only the nature of the health care workforce, but also the manner in which health care is provided.

## Working Conditions

***Hours.*** Average weekly hours of nonsupervisory workers in private health care varied among the different segments of the industry. Workers in offices of dentists averaged only 27.1 hours per week in 2006, while those in psychiatric and substance abuse hospitals averaged 35.7 hours, compared with 33.9 hours for all private industry.

Many workers in the health care industry are on part-time schedules. Part-time workers made up about 19 percent of the health care workforce as a whole in 2006, but accounted for 38 percent of workers in offices of dentists and 31 percent of those in offices of other health practitioners. Many health care establishments operate around the clock and need staff at all hours. Shift work is common in some occupations, such as registered nurses. Numerous health care workers hold more than one job.

*Work Environment.* In 2006, the incidence of occupational injury and illness in hospitals was 8.1 cases per 100 full-time workers, compared with an average of 4.4 for private industry overall. Nursing care facilities had a higher rate of 9.8. Health care workers involved in direct patient care must take precautions to prevent back strain from lifting patients and equipment; to minimize exposure to radiation and caustic chemicals; and to guard against infectious diseases, such as AIDS, tuberculosis, and hepatitis. Home care personnel who make house calls are exposed to the possibility of being injured in highway accidents, all types of overexertion when assisting patients, and falls inside and outside homes.

## Employment

As the largest industry in 2006, health care provided 14 million jobs—13.6 million jobs for wage and salary workers and about 438,000 jobs for self-employed and unpaid family workers. Of the 13.6 million wage and salary jobs, 40 percent were in hospitals; another 21 percent were in nursing and residential care facilities; and 16 percent were in offices of physicians. The majority of jobs for self-employed and unpaid family workers in health care were in offices of physicians, dentists, and other health practitioners—about 295,000 out of the 438,000 total self-employed.

Health care jobs are found throughout the country, but they are concentrated in the largest States—in particular, California, New York, Florida, Texas, and Pennsylvania.

Workers in health care tend to be older than workers in other industries. Health care workers also are more likely to remain employed in the same occupation, in part because of the high level of education and training required for many health occupations.

## Occupations in the Industry

Health care firms employ large numbers of workers in professional and service occupations. Together, these two occupational groups account for 3 out of 4 jobs in the industry (table 2). The next largest share of jobs, 18 percent, is in office and administrative support. Management, business, and financial operations occupations account for only 4 percent of employment. Other occupations in health care made up only 2 percent of the total.

Professional occupations, such as *physicians and surgeons, dentists, registered nurses, social workers,* and *physical therapists,* usually require at least a bachelor's degree in a specialized field or higher education in a specific health field, although *registered nurses* also enter through associate degree or diploma programs. Professional workers often have high levels of responsibility and complex duties. In addition to providing services, these workers may supervise other workers or conduct research.

Other health professionals and technicians work in many fast growing occupations, such as *medical records and health information technicians* and *dental hygienists.* These workers may operate technical equipment and assist health diagnosing and treating practitioners. Graduates of 1- or 2-year training programs often fill such positions; the jobs usually require specific formal training beyond high school, but less than 4 years of college.

Service occupations attract many workers with little or no specialized education or training. For instance, some of these workers are *nursing aides, home health aides, building cleaning workers, dental assistants, medical assistants,* and *personal and home care aides. Nursing* or *home health aides* provide health-related services for ill, injured, disabled, elderly, or infirm individuals either in institutions or in their homes. By providing routine personal care services, *personal and home care aides* help elderly, disabled, and ill persons live in their own homes instead of in an institution. Although some of these workers are employed by public or private agencies, many are self-employed. With experience and, in some cases, further education and training, service workers may advance to higher level positions or transfer to new occupations.

Most workers in health care jobs provide clinical services, but many also are employed in occupations with other functions. Numerous workers in management and administrative support jobs keep organizations running smoothly. Although many *medical and health services managers* have a background in a clinical specialty or training in health care administration, some enter these jobs with a general business education.

Each segment of the health care industry provides a different mix of wage and salary health-related jobs.

*Hospitals.* Hospitals employ workers with all levels of education and training, thereby providing a wider variety of services than is offered by other segments of the health care industry. About 3 in 10 hospital workers is a registered nurse. Hospitals also employ many physicians and surgeons, therapists, and social workers. About 1 in 5 hospital jobs are in a service occupation, such as nursing, psychiatric, and home health aides, or building cleaning workers. Hospitals also employ large numbers of office and administrative support workers.

*Nursing and residential care facilities.* About 2 out of 3 nursing and residential care facility jobs are in service occupations, primarily nursing, psychiatric, and home health aides. Professional and administrative support occupations make up a much smaller percentage of employment in this segment, compared to other parts of the health care industry. Federal law requires nursing facilities to have licensed personnel on hand 24 hours a day and to maintain an appropriate level of care.

*Offices of physicians.* Many of the jobs in offices of physicians are in professional and related occupations, primarily physicians, surgeons, and registered nurses. About two-fifths of all jobs, however, are in office and administrative support occupations, such as receptionists and information clerks.

*Offices of dentists.* Roughly one-third of all jobs in this segment are in service occupations, mostly dental assistants. The typical staffing pattern in dentists' offices consists of one dentist with a support staff of dental hygienists and dental assistants. Larger practices are more likely to employ office managers and administrative support workers.

*Home health care services.* About 3 in 5 jobs in this segment are in service occupations, mostly home health aides and personal and home care aides. Nursing and therapist jobs also account for substantial shares of employment in this segment.

*Offices of other health practitioners.* About 2 in 5 jobs in this industry segment are professional and related occupations, including physical therapists, occupational therapists, dispensing opticians, and chiropractors. Healthcare practitioners and technical occupations and office and administrative support occupations also accounted for a significant portion of all jobs—34 percent and 32 percent, respectively.

*Outpatient care centers.* This segment of the health care industry employs a high percentage of professional and related

**Table 2. Employment of wage and salary workers in health care by occupation, 2006 and projected change, 2006-2016.**
(Employment in thousands)

| Occupation | Employment, 2006 | | Percent change, 2006-16 |
|---|---|---|---|
| | Number | Percent | |
| **All occupations** | 13,621 | 100.0 | 21.7 |
| **Management, business, and financial occupations** | 579 | 4.2 | 18.2 |
| Top executives | 98 | 0.7 | 11.6 |
| Medical and health services managers | 185 | 1.4 | 18.6 |
| **Professional and related occupations** | 5,955 | 43.7 | 21.3 |
| Counselors | 169 | 1.2 | 29.3 |
| Social workers | 189 | 1.4 | 23.3 |
| Social and human service assistants | 97 | 0.7 | 28.9 |
| Dentists | 96 | 0.7 | 7.5 |
| Pharmacists | 64 | 0.5 | 22.2 |
| Physicians and surgeons | 468 | 3.4 | 17.1 |
| Physician assistants | 58 | 0.4 | 29.6 |
| Registered nurses | 2,072 | 15.2 | 25.2 |
| Occupational therapists | 66 | 0.5 | 28.4 |
| Physical therapists | 141 | 1.0 | 30.4 |
| Respiratory therapists | 91 | 0.7 | 23.4 |
| Clinical laboratory technologists and technicians | 266 | 2.0 | 14.3 |
| Dental hygienists | 163 | 1.2 | 30.4 |
| Cardiovascular technologists and technicians | 43 | 0.3 | 25.5 |
| Diagnostic medical sonographers | 44 | 0.3 | 19.2 |
| Radiologic technologists and technicians | 184 | 1.3 | 15.4 |
| Emergency medical technicians and paramedics | 130 | 1.0 | 22.3 |
| Pharmacy technicians | 60 | 0.4 | 31.6 |
| Psychiatric technicians | 48 | 0.4 | -5.2 |
| Surgical technologists | 82 | 0.6 | 24.6 |
| Licensed practical and licensed vocational nurses | 605 | 4.4 | 13.4 |
| Medical records and health information technicians | 142 | 1.0 | 18.6 |
| **Service occupations** | 4,334 | 31.8 | 27.1 |
| Home health aides | 582 | 4.3 | 46.9 |
| Nursing aides, orderlies, and attendants | 1,240 | 9.1 | 18.3 |
| Physical therapist assistants and aides | 100 | 0.7 | 29.7 |
| Dental assistants | 267 | 2.0 | 30.3 |
| Medical assistants | 390 | 2.9 | 36.1 |
| Medical transcriptionists | 76 | 0.6 | 10.5 |
| Cooks, institution and cafeteria | 115 | 0.8 | 17.2 |
| Food preparation workers | 107 | 0.8 | 15.4 |
| Food servers, nonrestaurant | 84 | 0.6 | 20.0 |
| Building cleaning workers | 362 | 2.7 | 17.5 |
| Personal and home care aides | 307 | 2.3 | 53.0 |
| Recreation workers | 54 | 0.4 | 15.9 |
| **Office and administrative support occupations** | 2,446 | 18.0 | 14.4 |
| Billing and posting clerks and machine operators | 192 | 1.4 | 10.2 |
| Bookkeeping, accounting, and auditing clerks | 120 | 0.9 | 20.9 |
| Interviewers, except eligibility and loan | 106 | 0.8 | 13.8 |
| Receptionists and information clerks | 363 | 2.7 | 22.7 |
| Executive secretaries and administrative assistants | 130 | 1.0 | 20.6 |
| Medical secretaries | 380 | 2.8 | 17.2 |
| Secretaries, except legal, medical, and executive | 190 | 1.4 | 6.3 |
| Office clerks, general | 335 | 2.5 | 21.5 |

Note: Columns may not add to totals due to omission of occupations with small employment

workers, including counselors, social workers, and registered nurses.

*Other ambulatory health care services.* Because this industry segment includes ambulance services, it employs about 2 out of every 5 *emergency medical technicians and paramedics* and *ambulance drivers and attendants.*

*Medical and diagnostic laboratories.* Professional and related workers, primarily clinical laboratory and radiologic technologists and technicians, make up 44 percent of all jobs in this industry segment. Service workers employed in this segment include medical assistants, medical equipment preparers, and medical transcriptionists.

## Training and Advancement

Most workers have jobs that require less than 4 years of college education, but health diagnosing and treating practitioners are among the most educated workers.

A variety of programs after high school provide specialized training for jobs in health care. Students preparing for health careers can enter programs leading to a certificate or a degree at the associate, baccalaureate, or graduate level. Two-year programs resulting in certificates or associate degrees are the minimum standard credential for occupations such as dental hygienist or radiologic technologist. Most therapists and social workers have at least a bachelor's degree. Health diagnosing and treating practitioners—such as physicians and surgeons, optometrists, and podiatrists—are among the most educated workers, with many years of education and training beyond college.

The health care industry also provides many job opportunities for people without specialized training beyond high school. In fact, more than half of workers in nursing and residential care facilities have a high school diploma or less, as do a fifth of workers in hospitals.

Some health care establishments provide on-the-job or classroom training, as well as continuing education. For example, in all certified nursing facilities, nursing aides must complete a State-approved training and competency evaluation program and participate in at least 12 hours of in-service education annually. Hospitals are more likely than other facilities to have the resources and incentive to provide training programs and advancement opportunities to their employees. In other segments of health care, the variety of positions and advancement opportunities are more limited. Larger establishments usually offer a broader range of opportunities.

Some hospitals provide training or tuition assistance in return for a promise to work at their facility for a particular length of time after graduation. Many nursing facilities have similar programs. Some hospitals have cross-training programs that train their workers—through formal college programs, continuing education, or in-house training—to perform functions outside their specialties.

Persons considering careers in health care should have a strong desire to help others, genuine concern for the welfare of patients and clients, and an ability to deal with people of diverse backgrounds in stressful situations.

Health specialists with clinical expertise can advance to department head positions or even higher level management jobs. Medical and health services managers can advance to more responsible positions, all the way up to chief executive officer.

## Outlook

Health care will generate 3 million new wage and salary jobs between 2006 and 2016, more than any other industry. Seven of the twenty fastest growing occupations are health care related. Job opportunities should be good in all employment settings.

*Employment change.* Wage and salary employment in the health care industry is projected to increase 22 percent through 2016, compared with 11 percent for all industries combined (table 3). Employment growth is expected to account for about 3 million new wage and salary jobs—20 percent of all wage and salary jobs added to the economy over the 2006-16 period. Projected rates of employment growth for the various segments of the industry range from 13 percent in hospitals, the largest and slowest growing industry segment, to 55 percent in the much smaller home health care services.

Employment in health care will continue to grow for several reasons. The number of people in older age groups, with much greater than average health care needs, will grow faster than the total population between 2006 and 2016; as a result, the demand for health care will increase. Employment in home health care and nursing and residential care should increase rapidly as life expectancies rise, and as aging children are less able to care for their parents and rely more on long-term care facilities. Advances in medical technology will continue to improve the survival rate of severely ill and injured patients, who will then need extensive therapy and care. New technologies will make it possible to identify and treat conditions that were previously not treatable. Medical group practices and integrated health systems will become larger and more complex, increasing the need for office and administrative support workers. Industry growth also will occur as a result of the shift from inpatient to less expensive outpatient and home health care because of improvements in diagnostic tests and surgical procedures, along with patients' desires to be treated at home.

Many of the occupations projected to grow the fastest in the economy are concentrated in the health care industry. For example, over the 2006-16 period, total employment of home health aides—including the self-employed—is projected to increase by 49 percent, medical assistants by 35 percent, physical therapist assistants by 32 percent, and physician assistants by 27 percent.

Rapid growth is expected for workers in occupations concentrated outside the inpatient hospital sector, such as pharmacy technicians and personal and home care aides. Because of cost pressures, many health care facilities will adjust their staffing patterns to reduce labor costs. Where patient care demands and regulations allow, health care facilities will substitute lower paid providers and will cross-train their workforces. Many facilities

have cut the number of middle managers, while simultaneously creating new managerial positions as the facilities diversify. Traditional inpatient hospital positions are no longer the only option for many future health care workers; persons seeking a career in the field must be willing to work in various employment settings. Hospitals will be the slowest growing segment within the health care industry because of efforts to control hospital costs and the increasing use of outpatient clinics and other alternative care sites.

Demand for dental care will rise due to population growth, greater retention of natural teeth by middle-aged and older persons, greater awareness of the importance of dental care, and an increased ability to pay for services. Dentists will use support personnel such as dental hygienists and assistants to help meet their increased workloads.

In some management, business, and financial operations occupations, rapid growth will be tempered by restructuring to reduce administrative costs and streamline operations. Office automation and other technological changes will slow employment growth in office and administrative support occupations; but because the employment base is large, replacement needs will continue to create substantial numbers of job openings. Slower growing service occupations also will provide job openings due to replacement needs.

*Job prospects.* Job opportunities should be good in all employment settings because of high job turnover, particularly from the large number of expected retirements and tougher immigration rules that are slowing the numbers of foreign health care workers entering the United States.

Occupations with the most replacement openings are usually large, with high turnover stemming from low pay and status, poor benefits, low training requirements, and a high proportion of young and part-time workers. Nursing aides, orderlies and attendants, and home health aides are among the occupations adding the most new jobs between 2006 and 2016, about 647,000 combined. By contrast, occupations with relatively few replacement openings—such as physicians and surgeons—are characterized by high pay and status, lengthy training requirements, and a high proportion of full-time workers.

Another occupation that is expected to have many openings is registered nurses. The median age of registered nurses is increasing, and not enough younger workers are replacing them. As a result, employers in some parts of the country are reporting difficulties in attracting and retaining nurses. Imbalances between the supply of and the demand for qualified workers should spur efforts to attract and retain qualified registered nurses. For example, employers may restructure workloads and job responsibilities, improve compensation and working conditions, and subsidize training or continuing education.

Health care workers at all levels of education and training will continue to be in demand. In many cases, it may be easier for jobseekers with health-specific training to obtain jobs and advance in their careers. Specialized clinical training is a requirement for many jobs in health care and is an asset even for many administrative jobs that do not specifically require it.

Office automation and other technological changes will slow employment growth in office and administrative support occupations; but because the employment base is large, replacement needs will continue to create substantial numbers of job openings. Slower growing service occupations also will provide job openings due to replacement needs.

**Table 3. Employment in health care by industry segment, 2006 and projected change, 2006-16**
(Employment in thousands)

| Occupation | 2006 Employment | 2006-16 Percent change |
|---|---|---|
| **Health services, total** | 13,621 | 21.7 |
| Hospitals, public and private | 5,438 | 13.0 |
| Nursing and residential care facilities | 2,901 | 23.7 |
| Offices of physicians | 2,154 | 24.8 |
| Home health care services | 867 | 55.4 |
| Offices of dentists | 784 | 22.4 |
| Offices of other health practitioners | 571 | 28.3 |
| Outpatient care centers | 489 | 24.3 |
| Other ambulatory health care services | 216 | 32.3 |
| Medical and diagnostic laboratories | 202 | 16.8 |

## Earnings

*Industry earnings.* Average earnings of nonsupervisory workers in most health care segments are higher than the average for all private industry, with hospital workers earning considerably more than the average and those employed in nursing and residential care facilities and home health care services earning less (table 4). Average earnings often are higher in hospitals because the percentage of jobs requiring higher levels of education and training is greater than in other segments. Those segments of the industry with lower earnings employ large numbers of part-time service workers.

As in most industries, professionals and managers working in health care typically earn more than other workers in the industry. Earnings in individual health care occupations vary as widely as the duties, level of education and training, and amount of responsibility required by the occupation (table 5). Some establishments offer tuition reimbursement, paid training, child day care services, and flexible work hours. Health care establishments that must be staffed around the clock to care for patients and handle emergencies often pay premiums for overtime and weekend work, holidays, late shifts, and time spent on call. Bonuses and profit-sharing payments also may add to earnings.

Earnings vary not only by type of establishment and occupation, but also by size; salaries tend to be higher in larger hospitals and group practices. Geographic location also can affect earnings.

*Benefits and union membership.* Health care workers generally receive standard benefits, such as health insurance, paid vacation and sick leave, and pension plans. However, benefits can vary greatly by occupation and by employer.

Although some hospitals have unions, the health care industry is not heavily unionized. In 2006, only 10 percent of workers in the industry were members of unions or covered by union contracts, compared with about 13 percent for all industries.

## Sources of Additional Information

For additional information on specific health-related occupations, contact:

➤ American Medical Association/Health Professions Career and Education Directory, 515 N. State St., Chicago, IL 60610. Internet: **http://www.ama-assn.org/go/alliedhealth**

For information on physician careers and applying to medical school, contact:

➤ Association of American Medical Colleges, 2450 N St. NW., Washington, DC 20037. Internet: **http://www.aamc.org/students**

### Table 4. Average earnings and hours of nonsupervisory workers in health services by industry segment, 2006

| Industry segment | Earnings | | Weekly hours |
|---|---|---|---|
| | Weekly | Hourly | |
| **Total, private industry**...................... | $568 | $16.76 | 33.9 |
| **Health services** ................................ | 623 | 18.73 | 33.3 |
| Hospitals, public and private............. | 794 | 22.19 | 35.8 |
| Medical and diagnostic laboratories ... | 715 | 19.48 | 36.7 |
| Offices of physicians.......................... | 669 | 19.98 | 33.5 |
| Outpatient care centers .................... | 658 | 19.33 | 34.1 |
| Offices of dentists ............................. | 557 | 20.51 | 27.1 |
| Other ambulatory health care services ......................................... | 555 | 15.58 | 35.7 |
| Offices of other health practitioners .. | 498 | 17.27 | 28.8 |
| Home health care services............... | 429 | 14.78 | 29.0 |
| Nursing and residential care facilities.. | 415 | 12.84 | 32.3 |

General information on health careers is available from:
➤ Bureau of Health Professions, Parklawn Rm. 8A-09, 5600 Fishers Lane, Rockville, MD 20857. Internet: **http://bhpr.hrsa.gov/kidscareers**

For a list of accredited programs in allied health fields, contact:
➤ Commission on Accreditation of Allied Health Education Programs, 1361 Park St., Clearwater, FL 333756. Internet: **http://www.caahep.org**

A wealth of information on health careers and job opportunities also is available through the Internet, schools, libraries, associations, and employers.

Information on the following occupations may be found in the 2008-09 *Occupational Outlook Handbook*:
• Audiologists
• Cardiovascular technologists and technicians
• Chiropractors
• Clinical laboratory technologists and technicians
• Dental assistants
• Dental hygienists
• Dentists
• Diagnostic medical sonographers
• Dietitians and nutritionists
• Emergency medical technicians and paramedics
• Licensed practical and licensed vocational nurses
• Medical and health services managers
• Medical assistants
• Medical, dental, and ophthalmic laboratory technicians

### Table 5. Median hourly earnings of the largest occupations in health care, May 2006

| Occupation | Ambulatory health care services | Hospitals | Nursing and residential care services | All industries |
|---|---|---|---|---|
| Registered nurses................................................................... | $26.25 | $28.12 | $25.03 | $27.54 |
| Licensed practical and licensed vocational nurses..................... | 16.78 | 16.89 | 18.35 | 17.57 |
| Dental assistants ................................................................... | 14.50 | 14.76 | — | 14.53 |
| Medical secretaries................................................................ | 13.62 | 13.30 | 12.66 | 13.51 |
| Medical assistants.................................................................. | 12.58 | 13.14 | 11.60 | 12.64 |
| Receptionists and information clerks........................................ | 11.55 | 11.74 | 10.07 | 11.01 |
| Office clerks, general.............................................................. | 11.47 | 12.55 | 11.12 | 11.40 |
| Nursing aides, orderlies, and attendants ................................. | 10.76 | 11.06 | 10.30 | 10.67 |
| Home health aides.................................................................. | 9.15 | 10.64 | 9.23 | 9.34 |
| Personal and home care aides ............................................... | 7.23 | 9.17 | 9.36 | 8.54 |

- Medical records and health information technicians
- Medical secretaries
- Medical transcriptionists
- Nuclear medicine technologists
- Nursing, psychiatric, and home health aides
- Occupational therapist assistants and aides
- Occupational therapists
- Opticians, dispensing
- Optometrists
- Personal and home care aides
- Pharmacists
- Pharmacy aides
- Pharmacy technicians
- Physical therapist assistants and aides
- Physical therapists
- Physician assistants
- Physicians and surgeons
- Podiatrists
- Psychologists
- Radiologic technologists and technicians
- Receptionists and information clerks
- Recreational therapists
- Registered nurses
- Respiratory therapists
- Social and human service assistants
- Social workers
- Speech-language pathologists
- Surgical technologists
- Veterinarians

# Social Assistance, Except Child Day Care

(NAICS 624, except 6244)

## SIGNIFICANT POINTS

- About 4 out of 10 jobs are in professional and service occupations.

- Job opportunities in social assistance should be numerous through the year 2016 because of job turnover and rapid employment growth.

- Some of the fastest growing occupations in the Nation, such as home health aides, personal and home care aides and social and human service assistants, are concentrated in social assistance.

- Average earnings are low because of the large number of part-time and low-paying service jobs.

## Nature of the Industry

At times, people need help to live a full and productive life. They may need assistance finding a job or appropriate child care, learning skills to find employment, locating safe and adequate housing, and getting nutritious food for their family. The social assistance industry provides help to individuals and families to aid them in becoming healthy and productive members of society.

*Goods and services.* Social assistance establishments provide a wide array of services that include helping the homeless, counseling troubled and emotionally disturbed individuals, training the unemployed or underemployed, and helping the needy to obtain financial assistance. In general, organizations in this industry work to improve the lives of the individuals and families they serve and to enrich their communities. The specific services provided vary greatly depending on the population the establishment is trying to serve and its goals or mission.

Social assistance consists of four segments—individual and family services; community food and housing, and emergency and other relief services; vocational rehabilitation services; and child day care services. (The child day care services segment, including day care and preschool care centers, is covered separately in the *Career Guide.*)

Establishments in the *individual and family services* sector work to provide the skills and resources necessary for individuals to be more self-sufficient and for families to live in a stable and safe environment. Many of the services in this sector are often aimed at a particular population, such as children, the elderly, or those with mental or physical disabilities. Services targeted at children can vary greatly based on the goal of the establishment providing the assistance. Some programs provide youth services such as after-school programs or youth centers. These programs are generally aimed at giving children a safe, supportive environment to spend their time after school or on weekends. There are often planned activities such as field trips, tutors to assist with homework, and games and sports equipment. Foster care and adoption agencies also provide services that are directly aimed at assisting children. These organizations are responsible for locating safe families and environments for children who are in the foster care system. Other services aimed at children include drug prevention and mentoring programs.

Services provided to the elderly include senior centers, which hold activities geared towards senior citizens and are often used as a place for seniors to gather to talk or play games. Some services, like adult day care, home care services, and support groups, are aimed at assisting both the elderly and disabled population. This sector of the industry also provides various support services to individuals and families. These often include programs for people addicted to drugs or alcohol, parenting support groups, and rape or abuse crisis centers.

*Community food and housing, and emergency and other relief services* establishments provide various types of assistance to members of the community. It consists of three subsectors: Community food services, community housing services, and emergency and other relief services.

Establishments in the *community food services* subsector collect, prepare, and deliver food for the needy. They may prepare and deliver meals to persons who by reason of age, disability, or illness are unable to prepare meals for themselves. They may also collect and distribute salvageable or donated food, or prepare and provide meals at fixed or mobile locations, and distribute clothing and blankets. Food banks, meal delivery programs, and soup kitchens are included in this industry.

Establishments in the *community housing services* sector provide short-term emergency shelter for victims of domestic violence, sexual assault, or child abuse. These establishments may operate their own shelter or may provide subsidized housing using existing homes. Also included in this sector are establishments that provide transitional housing for low-income individuals and families as well as temporary residential shelter for the homeless, runaway youths, and patients and families caught in medical crises. Community housing establishments also perform volunteer construction or repair of homes of the elderly or disabled, or of low-cost housing—sometimes in partnership with the future homeowner, who may assist in construction or repair work.

Establishments in the *emergency and other relief services* sector provide assistance to those that have been directly affected by a disaster. These establishments may set up emergency shelters for those who have been evacuated from their homes. They may also provide medical assistance to those who have been injured by the disaster. In the aftermath, they may supply food and clothing, assist with resettlement, and provide counseling to victims of domestic or international disasters or conflicts.

*Vocational rehabilitation services* establishments provide vocational rehabilitation or life skills services. They generally work with people who are disabled, either from birth or as a result of an illness or injury. They work to teach the client the skills necessary to live independently and find employment. Often, their services include assessing the abilities of their clients to determine what occupations they should pursue. They may also provide job counseling and assist in locating training and educational programs.

Thousands of other establishments, mainly in State and local government, provide additional social assistance. (For information about government social assistance, see the sections of the *Career Guide* on Federal Government, and State and local government, excluding education and hospitals.)

*Industry organization.* About 77,000 establishments in the private sector provided social assistance in 2006. Of that, 59,000 establishments were in individual and family services, about 9,000 in community food and housing, and emergency and other relief services, and 9,000 in vocational rehabilitation service organizations. Establishments in this industry tend to be smaller than the average for all establishments. In 2006, half of social assistance establishments employed fewer than 5 workers; however, larger establishments accounted for most jobs (chart).

## Working Conditions

*Hours.* Some social assistance establishments operate around the clock, and evening, weekend, and holiday work is common. Some establishments may be understaffed, resulting in large caseloads for each worker. Jobs in voluntary, nonprofit agencies often are part time.

*Work Environment.* Some workers spend a substantial amount of time traveling within the local area. For example, home health and personal care aides routinely visit clients in their homes; social workers and social and human service assistants also may make home visits.

## Employment

Social assistance provided 1.5 million nongovernment wage and salary jobs in 2006. About 65 percent were in individual and family services (table 1).

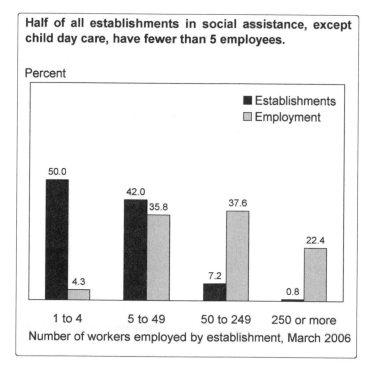

**Half of all establishments in social assistance, except child day care, have fewer than 5 employees.**

Percent

- ■ Establishments
- □ Employment

Number of workers employed by establishment, March 2006

Table 1. Employment in social assistance, except child day care by industry segment, 2006 and projected change, 2006-16
(Employment in thousands)

| Occupation | 2006 Employment | 2006-16 Percent change |
|---|---|---|
| **Social assistance, except child day care, total** | 1,502 | 54.8 |
| Individual and family services | 974 | 73.3 |
| Vocational rehabilitation services | 399 | 21.5 |
| Community food and housing, and emergency and other relief services | 129 | 18.6 |

Jobs in social assistance are concentrated in large States with heavily populated urban areas, such as New York and California.

## Occupations in the Industry

Careers in social assistance appeal to people with a strong desire to make life better and easier for others. Workers in this industry are usually good communicators and enjoy interacting with people. Many jobs in this industry are professional positions that require at least a bachelor's degree, while other occupations require little education beyond a high school diploma.

*Professional and related occupations.* More than 35 of all nongovernment social assistance jobs were in professional and related occupations in 2006 (table 2). Some of these workers may have direct interaction with clients while others have limited interaction with the population they serve. These workers may spend their time on tasks like planning programs or events, organizing classes or workshops, grant writing, or creating educational material to be used by clients. Professional and related occupations within this industry includes: social workers, counselors, health educators, teachers-adult literacy and remedial education, and social and human service assistants.

*Social workers* help clients function within the limitations of their environment, improve their relationships, and solve personal and family problems. Often, this includes counseling and assessing the needs of clients, referring them to the appropriate sources of help, and monitoring their progress. Many social workers specialize in a particular field. *Child, family and school social workers* aim to improve the social and psychological functioning of children and their families. This may involve work with single parents, parents seeking to adopt a child, or children in foster care. *Medical and public health social workers* provide support to individuals or families coping with illness or diseases; at times, this may include both terminal and chronic illnesses. They may help arrange for additional services to assist in caring for patients, including services such as meals-on-wheels or other home care services. *Mental health and substance abuse social workers* evaluate and treat individuals with mental health and substance abuse problems. They may provide treatment through group or individual therapy or work on community outreach and crisis intervention.

*Counselors* help people evaluate their interests and abilities, and advise and assist them with personal and social problems. Counselors generally specialize so their job duties to vary greatly based on the population they serve. *Educational, vocational, and school counselors* in this industry generally work in what is more commonly known as career counseling. They assist clients in determining what field of work they should enter and help them with job-seeking activities, like locating job openings for which they might apply or coaching them on proper interview conduct. *Rehabilitation counselors* assist people in living with the social, personal and vocational effects of a disability. In some cases, they assist people who are adjusting to a disability caused by injury or illness, but they also counsel those who have had disabilities from birth. These counselors evaluate the abilities and limitations of the individual and arrange for vocational training, medical care and job placement. *Mental health counselors* work with individuals and families to treat mental and emotional disorders. This is, often, done through individual or group therapy. *Substance abuse and behavioral disorder counselors* work with individual who are addicted to substances, such alcohol, tobacco or other drugs, or a behavior, like gambling or an eating disorder. They often use techniques such as group and individual therapy and, in some settings, they may be involved in crisis intervention and community outreach. *Marriage and family therapists* aim to improve an individual's or family's mental and emotional health through therapeutic techniques that focus on the family system. This is frequently done through individual, family or group therapy.

*Health educators* encourage healthy lifestyles and wellness by educating individuals and communities about behaviors that promote health and prevent illness and diseases. They use many different mediums and methods to get their message to their target audience. They often teach classes or entire courses, plan events or programs on health related topics, create pamphlets and other written materials, and organize screenings for illnesses. In the social assistance industry, they may often be responsible for writing applications for grants.

*Adult literacy and remedial education teachers* instruct adults and out-of-school youth in reading, writing, speaking English, and basic math skills. These workers may work with adults who are in need of basic education or who are pursuing their General Educational Development (GED) certificate. They may also work with adults and children who are learning English as a second language.

*Social and human service assistants* work in a variety of social and human service delivery settings. However, in general, they provide services, both directly and indirectly, to ensure that individuals in their care can function to the best of their ability. Job titles and duties of these workers vary, but they include human service worker, case management aide, social work assistant, mental health aide, child abuse worker, community outreach worker, and gerontology aide.

*Service occupations.* About 36 percent of the jobs in the social assistance industry are in service occupations. These workers generally provide direct services to their clients. Many do work that requires hands-on interaction with clients. These workers include personal and home care aides and home health aides who help elderly, disabled, and ill persons live in their own homes, instead of in an institution. *Personal and home care aides* provide routine personal care services. They generally do non-medical tasks, such as cooking meals, basic cleaning, assisting the client to bathe or dress and, in some cases, accompanying the client to appointments. *Home health aides* provide health related services, like administering oral medication, or checking the client's pulse rate or temperature. They may assist the client in performing exercises and help them bathe, dress, and groom.

*Other occupations.* *Social and community service managers* plan, organize and coordinate the activities of a social service program or community outreach program. This generally includes overseeing the budget and the execution of programs, events, and services. They often may direct and supervise those who are providing both direct and indirect services to the population they serve. In some situations, they may be responsible for fundraising activities or speaking to donors.

As in most industries, office and administrative support workers—secretaries and bookkeepers, for example—help with recordkeeping and other administrative tasks.

## Training and Advancement

Training requirements within this industry vary greatly based on occupation, state licensure requirements, and the setting in which the work is done. Many workers begin in this industry by working as a volunteer. Volunteering with a student, religious, or charitable organization is a good way for jobseekers to test their interest in social assistance, and may provide an advantage when applying for jobs in this industry. However, for many occupations, a bachelor's or master's degree is required for entrance into the industry.

*Professional and related occupations.* Entry requirements vary based on occupational specialty and State licensure and certification requirements. A bachelor's degree is the minimum educational requirement for entry-level positions as social workers, health educators, marriage and family therapists and counselors. However, some specialties and employers may require additional education, like a master's degree, or some previous experience. In some settings and specialties, social workers, marriage and family therapists and counselors may be required to obtain a State-issued license. Licensure requirements vary from State to State, but most States require a master's degree and 2 years or 3,000 hours of supervised clinical experience.

Educational requirement are less stringent for social and human service assistants. Some employers do not require any education beyond high school, but they may prefer some related work experience. Other employers favor workers who have completed some coursework in human services, social work, or another social or behavioral science. Other employers prefer an associate degree or a bachelor's degree in human services or social work. A number of employers also provide in-service training, such as seminars and workshops.

Professional workers in this industry often advance to a supervisory position, such as supervisor, program manager, assistant director, or executive director. Generally, advancing to this level requires a master's degree and the appropriate licenses. Some workers opt to move away from positions that provide services directly to clients and become involved in policymaking, grant writing, or research. Others enter private practice and provide psychotherapeutic counseling and other services on a contract basis.

*Service occupations.* Service occupations within this industry generally require little to no education beyond a high school diploma. Personal and home care aides generally receive some basic on-the-job training. The Federal Government has guidelines for home health aides whose employers receive reimbursement from Medicare and requires home health aides to pass a competency test covering a wide range of topics, including documentation of patient status and care provided; reading and recording of vital signs; basic infection-control procedures, and basic bodily functions. As result, many home health aides receive some training prior to taking the exam.

Workers in service occupations may opt to get some additional training and may advance to, for example, licensed practical nurse. Some personal and home care aides may opt to open their own business.

## Outlook

Job opportunities in social assistance should be plentiful because employment is expected grow rapidly and many workers leave the industry and need to be replaced.

***Employment Change.*** Employment within this industry is expected to grow rapidly relative to all other industries through 2016. The number of nongovernment wage and salary jobs is expected to increase 59 percent, compared with only 11 percent for all industries combined. However, growth will not be evenly distributed amongst the industry's subsectors. The individual and family services industry is expected to grow by 73 percent, making it one of the fastest growing industries in the economy. Community food and house and emergency and other relief services is expected to grow by 19 percent and vocational rehabilitation services is expected to grow 22 percent over the 2006-2016 projection period.

Growth of employment in the social assistance industry may depend, in large part, on the amount of funding made available by the government and managed-care organizations. Employment in private social service agencies may grow if State and local governments contract out some of their social services functions in an effort to cut costs.

Projected job growth in individual and family services will be due mostly to an increase in the population that will demand additional services from this sector. As baby boomers age, there is expected to be an increase in the elderly population, one of the primary segments of the populations that requires services from this industry. As a result, there will be an expansion in programs that serve the elderly, such as adult day care or services that provide home care, allowing the elderly to remain in their home for as long as possible. Furthermore, the number of small children and immigrants is expected to rise during the projections decade, increasing demand for programs aimed at assisting families. These may include after-school programs and mentoring programs or classes in English as a Second Language. Similarly, services for the mentally ill, the physically disabled, and families in crisis will be expanded and demand will increase for drug and alcohol abuse prevention programs.

Growth in community housing and food and emergency and other services will result from an increase in urbanization. As the population becomes more densely populated, more people will be affected by natural disasters, increasing the demand for disaster relief. Furthermore, demand for housing and food assistance will remain steady. However, charitable giving has been on the rise in recent years, so shelters and food banks may be able to respond to some of the growing demand for assistance.

Employment growth in vocational rehabilitation services is expected due to a steady demand for services from individuals with some form of physical or mental disability. Workers in this sector will continue to serve people who are injured on the job and need assistance moving back into the work environment. The main source of demand for this sector is injuries that are covered by worker's compensation, which are expected to grow as the population expands.

Some of the fastest growing occupations in the Nation are concentrated in social assistance. The number of home health aides within social assistance is projected to grow 79 percent and

employment of personal and home care is expected to grow by 79 percent between 2006 and 2016. Employment growth for these two occupations is driven predominantly by the need to provide services to the elderly and ill in their homes and avoid expensive hospital or nursing home care. The number of social and human

**Table 2. Employment of wage and salary workers in social assistance, except child day care by occupation, 2006 and projected change, 2006-2016.**

(Employment in thousands)

| Occupation | Employment, 2006 | | Percent change, 2006-16 |
|---|---|---|---|
| | Number | Percent | |
| **All occupations** | 1,502 | 100.0 | 54.8 |
| **Management, business, and financial occupations** | 132 | 8.8 | 43.1 |
| General and operations managers | 20 | 1.3 | 31.7 |
| Social and community service managers | 40 | 2.6 | 48.4 |
| Human resources, training, and labor relations specialists | 22 | 1.5 | 36.3 |
| **Professional and related occupations** | 532 | 35.4 | 56.7 |
| Clinical, counseling, and school psychologists | 9 | 0.6 | 57.2 |
| Substance abuse and behavioral disorder counselors | 13 | 0.9 | 58.4 |
| Educational, vocational, and school counselors | 23 | 1.6 | 33.8 |
| Marriage and family therapists | 9 | 0.6 | 63.6 |
| Mental health counselors | 19 | 1.2 | 58.3 |
| Rehabilitation counselors | 59 | 3.9 | 34.7 |
| Child, family, and school social workers | 61 | 4.1 | 58.0 |
| Medical and public health social workers | 16 | 1.1 | 57.0 |
| Mental health and substance abuse social workers | 26 | 1.7 | 56.0 |
| Health educators | 10 | 0.7 | 78.1 |
| Social and human service assistants | 107 | 7.1 | 76.4 |
| Preschool teachers, except special education | 16 | 1.1 | 57.5 |
| Adult literacy, remedial education, and GED teachers and instructors | 6 | 0.4 | 42.3 |
| Self-enrichment education teachers | 11 | 0.8 | 40.4 |
| Teacher assistants | 23 | 1.5 | 53.4 |
| Registered nurses | 17 | 1.1 | 52.8 |
| Therapists | 11 | 0.7 | 45.2 |
| **Service occupations** | 539 | 35.9 | 67.0 |
| Home health aides | 123 | 8.2 | 79.0 |
| Nursing aides, orderlies, and attendants | 14 | 0.9 | 55.6 |
| Cooks, institution and cafeteria | 11 | 0.7 | 46.6 |
| Janitors and cleaners, except maids and housekeeping cleaners | 31 | 2.1 | 36.3 |
| Child care workers | 26 | 1.7 | 54.3 |
| Personal and home care aides | 233 | 15.5 | 79.0 |
| Recreation workers | 23 | 1.5 | 47.5 |
| Residential advisors | 10 | 0.7 | 34.2 |
| **Office and administrative support occupations** | 180 | 12.0 | 38.9 |
| Bookkeeping, accounting, and auditing clerks | 18 | 1.2 | 47.2 |
| Receptionists and information clerks | 19 | 1.2 | 47.4 |
| Secretaries and administrative assistants | 45 | 3.0 | 40.7 |
| Office clerks, general | 40 | 2.7 | 44.8 |
| **Transportation and material moving occupations** | 54 | 3.6 | 31.5 |
| Bus drivers, school | 13 | 0.9 | 49.2 |
| Taxi drivers and chauffeurs | 10 | 0.7 | 47.4 |
| Laborers and material movers, hand | 18 | 1.2 | 8.5 |

Note: Columns may not add to totals due to omission of occupations with small employment

**Table 4. Median hourly earnings of the largest occupations in social assistance, except child day care, May 2006**

| Occupation | Individual and family services | Community food and housing and emergency and other services | Vocational rehabilitation services | All industries |
|---|---|---|---|---|
| Social and community service managers | $23.58 | $22.62 | $22.83 | $25.03 |
| Mental health and substance abuse social workers | 16.79 | 15.38 | 15.76 | 17.02 |
| Child, family, and school social workers | 15.71 | 14.29 | 14.61 | 18.02 |
| Rehabilitation counselors | 13.10 | 13.84 | 13.73 | 14.04 |
| Social and human service assistants | 11.78 | 11.67 | 10.83 | 12.30 |
| Office clerks, general | 10.48 | 10.33 | 10.29 | 11.40 |
| Child care workers | 9.32 | 9.65 | 9.10 | 8.48 |
| Home health aides | 9.27 | 8.51 | 9.41 | 9.34 |
| Personal and home care aides | 9.19 | 8.83 | 9.29 | 8.54 |
| Janitors and cleaners, except maids and housekeeping cleaners | 8.73 | 9.43 | 8.62 | 9.58 |

service assistants is expected to grow by 76 percent as the work of many social services is restructured to employ more assistants and fewer higher-paid social workers and counselors.

*Job prospects.* Besides job openings arising from employment growth, many additional openings will stem from the need to replace workers who transfer to other occupations or stop working. Workers leave jobs in this industry at a higher rate than the rest of the economy, making job prospects excellent.

# Earnings

*Industry earnings.* Average earnings in the social assistance industry are lower than the average for all industries, as shown in table 3. Earnings in selected occupations in the social assistance, except child day care industry in May 2006 appear in table 4. As in most industries, professionals and managers commonly earn more than other workers, reflecting higher education levels, broader experience, and greater responsibility.

*Benefits and union membership.* Professional workers in this industry typically receive benefits, such as medical insurance and paid time off. However, those working in service occupations generally receive no benefits. About 12 percent of workers

**Table 3. Average earnings of nonsupervisory workers in social assistance, 2006**

| Industry segment | Weekly | Hourly |
|---|---|---|
| **Total, private industry** | $568 | $16.76 |
| **Social assistance** | 353 | 11.76 |
| Community food and housing, and emergency and other relief services | 422 | 14.22 |
| Individual and family services | 385 | 12.79 |
| Vocational rehabilitation services | 330 | 11.05 |

in the social assistance industry were union members or were covered by union contracts in 2006, about the same as workers throughout all industries.

## Sources of Additional Information

For information about careers in social work and voluntary credentials for social workers, contact:
➢ National Association of Social Workers, 750 First St. NE., Suite 700, Washington, DC 20002-4241. Internet: **http://www.socialworkers.org**

For information on programs and careers in human services, contact:
➢ Council for Standards in Human Services Education, Harrisburg Area Community College, Human Services Program, One HACC Dr., Harrisburg, PA 17110-2999. Internet: **http://www.cshse.org**
➢ National Human Services Assembly 1319 F Street, NW, Suite 402, Washington, DC 20004. Internet: **http://www.nassembly.org**

For information regarding jobs in nonprofit organizations and voluntary credential information, contact:
➢ American Humanics, Inc. 1100 Walnut Ave, Suite 1900, Kansas City, MO 64106. Internet: **http://www.humanics.org**.

State employment service offices also may be able to provide information on job opportunities in social assistance.

Information on many occupations in social assistance, including the following, may be found in the 2008-09 *Occupational Outlook Handbook*:
- Counselors
- Health educators
- Nursing, psychiatric, and home health aides
- Personal and home care aides
- Social and human service assistants
- Social workers
- Teachers—adult literacy and remedial education
- Teachers—self-enrichment education

# Leisure and Hospitality

# Arts, Entertainment, and Recreation

## SIGNIFICANT POINTS

- The industry is characterized by a large number of seasonal and part-time jobs and relatively young workers.

- About 40 percent of all workers have no formal education beyond high school.

- Rising incomes, more leisure time, and growing awareness of the health benefits of physical fitness will increase the demand for arts, entertainment, and recreation services.

- Earnings are relatively low.

## Nature of the Industry

As leisure time and personal incomes have grown across the Nation, so has the arts, entertainment, and recreation industry. The industry includes about 122,000 establishments, ranging from art museums to fitness centers. Practically any activity that occupies a person's leisure time, excluding the viewing of motion pictures and video rentals, is part of this industry.

*Industry organization.* The diverse range of activities offered by this industry can be categorized into three broad groups— live performances or events; historical, cultural, or educational exhibits; and recreation or leisure-time activities.

The *live performances or events* segment of the industry includes professional sports, as well as establishments providing sports facilities and services to amateurs. Commercial sports clubs operate professional and amateur athletic clubs and promote athletic events. All kinds of popular sports can be found in these establishments, including baseball, basketball, boxing, football, ice hockey, soccer, wrestling, and even auto racing. Professional and amateur companies involved in sports promotion also are part of this industry segment, as are sports establishments in which gambling is allowed, such as dog and horse racetracks and jai alai courts.

A variety of businesses and groups involved in live theatrical and musical performances are included in this segment. Theatrical production companies, for example, coordinate all aspects of producing a play or theater event, including employing actors and actresses and costume designers and contracting with lighting and stage crews who handle the technical aspects of productions. Agents and managers, who represent actors and entertainers and assist them in finding jobs or engagements, are also included. Booking agencies line up performance engagements for theatrical groups and entertainers.

Performers of live musical entertainment include popular music artists, dance bands, disc jockeys, orchestras, jazz musicians, and rock bands. Orchestras range from major professional orchestras with million-dollar budgets to community orchestras, which often have part-time schedules. The performing arts segment also includes dance companies, which produce all types of live theatrical dances. The majority of these dance troupes perform ballet, folk dance, or modern dance.

The *historical, cultural, or educational exhibits* segment includes privately owned museums, zoos, botanical gardens, nature parks, and historical sites. Publicly owned facilities are included in sections on Federal, State, or local government elsewhere in the *Career Guide.* Each institution in this segment preserves and exhibits objects, sites, and natural wonders with historical, cultural, or educational value.

The *recreation or leisure activities* segment includes a variety of establishments that provide amusement for a growing number of customers. Some of these businesses provide video game and gaming machines for the public at amusement parks, arcades, and casinos. Casinos and other gaming establishments offering off-track betting are a rapidly growing part of this industry segment. This segment also includes amusement and theme parks, which range in size from local carnivals to multiacre parks. These establishments may have mechanical rides, shows, and refreshment stands. Other recreation and leisure-time services include golf courses, skating rinks, ski lifts, marinas, day camps, gocart tracks, riding stables, waterslides, and establishments offering rental sporting goods.

This segment of the industry also includes physical fitness facilities that feature exercise and weight loss programs, gyms, health clubs, and day spas. These establishments also frequently offer aerobics, dance, yoga, and other exercise classes. Other recreation and leisure-time businesses include bowling centers that rent lanes and equipment for tenpin, duckpin, or candlepin bowling.

These facilities may be open to the public or available on a membership basis. Sports and recreation clubs, including community centers, that are open only to members and their guests include some golf courses, country clubs, and yacht, tennis, racquetball, hunting and fishing, and gun clubs. Unlike private clubs, public golf courses and marinas offer facilities to the general public on a fee-per-use basis.

Technology is a major part of producing arts, entertainment, and recreation activities; for example, lighting and sound are vital for concerts and themed events and elaborate sets often are required for plays. However, most of this work is contracted to firms outside of the arts, entertainment, and recreation industry. (For more information about entertainment technology jobs, see the sources of additional information at the end of this statement.)

## Working Conditions

*Hours.* Jobs in arts, entertainment, and recreation are more likely to be part time than those in other industries. In fact, the average nonsupervisory worker in the arts, entertainment, and recreation industry worked 25.1 hours a week in 2006, as compared to an average of 33.9 hours for all private industry. Musical groups and artists were likely to work the fewest hours due to the large number of performers competing for a limited number of engagements, which may require a great amount of travel. The majority of performers are unable to support themselves in this profession alone and often supplement their income through other jobs.

Many types of arts, entertainment, and recreation establishments dramatically increase employment during the summer and either scale back employment during the winter or close down completely. Workers may be required to work nights, weekends, and holidays because that is when most establishments are the busiest.

*Work Environment.* Some jobs require extensive travel. Music and dance troupes, for example, frequently tour or travel to major metropolitan areas across the country, in hopes of attracting large audiences.

Many people in this industry work outdoors, whereas others may work in hot, crowded, or noisy conditions. Some jobs, such as those at fitness facilities or in amusement parks, involve some manual labor and, thus, require physical strength and stamina. Also, athletes, dancers, and many other performers must be in particularly good physical condition. Many jobs include customer service responsibilities, so employees must be able to work well with the public.

In 2006, cases of work-related illness and injury averaged 5.3 for every 100 full-time workers, higher than the average of 4.4 for the entire private sector. Risks of injury are high in some jobs, especially those of athletes. Although most injuries are minor, including sprains and muscle pulls, they may prevent an employee from working for a period.

## Employment

The arts, entertainment, and recreation industry provided about 1.9 million wage-and-salary jobs in 2006.

About 58 percent of these jobs were in the industry segment *other amusement and recreation industries*, which include golf courses, membership sports and recreation clubs, and physical fitness facilities (table 1).

Although most establishments in the arts, entertainment, and recreation industry are small, 41 percent of all jobs were in establishments that employ more than 100 workers (chart 1).

The arts, entertainment, and recreation industry is character-

**Table 1. Employment in arts, entertainment, and recreation by detailed industry, 2006**
(Employment in thousands)

| Industry segment | Employment | Percent |
|---|---|---|
| Arts, entertainment, and recreation, total ...... | 1,927 | 100.0 |
| Other amusement and recreation industries .... | 1,115 | 57.9 |
| Amusement parks and arcades........................ | 153 | 7.9 |
| Gambling industries......................................... | 137 | 7.1 |
| Spectator sports .............................................. | 131 | 6.8 |
| Museums, historical sites, and other institutions.............................................. | 124 | 6.4 |
| Performing arts companies............................. | 121 | 6.3 |
| Promoters of performing arts, sports, and similar events............................................. | 83 | 4.3 |
| Independent artists, writers, and performers .... | 47 | 2.4 |
| Agents and managers for artists, athletes, entertainers, and other public figures ............. | 17 | 0.9 |

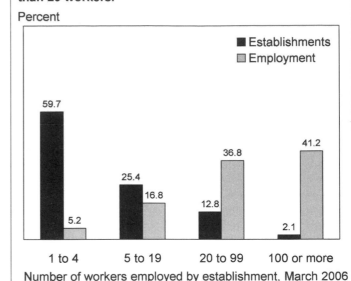

**Eighty-five percent of establishments in the arts, entertainment, and recreation industry employ fewer than 20 workers.**

Percent

Number of workers employed by establishment, March 2006

ized by a large number of seasonal and part-time jobs and by workers who are younger than the average for all industries. About 44 percent of all workers are under 35 (table 2). Many businesses in the industry increase hiring during the summer, often employing high school-age and college-age workers. Most establishments in the arts, entertainment, and recreation industry contract out lighting, sound, set-building, and exhibit-building work to firms not included in this industry.

## Occupations in the Industry

*Service occupations.* About 59 percent of wage-and-salary workers in the industry are employed in service occupations (table 3). *Amusement and recreation attendants*—the largest occupation in the arts, entertainment, and recreation industry—perform a variety of duties depending on where they are employed. Common duties include setting up games, handing out sports equipment, providing caddy services for golfers, collecting money, and operating amusement park rides.

*Fitness trainers and aerobics instructors* lead or coach groups or individuals in exercise activities and in the fundamentals of sports.

*Recreation workers* organize and promote activities, such as arts and crafts, sports, games, music, drama, social recreation, camping, and hobbies. They generally are employed by schools;

**Table 2. Percent distribution of employment, by age group, 2006**

| Age group | Arts, entertainment and recreation | All industries |
|---|---|---|
| Total ........................................................ | 100.0% | 100.0% |
| 16-19.......................................................... | 11.2 | 4.3 |
| 20-24.......................................................... | 12.8 | 9.6 |
| 25-34.......................................................... | 20.4 | 21.5 |
| 35-44.......................................................... | 19.1 | 23.9 |
| 45-54.......................................................... | 19.8 | 23.6 |
| 55-64.......................................................... | 11.5 | 13.4 |
| 65 and older................................................ | 5.2 | 3.7 |

theme parks and other tourist attractions; or health, sports, and other recreational clubs. Recreation workers schedule organized events to structure leisure time.

*Gaming services workers* assist in the operation of games, such as keno, bingo, and gaming table games. They may calculate and pay off the amount of winnings, or collect players' money or chips.

*Tour and travel guides* escort individuals or groups on sightseeing tours or through places of interest, such as industrial establishments, public buildings, and art galleries. They may also plan, organize, and conduct long-distance cruises, tours, and expeditions for individuals or groups.

*Animal care and service workers* feed, water, bathe, exercise, or otherwise care for animals in zoos, circuses, aquariums, or other settings. They may train animals for riding or performance.

Other service workers include *waiters and waitresses*, who serve food in entertainment establishments; *fast food and counter workers* and *cooks and food preparation workers,* who may serve or prepare food for patrons; and *bartenders,* who mix and serve drinks in arts, entertainment, and recreation establishments.

Building grounds, cleaning, and maintenance occupations include *building cleaning workers*, who clean up after shows or sporting events and are responsible for the daily cleaning and upkeep of facilities. *Landscaping and groundskeeping workers* care for athletic fields and golf courses. These workers maintain artificial and natural turf fields, mark boundaries, and paint team logos. They also mow, water, and fertilize natural athletic fields and vacuum and disinfect synthetic fields.

Establishments in this industry also employ workers in protective service occupations. *Security guards* patrol the property and guard against theft, vandalism, and illegal entry. At sporting events, guards maintain order and direct patrons to various facilities. *Gaming surveillance officers and gaming investigators* observe casino operations to detect cheating, theft, or other irregular activities by patrons or employees.

***Professional and related occupations.*** These workers account for 12 percent of all jobs in this industry. Some of the most well-known members of these occupations, *athletes and sports competitors,* perform in any of a variety of sports. Professional athletes compete in events for compensation, either through salaries or prize money. Organizations such as the Women's National Basketball Association (WNBA) and the National Football League (NFL) sanction events for professionals. Few athletes are able to make it to the professional level, where high salaries are common. In some professional sports, minor leagues offer lower salaries with a chance to develop skills through competition before advancing to major league play.

*Coaches and scouts* train athletes to perform at their highest level. Often, they are experienced athletes who have retired and are able to provide insight from their own experiences to players. Although some *umpires, referees, and other sports officials* work full time, the majority usually work part time and often have other full-time jobs. For example, many professional sport referees and umpires also officiate at amateur games.

*Musicians and singers* may play musical instruments, sing, compose, arrange music, or conduct groups in instrumental or vocal performances. The specific skills and responsibilities of musicians vary widely by type of instrument, size of ensemble, and style of music. For example, musicians can play jazz, classical, or popular music, either alone or in groups ranging from small rock bands to large symphony orchestras.

*Actors* entertain and communicate with people through their interpretation of dramatic and other roles. They can belong to a variety of performing groups, ranging from those appearing in community and local dinner theaters to those playing in full-scale Broadway productions. *Dancers* express ideas, stories, rhythm, and sound with their bodies through different types of dance, including ballet, modern dance, tap, folk, and jazz. Dancers usually perform in a troupe, although some perform solo. Many become teachers when their performing careers end. *Choreographers* create and teach dance, and they may be called upon to direct and stage presentations. *Producers and directors* select and interpret plays or scripts, and give directions to actors and dancers. They conduct rehearsals, audition cast members, and approve choreography. They also arrange financing, hire production staff members, and negotiate contracts with personnel.

*Archivists, curators, and museum technicians* play an important role in preparing museums for display. Archivists appraise, edit, and direct safekeeping of permanent records and historically valuable documents. They may also participate in research activities based on archival materials. Curators administer a museum's affairs and conduct research programs. Museum technicians and conservators prepare specimens, such as fossils, skeletal parts, lace, and textiles, for museum collection and exhibits. They may also take part in restoring documents or installing and arranging materials for exhibit.

***Sales and related occupations.*** About 8 percent of all jobs in this industry are in sales and related occupations. The largest of these, *cashiers,* often use a cash register to receive money and give change to customers. In casinos, *gaming change persons* and *booth cashiers* exchange coins and tokens for patrons' money. *Counter and rental clerks* check out rental equipment to customers, receive orders for service, and handle cash transactions.

***Office and administrative support occupations.*** Another 10 percent of jobs in this industry are in office and administrative support occupations. *Receptionists and information clerks*, one of the larger occupations in this category, answer questions and provide general information to patrons. Other large occupations in this group include *general office clerks* and *secretaries and administrative assistants. Gaming cage workers* conduct financial transactions for patrons in gaming establishments. For example, they may accept a patron's credit application and verify credit references to provide check-cashing authorizations or to establish house credit accounts. Also, they may reconcile daily summaries of transactions to balance books or sell gambling chips, tokens, or tickets to patrons. At a patron's request, gaming cage workers may convert gaming chips, tokens, or tickets to currency.

***Management, business, and financial occupations.*** These workers make up 5 percent of employment in this industry. Managerial duties in the performing arts include marketing, business management, event booking, fundraising, and public outreach. *Agents and business managers of artists, performers, and athletes* represent their clients to prospective employers and may handle contract negotiations and other business matters. *Recreation supervisors* and *park superintendents* oversee personnel, budgets, grounds and facility maintenance, and land and wildlife resources. Some common administrative jobs in sports are *tournament director, health club manager,* and *sports program director.*

*Installation, maintenance, and repair occupations.* These workers make up 4 percent of this industry's employment. *General maintenance and repair workers* are the largest occupation in this group.

*Media and communication equipment workers.* These workers set up and operate sound and lighting for shows and exhibits in theaters, amusement parks, and other arts and entertainment venues.

*Audio and video equipment technicians* set up and operate audio and video equipment—including microphones, sound speakers, video screens, projectors, connecting wires and cables, and sound and mixing boards—for theme parks, concerts, theaters, and sports events. They may also set up and operate spotlights and other custom lighting systems.

*Sound engineering technicians* operate machines and equipment to produce or project sound effects, music, or voices in theater productions, sporting arenas, amusement parks, or other arts and entertainment locations. They set up and test sound equipment and work with producers, performers, and others to achieve the desired sound.

## Training and Advancement

About 40 percent of all workers in the arts, entertainment, and recreation industry have no formal education beyond high school. In the case of performing artists or athletes, talent and years of training are more important than education. However, upper-level management jobs usually require a college degree.

*Service occupations.* Most service jobs require little or no previous training or education beyond high school. Many companies hire young, lesser skilled workers, such as students, to perform low-paying seasonal jobs. Employers look for people with the interpersonal skills necessary to work with the public.

In physical fitness facilities, fitness trainer and aerobic instructor positions usually are filled by persons who develop an avid interest in fitness and then become certified to teach. Certification from a professional organization may require knowledge of cardiopulmonary resuscitation (CPR); an associate degree or experience as an instructor at a health club; and successful completion of written and oral exams covering a variety of areas, including anatomy, nutrition, and fitness testing. Sometimes, fitness workers become health club managers or owners. To advance to a management position, a degree in physical education, sports medicine, or exercise physiology is useful.

*Professional and related occupations.* In the arts and professional sports, employment in professional and related occupations usually requires a great deal of talent, desire, and dedication. There are many highly talented performers and athletes, creating intense competition for every opening. Professional athletes usually begin competing in their sports during elementary or middle school. They play in amateur tournaments and on high school teams to get the attention of scouts. Performers such as musicians, dancers, and actors often study their professions most of their lives, taking private lessons and spending hours practicing. Usually, performers have completed some college or related study.

Musicians, dancers, and actors often go on to become teachers after completing the necessary requirements for at least a bachelor's degree. Musicians who complete a graduate degree in music sometimes move on to a career as a conductor. Dancers sometimes become choreographers, and actors can advance into producer and director jobs.

Table 3. Employment of wage and salary workers in arts, entertainment, and recreation by occupation, 2006 and projected change, 2006-2016. (Employment in thousands)

| Occupation | Employment, 2006 | | Percent change, 2006-16 |
|---|---|---|---|
| | Number | Percent | |
| **All occupations** | 1,927 | 100.0 | 30.9 |
| **Management, business, and financial occupations** | 101 | 5.2 | 26.4 |
| General and operations managers | 32 | 1.6 | 17.0 |
| Agents and business managers of artists, performers, and athletes | 8 | 0.4 | 14.0 |
| **Professional and related occupations** | 231 | 12.0 | 24.2 |
| Self-enrichment education teachers | 11 | 0.6 | 26.7 |
| Archivists, curators, and museum technicians | 11 | 0.6 | 36.0 |
| Artists and related workers | 8 | 0.4 | 36.6 |
| Designers | 8 | 0.4 | 26.9 |
| Actors | 17 | 0.9 | 12.0 |
| Producers and directors | 9 | 0.5 | 16.6 |
| Athletes and sports competitors | 12 | 0.6 | 25.7 |
| Coaches and scouts | 33 | 1.7 | 30.0 |
| Dancers | 9 | 0.4 | 14.9 |
| Musicians and singers | 32 | 1.7 | 6.7 |
| Public relations specialists | 10 | 0.5 | 28.6 |
| **Service occupations** | 1,132 | 58.8 | 33.7 |
| Security guards | 39 | 2.0 | 40.9 |
| Lifeguards, ski patrol, and other recreational protective service workers | 32 | 1.7 | 32.0 |
| Cooks | 51 | 2.6 | 36.7 |
| Food preparation workers | 15 | 0.8 | 34.2 |
| Bartenders | 40 | 2.1 | 32.4 |
| Fast food and counter workers | 63 | 3.3 | 40.0 |
| Waiters and waitresses | 91 | 4.7 | 33.4 |
| Dining room and cafeteria attendants and bartender helpers | 17 | 0.9 | 37.8 |
| Dishwashers | 18 | 0.9 | 33.8 |
| Janitors and cleaners, except maids and housekeeping cleaners | 43 | 2.2 | 38.8 |
| Landscaping and groundskeeping workers | 117 | 6.1 | 30.0 |
| Animal care and service workers | 19 | 1.0 | 29.3 |
| Gaming dealers | 26 | 1.4 | 32.2 |
| Gaming and sports book writers and runners | 8 | 0.4 | 39.2 |
| Ushers, lobby attendants, and ticket takers | 40 | 2.1 | 31.4 |
| Amusement and recreation attendants | 156 | 8.1 | 30.3 |
| Tour guides and escorts | 16 | 0.8 | 34.1 |
| Child care workers | 32 | 1.7 | 32.8 |
| Fitness trainers and aerobics instructors | 145 | 7.5 | 33.1 |
| Recreation workers | 25 | 1.3 | 25.6 |
| **Sales and related occupations** | 154 | 8.0 | 28.1 |
| Cashiers, except gaming | 52 | 2.7 | 19.3 |
| Gaming change persons and booth cashiers | 11 | 0.6 | 19.4 |
| Counter and rental clerks | 24 | 1.2 | 43.0 |
| Retail salespersons | 36 | 1.9 | 31.0 |
| Sales representatives, services | 11 | 0.6 | 44.0 |
| **Office and administrative support occupations** | 183 | 9.5 | 28.3 |
| Bookkeeping, accounting, and auditing clerks | 27 | 1.4 | 33.4 |
| Gaming cage workers | 8 | 0.4 | 29.9 |
| Receptionists and information clerks | 40 | 2.1 | 31.7 |
| Secretaries and administrative assistants | 36 | 1.9 | 21.0 |
| Office clerks, general | 34 | 1.8 | 27.6 |
| **Installation, maintenance, and repair occupations** | 68 | 3.5 | 30.9 |
| Maintenance and repair workers, general | 35 | 1.8 | 32.2 |
| Coin, vending, and amusement machine servicers and repairers | 9 | 0.4 | 31.3 |
| **Transportation and material moving occupations** | 36 | 1.9 | 23.4 |
| Parking lot attendants | 8 | 0.4 | 25.2 |
| Laborers and material movers, hand | 18 | 0.9 | 17.2 |

Note: Columns may not add to totals due to omission of occupations with small employment

*Management, business, and financial occupations.* Almost all arts administrators have completed 4 years of college, and the majority possess a master's or a doctoral degree. Experience in marketing and business is helpful because promoting events is a large part of the job.

Entry-level supervisory or professional jobs in recreation sometimes require completion of a 2-year associate degree in parks and recreation at a community or junior college. Completing a 4-year bachelor's degree in this field is necessary for high-level supervisory positions. Students can specialize in such areas as aquatics, therapeutic recreation, aging and leisure, and environmental studies. Those who obtain graduate degrees in the field and have years of experience may obtain administrative or university teaching positions. The National Recreation and Parks Association (NRPA) certifies individuals who meet eligibility requirements for professional and technical jobs. Certified park and recreation professionals must pass an exam; earn a bachelor's degree with a major in recreation, park resources, or leisure services from a program accredited by the NRPA or by the American Association for Leisure and Recreation; or earn a bachelor's degree and have at least 5 years of relevant full-time work experience, depending on the major field of study.

The education and experience of top executives varies widely, but many have a bachelor's degree or higher in business administration or liberal arts. Many positions are filled from within the organization by promoting experienced managers. They may help their advancement by participating in company and outside training programs to learn management techniques. Top executives must have excellent interpersonal skills, an analytical mind, decisiveness, and leadership ability.

*Media and communication equipment workers.* There are multiple training and education options for these workers, including technical school, an associate degree, an apprenticeship, and on-the-job training. Sound engineering technicians can best prepare by getting technical school, community college, or college training in broadcast technology, sound engineering technology, communications technology, electronics, or computer networking. They may then begin working and learn from more experienced technicians. Less formal training is required for audio and video equipment technicians. Many workers have community college degrees, but they are not always required. Workers may substitute on-the-job training for education and may gain experience by working as an assistant to audio and video equipment technicians.

## Outlook

Rising incomes, leisure time, and awareness of the health benefits of physical fitness will increase the demand for arts, entertainment, and recreation services. Opportunities should be available for young, seasonal, part-time, and lesser skilled workers, but there will continue to be intense competition for jobs as performing artists and professional athletes.

*Employment change.* Wage and salary jobs in arts, entertainment, and recreation are projected to grow about 31 percent over the 2006-16 period, compared with 11 percent for all industries combined. Rising incomes, leisure time, and awareness of the health benefits of physical fitness will increase the demand for arts, entertainment, and recreation services.

Employment in fitness centers and similar establishments will grow substantially, driven by several factors. Aging baby boomers are concerned with staying healthy, physically fit, and

independent, and have become the largest demographic group of health club members. The reduction of physical education programs in schools, combined with parents' growing concern about child obesity, has rapidly increased child health club membership. Membership among young adults has also grown steadily, driven by concern about physical fitness and funded by rising incomes. The proliferation of group exercise classes and the focus on overall wellness in health clubs should also increase the demand for workers in this industry.

Strong employment growth is expected in the gaming industry, spurred by the increase in casinos on American Indian reservations and the introduction of slot machines at racetracks. Many States are looking to relax gambling regulations so that they can increase State revenues from gaming establishment taxes.

Employment in museums, historical sites, and similar institutions is expected to grow rapidly, as these institutions increasingly create exhibits and provide services that appeal to the public. Bolstered by healthy public support and increasing funding in recent years, many museums have recently or are currently expanding their facilities.

Due to competition from competing forms of entertainment, employment in the performing arts is not expected to grow.

*Job prospects.* Employment opportunities should be available in a wide range of settings, including golf courses, parks and outdoor recreational facilities, and amusement parks. The arts, entertainment, and recreation industry has relied heavily on workers under the age of 25 to fill seasonal and lesser skilled positions. About 24 percent of all jobs in this industry are held by workers under age 25, compared to 14 percent in all industries combined. Opportunities should be available for young, seasonal, part-time, and lesser skilled workers. In addition, the industry is expected to hire a growing number of workers in other age groups. Because of the appeal of jobs as performing artists and professional athletes, the supply of workers in these occupations will expand, ensuring continued intense competition.

## Earnings

*Industry earnings.* Earnings in arts, entertainment, and recreation are relatively low, reflecting the large number of part-time and seasonal jobs. Nonsupervisory workers in arts, entertainment, and recreation averaged $332 a week in 2006, compared with $568 throughout private industry.

Earnings vary according to occupation and segment of the industry. For example, some professional athletes earn millions, but competition for these positions is intense, and most athletes are unable to reach even the minor leagues. Many service workers make the minimum wage or a little more. Actors often go long periods with little or no income from acting, so they are forced to work at second jobs. Earnings in selected occupations in arts, entertainment, and recreation appear in table 4.

Because many amusement and theme parks dramatically increase employment during vacation periods, employment for a number of jobs in the industry is seasonal. Theme parks, for example, frequently hire young workers, often students, for summer employment. Also, many sports are not played all year, so athletes and people in the service jobs associated with those sports often are seasonally employed.

*Benefits and union membership.* Employers in some segments of this industry offer benefits that are not available in other in-

**Table 4. Median hourly earnings of the largest occupations in arts, entertainment, and recreation, May 2006**

| Occupation | Performing arts, spectator sports, and related industries | Museums, historical sites, and similar institutions | Amusement, gambling and recreation industries | All industries |
|---|---|---|---|---|
| Security guards.......................................................... | $10.69 | $10.66 | $10.11 | $10.35 |
| Receptionists and information clerks................................ | 10.65 | 9.27 | 8.80 | 11.01 |
| Landscaping and groundskeeping workers ....................... | 9.80 | 10.67 | 9.48 | 10.22 |
| Janitors and cleaners, except maids and housekeeping cleaners...... | 9.60 | 9.49 | 8.81 | 9.58 |
| Cashiers.................................................................. | 8.93 | 8.47 | 8.06 | 8.08 |
| Bartenders............................................................... | 8.81 | 12.97 | 8.09 | 7.86 |
| Ushers, lobby attendants, and ticket takers ..................... | 8.33 | 8.32 | 7.54 | 7.64 |
| Fitness trainers and aerobics instructors ......................... | 8.31 | — | 13.05 | 12.46 |
| Amusement and recreation attendants............................. | 8.01 | 8.04 | 7.61 | 7.83 |
| Waiters and waitresses................................................ | 7.01 | 8.57 | 7.99 | 7.14 |

dustries. For example, benefits for workers in some theme parks include free passes to the park, transportation to and from work, housing, scholarships, and discounts on park merchandise.

Although unions are not common in most segments of this industry, they are important in professional sports and the performing arts. Many professional athletes, actors, and performers are members of unions. Consequently, earnings of athletes and performers are often determined by union contracts that specify minimum salary rates and working conditions.

## Sources of Additional Information

For additional information about careers in the parks and recreation industry and a listing of colleges and universities offering accredited programs in parks and recreation studies, contact:
➤ National Recreation and Parks Association, 22377 Belmont Ridge Rd., Ashburn, VA 20148. Internet: **http://www.nrpa.org**

For more information about a career in the field of dance, contact:
➤ Dance/USA, 1156 15th St. NW., Suite 820, Washington, DC 20005-1726. Internet: **http://www.danceusa.org**

For more information on employment with carnivals and other outdoor amusement businesses, contact:
➤ Outdoor Amusement Business Association, 1035 S. Semoran Blvd., Suite 1045A, Winter Park, FL 32792. Internet: **http://www.oaba.org**

For more information about starting or managing a small business in the leisure and entertainment industry, contact:
➤ International Association for the Leisure and Entertainment Industry, 10 Briarcrest Square, Hershey, PA 17033. Internet: **http://www.ialei.org**

For information about the fitness industry, contact:
➤ International Health, Racquet, and Sportsclub Association, 263 Summer St., Boston, MA 02210. Internet: **http://www.ihrsa.org**

For information about careers in museums, contact:
➤ American Association of Museums, 1575 Eye St. NW., Suite 400, Washington, DC 20005. Internet: **http://www.aam-us.org**

For more information about careers in entertainment services and technology, contact:
➤ Entertainment Services and Technology Association, 875 Sixth Ave., Suite 1005, New York, NY 10001. Internet: **http://www.esta.org**
➤ U.S. Institute for Theater Technology, Inc., 6433 Riddings Rd., Syracuse, NY 13206-1111. Internet: **http://www.usitt.org**

Information on the following occupations found in arts, entertainment, and recreation appears in the 2008-09 *Occupational Outlook Handbook*:
- Actors, producers, and directors
- Animal care and service workers
- Archivists, curators, and museum technicians
- Artists and related workers
- Athletes, coaches, umpires, and related workers
- Broadcast and sound engineering technicians and radio operators
- Dancers and choreographers
- Fitness workers
- Gaming cage workers
- Gaming services occupations
- Grounds maintenance workers
- Musicians, singers, and related workers
- Recreation workers
- Security guards and gaming surveillance officers

# Food Services and Drinking Places

(NAICS 722)

- Food services and drinking places provide many young people with their first jobs; more than 1 in 5 workers were aged 16 to 19 in 2006, about 5 times the proportion for all industries.

- Cooks, waiters and waitresses, and combined food-preparation and serving workers comprised nearly 3 out of 5 workers in this industry.

- About 2 out of 5 employees work part time, more than twice the proportion for all industries.

- Job opportunities will be plentiful because large numbers of young and part-time workers will leave their jobs in the industry, creating substantial replacement needs.

## Nature of the Industry

*Goods and services.* Food services and drinking places may be the world's most widespread and familiar industry. These establishments include all types of restaurants, from fast-food eateries to formal dining establishments. They also include cafeterias, caterers, bars, and food service contractors that operate the food services at places such as schools, sports arenas, and hospitals.

*Industry organization.* In 2006, there were 524,000 privately owned food service and drinking places across the United States. As shown in table 1, about 46 percent of establishments in this industry are *limited-service eating places*, such as fast-food restaurants, cafeterias, and snack and nonalcoholic beverage bars, that primarily serve patrons who order or select items and pay before eating. *Full-service restaurants* account for about 39 percent of establishments and cater to patrons who order, are served, and consume their food while seated, and then pay after eating. *Drinking places (alcoholic beverages)*—bars, pubs, nightclubs, and taverns—primarily prepare and serve alcoholic beverages for consumption on the premises. Drinking places comprise about 9 percent of all establishments in this industry. *Special food services*, such as food-service contractors, caterers, and mobile food-service vendors, account for 5 percent of establishments in the industry.

The most common type of a limited-service eating place is a franchised operation of a nationwide restaurant chain that sells fast food. Features that characterize these restaurants include a limited menu, the absence of waiters and waitresses, and emphasis on limited service. Menu selections usually offer limited variety and are prepared by workers with minimal cooking or food handling skills. Food typically is served in disposable, take-out containers that retain the food's warmth, allowing restaurants to prepare orders in advance of customers' requests. A growing number of fast-food restaurants provide drive-through and walk-up services.

Cafeterias are another type of limited-service eating place and usually offer a somewhat limited selection that varies daily. Cafeterias also may provide separate serving stations for salads or short-order grill items, such as grilled sandwiches or hamburgers. Patrons select from food and drink items on display in a continuous cafeteria line. Cafeteria selections may include foods that require more complicated preparations and greater culinary skills than are required in fast-food restaurants. Selec-

tions usually are prepared ahead in large quantities and seldom are cooked to the customer's order.

Limited-service snack and nonalcoholic beverage bars carry and sell a combination of snacks, pastries, nonalcoholic beverages, and other related products but generally promote and sell a unique snack or beverage for consumption on or near the premises. For example, some prepare and serve specialty snacks including ice cream, frozen yogurt, cookies, or popcorn. Others serve primarily coffee, juices, or soda.

Full-service restaurants offer more menu categories, including appetizers, entrées, salads, side dishes, desserts, and beverages, and varied choices within each category. Chefs and cooks prepare items to order, which may run from grilling a simple hamburger to composing a more complex and sophisticated menu item. Waiters and waitresses offer table service in comfortable surroundings.

Cost-conscious and time-strapped patrons increasingly eat at midscale or family-type restaurants, typically run by a national chain. These restaurants usually offer efficient table service, well-priced familiar menu items prepared by moderately skilled kitchen workers. By contrast, customers at upscale dining places tend to seek a nicer atmosphere with skillfully prepared cuisine and leisurely, professional service. While chains are an important segment of the restaurant market, many restaurants remain independently owned and locally operated.

Some drinking places also offer patrons limited dining services in addition to providing alcoholic beverages. In some States, they also sell packaged alcoholic beverages for consumption off the premises. Establishments selling alcoholic beverages are closely regulated by State and local alcoholic beverage control authorities.

Finally, the food services and drinking places industry covers

**Table 1. Percent distribution of employment and establishments in food services and drinking places by detailed industry sector, 2006**

| Industry segment | Employment | Establishments |
|---|---|---|
| Total | 100.0 | 100.0 |
| Full-service restaurants | 47.5 | 39.0 |
| Limited-service eating places | 42.9 | 46.4 |
| Special food services | 5.8 | 5.4 |
| Drinking places (alcoholic beverages) | 3.8 | 9.2 |

a variety of special food services establishments, including food service contractors, concession stands at sporting events, catering firms, and mobile food services, such as ice cream trucks and other street vendors who sell food.

*Recent developments.* Technology influences the food services and drinking places industry in many ways, enhancing efficiency and productivity. Many restaurants use computers to track orders, inventory, and patron seating. Point-of-service (POS) systems allow servers to key in a customer's order, either tableside using a hand-held device or from a computer terminal in the dining room, and send the order to the kitchen instantaneously so preparation can begin. The same system totals and prints checks, functions as a cash register, connects to credit card authorizers, and tracks sales. Many managers use inventory-tracking software to compare the record of sales from the POS with a record of present inventory to minimize food costs and spoilage. Some establishments enter an inventory of standard ingredients and suppliers into their POS system. When supplies of particular ingredients run low, additional inventory can be ordered directly from the supplier using this preprogrammed information. Computers also allow restaurant and food service managers to more efficiently keep track of employee schedules and pay.

Food service managers use the Internet to track industry news, find recipes, conduct market research, purchase supplies or equipment, recruit employees, and train staff. Internet access also makes service to customers more efficient. Many restaurants maintain websites that include menus and online promotions, provide information about the restaurant's location, and offer the option to make a reservation. Wireless communication headsets are now being used by some managers, hosts and hostesses, and chefs. Headsets allow a means of hands-free communications with other staff so that they can prevent order backups in the kitchen, better serve patrons in the dining room, or more easily accommodate special requirements, such as large groups, diners with special dietary needs, or disability accessible seating requirements. Other wireless technology systems allow managers to monitor orders placed through individual terminals or by particular employees, instantly check inventories, and ensure timely preparation of customers' orders.

## Working Conditions

*Hours.* Many food services and drinking places establishments in this industry are open long hours. Staff typically are needed to work during evening, weekend, and holiday hours. Full-time employees, often head or executive chefs and food service managers, typically work longer hours—12-hour days are common—and also may be on call to work at other times when needed. Part-time employees, usually waiters and waitresses, dining room attendants, hosts and hostesses, and fast-food employees, typically work shorter days (4–6 hours per day) or fewer days per week than most full-time employees.

Food services and drinking places employ more part-time workers than other industries. One-third of workers in food services and drinking places worked part time in 2006, more than twice the proportion for all industries. This allows some employees flexibility in setting their work hours, affording them a greater opportunity to tailor work schedules to personal or family needs. Some employees may rotate work on some shifts to ensure proper coverage at unpopular work times or to fully staff restaurants during peak demand times.

*Work Environment.* Food services and drinking places must comply with local fire, safety, and sanitation regulations. They also must provide appropriate public accommodations and ensure that employees use safe food-handling measures. These practices require establishments to maintain supplies of chemicals, detergents, and other materials that may be harmful if not used properly.

Typical establishments have well-designed kitchens with state-of-the-art cooking and refrigeration equipment and proper electrical, lighting, and ventilation systems to keep everything functioning. However, kitchens usually are noisy, and may be very hot near stoves, grills, ovens, or steam tables. Chefs, cooks, food preparation workers, dishwashers, and other kitchen staff may suffer minor cuts or burns, be subject to scalding or steaming liquids, and spend most of their time standing in a relatively confined area. Chefs and cooks are under extreme pressure to work quickly to stay on top of orders in a busy restaurant. The fast pace requires employees to be alert and quick-thinking, but also may result in muscle strains from trying to move heavy pots or force pressurized containers open without taking the proper safety precautions.

Dining areas also may be well-designed, but can become crowded and noisy when busy. Servers, attendants, and other dining-room staff, such as bartenders and hosts or hostesses, need to protect against falls, spills, or burns while serving diners and keeping service areas stocked.

Most food services and drinking places workers spend most of their time on their feet—preparing meals, serving diners, or transporting dishes and supplies throughout the establishment. Upper body strength often is needed to lift heavy items, such as trays of dishes, platters of food, or cooking pots. Work during peak dining hours can be very hectic and stressful.

Employees who have direct contact with customers, such as waiters and waitresses or hosts and hostesses, should have a neat appearance and maintain a professional and pleasant manner. Professional hospitality is required from the moment guests enter the restaurant until the time they leave. Sustaining a proper demeanor during busy times or over the course of a long shift may be difficult.

Kitchen staff also needs to be able to work as a team and to communicate with each other. Timing is critical to preparing more complex dishes. Coordinating orders to ensure that an entire table's meals are ready at the same time is essential, particularly in a large restaurant during busy dining periods.

In 2006, the rate of work-related injuries and illnesses was 4.2 per 100 full-time workers in eating and drinking places, slightly less than the average of 4.4 for the private sector. Work hazards include the possibility of burns from hot equipment, sprained muscles, and wrenched backs from heavy lifting and falls on slippery floors.

## Employment

The food services and drinking places industry, with about 9.4 million wage and salary jobs in 2006, ranks among the Nation's leading employers. Food services and drinking places tend to be small; about 70 percent of the establishments in the industry employed fewer than 20 workers (see chart). As a result, this industry often is considered attractive to individuals who want to own and run their own businesses. An estimated 248,000 self-employed and unpaid family workers were employed in the industry, representing about 3 percent of total employment.

Establishments in this industry, particularly fast-food estab-

**About 7 out of 10 establishments in the food services and drinking places industry employ fewer than 20 workers.**

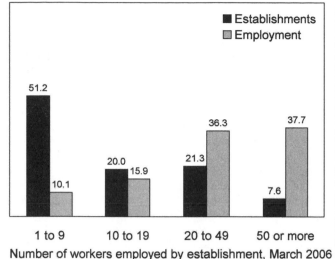

Percent

■ Establishments
■ Employment

Number of workers employed by establishment, March 2006

lishments, are leading employers of teenagers—aged 16 through 19—providing first jobs for many new entrants into the labor force. In 2006, about 21 percent of all workers in food services and drinking places were teenagers, about 5 times the proportion in all industries (table 2). About 43 percent were under age 25, more than 3 times the proportion in all industries.

## Occupations in the Industry
Workers in this industry perform a variety of tasks. They prepare food items from a menu or according to a customer's order, keep food preparation and service areas clean, accept payment from customers, and provide the establishment managerial or office services, such as bookkeeping, ordering, and advertising. Cooks, waiters and waitresses, and combined food preparation and serving workers accounted for 3 out 5 food services jobs (table 3).

*Service occupations.* Over 80 percent of workers in this industry are in food preparation and serving-related occupations. Most serving-related workers deal with customers in a dining area or at a service counter. *Waiters and waitresses* take customers' orders, serve food and beverages, and prepare itemized checks. They may describe chef's specials and take alcoholic beverage orders. In some establishments, they escort customers to their seats, accept payments, and set up and clear tables. In many larger restaurants, however, these tasks may be assigned to, or

shared with, other workers.

Other serving-related occupations include *hosts and hostesses,* who welcome customers, show them to their tables, and offer them menus. *Bartenders* fill drink orders for waiters and waitresses and from customers seated at the bar. *Dining room attendants and bartender helpers* assist waiters, waitresses, and bartenders by clearing, cleaning, and setting up tables, as well as keeping service areas stocked with supplies. *Counter attendants* take orders and serve food at counters, cafeteria steam tables, and fast-food counters. Depending on the size and type of establishment, attendants also may operate cash registers.

*Combined food preparation and serving workers, including fast food,* prepare and serve items in fast-food restaurants. Most take orders from customers at counters or drive-through windows at fast-food restaurants. They assemble orders, hand them to customers, and accept payment. Many of these workers also cook and package food, make coffee, and fill beverage cups using drink-dispensing machines.

Workers in the various food preparation occupations prepare food in a kitchen. *Institution and cafeteria cooks* work in the kitchens of schools, hospitals, industrial cafeterias, and other institutions where they prepare large quantities of a small variety of menu items. *Restaurant cooks* usually prepare a wider selection of dishes for each meal, cooking individual servings to order. *Short-order cooks* prepare grilled items and sandwiches in establishments that emphasize fast service. *Fast-food cooks* prepare and package a limited selection of food that either is prepared to order or kept warm until sold in fast-food restaurants. *Food preparation workers* clean and prepare basic food ingredients, such as meats, fish, and vegetables for use in making more complex meals, assemble salads and sandwiches using readily available ingredients, perform simple cooking tasks under the direction of the chef or head cook, and keep work areas clean. *Dishwashers* clean dishes, glasses, pots, and kitchen accessories by hand or by machine.

*Managerial and all other occupations.* Food service managers hire, train, supervise, and discharge workers in food services and drinking places establishments. They also purchase supplies, deal with vendors, keep records, and help whenever an extra hand is needed. *Executive chefs* oversee the kitchen, select the menu, train cooks and food preparation workers, and direct the preparation of food. In fine-dining establishments, *maitre d's* may serve as hosts or hostesses while overseeing the dining room. Larger establishments may employ *general managers,* as well as a number of assistant managers. Many managers and executive chefs are part owners of the establishments they manage.

Food services and drinking places may employ a wide range of other workers, including accountants, advertising and public relations workers, bookkeepers, dietitians, mechanics and other maintenance workers, musicians and other entertainers, human resources workers, and various clerks. However, many establishments may choose to contract this work to outside establishments who also perform these tasks for several food services and drinking places outlets.

## Training and Advancement
The skills and experience required by workers in food services and drinking places differ by occupation and type of establishment. Many entry-level positions, such as waiters and waitresses or food preparation workers, require little or no formal education or previous training. Managerial occupations, though, require

**Table 2. Percent distribution of employment, by age group, 2006**

| Age group | Food services and drinking places | All industries |
|---|---|---|
| **Total** ...................................................... | 100.0% | 100.0% |
| 16-19.......................................................... | 21.1 | 4.3 |
| 20-24.......................................................... | 22.1 | 9.6 |
| 25-34.......................................................... | 22.7 | 21.5 |
| 35-44.......................................................... | 15.8 | 23.9 |
| 45-54.......................................................... | 11.9 | 23.6 |
| 55-64.......................................................... | 4.7 | 13.4 |
| 65 and older................................................ | 1.8 | 3.7 |

prior experience working in food service, which may be acquired through summer or part-time employment in the industry, or through formal internships or other work opportunities while pursuing a culinary or hospitality management degree. Similarly, work in limited-service eating places generally requires less training and experience than work in full-service restaurants, particularly at higher end restaurants.

**Table 3. Employment of wage and salary workers in food services and drinking places by occupation, 2006 and projected change, 2006-2016.**
(Employment in thousands)

| Occupation | Employment, 2006 | | Percent change, 2006-16 |
| --- | --- | --- | --- |
| | Number | Percent | |
| **All occupations** | 9,383 | 100.0 | 10.9 |
| **Management, business, and financial occupations** | 227 | 2.4 | 3.7 |
| Top executives | 55 | 0.6 | 0.0 |
| Food service managers | 149 | 1.6 | 4.1 |
| **Service occupations** | 8,527 | 90.9 | 11.8 |
| Chefs and head cooks | 76 | 0.8 | 5.0 |
| First-line supervisors/managers of food preparation and serving workers | 592 | 6.3 | 10.8 |
| Cooks, fast food | 586 | 6.2 | 8.0 |
| Cooks, institution and cafeteria | 55 | 0.6 | 21.5 |
| Cooks, restaurant | 732 | 7.8 | 10.4 |
| Cooks, short order | 146 | 1.6 | 1.9 |
| Food preparation workers | 457 | 4.9 | 15.8 |
| Bartenders | 358 | 3.8 | 8.3 |
| Combined food preparation and serving workers, including fast food | 2,001 | 21.3 | 18.3 |
| Counter attendants, cafeteria, food concession, and coffee shop | 346 | 3.7 | 10.0 |
| Waiters and waitresses | 2,005 | 21.4 | 9.4 |
| Food servers, nonrestaurant | 43 | 0.5 | 12.3 |
| Dining room and cafeteria attendants and bartender helpers | 289 | 3.1 | 9.9 |
| Dishwashers | 405 | 4.3 | 8.5 |
| Hosts and hostesses, restaurant, lounge, and coffee shop | 310 | 3.3 | 9.8 |
| Building cleaning workers | 62 | 0.7 | 11.7 |
| **Sales and related occupations** | 282 | 3.0 | -0.3 |
| Cashiers | 259 | 2.8 | -1.4 |
| **Office and administrative support occupations** | 76 | 0.8 | 5.7 |
| **Transportation and material moving occupations** | 197 | 2.1 | 0.4 |
| Driver/sales workers | 155 | 1.7 | -1.6 |

Note: Columns may not add to totals due to omission of occupations with small employment

*Service occupations.* Many fast-food worker or server jobs are held by young or part-time workers. On-the-job training, typically under the close supervision of an experienced employee or manager, often lasts a few weeks or less. Some large chain operations require formal training sessions for new employees, many using on-line or video training programs. This type of corporate training generally covers the restaurant's history, menu, organizational philosophy, and daily operational standards.

Training options for chefs and other kitchen staff are more varied. Many food service workers start as untrained food preparation workers. As they acquire kitchen skills, and demonstrate greater responsibility, they may advance to cook positions pre-

paring routine or simple dishes. Advancement opportunities for food preparation workers, as well as for cafeteria and institution cooks and short-order cooks, generally require that they move into positions in full-service restaurants. In full-service restaurants, kitchen workers at all levels may acquire the appropriate experience and expand their skills, which may lead to work as a line cook. Line cooks also develop and acquire new skills, moving to more demanding stations and eventually to more challenging chef positions. As chefs improve their culinary skills, the opportunities for professional recognition and higher earnings increase. Chefs may advance to executive chef positions and oversee several kitchens within a food service operation, open their own restaurants as chef-proprietors, or move into training positions as teachers or culinary educators. Other chefs may go into sales or demonstrator careers, testing recipes, products, or equipment for sale to chefs and restaurateurs.

Formal culinary training for chefs and cooks is available through a wide variety of sources—independent cooking schools or academies, community and junior colleges, trade and vocational schools, and 4-year colleges and universities. Many trade associations and unions also certify cooking programs conducted at selected schools or sponsor Federally-approved apprenticeship programs that combine formal classroom instruction with on-the-job experience in a working kitchen. Many formal training programs offer job placement opportunities that help recent graduates find work in kitchens.

Most culinary programs now offer more business courses and computer training to better prepare chefs to assume greater leadership and managerial roles in the industry and to manage large, complex food service operations. Culinary training also has adapted to reflect changing food trends and eating habits. For example, chefs and cooks must know a wide variety of food preparation techniques and cooking styles. They also must know how to prepare foods to accommodate various dietary restrictions to satisfy health-conscious eating styles and to meet the needs of an increasingly international clientele. Chefs and cooks also need to be creative and know how to inspire other kitchen staff to develop new dishes and create inventive recipes.

Promotion opportunities in food services and drinking places vary by occupation and the size of individual establishments. As in other industries, larger establishments and organizations usually offer better advancement opportunities. As beginners gain experience and basic skills, those who choose to pursue careers in food services and drinking places can transfer to other jobs that require greater skill and offer higher earnings. Many workers earn progressively higher incomes as they gain experience or switch to jobs in establishments offering higher pay. For example, waiters and waitresses may transfer to jobs in more expensive or busier restaurants where larger tips are more likely.

*Managerial occupations.* Many managers of food services and drinking places obtain their positions through hard work and years of restaurant experience. Dining room workers, such as hosts and hostesses or waiters and waitresses, often are promoted to *maitre d'* or into managerial jobs. Many managers of fast-food restaurants advanced from the ranks of hourly workers.

Completion of postsecondary training, however, is increasingly important for advancement into management in this industry. Whether it is in the form of a bachelor's degree or as specialized training in culinary arts or hospitality management, completion of such programs demonstrates both the maturity and motivation required for work in a hectic, fast-paced industry. Appropriate training often enables graduates to start as assistant managers. Management programs may last from 18 months, for tailored certificate or associate degree programs, to 4 years, for more comprehensive bachelor's degree programs. A growing number of master's degree programs in hospitality management provide training for corporate-level management involving site selection and feasibility assessments, in addition to training for restaurant-level customer service responsibilities. Courses are available through community and junior colleges, trade and vocational schools, 4-year colleges and universities, hotel or restaurant associations, and trade unions. The Armed Forces are another source of training and experience in food service work.

Nationwide chains often operate their own schools for prospective assistant managers, so that they can attend training seminars before acquiring additional responsibilities. Eventually, successful assistant managers may advance to general manager of one of the chain's establishments, to a top management position in another large chain operation, or to a management position in an independent restaurant. Assistant managers in smaller, independent restaurants may learn their duties on the job, while assistant mangers in most chain-affiliated establishments receive training through more formal programs. Managers often are required to keep up with the latest food safety regulations, computer management systems, and hiring issues by attending industry or chain-sponsored seminars and classes.

## Outlook

Wage and salary jobs in food services and drinking places are expected to increase by 11 percent over the 2006–16 period, the same as that projected for wage and salary employment in all industries combined. Numerous job opportunities will be available for people with limited job skills, first-time job seekers, senior citizens, and those seeking part-time or alternative work schedules.

*Employment change.* A growing population that increasingly prefers the convenience of eating out and having their meals prepared for them will contribute to job growth and a wider variety of employment settings in which to work. All sectors of the industry are expected to grow and generate numerous jobs. The numbers of limited-service eateries and fast-casual restaurants that specialize in serving soups, salads and sandwiches made to order on the spot will grow as time-strapped diners seek out healthful menu alternatives while on the go. In contrast, traditional fast-food and quick-service restaurants that appeal to younger diners and those whose first priority is convenience should increase more slowly than in the past.

Moderately-priced restaurants that offer table service will afford increasing job opportunities, as these businesses expand to accommodate the needs of a more mobile population and families with young children. Fine dining establishments, which appeal more to affluent, often older, customers, also should grow as this part of the population increases over the decade.

The food service contracting sector of this industry will continue to grow as more schools, hospitals, and company cafeterias contract out their food services to these firms. Additionally, the contracting out of personal chefs, who prepare and store meals in clients' homes for later reheating and serving, is becoming more common.

Those who qualify—either through experience or formal culinary training—for skilled head cook and chef positions should be in demand, because of the need for skilled cooks to work in the growing number of new restaurants and to replace chefs that leave the occupation due to the long hours. Employment of salaried managers is projected to increase more slowly than the average for the industry, as more chain restaurants concentrate these workers in regional offices. Employment of self-employed managers in independent food services and drinking places is expected to grow more slowly.

*Job prospects.* Job opportunities in food services and drinking places should be very good, because the large number of young and part-time workers in the industry will generate substantial replacement needs. A large number of job openings will be created for new entrants as experienced workers find jobs in other, higher-paying establishments, seek full-time opportunities outside the industry, or stop working. Industry expansion also will create many new jobs as diners continue to seek the convenience of prepared meals. The greatest number of job openings will be in the largest occupations—waiters and waitresses and combined food-preparation and serving workers—which also have high replacement needs.

Graduates of college hospitality programs, particularly those with good computer skills, should have especially good opportunities at higher-end full service establishments. The growing dominance of chain-affiliated food services and drinking places also should enhance opportunities for advancement from food-service manager positions into general manager and corporate administrative jobs.

## Earnings

*Industry earnings.* Earnings in food services and drinking places usually are much lower than the average for all industries (table 4). In 2006, average weekly earnings for nonsupervisory workers in this industry were $215, which is much lower than the average for all private sector workers of $533. Average weekly hours in all food service sectors also were lower than the average for private industry. Low earnings are supplemented for many workers by tips from customers. Waiters, waitresses, and bartenders, for example, often derive the majority of their earnings from tips, which depend on menu prices and the volume of customers served. In some establishments, workers who receive tips share a portion of their gratuities with other workers in the dining room and kitchen.

Earnings vary by occupation, geographic area, and by type and size of establishment. Usually skilled workers, such as chefs, have the highest wages, and workers who are dependent upon tips to supplement earnings have the lowest. Many workers in the industry in 2006 earned the Federal minimum wage of $5.85 an hour, or less, if tips are included as a substantial part of earnings. Workers in these lower paying occupations will see their future earnings increase on a phased-in basis to $7.25

**Table 4. Average earnings of nonsupervisory workers in food services and drinking places by industry segment, 2006**

| Industry segment | Weekly | Hourly |
|---|---|---|
| **Total, private industry**............................... | $568 | $16.76 |
| **Food services and drinking places**................... | 215 | 8.69 |
| Special food services....................................... | 275 | 10.89 |
| Full-service restaurants.................................... | 232 | 9.23 |
| Limited-service eating places ........................... | 190 | 7.77 |
| Drinking places, alcoholic beverages................. | 185 | 8.39 |

per hour by 2009. A number of employers provide free or discounted meals and uniforms to employees. Earnings in the largest occupations employed in food services and drinking places appear in table 5.

*Benefits and union membership.* Unionization is not widespread in the food services and drinking places industry. In 2006, 1 percent of all employees were union members or covered by union contracts, compared with about 13 percent for all industries.

**Table 5. Median hourly earnings of the largest occupations in food services and drinking places, May 2006**

| Occupation | Food services and drinking places | All industries |
|---|---|---|
| First-line supervisors/managers of food preparation and serving workers ..... | $12.55 | $12.97 |
| Cooks, restaurant ................................... | 9.63 | 9.78 |
| Food preparation workers...................... | 7.99 | 8.37 |
| Bartenders............................................. | 7.78 | 7.86 |
| Counter attendants, cafeteria, food concession, and coffee shop .............. | 7.69 | 7.76 |
| Hosts and hostesses, restaurant, lounge, and coffee shop ...................... | 7.69 | 7.78 |
| Dishwashers......................................... | 7.47 | 7.57 |
| Cooks, fast food.................................... | 7.39 | 7.41 |
| Waiters and waitresses......................... | 7.08 | 7.14 |
| Combined food preparation and serving workers, including fast food ................ | 7.04 | 7.24 |

## Sources of Additional Information

For additional information about careers and training in the food-services and drinking-places industry, contact:

➢ National Restaurant Association, 1200 17th St. NW., Washington, DC 20036. Internet: **http://www.restaurant.org**
➢ National Restaurant Educational Foundation, 175 West Jackson Boulevard, Suite 1500, Chicago, Illinois 60604-2702. Internet: **http://www.nraef.org**
➢ The American Culinary Federation, 180 Center Place Way, St. Augustine, FL 32095. Internet: **http://www.acfchefs.org**

For a list of educational programs in the food services and drinking places industry, contact:

➢ The International Council on Hotel, Restaurant, and Institutional Education, 2810 North Parham Rd., Suite 230, Richmond, VA 23294. Internet: **http://www.chrie.org**

Information on vocational education courses for food preparation and service careers may be obtained from your State or local director of vocational education or superintendent of schools.

Information on these and other occupations found in food services and drinking places appears in the 2008–09 edition of the *Occupational Outlook Handbook*:

• Cashiers
• Chefs, cooks, and food preparation workers
• Food and beverage serving and related workers
• Food service managers

# Hotels and Other Accommodations

## SIGNIFICANT POINTS

- Service occupations, by far the largest occupational group, account for two-thirds of the industry's employment.

- Hotels employ many young workers and first-time job holders in part-time and seasonal jobs.

- Job opportunities should be excellent as a number of new hotels are expected to open.

## Nature of the Industry

People travel for a variety of reasons, including for vacations, business, and visits to friends and relatives. For many of these travelers, hotels and other accommodations will be where they stay while out of town. For others, hotels may be more than just a place to stay, but destinations in themselves. Resort hotels and casino hotels, for example, offer a variety of activities to keep travelers and families occupied for much of their stay.

*Goods and services.* Hotels and other accommodations are as different as the many family and business travelers they accommodate. The industry includes all types of lodging, from luxurious 5-star hotels to youth hostels and RV parks. While many provide simply a place to spend the night, others cater to longer stays by providing food service, recreational activities, and meeting rooms. In 2006, approximately 62,000 establishments provided overnight accommodations to suit many different needs and budgets.

Hotels and motels comprise the majority of establishments in this industry and are generally classified as offering either full-service or limited service. Full-service properties offer a variety of services for their guests, but they almost always include at least one or more restaurant and beverage service options—from coffee bars and lunch counters to cocktail lounges and formal restaurants. They also usually provide room service. Larger full-service properties usually have a variety of retail shops on the premises, such as gift boutiques, newsstands, and drug and cosmetics counters, some of which may be geared to an exclusive clientele. Additionally, a number of full-service hotels offer guests access to laundry and valet services, swimming pools, beauty salons, and fitness centers or health spas. A small, but growing, number of luxury hotel chains also manage condominium units in combination with their transient rooms, providing both hotel guests and condominium owners with access to the same services and amenities.

The largest hotels often have banquet rooms, exhibit halls, and spacious ballrooms to accommodate conventions, business meetings, wedding receptions, and other social gatherings. Conventions and business meetings are major sources of revenue for these properties. Some commercial hotels are known as conference hotels—fully self-contained entities specifically designed for large-scale meetings. They provide physical fitness and recreational facilities for meeting attendees, in addition to state-of-the-art audiovisual and technical equipment, a business center, and banquet services.

Limited service hotels are free-standing properties that do not have on-site restaurants or most other amenities that must be provided by a staff other than the front desk or housekeeping.

They usually offer continental breakfasts, vending machines or small packaged items, Internet access, and sometimes unattended game rooms or swimming pools in addition to daily housekeeping services. The numbers of limited-service properties have been growing. These properties are not as costly to build and maintain. They appeal to budget-conscious family vacationers and travelers who are willing to sacrifice amenities for lower room prices.

Hotels can also be categorized based on a distinguishing feature or service provided by the hotel. *Conference hotels* provide meeting and banquet rooms, and usually food service, to large groups of people. *Resort hotels* offer luxurious surroundings with a variety of recreational facilities, such as swimming pools, golf courses, tennis courts, game rooms, and health spas, as well as planned social activities and entertainment. Resorts typically are located in vacation destinations or near natural settings, such as mountains, seashores, theme parks, or other attractions. As a result, the business of many resorts fluctuates with the season. Some resort hotels and motels provide additional convention and conference facilities to encourage customers to combine business with pleasure. During the off season, many of these establishments solicit conventions, sales meetings, and incentive tours to fill their otherwise empty rooms; some resorts even close for the off-season.

*Extended-stay hotels* typically provide rooms or suites with fully equipped kitchens, entertainment systems, office space with computer and telephone lines, fitness centers, and other amenities. Typically, guests use these hotels for a minimum of 5 consecutive nights often while on an extended work assignment or lengthy vacation or family visit. *All-suite hotels* offer a living room or sitting room in addition to a bedroom.

*Casino hotels* combine both lodging and legalized gaming on the same premises. Along with the typical services provided by most full-service hotels, casino hotels also contain casinos where patrons can wager at table games, play slot machines, and make other bets. Some casino hotels also contain conference and convention facilities.

In addition to hotels, *bed-and-breakfast inns, recreational vehicle (RV) parks, campgrounds,* and *rooming and boarding houses* provide lodging for overnight guests and are included in this industry. *Bed-and-breakfast inns* provide short-term lodging in private homes or small buildings converted for this purpose and are characterized by highly personalized service and inclusion of breakfast in the room rate. Their appeal is quaintness, with unusual service and decor.

*RV parks and campgrounds* cater to people who enjoy recreational camping at moderate prices. Some parks and campgrounds provide service stations, general stores, shower and toilet facilities, and coin-operated laundries. While some are designed for overnight travelers only, others are for vacationers who stay longer. Some camps provide accommodations, such as cabins and fixed campsites, and other amenities, such as food services, recreational facilities and equipment, and organized recreational activities. Examples of these overnight camps include children's camps, family vacation camps, hunting and fishing camps, and outdoor adventure retreats that offer trail riding, white-water rafting, hiking, fishing, game hunting, and similar activities.

Other short-term lodging facilities in this industry include *guesthouses*, or small cottages located on the same property as a main residence, and *youth hostels*—dormitory-style hotels with few frills, occupied mainly by students traveling on limited budgets. Also included are *rooming and boarding houses*, such as fraternity houses, sorority houses, off-campus dormitories, and workers' camps. These establishments provide temporary or longer term accommodations that may serve as a principal residence for the period of occupancy. These establishments also may provide services such as housekeeping, meals, and laundry services.

*Industry organization.* In recent years, the hotel industry has become dominated by a few large national hotel chains. To the traveler, familiar chain establishments represent dependability and quality at predictable rates. Many chains recognize the importance of brand loyalty to guests and have expanded the range of lodging options offered under one corporate name to include a full range of hotels from limited service, economy-type hotels to luxury inns. While these national corporations own some of the hotels, many properties are independently owned but affiliated with a chain through a franchise agreement or management contract. As part of a chain, individual hotels can participate in the company's national reservations service or incentive program, thereby appearing to belong to a larger enterprise.

For those who prefer more personalized service and a unique experience, *boutique hotels* are becoming more popular. These smaller hotels are generally found in urban locations and provide patrons good service and more distinctive décor and food selection.

While there are nationwide RV parks and campgrounds, most small lodging establishments are individually owned and operated by a single owner, who may employ a small staff to help operate the business

*Recent developments.* The lodging industry is moving towards more limited-service properties mostly in suburban, residential, or commercial neighborhoods, often siting hotels near popular restaurants. Many full-service properties are limiting or quitting the food service business altogether, choosing to contract out their food service operations to third party restaurateurs, including long-term arrangements with chain restaurant operators. Urban business and entertainment districts are providing a greater mix of lodging options to appeal to a wider range of travelers.

Increased competition among establishments in this industry has spurred many independently owned and operated hotels and other lodging places to join national or international reservation systems. This allows travelers to make multiple reservations for lodging, airlines, and car rentals with one telephone call or Internet search. Nearly all hotel chains and many independent lodging facilities operate online reservation systems through the Internet or maintain websites that allow individuals to book

rooms. Online marketing of properties is so popular with guests that many hotels promote themselves with elaborate websites and allow people to investigate availability and rates.

## Working Conditions

*Hours.* Because hotels are open around the clock, employees frequently work varying shifts or variable schedules. Employees who work the late shift generally receive additional compensation. Many employees enjoy the opportunity to work part-time, nights or evenings, or other schedules that fit their availability for work and the hotel's needs. Hotel managers and many department supervisors may work regularly assigned schedules, but they also routinely work longer hours than scheduled, especially during peak travel times or when multiple events are scheduled. Also, they may be called in to work on short notice in the event of an emergency or to cover a position. Those who are self-employed, often owner-operators of small inns, camp sites, or RV parks, tend to work long hours and often live at the establishment or nearby.

Office and administrative support workers generally work scheduled hours in an office setting, meeting with guests, clients, and hotel staff. Their work can become hectic processing orders and invoices, dealing with demanding guests, or servicing requests that require a quick turnaround, but job hazards typically are limited to muscle and eye strain common to working with computers and office equipment.

Computer specialists, information technology and audiovisual technicians who are employed mostly by larger convention hotels typically maintain standard hours servicing the property's websites and computer and communications networks. However, they often work long hours setting up and testing equipment for events that require their services.

*Work environment.* Work in hotels and other accommodations can be demanding and hectic. Hotel staffs provide a variety of services to guests and must do so efficiently, courteously, and accurately. They must maintain a pleasant demeanor even during times of stress or when dealing with an impatient or irate guest. Alternately, work at slower times, such as the off-season or overnight periods, can seem slow and tiresome. Still, hotel workers must be ready to provide guests and visitors with gracious customer service at any hour.

Food preparation and food service workers in hotels must withstand the strain of working during busy periods and being on their feet for many hours. Kitchen workers lift heavy pots and kettles and work near hot ovens and grills. Job hazards include slips and falls, cuts, and burns, but injuries are seldom serious. Food service workers often carry heavy trays of food, dishes, and glassware. Many of these workers work part time, including evenings, weekends, and holidays.

In 2006, work-related injuries and illnesses averaged 5.8 for every 100 full-time workers in hotels and other accommodations, compared with 4.4 for workers throughout private industry. Work hazards include burns from hot equipment, sprained muscles and wrenched backs from heavy lifting, and falls on wet floors.

## Employment

Hotels and other accommodations provided 1.8 million wage and salary jobs in 2006. In addition, there were about 40,000 self-employed and unpaid family workers in the industry, who

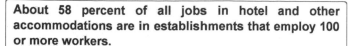

**About 58 percent of all jobs in hotel and other accommodations are in establishments that employ 100 or more workers.**

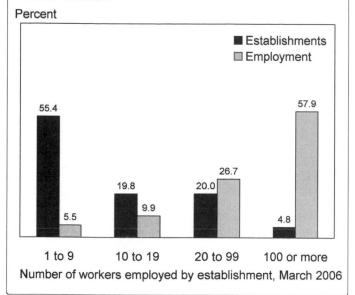

Percent

Number of workers employed by establishment, March 2006

worked in bed-and-breakfast inns, camps, and small inns and hotels.

Employment is concentrated in cities and resort areas. Compared with establishments in other industries, hotels and other accommodations tend to be small. About 75 percent employed fewer than 20 workers and 55 percent employed fewer than 10 (chart). As a result, lodging establishments offer opportunities for those who are interested in owning and running their own business. Although establishments tend to be small, the majority of jobs are in larger hotels with more than 100 employees.

Hotels and other lodging places often provide first jobs to many new entrants to the labor force. In 2006, about 17 percent of the workers were younger than age 25, compared with about 14 percent across all industries.

## Occupations in the Industry

The vast majority of workers in this industry—more than 4 out of 5 in 2006—were employed in service and office and administrative support occupations (table 1). Workers in these occupations usually learn their skills on the job. Postsecondary education is not required for most entry-level positions; however, college training may be helpful for advancement in some of the occupations. For those in administrative support—mainly hotel desk clerks—and service occupations, positive personality traits and a customer-service orientation may be more important than formal schooling. Traits most important for success in the hotels and other accommodations industry are good communication skills; the ability to get along with people in stressful situations; a neat, clean appearance; and a pleasant manner.

*Service occupations.* Service workers are by far the largest occupational group in the industry, accounting for 65 percent of the industry's employment. Most service jobs are in housekeeping occupations—including *building cleaning workers*, *maids and housekeeping cleaners*, and *janitors and cleaners*—and in food preparation and serving jobs—including *chefs and head cooks*, *waiters and waitresses*, *bartenders*, *fast food and counter workers*, and various other kitchen and dining room workers. The industry also employs many *baggage porters and bellhops*, *gam-*

**Table 1. Employment of wage and salary workers in hotels and other accommodations by occupation, 2006 and projected change, 2006-2016.**
(Employment in thousands)

| Occupation | Employment, 2006 Number | Employment, 2006 Percent | Percent change, 2006-16 |
|---|---|---|---|
| **All occupations** | 1,833 | 100.0 | 13.9 |
| **Management, business, and financial occupations** | 94 | 5.1 | 17.1 |
| General and operations managers | 12 | 0.7 | 4.0 |
| Lodging managers | 29 | 1.6 | 26.6 |
| Meeting and convention planners | 8 | 0.5 | 15.8 |
| Accountants and auditors | 8 | 0.4 | 16.0 |
| **Service occupations** | 1,184 | 64.6 | 13.5 |
| Security guards | 30 | 1.7 | 9.5 |
| Chefs and head cooks | 13 | 0.7 | 10.2 |
| First-line supervisors/managers of food preparation and serving workers | 23 | 1.3 | 16.2 |
| Cooks, restaurant | 57 | 3.1 | 12.8 |
| Food preparation workers | 21 | 1.1 | 16.1 |
| Bartenders | 36 | 2.0 | 16.3 |
| Fast food and counter workers | 28 | 1.5 | 23.9 |
| Waiters and waitresses | 133 | 7.2 | 6.9 |
| Food servers, nonrestaurant | 41 | 2.3 | 9.5 |
| Dining room and cafeteria attendants and bartender helpers | 46 | 2.5 | 7.9 |
| Dishwashers | 33 | 1.8 | 7.1 |
| Hosts and hostesses, restaurant, lounge, and coffee shop | 19 | 1.0 | 6.7 |
| First-line supervisors/managers of housekeeping and janitorial workers | 32 | 1.7 | 16.4 |
| Janitors and cleaners, except maids and housekeeping cleaners | 52 | 2.9 | 18.9 |
| Maids and housekeeping cleaners | 424 | 23.1 | 15.8 |
| Landscaping and groundskeeping workers | 22 | 1.2 | 16.1 |
| Gaming supervisors | 11 | 0.6 | 18.8 |
| Gaming dealers | 34 | 1.9 | 18.8 |
| Amusement and recreation attendants | 12 | 0.6 | 15.9 |
| Baggage porters and bellhops | 25 | 1.4 | 6.2 |
| Concierges | 8 | 0.4 | 4.9 |
| Recreation workers | 10 | 0.5 | 9.7 |
| **Sales and related occupations** | 52 | 2.9 | 12.0 |
| Cashiers, except gaming | 15 | 0.8 | 5.1 |
| Gaming change persons and booth cashiers | 7 | 0.4 | -5.0 |
| Sales representatives, services | 12 | 0.7 | 27.2 |
| **Office and administrative support occupations** | 345 | 18.8 | 13.8 |
| First-line supervisors/managers of office and administrative support workers | 25 | 1.3 | 8.0 |
| Switchboard operators, including answering service | 9 | 0.5 | -7.1 |
| Bookkeeping, accounting, and auditing clerks | 23 | 1.3 | 16.0 |
| Hotel, motel, and resort desk clerks | 207 | 11.3 | 17.2 |
| Reservation and transportation ticket agents and travel clerks | 13 | 0.7 | 4.6 |
| Secretaries and administrative assistants | 16 | 0.9 | 10.0 |
| **Installation, maintenance, and repair occupations** | 82 | 4.5 | 15.5 |
| Maintenance and repair workers, general | 70 | 3.8 | 15.7 |
| **Production occupations** | 38 | 2.1 | 18.2 |
| Laundry and dry-cleaning workers | 31 | 1.7 | 18.9 |
| **Transportation and material moving occupations** | 24 | 1.3 | 9.3 |
| Taxi drivers and chauffeurs | 8 | 0.4 | 14.2 |
| Parking lot attendants | 8 | 0.5 | 5.2 |

Note: Columns may not add to totals due to omission of occupations with small employment

*ing services workers*, and *grounds maintenance workers*.

Workers in cleaning and housekeeping occupations ensure that the lodging facility is clean and in good condition for the comfort and safety of guests. *Maids and housekeeping cleaners* clean lobbies, halls, guestrooms, and bathrooms. They make sure that guests not only have clean rooms, but have all the necessary furnishings and supplies. They change sheets and towels, vacuum carpets, dust furniture, empty wastebaskets, and mop bathroom floors. In larger hotels, the housekeeping staff may include assistant housekeepers, floor supervisors, housekeepers, and executive housekeepers. *Janitors* help with the cleaning of the public areas of the facility, empty trash, and perform minor maintenance work.

Workers in the various *food preparation and serving* occupations deal with customers in the dining room or at a service counter. *Waiters and waitresses* take customers' orders, serve meals, and prepare checks. In smaller establishments, they often set tables, escort guests to their seats, accept payment, and clear tables. In larger restaurants, some of these tasks are assigned to other workers.

*Hosts and hostesses* welcome guests, show them to their tables, and give them menus. *Bartenders* fill beverage orders for customers seated at the bar or from waiters and waitresses who serve patrons at tables. *Dining room and cafeteria attendants* and *bartender helpers* assist waiters, waitresses, and bartenders by clearing, cleaning, and setting up tables, replenishing supplies at the bar, and keeping the serving areas stocked with linens, tableware, and other supplies. *Fast food and counter workers* take orders and serve food at fast-food counters and in coffee shops; they also may operate the cash register.

*Chefs, cooks and food preparation* workers prepare food in the kitchen. Larger hotels employ chefs and cooks who specialize in the preparation of many different kinds of food. They may have titles such as salad chef, grill chef, or pastry chef. Individual chefs may oversee the day-to-day operations of different kitchens in a hotel, such as a fine-dining full-service restaurant, a casual or counter-service establishment, or banquet operations. Chef positions generally are attained after years of experience and, sometimes, formal training, including apprenticeships. Larger establishments also employ *executive chefs* and *food and beverage directors* who plan menus, purchase food, and supervise kitchen personnel for all of the kitchens in the property. *Food preparation workers* shred lettuce for salads, cut up food for cooking, and perform simple cooking steps under the direction of the chef or head cook. Beginners may advance to more skilled food preparation jobs with experience or specialized culinary training.

Many full-service hotels employ a uniformed staff to assist arriving and departing guests. *Baggage porters and bellhops* carry bags and escort guests to their rooms. *Concierges* arrange special or personal services for guests. They may take messages, arrange for babysitting, make restaurant reservations, provide directions, arrange for or give advice on entertainment and local attractions, and monitor requests for housekeeping and maintenance. *Doorkeepers* help guests into and out of their cars, summon taxis, and carry baggage into the hotel lobby.

Hotels also employ the largest percentage of *gaming services* workers because much of gaming takes place in casino hotels. Some gaming services positions are associated with oversight and direction—supervision, surveillance, and investigation—while others involve working with the games or patrons themselves, by tending the slot machines, handling money, writing and running tickets, dealing cards, and performing related duties.

The industry also employs a large number of *recreation and fitness workers*. At resort hotels and at vacation and recreational camps, recreation workers organize and conduct recreation activities for guests and campers. *Camp counselors* lead and instruct children and teenagers in outdoor-oriented forms of recreation, such as swimming, hiking, horseback riding, and camping. In addition, counselors at vacation and resident camps also provide guidance and supervise daily living and general socialization. Other types of campgrounds may employ trail guides for activities such as hiking, hunting, and fishing.

***Office and administrative support occupations.*** These positions accounted for 19 percent of the jobs in hotels and other accommodations in 2006. Hotel desk clerks, bookkeeping and accounting clerks, and switchboard operators ensure that the front office operates smoothly. *Hotel, motel, and resort desk clerks* process reservations and guests' registrations and checkouts, monitor arrivals and departures, handle complaints, and receive and forward mail. The duties of hotel desk clerks depend on the size of the facility. In smaller lodging places, one clerk or a manager may do everything. In larger hotels, a larger staff divides the duties among several types of clerks.

***Management, business, and financial operations occupations.*** Hotels and other lodging places employ many different types of managers to direct and coordinate the activities of the front office, kitchen, dining room, and other departments, such as housekeeping, accounting, personnel, purchasing, publicity, sales, security and maintenance. *Lodging managers*, typically the general manager and assistant managers, make decisions that affect the general operations of the hotel, including setting room rates, establishing credit policy, and having ultimate responsibility for resolving problems. In smaller establishments, lodging managers also may perform many of the front-office clerical tasks. In the smallest establishments, the owners—sometimes a family team—do all the work necessary to operate the business.

Other managers are responsible for different phases of hotel operations. For example, *food and beverage managers* oversee restaurants, lounges, and catering or banquet operations. *Rooms managers* look after reservations and occupancy levels to ensure proper room assignments and authorize discounts, special rates, or promotions. Large hotels, especially those with conference centers, use an executive committee structure to improve departmental communications and coordinate activities. Other managers who may serve on a hotel's executive committee include *public relations* or *sales managers, human resource directors, executive housekeepers*, and *heads of hotel security*.

***Other occupations.*** Hotels and other accommodations employ a variety of workers found in many other industries. *General maintenance and repair workers* fix leaky faucets, do some painting and carpentry, make sure that heating and air-conditioning equipment works properly, mow lawns, and exterminate pests. The industry also employs cashiers, accountants, personnel workers, and entertainers. As properties acquire and use more sophisticated computer systems, they employ more *computer specialists* to help maintain these systems as well as the hotel's website, and computer connections for guests. Also, many additional workers inside a hotel may work for other companies under contract to the hotel or may provide personal or retail services directly to hotel guests from space rented by the hotel. This group includes guards and security officers, barbers, cosmetologists, fitness trainers and aerobics instructors, valets, gardeners, and parking attendants.

## Training and Advancement

Most large hotel properties employ persons in occupations that require a wide range of skills and experience. Most entry-level jobs require little or no previous training; basic tasks usually can be learned in a short time. Lodging managers and many department heads conversely usually require some formal training or years of hospitality industry experience, or both. All positions though require employees to maintain a customer-service orientation. Yet, almost all workers in the hotel and other accommodations industry undergo some on-the-job training provided under the supervision of an experienced employee or manager to acclimate new employees to any unique characteristics of the property or the local area.

Hotel managers and owners recognize the importance of personal service and attention to guests; so they look for persons with positive personality traits and good communication skills when filling many guest services positions, such as desk clerk and host and hostess positions. Many hotel managers place a greater emphasis on customer service skills while providing specialized training in other skill areas, such as computer technology and software. Vocational courses and apprenticeship programs in food preparation, catering, and hotel and restaurant management, offered through restaurant and lodging associations and trade unions, provide training opportunities. Programs range in length from a few months to several years.

*Service workers.* Most service workers need only a high school diploma or equivalent to get hired, but some can be hired with even less. Some entry-level jobs are filled by students looking for part-time or seasonal work. Most hotels, particularly the chain hotels, have some formal training sessions for new employees that may include video or on-line training. Advancement opportunities for service workers in the hotel industry vary widely. Some workers, such as housekeepers and janitors, generally have few opportunities for advancement. In large properties, some may advance to supervisory positions. Advancement opportunities for chefs and cooks are better than those for most other service occupations. Cooks often advance to chef or to supervisory and management positions, such as executive chef, restaurant manager, or food service manager. Hotel desk clerks sometimes advance to supervisory or managerial front-office positions.

Promotional opportunities often are greatest for those who are willing to take on a new assignment in a different department. Advancement for those who excel at customer service and demonstrate a willingness to learn front-office jobs can serve as a steppingstone to jobs in public relations, advertising, sales, and management.

*Management, business, and financial operations occupations.* Many hotels fill first-level manager positions by promoting staff from within—particularly those with good communication skills, a solid educational background, tact, loyalty, and a capacity to endure hard work and long hours. People with these qualities still advance to manager jobs but, more recently, lodging chains have primarily been hiring persons with 4-year college degrees in the liberal arts or other fields and starting them in assistant manager or management trainee positions. Bachelor's and Master's degree programs in hotel, restaurant, and hospitality management provide the strongest background for a career as a hotel manager, with nearly 150 colleges and universities offering such programs. Graduates of these programs are highly sought by employers in this industry, because of their familiarity with technical issues and their ability to learn related skills quickly. Eventually, they may advance to a top management position in a hotel or a corporate management position in a large chain operation.

Upper management positions, such as general manager, food service manager, or sales manager, generally require considerable formal training and job experience. Some department managers, executive housekeepers, and executive chefs, generally require some specialized training and extensive on-the-job experience. To advance to positions with more responsibilities, lodging managers frequently change employers or relocate within a chain to a property in another area.

*Office and administrative support occupations.* For office and administrative support workers, advancement opportunities in the hotel industry vary widely. These occupations offer excellent entry-level job prospects and can serve as a steppingstone to jobs in hospitality, public relations, advertising, sales, and management.

## Outlook

The hotels and other accommodations industry is expected to provide many new jobs over the 2006-16 period. New hotel construction and steady strength in the business and international travel segments will create job opportunities in an array of occupations in this industry.

*Employment change.* Wage and salary employment in hotels and other accommodations is expected to increase by 14 percent, compared with 11 percent growth projected for all industries combined. Travel and tourism, having rebounded since the recession following 9/11, is expected to continue growing and result in a greater need for transient rooms. All segments of the hotel market are expected to see increases in the number of rooms, but the greatest number of rooms coming on line will be in limited service hotels that do not provide food service. Many of these newer hotels are being built in the suburbs where a growing population is increasingly based and a base of business establishments is being developed.

Employment outlook varies somewhat by service class of hotel and occupation. Growth of full-service hotels, casino hotels, and the small, but burgeoning, luxury hotel market that specializes in personal service will cause employment of lodging managers to grow much faster than the average. The accelerating trend toward chain-affiliated hotels should provide managers with opportunities for advancement into general manager positions, manager jobs at larger and busier properties, and corporate administrative jobs. Opportunities should be more limited for self-employed managers or owners of small lodging places, such as bed-and-breakfast inns, because of the competition from long-established chains as they move into new markets once friendly to the quainter properties. Job opportunities at outdoor recreation and RV parks should grow as RVs and driving vacations gain popularity in the United States. Also, gaming services and gaming manager occupations should grow as more casino hotels are built.

Employment of hotel, motel, and resort desk clerks is expected to grow faster than some other occupations in the industry in part because the growing numbers of limited-service hotels still require desk clerks. Employment of waiters and waitresses will grow more slowly—reflecting the increasing number of hotels and other accommodations that either do not offer full-service restaurants or contract them out to other food service establishments.

*Job prospects.* Although most of the hotels opening over the next decade will be limited service hotels, most of the job openings will arise in full-service hotels, including convention, casino, and resort hotels, because they employ the most workers. Limited-service properties do not operate restaurants, or lounges; therefore, these establishments offer a narrower range of employment opportunities; however, the streamlined organizational structure offers a faster route to the general manager level for those more interested in running or owning their own hotel. Job opportunities will be concentrated in the largest hotel occupations, such as building cleaning workers and hotel, motel, and resort desk clerks. These workers are found in all types of hotels and accommodations, from the limited service economy hotels to posh casino hotels. They also are important to the growing luxury hotel segment that emphasizes personal service.

Some occupations in this industry have relatively high numbers of workers who leave their jobs and must be replaced. Many young people and those looking only for seasonal or part-time work, and not a career, take food service and clerical jobs that require little or no previous training. To attract and retain workers, the hotel and other accommodations industry is placing more emphasis on training and retaining employees. Therefore, job opportunities in this industry should be plentiful for first-time jobseekers and people with limited skills.

## Earnings

*Industry earnings.* Earnings in hotels and other accommodations generally are much lower than the average for all industries. In 2006, average earnings for all nonsupervisory workers in this industry were $353 a week, compared with $533 a week, for workers throughout private industry. Many workers in this industry earn the Federal minimum wage of $5.85 an hour or less, if tips are included as a substantial part of earnings. Workers in these lower paying occupations will see their future earnings increase on a phased-in basis to $7.25 per hour by 2009. Some States have laws that establish a higher minimum wage.

Food and beverage service workers, as well as hosts and hostesses, maids and housekeeping cleaners, concierges, and baggage porters and bellhops, derive their earnings from a combination of hourly earnings and customer tips. Waiters and waitresses often derive the majority of their earnings from tips, which vary greatly depending on menu prices and the volume of customers served. Many employers also provide free meals and furnish uniforms. Food service personnel may receive extra pay for working at banquets and on other special occasions. In general, workers with the greatest skills, such as restaurant cooks, have the highest earnings, and workers who receive tips have the lowest. Earnings in the largest occupations in hotels and other lodging places appear in table 2.

Salaries of lodging managers are dependent upon the size and sales volume of the establishment and their specific duties and responsibilities. Managers may earn bonuses ranging up to 50 percent of their basic salary. In addition, they may be furnished with meals, parking, laundry, and other services, and sometimes on-site lodging for themselves and their families. Some hotels offer profit-sharing plans, tuition reimbursement, and other benefits to their employees.

*Benefits and union membership.* About 10 percent of the workers in hotels and other accommodations are union members or are covered by union contracts, compared with 13 percent of workers in all industries combined.

## Sources of Additional Information

For information on hospitality careers and a directory of academic programs in hospitality management, write to:
➤ International Council on Hotel, Restaurant, and Institutional Education, 2810 North Parham Rd., Suite 230, Richmond, VA 23294. Internet: http://www.chrie.org
➤ American Hotel and Lodging Association, 1201 New York Ave. NW, Suite 600, Washington, DC 20005-3931.

General information on food and beverage service jobs is available from:
➤ National Restaurant Association, 1200 17th St. NW., Washington, DC 20036-3097. Internet: **http://www.restaurant.org**

For information on the American Culinary Federation's apprenticeship and certification programs for chefs, write to:
➤ American Culinary Federation, 180 Center Place Way, St. Augustine, FL 32095. Internet: **http://www.acfchefs.org**

Detailed information on the following hotels and other accommodations occupations may be found in the 2008-09 *Occupational Outlook Handbook*:
• Building cleaning workers
• Chefs, cooks, and other food preparation workers
• Food and beverage serving and related workers
• Food service managers
• Gaming cage workers
• Gaming services occupations
• Hotel, motel, and resort desk clerks
• Lodging managers
• Recreation and fitness workers
• Security guards and gaming surveillance officers

**Table 2. Median hourly earnings of the largest occupations in hotels and other accommodations, May 2006**

| Occupation | Accommodations | All industries |
|---|---|---|
| Maintenance and repair workers, general | $11.63 | $15.34 |
| Cooks, restaurant | 11.24 | 9.78 |
| Janitors and cleaners, except maids and housekeeping cleaners | 9.66 | 9.58 |
| Hotel, motel, and resort desk clerks | 8.84 | 8.88 |
| Bartenders | 8.76 | 7.86 |
| Food servers, nonrestaurant | 8.59 | 8.70 |
| Dining room and cafeteria attendants and bartender helpers | 8.14 | 7.36 |
| Maids and housekeeping cleaners | 8.07 | 8.45 |
| Waiters and waitresses | 7.81 | 7.14 |
| Gaming dealers | 6.60 | 7.08 |

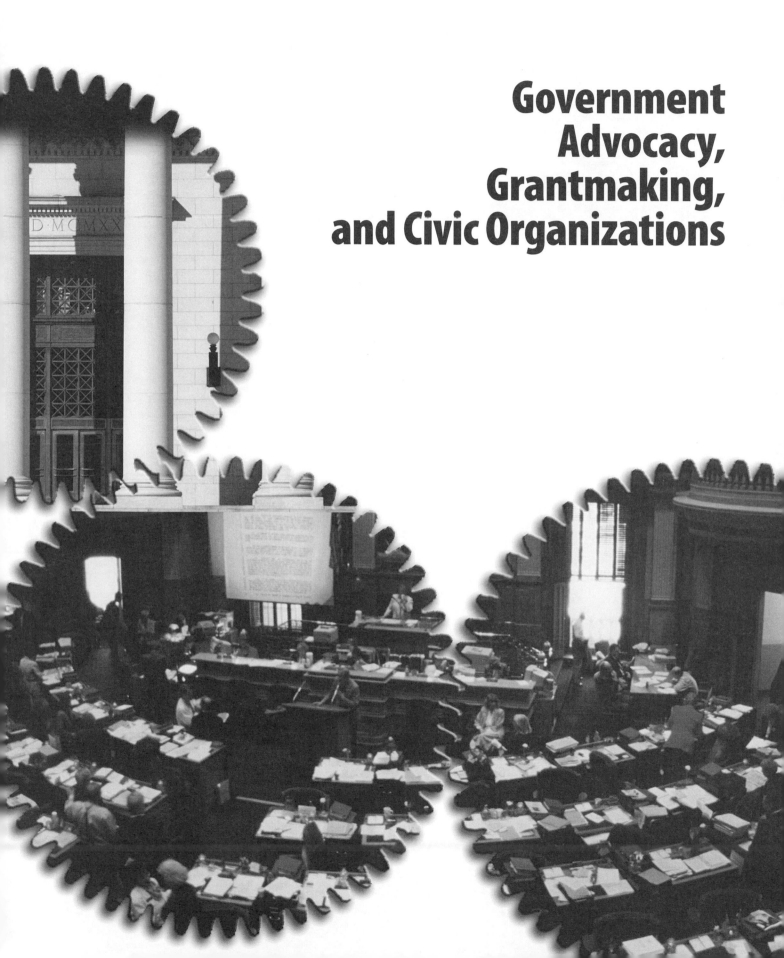

# Government Advocacy, Grantmaking, and Civic Organizations

# Advocacy, Grantmaking, and Civic Organizations

**(NAICS 8132, 8133, 8134, 8139)**

## SIGNIFICANT POINTS

- Advocacy, grantmaking, and civic organizations had 1.2 million wage and salary jobs in 2006, with 74 percent in civic, social, professional and similar organizations.

- Employers need individuals with strong communication and fundraising skills, because organizations must constantly mobilize public support for their activities.

- Social and demographic shifts should increase demand for services and spur job growth.

- A large number of job openings should result from employment growth and turnover, partially due to relatively low wages.

## Nature of the Industry

*Goods and services.* Advocacy, grantmaking, and civic organizations in the United States are distinct and, at some point, affect everyone's life. In every State these types of organizations are working to better their communities by directly addressing issues of public concern through service, independent action, or civic engagement. These organizations span the political spectrum of ideas and encompass every aspect of human endeavor, from symphonies to little leagues, and from homeless shelters and day care centers to natural resource conservation advocates. These organizations are collectively called "nonprofits," a name that is used to describe institutions and organizations that are neither government nor business. Other names often used include the not-for-profit sector, the third sector, the independent sector, the philanthropic sector, the voluntary sector, or the social sector. Outside the United States, these organizations often are called nongovernmental organizations (NGOs) or civil society organizations.

These other names emphasize the characteristics that distinguish advocacy, grantmaking, and civic organizations from businesses and government. Unlike businesses, these organizations do not exist to make money for owners or investors, but that doesn't mean that they cannot charge fees or sell products that generate revenue, or that revenue must not exceed expenses. Instead, these groups are dedicated to a specific mission that enhances the social fabric of society. Unlike government, these organizations are not able to mandate changes through legislation or regulations enforceable by law. Instead, they work toward the mission of their organization by relying on a small group of paid staff and voluntary service and financial support by large numbers of their members or the public. This industry includes four main segments: business, professional, labor, political, and similar organizations; civic and social organizations; social advocacy organizations; and grantmaking and giving services. (Religious organizations, which also have legal status as nonprofits, are not included this section of the *Career Guide*.)

*Industry organization.* *Business, professional, labor, political, and similar organizations* comprised about one-half of the advocacy, grantmaking, and civic organizations industry establishments in 2006 (table 1). Business associations are primarily engaged in promoting the business interests of their members. They include organizations such as chambers of commerce, real estate

boards, and manufacturers' and trade associations. They may conduct research on new products and services; develop market statistics; sponsor quality and certification standards; lobby public officials; or publish newsletters, books, or periodicals for distribution to their members. Professional organizations seek to advance the interests of their members and their profession as a whole. Examples of professional associations are health professional and bar associations. Labor organizations promote the interests of the labor union members they represent by negotiating improvement in wages, benefits, and working conditions. They persuade workers to become members of a union and then seek to win the right to represent them in collective bargaining with their employer. Political organizations promote the interests of national, State, or local political parties and their candidates for elected public positions. Included are political groups organized to raise funds for a political party or individual candidates, such as political action committees (PACs). A variety of other similar organizations also are included in this segment of the advocacy, grantmaking, and civic organizations industry. They include athletic associations that regulate or administer various sports leagues, conferences, or even entire sports at the amateur or professional level. Also included in this segment are condominium and homeowners' associations, property owners' associations, and tenant associations.

More than one-fourth of the establishments in the advocacy, grantmaking, and civic organizations industry are associated with *civic and social organizations* engaged in promoting the civic and social interests of their members. These organizations include alumni associations, automobile clubs, booster clubs, youth scouting organizations, and parent-teacher associations. This segment also includes social clubs, fraternal lodges, ethnic associations, and veterans' membership organizations, some of which may operate bars and restaurants for their members.

*Social advocacy organizations*, which comprise 14 percent of advocacy, grantmaking, and civic organization establishments, promote a particular cause or work for the realization of a specific social or political goal to benefit either a broad segment of the population or a specific constituency. They often solicit contributions and offer memberships to support their activities. There are three types of social advocacy organizations: human rights organizations; environment, conservation, and wildlife organizations; and all other social advocacy organizations. Human rights organizations address issues, such as protecting and promoting the broad constitutional rights and civil liberties of individuals and those suffering from neglect, abuse, or exploitation. They also may promote the interests of specific groups, such as children, women, senior citizens, or persons with disabilities; work to improve relations between racial, ethnic, and cultural groups; or promote voter education and registration. Environment, conservation, and wildlife organizations promote the preservation and protection of the environment and wildlife. They address issues such as clean air and water; conserving and developing natural resources, including land, plant, water, and energy resources; and protecting and preserving wildlife and endangered species. Other social advocacy organizations address issues such as peace and international understanding; organize and encourage community action; or advance social causes, such as firearms safety, drunk driving prevention, and drug abuse awareness.

*Grantmaking and giving services* comprised about 10 percent of advocacy, grantmaking, and civic organizations establishments and include grantmaking foundations, voluntary health organizations, and establishments primarily engaged in raising funds for a wide range of social welfare activities, such as health, educational, scientific, and cultural activities. Grantmaking foundations, also called charitable trusts, award grants from trust funds based on a competitive selection process or on the preferences of the foundation managers and grantors; some fund a single entity, such as a museum or university. There are two types of grantmaking foundations: private foundations and public foundations. Most of the funds of a private foundation come from one source—an individual, a family, or a corporation. Public foundations, in contrast, normally receive their funds from multiple sources, which may include private foundations, individuals, government agencies, and fees for services. Moreover, public foundations must continue to seek money from diverse sources in order to retain their public status. Voluntary health organizations are primarily engaged in raising funds for health-related research, such as the development of new treatments for diseases like cancer or heart disease, disease awareness and prevention, or health education.

*Recent developments.* Advocacy, grantmaking, and civic organizations receive the revenue that makes possible their operations from a variety of sources. Some organizations receive most of their funds from private contributions. Many organizations have experienced an increase in donors, stemming partially from more favorable treatment of donations by tax laws. Also, estates of many members of the Depression generation (those born during the 1920s and 1930s) have donated large sums to these organizations. However, many advocacy, grantmaking, and civic organizations—such as nonprofit hospitals and universities—generate revenue by charging fees for the services they provide, earning interest on investments, or producing and selling goods.

The formation of joint ventures or partnerships between advocacy, grantmaking, and civic organizations and corporations also has risen. The last few years also have seen a rise in three-sector partnerships formed between an advocacy, grantmaking, and civic organization, a corporation, and a government agency. These partnerships have ensured a steady flow of income to the advocacy, grantmaking, and civic organizations industry and increased public awareness of these organizations and the importance of their missions. On the corporate side, partnerships help sell corporate products, enhance the civic image of the corporation, and allow corporations to provide additional revenue to advocacy, grantmaking, and civic organizations, which have traditionally relied on simple donations.

New information technology also is increasing the capacity of advocacy, grantmaking, and civic organizations to advocate their causes and to raise funds. Interactive Web sites, e-mail and electronic philanthropy, and electronically generated databases have transformed the way these organizations communicate with the public, grantmakers, and donors. These advancements have reduced the costs of gathering constituents and connecting to policymakers and allies. These technological advancements also have changed the way charitable organizations interact with government and its agencies as they continue to use "e-services" in order to remain efficient. For advocacy, grantmaking, and civic organizations, these advances provide an opportunity to reduce their paperwork, increase their efficiency in responding to regulatory demands, and improve their organizational capabilities. The Internet will continue to change the way these organizations collect and report data, and lead to greater consolidation of Federal and State regulatory demands on the industry.

## Working Conditions

*Hours.* In 2006, about three-fourths of the workers in advocacy, grantmaking, and civic organizations worked full time; the remainder worked part-time or variable schedules.

*Work Environment.* Most workers spend the majority of their time in offices functioning in a team environment, often working with volunteers. The work environment may differ depending on the size of the organization. For those who work in small organizations, the equipment is sometimes outdated and their workspace cramped. But, in larger, well-funded organizations, conditions are very similar to those in most business offices. The work environment generally is positive—workers know that their work helps people and improves their communities.

Top executives and workers responsible for fundraising may travel frequently to meet with supporters and potential donors, often in evenings and on weekends. Fundraising can be highly stressful because the financial health of the organization depends on being successful. Workers employed in the delivery of social services also work in very stressful environments because many of their clients are struggling with a wide range of problems related to child care, child welfare, juvenile justice, addiction, health, unemployment, and inadequate workforce skills.

Work in the advocacy, grantmaking, and civic organizations industry is rarely hazardous. In 2006, the industry had only 2.7 injuries and illnesses per 100 full-time workers, compared with an average of 4.4 throughout private industry.

## Employment

Advocacy, grantmaking, and civic organizations had 1.2 million wage and salary jobs in 2006. About 74 percent of them were

**Table 1. Percent distribution of employment and establishments in advocacy, grantmaking, and civic organizations by detailed industry sector, 2006**

| Industry segment | Employment | Establishments |
|---|---|---|
| Total | 100.0 | 100.0 |
| Business, professional, labor, political, and similar organizations | 38.0 | 50.7 |
| Civic and social organizations | 36.7 | 25.1 |
| Social advocacy organizations | 14.8 | 13.9 |
| Grantmaking and giving services | 10.5 | 10.3 |

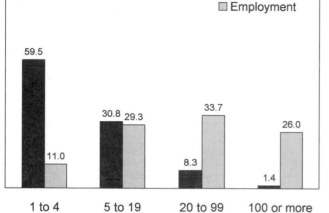

**About 9 out of 10 advocacy, grantmaking, and civic organizations establishments employ fewer than 20 employees.**

Percent

- ■ Establishments
- ☐ Employment

59.5

30.8  29.3

33.7

26.0

11.0

8.3

1.4

| 1 to 4 | 5 to 19 | 20 to 99 | 100 or more |

Number of workers employed by establishment, March 2006

in civic and social organizations or professional and similar organizations.

Advocacy, grantmaking, and civic organizations establishments are found throughout the nation, but the greatest numbers of jobs are found in California and New York, the States with the greatest population. Most establishments in this industry are small (chart). The vast majority of jobs are in establishments that employ fewer than 5 people.

## Occupations in the Industry

Advocacy, grantmaking, and civic organizations employ many different types of workers, but 75 percent of the jobs are in management, business, and financial occupations; service occupations; or office and administrative support occupations (table 2).

*Management, business, and financial occupations.* Chief executives in advocacy, grantmaking, and civic organizations formulate policies and direct daily operations. In publicly held and nonprofit corporations, the board of directors ultimately is accountable for the success or failure of the enterprise, and the chief executive officer reports to the board. Chief executives perform a variety of duties depending the size of their association and how it is organized. In a larger association, they may direct a number of operations specialty managers, each of whom is responsible for part of the organization's operations. In a small association, executives are likely to direct many or all of these functions themselves and be required to wear many hats at one time. The most common type of operations specialty managers in advocacy, grantmaking, and civic organizations is *social and community service managers,* who plan, organize, or coordinate the activities of a social service program or community outreach organization. They oversee the program or organization's budget and polices regarding participant involvement, program requirements, and benefits. Work may involve directing social workers, counselors, or probation officers. Larger organizations employ a variety of business and financial operations specialists. For example, *accountants and auditors* handle the financial affairs of an association. They also prepare financial statements,

**Table 2. Employment of wage and salary workers in advocacy, grantmaking, and civic organizations by occupation, 2006 and projected change, 2006-2016.**
(Employment in thousands)

| Occupation | Employment, 2006 | | Percent change, 2006-16 |
|---|---|---|---|
| | Number | Percent | |
| **All occupations** | 1,234 | 100.0 | 12.8 |
| **Management, business, and financial occupations** | 281 | 22.8 | 11.8 |
| Top executives | 43 | 3.5 | 2.9 |
| Public relations managers | 8 | 0.7 | 16.5 |
| Property, real estate, and community association managers | 6 | 0.5 | 20.2 |
| Social and community service managers | 17 | 1.4 | 14.7 |
| Human resources, training, and labor relations specialists | 65 | 5.3 | 6.3 |
| Meeting and convention planners | 11 | 0.9 | 18.5 |
| Accountants and auditors | 17 | 1.4 | 15.2 |
| **Professional and related occupations** | 233 | 18.9 | 15.7 |
| Computer specialists | 21 | 1.7 | 23.5 |
| Counselors | 5 | 0.4 | 14.6 |
| Social workers | 20 | 1.6 | 14.3 |
| Health educators | 5 | 0.4 | 31.8 |
| Social and human service assistants | 17 | 1.3 | 5.1 |
| Lawyers | 5 | 0.4 | 16.2 |
| Preschool teachers, except special education | 15 | 1.2 | 12.2 |
| Self-enrichment education teachers | 9 | 0.7 | 12.1 |
| Teacher assistants | 14 | 1.1 | 12.8 |
| Coaches and scouts | 9 | 0.7 | 12.0 |
| Public relations specialists | 40 | 3.2 | 17.1 |
| Writers and editors | 12 | 1.0 | 12.0 |
| **Service occupations** | 356 | 28.8 | 13.3 |
| Security guards | 18 | 1.5 | 18.3 |
| Lifeguards, ski patrol, and other recreational protective service workers | 25 | 2.0 | 11.7 |
| Cooks and food preparation workers | 16 | 1.3 | 11.8 |
| Bartenders | 46 | 3.8 | 10.7 |
| Waiters and waitresses | 16 | 1.3 | 11.4 |
| Janitors and cleaners, except maids and housekeeping cleaners | 26 | 2.1 | 16.1 |
| Landscaping and groundskeeping workers | 14 | 1.1 | 19.6 |
| Nonfarm animal caretakers | 9 | 0.7 | 14.7 |
| Amusement and recreation attendants | 9 | 0.8 | 12.9 |
| Child care workers | 37 | 3.0 | 21.0 |
| Personal and home care aides | 10 | 0.8 | 14.6 |
| Fitness trainers and aerobics instructors | 34 | 2.8 | 10.9 |
| Recreation workers | 36 | 2.9 | 6.4 |
| **Sales and related occupations** | 34 | 2.8 | 12.9 |
| **Office and administrative support occupations** | 288 | 23.4 | 10.4 |
| Bookkeeping, accounting, and auditing clerks | 34 | 2.7 | 12.8 |
| Customer service representatives | 26 | 2.1 | 26.5 |
| Receptionists and information clerks | 24 | 1.9 | 14.1 |
| Executive secretaries and administrative assistants | 48 | 3.9 | 15.3 |
| Secretaries, except legal, medical, and executive | 47 | 3.8 | 0.7 |
| Office clerks, general | 56 | 4.5 | 12.6 |
| **Installation, maintenance, and repair occupations** | 26 | 2.1 | 18.4 |
| Maintenance and repair workers, general | 24 | 1.9 | 18.4 |

Note: Columns may not add to totals due to omission of occupations with small employment

records, and reports. Accountants also contribute to fundraising efforts by figuring the costs of new programs and including those estimates in grant proposals. Larger organizations also may have *human resources, training, and labor relations specialists.*

*Professional and related occupations.* Among professional specialty occupations that play an important role in advocacy, grantmaking, and civic organizations, *public relations specialists* handle functions such as media, community, consumer, and governmental relations; political campaigns; interest-group representation; conflict mediation; or employee and investor relations. They prepare press releases and contact people in the media who might print or broadcast their material. Many public relations specialists go on to specialize in fundraising, sometimes having the title director of development. Fundraisers find the money and other gifts needed to keep an organizations operations operating by asking for large gifts from individual donors, soliciting bequests, hosting special events, applying for grants, and launching phone and letter appeals. In small organizations, the director of development does all these things; in large ones, fundraisers specialize. *Social and human service assistants* provide direct and indirect client services to ensure that individuals in their care reach their maximum level of functioning. They assess clients' needs, establish their eligibility for benefits, and help them obtain services such as food stamps, Medicaid, or welfare.

Many advocacy, grantmaking, and civic organizations play an important role in education. *Self-enrichment education teachers* teach courses that students take for pleasure or personal enrichment; these classes usually are not intended to lead to a particular degree or vocation. Self-enrichment teachers may instruct children or adults in a wide variety of areas, such as cooking, dancing, creative writing, photography, or personal finance. If working for an association, for example, educators will be expected to possess strong management skills, exceptional people skills, event planning knowledge, extensive marketing talents, and an ability to work effectively with volunteers. *Teacher assistants* provide instructional and clerical support for classroom teachers, allowing teachers more time for lesson planning and teaching.

*Service occupations.* Among service occupations, *recreation workers* and *fitness trainers and aerobics instructors* plan, organize, and direct leisure and athletic activities, such as aerobics, arts and crafts, the performing arts, camping, and sports. Many work at playgrounds and recreation areas, community centers, health clubs, and fitness centers run by advocacy, grantmaking, and civic organizations. *Waiters and waitresses* take customers' orders, serve food and beverages, prepare itemized checks, and sometimes accept payment at food service facilities. *Janitors and cleaners* clean floors, shampoo rugs, wash walls and glass, and remove rubbish. They may fix leaky faucets, empty trash cans, do painting and carpentry, replenish bathroom supplies, mow lawns, and see that heating and air-conditioning equipment works properly. While janitors typically perform a range of duties, cleaners tend to work for organizations that specialize in one type of cleaning activity, such as washing windows. *Security guards* patrol and inspect property to protect against fire, theft, vandalism, terrorism, and illegal activity. They protect their employer's investment, enforce laws on the property, and deter criminal activity or other problems. Security guards may be required to write comprehensive reports outlining their observations and activities during their assigned shift. They also may interview witnesses or victims, prepare case reports, and testify in court.

*Office and administrative support occupations.* The larger the organization, the more administrative support occupations it needs. Advocacy, grantmaking, and civic organizations also employ *bookkeeping, accounting, and auditing clerks, receptionists and information clerks, executive secretaries and administrative assistants, office clerks,* and *first-line supervisors/managers of office and administrative support workers* commonly found in most business organizations.

*Installation, maintenance, and repair occupations.* Many advocacy, grantmaking, and civic organizations have buildings and other facilities, vehicles, and equipment that must be kept in good working order. *Maintenance and repair workers* maintain heating, air-conditioning, and ventilation systems; service and repair vehicles and outdoor power equipment; and restore residential facilities, including senior center and low income housing units.

## Training and Advancement

The types of jobs and skills required for advocacy, grantmaking, and civic organizations vary with the type and size of the organization. But all organizations need individuals with strong communication and fundraising skills, because they must constantly mobilize public support for their activities. Creativity and initiative are important as many workers are responsible for a wide range of activities, such as creating new events designed to communicate and sell an organizations goals and objectives. Basic knowledge about accounting, finance, management, information systems, advertising, and marketing provide an important advantage for those trying to enter the advocacy, grantmaking, and civic organizations industry. In some cases, a second language may be needed for jobs that involve international activities. The highly competitive industry also needs individuals who have adequate technical skills to efficiently operate and maintain their computer systems.

There are many ways that a person can enter the advocacy, grantmaking, and civic organizations industry. One way to prepare for a job is to gain experience as a volunteer. Volunteering allows a person to try out an organization to see if he or she likes it, to make good contacts in the industry, and to demonstrate a commitment to a cause. Volunteer work can be found through career and guidance counselors at high schools and colleges, as they often maintain a database of opportunities. County libraries and governments often have lists of opportunities as well. Many local schools and community groups also can identify organizations that need volunteers. The Internet is another good way to find volunteer openings. Paid work also can prepare job seekers for advocacy, grantmaking, and civic organizations. Many professionals in the industry began their careers in for-profit business. Many organizations need marketing or technological expertise and often hire someone from the for-profit sector-especially if that person has volunteer experience.

As of 2006, more than 250 colleges and universities offered courses on the management of nonprofit organizations. In addition, about 70 programs offered noncredit courses in fundraising and nonprofit management and more than 50 programs offered continuing education courses. About 119 schools offered at least one course for undergraduate credit and more than 90 were affiliated with American Humanics (an alliance of colleges, universities and nonprofit organizations preparing undergraduates for careers with youth and human service agencies).

In 2006, there were more than 90 master's degree programs, usually in business administration or in public administration, with a focus on nonprofit or philanthropic studies. About 160 colleges and universities had at least one course related to management of nonprofits within a graduate department. Of these programs, more than 110 offered a graduate degree with a concentration in the management of nonprofit organizations and about 40 offered one or two graduate courses, usually in financial management and generic nonprofit management.

*Management, business, and financial occupations.* The formal education and experience of chief executives or executive directors varies as widely as the nature of their responsibilities. There are many ways to prepare for the job of running an advocacy, grantmaking, and civic organization. Most paid executive directors in large organizations have graduate degrees, often in business or public administration, some specifically in nonprofit management. Some executive directors start their careers in other positions, such as fundraiser or communications director. Others start on the program side of an organization, offering services directly to the public. They might be teachers, health care workers, ecologists, or another type of professional. Accountants and auditors need a good understanding of business computer systems and some hands-on knowledge of accounting software. An accounting or finance degree with some management course work or a business administration degree with some accounting course work is a good background to have. A master of business administration or other advanced degree may be desirable for more senior positions. The certified nonprofit accounting professional (CNAP) accreditation also provides the additional credibility needed in some larger organizations. Social community service managers need a bachelor's degree. They must possess knowledge of principles and procedures for personnel recruitment, selection, training, compensation and benefits, labor relations and negotiation, and personnel information systems.

*Professional and related occupations.* A bachelor's degree usually is not required to work as a social and human service assistant. However, employers increasingly seek individuals with relevant work experience or education beyond high school. Certificates or associate degrees in subjects such as social work, human services, gerontology, or one of the social or behavioral sciences meet most employers' requirements. Employers try to select applicants who have effective communication skills, a strong sense of responsibility, and the ability to manage time effectively. Employers usually provide on-the-job training, often in the form of seminars and workshops, to prepare employees for particular position. Formal education almost always is necessary for advancement. In general, advancement requires a bachelor's or master's degree in human services, counseling, rehabilitation, social work, or a related field. There are no defined standards for entry into a public relations career. A college degree combined with public relations experience, usually gained through an internship, is considered excellent preparation for public relations work. People who choose public relations as a career need an outgoing personality, self-confidence, an understanding of human psychology, and an enthusiasm for motivating people. Many public relations specialists advance to become directors of development or fundraisers. Directors of development find the money and other gifts needed to keep the organizations operations thriving. For self-enrichment teachers working in the advocacy, grantmaking, and civic organizations industry, a college degree that encompasses education or human resources courses and general business courses is good preparation. Opportunities for advancement as a self-enrichment teacher vary from State to

State and program to program. They may advance to administrative positions, or experienced self-enrichment teachers may mentor new instructors and volunteers. Educational requirements for teacher assistants vary by State or school district and range from a high school diploma to some college training, although employers increasingly prefer applicants with some college training. Teacher assistants must have good writing skills and be able to communicate effectively with students and teachers. Advancement for teacher assistants—usually in the form of higher earnings or increased responsibility—comes primarily with experience or additional education.

*Office and administrative support occupations.* Office and administrative support occupations in the advocacy, grantmaking, and civic organizations industry generally require a high school diploma or its equivalent. However, many employers prefer those who have familiarity or experience with computers. Good interpersonal skills also are becoming increasingly important to employers. Some employers may require previous office or business experience. Those who exhibit strong communication, interpersonal, and analytical skills may be promoted to supervisory positions. Advancement to professional occupations within an organization normally requires additional formal education, such as a college degree. While most workers receive on-the-job training, executive secretaries and administrative assistants acquire skills in various ways. Training ranges from high school vocational education programs that teach office skills and keyboarding to 1-year and 2-year programs in office administration offered by business schools, vocational-technical institutes, and community colleges.

*Service occupations.* Some service workers in the advocacy, grantmaking, and civic organizations industry, such as waiters and waitresses and janitors, don't require any formal education and are trained on the job. Opportunities for advancement for waiters and waitresses are limited, but those workers who excel at their work can become food service managers. Food service managers supervise the work of cooks; they plan meals and oversee food safety. Educational requirements for recreation and fitness workers range from a high school diploma to a graduate degree for some administrative positions in large public recreation systems. Recreation and fitness workers need managerial skills in order to advance to supervisory or managerial positions. College courses in management, business administration, accounting, and personnel management are helpful for advancement to supervisory or managerial jobs. Most States require that security guards be licensed. Some security guards may advance to supervisor or security manager positions. Guards with management skills may open their own contract security guard agencies.

## Outlook

Turnover and employment growth should result in a large number of job openings.

*Employment change.* Wage and salary jobs in advocacy, grantmaking, and civic organizations are projected to increase 13 percent over the 2006-16 period, compared to 11 percent growth projected for all industries combined (table 3).

Social and demographic shifts will continue to increase the demand for services offered by advocacy, grantmaking, and civic organizations and spur job growth. For example, rapid growth of the elderly population will increase the demand for home health and nursing home care. Other demographic shifts include the

**Table 3. Employment in advocacy, grantmaking, and civic organizations by industry segment, 2006 and projected change, 2006-1**
(Employment in thousands)

| Industry segment | 2006 Employment | 2006-16 Percent change |
|---|---|---|
| **Advocacy, grantmaking, and civic organizations, total** .............. | 1,234 | 12.8 |
| Grantmaking and giving services .............. | 142 | 14.4 |
| Social advocacy organizations .................. | 178 | 13.9 |
| Civic and social organizations ................... | 413 | 10.7 |
| Business, professional, labor, political, and similar organizations......................... | 500 | 13.6 |

growing numbers of immigrants and refugees; a high divorce rate creating more single parent households; more out-of-wedlock births; and greater ethnic and cultural diversity. These shifts will increase the demand for many services such as child day care, home health and nursing home care, family counseling, foster care, relocation assistance, and substance abuse treatment and prevention.

State and local governments usually are expected to fulfill new and growing social service roles, but many lack the resources to meet the rising demands. As a result, governments will increasingly turn to advocacy, grantmaking, and civic organizations, utilizing their experience at offering efficient and effective social services. In other cases, governments will form joint ventures or partnerships with these organizations to operate services more effectively. Governments also are expected to contract out some services, which will continue to be a major source of employment growth in the advocacy, grantmaking, and civic organizations industry.

Projected growth for some occupations in advocacy, grantmaking, and civic organizations differs from the 13 percent average growth projected for the industry as a whole (table 2). For example, employment of social and human service assistants is expected to grow faster than the industry because of the increased need for the services that these workers provide to the public. Employment of bookkeeping, accounting, and auditing clerks, on the other hand, is expected to grow more slowly than the industry because of the increasing use of office automation.

***Job prospects.*** A large number of job openings should result from employment growth and turnover, partially due to the industry's relatively low wages, as workers retire or leave the industry for other reasons.

## Earnings

***Industry earnings.*** Earnings of wage and salary workers in advocacy, grantmaking, and civic organizations averaged $15.81

**Table 4. Average earnings of production or nonsupervisory workers in advocacy, grantmaking, and civic organizations by industry segment, 2006**

| Industry segment | Weekly | Hourly |
|---|---|---|
| **Total, private industry**........................ | $568 | $16.76 |
| **Nonprofit organizations** ...................... | 471 | 15.81 |
| Business, professional, labor, political, and similar organizations............................ | 637 | 19.65 |
| Civic and social organizations ............................ | 232 | 11.38 |
| Social advocacy organizations ........................ | 470 | 14.52 |
| Grantmaking and giving services ........................ | 620 | 19.94 |

an hour, compared with $16.76 per hour for all workers in private industry in 2006 (table 4). The lower earnings reflect the large proportion of entry-level, part-time jobs. Weekly earnings among civic and social organizations were significantly lower than average, $232, compared with $568 for all workers in private industry in 2006.

Median hourly earnings of the occupations in advocacy, grantmaking, and civic organizations with the highest employment appear in table 5.

Directors and upper-level managers usually receive a salary. Entry-level salaries vary based on education, experience, and the size, budget, and geographic location of the association. The Nonprofit Times Annual Salary Survey reported the following average total compensation in 2006:

| | |
|---|---|
| Executive director ..................................................... | $149,427 |
| Chief financial officer ................................................ | 97,248 |
| Chief of direct marketing............................................ | 89,032 |
| Program director ........................................................ | 80,228 |
| Development director................................................... | 76,770 |
| Planned giving officer and major gifts officer ........................... | 73,325 |
| Director of human resources ...................................... | 66,755 |
| Webmaster ................................................................ | 57,085 |
| Director of volunteers................................................. | 41,894 |

***Benefits and union membership.*** Fringe benefits vary by region, sector, organization budget, geographic scope, number of employees, and type of organization. Most organizations appear to provide long-term disability, extended health care, dental, prescription drug, and life insurance coverage to all employees. Vision care has become a common benefit in the industry. Most employers pay all of their employees' insurance benefit premiums, but none of the coverage for their dependents. Only some organizations allow their employees to purchase additional life insurance beyond the basic benefit amount provided, but most hold the line at somewhat less than one year's salary, with one and two years' salary being common as well.

Many advocacy, grantmaking, and civic organizations provide an automobile or car allowance to their senior managers, with most of them paying the entire cost for chief executive officers. Publication subscriptions and professional society and association memberships are generally provided for managers at all levels, and the overwhelming practice is to pay the entire registration fee to attend conferences, as well as associated travel, room, and meal expenses for the chief executive and other administrative and professional employees. Organizations rarely pay for club/social membership dues, first-class air travel, or travel expense for spouses. Most employers allow staff education leave without pay and contribute to tuition expenses for training considered relevant to the employee's job or the organization's current mission. Some workers have access to a sabbatical leave program.

About 11 percent of workers in the advocacy, grantmaking, and civic organizations industry were union members or were covered by a union contract in 2006, less than the 13 percent rate throughout all industries.

## Sources of Additional Information

For more information about career opportunities in advocacy, grantmaking, and civic organizations, contact:
➤ American Society of Associate Executives, 1575 I St. NW., Washington, DC 20005. Internet: **http://www.asaenet.org**

**Table 5. Median hourly earnings of the largest occupations in advocacy, grantmaking, and civic organizations, May 2006**

| Occupation | Grantmaking and giving services | Social advocacy organizations | Civic and social organizations | Business, professional, labor, political, and similar organizations | All industries |
|---|---|---|---|---|---|
| Human resources, training, and labor relations specialists, all other | $25.29 | $19.04 | $6.91 | $21.33 | $25.13 |
| Business operations specialists, all other | 24.58 | 19.81 | 18.81 | 21.18 | 26.76 |
| Public relations specialists | 22.23 | 22.33 | 19.06 | 24.71 | 22.76 |
| Executive secretaries and administrative assistants | 18.01 | 16.90 | 15.98 | 18.33 | 17.90 |
| Secretaries, except legal, medical, and executive | 13.57 | 13.16 | 11.21 | 13.80 | 13.20 |
| Fitness trainers and aerobics instructors | 13.29 | 15.27 | 10.88 | 15.01 | 12.46 |
| Office clerks, general | 10.71 | 11.11 | 8.95 | 11.46 | 11.40 |
| Recreation workers | 9.86 | 8.81 | 8.62 | 10.49 | 9.84 |
| Bartenders | 9.47 | 7.43 | 7.56 | 7.68 | 7.86 |
| Child care workers | 9.43 | 8.91 | 7.91 | 7.94 | 8.48 |

➢ Independent Sector, 1200 18th St. NW., Suite 200, Washington, DC 20036. Internet: **http://www.independentsector.org**

➢ The Foundation Center, 79 Fifth Ave., New York, NY 10003. Internet: **http://fdncenter.org**

Information on the following occupations may be found in the 2008-09 *Occupational Outlook Handbook*:

- Accountants and auditors
- Administrative services managers
- Athletes, coaches, umpires, and related workers
- Bookkeeping, accounting, and auditing clerks
- Child care workers
- Customer service representatives
- Human resources, training, and labor relations managers and specialists
- Maintenance and repair workers, general
- Office clerks, general
- Public relations specialists
- Receptionists and information clerks
- Recreation workers
- Secretaries and administrative assistants
- Security guards and gaming surveillance officers
- Social and human service assistants
- Social workers
- Teacher assistants
- Teachers—preschool, kindergarten, elementary, middle, and secondary
- Teachers—self-enrichment education
- Top executives

# Federal Government, Excluding the Postal Service

- With 1.8 million civilian employees, the Federal Government, excluding the Postal Service is the Nation's largest employer.

- About 4 out of 5 Federal employees work outside the Washington, DC metropolitan area.

- Job growth generated by increased homeland security needs will be offset by projected declines in other Federal sectors; however, many job openings should arise from the need to replace workers who retire or leave the Federal Government for other reasons.

- Competition is expected for many Federal positions, especially during times of economic uncertainty, when workers seek the stability of Federal employment.

## Nature of the Industry

The Federal Government is an organization formed to produce public services. We use some of these services every day, such as streets and sidewalks, police to maintain order, and parks, to name a few.

*Goods and services.* The Federal Government's essential duties include defending the United States from foreign aggression and terrorism, representing U.S. interests abroad, enforcing laws and regulations, and administering domestic programs and agencies. U.S. citizens are particularly aware of the Federal Government when they pay their income taxes each year, but they usually do not consider the government's role when they watch a weather forecast, purchase fresh and uncontaminated groceries, travel by highway or air, or make a deposit at their bank. Workers employed by the Federal Government play a vital role in these and many other aspects of our daily lives. (While career opportunities in the U.S. Postal Service and the Armed Forces are not covered here, both are described in the 2008-09 edition of the *Occupational Outlook Handbook*. See the *Handbook* statements on Postal Service workers and job opportunities in the Armed Forces.)

*Industry organization.* More than 200 years ago, the founders of the United States gathered in Philadelphia, PA, to create a constitution for a new national government and lay the foundation for self-governance. The Constitution of the United States, ratified by the last of the 13 original States in 1791, created the three branches of the Federal Government and granted certain powers and responsibilities to each. The legislative, judicial, and executive branches were created with equal powers but very different responsibilities that act to keep their powers in balance.

The legislative branch is responsible for forming and amending the legal structure of the Nation. Its largest component is Congress, the primary U.S. legislative body, which is made up of the Senate and the House of Representatives. This body includes senators, representatives, their staffs, and various support workers. The legislative branch employs only about one percent of Federal workers, nearly all of whom work in the Washington, DC area.

The judicial branch is responsible for interpreting the laws that the legislative branch enacts. The Supreme Court, the Na-

tion's definitive judicial body, makes the highest rulings. Its decisions usually follow the appeal of a decision made by the one of the regional Courts of Appeal, which hear cases appealed from U.S. District Courts, the Court of Appeals for the Federal Circuit, or State Supreme Courts. U.S. District Courts are located in each State and are the first to hear most cases under Federal jurisdiction. The judicial branch employs more than one percent of Federal workers; unlike the legislative branch, its offices and employees are dispersed throughout the country.

Of the three branches, the executive branch—through the power vested by the Constitution in the office of the President—has the widest range of responsibilities. Consequently, it employed about 98 percent of all Federal civilian employees (excluding Postal Service workers) in 2005. The executive branch is composed of the Executive Office of the President, 15 executive Cabinet departments—including the newly created Department of Homeland Security—and nearly 90 independent agencies, each of which has clearly defined duties. The Executive Office of the President is composed of several offices and councils that aid the President in policy decisions. These include the Office of Management and Budget, which oversees the administration of the Federal budget; the National Security Council, which advises the President on matters of national defense; and the Council of Economic Advisers, which makes economic policy recommendations.

Each of the 15 executive Cabinet departments administers programs that oversee an aspect of life in the United States. The highest departmental official of each Cabinet department, the Secretary, is a member of the President's Cabinet. Each, listed by employment size, is described below and in table 1.
- *Defense:* Manages the military forces that protect our country and its interests, including the Departments of the Army, Navy, and Air Force and a number of smaller agencies. The civilian workforce employed by the Department of Defense performs various support activities, such as payroll and public relations.
- *Veterans Affairs:* Administers programs to aid U.S. veterans and their families, runs the veterans' hospital system, and operates our national cemeteries.
- *Homeland Security:* Works to prevent terrorist attacks within the United States, reduce vulnerability to terrorism, and minimize the damage from potential attacks and natural disasters. It also administers the country's immigration policies and oversees the Coast Guard.

278

- *Treasury:* Regulates banks and other financial institutions, administers the public debt, prints currency, and collects Federal income taxes.
- *Justice:* Works with State and local governments and other agencies to prevent and control crime and ensure public safety against threats both domestic and foreign. It also enforces Federal laws, prosecutes cases in Federal courts, and runs Federal prisons.
- *Agriculture:* Promotes U.S. agriculture domestically and internationally, manages forests, researches new ways to grow crops and conserve natural resources, ensures safe meat and poultry products, and leads the Federal anti-hunger programs, such as Food Stamps and School Lunch.
- *Interior:* Manages Federal lands, including the national parks; runs hydroelectric power systems; and promotes conservation of natural resources.
- *Health and Human Services:* Performs health and social science research, assures the safety of drugs and foods other than meat and poultry, and administers Medicare, Medicaid, and numerous other social service programs.
- *Transportation:* Sets national transportation policy; plans and funds the construction of highways and mass transit systems; and regulates railroad, aviation, and maritime operations.
- *Commerce:* Forecasts the weather, charts the oceans, regulates patents and trademarks, conducts the census, compiles statistics, and promotes U.S. economic growth by encouraging international trade.
- *State:* Oversees the Nation's embassies and consulates, issues passports, monitors U.S. interests abroad, and represents the United States before international organizations.
- *Labor:* Enforces laws guaranteeing fair pay, workplace safety, and equal job opportunity; administers unemployment insurance; regulates pension funds; and collects and analyzes economic data.
- *Energy:* Coordinates the national use and provision of energy, oversees the production and disposal of nuclear weapons, and plans for future energy needs.
- *Housing and Urban Development:* Funds public housing projects, enforces equal housing laws, and insures and finances mortgages.
- *Education*: Monitors and distributes financial aid to schools and students, collects and disseminates data on schools and other education matters, and prohibits discrimination in education.

Numerous independent agencies perform tasks that fall between the jurisdictions of the executive departments are more efficiently executed by an autonomous agency. Some smaller, but well- known, independent agencies include the Peace Corps, the Securities and Exchange Commission, and the Federal Communications Commission. Although the majority of these agencies are fairly small, employing fewer than 1,000 workers (many employ fewer than 100 workers), some are quite large. The largest independent agencies are:

- *Social Security Administration:* Operates various old age, survivor, and disability insurance programs.
- *National Aeronautics and Space Administration:* Oversees aviation research and conducts exploration and research beyond the Earth's atmosphere.
- *Environmental Protection Agency:* Runs programs to control and reduce pollution of the Nation's water, air, and lands.
- *Tennessee Valley Authority:* Operates the hydroelectric power system in the Tennessee River Valley.
- *General Services Administration:* Manages and protects

Federal Government property and records.
- *Federal Deposit Insurance Corporation:* Maintains stability of and public confidence in the Nation's financial system, by insuring deposits and promoting sound banking practices.

**Table 1. Federal Government executive branch civilian employment, except U.S. Postal Service, January 2007**
(Employment in thousands)

| | United States | Washington, DC area |
|---|---|---|
| **Total** | 1,774 | 284 |
| | | |
| **Executive departments** | 1,593 | 234 |
| Defense, total | 623 | 65 |
| Army | 223 | 19 |
| Navy | 168 | 24 |
| Air Force | 152 | 6 |
| Other | 80 | 16 |
| Veterans Affairs | 239 | 7 |
| Homeland Security | 149 | 20 |
| Treasury | 109 | 14 |
| Justice | 105 | 23 |
| Agriculture | 92 | 11 |
| Interior | 66 | 7 |
| Health and Human Services | 60 | 28 |
| Transportation | 53 | 9 |
| Commerce | 39 | 21 |
| Labor | 16 | 6 |
| Energy | 15 | 5 |
| State | 14 | 12 |
| Housing and Urban Development | 10 | 3 |
| Education | 4 | 3 |
| | | |
| **Independent agencies** | 179 | 48 |
| Social Security Administration | 62 | 2 |
| National Aeronautics and Space Administration | 18 | 4 |
| Environmental Protection Agency | 18 | 5 |
| Tennessee Valley Authority | 12 | 0 |
| General Services Administration | 12 | 4 |
| Small Business Administration | 6 | 1 |
| Office of Personnel Management | 5 | 2 |
| Other | 45 | 30 |

SOURCE: U.S. Office of Personnel Management.

## Working Conditions

*Hours.* The vast majority of Federal employees work full time; some work on flexible or "flexi-time" schedules that allow workers more control over their work schedules. Some agencies also offer telecommuting or "flexi-place" programs, which allow selected workers to perform some job duties at home or from regional centers.

*Work Environment.* Some Federal workers spend much of their time away from the offices in which they are based. For example, inspectors or compliance officers often visit businesses and worksites to ensure that laws and regulations are obeyed. Some Federal workers frequently travel long distances, spending days or weeks away from home. Auditors, for example, may spend weeks at a time in distant locations.

Because of the wide range of Federal jobs, working conditions are equally variable. Most Federal employees work in office buildings, hospitals, or laboratories; but a large number also can be found at border crossings, airports, shipyards, military bases, construction sites, and national parks. Work environments vary from comfortable and relaxed to hazardous and stressful, such as those experienced by law enforcement officers, astronauts, and air traffic controllers.

## Employment
In January 2007, the Federal Government, excluding the Postal Service employed about 1.8 million civilian workers. The Federal Government is the Nation's single largest employer. Because data on employment in certain agencies cannot be released to the public for national security reasons, this total does not include employment for the Central Intelligence Agency, National Security Agency, Defense Intelligence Agency, and National Imagery and Mapping Agency.

The Federal Government makes an effort to have a workforce as diverse as the Nation's civilian labor force. The Federal Government serves as a model for all employers in abiding by equal employment opportunity legislation, which protects current and potential employees from discrimination based on race, color, religion, sex, national origin, disability, or age. The Federal Government also makes a special effort to recruit and accommodate persons with disabilities.

Even though the headquarters of most Federal departments and agencies are based in the Washington, DC, area, only 16 percent of Federal employees worked in the vicinity of the Nation's Capital in 2007. In addition to Federal employees working throughout the United States, about 92,000, which includes foreign nationals, are assigned overseas, mostly in embassies or defense installations.

## Occupations in the Industry
Although the Federal Government employs workers in every major occupational group, workers are not employed in the same proportions in which they are employed throughout the economy as a whole (table 2). The analytical and technical nature of many government duties translates into a much higher proportion of professional, management, business, and financial occupations in the Federal Government, compared with most industries. Conversely, the Government sells very little, so it employs relatively few sales workers.

*Management, business, and financial occupations.* Management, business, and financial workers made up about 33 percent of Federal employment and were primarily responsible for overseeing operations. Managerial workers include a broad range of officials who, at the highest levels, may head Federal agencies or programs. Middle managers, on the other hand, usually oversee one activity or aspect of a program. One management occupation—*legislators*—is responsible for passing and amending laws and overseeing the executive branch of the government. Within the Federal Government, legislators are entirely found in Congress.

Other occupations in this occupational group are *accountants and auditors*, who prepare and analyze financial reports, review and record revenues and expenditures, and investigate operations for fraud and inefficiency. *Management analysts* study government operations and systems and suggest improvements. *Purchasing agents* handle Federal purchases of supplies and *tax examiners, collectors, and revenue agents* determine and collect taxes.

*Professional and related occupations.* Professional and related occupations accounted for about 33 percent of Federal employment in 2006 (table 3). The largest groups of professional workers were in life, physical, and social science occupations, such as *biological scientists, conservation scientists and foresters, en-*

**Table 2.  Percent distribution of employment in the Federal Government, excluding the Postal Service, and for all industries by major occupational group, 2006**

| Occupational group | Federal Government | All industries |
|---|---|---|
| **Total** ................................................ | 100.0 | 100.0 |
| Management, business, and financial ...... | 33.2 | 10.2 |
| Professional and related ............................ | 32.8 | 19.8 |
| Office and administrative support ............. | 14.3 | 16.2 |
| Service ................................................ | 8.0 | 19.2 |
| Installation, maintenance, and repair........ | 4.7 | 3.9 |
| Transportation and material moving ......... | 2.9 | 6.8 |
| Construction and extraction...................... | 1.7 | 5.5 |
| Production.............................................. | 1.5 | 7.1 |
| Sales and related.................................... | 0.5 | 10.6 |
| Farming, fishing, and forestry .................. | 0.4 | 0.7 |

*vironmental scientists and geoscientists,* and *forest and conservation technicians.* They performed tasks such as determining the effects of drugs on living organisms, preventing fires in the National forests, and predicting earthquakes and hurricanes.

Many health professionals, such as *licensed practical and licensed vocational nurses*, *registered nurses*, and *physicians and surgeons*, were employed by the Department of Veterans Affairs (VA) in VA hospitals.

Large numbers of Federal workers also held jobs as engineers, including *aerospace, civil, computer hardware, electrical and electronics, environmental, industrial, mechanical,* and *nuclear engineers.* Engineers were found in many departments of the executive branch, but the vast majority worked in the Department of Defense. Some worked in the National Aeronautics and Space Administration as well as other agencies. In general, they solve problems and provide advice on technical programs, such as building highway bridges or implementing agency wide computer systems.

The Federal Government hires many *lawyers, judges and related workers,* as well as *law clerks* to write, administer, and enforce many of the country's laws and regulations.

Computer specialists—primarily *computer software engineers, computer systems analysts,* and *network and computer systems administrators*—are employed throughout the Federal Government. They write computer programs, analyze problems related to data processing, and keep computer systems running smoothly.

*Office and administrative support occupations.* About 14 percent of Federal workers were in office and administrative support occupations. These employees aid management staff with administrative duties. Administrative support workers in the Federal Government include *information and record clerks, general office clerks,* and *secretaries and administrative assistants.*

*Service occupations.* Compared with the economy as a whole, workers in service occupations were relatively scarce in the Federal Government. About half of Federal workers in service occupations were protective service workers, such as *correctional officers and jailers, detectives and criminal investigators,* and *police officers.* These workers protect the public from crime and oversee Federal prisons.

*Installation, maintenance, and repair occupations.* Federally employed workers in installation, maintenance, and repair occupations include *aircraft mechanics and service technicians* who fix and maintain all types of aircraft, and *electrical and electronic*

Table 3. Employment of wage and salary workers in Federal Government by occupation, 2006 and projected change, 2006-2016.
(Employment in thousands)

Table 3. Employment of wage and salary workers in Federal Government by occupation, 2006 and projected change, 2006-2016.
(Employment in thousands)

| Occupation | Employment, 2006 | | Percent change, 2006-16 |
|---|---|---|---|
| | Number | Percent | |
| **All occupations** | 1,958 | 100.0 | -4.6 |
| **Management, business, and financial occupations** | 650 | 33.2 | -2.9 |
| General and operations managers | 29 | 1.5 | -0.4 |
| Financial managers | 12 | 0.6 | -5.5 |
| Purchasing agents, except wholesale, retail, and farm products | 30 | 1.5 | -14.9 |
| Claims adjusters, examiners, and investigators | 42 | 2.2 | -5.5 |
| Compliance officers, except agriculture, construction, health and safety, and transportation | 91 | 4.6 | -5.5 |
| Human resources, training, and labor relations specialists | 23 | 1.2 | 3.8 |
| Logisticians | 23 | 1.2 | 4.0 |
| Management analysts | 45 | 2.3 | -5.5 |
| Accountants and auditors | 24 | 1.2 | -14.9 |
| Budget analysts | 14 | 0.7 | -5.5 |
| Tax examiners, collectors, and revenue agents | 36 | 1.8 | 1.2 |
| **Professional and related occupations** | 642 | 32.8 | -3.2 |
| Computer specialists | 77 | 3.9 | 2.0 |
| Engineers | 90 | 4.6 | -4.4 |
| Engineering technicians, except drafters | 29 | 1.5 | -5.1 |
| Biological scientists | 23 | 1.2 | -5.5 |
| Conservation scientists | 8 | 0.4 | 12.2 |
| Chemists | 6 | 0.3 | -5.5 |
| Environmental scientists and specialists, including health | 6 | 0.3 | -5.5 |
| Biological technicians | 12 | 0.6 | -5.5 |
| Forest and conservation technicians | 26 | 1.3 | -4.9 |
| Lawyers | 31 | 1.6 | -5.5 |
| Paralegals and legal assistants | 14 | 0.7 | 5.5 |
| Education, training, and library occupations | 32 | 1.6 | -5.5 |
| Physicians and surgeons | 25 | 1.3 | -5.5 |
| Registered nurses | 54 | 2.7 | 4.0 |
| Health technologists and technicians | 40 | 2.1 | -5.6 |
| Licensed practical and licensed vocational nurses | 14 | 0.7 | -5.5 |
| Occupational health and safety specialists | 7 | 0.3 | -5.5 |
| **Service occupations** | 157 | 8.0 | 2.9 |
| Fire fighters | 8 | 0.4 | -5.5 |
| Correctional officers and jailers | 16 | 0.8 | 13.4 |
| Detectives and criminal investigators | 39 | 2.0 | 13.4 |
| Police and sheriff's patrol officers | 12 | 0.6 | 3.9 |
| Building cleaning workers | 12 | 0.6 | -3.4 |
| **Office and administrative support occupations** | 279 | 14.3 | -15.5 |
| Bookkeeping, accounting, and auditing clerks | 21 | 1.1 | -5.5 |
| Procurement clerks | 15 | 0.7 | -14.9 |
| Eligibility interviewers, government programs | 26 | 1.3 | 6.3 |
| Human resources assistants, except payroll and timekeeping | 14 | 0.7 | -5.5 |
| Secretaries and administrative assistants | 34 | 1.7 | -15.4 |
| Word processors and typists | 14 | 0.7 | -24.4 |
| **Farming, fishing, and forestry occupations** | 9 | 0.4 | -11.5 |
| Agricultural inspectors | 6 | 0.3 | -14.7 |

(continued on next column)

(continued from previous column)

Table 3. Employment of wage and salary workers in Federal Government by occupation, 2006 and projected change, 2006-2016.
(Employment in thousands)

| Occupation | Employment, 2006 | | Percent change, 2006-16 |
|---|---|---|---|
| | Number | Percent | |
| **Installation, maintenance, and repair occupations** | 93 | 4.7 | -6.1 |
| Electrical and electronic equipment mechanics, installers, and repairers | 15 | 0.8 | -2.0 |
| Aircraft mechanics and service technicians | 19 | 1.0 | -14.9 |
| **Transportation and material moving occupations** | 56 | 2.9 | -1.0 |
| Air traffic controllers | 22 | 1.1 | 9.1 |

Note: Columns may not add to totals due to omission of occupations with small employment

*equipment mechanics, installers, and repairers,* who inspect, adjust, and repair electronic equipment such as industrial controls, transmitters, antennas, radar, radio, and navigation systems.

***Other occupational groups.*** The Federal Government employed a relatively small number of workers in transportation; production; construction; sales and related; and farming, fishing, and forestry occupations. However, the Government employs almost all or a significant number of some occupations, such as *air traffic controllers*, *agricultural inspectors*, and *bridge and lock tenders*.

## Training and Advancement

The educational and training requirements for jobs in the Federal Government mirror those in the private sector for most major occupational groups. Many jobs in managerial or professional and related occupations, for example, require a 4-year college degree. Some, such as engineers, physicians and surgeons, and biological and physical scientists, require a bachelor's or higher degree in a specific field of study. However, registered nurse and many technician occupations may be entered with 2 years of training after high school. Office and administrative support workers in the government usually need only a high school diploma, although any further training or experience, such as a junior college degree or a couple of years of relevant work experience, is an asset. Most Federal jobs in other occupations require no more than a high school degree, although most departments and agencies prefer workers with vocational training or previous experience.

In all but a few cases, applicants for Federal jobs must be U.S. citizens. Applicants who are veterans of military service also may be able to claim veteran's preference which gives them preferred status over other candidates with equal qualifications. For jobs requiring access to sensitive or classified materials, applicants must undergo a background investigation in order to obtain a security clearance. This investigation covers an individual's criminal, credit, and employment history, as well as other records. The scope of the investigation will vary, depending on the nature of the position in the government and the degree of harm that an individual in that position could cause. Generally, the higher the level of clearance needed, the greater the scope of investigation.

Once employed, each Federal department or agency determines its own training requirements and offers workers opportunities to improve job skills or become qualified to advance to other jobs. These may include technical or skills training, tuition assistance or reimbursement, fellowship programs, and executive leadership and management training programs, seminars, and workshops. This training may be offered on the job, by another agency, or at local colleges and universities.

Advancement for most workers in the Federal Government is currently based on a system of occupational pay levels, or "grades," although more departments and agencies are being granted waivers to utilize different pay and promotion strategies. Workers typically enter the Federal civil service at the starting grade for an occupation and begin a "career ladder" of promotions until they reach the full-performance grade for that occupation. This system provides for a limited number of non-competitive promotions, which usually are awarded at regular intervals, assuming job performance is satisfactory. The exact pay grades associated with a job's career track depend upon the occupation.

Typically, workers without a high school diploma who are hired as clerks start at grade 1, and high school graduates with no additional training hired at the same job start at grade 2 or 3. Entrants with some technical training or experience who are hired as technicians may start at grade 4. Those with a bachelor's degree generally are hired in professional occupations, such as economist, with a career ladder that starts at grade 5 or 7, depending on academic achievement. Entrants with a master's degree or Ph.D. may start at grade 9. Individuals with professional degrees may be hired at the grade 11 or 12 level. Those with a combination of education and substantive experience may be hired at higher grades than those with education alone.

Once nonsupervisory Federal workers reach the full-performance level of the career track, they usually receive periodic step increases within their grade if they are performing their job satisfactorily. They must compete for subsequent promotions, and advancement becomes more difficult. At this point, promotions occur as vacancies arise, and they are based solely on merit and in competition with other qualified candidates. In addition to within-grade longevity increases, Federal workers are awarded bonuses for excellent job performance.

Workers who advance to managerial or supervisory positions may receive within-grade longevity increases, bonuses, and promotions to higher grades. The top managers in the Federal civil service belong to the Senior Executive Service (SES), the highest positions that Federal workers can reach without being specifically nominated by the President and confirmed by the U.S. Senate. Relatively few workers attain SES positions, and competition is intense. Bonus provisions for SES positions are even more performance-based than are those for lower-level positions. Because it is the headquarters for most Federal agencies, the Washington, DC, metropolitan area offers the best opportunities to advance to upper-level managerial and supervisory jobs.

## Outlook

Wage and salary employment in the Federal Government is projected to decline by 4.6 percent over the 2006-16 period. Some job growth will be generated by increased homeland security needs. There is projected slow growth or declines in other Federal sectors due to governmental cost-cutting, the growing use of private contractors, and continuing devolution—the practice of turning over the development, implementation, and manage-

ment of some programs of the Federal Government to State and local governments. However, many job openings should arise from the need to replace workers who retire or leave the Federal Government for other reasons.

*Employment change.* Staffing levels in Federal Government, while relatively stable in the short run, can be subject to change in the long run primarily because of changes in public policies as legislated by the Congress, which affect spending levels and hiring decisions for the various departments and agencies. In general, over the coming decade, domestic programs are likely to see cuts in their budgets as Congress seeks to reduce the Federal budget deficit, but the cuts will likely affect some agencies more than others. Any employment declines, however, generally will be carried out through attrition—simply not replacing workers who retire or leave the Federal Government for other reasons. Layoffs, called "reductions in force," have occurred in the past, but they are uncommon and usually affect relatively few workers.

While there will be job openings in all types of jobs over the coming decade, demand will continue to grow for specialized workers in areas related to border and transportation security, emergency preparedness, public health, and information analysis.

A study by the Partnership for Public Service, which surveyed Federal department and agency hiring needs through September 2009, found that most new hires in the Federal Government will come in five major areas: security, enforcement, and compliance, which includes inspectors, investigators, police officers, airport screeners, and prison guards; medical and public health fields; engineering and the sciences, including microbiologists, botanists, physicists, chemists, and veterinarians; program management and administration; and accounting, budget, and business, which includes revenue agents and tax examiners needed mainly by the Internal Revenue Service. The Department of Health and Human Services will need health insurance specialists and claims and customer service representatives to implement the Medicare Prescription Drug benefit. Patent examiners, foreign service officers, and lawyers also are in high demand.

*Job prospects.* In spite of legislative budget cuts, there still will be numerous employment opportunities in many agencies from the need to replace workers who leave the workforce, retire, or accept employment elsewhere. In fact, the need for replacement for workers will be significant in the coming years. For example, the U.S. Office of Personnel Management (OPM) estimates that among all full-time permanent employees in the Federal workforce as of October 2004, 58 percent of supervisory and 42 percent of nonsupervisory workers will be eligible to retire by the end of 2010.

Competition is expected for many Federal positions, especially during times of economic uncertainty, when workers seek the stability of Federal employment. In general, Federal employment is considered to be relatively stable because it is not affected by cyclical fluctuations in the economy, as are employment levels in many private sector industries.

The distribution of Federal employment will continue to shift toward a higher proportion of professional, business, and financial operations, and protective service workers. Employment declines will be the greatest among office and administrative support occupations and production occupations because of increasing office automation and contracting out of these jobs.

## Earnings

*Industry earnings.* In an effort to give agencies more flexibility in how they pay their workers, there are different pay systems in effect, or planning to be implemented over the next few years, within the Federal Government. The new systems incorporate fewer, but wider, pay "bands," instead of grade levels. Pay increases, under these new systems, are almost entirely based on performance, instead of length of service.

The majority of professional and administrative Federal workers are still paid under the General Schedule (GS). The General Schedule, shown in table 4, has 15 grades of pay for civilian white-collar and service workers, and smaller within-grade step increases that occur based on length of service and quality of performance. New employees usually start at the first step of a grade; however, if the position in question is difficult to fill, entrants may receive somewhat higher pay or special rates. Almost all physician and engineer positions, for example, fall into this category. In an effort to make Federal pay more responsive to local labor market conditions, Federal employees working in the continental United States receive locality pay. The specific amount of locality pay is determined by survey comparisons of private sector wage rates and Federal wage rates in the relevant geographic area. At its highest level, locality pay can lead to an increase of as much as 30 percent above the base salary in 2007. Every January, a pay adjustment tied to changes in private sector pay levels is divided between an across-the-board pay increase in the General Schedule and locality pay increases.

In March 2007, the average earnings for full-time workers paid under the General Schedule were $65,463. (See table 5).

For those in craft, repair, operator, and laborer jobs, the Federal Wage System (FWS) is used to pay these workers. This schedule sets Federal wages so that they are comparable with prevailing regional wage rates for similar types of jobs. As a result, wage rates paid under the FWS can vary significantly from one locality to another.

In addition to base pay and bonuses, Federal employees may receive incentive awards. These incentive awards can be in the form of cash rewards, quality step increase (a faster than normal progression of steps on the GS pay scale), and time off awards (allowing time off without using leave or loss of pay). The one-time cash awards can be up to $25,000, but are typically significantly smaller, are bestowed for a significant suggestion, a

**Table 5. Average annual salaries for full-time workers under the General Schedule in the Federal Government in selected occupations, 2007**

| Occupation | Salary |
|---|---|
| All occupations | $65,463 |
| General attorney | 111,304 |
| Financial management | 101,022 |
| General engineering | 100,051 |
| Economist | 94,098 |
| Computer science | 90,929 |
| Chemistry | 89,954 |
| Criminal investigating | 88,174 |
| Microbiology | 87,206 |
| Architecture | 87,128 |
| Statistics | 85,690 |
| Information technology management | 81,524 |
| Librarian | 80,873 |
| Accounting | 78,665 |
| Chaplain | 78,030 |
| Ecology | 76,511 |
| Human resources management | 76,503 |
| Mine safety and health | 73,003 |
| Air traffic control | 72,049 |
| Budget analysis | 71,267 |
| Correctional officer | 67,140 |
| Nurse | 65,345 |
| Engineering technical | 63,951 |
| Border patrol agent | 63,550 |
| Medical technologist | 59,840 |
| Customs and border protection | 59,248 |
| Legal assistance | 46,912 |
| Fire protection and prevention | 43,407 |
| Secretary | 42,334 |
| Police | 42,150 |
| Tax examining | 38,290 |
| Human resources assistance | 37,835 |
| Nursing assistant | 33,134 |

SOURCE: U.S. Office of Personnel Management

special act or service, or sustained high job performance. Some workers also may receive "premium" pay, which is granted when the employee must work overtime, on holidays, on weekends, at night, or under hazardous conditions.

*Benefits and union membership.* Benefits are an important part of Federal employee compensation. Federal employees may choose from a number of health plans and life insurance options; premium payments for these policies are partially offset by the Government. In addition, workers hired after January 1, 1984, participate in the Federal Employees Retirement System (FERS), a three-tiered retirement plan including Social Security, a pension plan, and an optional Thrift Savings Plan. Worker participation in the Thrift Savings Plan is voluntary, but any contributions made are tax-deferred and, up to a point, matched by the Federal Government. In addition to other benefits, some Federal agencies provide public transit subsidies in an effort to encourage employee use of public transportation.

Federal employees receive both vacation and sick leave. They earn 13 days of vacation leave a year for the first 3 years, 20 days a year for the next 12 years, and 26 days a year after their 15th year of service. Workers also receive 13 days of sick leave a year, which may be accumulated indefinitely.

The American Federal Government Employees union represents nonsupervisory Federal employees. About 22 percent of all Federal civilian employees outside the Postal Service were union members or covered by union contract in 2006.

**Table 4. Federal Government General Schedule base pay rates, 2007**

| GS level | Entrance level | Step increase | Maximum level |
|---|---|---|---|
| 1 | $16,630 | varies | $20,798 |
| 2 | 18,698 | varies | 23,527 |
| 3 | 20,401 | $680 | 26,521 |
| 4 | 22,902 | 763 | 29,769 |
| 5 | 25,623 | 854 | 33,309 |
| 6 | 28,562 | 952 | 37,130 |
| 7 | 31,740 | 1,058 | 41,262 |
| 8 | 35,151 | 1,172 | 45,699 |
| 9 | 38,824 | 1,294 | 50,470 |
| 10 | 42,755 | 1,425 | 55,580 |
| 11 | 46,974 | 1,566 | 61,068 |
| 12 | 56,301 | 1,877 | 73,194 |
| 13 | 66,951 | 2,232 | 87,039 |
| 14 | 79,115 | 2,637 | 102,848 |
| 15 | 93,063 | 3,102 | 120,981 |

SOURCE: U.S. Office of Personnel Management

## Sources of Additional Information

Information on obtaining a position with the Federal Government is available from the Office of Personnel Management (OPM) through USAJOBS, the Federal Government's official employment information system. This resource for locating and applying for job opportunities can be accessed through the Internet at **http://www.usajobs.opm.gov** or through an interactive voice response telephone system at (703) 724-1850 or TTY (978) 461-8404. These numbers are not tollfree, and charges may result.

For advice on finding a job with the Federal Government and more information on the Federal hiring process and employment system, contact:

➢ Partnership for Public Service, 1725 Eye St. NW., Suite 900, Washington, DC 20006. Internet: **http://www.makingthedifference.org**

For more information on union membership for Federal government employees, contact:

➢ American Federation of Government Employees, 80 F St. NW., Washington, DC 20001.

The duties of Federal Government workers are similar to those of their private sector counterparts. Further information on many Federal Government occupations, including those listed below, can be found in the 2008-09 edition of the *Occupational Outlook Handbook*.

- Accountants and auditors
- Air traffic controllers
- Aircraft and avionics equipment mechanics and service technicians
- Biological scientists
- Computer software engineers
- Computer support specialists and systems administrators
- Computer systems analysts
- Conservation scientists and foresters
- Correctional officers
- Electrical and electronics installers and repairers
- Engineers
- Environmental scientists and hydrologists
- Geoscientists
- Inspectors, testers, sorters, samplers, and weighers
- Judges, magistrates, and other judicial workers
- Lawyers
- Licensed practical and licensed vocational nurses
- Management analysts
- Office clerks, general
- Physicians and surgeons
- Police and detectives
- Probation officers and correctional treatment specialists
- Purchasing managers, buyers, and purchasing agents
- Registered nurses
- Science technicians
- Secretaries and administrative assistants
- Tax examiners, collectors, and revenue agents
- Top executives
- Job opportunities in the Armed Forces

# State and Local Government, Except Education and Hospitals

## SIGNIFICANT POINTS

- Local governments employ more than twice as many workers as State governments.

- Professional and service occupations accounted for more than half of all jobs; fire fighters and law enforcement workers, concentrated in local government, are the largest occupations.

- Although job prospects vary by State and region, overall prospects are expected to be favorable.

- Employer-provided benefits are more common among State and local government employees than among workers in the private sector.

## Nature of the Industry

***Goods and services.*** State and local governments provide their constituents with vital services, such as transportation, public safety, health care, education, utilities, and courts.

***Industry organization.*** Excluding education and hospitals, State and local governments employ about 8.0 million workers, placing them among the largest employers in the economy. Seven out of 10 of these employees work for local governments, such as counties, cities, special districts, and towns. In addition, large numbers of State and local workers work in public education; they are not included in these figures. These workers form a major part of the educational services industry, which is discussed elsewhere in the *Career Guide.* Many State and local workers also work in public hospitals, which are included in the health care industry elsewhere in the *Career Guide.*

In addition to the 50 State governments, there were about 87,500 local governments in 2002, according to the U.S. Census Bureau. These included about 3,000 county governments; 19,400 municipal governments; 16,500 townships; 13,500 school districts; and 35,100 special districts. Illinois had the most local government units, with more than 6,900; Hawaii had the fewest, with 20.

In many areas of the country, citizens are served by more than one local government unit. For example, most States have *counties,* which may contain various municipalities such as cites or towns, but which also often include unincorporated rural areas. *Townships,* which do not exist in some States, may or may not contain municipalities and often consist of suburban or rural areas. Supplementing these forms of local government, *special district* government bodies are independent, limited purpose governmental units that usually perform a single function or activity. For example, a large percentage of special districts manage the use of natural resources. Some provide drainage and flood control, irrigation, and soil and water conservation services.

## Working Conditions

***Hours.*** Working conditions vary by occupation and, in some instances, by size and location of the State or local government. For example, chief executives in very small jurisdictions may work less than 20 hours a week; in larger jurisdictions, they often work more than 40 hours per week. Chief executives in large jurisdictions work full time year round, as do most county and city managers. Most State legislators work full time only when in session, usually for a few months a year, and work part time the rest of the year. Local elected officials in some small jurisdictions work part time.

Most professional, financial operations, and office and administrative support workers in State and local government work a standard 40-hour week in an office environment. However, workers in some of the most visible local government jobs have very different working conditions and schedules. Fire fighters' hours are longer and vary more widely than those of most workers. Many professional fire fighters are on duty for several days in a row, working over 50 hours a week, because some must be on duty at all times to respond to emergencies. They often eat and sleep at the fire station. Following this long shift, they are then off for several days in a row or for the entire next week. Some local fire districts also use the services of volunteer fire fighters, who tend to work shorter, regularly scheduled shifts.

Most police and detectives work 40 hours a week, with paid overtime when they testify in court or work on an investigation. Because police protection must be provided around the clock, some officers work weekends, holidays, and nights. Many officers are subject to call any time their services are needed and are expected to intervene whenever they observe a crime, even if they are off duty.

Bus drivers with regular routes and subway operators generally have consistent weekly work schedules. Those who do not have regular schedules may be on call and must be prepared to report for work on short notice. To accommodate commuters, many operators work split shifts, such as 6 a.m. to 10 a.m. and 3 p.m. to 7 p.m., with time off in between.

A number of other State and local government jobs also require weekend or night work. For example, split, weekend, and night shifts are common for water and other public utility workers.

***Work environment.*** Law enforcement work is potentially dangerous. The injury and fatality rates among law officers are higher than in many occupations, reflecting risks taken in apprehending suspected criminals and responding to various emergency situations such as traffic accidents. In addition to irregular hours, firefighting can involve the risk of death or injury.

Most driver/operator jobs in public transit systems are stressful and fatiguing because they involve dealing with passengers, tight schedules, and heavy traffic.

**Table 1. Wage and salary employment in State and local government, excluding education and hospitals, 2006**
(Employment in thousands)

| Jurisdiction | Employment | Percent |
|---|---|---|
| State and local government, total ................. | 8,018 | 100.0 |
| Local government............................................. | 5,594 | 69.8 |
| State government .............................................. | 2,424 | 30.2 |

## Employment

State and local governments, excluding education and hospitals, employed about 8 million people in 2006. Seven out of 10 of these workers were employed in local government (table 1).

## Occupations in the Industry

Service occupations made up the largest share of employment in State and local governments, accounting for 31 percent of all jobs (table 2). Of these, *police and sheriff's patrol officers, bailiffs, correctional officers and jailers,* and *fire fighters,* concentrated in local government, were the largest occupations (chart). Professional and related occupations accounted for 21 percent of employment; office and administrative support occupations accounted for 20 percent; and management, business, and financial occupations constituted 12 percent.

State and local governments employ people in occupations found in nearly every industry in the economy, including chief executives, managers, engineers, computer specialists, secretaries, and health technicians. Certain occupations, however, are mainly or exclusively found in these governments, such as legislators; tax examiners, collectors, and revenue agents; urban and regional planners; judges, magistrates, and other judicial workers; police and sheriff's patrol officers; and correctional officers and jailers.

*Chief executives, general and operations managers,* and *legislators* establish government policy and develop laws, rules, and regulations. They are elected or appointed officials who either preside over units of government or make laws. Chief execu-

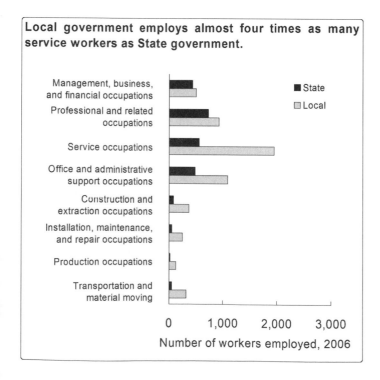

**Local government employs almost four times as many service workers as State government.**

Number of workers employed, 2006

tives include governors, lieutenant governors, mayors, and city managers. General and operations managers include district managers and revenue directors. Legislators include State senators and representatives, county commissioners, and city council members.

*Tax examiners, collectors, and revenue agents* determine tax liability and collect past-due taxes from individuals or businesses. *Urban and regional planners* draft plans and recommend programs for the development and use of resources such as land and water. They also propose construction of physical facilities, such as schools and roads, under the authority of cities, counties, and metropolitan areas. Planners devise strategies outlining the best use of community land and identify the places in which residential, commercial, recreational, and other types of development should be located.

*Judges* arbitrate, advise, and administer justice in a court of law. They oversee legal processes in courts and apply the law to resolve civil disputes and determine the sentence when guilt has been established in criminal cases. *Magistrates* resolve criminal cases not involving penitentiary sentences, as well as civil cases involving damages below a sum specified by State law.

*Social workers* counsel and assess the needs of clients, refer them to the appropriate sources of help, and monitor their progress. *Eligibility interviewers, government programs* interview and investigate applicants and recipients to determine eligibility to receive, or continue receiving, welfare and other types of social assistance. *Social and human service assistants'* duties vary with specific job titles. These workers include social service technicians, case management aides, social work assistants, residential counselors, alcoholism or drug abuse counseling aides, child abuse workers, community outreach workers, and gerontology aides. *Probation officers and correctional treatment specialists* assist in rehabilitation of law offenders in custody or on probation or parole.

*Court, municipal, and license clerks* perform a variety of State and local government administrative tasks. *Court clerks* prepare dockets of cases to be called, secure information for judges, and contact witnesses, lawyers, and attorneys to obtain information for the court. *Municipal clerks* draft agendas for town or city councils, record minutes of council meetings, answer official correspondence, keep fiscal records and accounts, and prepare reports on civic needs. *License clerks* keep records and help the public obtain motor vehicle ownership titles, operator permits, and a variety of other permits and licenses. State and local governments also employ many *secretaries and administrative assistants* and *general office clerks.*

*Fire fighters* control and extinguish fires, assist with emergency medical treatment, and help with the recovery from natural disasters such as earthquakes and tornadoes. *Fire inspectors* inspect public buildings for conditions that might present a fire hazard. *Emergency medical technicians and paramedics* assess injuries, administer emergency medical care, and extricate trapped individuals. They transport injured or sick persons to medical facilities.

*Police and sheriff's patrol officers* and *detectives and criminal investigators* have duties that range from controlling traffic to preventing and investigating crimes. They maintain order; enforce laws and ordinances; issue traffic summonses; investigate accidents; give evidence in court; serve legal documents for the court system; and apprehend, arrest, and process prisoners. State and local *correctional officers* guard inmates in jails, prisons, or juvenile detention institutions. *Bailiffs* keep order in courts.

*Highway maintenance workers* maintain highways, municipal and rural roads, airport runways, and rights-of-way. They patch broken or eroded pavement, repair guard rails and highway markers, plow snow, and mow or clear brush from along roads. *Bus drivers* pick up and deliver passengers at prearranged stops throughout their assigned routes. Operators may collect fares, answer questions about schedules and transfer points, and announce stops.

## Training and Advancement

The educational level and experience needed by workers in State and local government varies by occupation. Voters elect most chief executives and legislators, so local support is very important. Taking part in volunteer work and helping to provide community services are good ways to establish vital community support. Those elected to chief executive and legislator positions come from a variety of backgrounds, but must conform to age, residency, and citizenship regulations regarding the positions that they seek. Advancement opportunities for most elected public officials are limited to other offices in the jurisdictions in which they live. For example, a local council member may run for mayor or for a position in State government, and State legislators may decide to run for State governor or for the U.S. Congress.

For city managers, a master's degree in public administration is widely recommended. Many cities prefer but do not require a master's degree. A bachelor's degree in business administration, public administration, finance, or a related field is usually required. City manager candidates may gain experience as management analysts or assistants in government departments, working with councils and mayors. They may also gain experience by moving to an executive position in a government agency or becoming a deputy or assistant city manager. They may initially be hired to manage a town or a small city and eventually become manager of larger cities.

For most professional jobs, a college degree is required. To obtain an entry-level urban or regional planning position, most State and local government agencies require 2 years of graduate study in urban and regional planning or the equivalent in work experience. To become a judge, particularly a State trial or appellate court judge, one usually is required to be a lawyer. Some State judges are appointed, while others are elected in partisan or nonpartisan elections. Most State and local judges serve fixed terms, usually ranging from 2 to 14 years. Appellate judges commonly serve longer terms than lower court judges.

Most applicants for firefighting jobs must have a high school education or its equivalent and pass a civil service examination. In addition, they need to pass a medical examination and tests of strength, physical stamina, coordination, and agility. Experience as a volunteer fire fighter or as a fire fighter in the Armed Forces is helpful, as is completion of community college courses in fire science. Recruits study firefighting techniques, fire prevention, local building codes, emergency procedures, and the proper use of rescue equipment. Fire fighters may be promoted depending on written examination results and job performance.

Bus drivers must comply with Federal regulations that require drivers who operate vehicles designed to transport 16 or more passengers to obtain a commercial driver's license from the State in which they live. To qualify for a commercial driver's license, applicants must pass a written test on rules and regulations and demonstrate that they can operate a commercial vehicle safely. For subway and streetcar operator jobs, applicants with at least a high school education have the best chance. In some cities, prospective subway operators are required to work as bus driv-

ers for a specified period. Successful applicants generally are in good health, possess good communication skills, and are able to make quick, sound judgments. Because bus drivers and subway operators deal with passengers, they need an even temperament and emotional stability. Driving in heavy, fast-moving, or stop-and-go traffic and dealing with passengers can be stressful.

Police departments in most areas require applicants to be U.S. citizens of good character, at least 20 years old, and able to meet rigorous physical and mental standards. Police departments increasingly encourage applicants to take college courses, and some require a college degree. Many community and junior colleges, as well as colleges and universities, offer programs in law enforcement or criminal justice. Officers usually attend a local or regional police academy that includes classroom instruction in constitutional law, civil rights, and State and local law. They also receive training in patrol, accident investigation, traffic control, using firearms, self-defense, first aid, and emergency management. Promotions for police officers are highly influenced by scores on a written civil service examination and subsequent performance evaluations by their superiors.

## Outlook

Although job prospects vary by State and region, overall prospects are expected to be favorable.

*Employment change.* Wage and salary employment in State and local government is projected to increase 8 percent during the 2006-16 period, slower than the 11 percent growth projected for all sectors of the economy combined.

Job growth will stem from the rising demand for services at the State and local levels particularly demand for public safety and health services. An increasing population and State and local government assumption of responsibility for some services previously provided by the Federal Government are fueling the growth of these services. Despite the increased demand for the services of State and local governments, employment growth will be dampened by budgetary constraints due to the rapidly increasing proportion of revenues devoted to the Medicaid program, and public resistance to tax increases. Outsourcing of government jobs to the private sector will also limit employment in State and local government. When economic times are good, many State and local governments increase spending on programs and employment.

Professional and service occupations accounted for over half of all jobs in State and local government. Most new jobs will stem from steady demand for community and social services, health services, and protective services. For example, increased demand for services for the elderly, the mentally impaired, and children will result in steady growth in the numbers of social workers, registered nurses, and recreation workers. There will also be strong demand for information technology workers.

Employment of management, business, and financial occupations is projected to grow at about the same rate as overall employment in State and local government. Employment in office and administrative support occupations in State and local government is expected to remain close to current levels as these functions are increasingly outsourced to the private sector.

*Job prospects.* Although job prospects vary by State and region, overall prospects are expected to be favorable. In addition to job openings from employment growth, many opportunities will be created by workers who retire from the industry. Additionally, many State and local governments are considering cuts in

**Table 2. Employment of wage and salary workers in State and local government, except education and health by occupation, 2006 and projected change, 2006-2016**
(Employment in thousands)

| Occupation | Employment, 2006 Number | Employment, 2006 Percent | Percent change, 2006-16 |
|---|---|---|---|
| All occupations ..................................... | 8,018 | 100.0 | 7.7 |
| **Management, business, and financial occupations**.............................. | 942 | 11.7 | 6.3 |
| General and operations managers ............ | 73 | 0.9 | -3.4 |
| Legislators .......................................... | 64 | 0.8 | 1.0 |
| Compliance officers, except agriculture, construction, health and safety, and transportation ...................................... | 58 | 0.7 | 3.7 |
| Human resources, training, and labor relations specialists ............................... | 71 | 0.9 | 9.1 |
| Accountants and auditors ........................... | 81 | 1.0 | 16.1 |
| Appraisers and assessors of real estate . | 28 | 0.4 | 6.6 |
| Tax examiners, collectors, and revenue agents ........................................ | 45 | 0.6 | 2.9 |
| **Professional and related occupations** ...... | 1,655 | 20.6 | 8.0 |
| Computer specialists .................................... | 142 | 1.8 | 12.7 |
| Civil engineers ............................................ | 59 | 0.7 | 5.2 |
| Civil engineering technicians ...................... | 39 | 0.5 | 3.9 |
| Urban and regional planners ...................... | 26 | 0.3 | 10.7 |
| Counselors ................................................. | 71 | 0.9 | 4.7 |
| Social workers ............................................ | 175 | 2.2 | 5.4 |
| Probation officers and correctional treatment specialists................................. | 92 | 1.1 | 9.9 |
| Social and human service assistants ......... | 90 | 1.1 | -0.5 |
| Lawyers ..................................................... | 88 | 1.1 | 27.6 |
| Judges, magistrate judges, and magistrates .. | 27 | 0.3 | 5.1 |
| Legal support workers ............................... | 58 | 0.7 | 8.2 |
| Librarians .................................................. | 45 | 0.6 | 0.9 |
| Library technicians..................................... | 60 | 0.8 | 12.0 |
| Registered nurses...................................... | 90 | 1.1 | 5.9 |
| Health technologists and technicians ......... | 123 | 1.5 | 8.4 |
| **Service occupations**................................. | 2,508 | 31.3 | 10.9 |
| Nursing, psychiatric, and home health aides ........................................... | 107 | 1.3 | 4.9 |
| First-line supervisors/managers of correctional officers................................ | 37 | 0.5 | 11.9 |
| First-line supervisors/managers of police and detectives................................... | 84 | 1.1 | 10.3 |
| Fire fighters............................................... | 276 | 3.4 | 12.1 |
| Correctional officers and jailers.................. | 409 | 5.1 | 15.8 |
| Detectives and criminal investigators.......... | 66 | 0.8 | 19.8 |
| Police and sheriff's patrol officers .............. | 618 | 7.7 | 10.9 |
| Crossing guards......................................... | 48 | 0.6 | 1.1 |
| Lifeguards, ski patrol, and other recreational protective service workers..... | 43 | 0.5 | 12.2 |
| Building cleaning workers............................ | 111 | 1.4 | 3.6 |
| Landscaping and groundskeeping workers ................................................. | 91 | 1.1 | 4.3 |
| Gaming services workers ........................... | 32 | 0.4 | 21.4 |
| Recreation workers ..................................... | 105 | 1.3 | 6.9 |
| **Office and administrative support occupations** ............................................. | 1,572 | 19.6 | 2.0 |
| Bookkeeping, accounting, and auditing clerks .................................................... | 104 | 1.3 | 8.5 |
| Court, municipal, and license clerks........... | 108 | 1.3 | 8.2 |
| Eligibility interviewers, government programs... | 80 | 1.0 | 0.0 |
| Library assistants, clerical .......................... | 61 | 0.8 | 12.2 |
| Police, fire, and ambulance dispatchers ..... | 87 | 1.1 | 12.5 |
| Secretaries and administrative assistants .. | 308 | 3.8 | 2.2 |
| Office clerks, general................................. | 317 | 4.0 | 3.1 |

(continued on the next column)

(continued from previous column)

**Table 2. Employment of wage and salary workers in State and local government, except education and health by occupation, 2006 and projected change, 2006-2016**
(Employment in thousands)

| Occupation | Employment, 2006 Number | Employment, 2006 Percent | Percent change, 2006-16 |
|---|---|---|---|
| **Construction and extraction occupations** ............................................. | 447 | 5.6 | 9.9 |
| Construction equipment operators.............. | 83 | 1.0 | 10.3 |
| Highway maintenance workers................... | 138 | 1.7 | 8.8 |
| **Installation, maintenance, and repair occupations** ............................................. | 302 | 3.8 | 10.6 |
| Maintenance and repair workers, general... | 124 | 1.5 | 9.8 |
| **Production occupations**............................. | 143 | 1.8 | 10.7 |
| Water and liquid waste treatment plant and system operators .............................. | 89 | 1.1 | 12.1 |
| **Transportation and material moving occupations** ............................................. | 366 | 4.6 | 7.4 |
| Bus drivers, transit and intercity................. | 117 | 1.5 | 11.5 |
| Refuse and recyclable material collectors .. | 49 | 0.6 | 1.0 |

Note: Columns may not add to totals due to omission of occupations with small employment

their retiree pension and benefits programs. Such cuts may make State and local government jobs attractive to fewer people, reducing competition for available jobs.

## Earnings

*Industry earnings.* Earnings vary by occupation, size of the State or locality, and region of the country. As in most industries, professionals and managers earn more than other workers. Earnings in the occupations having the largest employment in State and local government appear in table 3.

The International City/County Management Association (ICMA) reported the 2006 median annual salaries of selected executive and managerial occupations in local government (see table 4).

*Benefits and union membership.* Employer-provided benefits—including health and life insurance and retirement benefits—are

**Table 3. Median hourly earnings of the largest occupations in State and local government, excluding education and hospitals, May 2006**

| Occupation | State government | Local government | All industries |
|---|---|---|---|
| Business operations specialists, all other........................................ | $26.82 | $25.73 | $26.76 |
| Police and sheriffs patrol officers .... | 25.26 | 22.69 | 22.82 |
| Child, family, and school social workers ............................... | 18.75 | 20.91 | 18.02 |
| Fire fighters.................................... | 17.79 | 20.00 | 19.80 |
| Correctional officers and jailers....... | 17.37 | 16.74 | 17.19 |
| Executive secretaries and administrative assistants.............. | 17.23 | 18.59 | 17.90 |
| Highway maintenance workers....... | 15.77 | 14.99 | 15.17 |
| Secretaries, except legal, medical, and executive................................ | 15.21 | 14.59 | 13.20 |
| Maintenance and repair workers, general........................................ | 14.90 | 15.85 | 15.34 |
| Office clerks, general ..................... | 13.17 | 12.78 | 11.40 |

**Table 4. Median annual salary for selected executive and managerial occupations in local government, 2006**

| Occupation | Salary |
|---|---|
| City manager/Chief administrative officer | $92,799 |
| Assistant chief administrative officer | 83,155 |
| Engineer | 79,648 |
| Chief financial officer | 76,101 |
| Fire chief | 75,645 |
| Information services director | 75,118 |
| Economic development director | 73,140 |
| Human resources director | 72,527 |
| Public works director | 71,360 |
| Human services director | 70,958 |
| Chief law enforcement official | 69,600 |
| Parks and recreation director | 68,284 |
| Health officer | 67,275 |
| Purchasing director | 63,043 |
| Chief librarian | 58,750 |
| Treasurer | 54,803 |
| Clerk | 45,497 |
| Chief elected official | 25,000 |

more common among State and local government employees than among workers in the private sector.

Although union membership data are not available, workers in State and local government have a relatively high rate of union membership.

## Sources of Additional Information

Individuals interested in working for State or local government agencies should contact the appropriate agencies. City, county, and State personnel and human resources departments, and local offices of State employment services have applications and additional information.

Information about careers related to human resources at the Federal, State and local levels of government is available from:

➤ International Public Management Association for Human Resources, 1617 Duke St., Alexandria, VA 22314. Internet: **http://www.ipma-hr.org**

For more information about careers in local government management, including local government management internship programs, contact:

➤ International City/County Management Association, 777 North Capitol St. NE., Suite 500, Washington, DC 20002. Internet: **http://www.jobs.icma.org**

Information on many occupations commonly found in State and local governments is available in the 2008-09 *Occupational Outlook Handbook*:

- Bus drivers
- Correctional officers
- Court reporters
- Firefighting occupations
- Judges, magistrates, and other judicial workers
- Lawyers
- Police and detectives
- Probation officers and correctional treatment specialists
- Social and human service assistants
- Social workers
- Tax examiners, collectors, and revenue agents
- Top executives
- Urban and regional planners

# Sources of State and Local Job Outlook Information

Most States have career information delivery systems (CIDS), which may be found in secondary and postsecondary institutions, as well as libraries, job training sites, vocational-technical schools, and employment offices. A wide range of information is provided, from employment opportunities to unemployment insurance claims.

Whereas the Career Guide provides information for industries on a national level, each State has detailed information on industries and labor markets within their respective jurisdictions. State occupational projections are available at: http://www.projectionscentral. com  Listed below are the addresses and telephone numbers of the directors of research and analysis in these agencies and Internet addresses of these agencies.

**Alabama**
Labor Market Information Division, Alabama Department of Industrial Relations, 649 Monroe St., Room 422, Montgomery, AL 36131.
Telephone: (334) 242-8859.
Internet: **http://dir.alabama.gov**

**Alaska**
Research and Analysis Section, Department of Labor and Workforce Development, P.O. Box 25501, Juneau, AK 99802-5501.
Telephone: (907) 465-4500.
Internet: **http://www.jobs.state.ak.us**

**Arizona**
Arizona Department of Economic Security, P.O. Box 6123 SC 733A, Phoenix, AZ 85005-6123.
Telephone: (602) 542-5984.
Internet: **http://www.workforce.az.gov**

**Arkansas**
Labor Market Information, Department of Workforce Services, #2 Capital Mall, Little Rock, AR 72201.
Telephone: (501) 682-3198.
Internet: **http://www.arkansas.gov/esd**

**California**
State of California Employment Development Department, Labor Market Information Division, P.O. Box 826880, Sacramento, CA 94280-0001.
Telephone: (916) 262-2162.
Internet: **http://www.labormarketinfo.edd.ca.gov**

**Colorado**
Labor Market Information, Colorado Department of Labor and Employment, 633 17th St., Suite 201, Denver, CO 80202-3660.
Telephone: (303) 318-8000.
Internet: **http://www.coworkforce.com/lmi**

**Connecticut**
Office of Research, Connecticut Department of Labor, 200 Folly Brook Blvd., Wethersfield, CT 06109-1114.
Telephone: (860) 263-6275.
Internet: **http://www.ctdol.state.ct.us/lmi**

**Delaware**
Office of Occupational and Labor Market Information, Department of Labor, 19 West Lea Blvd., Wilmington, DE 19802-.
Telephone: (302) 761-8069.
Internet:
**http://www.delawareworks.com/oolmi/welcome.shtml**

**District of Columbia**
DC Department of Employment Services, 609 H St. NE., Washington, D.C. 20002.
Telephone: (202) 724-7000.
Internet: **http://www.does.dc.gov/does**

**Florida**
Labor Market Statistics, Agency for Workforce Innovation, MSC G-020, 107 E. Madison St., Tallahassee, FL 32399-4111.
Telephone: (850) 245-7205.
Internet: **http://www.labormarketinfo.com**

**Georgia**
Workforce Information and Analysis, Room 300, Department of Labor, 223 Courtland St., CWC Building, Atlanta, GA 30303.
Telephone: (404) 232-3875.
Internet:
**http://www.dol.state.ga.us/em/get_labor_market_information.htm**

Guam
Guam Department of Labor, 504 D St., Tiyan, Guam 96910.
Telephone: (671) 475-0101.

**Hawaii**
Research and Statistics Office, Department of Labor and Industrial Relations, 830 Punchbowl St., Room 304, Honolulu, HI 96813.
Telephone: (808) 586-8999.
Internet: **http://www.hiwi.org**

**Idaho**
Research and Analysis Bureau, Department of Commerce and Labor, 317 West Main St., Boise, ID 83735-0670.
Telephone: (208) 332-3570.
Internet: **http://lmi.idaho.gov**

**Illinois**
Illinois Department of Employment Security, Economic Information and Analysis Division, 33 S. State St., 9th Floor , Chicago, IL 60603.
Telephone: (312) 793-2316.
Internet: **http://lmi.ides.state.il.us**

**Indiana**
Research and Analysis—Indiana Workforce Development, Indiana Government Center South, 10 North Senate Ave., Indianapolis, IN 46204.
Telephone: (800) 891-6499.
Internet: **http://www.in.gov/dwd**

**Iowa**
Policy and Information Division, Iowa Workforce Development, 1000 East Grand Ave., Des Moines, IA 50319-0209.
Telephone: (515) 281-5116
Internet: **http://www.iowaworkforce.org/lmi**

**Kansas**
Kansas Department of Labor, Labor Market Information Services, 401 SW Topeka Blvd., Topeka, KS 66603-3182.
Telephone: (785) 296-5000.
Internet: **http://laborstats.dol.ks.gov**

**Kentucky**
Research and Statistics Branch, Office of Employment and Training, 275 East Main St., Frankfort, KY 40621.
Telephone: (502) 564-7976.
Internet: **http://www.workforcekentucky.ky.gov**

**Louisiana**
Research and Statistics Division, Department of Labor, 1001 North 23rd St., Baton Rouge, LA 70802-3338.
Telephone: (225) 342-3111.
Internet: **http://www.laworks.net**

**Maine**
Labor Market Information Services Division, Maine Department of Labor, State House Station 54, P.O. Box 259 45 Commerce Dr., Augusta, ME 04330.
Telephone: (207) 621-5182.
Internet: **http://www.state.me.us/labor/lmis/index.html**

**Maryland**
Maryland Department of Labor Licensing and Regulation, Office of Labor Market Analysis and Information, Room 316, 1100 N. Eutaw, Baltimore, MD 21201.
Telephone: (410) 767-2250.
Internet: **http://www.dllr.state.md.us/lmi/index.htm**

**Massachusetts**
Executive Office of Labor and Workforce Development, Division of Career Services, 19 Staniford St., Boston, MA 02114.
Telephone: (617) 626-5300.
Internet: **http://www.detma.org/LMIdataprog.htm**

**Michigan**
Bureau of Labor Market Information and Strategic Initiatives, Department of Labor and Economic Growth, 3032 West Grand Blvd., Suite 9-100, Detroit, MI 48202.
Telephone: (313) 456-3090.
Internet: **http://www.milmi.org**

**Minnesota**
Department of Employment and Economic Development, Labor Market Information Office, 1st National Bank Building, 332 Minnesota St., Suite E200, St. Paul, MN 55101-1351.
Telephone: (888) 234-1114.
Internet: **http://www.deed.state.mn.us/lmi**

**Mississippi**
Labor Market Information Division, Mississippi Department of Employment Security , 1235 Echelon Pkwy., P.O. Box 1699, Jackson, MS 39215.
Telephone: (601) 321-6000.
Internet: **http://mdes.ms.gov**

**Missouri**
Missouri Economic Research and Information Center, P.O. Box 3150, Jefferson City, MO 65102-3150.
Telephone: (866) 225-8113.
Internet: **http://www.missourieconomy.org**

**Montana**
Research and Analysis Bureau, P.O. Box 1728, Helena, MT 59624.
Telephone: (800) 541-3904.
Internet: **http://www.ourfactsyourfuture.org**

**Nebraska**
Nebraska Workforce Development—Labor Market Information, Nebraska Department of Labor, 550 South 16t'h St., P.O. Box 94600, Lincoln, NE 68509.
Telephone: (402) 471-2600.
Internet: **http://www.dol.state.ne.us/nelmi.htm**

**Nevada**
Research and Analysis, Department of Employment Training and Rehabilitation, 500 East Third St., Carson City, NV 89713.
Telephone: (775) 684-0450.
Internet: **http://www.nevadaworkforce.com**

**New Hampshire**
Economic and Labor Market Information Bureau, New Hampshire Employment Security, 32 South Main St., Concord, NH 03301-4857.
Telephone: (603) 228-4124.
Internet: **http://www.nhes.state.nh.us/elmi**

**New Jersey**
Division of Labor Market and Demographic Research, Department of Labor and Workforce Development, P.O. Box 388, Trenton, NJ 08625-0388.
Telephone: (609) 984-2593.
Internet: **http://www.wnjpin.net**

**New Mexico**
New Mexico Department of Labor, Economic Research and Analysis, 401 Broadway NE., Albuquerque, NM 87102.
Telephone: (505) 222-4683.
Internet: **http://www.dol.state.nm.us/dol_lmif.html**

**New York**
Research and Statistics, New York State Department of Labor, State Office Campus, Room 490, Albany, NY 12240.
Telephone: (518) 457-2919.
Internet:
**http://www.labor.state.ny.us/workforceindustrydata/index.asp**

**North Carolina**
Labor Market Information Division, Employment Security Commission, 700 Wade Ave., Raleigh, NC 27605.
Telephone: (919) 733-4329.
Internet: **http://www.ncesc.com**

**North Dakota**
Labor Market Information Manager, Job Service North Dakota, 1000 East Divide Ave., Bismarck, ND 58506.
Telephone: (800) 732-9787.
Internet: **http://www.ndworkforceintelligence.com**

**Ohio**
Bureau of Labor Market Information, Office of Workforce Development, Ohio Department of Job and Family Services, P.O. Box 1618, Columbus, OH 43216-1618.
Telephone: (614) 752-9494.
Internet: **http://www.ohioworkforceinformer.org**

**Oklahoma**
Labor Market Information, Oklahoma Employment Security Commission, 2401 N. Lincoln Blvd., Oklahoma City, OK 73105.
Telephone: (405) 557-7100.
Internet: **http://www.oesc.state.ok.us/lmi/default.htm**

**Oregon**
Oregon Employment Department, Research Division, 875 Union St. NE., Salem, OR 97311.
Telephone: (503) 947-1200.
Internet: **http://www.qualityinfo.org/olmisj/OlmisZine**

**Pennsylvania**
Center for Workforce Information & Analysis, Pennsylvania Department of Labor and Industry, 220 Labor and Industry Building, Seventh and Forster Sts., Harrisburg, PA 17121.
Telephone: (877) 493-3282.
Internet: **http://www.paworkstats.state.pa.us**

**Puerto Rico**
Labor Market Information Office, P.O. Box 195540, San Juan, Puerto Rico 00919-5540.
Telephone: (787) 281-5760.
Internet:
**http://www.dtrh.gobierno.pr/oficina_procurador_del_trabajo.asp**

**Rhode Island**
Labor Market Information, Rhode Island Department of Labor and Training, 1511 Pontiac Ave., Cranston, RI 02920.
Telephone: (401) 462-8740.
Internet: **http://www.dlt.ri.gov/lmi**

**South Carolina**
Labor Market Information Department, South Carolina Employment Security Commission, 631 Hampton St., Columbia, SC 29202.
Telephone: (803) 737-2660.
Internet: **http://www.sces.org/lmi/index.asp**

**South Dakota**
Labor Market Information Center, Department of Labor, P.O. Box 4730, Aberdeen, SD 57402-4730.
Telephone: (605) 626-2314.
Internet: **http://www.state.sd.us/dol/lmic/index.htm**

**Tennessee**
Research and Statistics Division, Department of Labor and Workforce Development, 710 James Robertson Pkwy., Nashville, TN 37243.
Telephone: (615) 741-6642.
Internet: **http://www.state.tn.us/labor-wfd/lmi.htm**

**Texas**
Labor Market Information, Texas Workforce Commission, 9001 North IH-35, Suite 103A, Austin, TX 75753.
Telephone: (866) 938-4444.
Internet: **http://www.tracer2.com**

**Utah**
Director of Workforce Information, Utah Department of Workforce Services, P.O. Box 45249, Salt Lake City, UT 84145-0249.
Telephone: (801) 526-9675.
Internet: **http://jobs.utah.gov/opencms/wi**

**Vermont**
Research and Analysis, Vermont Department of Labor, P.O. Box 488, Montpelier, VT 05601-0488.
Telephone: (802) 828-4000.
Internet: **http://www.labor.vermont.gov**

**Virgin Islands**
Bureau of Labor Statistics, Department of Labor, P.O. Box 302608, St Thomas, VI 00803-2608.
Telephone: (340) 776-3700.
Internet: **http://www.vidol.gov**

**Virginia**
Economic Information Services, Virginia Employment Commission, P.O. Box 1358, Richmond, VA 23218-1358.
Telephone: (804) 786-8223.
Internet: **http://velma.virtuallmi.com**

**Washington**
Labor Market and Economic Analysis, Washington Employment Security Department, PO Box 9046, Olympia, WA 98507-9046.
Telephone: (800) 215-1617.
Internet: **http://www.workforceexplorer.com**

**West Virginia**
WORKFORCE West Virginia, Research, Information and Analysis Division, 112 California Ave., Charleston, WV 25303-0112.
Telephone: (304) 558-2660.
Internet: **http://www.wvbep.org/bep/lmi**

**Wisconsin**
Bureau of Workforce Information, Department of Workforce Development, P.O.Box 7944, Madison, WI 53707-7944.
Telephone: (608) 266-8212.
Internet: **http://worknet.wisconsin.gov/worknet**

**Wyoming**
Research and Planning, Wyoming Department of Employment, 246 S. Center St., Casper, WY 82602.
Telephone: (307) 473-3807.
Internet: **http://doe.state.wy.us/lmi**

# Index

GPO U.S. GOVERNMENT PRINTING OFFICE: 2008-342-263

# BLS Employment Projections Online

## http://www.bls.gov/emp

### Federal Government's Premier Career Guidance Publications
→ Occupational Outlook Handbook
→ Career Guide to Industries
→ Occupational Outlook Quarterly
→ Occupational Projections and Training Data

### People Are Asking
→ What are the fastest growing occupations and industries?
→ Which occupations will add the most new jobs?

### Publications
→ Projections-related articles
→ Special features: "Charting the projections"
→ and "The job outlook in brief"

### Searchable Databases
→ Occupational Employment, Training, and
→ Earnings
→ National Employment Matrix
→ Tables created by BLS

### Related Links
→ BLS career information for young people
→ State employment projections

### Contacts
→ Telephone listings for industry and occupational experts atthe Office of Occupational Statistics and Employment Projections

# Related Publications

## Occupational Projections and Training Data, 2008-09 Edition
### BLS Bulletin 2702

This publication is a research and statistical supplement to the *Occupational Outlook Handbook*. Education and training planners, career counselors, and jobseekers can compare hundreds of occupations on characteristics such as projected employment change, self-employed and part-time workers, earnings, the unemployment rate, and education and training. Users also will find information on factors affecting occupational utilization, and data on awards and degrees by field of study.

## Occupational Outlook Handbook, 2008-09 Edition
### BLS Bulletin 2700

The *Handbook* has been the Federal Government's premier publication on tomorrow's job market since the late 1940s. The *Handbook* covers hundreds of occupations, accounting for 9 of every 10 jobs in the Nation, and discusses nature of the work; training, other qualifications, and advancement; job outlook; earnings; and sources of additional information. The *Handbook* also includes information on finding and applying for jobs and evaluating offers, and sources of financial aid.